Monongalia County, (West) Virginia, Deedbook Records, 1784-1810 (Old Series Volumes 1-4)

by
Rick Toothman

HERITAGE BOOKS
2008

HERITAGE BOOKS
AN IMPRINT OF HERITAGE BOOKS, INC.

Books, CDs, and more—Worldwide

For our listing of thousands of titles see our website at
www.HeritageBooks.com

Published 2008 by
HERITAGE BOOKS, INC.
Publishing Division
100 Railroad Avenue #104
Westminster, Maryland 21157

Copyright © 1994 Rick Toothman

Other books by the author:

Pendleton County, (West) Virginia, Deedbook Records, 1788-1813
Pendleton County, (West) Virginia, Probate Records: Wills, 1788-1866;
Inventories, Sale Bills, Settlements, 1788-1846

All rights reserved. No part of this book may be reproduced or transmitted in any form or by any means, electronic or mechanical, including photocopying, recording or by any information storage and retrieval system without written permission from the author, except for the inclusion of brief quotations in a review.

International Standard Book Number: 978-0-7884-0000-1

To my parents, and to my niece Rebecca, with love

TABLE OF CONTENTS

Editorial Notes...........................vii

Deedbook OS 1..............................1

Deedbook OS 2.............................77

Deedbook OS 3............................181

Deedbook OS 4............................281

Appendix: Other Early Monongalia Land Transfers
..........................377

Index....................................387

EDITORIAL NOTES

The deeds and other instruments abstracted in this volume are from the OS, or Old Series, record books at Morgantown. There are 21 volumes in the Old Series. In 1856 a new series of deedbooks was begun, whose volume numbers started again from 1 (without prefix). "OS" should be included in any citation of these deeds and must be included by anyone attempting to acquire a particular instrument from the county clerk's office.

Except where noted, all instruments are general warranty conveyances. However, wills, deeds of trust, powers of attorney, bills of sale, mortgages, manumissions, and other miscellaneous items are also recorded. Not all of these documents are listed in the general index to deedbooks.

All principals are identified as "of Monongalia County, VA," unless otherwise specified, though not all persons named as residents actually were. All counties mentioned are in VA unless otherwise specified. The original deeds normally name "John Doe and Jane his wife" as grantors. I have identified married couples as "John and Jane Doe," giving full names ("John Doe" and "Jane Doe") for parties who are not stated to be husband and wife.

Standard USPS abbreviations for states are used throughout. Otherwise, spelling follows the original as closely as possible, variations included. I have not attempted to "[sic]" every dubious spelling, of which there are many.

Identification of parties involved follows the spelling in the deed's preamble. Signatures are often different, and many names are spelled discrepantly within the same document. I have tried to indicate significant variations. Marks which can be duplicated on the keyboard are so shown. Others (some of them quite distinctive) are indicated by [mark]. The earlier scribes take some pains to copy individual marks, but almost never duplicate German script signatures, which are usually noted as "signed in Dutch."

Names of places and of adjoiners and previous owners are indicated whenever mentioned in the originals, as is any information regarding original patents or surveys. Metes and bounds are omitted. Money values are expressed as £.s.d [or s.d. in some cases] before dollar values become universal. Frequently currency is of a particular state. Money values differed from one state to another in this period.

Witnesses are named where they appear, but are absent from many instruments. No inferences as to relationships can be derived automatically from names of witnesses. Most typically, witnesses were justices of the peace or the courthouse regulars whose names will become quite familiar to readers of this book.

Acknowledgement of the deed was required, and was sometimes done via the testimony of witnesses rather than by the grantors, for various reasons. Numerous early instruments bear no recorded acknowledgement. All acknowledgements were made in Monongalia County unless otherwise specified.

"Delivery" [abbreviated Del: in my text] is the return of the original instrument after it had been recorded and the fees paid. Normally, but not always, delivery was made to the grantee.

The Monongalia Clerk's office burned in 1796, destroying such deedbooks as then existed. The horizon of instruments presently of record is about 1794/95, since not all deeds made by the time of the fire had been recorded, but numerous pre-1796 instruments were recorded again, from the originals. These bear a formula notation which I have abbreviated below as "Re-recording of burned instrument." Still other lands were conveyed anew, with reference to burning of the record.

The earliest items in the text are 1784 and 1785 conveyances of lots in Morgantown, and I have used 1784 as the starting date in the title of this volume although it does not include a *complete* set of Monongalia deedbook information from that date.

The appendix contains memoranda on many pre-1797 conveyances, taken from the land books. This is strongest for the portion of Monongalia which later became Preston County, WV. With the re-recordings, reconveyances, chains of title given in later deeds, and the assessors' notes, it would appear that a significant amount of pre-1796 data is recoverable, despite loss of the records themselves.

These abstracts were made from the original records in the office of the Monongalia County Clerk at Morgantown, WV, and from Family History Library films 0840572 and 0840573. My editorial comments appear in [brackets]. Some information from the original documents is enclosed in (parentheses) for purposes of clarity.

RICK TOOTHMAN

11 December 1796. William and Margret ICE to James EDGELL. 100 acres on Buffalow Creek, part of a larger tract granted to John Ice, deceased, to whom William Ice is heir at law. No adjoiners named. Consideration: £12, VA. Signed: William [X] Ice, Margret [M] Ice. Witnesses: Joseph Cox, Hedgman Triplett. No acknowledgement recorded. Del: to [name obscured by binding tape], 16 March 1803. Recorded: OS 1:1.

11 January 1796. William and Margret ICE to Eden BAYLES. 100 acres on Buffalow Creek, part of a larger tract granted to John Ice, adjoining Adam Ice's survey and Anthony Mahan. Consideration: £30, VA. Signed: William [X] Ice, Margret [M] Ice. Witnesses: Joseph Cox, Hedgman Triplett. No acknowledgement recorded. No delivery shown. Recorded: OS 1:2.

8 February 1796. Henry and Lydia BARNES to John CASSATY. 319 acres on Three Forks Creek, patented 10 February 1787. No adjoiners named. Consideration: $150.50. Signed: Henry Barnes, Lydia Barnes. Witnesses: Thomas Barnes, Nathan Springer. No acknowledgement recorded. No delivery shown. Recorded OS 1:3.

2 March 1796. John ROBESON, Nelson Co, KY, heir at law of William ROBESON, deceased, to Elijah BEALL, Morgantown. Power of attorney to convey any and all lands in Monongalia, Harrison, Randolph, Greenbriar, and Kanhawa. Excepted are 2 tracts in Monongalia, held by entry, on the east branch of Booths Creek adjoining the middle fork, about 3 miles from the mouth, at a place called Raleighs Camp, adjoining Thomas Miller. Witnesses: J H Williams, Hugh McNeely, John Willey, Hugh Masterson. No acknowledgement recorded. No delivery shown. Recorded: OS 1:4.

[blank] June 1795. Thomas and Rebecca BUTLER to John SHAY. 100 acres on Roaring Creek, part of Butler's pre-emption survey, adjoining lands of Amos Roberts. Consideration: £25, VA. Signed: Thomas Butler, Rebecca [X] Butler. Witnesses: Thos Burchinal, James Morgan. No acknowledgement recorded. No delivery shown. Recorded: OS 1:5.

10 January 1796. Richard and Phebe MERRIFIELD to William BAMBRIDGE. 150 acres on White Day Creek, at head of Laurel Run, adjoining Achilles Morgan, Rice Bullock, and Robert Beall. Consideration: £75. Signed: Richard Merrifield, Phebe [mark] Merrifield. Witnesses: none. Acknowledged in court. No delivery shown. Recorded: OS 1:6.

11 December 1796. William and Margret ICE to Anthony MAHON. 100 acres on Buffalow Creek, part of a larger tract granted to John Ice, deceased. No adjoiners named. Consideration: £25, VA. Signed: William [X] Ice, Margret [M] Ice. Witnesses: Joseph Cox, Hedgman Triplett. No acknowledgement recorded. No delivery shown. Recorded: OS 1:7.

14 March 1796. Leonard and Kisshey TETSOARD to Jesse HANWAY. 469 acres on east side of Deckers Creek, below the mouth of Laurel Run. Part of 2 patents totaling 777 acres. Consideration: £250. Signed: Leonard [mark] Tetsoard. [Kisshey does not sign.] Witnesses: none. Acknowledged in court. No delivery shown. Recorded: OS 1:8.

20 April 1795. Anthony and Dianah WORLEY to Ezekiel WORLEY. 400 acres on Little Sandy Creek, near mouth of Chenies Run and Mill Run, adjoining John Hartness. Patented to Anthony on 10 May 1781, and including his 1770 improvement. Consideration: £287. Signed: Anthony Worley, Dianah [mark] Worley. Witnesses: Thomas Chipps, Edwd Jones. No acknowledgement recorded. No delivery shown. Recorded: OS 1:9.

15 February 1796. Joseph and Elisabeth BUTLER to Thomas BURCHINAL. 150 acres at Butlers Mill Run, adjoining Thomas Chipps and extending toward the Briary Mountain. [Patented?] 12 April 1793. Consideration: £36, VA. Signed: Joseph [mark] Butler, Elizabeth [D] Butler. Witnesses: Thos Butler, Edward Jones, Thos Smout. No acknowledgement recorded. No delivery shown. Recorded: OS 1:10.

12 January 1796. William and Margret ICE to Adam ICE. 100 acres on Buffalo, part of a larger tract formerly property of John Ice, deceased, and adjoining Anthony Mahan. Consideration: £25, VA. Signed: William [X] Ice, Margret [M] Ice. Witnesses: Joseph Cox, Hedgman Triplett. No acknowledgement recorded. Del: to Jasper Wayatt, 16 March 1803. Recorded: OS 1:11.

12 March 1796. James and Mary STINSON to John KEELER. 195 acres, including the rich hill on Worleys Mill Run, surveyed 8 November 1785. No adjoiners named. Consideration: £56, VA. Signed: James Stinson, Mary Stinson. Witnesses: none. Acknowledged in court. No delivery shown. Recorded: OS 1:12.

14 March 1796. James and Mary STINSON to James GUTHRIE. 126 acres on a branch of Little Sandy Creek, in Sandy Creek Glades. No adjoiners named. Surveyed 26 March 1784. Consideration: £100, VA. Signed: James Stinson, Mary Stinson. Witnesses: none. Acknowledged in

court. No delivery shown. Recorded: OS 1:13.
28 November 1795. Andrew RAMSEY to his brother John RAMSEY. Power of attorney to demand and recover debts and to assign one location to Joseph Butler Junr and two plats or surveys to Nicholas Casey. Signed: Andrew Ramsey. Witnesses: F Warman, Jas Henthorn, Jas Shaw. Recorded: OS 1:14.
9 October 1794. Zephor and Elizabeth BLATCHLEY to Joseph CASEY. Mortgage on 121 3/4 acres at Big Sandy Creek. No adjoiners named. Consideration: £113, PA. Blatchley may repay the money with interest from 19 October 1796 and redeem the land. Signed: Zephor Blatchley, Elizabeth Blatchley. Witnesses: Martin Judy, John McClain, Russell Potter. No acknowledgement recorded. Del: to Russell Potter, 7 September 1805. Recorded: OS 1:15.
16 October 1794. Joseph CORY to Samuel DARBY. Power of attorney to demand and recover all debts and to transact all my business. Signed: Joseph Cory. Witnesses: John Gribble, Russell Potter. Recorded: OS 1:15.
12 January 1796. Jonathan and Drusilla DOWNAR, Fayette Co, PA, to Silas LORD. Lot #84 in Morgan Town. Consideration: £24. Signed: Jonathan Downar, Drusilla Downar. Witnesses: Peregrine Foster, Hedgman Triplett, Hugh McNeely. Acknowledged by Drusilla Downar, 15 April 1796, in Union Twp, Fayette Co, PA, certified by Jonathan Rowland and Abraham Stuart. No delivery shown. Recorded: OS 1:15-16.
12 April 1794. William WORTH, yeoman, Pitsgrove Twp, Salem Co, NJ, to David EVANS, yeoman, New Brittan Twp, Bucks Co, PA. 1000 acres adjoining William Pettyjohn, Samuel Conley, Samuel Ruble, and Arthur Trader. Patented to Worth 26 February 1794. Consideration: 100 silver dollars. Signed: William Worth. Witnesses: Thomas Morris, James Evans. Receipt for $100, signed by Worth and certified 27 February 1796 by John Barcley, associate judge of common pleas, Bucks Co, PA. Certificate of William Linton, Bucks Co prothonotary, 20 April 1796. No delivery shown. Recorded: OS 1:17-18.
27 January 1795. Francis DEAKINS and William DEAKINS Jr, Montgomery Co, MD, to John CALLAHAN, Annapolis Co, MD. 141 acres on the south side of Salt Lick Creek. Consideration: 20 shillings. Signed: Francis Deakins, William Deakins Junr. Witnesses: Daniel Reintzel, George French. Receipt for 20 shillings, dated 27 January 1795. Jane, wife of William Deakins Jr,

acknowledges at the same time. Elenor, wife of Francis
Deakins, acknowledges 5 February 1795, before Aeneas
Campbell and Lawrence Oneall, justices of Montgomery Co.
Certificate of Brooke Beall, clerk of Montgomery Co, 12
March 1795. No delivery shown. Recorded: OS 1:18-19.

13 July 1795. James and Susannah DAUGHERTY to
William TINGLE. Lot # [blank] in Morgan's Town,
adjoining Daugherty's store house, John Stealey's
corner. Consideration: $50. Signed: James Daugherty,
Susannah Daugherty. Witnesses: none. Acknowledged in
court. Del: to William Tingle. Recorded: OS 1:20.

26 September 1795. Jonas and Dorothy DUNKIN,
Fayette Co, PA, to Philip HORNER. 83 acres adjoining
Jacob Jones. No place names mentioned. Consideration:
£50. Signed: Jonas Dunkin, Dorothy [+] Dunkin.
Witnesses: Francis Warman, Wm Norris, Josiah [+]
Jenkins. No acknowledgement recorded. Del: to Philip
Horner, 16 February 1805. Recorded: OS 1:20-21.

[blank] 1796. Jacob and [blank] NOOSE, Jacob (Junr)
and Phebe NOOSE to John STEALEY. 192 acres between the
lands of Lott Ridgway and Nicholas Vandervort, adjoining
lands of Samuel Hanway. Consideration: $600. Signed:
Jacob [mark] Noose Junr, Phebe [+] Noose. [Jacob and
(blank) do not sign.] Witnesses: none. Acknowledged in
court. Del: to Stealey, 19 December 1821. Recorded:
OS 1:22.

9 October 1796. James SCOTT to William TANNAHILL.
100 acres on Laurel Run, left to Scott by the will of
William Hamilton. No adjoiners named. Consideration:
£12.16, VA. Signed: James [+] Scott. Witnesses: James
Clark, James Hamilton, John Clark. No acknowledgement
recorded. Del: to Taneyhill, 23 [?] March 1800.
Recorded: OS 1:23.

11 April 1796. Thomas and Sarah LAIDLEY, Samuel
HANWAY, John and Prudence STEALEY, and Peregrine and
Polly FOSTER to Thomas WILSON, Esqr. 4 acres, 4 poles on
northwesterly side of Back Street, Morgan Town.
Consideration: £200, VA. Signed: Thos Laidley, John
Stealey, Prudence [-] Stealey, Peregrine Foster, Polly
Foster. [Sarah does not sign] Witnesses: none.
Acknowledged in court. No delivery shown. Recorded:
OS 1:24.

11 April 1796. John and Prudence STEALEY to John
WATSON, Fayette Co, PA. 192 acres between lands of Lott
Ridgway and Nicholas Vandervort, adjoining lands of
Samuel Hanway. Consideration: £240, VA. Signed: John
Stealey, Prudence [-] Stealey. Witnesses: none.
Acknowledged in court. Del: to the widow of the grantee,

26 August 1820. Recorded: OS 1:25.
9 May 1796. Henry and Jane ROBESON, Fayette Co, PA, to Hugh SIDWELL. 174 acres on Wests Run, moiety of a tract patented to Robinson 16 September 1784, adjoining another moiety of the same tract previously sold to Rees Hastings. Consideration: £150, VA. Signed: Henry Robinson, Jane [+] Robinson. Witnesses: John Evans, Wm McCleery, Dudley Evans. Receipt for £150, witnessed by John Evans and Wm McCleery. Del: to H Sidwell. Recorded: OS 1:26.
9 May 1796. Henry and Jane ROBINSON, Fayette Co, PA, to Reece HASTINGS. 174 acres on Wests Run, moiety of a tract patented to Robinson 16 September 1784. Consideration: £150, VA. Signed: Henry Robinson, Jean [X] Robinson. Witnesses: John Evans, Wm McCleery, Dudley Evans. Receipt for £150, witnessed by Evans and McCleery. Del: to H Sidwell, 15 November 1800. Recorded: OS 1:27.
24 March 1796. Ezekiel JACOB, Prince Georges Co, MD, to Samuel JACOB, Anne Arundel Co, MD. 300 acres adjoining the settlement of Charles Donaldson on Martins Run. Consideration: £300. Signed: Ezekiel Jacob. Witnesses: Hend Magruder, Turner Wootton. Acknowledged 24 March 1796, Prince Georges Co, MD. Certificate of Allen Quynn, mayor of Annapolis. No delivery shown. Recorded: OS 1:28.
16 May 1796. WILL of John PEIRPOINT. Wife Ann: personalty, 2 lots in Morgantown, plantation while she remains unmarried. Son Larkin: one half of my land, he to pay £100 to daughter Ann when he is 18. Son Zackquill: the other half of my land, he to pay daughter Temperance £100 when he is 18. Daughter Sarah Watson: 150 acres in Harrison Co, purchased of Samuel Hanway. Son Francis: 400 acres between the Tyger Valley and West Fork Rivers, in Harrison Co, he to pay son John £50, 15 years after taking possession of the land. Son John: 324 acres that I own in partners with Samuel Hanway, near the Monongalia Glades. Daughters Ann and Temperance: 200 acres at the forks of Bingermons Creek. Executors: wife Ann and Nicholas Vandervort. Signed: John Peirpoint. Witnesses: Paul Vandervort, Jonah Vandervort, Jacob Scott. No probate data. Recorded: OS 1:29-30. [Also recorded in Wills, 1:297-298.]
22 December 1794. Stephen (Esqr) and Mary Rickets MOYLAN, Philadelphia, PA, to William Stevens SMITH, Esqr, New York City. 8000 acres, adjoining surveys of Richard Claiborne, John Moylan, and including 4000 acres conveyed to Stephen by his brother John Moylan, 17 July

1794. No place names mentioned. Consideration: $5500. Signed: Stephen Moylan, Mary Rickets Moylan. Witnesses: William Sighman [?], Andrew Ross. Receipt for $5500. Certificate of Mathew Clarkson, Mayor of Philadelphia. No delivery shown. Recorded: OS 1:31-33.

9 June 1796. Keziah LITTLE, Keziah VERDEN, Henry and Elizabeth BATTEN, James and Mary LONGWELL, and Charles SNODGRASS, attorney in fact for Jehu LITTLE, to John EVANS Jr and Benjamin REEDER. 400 acres on the west side of the Monongahela River, patented to Adonijah Little 15 May 1787. Consideration: $1000. Signed: Kisia Verdin, Henry [mark] Batten, Elizabeth [mark] Batten, James [0] Longwell, Mary [mark] Longwell, Charles Snodgrass. [Keziah Little does not sign.] Witnesses: Calder Haymon, Josiah Prickett, Wm Jolliff. Power of attorney from Jehu Little, Bourbon Co, KY, to Charles Snodgrass, dated 11 November 1795 and witnessed by Calder Haymon and Josiah Prickett. No acknowledgement recorded. No delivery shown. Recorded: OS 1:34-36.

13 June 1796. William and Mary JOHN to Asa DUDLEY. Half lot in Morgan Town where Dudley has built a framed house. Includes quit rent of 1.6d per annum to be paid to the heirs of Zack'll Morgan deceased. Consideration: $100. Signed: Wm John, Mary [+] John. Witnesses: none. Acknowledged in court. Del: to Asa Dudley, 12 March 1810. Recorded: OS 1:36-37.

13 June 1796. Joseph and Ann Skinner WILSON to Thos WILSON. Lot #104 in Morgan Town. Consideration: £15. Signed: Joseph Wilson. [Ann does not sign.] Witnesses: none. Acknowledged in court. Del: to Thos Wilson, 4 August 1803. Recorded: OS 1:38-39.

21 May 1796. Richard and Mary LEE to Alexander McINTIRE. 2 acres on the road from Morgan Town to Colo Evans', adjoining Thomas Wilson and Colo Evans. Part of a larger tract conveyed by Thomas and Judah Pindall to Richard Lee, 10 March 1794. Consideration: £8, VA. Signed: Richard Lee. [Mary does not sign.] Witnesses: none. Acknowledged in court. No delivery shown. Recorded: OS 1:39-40.

9 June 1794. Thomas and Judeth PINDALL to Alexander Ferguson LANHAM. 3¼ acres on the road from Morgantown to Suels Ferry, adjoining Thomas Wilson. Consideration: £6. Signed: Thomas Pindall, Juda [X] Pindall. Witnesses: none. No acknowledgement recorded. No delivery shown. Recorded: OS 1:40-41. Re-recording of burned instrument.

13 March 1796. John and Eve STATLAR to John JOHNSTON. 100 acres on Dunker Creek, adjoining Michael Core. Part of a larger tract patented 7 February 1787.

Consideration: £50. Signed: John [mark] Statler, Eve [+] Statler. Witnesses: George Snyder, John Downer. No acknowledgement recorded. No delivery shown. Recorded: OS 1:41-42.

26 June 1795. John SIMSON to Benjamin REEDER. 400 acres in Monongalia Glades, adjoining Benjamin Reeder and George Zinn. Surveyed for Simpson 22 June 1781 and patented to him on an improvement right of Isaac Dillon. Consideration: £120. Signed: John Simpson. Witnesses: Hedgman Triplett, Jesse Hanway, Joseph Southworth. No acknowledgement recorded. Del: to H Reeder, 14 February 1807. Recorded: OS 1:42-43. Re-recording of burned instrument.

12 November 1792. Faquire and Susanah McCREA to William LANHAM. Lot #108 in Morgan Town. Includes quit rent of 3 shillings per annum to Zackll Morgan, his heirs and assigns forever. Consideration: £12. Signed: Farquir McCrea, Susannah [mark] McCrea. Witnesses: none. Acknowledged in court. No delivery shown. Recorded: OS 1:43. Re-recording of burned instrument.

13 March 1796. Michael and Catherine CORE to Patrick KELLY. 2 tracts: 100 acres from a larger tract patented 13 October 1785, and 67 acres from a 22 August 1792 patent for 170 acres. No place names or adjoiners mentioned. Consideration: £100, VA. Signed: Michael Core, Catherine [mark] Core. Witnesses: George Snyder, John Downer. No acknowledgement recorded. No delivery shown. Recorded: OS 1:44-45.

11 August 1788. John and Nancy PEIRPOINT to William LANHAM. Lot #107 in Morgan Town. Includes quit rent of 3 shillings per annum to Zackquill Morgan, his heirs and assigns forever. Consideration: £20. Signed: John Peirpoint, Nancy [A] Peirpoint. Witnesses: none. Acknowledged in court. No delivery shown. Recorded: OS 1:45-46.

11 June 1796. William and Mary JOHN to Alexander McINTIRE. Lot [# blank] in Morgantown, northward side of courthouse lot. Consideration: $253. Signed: Wm John, Mary [X] John. Witnesses: none. Acknowledged in court. No delivery shown. Recorded: OS 1:47-48.

9 December 1794. William PETTY JOHN to Benjamin REEDER. 100 acres in the Monongalia Glades, adjoining Thomas Chipps. Patented to Petty John on [blank]. Consideration: £25. Signed W Petty John. Witnesses: Henry Dering Junr, Baldwin Weaver, Saml Hanway. No acknowledgement recorded. No delivery shown. Recorded: OS 1:48-49. Re-recording of burned instrument.

10 October 1790. Hugh McCLANAHAN, Allegany Co, PA,

executor of the last will and testament of James BULLAN Dec'd to Joseph KERSON, Fayette Co, PA. James Bullan's will, dated 11 March 1791 [sic] appointed Hugh executor for all affairs of James Bullan on the west side of the mountains. Hugh has this day exposed at public vendue in Morgan Town 3290 acres on Wickwars Creek and Threefork Creek, part of a tract of 3635 acres patented to Bulland on 9 April 1789. This land previously mortgaged by Bullan to James Lang, 16 August 1788 (of record in Monongalia Co), and Lang consents to its sale to Kerson. Consideration: £123.14.3, VA. Signed: Hugh McClenahan. Witnesses: Henry Dering Junr, Thomas Laidley, John Davis, Henry Perviance. No acknowledgement recorded. No delivery shown. Recorded: OS 1:49-51. Re-recording of burned instrument.

9 July 1792. Conrad HOGMIER, Washington Co, MD, to John and Elizabeth STOUGH [also spelled STUFF in the instrument]. 254 acres adjoining Henry Hogmire and Daniel Hogmire, part of an 820 acre tract conveyed to Conrad Hogmire by Francis and William Deakins. Consideration: Natural love and affection for my daughter Elizabeth and her husband John Stough. Signed: Conrod Hogmire. Witnesses: David Semple, -- ["name written in Dutch,"] George Stough. No acknowledgement recorded. No delivery shown. Recorded: OS 1:51-52. Re-recording of burned instrument.

13 March 1788. Samuel SHAW, Harrison Co, to William JOHN. Lot [blank] on the northward side of the courthouse lot in Morgantown. Including a quit rent of 3s per year to Zackll Morgan, his heirs and assigns for ever. Consideration: [£?]42. Signed: Samuel Shaw. Witnesses: none. Acknowledged in court. No delivery shown. Recorded: June 1796, OS 1:53-54. Re-recording of burned instrument.

14 March 1787. Francis DEAKINS and William DEAKINS, Montgomery Co, MD, to Philip HESL [?], Washington Co, MD. 200 acres in forks of Horse Shoe Run, surveyed for Deakins 20 October 1783. Consideration: £60.13.4. Signed: Francis Deakins. William Deakins. Witnesses: Aens Campbell, Laurance Oneal. Receipt for £60.13.4. Acknowledged by William and Francis Deakins 14 March 1787 in Montgomery Co before Campbell and Oneal. Acknowledged by Jane Deakins, wife of William, 21 March 1787 in Montgomery Co before Saml W Magruder and Richard Thompson. Certificate of Brooke Beall, clerk of Montgomery Co, MD, 21 March 1787. No delivery shown. Recorded: June 1796, OS 1:54-56. Re-recording of burned instrument.

19 September 1794. William Ward and Mary BURROWS, Philadelphia Co, PA, and Jane BOND (widow of Dr Thomas Bond) and David and Sarah EASTON, all of Alexandria, VA, to William CRAMOND, Philadelphia. Grantors are heirs of Dr Thomas Bond, now deceased. 47,000 acres adjoining Rawley Evans, Jeremiah Clark, on a drain of Greens Run, a drain of Cheat River, patented to William McCleery 24 January 1793. Excepting 1200 acres of older rights, 10,000 acres sold to Patten and Foley by Bond during his lifetime, 200 acres already conveyed by William and Isabella McCleery to Michael Lord, 600 acres sold by Burrows to Alexander Hawthorn, Robert Hawthorn and James Brown, and 400 acres sold but not yet conveyed to [blank] Parkyns, for a total of 34,600 acres now conveyed to Craig. Consideration: £6487.10, PA. Signed: WW Burrows, Mary Burrows, Jane Bond, David Easton, Sarah Easton. Witnesses: John Brown, Francis Peyton, James McCitten [?]. Receipt for consideration money, 19 September 1794. Certificate of Mathew Clarkson, Mayor of Philadelphia. Acknowledged by Sarah Easton in Alexandria, before Francis Payton and James Laurason. Certificate of Robert Mean, Mayor of Alexandria, 8 October 1794. Del: to Noah Linsley, agent for Robert Troop and John Johnston of New York State, 15 March 1805. Recorded; OS 1:56-59. Re-recording of burned instrument.

13 June 1795. Alexander and Catherine McINTIRE to James STAFFORD. 95 acres on Little Creek, part of a 1000 acre patent to Richard Merrifield and Rice Bullock, 9 April 1793. No adjoiners named. Consideration: £50. Signed: Alexander McIntire, Catherine McIntire. Witnesses: none. Acknowledged in court. No delivery shown. Recorded: OS 1:61.

9 June 1795. Thomas and Joannah CHIPPS to Benjamin REEDER. 400 acres on Deckers Creek, patented to Chipps 9 July 1787. No adjoiners named. Consideration: £200, VA. Signed: Thomas Chipps, Joanna Chipps. Witnesses: none. Acknowledged in court. Receipt for £200, signed by Thomas Chipps and witnessed by J Williams. No delivery shown. Recorded: OS 1:62-63. Re-recording of burned instrument.

9 March 1794. Thomas and Judith PINDALL to Richard LEE. 2 tracts. 23½ acres on the east side of the county road from Morgan Town to Martins ferry, adjoining John Stealey, Alexander McIntire, William Lanham, Thomas Wilson, John Evans. 6 acres in the same location, adjoining Thomas Wilson and Alexander McIntire. Consideration: £54. Signed: Thomas Pindall, Judith [X]

Pindell. Witnesses: none. Acknowledged in court. No delivery shown. Recorded: OS 1:63-64. Re-recording of burned instrument.

17 July 1794. John MOYLAN to Stephen MOYLAN, Esqr, both of Philadelphia, PA. 2000 acres surveyed 12 April 1784 and patented 22 [blank] 1791, adjoining Moylan's fifth entry. 1000 acres surveyed 12 April 1784 and patented 22 [blank] 1791, adjoining Richard Claiborne's third entry. Consideration: £500. Signed: John Moylan. Witnesses: Moses North, Jesse Morris, Clement Bidle. Receipt for consideration money. Certificate of Mathew Clarkson, Mayor of Philadelphia, 26 July 1794. No delivery shown. Recorded: OS 1: 64-66. Re-recording of burned instrument.

19 November 1794. William (merchant) and Sarah CRAMOND, Philadelphia, PA, to William SMITH, Esqr, New York City. Whereas Cramond bought a tract of land from the heirs of Dr Thomas Bond and has not paid the purchase money, the heirs are agreeable to sell the land to Smith at the same price, and Cramond releases title. Consideration: none stated. Signed: Wm Cramond, Sarah Cramond. Witnesses: Joseph Pemberton, Thomas Smith. Certificate of Mathew Clarkson, Mayor of Philadelphia, 3 January 1795. No delivery shown. Recorded: OS 1:66-68.

10 October 1790. John and Elizabeth JOHNSTON to Weightman FURBY, Kent Co, DE. 230 acres on Wests Run, including Johnston's 1771 settlement, surveyed 17 January 1787. Adjoining William Joseph, Samuel Hanway Esqr, Thomas Evans. Consideration: £208, VA. Signed: John Johnston, Elizabeth [+] Johnston. Witnesses: David Scott, F Warman, John Downer. No acknowledgement recorded. No delivery shown. Recorded: OS 1:69-70. Re-recording of burned instrument.

25 May 1796. Benjamin and Susannah BRANE to Paul DEWIT. 58½ acres. No adjoiners or place names mentioned. Consideration: £23.8, VA. Signed: Benjamin Brane, Susannah [X] Brane. Witnesses: none. Acknowledged in court. No delivery shown. Recorded: OS 1:71.

11 July 1796. Benjamin and Susannah BRANE to Thomas MAGEE. 79 acres on Threeforks and near the Clarksburg road. Part of a tract granted to Brane by settlement right. No adjoiners named. Consideration: £50. Signed: Benjamin Brane, Susannah [+] Brain. Witnesses: none. Acknowledged in court. No delivery shown. Recorded: OS 1:72.

12 August 1795. Grafton and Margret WHITE to Barney HANEY. 100 acres on Robesons Run, part of a 400-acre tract where White now lives, and adjoining Michael

Courtney. Consideration: £20. Signed: Grafton [+] White, Margret [0] White. Witnesses: David Scott, John Collens. Receipt for consideration money. Del: to B Haney, 27 Septr 1801. Recorded: OS 1:73-74.

10 August 1795. Grafton and Margrett WHITE to Michael COURTNEY. 100 acres on Robinsons Run, adjoining Barney Haney. Consideration: £42.10. Signed: Grafton [+] White, Margrett [mark] White. Witnesses: David Scott, John Collins. Receipt for consideration money. Del: to Michael Courtney, 27 June 1807. Recorded: OS 1:74-76.

11 July 1796. Richard and Nancy LEE to Robert LEE. 2 acres, part of a 29½ acre tract conveyed to Richard Lee by Thomas Pindell, adjoining Thomas Wilson and Alexander McIntire. Consideration: £6.12, VA. Signed: Richard Lee, Nancy [X] Lee. Witnesses: none. Acknowledged in court. No delivery shown. Recorded: OS 1:76-77.

11 July 1796. Richard and Nancy LEE to John BAKER. 25 acres, part of two separate surveys, adjoining John Stealey and Alexander McIntire, the road from Morgan Town to Martins ferry, William Lanham, Thomas Wilson, and John Evans. Consideration $416.66 2/3. Signed: Richard Lee, Ann [+] Lee. Witnesses: none. Acknowledged in court. No delivery shown. Recorded: OS 1:77-79.

29 August 1796. Thomas BOYLE to Robert GIBSON, Bedford Co, PA. Power of attorney to act for Boyle in the state of Pennsylvania. Signed: Thomas [X] Boyle. Witnesses: none. Acknowledged in court. Recorded: OS 1:79.

4 April 1796. Joseph KRESSER to James LANG, both of Fayette Co, PA. 3299 acres on Wickwares Creek and Three Forks, part of a James Bulland patent which Kresser bought at executor's sale. Consideration: $412.37½. Signed: Joseph Kressor. Witnesses: none. Acknowledged 13 May 1796, before Nathaniel Breeding, Fayette Co, PA. Receipt for consideration money. Certificate of Ephraim Douglass, prothonotary, 28 June 1796. No delivery shown. Recorded: OS 1:80-81.

22 September 1796. John and Ann EVANS and William and Ruth PETTYJOHN to Davis MERIDYTH. Tract on Stacks Run, adjoining Jeremiah Clark survey. [This deed is unfinished here and has been overscored and canceled. Recorded in full below.] Recorded: OS 1:81 [incompletely].

12 September 1796. Charles LARSH, Nelson Co, KY, to John HUGHN [?], Fayette Co, PA. 400 acres on Papaw Creek, adjoining Thomas Pindall, John Carberry, Elias Brumegin. Patented 10 July 1789 to John Robins and

Charles Larsh, a moiety of which had previously been conveyed to Paul Larsh, to whom Charles Larsh is heir at law. Charles owns a moiety of the tract in fee simple and another as the heir of Paul Larsh. Consideration: £40. Signed: Chs Larsh. Witnesses: none. Acknowledged in court. No delivery shown. Recorded: OS 1:82.

22 September 1796. John and Ann EVANS and William and Ruth PETTE JOHN to Davis MARIDYTH. 400 acres on a branch of Stacks Run, adjoining Jeremiah Clark's survey on his settlement certificate. Consideration: £100, VA. Signed: John Evans, Ann Evans, W Petty John, Ruth PettyJohn. Witnesses: Thomas McKinley, John Doyle, Elihu Horton. No acknowledgement recorded. No delivery shown. Recorded OS 1:83-84.

10 October 1796. Nicholas HAWK, late of Randolph Co, to Matthias HITE, Monongalia Co, and Mark HAWK, Hardy Co. Power of attorney to recover any money or property due Hawk from James Bruff of Randolph Co, regarding land Bruff bought of Hawk on Clover Run, a drain of Cheat River. Signed: Nicholas [X] Hawk. Witness: J Williams. Recorded: OS 1:85.

10 April 1796. Thomas and Elizabeth PINDELL to Richard PRICE. 400 acres on Poppaw Creek, part of a patent to Pindell. No adjoiners named. Consideration: [£?$?]80, VA. Signed: Thomas [+] Pindell, Elizabeth Pindell. Witnesses: John Harris, John Dawson, William Cannedy, John Linch, WIlliam Jenkins, John Longwell, J Williams, Reuben Squires, Joseph [mark] Barker. No acknowledgement recorded. Del: to grantee, 2 November 1816. Recorded: OS 1:86-87.

20 August 1796. Edward and Sarah HAYMOND to James HICKMAN, Frederick Co. 100 acres on right fork of Wickwares Creek and Haw Run, part of the tract on which Haymond now lives, adjoining James Bulland. Consideration: £30. Signed: Edward Haymond, Sarah Haymond. Witnesses: John Haymond, William Hoult, Calder Haymond, Josiah Prickett. No acknowledgement recorded. No delivery shown. Recorded: OS 1:88.

8 August 1796. William PETTY JOHN to John NUZUM and Silas STEVENS. 100 acres on Monongahela River. No adjoiners named. Consideration: £140. Signed: Wm Petty John. Witnesses: John Dent, Nathan Springer, Empson Brownfield. No acknowledgement recorded. No delivery shown. Recorded: OS 1:89-90.

9 September 1796. John and Mary FLEMING to James HAMILTON, planter. 100 acres on Sandy Creek. No adjoiners named. Consideration: £100.9.7, VA. Signed: John Fleming, Mary [X] Fleming. Witnesses: James Clark,

Elias [mark] Leaton. No acknowledgement recorded. No delivery shown. Recorded: OS 1:90-92.
13 April 1796. Martin and Ann JUDY to Joseph BRANDON. 200 acres near Glade Run. No adjoiners named. Consideration: £75, PA. Signed: Martin Judy, Ann Judy ["both signed in dutch"]. Witnesses: Abam Brandon, Godfrey Wagener, Robert Woods. No acknowledgement recorded. No delivery shown. Recorded: OS 1:92-93.
14 November 1796. James and Margrett MORGAN to Elisha TRIMBLE, [illegible] Co, MD. Tract on Kings Cabbon Run, acreage and adjoiners not mentioned. Consideration: £100, VA. Signed: James Morgan, Margret Morgan. Witnesses: none. Acknowledged in court. No delivery shown. Recorded: OS 1:94- 95.
13 July 1796. Thomas and Margaret LAIDLEY to Jonathan DAVIS, Morgantown. Two adjoining lots [# not shown] in Morgantown, joining High Street, Pleasant Street, and Spruce Street. Also, 6 acres previously purchased by Laidley from Robert Parks, near the wagon road from Morgans Town to the house lately occupied by Thomas Pindell, now occupied by Moses Williams. Consideration: £150. Signed: Thos Laidley, Sarah Laidley. Witnesses: B Reeder, Nimrod Evans, M Hite. Acknowledged by Sarah Laidley, 6 August 1796, before B Reeder and H Triplett, justices. No delivery shown. Recorded: OS 1:95-96.
12 September 1796. David WADKINS, Southwestern Territory, to William WILLEY. 400 acres on Scotts Mill Run, adjoining John Harden and William Watkins. Patented to David 1 December 1784, and previously conveyed by him to Willey, the deed consumed by fire. Consideration: $5. Signed: David [mark] Wadkins. Witnesses: none. Acknowledged in court. Del: to Wm Willey, 12 May 1802. Recorded: OS 1:97.
12 September 1785. Zackquill and Drusilla MORGAN to George JACKSON, Harrison Co. Lot [# not shown] in Morgantown, adjoining the main street next to the river and lots of William Robeson, Thomas Laidley, Thomas Evans. Consideration: £4. Signed: Zackll Morgan, Drusilla Morgan. Witnesses: none. Acknowledged in court. No delivery shown. Recorded: OS 1:99. [page 98 omitted in the original numbering]
8 September 1796. John and Catherine COROTHERS to John CUNNINGHAM. 200 acres on Indian Creek, part of a 400-acre patent of 20 October 1786. Consideration: £[blank]00. Signed: John [X] Corothers, Catherine [X] Corothers. Witnesses: none. Acknowledged in court. Del: to Ezekiel Cunningham, 28 October 1811. Recorded:

13

OS 1:100.
9 April 1796. Martin and Ann JUDY to Godfrey WAGENER. 200 acres on Big Sandy, part of Judy's "bigg survey." No adjoiners named. Consideration: £60, VA. Signed: Martin Judy, Ann Judy. Witnesses: Alexr Brandon, Robert Woods, Joseph Brandon. No acknowledgement recorded. No delivery shown. Recorded: OS 1:101.

11 October 1796. Isaiah and Hannah HOSKINSON to James THOMPSON. Acreage not stated, adjoining heirs of Azariah Hoskinson, Isaac Van Camp, Allen Hall. Tract patented to Isaiah 15 October 1789. Consideration: £52. Signed: Isaiah Hoskinson, Hannah Hoskinson. Witnesses: none. Acknowledged in court. Del: to James Thompson Jr, 12 October 1802. Recorded: OS 1:102.

12 September 1796. John BURK, Kentucky, by Joseph TRICKETT, his attorney in fact, to Augustine WELLS. 133 acres on the west bank of Deckers Creek, adjoining George Hoskins, the moiety of a tract patented to Burk 20 April 1784. Consideration: £50. Signed: Joseph Trickett. Witnesses: none. No acknowledgement recorded. No delivery shown. Recorded: OS 1:103.

3 November 1796. David and Dorkas CUSHMAN, Kentucky, to Hedgman TRIPLETT. 400 acres patented to Thomas Cushman, including his 1770 settlement, on a drain of Little Sandy Creek, David being heir at law of Thomas. Adjoining David Frazee, Ephraim Frazee. Also, 327 acres patented to David Cushman, adjoining the Pennsylvania line. Also, 50 acres patented to Mary Cushman and conveyed by her to David Cushman, adjoining Ephraim Frazee. Total of 700 acres [sic]. Consideration: [£?$?]500, VA. Signed: David Cushman, Darkas Cushman. Witnesses: Samuel Hanway, Jona Davis, B Reeder, Wm McCleery. No acknowledgement recorded. Del: to H Triplett, 18 September 1801. Recorded: OS 1:104-106.

12 December 1796. David SCOTT to Philip SHIBLEY. 130 acres on a branch of Scotts Mill Run, part of a 250 acre patent. Adjoining Shibley's other land and James Denny. Consideration: £60. Signed: David Scott. Witnesses: none. Acknowledged in court. Del: to grantee, 18 May 1815. Recorded: OS 1:107.

12 December 1796. David ROBE to John FOURGUSSON [the name is variously spelled in the instrument]. Lot [number omitted] in Morgantown, adjoining lots of Thomas Wilson and William Petty John. Consideration: $100, VA. Signed: David Robe. Witnesses: none. Acknowledged in court. No delivery shown. Recorded: OS 1:108.

12 December 1796. David HANWAY, Hartford Co, MD, by Jesse HANWAY, his attorney in fact, to Michael

HYLDERBRAND. 382 acres on Little Creek, near Sandy Creek and Threefork Cree, adjoining John Harden. Patented to Hanway 3 September 1788. Consideration: £60. Signed: Jesse Hanway. Witnesses: none. Acknowledged in court. No delivery shown. Recorded: OS 1:109-110.

12 December 1796. William and Mary DAWSON, Kentucky, by Charles DAWSON, their attorney in fact, to Anthony AMMON. 50 acres adjoining Caleb Hurley, Samuel Everley. Part of a 225-acre patent. Consideration: £80. Signed: Charles [X] Dawson. Witnesses: none. Acknowledged in court. No delivery shown. Recorded: OS 1:111.

11 February 1793. Samuel HANWAY and Thomas and Sarah LAIDLEY to James THOMPSON. Lot [# not shown] in northwest corner of Morgan Town, adjoining Back Street and Front Street. Consideration: £12. Signed: Samuel Hanway, Thos Laidley, Sarah Laidley. Witnesses: none. Acknowledged in court. Del: to James Thompson, 12 October 1802. Recorded: OS 1:112.

12 December 1796. William and Mary DAWSON, Kaintuckey, by Charles DAWSON, their attorney in fact, to Caleb HURLEY. 50 acres, adjoining Anthony Ammons. Part of a 225-acre patent to William Dawson. Consideration: £80, VA. Signed: Chas Dawson. Witnesses: none. Acknowledged in court. Del: to Hurley. Recorded: OS 1:113.

12 December 1796. David HANWAY, Hartford Co, MD, by Jesse HANWAY, his attorney in fact, to John NEAXON. 392 acres on Sandy Creek, adjoining Edward Goodridge, Michael Hylder Brand, John Barry. Part of a 2000-acre patent to David Hanway. Consideration: £70. Signed: Jesse Hanway. Witnesses: none. Acknowledged in court. No delivery shown. Recorded: OS 1:114-115.

9 April 1795. Martin and Ann JUDY to John HARRUDER [Harreider? Harrcider?]. 6[4?8?]2 acres on east side of Sandy Creek, adjoining Russell Potter, John Judah's settlement survey and Joseph Brandon, on Little and Big Sandy Creeks. Consideration: £842, PA. Signed: Martin Judah, Ann Judah [both "signed in Dutch"]. Witnesses: Edward Jones, Russell Potter, Elihu Horton. No acknowledgement shown. Del: to Russell Potter, 12 March 1805. Recorded: OS 1:115-116.

14 June 1795. Adley and Margrett RAY to Isaac REED. 117½ acres adjoining John Summers, David Sayre, John Fillips, part of a 185½ acre tract Adley now lives on, patented 11 April 1793 to Richard [blank]. Consideration: £35, VA. Signed: Adley Rea, Margrett [mark] Rea. Witnesses: none. Acknowledged in court. No

delivery shown. Recorded: OS 1:117-118.

15 April 1796. Denune and Anne HOWARD to Luke HARMESON. 189 acres on one of the head branches of Scotts Mill Run, with reference to "beginning tree of William Haynes part of said tract." Part of a larger tract granted to Denune. Consideration: £30. Signed: Denune Howard, Ann Howard. Witnesses: none. Acknowledged in court. No delivery shown. Recorded: OS 1:119-120.

9 May 1796. Alexander BRANDON to Jacob PINDALL. 157 acres on the west side of Peter Cook's land on which he now lives, adjoining Thomas Hayton. Part of a 314-acre survey. Consideration: £100, VA. Signed: Alexander Brandon. Witnesses: Thos Chipps, Russell Potter, Joseph Brandon, Godfrey Wagener. No acknowledgement recorded. No delivery shown. Recorded: OS 1:121.

12 December 1796. Enoch and Charity JENKINS to Henry HAMILTON. 384 acres, adjoining Rees Wolf. Consideration: £400. Signed: Enoch Jenkins, Charity [+] Jenkins. Witnesses: none. Acknowledged in court. Del: to Henry Hamilton, 10 March 1802. Recorded: OS 1:122.

12 December 1796. John GELLESPIE, Fayette Co, PA, to William JENKINS. 355 acres on Indian Creek, formerly conveyed by Gellespie to Jenkins but the deed destroyed by fire in the clerk's office. Consideration: £177. Signed: John Gellespie. Witnesses: Philip Pearse, Samuel Crane, Nancy [X] Lynch, Richd Merrefield, William Tenehill, JH Williams. No acknowledgement recorded. No delivery shown. Recorded: OS 1:123.

13 November 1796. WILL of Joseph JOSEPH. Wife Jemima: 30 acres for life, plus Negro girl Joan. Son Eli: the 30 acres after Jemima's death, plus 105 acres of other land. Son-in-law John Simpler, 50 acres. Uriah Joseph [relationship not stated]: one great coat. Daughter Delilah Atkin: bell and pewter basen. Daughter Pethena Simpler: Negro girl Joan after Jemima's death. Executor: wife Jemima. Witnesses: Joshua Walls Senr, Joshua Walls Junr, Manlove Walls. No probate data. Recorded: OS 1:124. [Also recorded in Wills, 1:296.]

4 August 1796. William and Mary DAWSON, Washington Co, KY, to Charles DAWSON. Power of attorney to convey land heretofore sold by William and Mary to John Dawson. Signed: William [mark] Dawson, Mary [W] Dawson. Witnesses: Bendt Spalding, Joseph Seay. Certificate, 27 August 1796, from John Reed, clerk of Washington Co, KY. Recorded: OS 1:125.

13 January 1794. Thomas and Elisabeth JOHN to Fidelles FOSTER. 95 acres, 2 quarters, 34 poles,

adjoining Lewis Rodgers, Thomas Evans, Thomas John, and Lemuel John. Consideration: £100, VA. Signed: Thomas John, Elisabeth John. Witnesses: none. Acknowledged in court. Del: to Frank Brand, 2 January 1959. Recorded: OS 1:125-126.

27 October 1787. Reece WOOLF, Sussex Co, DE, yeoman, executor of the will of his son Francis Woolf (dated 8 May 1785 and proven in Sussex Co, DE), to his son Reece WOOLF Junr. Power of attorney to sell properties of Francis Woolf located in PA and VA. Signed: Reece Woolf. Witnesses: Henry Neill, Peter Marsh. Certificate of William Peiry, 27 October 1787, for witnesses, and of David Hall, prothonotary of Sussex Co, 27 October 1787. Recorded: OS 1:126-128.

15 December 1796. Jacob PRICKETT, Sr, by his attorney in fact James PRICKETT, both of the North West Territory, to James MORGAN. 120 acres on Pricketts Creek, adjoining Josiah Prickett, Joseph Heartley, Jacob Prickett Jr, Nancy Graham. Consideration: £100, VA. Signed: James Prickett. Witnesses: Nathan Springer, John Hoult, Colder Haymond. No acknowledgement recorded. No delivery shown. Recorded: OS 1:128-129.

10 May 1796. Robert RALSTON and James VANUSCEN [?], merchants, Philadelphia, PA, to William DEAKINS Junr and Francis DEAKINS, Prince Georges Co, MD. Bartholomew Terrison, merchant of Philadelphia, owned several tracts of land in Monongalia. At his bankruptcy, 1 April 1790, all of his property, debts and credits, both in and out of PA, were conveyed to the grantors to secure his debts. They convey 2000 acres on Cheet River below Dunker Bottom settlement, adjoining John Evans; 1000 acres adjoining Richard Claiborne's second entry; 2000 acres adjoining Richard Claiborne's third entry; and 2000 acres adjoining Claiborne's second entry and John Evans. This property was first conveyed to the Deakins on 15 August 1794 for $1400, the deed later burned in the clerk's office of Monongalia. The property is now reconveyed. Consideration: $1. Signed: Robt Ralston, James Vanuxen [?]. Witnesses: Thomas Biddle, Fras Munhall, G W Biddle. Receipt for $1. Certificate of Mathew Clarkson, Mayor of Philadelphia, 12 July 1796. Del: to J Hoy, 22 November 1800. Recorded: OS 1:130-131, 134-135 [132 and 133 are blank].

15 June 1796. William DEAKINS Junr, Montgomery Co, MD, to Thomas RINEHART. 350 acres, adjoining Jacob Ridenever, a tract surveyed for Francis and William Deakins, and Goff's tract. Consideration: £105, MD. Signed: Will Deakins Jur. Witnesses: Lloyd Beall, Thos

Corcoran. Receipt for £105. Acknowledgement of Jane, wife of William Deakins. Certificate of Upton Beall, Clerk of Montgomery Co, MD, 7 July 1796. No delivery shown. Recorded: OS 1:135-137.

15 June 1796. Francis DEAKINS and William DEAKINS Junr, Montgomery Co, MD, to Christian SHAFFER, Washington Co, MD. 186 acres adjoining William Wilds, part of a 908-acre survey. Consideration: £62, MD. Signed: Francis Deakins, Will Deakins Junr. Witnesses: Lloyd Beall, Thos Corcoran. Receipt for consideration money. Acknowledgement by Jane, wife of William Deakins. Certificate of Upton Beall, Clerk of Montgomery Co MD, 7 July 1796. Del: "to H.K. Town M.Y. W. G cty" [sic]. Recorded: September 1796, OS 1:137-139.

2 January 1795. Joseph (Sr) and Olley SEVERNS to Joseph SEVERNS the 2d. 118 acres on Little Sandy Creek, the same survey that Joseph 2d now lives on, adjoining James Dunwoody. Consideration: £5, VA. Signed: Joseph Severns, Olley [X] Severns. Witnesses: James Webster, Joseph Severns, Robert Conner. Proved by witnesses, February 1797. Del: to Moses Matheny, 25 February 1805. Recorded: OS 1:139-140.

13 February 1797. Daniel and Sarah SAYRE to Godfrey STONEMAN. 300 acres on a pre-emption survey adjoining Morgan Morgan Sr. Tract sold by Richard Merrifield to Sayre in May or June 1795. Consideration: £90. Signed: Daniel Sayre, Sarah Sayre. Witnesses: none. No acknowledgement recorded. No delivery shown. Recorded: OS 1:140-141.

2 December 1796. WILL of John CONNER. Wife [illegible in this copy; "Mary" in willbook]. Son Robert: 204 acres, farm tools. Daughter Elizabeth, daughter Grace Webster, son John, son James, daughter Sarah Trader, son William: cash. Executors: sons John (of Fayette Co, PA) and Robert. Witnesses: John McClain, Alexr Brandon, Jonathan Brandon. No probate data. Recorded: OS 1:142-143. [Also recorded in Wills, 1:292.]

17 November 1796. Ruben and Elenor SQUIRES to William ANDERSON, yeoman. 200 acres adjoining Jonathan Roberts. Part of a 400-acre tract sold by John Prickett to Ruben Squires. Consideration: £80, VA. Signed: Reuben Squires, Ellender [X] Squires. Witnesses: David Scott, James Scott. No acknowledgement recorded. No delivery shown. Recorded: OS 1:143-144.

13 February 1797. John and Elizabeth FERGUSON to Samuel NIXON. Half-lot in Morgantown [# not shown], purchased by Ferguson from John Wily and adjoining lot of Thomas Wilson. Consideration: $50, VA. Signed: John

Ferguson, Elizabeth Ferguson. Witnesses: none. Acknowledged in court. No delivery shown. Recorded: OS 1:145-146.

15 December 1796. Jacob (Jr) and Jemimah PRICKETT to James MORGAN. 53 acres, adjoining Nathan Springer. Part of a 28 June 1791 patent for 180 acres. Consideration: £40, VA. Signed: Jacob Prickett, Jemimah Prickett. Witnesses: Nathan Springer, John Hoult, Colder Haymond. No acknowledgement recorded. Del: to James Morgan, 10 March 1804. Recorded: OS 1:146-147.

11 October 1796. James and Linny DONALDSON to William NEIGHBOURS. 31 acres, 28 poles, part of a tract of 200 acres on which Donaldson now lives, adjoining John Fowler. Consideration: £23.7. Signed: James Donaldson, Linney Donaldson. Witnesses: James Robison, John Wimp, Jacob Smith. No acknowledgement recorded. No delivery shown. Recorded: OS 1:147.

21 September 1796. John P DUVALL, Kentucky, to William DEEKINS, Gentleman, Maryland. 400 acres on the run above Pringles Run, on west side of Cheat River, a survey of 8 April 1785 for Duvall, assignee of Basil Brown. Consideration: $200. Signed: John P Duvall. Witnesses: John Evans, Dudley Evans, John Fairfax, B Reeder. No acknowledgement recorded. No delivery shown. Recorded: OS 1:148.

8 August 1796. George and Elizabeth BAKER to John DOYLE. Lot #83 in Morgan Town. Consideration: £4. Signed: George Baker, Elizabeth Baker. Witnesses: F Warman, Robt Hawthorne, Nichlas Madera. No acknowledgement recorded. No delivery shown. Recorded: OS 1:149.

13 February 1797. David HANWAY, Hartford Co, MD, by Jesse HANWAY, his attorney in fact, to Joseph SOUTHWERTH. 350 acres, adjoining Samuel Cobb, part of a 2000-acre patent of 3 September 1788. Consideration: £100. Signed: Jesse Hanway. Witnesses: none. Acknowledged in court. No delivery shown. Recorded: OS 1:150.

13 February 1797. John and Elizabeth FERGUSON to Henry FESLAR. Half lot in Morgan Town, purchased by John Ferguson from John Wiley, adjoining half lot sold to Samuel Nixon. Consideration: $50, VA. Signed: John Ferguson, Elizabeth Ferguson. Witnesses: Acknowledged in court. No delivery shown. Recorded: OS 1:151-152.

7 November 1796. Daniel and Elizabeth MARTIN, Harrison Co, to James GEFFS. 271 acres on a lefthand drain of Buffalo Creek, part of a land office preemption warrant of 9 April 1785. No adjoiners named.

Consideration: £81. Signed: Daniel Martin, Elizabeth Martin. Witnesses: teste John Evans. No acknowledgement recorded. No delivery shown. Recorded: OS 1:152-153.

13 February 1797. Jacob and Catherine SCOTT to Joseph DONLAP. 161½ acres on Scotts Run. Patented to Scott 5 July 1791, "perhaps enterlocking with" the survey Scott lives on. Consideration: £175, VA. Signed: Jacob Scott, Catherine Scott. Witnesses: teste John Evans. No acknowledgement recorded. No delivery shown. Recorded: OS 1:153-154.

13 February 1797. Daniel and Sarah SAYRE to John P PLEASANTS, Robt PLEASANTS, and Benjamin REEDER. 985 acres on the west side, including the mouth of Bingamon Creek. Patented to Daniel Sayre (assignee of John Gray) 14 October 1796. Consideration: $2400, VA. Signed: Daniel Sayre, Sarah Sayre. Witnesses: none. Acknowledged in court. No delivery shown. Recorded: OS 1:155-157.

26 September 1796. Joseph and Mary BATTEN to Thomas BATTEN Junr. Thomas Batten of Springhill Twp, Fayette Co, PA, willed 95 acres to his son Joseph, adjoining Martin Harden, and James Neel, part of a tract called Battens Grove. Thomas Batten Jr [illegible words] a patent for the said tract. Joseph conveys all his interest in the land to Thomas Jr. Consideration: 5 shillings. Signed: Joseph [B] Batten, Mary [0] Batten. Witnesses: William Snodgrass, Henry Batten, Charles Snodgrass. No acknowledgement recorded. No delivery shown. Recorded: OS 1:157.

10 April 1797. William and Silance LAYCOCK to Gabriel WILSON and Jesse WILSON. 100 acres by survey, part of the Nehemiah Harper tract. No adjoiners or place names mentioned. Consideration: £200. Signed: William Laycock, Silance [mark] Laycock. Witnesses: none. Acknowledged in court. No delivery shown. Recorded: OS 1:158.

4 April 1796. John and Rachel ALDREDGE to Amos WORKMAN, Algania Co, MD. 100 acres, adjoining the south side of lands surveyed for Richard Conner. Consideration: £50. Signed: John Aldredge, Rachel [mark] Aldredge. Witnesses: Nathan Metheny, John Fleming, John Floyd. No acknowledgement recorded. Del: "to him", 2 April 1811. Recorded: OS 1:159.

14 November 1796. Aaron MILLS and James MILLS Junr, both of Burbon Co, KY, to Samuel WILSON, Fyette Co, PA. 156 acres on right fork of Maricals Run. No adjoiners named. Consideration: £40, PA. Signed: Aaron Mills, James Mills Junr. Witnesses: teste John Evans. No delivery shown. Recorded: OS 1:160.

[blank] 1796. Jacob and Hannah JACOBS to Henry SHAVER. 40 acres on Deckers Creek, part of a 250-acre patent of [date blank]. No adjoiners named. Consideration: £80. Signed: Jacob Jacobs, Hannah Jacobs. Witnesses: none. Acknowledged in court. Del: to Henry Shaver, 3 September 1806. Recorded: OS 1:161.

9 May 1797. James GELLESPIE [residence not stated] to John GELLESPIE, Fayette Co, PA. Power of attorney to sell land put into his hands. Signed: James Gillespie. Witnesses: Moses Williams, Isaiah Hoskinson, Joseph Downing. Recorded: OS 1:162.

9 January 1797. Jacob and Elizabeth NOOSE to John WILSON [also WHITSON in text], Fyette Co, PA. 732 acres on Sandy Creek, at the mouth of Hazel Run, adjoining Charles Donaldson. Patented 11 September 1789. Consideration: £160. Signed: Elizabeth [mark] Noose [Jacob's signature not recorded.] Witnesses: James Daugherty, Wm Tingle, Alexr Hawthorn, Frederick Gebler. Acknowledged by Elizabeth Noose, 9 January 1797, before Wm Tingle and John Dent. No delivery shown. Recorded: OS 1:162-163.

8 August 1796. William and Hannah MORGAN to David MORGAN. 100 acres on west side of Cheat River, opposite Dunkard Bottom, part of a settlement right assignee James Morgan to the said William [sic]. Consideration: £5, VA. Signed: William Morgan, Hannah Morgan. Witnesses: none. Acknowledged in court. No delivery shown. Recorded: OS 1:164.

10 August 1786. Andrew and Elizabeth DAVISSON to William HAYMOND, all of Harrison Co. 330 acres near the east side of the Monongalia River, adjoining Tegal Trader's heirs and John Vandroof, and including settlement made in 1774. Consideration: £100. Signed: Andrew Davisson, Elizabeth Davisson. Witnesses: none. Acknowledged in court. No delivery shown. Recorded: OS 1:165-166.

4 December 1793. WILL of John FERGUSON. Daughter Catherine, wife of William Lanham: 5s. Daughter Ann Skiner, wife of Joseph Wilson: 100 acres, lower end of plantation between Deckers and Aarons Creeks. Daughter Rebeca, wife of William Wilson: 5s. Daughter Susanna, wife of Fauquire McCrea: 5s. Daughter Lydia, wife of Zephaniah Bell: 5s. Son John and daughter Margaret: all other lands, upper end of the plantation. Wife Barshaba: full use of land during her lifetime. Executor: wife Barshaba. Signed: John Forguson. Witnesses: Daniel Dugan, James Thompson Junr, Richard Lee, Peregrine Foster. No probate data. Recorded: OS 1:167-168. [Also

recorded in Wills, 1:293-294]
[blank] November 1796. Balser and Nancy KRETZER to Jacob ZINN. 200 acres on both sides of Lick Creek and Three Fork Creek. No adjoiners named. Consideration: £55. Signed: Balser Kretzer [Nancy does not sign]. Witnesses: none. Acknowledged in court. No delivery shown. Recorded: OS 1:169.

10 June 1797. William WOOD, merchant, Philadelphia, PA, to Timothy SMITH, Fayette Co, PA. Power of attorney to deliver to David Dunham a deed and title papers for 900 acres in the Genesee country of New York state. Dunham to pay $850 for the land. Signed: William Wood. Witnesses: Wm McCleery, Hugh McNeely, John Evans. Recorded: OS 1:170.

13 November 1796. Joseph and Margret TRICKETT to Jacob NOOS. 39 acres, part of a larger tract of 89 acres, adjoining Noos' other land, David Crool, and John Standley. Consideration: £50. Signed: Joseph Trickett, Margrett Trickett. Witnesses: none. Acknowledged in court. Del: to J Nuess, 27 July 1805. Recorded: OS 1:171-172.

10 August 1786. Andrew and Elizabeth DAVIDSON to William HAYMOND, all of Harrison Co. Incomplete copy of deed recorded OS 1:165-166. Recorded: OS 1:172.

13 September 1790. William and Elizabeth ROARK to Henry AMOS. 200 acres on Indian Creek, part of a 400-acre survey of 5 September 1785. No adjoiners named. Consideration: £60. Signed: William Roark, Elizabeth [mark] Roark. Witnesses: none. Acknowledged in court. No delivery shown. Recorded: OS 1:173.

14 November 1796. John and Elizabeth BERRY to Lewis WOLFF, Frederick Co, MD. 100 acres on Little Sandy. No adjoiners named. Consideration: £37.10, VA. Signed: John [mark] Berry, Elizabeth [mark] Berry. Witnesses: none. Acknowledged in court. No delivery shown. Recorded: OS 1:173-174.

10 November 1796. Arthur and Sarah TRADER to John McCLANE. 200 acres on Sandy Creek, adjoining James Dunwoodie. Consideration: £120, VA. Signed: Arthur [mark] Trader, Sarah [X] Trader. Witnesses: Patrick Magraw, Jonath Brandon, Russel Potter. No acknowledgement recorded. No delivery shown. Recorded: OS 1:174.

8 November 1796. Robert MINNIS to Benjamin REEDER. 400 acres on Deckers Creek, adjoining Richard Powell, Jonathan Rees, Richard Cain. Surveyed 16 August 1785, patented to Minnis as assignee of Joseph Cox, 2 December 1791. Consideration: £300, VA. Signed: Robt Minnis.

Witnesses: J H Williams, Nimrod Evans, John C Williams. No acknowledgement recorded. Del: to H Reeder, 14 February 1807. Recorded: OS 1:175-176.

6 August 1794. James and Rachael POLLICK and John and Agnes POLLICK, all of Washington Co, PA, to John WADE. 52 acres adjoining Hezekiah Wade and James Pollick. Consideration: £20, VA. Signed: James Pollick, Rachael [X] Pollick, John Pollick, Agness [mark] Pollick. Witnesses: John Collins, George Wade Senr, Richd Wade, Thomas Wade. No acknowledgement recorded. Del: to John Wade, 23 June 1801. Recorded: OS 1:176-177.

10 October 1796. Elijah and Hannah PILES to William WINDSOR. 50 acres on Flagge Meadow Run, adjoining Elijah Piles, Phillip Pindell. Patented to Elijah 5 June 1787. Consideration: [blank]. Signed: Elijah [X] Piles, Hannah [X] Piles. Witnesses: none. Acknowledged in court. No delivery shown. Recorded: OS 1:177-178.

10 January 1797. Isaac and Nancy LEMASTERS to John GRAYHAM. 76 acres on Indian Creek, patented to Aaron Henry 10 July 1787, and conveyed by him to Richard Lemasters 12 May 1792, and conveyed by him to Isaac Lemasters [date is blank]. Consideration: £60. Signed: Isaac Lemasters, Ann [X] Lemasters. Witnesses: none. Acknowledged in court. No delivery shown. Recorded: OS 1:178-179.

12 April 1796. Joseph STEWART to Patrick McGREW. 100 acres on Sandy Creek, adjoining John Robenet, surveyed 25 September 1784. Consideration: £45, VA. Signed: Joseph Stewart. Witnesses: Augustin Wolf, Jonath Brandon Sr, Wm Biggs. No acknowledgement recorded. No delivery shown. Recorded: OS 1:180.

8 August 1796. William PETTY JOHN to John NUZUM and Silas STEPHENS. 100 acres on and near the Monongahela River. No adjoiners named. Consideration: £140. Signed: William PettyJohn. Witnesses: John Dent, Nathan Springer, Empson Brumfield. No acknowledgement recorded. No delivery shown. Recorded: OS 1:181.

14 March 1797. Rees and Sarah WOOLF, heir and executor of Francis WOOLF, deceased, to Thomas McGEE. 134 3/4 acres on a drain of Three Forks Creek, adjoining Benjamin Brain. Part of a tract patented to Francis Woolf, 14 October 1787. Consideration: £53. Signed: Reece Woolf, Sarah Woolf. Witnesses: none. Acknowledged in court. No delivery shown. Recorded: OS 1:182.

2 September 1796. WILL of Christopher GARLOW. Son John: horse. Daughter Christine: £10. My [blank; also blank in willbook copy] Mary Garlow: £10. Youngest

daughter Hannah under 18. Four sons, John, Andrew, Joseph, David: land, to be equally divided. Five daughters, Magdalen Partmus, Ann Partmus, Sarah Garlow, Elizabeth Garlow, Lavina [?] Garlow, Hanah Garlow: personalty, to be divided at a ratio equal to one-half of each son's share. Daughters to be paid at or upon 27 October 1814. Executors: wife Ann and son John. Signed: Christopher Garlow. Witnesses: Adam Sriver, John [I] Sriver, William Holson. Recorded: OS 1:183-184. No probate data. [Also recorded in Wills 1:294-295.]

15 April 1796. Denune and Ann HOWARD to James BUCHANNAN. 63 acres on a head branch of Scotts Mill Run, adjoining Luke Harmeson. Patented to Howard. Consideration: £18.18, VA. Signed: Denune Howard, Ann Howard. Witnesses: none. Acknowledged in court. No delivery shown. Recorded: OS 1:184-185.

4 May 1796. WILL of Hugh STEPHENSON. Wife Peggy: all property, including note on Josiah Jenkins. Son John, son James, daughter Liddy, daughter [blank], son William, daughter Janny: each "cut of" with one shilling. Signed: Hugh [mark] Stephenson. Witnesses: Samuel Hanna, Nancy [mark] Hanna, Elizabeth [mark] Draga. No probate data. Recorded: OS 1:186-187. [Also recorded in Wills 1:299-300]

15 April 1796. Denune and Ann HOWARD to William HOGUE. 151 acres, part of a larger tract on a head branch of Scotts Mill Run, adjoining William Dawson's old place, Luke Harmeson and James Buchannan. Consideration: £30, VA. Signed: Denune Howard, Anne Howard. Witnesses: none. Acknowledged in court. No delivery shown. Recorded: OS 1:187-188.

10 August 1796. Prudence POWELL (widow of Richard), Moses POWELL, Aron POWELL, and William and Elizabeth LINSAY, heirs of Richard POWELL, deceased, to Benjamin REEDER. 200 acres adjoining William Haymond and a survey for Richard Powell's heirs. Surveyed 16 July 1785 and patented 31 July 1788. Consideration: £100. Signed: Prudence [+] Powell, Moses Powell, Aaron Powell, William Linzia, Elizabeth [^] Linzia. Witnesses: Alexr Hawthorn, George Zinn, Jacob Zinn. No acknowledgement recorded. No delivery shown. Recorded: OS 1:189-190.

13 April 1791. Thomas (Esqr) and Judith PINDELL to James WEAVER, yeoman. 106 acres, 44 poles, adjoining William Robe and Ferguson. No place names mentioned. Consideration: £106.4, VA. Signed: Thos Pindell, Judith Pindell. Witnesses: none. Acknowledged in court. No delivery shown. Recorded: OS 1:190-191.

[blank] November 1796. Robert MINNIS to Mattias

DAVIS. 200 acres on dividing ridge between the two Popas about 3 miles from the Big Spring. No adjoiners named. Part of a 400-acre patent of 3 September 1788. Consideration: $200, VA. Signed: Robt Minnis. Witnesses: M Hite, J Williams, James Post [or Port?]. No acknowledgement recorded. No delivery shown. Recorded: OS 1:192-193.

19 March 1796. Charles and Mary DONALDSON to John EVANS. 100 acres, adjoining 200 acres laid off for Jacob Smith and Jacob Noos, adjoining east side of the road, part of the Blackburn Glade tract. Consideration: £15, VA. Signed: Charles [mark] Donaldson. [Mary does not sign.] Witnesses: Richard Lee, John Downer, Elizabeth [+] Sweleven. No acknowledgement recorded. No delivery shown. Recorded: OS 1:194.

6 September 1796. Jehu and Elizabeth LITTLE, Kentucky, and Hugh VERDIN, Washington Co, North West Territory, to John EVANS Jr and Benjamin REEDER. Moiety of a tract on upper side of Papaugh Creek and the Monongahela River, whereon Adonijah Little lived at the time of his death. Interest of Jehu as an heir at law of Adonijah and of Hugh by marriage settlement. Consideration: £60. Signed: Jehu Little, Elizabeth [mark] Little. [Verdin does not sign; see below.] Witnesses: Saml Wells, H Churchill. Acknowledged by Elizabeth Little, 6 September 1796, in Jefferson Co, KY, before Saml Wells and Henry Churchill. Certificate of Stephen Ormsby, clerk of Jefferson Co, KY. No delivery shown. Recorded: OS 1:195-196.

13 April 1790. Samuel HANWAY to Levi SPRINGER. 348 acres patented to Hanway 16 December 1784. No adjoiners or place names mentioned. Consideration: 5s. Signed: Samuel Hanway. Witnesses: none. Acknowledged in court. Del: to Peter Miller, 28 December 1803. Recorded: OS 1:197.

27 December 1796. Hugh and Keziah VERDIN to John EVANS Junr and Benjamin REEDER. Undivided interest in lands descended to Keziah from her father Adonijah Little, deceased, including the mouth of Papaw Creek and adjoining Henry Batton, James Longwell, Nicholas Wood. Consideration: £75, VA. Signed: Hugh [mark] Verdin, Keziah Verdin. Witnesses: J H Williams, Hugh McNeely, Fleming Jones; Witnesses for Keziah Verdin: Stephen Morgan, William Hoult, Benjamin Hayes. Acknowledged by Mary Longwell, Elizabeth Batton, Kesiah Verdin, 3 April 1797, before John Dent and Dudley Evans. No delivery shown. Recorded: OS 1:198-200.

9 January 1797. Abraham FRANKS, Nicholas and Mary

HELMICK, Fayette Co, PA, to Richard and Jesse BUSSEY. 308 acres adjoining the PA line, sold by James and Rachael Potterll [?] to Franks and Helmick, 6 August 1796. No adjoiners named. Consideration: £166, VA. Signed: Abraham [A] Franks, Nichlas Helmick, Mary [mark] Helmick. Witnesses: none. Acknowledged in court. No delivery shown. Recorded: OS 1:201-202.

[blank] February 1796. Arthur and Sarah TRADER to Henry MILLER and James MILLER, heirs of Andrew MILLER, deceased, of Cumberland Co, PA. 200 acres on Little Sandy Creek, at the east end of the survey Trader formerly lived on, now sold to John McClain. Consideration: £22.10. Signed: Arthor Trader, Sarah Trader. Witnesses: John Runyon, James Webster, John Connor, Jonath Brandon, Patrick Magrew. No acknowledgement recorded. No delivery shown. Recorded: OS 1: 203-204.

9 June 1794. John BURK by Joseph TRICKETT, his attorney in fact, to George HOSKINS. 130 acres on south side of Deckers Creek, adjoining heirs of Godfrey Goosman. Granted to Burk 20 April 1784. Consideration: £30. Signed: Joseph Trickett. Witnesses: none. Acknowledged in court. No delivery shown. Recorded: OS 1:204-205.

9 August 1796. James and Catherine JOHNSTON to John W DEAN. 333 acres on Wests Run, including Johnston's 1775 settlement, adjoining Elijah Burris, David Scott, Jesse Martin, Samuel Hanway. Surveyed 20 September 1788. Consideration: £100, VA. Signed: James Johnston, Caty Johnston. Witnesses: none. Acknowledged in court. No delivery shown. Recorded: OS 1:205-206.

26 July 1796. Lewis and Eliz [sic] ROGERS, North West Territory, to James JENKINS. 400 acres on Cheat River, including Lewis' 1772 settlement, adjoining James Stafford, John Peirpoint, and Sugar Camp Run. Patented 1 May 1784. Consideration: £425, KY. Signed: Lewis Rogers, Eliz Rogers. Witnesses: Charles Gallagher, Edwd Gallagher, F Taylor. Acknowledged by Elizabeth Rogers, 25 [sic] July 1796, in Mason Co, KY, before John Wilson and Thos Sloe. Certificate of T Marshall, Clerk of Mason Co, 4 March 1797. No delivery shown. Recorded: OS 1:207-209.

27 August 1796. Hugh and Hannah PHELPS, Harrison Co, to Ezekiel BARNS. 100 acres on the east side of Cheat River, adjoining the PA line. No adjoiners named. Same land formerly conveyed by Phelps to Barns but the deed was destroyed by fire. Consideration: £100. Signed: Hugh Phelps, Hannah Phelps. Witnesses: John Dent, John

Evans Junr, J Williams. Acknowledged by Hannah Phelps, 27 April 1796, before Benjamin Reeder and John Dent. Recorded: OS 1: 209-211.

4 November 1796. Articles of agreement between Aaron TICHENOR and James TICHENOR. James sells to Aaron a mare and cow; beds, bedclothes, bedsteads and furniture; pot mettle, pewter and other household furnishings, to the value of £38.8, plus various fabrics to the value of £37.19.1. Consideration: for value received. Signed: James Tichonor. Witnesses: Joel Smith, John Courtney. Recorded: OS 1:211.

10 October 1796. James and Mary ANDERSON, Fayette Co, PA, to Andrew MILLER, Randolph Co. Acreage not stated, on Sandy Creek, near falls of Swamp Mill Run. Consideration: £200, PA. Signed: James Anderson, Mary Anderson. Witnesses: none. Acknowledged in court. No delivery shown. Recorded: OS 1:211-213.

19 December 1794. Silvester FULLER, merchant, to Asher ROBINSON [also ROBBENS/ROBBINS in the body of the instrument], Esqr, both of Providence Town and Co, Providence Plantations. 2500 acres on a lefthand drain of Buffelow Creek, adjoining west side of Henry Banks' 33rd entry. No other adjoiners mentioned. Surveyed 17 May 1785, patented to Banks 28 [blank] 1787, and conveyed to Fuller 6 October 1787 by Alexander Boyd, attorney for Banks. Consideration: 750 Spanish mill dollars. Signed: Sylvester Fuller. Witnesses: Anthony Dyer, Jacob Westcott, Wm Tylor. Acknowledged by Affie B Fuller, wife of Sylvester, 19 December 1794. Certificate of Arthur Fenner, Governor of Rhode Island and Providence Plantations, 13 January 1795. No delivery shown. Recorded: OS 1:213-215.

2 November 1796. Joseph and Mary HUNT, Bedford Co, PA, to Charless [sic] ROSE. 299 acres on Wolf Pen Ridge, patented to Joseph Hunt 11 September 1787. No adjoiners mentioned. Consideration: £100, PA. Signed: Joseph Hunt, Mary Hunt. Witnesses: Barnard Mann, Samuel Graves. Receipt for £100, witnessed by Andrew Mann, 29 November 1796. Certificate of John Anderson, prothonotary of Bedford Co, PA, 1 December 1796. No delivery shown. Recorded: OS 1:216-216½.

12 April 1796. Joseph and Jamima STEWART [also SWART in body of instrument] to Augustine WOOL [also WOLF in body of instrument]. 90 acres on Little Sandy Creek, half a mile from the mouth of Beaver Creek, part of a tract granted to John Simpson. No adjoiners named. Consideration: £[blank], VA. Signed: Joseph Stewart, Jamima [X] Stewart. Witnesses: Patrick Megrew, Jona

Brandon, Wm Biggs. No acknowledgement recorded. No delivery shown. Recorded: OS 1:216½-217.

12 March 1790. Francis DEKENS and William DEAKENS Junr, Montgomery Co, MD, to Charles WALLACE, Anopolas City, MD, Joshua JOHNSTON, London, England, and John MINOR, Anopalia City, MD. 8 tracts in Monongalia (only 7 described), including 897 acres on Cheat River, surveyed 15 July 1784; 6000 acres on Snowy Glades Creek, surveyed 10 May 1788; 2080 acres, no location, surveyed 25 June 1786; 670 acres on east side of Cheat near the Big Island, surveyed 24 September 1786; 723 acres, no location, surveyed 29 April 1788; 1000 acres adjoining Limestone Hill and Cheat River, surveyed 17 May 1784; 1696 acres in the same location, surveyed the same date [noting that the 2 latter tracts will contain in full 3107 acres]. One undivided third share to each grantee. Consideration: £3000, MD. Signed: Francis Deakens, William Deakens Junr. Witnesses: Richard Thompson, Bernard ONiall, Laurance ONeill, Aens Campbell. Receipt for £3000. Acknowledged by William and Jean Deakins, 12 March 1790 before Richard Thompson. Acknowledged by Francis and Eleanor Deakins, 30 March 1790 before Laurance O'Neill and Aens Campbell. Certificate of Brooke Beall, Clerk of Montgomery Co, MD, 17 April 1796. No delivery shown. Recorded: OS 1:218-221.

19 November 1796. David DAVIS to Richard DAVIS [no addresses stated]. 100 acres in Loudoun Co, called Devers [?] Lot, adjoining the stone house that Richard Davis is now [renting?], plus 2000 acres in Monongalia Co, purchased from William Hebburn. Consideration: 5 shillings. Signed: David Davis. Witnesses: M Harrison Junr, A Russell, Lewes Elsey. Proved by witnesses, 9 January 1797, in Loudoun Co. Certificate of Chs Bens, Clerk of Loudoun Co. No delivery shown. Recorded: OS 1:221-222.

15 May 1797. James and Sarah BUCKHANAN to Davis SHOCKLEY. 36 3/4 acres on a drain of Dunker Creek, part of a 400-acre tract adjoining heirs of Joseph Wade, Luke Harmison, and the great road leading from Scotts Mill up Dunker Creek. Consideration: £60.10, VA. Signed: James Buchanon, Sarah [X] Buchanon. Witnesses: Alexr Hawthorn, Alexr Beatty, Thos McKinley. No acknowledgement recorded. No delivery shown. Recorded: OS 1:222-223.

21 December 1796. Ruth and John PETER to Mary BEALL, all of Frederick Co MD. Undivided moiety or half interest in 1000 acres in Sandy Creek Glades, on Sand Creek, between the lands of Thomas Cheney and John Morris. Patented 7 August 1787 by William Hilton and

John Orr. Also, moiety of land included in a resurvey of the same tract. Consideration: 5s. Signed: Ruthey Peter, John Peter. Witnesses: George Murdock, George Baer Jr. Acknowledged in Frederick Co, MD, before Murdock and Baer. Certificate of William Ritchie, clerk of Frederick Co, MD, 1 March 1797. No delivery shown. Recorded: OS 1 224-225.

12 June 1797. Jeremiah and Lettice TANNEHILL to James CLARK. 200 acres on Sandy Creek and Laurel Run, adjoining Jeremiah Tannehill. Consideration: $200, VA. Not signed. No witnesses, acknowledgement or delivery shown. Recorded: OS 1:226.

27 June 1797. Thomas POWELL, Bourbon Co, KY, to Blemus [?] HEYDON, Montgomery Co, KY. Power of attorney to sell land in Monongalia where Powell formerly lived. Signed: Thomas [T] Powell. Witnesses: none. Acknowledged 27 June 1797, Montgomery Co, KY, before William Robinson and William Caldwell. Nancy Powell, wife of Thomas, relinquishes dower in said lands. Certificate of Micajah Harrison, Clerk of Montgomery Co, KY. Recorded: OS 1:227-228.

13 June 1797. Jesse and Hannah MARTIN to William SLEDGER, Allegany Co, MD. 170 acres on Scotts Mill Run and Dunker Creek, adjoining John Golding and Jesse Martin. Part of a tract granted to Elizabeth Poppeno, assignee of William Robeson, 4 April 1792. Consideration: $85. Signed: Jesse Martin, Hannah Martin. Witnesses: Wm Tingle, George Hite, J Williams. No acknowledgement recorded. No delivery shown. Recorded: OS 1:228.

10 April 1797. Jacob and Elizabeth NOOS to John DOYLE. Lot #83 on High Street in Morgan Town, including 1.6d quitrent per annum payable to Zack Morgan, his heirs or assigns forever. Consideration: £50. Signed: "signed in Dutch," Elizabeth [X] Noos. Witnesses: none. Acknowledged in court. Recorded: OS 1:229.

15 June 1797. Jeremiah and Mary SIMPSON, Borbon Co, KY, to James Edmonston BEALL and James C BEALL (son of Jeremiah). 389½ acres on Cheat River and Buffaloe Run, part of a 395-acre tract patented [blank], adjoining Andrew Ramsey. [illegible]¼ acres reserved, having been already sold to Benjamin Reeder. Consideration: £200, VA. Signed: Jeremiah Simpson. Witnesses: J Williams, Hugh McNeely, John Dent, Asa Dudley. No acknowledgement recorded. Del: to Jas E Beall, 10 February 1807. Recorded: OS 1:230-231.

11 April 1797. Elizabeth POPPENO, by James POPPENO, her attorney in fact, to Jesse MARTIN. 500 acres on

Scotts Mill Run and Dol Snyder's Run. No adjoiners named. Refers to power of attorney dated 17 August 1796. Consideration: [blank]. Signed: James Poppeno. Witnesses: none. Acknowledged in court. No delivery shown. Recorded: OS 1:232-233.

1 January 1797. WILL of Job SIMS. Wife Sarah: all property real and personal. Executors: wife Sarah and her brother James Weaver. Signed: Job [mark] Sims. Witnesses: Jas Hamilton, Rees Hastings, Stephen McDade. Recorded: OS 1:233. No probate data. [Also recorded in Wills, 1:299]

[blank] June 1787. Benjamin SUTTON to Jacob NOOS. Lots #81, 82, and 83 in Morgan Town. Includes 4.6d quit rent per annum to Zackll Morgan, his heirs and assigns forever. Consideration: [blank]. Signed: Benjamin Sutton. Witnesses: John Evans, William Jolliff, John Davis. No acknowledgement recorded. No delivery shown. Recorded: OS 1:234.

22 August 1796. Rapheal and Margarett WATHEN, Randolph Co, to John CLARK, Montgomery Co, MD. 150 acres on Cheat River, 2 miles above Dunker Bottom, adjoining Wildie Taylor and William Morgan. Part of a 500-acre survey of Taylor's, conveyed by him to Wathen. Consideration: £45, VA. Signed: Raphael Wathin, Margarett Wathin. Witnesses: none. Acknowledged in court. Del: to J Clark, 24 April 1801. Recorded: OS 1:235-236.

19 November 1796. Joel and Margarett SMITH to John THOMPSON. 150 acres on Robinsons Run, adjoining Joel Smith, Boils [?] Run. Part of a 20 September 1785 patent to William Smith, bequeathed by him to Joel Smith in his last testament. Consideration: £45, VA. Signed: Joel Smith, Margarett [mark] Smith. Witnesses: Jona Davis, B Reeder, Nathan Hall. Acknowledged by Margarett Smith, 19 November 1796, before B Reeder, Jona Davis. Del: to J Thompson, 25 May 1802. Recorded: OS 1:236-237.

10 September 1796. Jonas and Susannah HOGMIRE, Washington Co, MD, to Francis and William DEAKINS, Montgomery Co, MD. 202 acres between Big and Little Sandy Creeks, adjoining John Conner and lands surveyed for Francis and William Deakins. Surveyed 10 May 1785 on Land Office preemption warrant. Consideration: £50, MD. Signed: Jonas Hogmire, Susannah Hogmire. Witnesses: I Taylor, Jacob Schnebly. Receipt for £50. Certificate of Elie Williams, Clerk of Washington Co, MD. Del: to J Hay, 22 November 1810. Recorded: OS 1:238-240.

19 June 1797. Charles and Mary MARTIN to William MARTIN. 400 acres on Buffalow Creek, no adjoiners named.

Patented to Charles Martin 16 December 1783 as assignee of Benjn Goodwin's settlement right. Consideration: £1, VA. Signed: Charles Martin, Mary Martin. Witnesses: Wm Tingle, David Scott, John Dent, Jas Scott. No acknowledgement recorded. Del: to Norman Randall, per order William Martin, 16 May 1805. Recorded: OS 1:240-241.

12 June 1797. James and Margaret MORRIS to William VEACH. 100 acres on Scotts Mill Run, the lower end of a tract purchased from William Dawson Senior. Consideration: £100, VA. Signed: James Morris, Margrett [M] Morris. Witnesses: none. Acknowledged in court. Del: to Wm Veatch, 6 November 1800. Recorded: OS 1:242.

7 August 1797. Alexander and Catherine McINTIRE to Cornelius VANHORN, Allegheny Co, PA. Lot in Morgantown [# not shown] adjoining the courthouse lot. Consideration: £500, PA, "the said sum being in lieu as mentioned for a tract of land Conveyed by the said Cornelius Vanhorn Catherine and [?] Vanhorn McIntire daughter of the said Alexr McIntire" [text appears to be defective]. Signed: Alexr McIntire, Catharine McIntire. Witnesses: [illegible] Davison, Thos Vanhorn, [torn] Huffragt [?]. No acknowledgement recorded. No delivery shown. Recorded: OS 1:243.

15 October 1796. Joseph and Sarah FRIEND, Allegania Co, MD, to Moses ROYSE. 100 acres on Buffalow Run, a drain on the west side of Cheat River. No adjoiners named. Part of a survey of the late John Green, patented to him 1 September 1783 and conveyed to Joseph and Sarah Friend, heirs of the said John Green, by order of Monongalia County court. Consideration: £60, VA. Signed: Joseph Friend. Witnesses: Thos Button, Thos Smoot, David Phillips. No acknowledgement recorded. No delivery shown. Recorded: OS 1:244.

12 June 1797. James HAMILTON to Jonathan DAVIS and Samuel TOPLIF, 100 acres on Big Sandy Creek, opposite the big falls, adjoining James Clark. Part of a larger tract patented to William Hamilton and left by his will to his oldest daughter Mary, assigned by her to James Hamilton. Consideration: £100, VA. Signed: James [JH] Hamilton. Witnesses: none. Acknowledged in court. No delivery shown. Recorded: OS 1:245-246.

12 June 1797. Samuel and Sarah BOWEN, Fayette Co, PA, to Asa HALL. 228 acres on Monongahela River, adjoining Asa Hall. Formerly claimed by David Sasto [?]. Consideration: £50. Signed: Samuel Bowen, Sarah Bowen. Witnesses: teste John Evans. No delivery shown. Recorded: OS 1:247.

11 April 1797. Zebulen and Mary HOGUE to Jacob NOOSE. Moiety of 150 acres, including the Camp Spring, adjoining David Crull, James Ross. Patented to Hogue and Noose 18 September 1787. Consideration: £50, VA. Signed: Zebulin Hoge, Mary [X] Hoge. Witnesses: John Evans, Alexr Hawthorn, Thos Wilson. No acknowledgement recorded. No delivery shown. Recorded: OS 1:248.

25 May 1797. George and Elizabeth MARTIN to Thomas BURCHANALD and Absalom MORRIS, both of Fayette Co, PA. 200 acres on Buffalow Creek, patented 14 September 1785. No adjoiners named. Consideration: $400. Signed: George Martin, Elizabeth Martin. Witnesses: Philip Pindell, John Dent, John Barker. Commission ordered to take Elizabeth Martin's acknowledgement but no action recorded here. Del: "to him", no date. Recorded: OS 1:249-250.

5 December 1796. Francis DEAKINS and William DEAKINS Junr, Montgomery Co, MD, to John HORSE. On or about 28 July 1795 the grantors conveyed to the grantee 310 acres in Monongalia Co, VA. The deed having later been burned, tract is now reconveyed. Part of a 908-acre tract, no adjoiners or place names mentioned. Consideration: £103, MD. Signed: Francis Deakins, William Deakins Junr. Witnesses: Chas A Beatty, Lloyd Beall. Receipt for £103. Acknowledged by Francis and William Deakins, 5 October [sic] 1796. Certificate of Upton Beall, Clerk of Montgomery Co, MD, 10 January 1797. Del: to J Horse, 2 November 1800. Recorded: OS 1:250-252.

12 June 1797. Luke and Easther HARMENSON to Davis SHOCKLEY. 87 acres, part of a larger tract adjoining Joseph Wade's heirs on a drain of Dunker Creek, near the great road from Scotts Mill up Dunker Creek, James Buchanan and William Hogue. Consideration: £21.15. Signed: Luke Harmenson, Hester [X] Harmenson. Witnesses: none. Acknowledged in court. No delivery shown. Recorded: OS 1:252-253.

9 May 1794. George and Elisabeth McMUNN, Alexandria, and Samuel LOVE, Winchester, to William GRUBB, Berkeley Co. 500 acres on the second right fork of Flatt Run, a branch of Buffelow Creek, adjoining and above lands entered for David Scott. Patented to McMunn and Love 20 October 1788, assignees of Golesmith Chandler, assignee of David Scott, assignee of William Robinson, assignee of John Busby [?]. Consideration: £40, VA. Signed: George Mc Munn, Elisa [X] McMunn, Saml Love. Witnesses: J Peyton, Obed Waite, Charles Perry. No acknowledgement recorded. No delivery shown. Recorded:

OS 1:254-255.
22 January 1796. Joseph BUTLER Senr to Thomas BUTLER Junr, his son. 228 acres on east side of Cheat River, patented [blank]. No adjoiners named. Consideration: £50, VA. Signed: Joseph [T] Butler. Witnesses: Amos Roberts, William Morgan, Willm Biggs, Peter Casey, Isaac Butler. No acknowledgement recorded. Del: to him, 28 February 1814. Recorded: OS 1:256-257.

12 June 1797. David [Jr] and Rachel SCOTT to Thomas, Lewis, Samuel, William, James, Jethro, and Joshua DEWEES. 200 acres on the west side of Monongalia River, part of a patent to James Scott deceased, David his heir at law. Conveyance agreeable to the last will and testament of Joshua Deweese, deceased, late of Fayette Co, PA. Consideration: £25, VA, previously paid by Joshua Deweese. Signed: David Scott. [Rachel does not sign] Witnesses: none. Acknowledged in court. Acknowledged June 1797, by Rachel Scott. No delivery shown. Recorded: June 1797, OS 1: 257-258.

12 June 1797. James and Aleathia CLARK to Jonathan DAVIS and Samuel TOPLIFF. 100 acres on Sandy Creek and Laurel Run, part of a larger tract bequeathed to the grantors in the last will and testament of William Hamilton, and adjoining James Hamilton. Consideration: £200, VA. Signed: James Clark, Aleathia Clark. Witnesses: none. Acknowledged in court. No delivery shown. Recorded: OS 1:258-259.

12 June 1797. William and Phebe POSTLE to John MOORE. 307.75 acres on Scotts Mill Run, adjoining William Dawson. Consideration: £150. Signed: William Postle, Phebe Postle. Witnesses: none. Acknowledged in court. No delivery shown. Recorded: OS 1:260-261.

10 or 11 February 1796 [?]. Testimony regarding the nuncupative WILL of Rudolph SNIDER. "William Martin heard Rudolph Snider say [to?] John Snider May 15th that he would have his will as followes. the land to be Divided in three parts between the Sons Moses to have the improvement part with paying three of the girls fifteen pounds apeas and the other two boys to pay the other two girls fifteen pounds each and as for the moveabel property be left with his famelly while they continue to gether for the Support of the small Children, Ditto as followeth Either the last of may or the first of June [A blank space follows in original, but succeeding text appears to begin at the word "Ditto" above] I Wm Lancaster heard as followeth that his land Should be Divided in three parts to the boys with the widows thirds in the Lower End which belongs to moses at

her death and the moveable property amongs the children with Moses paying 2 or 3 of the girls 14 pounds a peas the other 2 boys paying 2 girls 14 pounds a peas NB the Moveable property to be praised and Equally divided Amongst the Children." Recorded: OS 1:261. [Not recorded in Wills.]

20 April 1797. Jacob and Hannah SMITH to Daniel McCOLLUM. 100 acres, moiety of a 200-acre tract conveyed by Charles Donaldson. From a 268-acre patent of 11 September 1789, known as Blackbourn's Glades. No adjoiners named. Consideration: £100, VA. Signed: Jacob Smith, Hannah [X] Smith. Witnesses: John Fleming, James Hamilton, James Clark. No acknowledgement recorded. No delivery shown. Recorded: OS 1:262-263.

12 September 1797. William and Margarett ICE to Thomas SCOTT, Northwestern Territory. 35 acres on the north side of Buffeloe Creek, part of a larger tract granted to Ice and on which Ice now lives. No adjoiners named. Consideration: £12, VA. Signed: William [X] Ice, Margarett [M] Ice. Witnesses: none. Acknowledged in court. Del: to Thomas Scott, 3 April 1800. Recorded: OS 1:263-265.

11 September 1797. Richard and Phebe MERRIFIELD to David SAYRE Jr. 200 acres on middle fork of Booths Creek, about three miles from the river, adjoining John Phillips. Consideration: [£? $?]50. Signed: Richard Merrifield. [Phebe does not sign.] Witnesses: none. Acknowledged in court. Recorded: July 1797 [sic], OS 1:265.

11 September 1797. William and Peggy VEACH to Daniel DAVIS. 100 acres on Scotts Mill Run, adjoining James Morris. Part of a larger tract sold by William Dawson to James Morris and by James Morris to William Veach. Consideration: £150, VA. Signed: William Veach, Peggy Veach. Witnesses: none. Acknowledged in court. No delivery shown. Recorded: OS 1:266.

11 September 1797. Joseph and Elizabeth REED to Nicholas MADARA. Lot #102 in Morgantown. Consideration: £80. Signed: Joseph Reed, Elizabeth Reed. Witnesses: none. Acknowledged in court. Del: to Nich Madera, 29 July 1803. Recorded: OS 1:267-268.

11 September 1797. Joseph and Elizabeth REED to Thomas DOOLITTLE. Lot #103 in Morgantown. Consideration: £20. Signed: Joseph Reed, Elizabeth [mark called for but not recorded] Reed. Witnesses: none. Acknowledged in court. Del: to grantee, 14 October 1818. Recorded: OS 1:268-269.

11 March 1794. Rodham PETTY [PELLY?], Feyett Co,

PA, by Isaac SUTTON, his attorney in fact, to Samuel GANDY. 400 acres on Three Forks Creek, adjoining James Brane. Sold to Rodham by Benjamin Jenings, 10 February 178[9?]. Consideration: £35, PA. Signed: Isaac Sutton. Witnesses: none. Acknowledged in court. No delivery shown. Recorded: OS 1:269-270.

9 September 1797. Thomas and Deliah JENKINS to Henry HARDESTY. 4 acres at Glade Run, part of the survey on which Jenkins now lives. Consideration: $10, VA. Signed: Thomas Jenkins, Delilah [0] Jenkins. Witnesses: Daniel Hill, John Jenkins, Thomas Gibson. No acknowledgement recorded. No delivery shown. Recorded: OS 1:271-272.

26 March 1791. John and Margarett DENT to William WATKINS. 400 acres on Scotts Mill Run, including a 1776 settlement, and adjoining Philip Shively, Abraham Harden, and David Watkins. Surveyed 8 December 1781. Consideration: £25, VA. Signed: John Dent, Margarett Dent. Witnesses: David Scott, Thomas Pindell, Evan Watkins. No acknowledgement recorded. No delivery shown. Recorded: OS 1:273-274.

9 May 1795. Charles FERRY, Greensburgh, Washington Co, PA, to William McCLEERY. 101,212½ acres on main lefthand fork of Big Sandy River, a branch of the Ohio River, and about 35 miles above Vancover's old settlement at the junction of left and right forks of Big Sandy, in Kanaway Co. [Some illegible words in the text. Land was located via treasury land warrants issued in December 1794 for 63,000 and 38,212½ acres, in the name of Thomas Wilson, and assigned by Wilson to McCleery in January 1795.] Consideration: £607.4. Signed: Charles Ferrey. Witnesses: B Reeder, Thos McKinley, George Yeager. No acknowledgement recorded. No delivery shown. Recorded: OS 1:274-275.

11 September 1797. Larence and Hannah VN CAMP to Richard CHEW. 124 acres on Days and Maricles Run, branches of Dunker Creek. No adjoiners named. Part of a 228-acre tract patented to Van Camp. Consideration: £37. Signed: Larence Vn Camp, Hannah [X] Van Camp. Witnesses: none. Acknowledged in court. Del: to Richard Chew, 18 October 1805. Recorded: OS 1:276-277.

11 September 1797. Larence and Hannah VN CAMP to Elias HOSKINSON. 100 acres on Days and Maricles Run, branches of Dunker Creek, part of a 200 acre patent issued to Van Camp and adjoining Richard Chew's part of said survey. Consideration: £15. Signed: Larence Vn Camp, Hannah [X] Van Camp. Witnesses: none. Acknowledged in court. Del: to E Hoskinson, 16 March 1805. Recorded:

OS 1:277-278.

3 September 1793. David HANWAY, Harford Co, MD, to Bernard GILPIN, Berkeley Co. 255 acres on Monongalia River, adjoining Samuel Hanway and John Tucker's settlement survey. Surveyed 16 May [blank] for Hanway, assignee of John Hopkins on a treasury land warrant. Consideration: £50. Signed: David Hanway. Witnesses: John Rumsey, Edward Proll. Receipt for £50. Sarah Hanway, wife of David, acknowledges in Harford Co, MD, 3 September 1793. Certificate of John Lee Gibson, clerk of Harford Co, 3 September 1793. No delivery shown. Recorded: OS 1:279-280.

4 August 1797. Benjamin STODDERT to Doctr James Heighe BLAKE, both of Montgomery Co, MD. 1000 acres between the head of Mody Creek and waters of Cheat River, adjoining Stoddert's other survey. Patented 12 September 1797. Consideration: £250, MD. Signed: Benjamin Stoddert. Witness: Lloyd Beall. Acknowledged 4 August 1797 before Lloyd Beall, mayor of George Town, MD. Certificate of John Mountz Junr, clerk of George Town. No delivery shown. Recorded: OS 1:281-282.

11 September 1797. Robert and Messey DAVIS and John and Ann DAVIS to William VEACH. 106 acres on Robinsons Run, adjoining John Davis and Robert Davis. Part of a tract patented to Joseph Meal, 26 January 1787. Consideration: $100, VA. Signed: Robert Davis, Messey Davis, John Davis, Anna Davis. Witnesses: none. Acknowledged in court. Del: to Wm Veatch, 6 November 1800. Recorded: OS 1:282-283.

3 July 1797. Evan and Elizabeth JENKINS to Daniel HILL. 100 acres on Big Sandey Creek. No adjoiners named. Consideration: £100.19.9½, VA. Signed: Evan [/] Jenkins, Elisabeth [0] Jenkins. Witnesses: John Fleming, Henry Hardisty, Thomas [mark] Gibson. No acknowledgement recorded. No delivery shown. Recorded: OS 1:283-284.

[no date] Recording of statements regarding slaves of Alexander McINTIRE. McIntire, of New Jersey, has not moved into VA with intent to evade laws for preventing further import of slaves from Africa, nor has he brought any slaves with intent to sell them, nor has he brought any slaves who might have been imported from Africa or the West India islands after 1 November 1778. On 23 April 1793 Negro Sambo declares to Jacob Piatt, JP, of Susex Co, NJ, that he is willing to go to MD and elsewhere with his master. Signed: Sambo [X]. Jno Turner, JP, in [Berkeley?] Co, VA, attests McIntire's arrival, 13 May 1793, accompanied by Negro Sambo. On 30 July 1792 Robert Bolling, Alderman of Petersburgh, VA,

records McIntire's arrival there with slaves Betsy, Charles, and Jane. Richard Mayner made oath that McIntire reached Petersburg with the slaves on Saturday, 28 July 1792. Recorded: OS 1:285.

19 February 1796. Joseph BUTLER to John BUTLER, his son. 217 acres on the east side of Cheat River, part of a larger patent of 20 September 1785. No adjoiners named. Consideration: £50. Signed: Joseph [T] Butler. Witnesses: Peter Casy, Isaac Butler. No acknowledgement recorded. No delivery shown. Recorded: OS 1:286.

8 January 1798. William and Catharine JOLLIFF to Charles STEWART. 100 acres on the west side of Cheet River, adjoining Lewis Rogers and William Stewart. Patented to Henry Croll, 1 April 1784, and sold by him to Jacob Noose, who sold to Jolliff. Consideration: £55. Signed: William Jolliff, Catharine Jolliff. Witnesses: none shown. No acknowledgement recorded. Del: to Charles Stewart, 13 February 1809. Recorded: OS 1:287.

9 October 1797. Joseph and Sarah WISBEY to Elijah HERRYMAN. 100 acres on Gyces Run, part of the tract Wisbey now lives on, adjoining Simon Kratcher. Patented 9 May 1796. Consideration: $200. Signed: Joseph [mark] Wisbey, Sarah [mark] Wisbey. Witnesses: none. Acknowledged in court. No delivery shown. Recorded: OS 1:287-288.

10 October 1797. John and Elisabeth MOORE to John STAGG. 94½ acres on Scotts Mill Run, adjoining William Postle. Consideration: £170. Signed: John [X] Moore, Elisabeth [X] Moore. Witnesses: none. Acknowledged in court. No delivery shown. Recorded: OS 1:289.

11 October 1784. Zackquill and Drusilla MORGAN to Isabella EVANS. Lot [description blank, # not shown] in Morgan Town. Consideration: £3, plus annual rent of 3s per annum to Zackquill Morgan, his heirs and assigns forever. Signed: Zackll Morgan, Drusilla [+] Morgan. Witnesses: none. Acknowledged in court. No delivery shown. Recorded: OS 1:290.

27 September 1797. John and Elisabeth MILLER to John BUNNER. 123 acres on Monongalia River, above the mouth of Parkers Run, adjoining Henry Batton. Consideration: £61.10, VA. Signed: John Miller, Elisabeth [//] Miller. Witnesses: none. Acknowledged in court. Del: to J Bunner, 4 November 1809. Recorded: OS 1:291.

7 October 1797. John and Elisabeth MILLER to Stephen MORGAN. 83 acres on Monongalia River, including the mouth of Parkers Run. No adjoiners named. Patented to Miller 18 May 1793 as assignee of Thomas Dowthet.

Consideration: £14. Signed: John Miller, Elisabeth Miller. Witnesses: none. Acknowledged in court. Del: to S Morgan, 10 April 1810 [or 1816?]. Recorded: OS 1:291-292.

9 October 1797. John and Nicey EVANS to Daniel LANCE, Alleghany Co, MD. 100 acres, part of the Blackburn Glade tract. Adjoining 200 acres laid off for Jacob Smith and Jacob Noose and the east side of the road. Consideration: £40, VA. Signed: John Evans, Unise [+] Evans. Witnesses: none. Acknowledged in court. Del: to Daniel Lance, 24 June 1805. Recorded: OS 1:293.

9 October 1797. Anthony HARTLEY to James HARTLEY. 100 acres on Gises Run, now occupied by James. Part of a 200-acre patent to Anthony Hartley, 2 December 1791. Consideration: $100. Signed: Anthony Hartley. Witnesses: none. Acknowledged in court. No delivery shown. Recorded: OS 1:293-294.

5 June 1795. Jacob and Elisabeth BUSER, Earl Twp, Lancaster Co, PA, and Henry SHIBLEY, Leacock Twp, Lancaster Co, PA, to George DIFFENDOWER, late of the said twp, "Dealer." Power of attorney. Elisabeth Buser is the daughter of John Shibley, deceased, and Margaret his wife, late Margaret Peters. Henry Shibley is guardian for John and Margaret Shibley, two of the infant children of John Shibley deceased. Henry Peters, deceased, the brother of Margaret Peters Shibley, owned a lot in Morgantown. Diffendower is empowered to sell that lot, but no other part of the estate of Henry Peters. Signed: Jacob Busser, Elisabeth Busser, Henry Shibeley. Acknowledged in Lancaster Co, PA, before Frederick Seeger "and one other signed in Dutch." [A copy of the German signature reads "Jacob Scheibli."] Certificate of John Hubley, clerk of Lancaster Co, PA. Recorded: OS 1:294-295.

5 January 1798. Patrick and Martha McGREW to John WIMP. 97 acres on Big Sandy Creek, adjoining Russel Potter. Part of a larger tract surveyed for John [illegible], the remainder of the tract conveyed to Russel Potter. Consideration: £55, PA. Signed: Patrick McGrew, Martha McGrew. Witnesses: Robert Woods, William Woods, Mordecai Dunham. No acknowledgement recorded. No delivery shown. Recorded: OS 1:295.

5 June 1795. Certificate of Frederick Seeger, Lancaster Co, PA, stating that Margaret Sheibly, widow of John Sheibly, was a sister to Henry Peters, formerly of Lancaster Co, PA, and that there are no other heirs of Henry Peters besides the within-named children of Margaret Peters Sheibly. Del: to Wm Paul, Executor of

Wireman, 27 May 1805. Recorded: inserted between OS 1:295-296, on unnumbered leaf.

18 September 1797. Jacob and Elisabeth BUSSER and Henry SHIBELY, by George DIFFENDERVER, Washington Co, MD, their attorney in fact, to Christian WIREMAN. Lot in Morgan Town formerly owned by Henry Peters, deceased. Consideration: £100. Signed: George Diffenderffer. Witnesses: Jno Buchanan, R Sturgeon, Benjn Clagett. Receipt for £100, dated 18 September 1797, before Cephas Beall and Jacob Schnebly, Washington Co, MD. Certificate of Elie Williams, Clerk of Washington Co, MD, 18 September 1797. Del: to Wm Paul, Executor of Wireman, 27 May 1805. Recorded: OS 1:296-297.

5 February 1798. James and Mary METHENY to Francis AYERS. 64 3/4 acres near Roling Creek, part of the tract on which Metheny now lives. No adjoiners named. Consideration: £20.16, VA. Signed: James Metheny, Mary [X] Metheny. Witnesses: Henry Floyd, Amos Roberts, Michael Floyd. No acknowledgement recorded. Del: to Dennis Jeffers, 14 April 1806. Recorded: OS 1:297-298.

6 January 1798. James and Mary METHENY to Henry FLOYD. 110 acres on Cheat River, adjoining Nathan Metheny. Consideration: £100. Signed: James Metheny, Mary [X] Metheny. Witnesses: Thos Butler, Thos Smoot, Michael Floyd, Francis Ayers. No acknowledgement recorded. No delivery shown. Recorded: OS 1:298.

6 January 1798. James MORRIS to Henry HARDESTY. 90 acres on Muddy Creek, adjoining George Sipolt and Henry Criss. Consideration: £20, VA. Signed: James Morris. Witnesses: none. Acknowledged in court. No delivery shown. Recorded: OS 1:299.

5 September 1797. John and Phebe JUDY, formerly of Monongalia Co, to Patrick MAGREW. 97 acres on Sandy Creek, adjoining lands sold by Judy to Russel Potter. Consideration: £40. Signed: John Judy, Phebe Judy. Witnesses: Michael Frits, John Hatfield. No acknowledgement recorded. No delivery shown. Recorded: OS 1:300.

9 January 1798. William and Isabella McCLEERY to James HILL, Harrison Co. 300 acres on Booths Creek, Harrison Co, adjoining John Booth, James Currant, and John Anderson. Patented to McCleery 24 June 1791. Consideration: $5. Signed: Wm McCleery, Isabella McCleery. Witnesses: Henry Barnes, Simon Kratzer, Joseph [mark] Wisbey. No acknowledgement recorded. No delivery shown. Recorded: OS 1:301.

1 January 1798. Amos and Elisabeth ROBERTS to James METHENY. 400 acres, adjoining Joseph Butler.

Consideration: £135, VA. Signed: Amos Roberts, Elisabeth Roberts. Witnesses: Henry [mark] Floyd, Michael [0] Floyd, Francis Ayers. No acknowledgement recorded. No delivery shown. Recorded: OS 1:302.

9 January 1798. Jacob and Jenny VANKIRK to George Jacob BALTZEL and Ezekiel CHENEY. 200 acres on the south side of lands claimed by Henry Croll and east of Zebulon Hoge. Patented to Vankirk, assignee of James Jameson, 18 May 1793. Consideration: £100. Signed: Jacob Vankirk, Jane Vankirk. Witnesses: none. Acknowledged in court. Del: to Ezekiel Chaney, 20 May 1801. Recorded: OS 1:303.

28 January 1796. Richard SMYTH, Philadelphia PA, to Benjamin REEDER. Acreage not stated. Tract patented 28 June 1787 by Henry Banks and sold by him to Smyth, adjoining lands of Moylan and Clayborne and other lands of Henry Banks. No place names mentioned. Consideration: £376. Signed: R Smyth. Witnesses: William Duquid, Alexander Colden. Acknowledged 28 January 1796 before Matthew Clarkson, Mayor of Philadelphia. No delivery shown. Recorded: January 1798, OS 1:304.

5 June 1795. Margarett SHEIBLEY, late Peters, Lancaster Co, PA, sister of Henry Peters, deceased, of Morgantown, to Jacob and Elisabeth BUSSER and to her minor children. Release of all her title and claim to estate of Henry Peters. Consideration: none stated. Signed: Margaret [X] Sheibley. Witnesses: F Seeger, Jacob Shibley. Acknowledged 5 June 1795, Lancaster Co, PA. Certificate of John Hubley, Clerk of Lancaster Co. Recorded: OS 1:305.

6 January 1798. Christian and Elisabeth CALE to John JENKINS. 27 acres on Cheat River, adjoining Thomas Jenkins and David Porter's old line. Consideration: £6.1.6. Signed: Christian Cale, Elisabeth [X] Cale. Witnesses: Henry Hardesty, Jonathan Harriss, Thomas Gibson. No acknowledgement recorded. Del: grantee's order, 19 April 1824. Recorded: OS 1:306.

12 June 1797. David and Rachael SCOTT to John SAVARY, Gentleman, of Kentucky. 400 acres on the west side of the Monongahela, near the mouth of Robensons Run and adjoining David Scott. Land granted to David as heir at law of James Scott, deceased, who was assignee of William Robinson. This land previously conveyed and the deed burned. Consideration: £400. Signed: David Scott, Rachael [X] Scott. Witnesses: none. Acknowledged in court. No delivery shown. Recorded: OS 1:307-308.

12 January 1803. Commission to Zadock Springer and Robert Richey, Fayette Co, PA, to get acknowledgement of Mary BELL to a deed from John and Mary BELL to Thomas

FLEMING for 75 acres. Certificate of Richey and Springer as to Mary Bell's acknowledgement, 14 January 1803. Recorded: on unnumbered sheet interleaved between OS 1:307-308 [cf below, OS 1:336-337].

10 September 1796. Jonas and Susannah HOGMIRE, Washington Co, MD, to John SWAN, Baltimore, MD. 3400 acres on head of Laurel and Buffelow Runs, branches of Yohogania River, 3/4 mile above Jeremiah Bosley's dwelling house. No other adjoiners mentioned. Surveyed 30 May 1787 on a treasury warrant issued to John Hopkins 12 May 1783. Consideration: £648, MD. Signed: Jonas Hogmire, Susanah Hogmire. Witnesses: I Taylor, Jacob Schnebly. Acknowledged 12 April 1797 in Washington Co, MD. Certificate of Elie Williams, clerk of Washington Co. No delivery shown. Recorded: OS 1:308-309.

8 May 1797. Alexander and Deborah WILSON, Fayette Co, PA, to William LANKESTER. 281 acres on south side of Dunker Creek, adjoining lands claimed by John Cooper and including 1775 settlement right. Consideration: £200. Signed: Alexander Wilson, Deborah [+] Wilson. Witnesses: John Evans, Dudley Evans, John Fairfax. No delivery shown. Recorded: OS 1:309.

12 September 1797. Alexander and Catron [also Catherine] McINTIRE to Thomas McKINLEY. 8 acres, part of a larger tract conveyed by Thomas Pindell to Moses Williams and by Williams to McIntire. No adjoiners or place names mentioned. Consideration: $150, VA. Signed: Alexander McIntire, Catherine McIntire. Witnesses: none. Acknowledged in court. No delivery shown. Recorded: OS 1:310-311.

12 September 1797. John DOWNER and Robert MINNIS to Jonathan HARRISS. 400 acres on Big Sandy Creek, adjoining John Morris [?], tract known as Ruble's Improvement. Consideration: £250, VA. Signed: John Downer [Minnis' signature not recorded]. Witnesses: Thos Wilson, John Fleming, Michael Karn. No acknowledgement recorded. No delivery shown. Recorded: OS 1:311.

10 February 1797. Isaac and Nancey LEMASTERS to David SCOTT. 273 acres at a small run that empties into the Monongahela River at the long riffle, the tract that Lemasters now lives on. Patented 17 October 1791. Consideration: £700, VA. Signed: Isaac Lemasters [Nancey does not sign]. Witnesses: John Dent, David Scott, Otho Henry. No acknowledgement recorded. No delivery shown. Recorded: OS 1:312.

12 February 1798. John and Elisabeth LEETH to Joshua WALLS. 100 acres on Cheat River. No adjoiners or place names mentioned. Consideration: £100, VA. Signed:

John [mark] Leeth, Elisabeth [8] Leeth. Witnesses: none. Acknowledged in court. No delivery shown. Recorded: OS 1:313.

29 November 1792. George and Mary RIDDLE, Alleghany Co, MD, to John BUTLER. 240 acres on the east side of Cheat River, adjoining Henry Richards. Patented 5 January 1787. Consideration: £60. Signed: George Riddle, Mary [0] Riddle. Witnesses: Wildey Taylor, William Morgan. No acknowledgement recorded. No delivery shown. Recorded: OS 1:314.

10 September 1797. Alexander and Catherine McINTIRE to Mary WEAVER. Lot [# blank] in Morgan Town. Includes ground rent of 50¢ annually to the proprietor. Consideration: $300. Signed: Alexander McIntire, Catherine McIntire. Witnesses: none. Acknowledged in court. Del: to Joseph Griffith, 19 May 1811, fees pd by him. Recorded: OS 1:315.

20 September 1797. Thomas and Margaret BURCHENAL to John FIKE, Somerset Co, PA. Mortgage on 150 acres at Butlers Mill Run, including lots that have been laid off for a town. Burchenal may redeem on or before 20 September 1798. Consideration: $100. Signed: Thomas Burchenal, Margaret [mark indicated but not shown] Burchenal. Witnesses: George Lemon, John Runyon, Johannes [illegible, in poorly-copied German script]. No acknowledgement recorded. No delivery shown. Recorded: OS 1:316.

12 February 1798. Thomas and Martha TANEHILL to Leven OKEY. 112 acres near Cheat River Hill, below the mouth of Sandy Creek, part of the tract that Tanehill lives on. Consideration: £127.10, VA. Signed: Thomas Tanehill, Martha [+] Tanehill. Witnesses: none. Acknowledged in court. Del: to Okey, April 1800. Recorded: OS 1:317.

12 February 1798. Thomas and Martha TANNEHILL to Isaac HAYS. 61 acres adjoining Levin Okey, Hays' house. Part of the tract that Tannehill lives on. Consideration: £30. Signed: Thomas Tannehill, Martha [+] Tannehill. Witnesses: [blank]. No acknowledgement recorded. No delivery shown. Recorded: OS 1:318.

10 February 1798. Thomas and Rebeccah BUTLER to Ezra HORTON. 300 acres on the east side of Cheat River, opposite the lower end of Dunkard Bottom and half a mile from Cheat River. Surveyed 28 April 1785 and patented 25 October 1792. Consideration: £100, VA. Signed: Thos Butler, Rebeckah [+] Butler. Witnesses: Alexander Dalis [?], Thos Burchenal, Wildy Taylor, James Methena. No acknowledgement recorded. Del: to Ezra Horton, 16

September 1805. Recorded: OS 1:319.
12 February 1798. John and Ann DRAGOO to William STREIGHT. 25¼ acres on Finches Run, adjoining Jacob Strait. Consideration: £9, VA. Signed: John [mark] Dragoo, Anna [mark] Dragoo. Witnesses: none. Acknowledged in court. No delivery shown. Recorded: OS 1:320-321.
13 February 1798. Davis and Elizabeth MERIDITH to James Smallwood WILSON. 384 acres on a branch of Slacks Run, adjoining lands formerly claimed by Jeremiah Clark and now property of the heirs of Josiah Jenkins. Part of a 400-acre survey granted to William PettyJohn and John Evans [date blank]. Consideration: £175. Signed: Davis Meridith, Elisabeth [/] Meridith. Witnesses: none. Acknowledged in court. No delivery shown. Recorded: OS 1:321-322.
12 January 1789. David and Ann CROLL to John STANDLEY. 86 acres on Arons Creek, adjoining Joseph Trickett and John Burk. Part of a 400-acre survey. Consideration: £40. Signed: David Croll, Ann Croll. Witnesses: none. Acknowledged in court. No delivery shown. Recorded: OS 1:323-324.
11 February 1797. Ezekiel and Nelly BARNS to Neil GILLISPIE, Washington Co, PA. 95 acres, no adjoiners or place names mentioned. Patented to Hugh Phelps 25 October 1788. Consideration: $1000. Signed: Ezekiel Barns, Nelly [X] Barns. Witnesses: Francis Warman, Eh Evans, John Fowler. Proved by witnesses. Del: to Wm Gans, 11 October 18[30?38?]. Recorded: April 1798, OS 1:324, 327 [cf next entry].
21 July 1797. Christian WIREMAN to Richard LANGFORD, residences not stated. Title bond. On 6 December 1788 Martin Myers, assignee of Martin Judy, assignee of John Judy's heirs, patented 100 acres adjoining Judy's settlement survey, David More and Jacob Judy. On 13 February 1797 Myers sold this land to Wireman. Wireman conveys to Langford and covenants that he will make a more complete deed when necessary. Consideration: £60. Signed: Christian Wireman. Witnesses: Thomas Rhoads, Archibold Vanhorn. Acknowledged 21 July 1797, in Prince Georges Co, MD, before Richard Cramplin and Gabriel Peters Vanhorn. Receipt for £60, VA, witnessed by Archd Vanhorn and Bayley E Clark. Certificate of John B Magruder, clerk of Prince Georges Co, MD, 22 January 1798. Recorded: OS 1:325-326.
21 November 1797. Peter and Elizabeth STRATE to Elizabeth STRAIT Sr. 65 acres, one-third of a 195-acre

tract on Finches Run. No adjoiners named. Elizabeth Sr's dower in the real and personal property of Jacob Strate, deceased, her husband, is noted. This conveyance to her in fee simple. Consideration: love and affection for their mother. Signed: Peter [mark] Straight, Elizabeth [8] Straight. Witnesses: none. Acknowledged in court. Del: to Jasper Wayette, 16 March 1803. Recorded: OS 1:327, 329 [page 328 omitted in numbering].

14 August 1797. Gower THOMPSON, residence not stated, by Thomas BUTLER, his attorney in fact, to Aaron RYCE, Hampshire Co. 2 tracts on Muddy Creek. 232½ acres, adjoining Cole Lick Run, patented to Thomas Butler and sold by him to Thompson, and 50 acres, patented to Thompson. Consideration: $500, VA. Signed: Thomas Butler. Witnesses: M Hite, Asa Dudley, Joshua Warman, Joshua Stockton, John Williams. No acknowledgement recorded. No delivery shown. Recorded: OS 1:329-330.

12 February 1797. Philip PINDELL, farmer, to Thomas PINDELL. 100 acres on Dunker Mill Run, a branch of Buffelow Creek, a tract known as the Rock Camp, adjoining Joseph Davis, Jacob Pindell. Consideration: £30. Signed: Philip Pindell. Witnesses: none. Acknowledged in court. Del: to Jacob Pindle son of Tom, 26 February 1801. Recorded: OS 1:331.

9 April 1798. Samuel HANWAY to Samuel TOPLIFF, Norfolk Co, Massachusetts, and Jonathan DAVIS. Two tracts. 500 acres on both sides of Sandy Creek, including the mouth of Soverans Run and the great falls of Sandy Creek, patented 4 September 1788. 340 acres on the south side of Laurel Run, a branch of Sandy Creek, adjoining Jeremiah Tanehill and William Hamilton, patented to Hugh Marshall 7 August 1787 and conveyed by Hugh and Keziah Marshall to Hanway, 25 September 1797. Consideration: $2100. Signed: Samuel Hanway. Witnesses: none. Acknowledged in court. No delivery shown. Recorded: OS 1:332-333.

17 November 1789. John LOGAN, grubber, to William ORSON, farmer. Power of attorney to collect debts due in Logan's account books from persons "mostly all dwellers in and about Cusewago." Signed: John Logan. Acknowledged before William John, Gent, JP. Recorded: OS 1:333.

29 August 1789. George and Sarah ORSON, York Co, PA, to William ORSON. Acreage not stated, adjoining Robert Hill, Henry Robeson, Owen Davis, West's Run, William Joseph. Consideration: 5 shillings, VA. Signed: George Orson, Sarah Orson. Witnesses: Francis Brooks, Richard Tull, Thomas Pindell. No acknowledgement recorded. No delivery shown. Recorded: OS 1:334.

16 September 1797. Philip and Rachael PINDELL to Benjamin JENKINS. 60¼ acres, adjoining Philip Pindell, Jacob Pindell, William Windsor, John Coombs. Patented to Pindell, 1 July 1784. Consideration: £60.5, VA. Signed: Philip Pindell [Rachael does not sign]. Witnesses: John Dent, Thos Chipps, Joseph [mark] Barker. Acknowledged by Rachael Pindell, 16 September 1797, before John Dent and Thos Chipps. Del: to Benj Jenkins, 2 June 1803. Recorded: OS 1:335-336.

11 September 1797. John and Mary BEALL, Fayette Co, PA, to Thomas FLEMING. 275 acres on Monongalia River, adjoining John Bozarth. Patented 12 October 1789. Consideration: £260, VA. Signed: John Bell, Mary Bell. Witnesses: none. Acknowledged in court. Delivery not shown. Recorded: OS 1:336-337.

9 April 1798. Christian WHITEHARE to Abraham WOODRING Junr. Lot #40 in Salem town. Includes annual quit-rent of 50¢, due 1 July, to Francis Deakins, his heirs and assigns forever. Consideration: £22. Signed: Christian Whitehare. Witnesses: none. Acknowledged in court. No delivery shown. Recorded: OS 1:338.

21 February 1798. Robert MINNIS to Alexr McINTIRE. 200 acres on the north side of the West Fork River, adjoining James Morrison. Consideration: $200. Signed: Robert Minnis. Witnesses: Frederick Reed, John Melrose, [illegible] Melrose. No acknowledgement recorded. No delivery shown. Recorded: OS 1:339-340.

9 April 1798. Jacob and Eunice HAMPTON to Benjamin POWEL. 150 acres on Tigar Valley River, adjoining David Dunham and Thomas Hughs. Part of a 400-acre patent of 27 July 1796 to Jacob Hampton, assignee of James Mills, assignee of Simon Hendrickson. Consideration: £200, VA. Signed: Jacob Hampton, Eunice Hampton. Witnesses: Hugh McNeely, David Dunham, Francis Stanbury. No acknowledgement recorded. No delivery shown. Recorded: OS 1:341-342.

10 February 1798. James and Mary GUTHRIE to Nicholas GROVE. 200 acres adjoining Absalom Sovereign, James Guthrie. Consideration: [£? $?]200. Signed: James Guthrie, Mary Guthrie. Witnesses: Zopher Blatchley, Russel Potter, Samuel M Potter. No acknowledgement recorded. Del: to C [?] Grew [?]m 29 March 1805. Recorded: OS 1:344-345.

5 April 1798. John and Margaret McCLAIN to Henry DORROW. 365½ acres on left hand fork of Murreculs Run, including a 1777 improvement. No adjoiners named. Consideration: £131.4, VA. Signed: John McClain, Margaret McClain. Witnesses: John Wimp, Wm Biggs. No

acknowledgement recorded. No delivery shown. Recorded: OS 1:345-346.

22 January 1798. Commission to William Tingle and Alexander Hawthorn to take acknowledgement of Mary CHANEY, wife of Ezekiel CHANEY, regarding a deed of 20 January 1798 to Mary BENNETT. Certificate of Tingle and Hawthorn regarding her acknowledgement. Recorded: on sheet interleaved between OS 1:346-347.

20 January 1798. Ezekiel and Mary CHANEY to Mary BENNETT, Berkly Co. Half a lot in Morgan Town, adjoining Mr Thos Wilson's lot on which George Hite now lives, and the lot now owned by George R Tingle. Consideration: $50. Signed: Ezekiel Chiney, Mary [X] Chiny. Witnesses: George R Tingle, Thos Wilson, J[obscured by tape] Stockton. Acknowledged: see preceding entry. No delivery shown. Recorded: OS 1:347.

13 December 1797. Joseph and Sarah WHISBY to Joseph WHISBY his Eldest Son Thomas WHISBY Hugh WHISBY Samuel WHISBY. $67\frac{1}{2}$ acres, adjoining Vandgraft, Joseph Whisbey, and Hereyman's line. Consideration: £10. Signed: Joseph [mark] Whisby, Sarah [mark] Whisby. Witnesses: none. Acknowledged in court. Del: to Jos Whisbey, 13 August 1802. Recorded: OS 1:348-349.

23 March 1798. WILL of Elijah BURROUGHS. Sons John, Charles, William, and daughters Elizabeth, Catherine, and Ann. Elizabeth and Catherine to have 50 acres each from the back part, adjoining the big run, and Ann to have 50 acres at the fork of the road, adjoining Johnston's and Evans' lines. Remainder of land to be equally divided among the sons. Executors: John Evans Junr, John W Dean. Signed: Elijah Burroughs. Witnesses: John Evans, Thomas Bevin, John Davis. Codicil, same date and witnesses: Executors are to take all lawful means for recovery of land now claimed by David and Robert Scott. If the case be lost in county court it is to be appealed to the High Court of Chancery. Plantation to be rented at best rate and money used for the education of William and Charles. John to be bound to a suitable trade. No probate data. Recorded: OS 1:350-351. [Also recorded in Wills, 1:291.]

6 September 1797. Joshua WORLEY, Ohio Co, to Samuel HESLET. 200 acres on a branch of Little Sandy Creek, in Sandy Creek Glade, adjoining John Myre, Samuel Worall, and Thomas Chiney. Part of a survey of 11 May 1781. Consideration: £200, PA. Signed: Joshua [+] Worley. Witnesses: Hedgman Triplett, Alexr Sommerville, Amos Skinner [?]. No acknowledgement recorded. Del: to Samuel Haslet, 13 October 1800. Recorded: OS 1:351-352.

12 February 1798. James HENTHORN, of Mason Co, KY, by John HENTHORN, his attorney in fact, to Daniel KIGER. Cites a 1 October 1796 power of attorney authorizing John to sell 1000 acres in Monongalia, now Harrison, Co, on a righthand branch of Big Sandy, adjoining Samuel Lieuellen. Tract patented to Samuel Hanway, 20 June 1787, and sold by him to Christian Wireman, 9 August 1790; sold by Wireman to James Henthorn, 17 August 1790. Consideration: $1500. Signed: John Henthorn. Witnesses: none. Acknowledged in court. No delivery shown. Recorded: OS 1:353-354.

17 October 1796. Samuel HANWAY to Robt MAXWELL, Randolph Co. Power of attorney to convey a tract on Cherry Tree Fork of Elk River, adjoining Nehemiah Dunham. Signed: Samuel Hanway. Witnesses: Matt Hite, Dudley Evans. Recorded: OS 1:355.

12 February 1798. Joseph and Sarah WISBEY to Joseph WISBEY. 12 3/4 acres, 36 perches, on Gyses Run, adjoining Elijah Herriman. Patented 9 March 1796. Consideration: $1. Signed: Joseph [mark] Wisbey, Sarah [mark] Wisbey. Witnesses: none. Acknowledged in court. Del: to Jos Wisbey Jun, 9 April 1804. Recorded: OS 1:355-356.

22 February 1798. Eli and Susannah LEIGHTON to Daniel BOYCE. 70 acres on Sandy Creek and Laurel Run, part of Leighton's 400-acre settlement right. Consideration: £71, VA. Signed: Elias [mark] Leighton, Susanna [+] Leighton. Witnesses: none. Acknowledged in court. No delivery shown. Recorded: OS 1:357-358.

29 January 1788. Thomas and Mary DAVIS, Samuel and Sarah BOWERS, John and Catherine [elsewhere Rachael] WEBB, Jacob and Hulder COUNTS, and James and Hannah WALKER, heirs at law of Joseph DAVIS deceased, to Jordan HALL. 400 acres on Tiger Valley fork of Monongalia River, adjoining John Pettyjohn and including a 1770 settlement right. Consideration: £200. Signed: Thomas [+] Davis, Mary [+] Davis, Samuel Bowers, Sarah Bowers, John [mark] Webb, Rachael Webb, Jacob Counts, Hulder Counts, James Walker, Hannah [mark] Walker. Witnesses: Wm John, David Scott, Bazel Bowel, John Jenkins. Acknowledged by James and Hannah Walker, in Fayette Co, PA, 30 January 1798, before Robert Richey. No delivery shown. Recorded: OS 1:359-361.

6 October 1787. Henry BANKS, of VA, by Alexander BOYD, Gentleman, Portsmouth, VA, his attorney, to Sylvester FULLER, Providence Town and County, Rhode Island. 5000 acres on some of the head drains of the right fork of Buffalo Creek, adjoining on the west side

Henry Banks' 33rd entry. Patented to Banks 28 June 1787. Consideration: £320, silver money. Signed: Alexr Boyd. Witnesses: Randall Briggs, Theodore Foster, Olive Fuller. Acknowledged before Theodore Foster, Providence RI, 6 October 1787. Recorded in Kent Co, RI, October 1788. Certificate of Allen Fry, Clerk. Certificate of John Collins, Governor of Rhode Island. Del: to Sylvester Fuller, 7 March 1806. Recorded: OS 1:363-364.

3 April 1798. Jacob and Eunice HAMPTON to David DUNHAM. Two tracts. 113 acres, 30 poles. $63\frac{1}{2}$ acres, 30 poles is of a tract called "fereshaes [?] Levels," including a 1774 settlement right, patented 11 September 1789. 100; the remaining 50 acres from a 1775 settlement right, adjoining Benjamin Powell on the east and Jacob Hampton on the rest. Patented 27 July 1796. 100 acres adjoining Isaac Powell on the east and Benjamin Powell on the west, part of a survey called Simon Hendrickson's 1775 settlement, patented 27 July 1796. Consideration: £200, VA. Signed: Jacob Hampton, Eunice Hampton. Witnesses: Hugh McNeely, Francis Stanbrey, Thomas Hughes. No acknowledgement recorded. No delivery shown. Recorded: OS 1:364-367.

11 September 1797. Robt MINNIS to Samuel MERRIFIELD Junr. 181 acres on a ridge between Pricketts Creek and White Day Creek, adjoining John Springer. Consideration: £90. Signed: Robt Minnis. Witnesses: none. Acknowledged in court. Del: to Wm McCleery, 2 October 1806. Recorded: OS 1:367-368.

11 February 1797. Neal and Nancy GILLISPIE, Washington Co, PA, to James GILLISPIE. 350 acres on east side of Cheat River, adjoining Rubles Run, Morgans Run, Samuel Lewellen. Consideration: £1000. Signed: Neal Gillispie [Nancy does not sign]. Witnesses: Eh Evans, John Fowlar. No acknowledgement recorded. Del: to James Gillespie, 12 April 1803. Recorded: OS 1:368-369.

[blank] 1798. Joseph and Mary PARMER to John WIMP. 4 acres, 10 poles, adjoining Zacwell Morgan, James Cochran, and the main road near Thomas Pindell's cleared land. Part of an 8 October 17[blank] patent to Thomas Pindell. Consideration: $100. Signed: Joseph Palmer, Mary Palmer. Witnesses: none. Acknowledged in court. No delivery shown. Recorded: OS 1:370.

16 September 1797. Philip and Rachael PINDELL to Joseph BARKER. 89 acres on Indian Creek, adjoining William Winsor, Philip Pindell, Benjamin Jenkins. Part of a 1 May 1784 patent and part of a 1 May 1784 entry warrant. Consideration: £45, VA. Signed: Philip Pindell, Racheal Pindell. Witnesses: John Dent, Thos Chipps,

Benjamin Jenkins. Acknowledged by Rachael Pindell, 16 September 1797, before John Dent and Thomas Chipps. No delivery shown. Recorded: OS 1:371-373.

10 November 1788. John and Margarett DENT to James ROGERS. 363 acres on Scotts Mill Run, adjoining land claimed by William Robinson, Henry Martin, and John Ramsey. Surveyed 23 October 1781. Consideration: £100, VA. Signed: John Dent, Margrett Dent. Witnesses: none. Acknowledged in court. No delivery shown. Recorded: OS 1:373-374.

6 September 1797. Joshua WORLEY, Ohio Co, to John MYER. 200 acres on a branch of Little Sandy Creek, in Sandy Creek Glades, adjoining Anthony Worley, Chaneys Run. Part of Worley's old survey of 11 May 1781. Consideration: £250, PA. Signed: Joshua [+] Worley. Witnesses: Hedgman Triplett, Alexander Sommerville, Amos Spencer. No acknowledgement recorded. Del: to Saml Haslet, 13 October 18[blank]. Recorded: OS 1:374-375.

11 December 1797. James BEALL, son of Jeremiah, to William BEALL. One-fourth part of a 420-acre tract purchased from Jeremiah Simpson by James Edmunston Beall and James Beall son of Jeremiah. William's portion to be laid off on the end of the tract adjoining Cheat River. Consideration: $200. Signed: James Beall. Witnesses: none. Acknowledged in court. No delivery shown. Recorded: OS 1:375, 379.

4 January 1794. James and Jane ROGERS to James and Ann RANDALL with reversion to Henrietta Isabelle CLARK, Elisabeth CLARK, Ann CLARK, and Mary CLARK (all minors in 1794). 363 acres on Scotts Mill Run, adjoining lands claimed by William Robinson, Henry Martin, and John Ramsey. Surveyed 23 October 1781 and patented by John Dent. Conveyed by John and Margrett Dent to Rogers 10 November 1788. Land to Ann Randall, the wife of James, during her lifetime and after her "descease" to her four daughters, as tenants in common and not as joint tenants. Rogers covenants to give possession of the lands to James Randall 1 April 1794. Consideration: £150, VA, paid by Henry Purviance, Washington Co, PA, in behalf of the minors mentioned. Signed: James Rogers [Jane does not sign]. Witnesses: Henry Dering Junr, John J Cooper Junr, Wm McCleery. Receipt for £150. No acknowledgement recorded. Del: "to him", 10 November 1815. Recorded: OS 1:376, 378 [page 377 omitted in numbering].

31 March 1797. William WALLACE to Heal PICK, both of Montgomery Co, MD. 1000 acres on Warrior Fork of Dunker Creek, adjoining Esther Eastburn's survey. Land

heretofore conveyed by said Heal and Hannah Peck to Wallace. Consideration: £500. Signed: William Wallace. Witnesses: John L Summers, Elimelech Swearingen. Acknowledged 31 March 1797 in Montgomery Co, MD, before Summers and Swearingen. Certificate of Upton Beall, clerk of Montgomery Co, 1 April 1797. Del: to John Stealey, 4 August 1803. Recorded: June 1797, OS 1:379-380.

26 November 1796. Thomas and Catherine EVANS to Jno B ARMESTEAD, Prince William Co. 120 acres on both sides of Cheat River, near Quarry Run, adjoining Andrew Ice. Part of a 20 May 1787 survey for 250 acres and excepting 130 acres sold to Ramsey. [Acreage not expressed in the instrument.] Consideration: 5 shillings. Signed: Thos Evans, Caty Evans. Witnesses: Joh [sic] Sanders, Will Armistead, James Newman, Lewis Armistead, Thos Newman. Acknowledged in court. No delivery shown. Recorded: OS 1:381.

26 December 1796. Nicholas and Mary MARSTILLER, Randolph Co, to Abraham WOTRING Junr. Lotts #62 and 63 "in said Town [not named]." Includes annual rent of $1, due 1 July, to Francis Deakins and Conrad Hogmire, their heirs and assigns forever. Consideration: £6. Signed: Nicholas Marstiller, Mary Marstiller. Witnesses: none. Acknowledged in Randolph Co, 26 December 1796. Certificate of Jacob Westfall, Clerk. Recorded: OS 1:382.

9 August 1791. Savory DE VALCOLIN, Washington Co, PA, to Albert GALLATIN, Fayette Co, PA. Whereas both men own jointly and separately numerous tracts, they make this partial division of lands. Savory conveys to Albert 16,800 acres patented in Greenbrier, now lying in Kanhaway Co, VA, patent 17 March 1788. Also, 6 tracts in Harrison Co: 4000 acres patented 25 March 1786; 1500 acres patented same date; 1500 acres, patented same date; 1000 acres, patented 25 April 1786; 3500 acres on Mill Creek, adjoining Savary's 40th entry, patented 29 March 1786. Also, 3 tracts patented in Harrison and now lying in Kanhaway Co: 1500 acres on right main fork of Mill Creek, patented 10 February 1786 and 1500 acres, same location, same date [only 2 tracts described]. Albert conveys to Savory his interest in 2 tracts patented in Greenbrier and now lying in Kanhaway Co: 4900 acres on Big Sandy Creek of Elk River and 7000 acres, no location shown, patented 17 March 1788. Also, 3 tracts in Harrison Co: 4500 acres on Mill Creek, patent date not shown; 4375 acres, patented 25 March 1786; and 1600 acres, patented 9 May 1787. Also 6

tracts: 6000 acres, patented in Harrison and now lying in Kanhaway Co, patented 26 August 1788; 1500 acres, same location, adjoining Savory's 12th entry, patented 10 February 1786; 396 acres on Gnatty Creek, Harrison Co, patented 13 July 1789; 500 acres on Freemans Creek, Harrison Co, patented 13 July 1789; 400 acres on Cheat River, Monongalia Co, patented 13 July 1789; and 933 1/3 acres in the district set apart for officers and soldiers of the VA State Line, from 5 military warrants. Consideration: the exchanges of land and 5 shillings. Signed: Savary Devalcoalin, Albert Gallatin. Witnesses: Jno Minor, John Badollet [?], James Hughes, James Hannah, Daniel Duggan. No acknowledgement recorded. No delivery shown. Recorded: OS 1:383-385.

14 December 1789. Ann PHILLIPS, administratrix of Theophilus PHILLIPS, deceased, Fayette Co, PA, to Christopher REAVER. 380 acres adjoining Nicholas Horner. Patented to James Sterling and conveyed by James and Hester Sterling to Theophilus Phillips. Consideration: £250, VA. Signed: Ann Philips. Witnesses: none. Acknowledged in court. No delivery shown. Recorded: OS 1:385-386.

11 September 1798. John and Ann EVANS to Benjamin JONES. 140 acres on Three Forks Creek, part of a 372-acre patent of 7 October 1789. Consideration: $100. Signed: John Evans, Ann Evans. Witnesses: None. Acknowledged in court. No delivery shown. Recorded: OS 1:387.

29 July 1797. Alexander and Catherine McINTIRE, Morgan Town, to Daniel MARCHANT, Westmoreland Co, PA. 111 acres on the east side of Monongalia River, below the mouth of Falling Run, adjoining lands sold by Thomas Laidley to Benjamin Reeder, near the road from Morgan Town to Martins Ferry, adjoining John Evans. Land conveyed to McIntire by Thomas Pindell, 20 September 1793, excepting 8 acres sold to Thomas McKinley. Consideration: $1900. Signed: Alexr McIntire, Catharine McIntire. Witnesses: B Reeder, John Davis, Thos McKinley. No acknowledgement recorded. No delivery shown. Recorded: OS 1:388-389.

11 September 1798. John and Ann EVANS to Samuel JONES. 111 acres on Three Forks Creek, part of a 372-acre patent, 7 October 1789. Consideration: $100. Signed: John Evans, Ann Evans. Witnesses: none. Acknowledged in court. No delivery shown. Recorded: OS 1:390.

11 September 1798. John and Margret WIMP to John STAFFORD. 123 acres on Cheat River, known as Ignatius

Butlar's land. No adjoiners mentioned. Consideration: £150, VA. Signed: John Wimp, Margrett [mark] Wimp. Witnesses: none. Acknowledged in court. No delivery shown. Recorded: OS 1:391-392.

10 September 1798. Benjamin and Ellinor WILSON to Aron POWELL. 180 acres on Three Forks, adjoining George Moredock and others [not named]. Consideration: £6. Signed: Ben Wilson, Ellenor Wilson. Witnesses: none. Acknowledged in court. No delivery shown. Recorded: OS 1:393.

15 May 1798. Arthur and Sarah TRADER to Elisha GRIFFITH. 22 acres on Rubles Run, a branch of Cheat River. Part of a 322-acre patent of 3 March 1785. Consideration: £300 "(or part property)." Signed: Arthur Trader, Sarah [X] Trader. Witnesses: George Baker, Jacob Ruble, Docter [X] Lewellin. No acknowledgement recorded. Del: to J Evans Nailor, 27 January 1801. Recorded: OS 1:394-395.

21 November 1796. Robt MINNIS to Benjamin REEDER. Lot [# not shown] in Morgan Town, on the west side of High Street, conveyed to Minnis by Zaquel Morgan and wife in a deed now burned but proven by the oath of John Hall. Includes 3s quit rent to heirs of Zacuel Morgan "forEVER" [sic]. Consideration: £20, VA. Signed: Robt Minnis. Witnesses: An Hite, Thomas Forster, Barw Clark. No acknowledgement recorded. Del: to B G Reeder, 3 November 1952. Recorded: OS 1:395-396.

[blank] 1797. Abraham and Elizabeth LOWE to John WEST. 100 acres on Indian Creek, no adjoiners named. Part of a 400-acre patent of 29 June 1796. Consideration: £60. Signed: Abraham [A] Lowe, Elizabeth [mark] Lowe. Witnesses: Zackquill Morgan, William Scripps. No acknowledgement recorded. Del: to John West, 20 February 1802. Recorded: OS 1:397-398.

24 November 1796. Thomas and Catherine EVANS to John B ARMISTED, Prince William Co. 1000 acres on the east side of Cheat River, near Quarry Run, joining with and above Evans' land. Surveyed 20 May 1787, patented 26 July 1796. Consideration: 5 shillings. Signed: Thos Evans, Caty Evans. Witnesses: none. Acknowledged in court. No delivery shown. Recorded: OS 1:398-399.

11 June 1798. Joseph and Ann WILSON to Susana BEALL. 100 acres on Deckers Creek, adjoining John Reed, Samuel Hanway, James S Wilson. Patented 5 April 1784 to Henry Smith and sold by him to Ann Wilson, 12 May 1788. Consideration: £10. Signed: Joseph Wilson, Ann Wilson. Witnesses: none. No acknowledgement recorded. No delivery shown. Recorded: OS 1:399.

22 October 1794. Thomas and Mary DAWSON to Lott RIDGEWAY, administrator of Robert YOUNG, deceased. Acreage not stated. Land on the waters of Pappaw Creek, formerly property of John Webb and later of Philip Roberts. Conveyed to the use of Robert Young's estate. Consideration: £100. Signed: Thos [-] Dawson, Mary [X] Dawson. Witnesses: Baldn Weaver, William Roark, Jacob Noose. No acknowledgement recorded. No delivery shown. Recorded: OS 1:400.

14 August 1798. Edward and Sarah EVANS to Jacob PINDELL. Acreage not stated. Land adjoining John Hamilton and including Evans' 1773 settlement. Consideration: £200, VA. Signed: Edward [mark] Evans, Sarah [mark] Evans. Witnesses: none. Acknowledged in court. No delivery shown. Recorded: OS 1:401.

11 June 1798. Alexander BRANDON to James SMITH, Hampsher Co. 157 acres, adjoining Jacob Pindell. No other adjoiners or place names mentioned. Consideration: $157. Signed: Alexander brandon. Witnesses: none. Acknowledged in court. No delivery shown. Recorded: OS 1:402.

10 April 1798. William and Jean TINGLE, Morgan Town, to Hugh SIDWELL. 2 acres, 74 poles on Wests Run, the moiety of a tract sold to Tingle by Reece Hastings and adjoining Hastings and Sidwell. Consideration: $20, VA. Signed: Wm Tingle [Jean does not sign]. Witnesses: none. Acknowledged in court. Del: to Hugh Sidwell, 15 November 1800. Recorded: OS 1:403.

9 July 1798. David and Charity HALL to Henry AMOS. 205 acres on the head of Glady Creek, adjoining Absalom Little, Thomas Laidley, and Robert Faucet. Part of a 410-acre patent. Consideration: £50, VA. Signed: David Hall, Charity [+] Hall. Witnesses: none. Acknowledged in court. No delivery shown. Recorded: OS 1:405.

2 January 1798. David and Sarah EASTON to James PATTON, all of Alexandria, Fairfax Co. 1000 acres on Salt Lick Creek, east side of Cheat River, adjoining Thomas Laidley. Patented to Charles Gallagher, 15 November 1787, and sold by him to David Easton, 10 November 1795. Consideration: $1. Signed: David Easton, Sarah Easton. Witnesses: John Gill, James Cavare [?], Ben Wear, James Miller. Receipt for $1. Acknowledged 21 May 1798 in Fairfax Co. Certificate of G Deneale [?], Clerk. No delivery shown. Recorded: OS 1:405-406.

5 August 1797. John and Eve STATELER to Martin LOWDINSLAGER, Green Co, PA. Lots #30-40 and 43, Hampshire Town. Part of a 17 February 1787 patent to John Stateler. Includes annual quit rent of 2s per lot

to Stateler, his heirs and assigns, forever. Consideration: $30, VA. Signed: John [S] Stateler, Eve [+] Stateler. Witnesses: John Fairfax, David Scott. No acknowledgement recorded. No delivery shown. Recorded: OS 1:407.

 13 March 1797. Zebulon and Mary HOGUE to Alexr HAWTHORN. 196 acres adjoining Josiah Jenkins. Part of a 200-acre patent of [blank] 1787. Consideration: £100. Signed: Zebulon Hogue, Mary [X] Hogue. Witnesses: Jona Davis, Wm Tingle, Asa Dudley. Acknowledged 20 March 1797 by Mary Hogue, before Jonathan Davis and Wm Tingle, JPs. No delivery shown. Recorded: OS 1:407-408 [Acknowledgement and commission on sheet interleaved between 406 and 407.]

 22 November 1797. Francis and Catharine WARMAN to Bartholomew JENKINS. 76 acres, 15 poles, adjoining John Ramsey, Enoch Jenkins, Bartholomew Jenkins. Consideration: $677. Signed: F Warman, Ca Warman. Witnesses: Enoch Evans, Enoch Jenkins, Thos Warman. Acknowledged 19 November 1803 by Catherine Warman. No delivery shown. Recorded: OS 1:408-409. [Acknowledgement and commission on sheet interleaved between 408 and 409.]

 14 August 1798. William and Elizabeth HOGUE to George PICKINGPAUGH, Fyette Co, PA. 151 acres on head branches of Scotts Mill Run, adjoining land claimed by William Dawson, Luke Harminson, William Hogue, James Buchanan, excepting 6½ acres not sold. Consideration: £100. Signed: William Hogge, Elizabeth Hogge. Witnesses: none. Acknowledged in court. No delivery shown. Recorded: OS 1:409-410.

 23 November 1797. Henry and Vilender FESLER to George Roberts TINGLE. Half lot [# not shown] in Morgan Town, adjoining Thomas Wilson's lot (now occupied by George Hite) and the lot occupied by William Lanham. Consideration: $50. Signed: Henry Fesler, Vilinder Fesler. Witnesses: Wm Tingle, Robert Lee, Christopher [SS] Stealy, Thomas [X] Doolittle. No acknowledgement recorded. No delivery shown. Recorded: OS 1:410.

 8 December 1797. Elias and Amy PEARCE to Joshua HICKMAN. 33 acres on Buffalo Lick Run, a drain of Monongahalia River, adjoining James Dunn and John Magee. Part of a 400-acre patent. Consideration: £35, VA. Signed: Elias [X] Pearce, Amy [A] Pearce. Witnesses: James [mark] Dunn, Henry Dunn, Nathan Springer. No acknowledgement recorded. Del: to Joshua Hickman, 9 April 1805. Recorded: OS 1:411.

 19 June 1797. John GALLASPEY, Fayatte Co, PA, to

Samuel SMITH. 400 acres on Scotts Meadow Run, adjoining and below James Camp, David Scott, Isaac Camp. Consideration: £200. Signed: John Gillispey. Witnesses: Dudley Evans, Wm Hamilton, Graftin [+] White. No acknowledgement recorded. No delivery shown. Recorded: OS 1:412.

[Pages 413 and 414 are now missing from this volume. Index at the front of the book indicates that OS 1:413 contained a conveyance from William DAWSON to Joseph SAPP, and that OS 1:414 contained the WILL of John GRAHAM, which is also recorded in Wills 1:295.]

10 December 1798. James and Lucretia STAFFORD to Alexander McINTIRE. 370 acres on Buffalo Creek, adjoining Robert Campbell's survey and Charles Martin. Patented to Stafford, 9 February 1787. Consideration: $1500. Signed: James Stafford, Lucresa [mark] Stafford. Witnesses: None. Acknowledged in court. No delivery shown. Recorded: OS 1:415.

12 December 1798. James S and Susanna WILSON to Daniel FORTNEY. 380 acres on Three Forks, adjoining lands sold by James Jenkins to William McCleery. Consideration: £200, VA. Signed: James S Wilson, Susannah [X] Wilson. Teste: J Evans. No acknowledgement recorded. Del: to Daniel Fortney, 9 March 1807. Recorded: OS 1:416.

15 November 1798. Robert and Elisabeth THORNTON, Harrison Co, to Adam BROWN, Fayette Co, PA. 400 acres on Sandy Creek, adjoining Charles Donaldson. Tract conveyed by John Jacob Judy to Thornton. Consideration: £200. Signed: Robert [RT] Thornton. [Elisabeth does not sign.] Witnesses: Rawley Evans, Francis [mark] Tibbs, John Downer. Receipt for £200. No acknowledgement recorded. No delivery shown. Recorded: OS 1:417.

14 January 1799. Dudley and Annarah EVANS to Jabish BELL. 100 acres on Swamp Run, adjoining Theophilus Phillips' heirs. Part of a 1700-acre patent of 23 August 1797. Consideration: $100. Signed: Dudley Evans, Annarah Evans. Witnesses: none. Acknowledged in court. No delivery shown. Recorded: OS 1:417-418.

14 January 1799. Dudley and Annarah EVANS to William DRAGOO. 100 acres on Swamp Run, adjoining Andrew Miller. Part of a 1700-acre patent of 23 August 1797. Consideration: $100. Signed: Dudley Evans, Annarah Evans. Witnesses: none. Acknowledged in court. No delivery shown. Recorded: OS 1:418.

14 January 1799. Dudley and Annarah EVANS to John JONES. 100 acres on Three Fork, no adjoiners named. Part of a 1700-acre patent of 23 August 1797. Consideration:

$100. Signed: Dudley Evans, Annarah Evans. Witnesses: none. Acknowledged in court. No delivery shown. Recorded: OS 1:419.

12 November 1798. John and Hannah STAG to James MORRIS. 21½ acres on Scotts Mill Run, adjoining Morris, George Pickingpaugh. Consideration: £32, VA. Signed: John Stag, Hannah [X] Stag. Witnesses: John Dent, Edward Jones, Joseph Reed. No acknowledgement recorded. No delivery shown. Recorded: OS 1:420.

12 September 1798. Francis DEAKINS, George Town, Montgomery Co, MD, to Alexander SMITH, Alligany Co, MD. Francis Deakins, William Deakins Junr (deceased), and Clement Biddle were joint purchasers of lands, as tenants in common and not joint tenants, sold by Robert Ralston and James Vanuxen, the trustees of Bartholomew Tarrison, bankrupt merchant of Philadelphia. During the lifetime of William Deakins Junr the lands were bargained and sold to Alexander Smith. Under his last will and testament, William Deakins invested Francis with power to convey the lands to Smith. Property described as lots #1 and #2 on the west side of Cheat River, near Dunkard Bottom. Consideration: $1. Signed: Francis Deakins. Witnesses: John Reid, Chs Wayman, Clement Smith. Receipt for $1. Acknowledged by Francis and Eleanor Deakins, 12 September 1798, in George Town, MD. Certificate of Lloyd Beall, mayor of George Town. No delivery shown. Recorded: OS 1:420-423.

2 November 1798. Francis DEAKINS, George Town, Montgomery Co, MD, to Abraham WOODRING Junr. Lot #55 in the town of Mount Carmel. Consideration: $10. Signed: Francis Deakins. Witnesses: A Faw, Clemt Sewall, James D Barry. Acknowledged, 2 November 1798 in George Town, MD. Certificate of Lloyd Beall, mayor of George Town. No delivery shown. Recorded: OS 1:423-424.

2 November 1798. Francis DEAKINS, George Town, Montgomery Co, MD, to John HOYE and Abram WOODRING Junr. 103 acres on the west side of Cheat River, between Buffalo Lick Creek and the Jurdins Bottoms. No adjoiners named. Surveyed 5 June 1786 for Francis and William Deakins. Consideration: [£? $?]100. Signed: Francis Deakins. Witnesses: A Faw, Clemt Sewell, James D Barry. Acknowledged 2 November 1798 in George Town, MD. Certificate of Lloyd Beall, mayor of George Town. No delivery shown. Recorded: OS 1:424-425.

26 September 1798. Francis DEAKINS, George Town, Montgomery Co, MD, to Nicholas WOODRING. Lot #39 and #40 in town of Mount Carmel. Consideration: £6, MD. Signed: Francis Deakins. Witnesses: Edwn Jones, Willm Whaim,

John Mountz Junr. Acknowledged 26 September 1798 in Montgomery Co, MD. Certificate of Lloyd Beall, mayor of George Town. No delivery shown. Recorded: OS 1:425-426.
29 May 1798. Balzer KRETCHER to Samuel POSTLEWAIT. Power of attorney to convey 200 acres of a larger tract patented to Jeremiah Simpson and Thomas Bird. Signed: Baltzer Kretcher. Witnesses: Jas C Goff, William Asby. Acknowledged 29 May 1798 before John T Goff, JP. Recorded: OS 1:426.
10 October 1798. Jonathan DAVIS to Ezekiel CHANEY. Lot [# not shown] in Morgan Town, on main street opposite William McCleery's lot and adjoining a half-lot of John Melrose. Consideration: £30. Signed: Jona: Davis. Witnesses: Noah Linsley, J Evans, Nimrod Evans. Receipt for £30. No acknowledgement recorded. Del: "to him selfe", 3 August 1805. Recorded: OS 1:427.
5 April 1798. WILL of Margaret STEMPLE. Daughter Barbary: excluded from any share in the estate. Personalty and cash to sons John, David, and Martin, and to daughters Christeenah, Catherine, Rosanah, Susanah, Eve, and Polly. Executors: son John Stemple and son-in-law Jacob Ridinhour. Signed: Margarett [+] Stemple. Witnesses: David Ridenhour, William Wiles, John George Wiles [all?] "signed in dutch." No probate data. Recorded: OS 1:428-429. [Also recorded in Wills 1:298.]
6 October 1798. Samuel and Magdalen COBB to Benjamin WHITSTON [also written WHITSON and WHILSON in the instrument]. 125 acres on Little Sandy Creek, adjoining Robert Brownfield. Part of a 400-acre resident right conveyed by Thomas Berry Junr to Samuel Cobb. Consideration: £28.2.6. Signed: Samuel Cobb, Magdalin Cobb. Witness: teste John Evans. No acknowledgement recorded. No delivery shown. Recorded: OS 1:428.
30 October 1798. Bertrand EWELL, Prince William Co, to Isaac H WILLIAMS. Mortgage on 565 acres at Deckers Creek, near the mouth of Laurel Run in the Monongalia Glades. No adjoiners named. Land conveyed to Ewell by John and Mahitable Melrose, 29 October 1798. Consideration: £560, VA, with repayment and interest schedule. Signed: Bertrand Ewell. Witnesses: J Williams, Hugh McNeely, Noah Linsly, Nimrod Evans. No acknowledgement recorded. Del: to JHW, 25 May 1802. Recorded: OS 1:429-430.
29 October 1798. John and Mahitible MELROSE, Morgan Town, to Bertrand EWELL, Prince William Co. 565 acres on Deckers Creek, conveyed to Melrose by Jesse and Rachel Hanway, 12 December 1797. Consideration: £560, VA. Signed: John Melrose [Mahitible does not sign].

Witnesses: J Williams, Noah Linsly, Nimrod Evans, E Evans, Alexr Hawthorn. No acknowledgement recorded. No delivery shown. Recorded: OS 1:430-431.

[blank] 1796. John and Mary GRAY, Berkely Co, to Robert RUTHERFORD, Esq, residence not stated. 360 acres on Buffalo Creek, adjoining Rutherford's 1000-acre tract. Consideration: £190, VA. Signed: John Gray [Mary does not sign]. Witnesses: Geo Hite, Wythe Baylor, Robert Gates Hite. No acknowledgement recorded. Del: to James Brown, 1 June 1802. Recorded: OS 1:432-433.

3 December 1798. William SLIDGER, Alleghany Co, MD, to Jacob MYERS, son of George, Baltimore Co, MD. 170 acres on Scotts Mill Run and Dunkard Creek, adjoining John Gooding and Jesse Martin. Conveyed to Slidger by Jesse and Hannah Martin, 13 June 1797. Consideration: $175. Signed: Wm Slidger. Witness: J Winchester. Receipt for $175 and acknowledgement by William Slidger in Baltimore, 3 December 1798. Certificate of Jas Calhoun, mayor of Baltimore. Del: to John Stealey. Recorded: OS 1:434-435.

14 January 1799. Robert and Hannah FERREL to John SAYRE. 237½ acres, 31 poles on White Day Creek, adjoining Thomas Griggs, the "bigg road," and Ferrel's settlement right. Part of a larger tract including a settlement and preemption right. Consideration: £117, VA. Signed: Robert Ferrel, Hannah [+] Ferrel. Witnesses: Daniel Sayre, John Bunner, Reuben Bunner. No acknowledgement recorded. Del: to Sayre. Recorded: OS 1:436.

10 September 1798. Charles and Priscilla CONWAY, Executrix of Jonathan REES, deceased, of Fayette Co, PA, to George ZINN. During his lifetime Rees sold Zinn 400 acres on Deckers Creek, in the Monongalia Glades, and his will directed Priscilla, his executrix, to convey the land upon payment of the purchase money. Land adjoining John Simpson, surveyed for Rees 18 June 1784 and patented 2 May 1785. Consideration: £172, PA. Signed: Charles Conaway, Prisilla [X] Conaway. Witnesses: none. Acknowledged in court. Receipt for purchase money, signed by Charles Conaway. Del: to G Zinn. Recorded: OS 1:437-438.

[blank] 1797. Jacob and Elizabeth NUSE to Hugh McNEELY. Lot [# not shown] in Morgan Town, adjoining High St [remainder of description blank]. Consideration: [blank]. Signed: Jacob Noose, Elizabeth [mark] Noose. Witnesses: none. Acknowledged in court. Del: to Mrs McNeely, 27 May 1805. Recorded: OS 1:439-440.

26 May 1798. William (Sr) and Ann WILLEY to William

WILLEY Junr. 159 acres on Scotts Run, adjoining William Watkins, Booz Burrows. Part of a 400-acre patent to William Sr. Consideration: £[blank], VA. Signed: William Willy, Ann Willey. Witnesses: David Scott, John Dent, John Willey. Acknowledged 26 May 1798 by William and Ann Willey. No delivery shown. Recorded: OS 1:440-441.

12 June 1798. Coverdill and Suffia COLE to John WILLEY. 50½ acres on Scotts Mill Run, no adjoiners named. Part of a larger patent granted to John Shibley. Consideration: £88.7.6, VA. Signed: Coverdill Cole, Saphia [X] Cole. Witnesses: none. Acknowledged in court. Del: to Wm Willey Senr, 12 May 1802. Recorded: OS 1:442.

11 February 1799. John and Mary HUTSON to Harry STEVENS, Green Co, PA. 68 acres on the Camp Run, adjoining Casper Everly and Charles Martin. Part of a patent of 19 August 1794. Consideration: $204. Signed: John [0] Hutson, Mary [-] Hutson. Witnesses: none. Acknowledged in court. Del: to H Stevens, 21 June 180[1??]. Recorded: OS 1:443.

31 March 1797. Hiel and Hannah PECK to William WALLACE, all of Montgomery Co, MD. 1000 acres on Warrior Fork of Dunker Creek, adjoining Eastburn's survey. Granted to said Hannah Peck in the name of Hannah Eastburn, 31 October 1783. Consideration: £500. Signed: Heil Peck, Hannah Peck. Witness: John Summers, Elimelech Swearingen. Acknowledged 31 March 1797 in Montgomery Co, MD. Certificate of Upton Beall, clerk of Montgomery Co, 1 April 1797. No delivery shown. Recorded: OS 1:444-445.

24 March 1798. Rees and Mary HASTINGS to William TINGLE. 20¼ acres, 12 poles on Wests Run, adjoining Hugh Sidwell's meadow, William McCleery, and heirs of Edward Pindcll. Part of a larger tract granted to Henry Robertson and conveyed by him, to Rees Hastings and Hugh Sidwell. Consideration: $164. Signed: Rees Hastings, Mary [mark] Hastings. Witnesses: Asa Dudley, Alexr Hawthorn, Frederick Gibbler, James Daugherty. No acknowledgement recorded. No delivery shown. Recorded: OS 1:446.

12 February 1798. Simeon and Massa RIGGS to Richard SMITH. 21 acres on White Day Creek. Part of a 400-acre settlement survey of Robinson Lucas, who conveyed 189¼ acres to Riggs. Consideration: £50, VA. Signed: Simeon Riggs, Massa [X] Riggs. Witnesses: Thomas Gregs, Reuben Bunner, Henry Weaver Senr. No acknowledgement recorded. No delivery shown. Recorded: OS 1:447-448.

9 March 1798. John and Catherine MILLAR to Aron ROYCE. Lots #12 and #13 in the town of Kingwood, on the south side of Main Street. Consideration: £6, VA.

Signed: John Millar, Catherine Millar, "signed in Dutch." Witnesses: David Morgan, William Royce, Thomas Smoot. No acknowledgement recorded. Del: to D Morgan, 9 March 1802. Recorded: OS 1:448.

28 October 1797. Bartholomew and Susannah JENKINS to Joseph POPE, Prince Georges Co, MD. 400 acres on the ridge between Booths Creek and Cobuns Creek, no adjoiners named. Patented 20 September 1783. Consideration: $800. Signed: Barth Jenkins, Susanna Jenkins. Witnesses: Enoch Evans, Thos Chipps, Joseph Jenkins, F Warman. Certificate of Enoch Evans and Jonathan Davis for Susannah's acknowledgement, 17 June 1798. Del: to Joseph Jenkins, 25 August 1800. Recorded: OS 1:449-450.

23 April 1798. Augustin and Hannah FREIND [also written FRUND in the document] to John DAVIS. One undivided moiety of 50 acres at Snowey Glade Creek, adjoining George Ashby. Patented to Ashby 10 September 1787. One undivided moiety of another tract, acreage not stated, at Snowey Glade Creek. No adjoiners named. Consideration: $1190. Signed: Augustin [AF] Frund, Hannah [HF] Frund. Witnesses: Nimrod Evans, Noah Linsley, Robt Hawthorn. Acknowledged by Hannah before William Tingle and James Scott, 23 April 1798. No delivery shown. Recorded: OS 1:451-452.

12 July 1798. Richard CLAIBORNE, Esq, late of Richmond, VA, and now of Philadelphia PA, to John HOPKINS and George PICKETT, gentlemen, of Richmond, VA. 52,000 acres in 31 tracts. No place names or adjoiners mentioned. Consideration: $3819.86, the balance of an account due to Claiborne from Mrs Susan Baring, late Susan Heyward, now the wife of Charles Baring, Esq. The balance assigned by Baring to Hopkins and Pickett, 27 June 1798. Signed: Rd Claiborne. Witnesses: Michael Kitts, Chs Barring Junr, Hilary Baker. Receipt for purchase money. Acknowledged by Richard Claiborne, 5 July [sic] 1798, before Hilary Baker, Mayor of Philadelphia. Acknowledged by Anne Claiborne, wife of Richard, 11 February 1799 in Monongalia. No delivery shown. Recorded: OS 1:453-455, 458 [pp 456-457 omitted in numbering].

13 March 1798. Elias and Susanna LEIGHTON to John STEWART, Washington Co, PA. 320 acres on Sandy Creek and Laurel Run, part of Leighton's settlement right. No adjoiners named. Consideration: £240, VA. Signed: Elias [mark] Layton, Susanna [mark called for but not shown] Layton. Witnesses: none. Acknowledged in court. No delivery shown. Recorded: OS 1:459.

No date. Account of Mrs Chas BARRING with Richard CLAIBORNE. Recorded: unnumbered sheet interleaved between OS 1:459-460.

29 February 1798. Adam HELMICK, Fayette Co, PA, to George McDANIELS, Hampshier Co. 185 acres on Laurel Run, adjoining Elias Leghton and Patrick Johnson. Consideration: £30, VA. Signed: Adam [mark] Helmick. Witnesses: Joseph Lane, Levi Potter, Russel Potter. No acknowledgement recorded. No delivery shown. Recorded: OS 1:460.

10 October 1796. Philip and Rachel PINDELL to William WINDSOR. 40 acres on Flagy Meadow Run, on the west side of Monongalia, adjoining Joseph Barker. Patented 1 May 1785. Consideration: [£?$?]100, VA. Signed: Philip Pindell, Rachel Pindell. Witnesses: Peter Hess, Elijah [X] Piles. No acknowledgement recorded. No delivery shown. Recorded: OS 1:461.

8 January 1798. Jesse and Rachel HANWAY to Henry CRISS. 300 acres on Deckers Creek, no adjoiners named. Consideration: £110, VA. Signed: Jesse Hanway, Rachel [mark] Hanway. Witnesses: Elihu Horton, Thomas [+] Doolittle, John Melrose. No acknowledgement recorded. Del: to H Criss, 20 June 1809. Recorded: OS 1:462.

9 April 1798. Septamus and Sarah CADWALLADER, Fayette Co, PA, to William DARLING. Acreage not stated, on west side of Cheat River, adjoining William Morgan, James Morgan, John Daugherty, William Darling, and including an improvement made by Septamus Cadwallader. Consideration: $200. Signed: Septemus Cadwallader [Sarah does not sign]. Witnesses: J Williams, J Evans, E Evans. No acknowledgement recorded. No delivery shown. Recorded: OS 1:463.

28 December 1797. Francis BURREL Senr to Francis BURREL Junr. 310 acres on Cobuns Creek, no adjoiners named. Patented 14 December 1784. Consideration: £50, VA. Signed: Francis [X] Burrel Senr. Witnesses: Evan Morgan, Henry Hamilton, And Frazer. No acknowledgement recorded. Del: to Mtt Hite, 4 March [blank]. Recorded: OS 1:464.

20 October 1797. Aden and Margarett BAYLES to George NORTH, Fayette Co, PA. 100 acres on Buffalo, adjoining Adam Ice, Anthony Mahon. Part of a larger tract patented to John Ice and conveyed by his heir at law, William Ice, to Bayles, 11 January 1796. Consideration: £50. Signed: Aden Bayles, Margarett [X] Bayles. Witnesses: J Williams, J Evans junr, Joshua Stockton. Acknowledged by Margaret Bayles before B Reeder and J Davis, JPs, 28 October 1797. No delivery

shown. Recorded: OS 1:465-466.

25 September 1797. Hugh and Kisiah MARSHALL, Braking Co, KY, to Samuel HANWAY. 340 acres on the south side of Laurel Run, a branch of Sandy Creek, adjoining Jeremiah Tanehill and William Hamilton. Patented 7 August 1787. Consideration: £100. Signed: Hugh Marshall, Kesiah Marshall. Witness: none named. Receipt for £100. Acknowledged by Hugh and Keziah in Mason Co, KY, 25 September 1797. Certificate of Thos Marshall Junr, Clerk of Mason Co. No delivery shown. Recorded: OS 1:467.

10 September 1798. John and Barthseba ["Bashy" in body of the instrument] SPRINGER to the heirs of Joseph BATTEN, deceased [grantees are not named individually]. 200 acres west of the Monongalia River and part of Springer's patent of 8 October 1789. No adjoiners named. Consideration: £120, specie, paid by Joseph Batten. Signed: John Springer, Barshaba Springer. Witnesses: none. Acknowledged in court. Del: to George Lowe, 4 September 1810. Recorded: OS 1:468-469.

5 December 1796. Robert MINNIS to Bartholomew CLARK. Lot [# not shown] in Morgan Town, adjoining Widow Peirpoint's lot. Consideration: £20. Signed: Robert Minnis. Witnesses: James Miller, Alexr Hawthorn, George Hite. Acknowledged in court. Del: to B Clark, 12 July 1804. Recorded: OS 1:469.

[blank] 1798. Thomas and Martha TANEHILL to Samuel DEWESE. 100 acres on Sandy Creek, adjoining Thomas Tanehill. Patented 8 June 1796. Consideration: £100, VA. Signed: Thos Tanehill, Martha [X] Tanehill. Witnesses: none. Acknowledged in court. Del: to Saml Dewees, 26 February 1806. Recorded: OS 1:470.

10 August 1795. Moses MUSGRAVE to Jonathan ROBERTS. 200 acres on a branch of Tygers Valley River, adjoining Jacob Prickett and William Petty John. Part of a 28 June 1791 patent to Jacob Prickett for 400 acres. Consideration: £40, VA. Signed: Moses Musgrave. Witnesses: Robert Ferrel, Nathan Springer, Richard Merrefield. No acknowledgement recorded. Del: to Thomas Anderson, 14 December 1801. Recorded: OS 1:471.

29 February 1796. Thomas BERRY, Harrison Co, to Samuel COBB. 400 acres on Sandy Creek, adjoining Thomas Berry Senr. Patented 31 October 1792. Consideration: £100, VA. Signed: Thomas Berry. Witnesses: Daniel Davisson, Josiah Davisson, John Prunty. Proved by witnesses, 20 June 1796 in Harrison Co. Certificate of Benj Wilson, Clerk of Harrison Co. No delivery shown. Recorded: OS 1:472.

3 September 1795. David HANWAY, Harford Co, MD, to

Jesse HANWAY. Power of attorney to recover debts and to convey 2000 acres on Little Sandy. Signed: David Hanway. Witnesses: Wm Smithson, John Guyton. Acknowledged by David Hanway, 3 September 1795, in Harford Co, MD. Certificate of John Lee Gibson, Clerk of Harford Co. Recorded: OS 1:473.

19 July 1797. Conrad HOGMIRE, Washington Co, MD, to Francis and Wm DEAKINS, both of Montgomery Co, MD. 127 lots in the town of Salem, Monongalia Co, laid out on Hogmire's own property. Excepts lots #42, 62 and 63, already conveyed to Nicholas Marstiller, and #43, 73, 74, 85, 115 and 120, for his own use. Lots #22, 56, 60, and 84 formerly promised for churches and a school. Also conveys 3/8 interest in lots held by David Ridenour and Thomas Rinehart. Also conveys 279 acres adjoining the town. 91 acres, previously conveyed to Hogmire by Deakins, appear by an older survey to be within the lands of Thomas Goff. Adjoiners include tracts conveyed by Hogmire to Jacob Teter and to John and Elizabeth Stough. Consideration: £265.13.1 for the town and lots, £279 for the adjoining acreage, and £22.15 for Hogmire's expenses re: the land disputed with Goff, for a total of £544.13.1, MD. Signed: Conrad Hogmire. Witness: William Fitzhugh. Acknowledged by Conrad and Mary Hogmire, 19 July 1797, in Washington Co, MD. Certificate of E Williams, Clerk of Washington Co, 9 August 1797. No delivery shown. Recorded: OS 1:474-476.

14 November 1796. Robert MINNIS to Moses WILLIAMS. Half-lot in Morgantown, adjoining lot belonging to Henry Peters' heirs and where Frederick Reed now lives. Including ground rent, terms not stated. Consideration: £101, VA. Signed: Robt Minnis. Witnesses: none. Acknowledged in court. No delivery shown. Recorded: OS 1:476-477.

14 February 1797. Robert MINNIS to James SNODGRASS, son to Wm Snodgrass. 100 acres on Buffaloe Creek, adjoining Morgans Run. Consideration: £10. Signed: Robt Minnis. Witnesses: Charles Snodgrass, Philip Roberts, Wm Snodgrass, Isaac Eddy. Receipt for purchase money. Del: to Wm Snodgrass father of James, 13 August 1805. Recorded: OS 1:478.

31 December 1796. WILL of James McCOLLUM. Wife Elizabeth: one-third of estate real and personal during her lifetime. Daughter Mary: household furniture. Son Daniel: all other real and personal estate; he to pay Mary £100, PA, in 5 years after my death @ £20 per year. Executors: wife Elizabeth and son Daniel. Signed: James [mark] McCollum. Witnesses: Samuel Darby, Joseph Martin,

Russel Potter. No probate data. Recorded: OS 1:479. [Also recorded in Wills 1:296-297.]

25 December 1797. WILL of Thomas HELLIN. Daughter Anne Coon: all estate, real and personal, during her lifetime, including debt due me from Joshua Oatley. After her death, land to grandchildren Mary and Jacob Koon. Executors: Anthony Koon, Benjamin J Brice. Signed: Thomas [X] Hellin. Witnesses: Nathaniel Cochran, Spencer Martin, Norman Randall. No probate data. Recorded: OS 1:480. [Also recorded in Wills 1:295-296.]

12 January 1789. David and Ann CROLL to John STANLEY. 86 acres on Arons Creek, adjoining Joseph Tricket and John Burk. Part of a 400-acre patent of 20 September 1785. Consideration: £40. Signed: David Croll, Ann [mark] Croll. Witnesses: none. Acknowledged in court. No delivery shown. Recorded: OS 1:481.

26 September 1798. Francis DEAKINS, to Thomas TOLBOTT, both of George Town, Montgomery Co, MD. Lot #38 in town of Mount Carmel. Consideration: £3. Signed: Francis Deakins. Witnesses: Edw Jones, Willm Whaim, John Mountz Junr. Acknowledged 26 September 1798. Certificate of Lloyd Beall, mayor of George Town. No delivery shown. Recorded: OS 1:482.

9 July 1798. David and Nancy CROLL to Jacob NOOSE. 22 acres on Aarons Creek, no adjoiners named. Part of a larger patent. Consideration: £11. Signed: David Croll, Ann Croll. Witnesses: none. Acknowledged in court. Del: to Jacob Neuss, 27 July 1805. Recorded: OS 1:483.

4 February 1797. Francis DEAKINS and William DEAKINS Junr, Montgomery Co, MD, to Henry DILMAN, Washington Co, MD. On 28 May 1792 the grantors conveyed to Everhart Michael 100 acres in Monongalia Co. The deed was later destroyed by fire. Michael sold to his nephew Henry Dilman, to whom the grantors now make conveyance. 100 acres, part of a 1094-acre patent. No adjoiners or place names mentioned. Consideration: £31, MD. Signed: Francis Deakins, Will Deakins Junr. Witnesses: Aens Campbell, Greeny Howard, Thos Corcoran, Lloy [sic] Beall [the two latter witnesses for William Deakins]. Acknowledged by Francis and Eleanor Deakins, 4 February 1797, in Montgomery Co, MD. Certificate of Upton Beall, Clerk, 9 February 1797. Acknowledged by William Deakins. Certificate of Upton Beall, 11 March 1797. No delivery shown. Recorded: OS 1:484-485.

13 March 1798. Joseph and Jemima DOWNING to George ROBERTS. 328 acres on the Hazel Run, adjoining Joseph Martin. Patented 20 April 1784. Consideration: $400. Signed: Joseph Downing, Jemmimah [+] Downing. Witnesses:

none. Acknowledged in court. Del: to G Roberts, 19 February 1800. Recorded: OS 1:486-487.

13 February 1798. Francis DEAKINS and William DEAKINS Junr, George Town, Montgomery Co, MD, to Nicholas MARSTILLER. 152 acres on Salt Lick Creek, about 3 miles east from the mouth. No adjoiners named. Consideration: $152. Signed: Francis Deakins, Will Deakins Junr. Witnesses: Lloyd Beall, Washington Bowie, Leonard H Johns. Receipt for $152. Acknowledged by William and Jane Deakins and Francis and Eleanor Deakins, 13 February 1798. Certificate of Lloyd Beall, mayor of Georgetown. No delivery shown. Recorded: OS 1:487-488.

22 February 1798. Thomas and Rebeccah BUTLAR to James ROSE. 100 acres on the east side of Cheat River, adjoining William Daugherty. Patented 10 October 1782. Signed: Thomas Bullar [sic; Rebeccah does not sign]. Witnesses: Ezra Horton, James Morgan, Levi Knotts. No acknowledgement recorded. Del: to James Rose, 13 September 1809. Recorded: OS 1:489.

8 June 1798. Enoch and Sarah JAMES to John ROSE, all of Harrison Co. 110¼ acres on the west side of the West Fork River, just above the mouth of Tevebaugh Run and adjoining John Dunham. Consideration: £50. Signed: Enoch James, Sarah James. Witnesses: none. Acknowledged in court. Certificate of Thos Cheney and John Hall, JPs, as to Sarah's acknowledgement. Del: to Saml Freeman, 2 June 1807. Recorded: OS 1:491. [Page 490 is blank.]

9 June 1798. John and Rebeccah ROSE, Harrison Co, to Samuel FREEMAN. 110¼ acres on the west side of the West Fork River, just above the mouth of Tevebaugh Run and including the mouth of the Camp Run. Consideration: £65. Signed: John Rose, Rebecca Rose. Witnesses: Thomas Laidley, Thomas McKinley, Anthony Coon. Acknowledged in court. Del: to Saml Freeman, 2 January 1807. Recorded: OS 1:492.

13 February 1798. Francis DEAKINS and William DEAKINS Junr, George Town, Montgomery Co, MD, to Benjamin MARSTILLER. 152 acres adjoining Nicholas Marstiller. Part of a 281-acre patent. No other adjoiners or place names mentioned. Consideration: $152. Signed: Francis Deakins, Will Deakins Jur. Witnesses: Lloyd Beall, Leonard H Johns, Washington Bowie. Receipt for $152. Acknowledged by Francis and Eleanor Deakins and William and Jane Deakins, 13 February 1798. Certificate of Lloyd Beall, mayor of George Town. Del: to [illegible] Marstiller's order, 3 March 180[1?]7?]. Recorded: OS 1:492-493.

8 April 1799. Absalom and Mary LITTLE, Fayette Co, PA, to Henry TUCKER. 400 acres on both sides of Glady Creek, adjoining and above Mason Poor, including a 1776 settlement. Patented 4 December 1785. Consideration: £200, VA. Signed: Absalom Little, Mary Little. Witnesses: none. Acknowledged in court. Del: to H Tucker, 9 October 1800. Recorded: OS 1:494.

29 October 1798. Alpheus and Mary GUSTIN to Bertrand EWELL, Prince William Co. 1000 acres on head drains of Scotts Mill Run and Dunkard Creek, adjoining William Anderson's survey. Entered 3 January 1785 and surveyed 3 February 1786 for William Anderson assignee. Patented to Alpheus Gustin, assignee of George Dent, assignee of Robt Minnis, assignee of William Anderson. Consideration: £500, VA. Signed: Alpheus Gustin, Mary Gustin. Witnesses: B Reeder, John Davis, Alexr Hawthorn, Asa Dudley, Hugh McNeely. Receipt for purchase money. Certificate of Alex Hawthorn and Asa Dudley as to Mary Gustin's acknowledgement, 29 October 1798. Del: to Ewell's brother. Recorded: OS 1:495-496.

12 December 1797. Jesse and Rachel HANWAY to John MELROSE. 565 acres on Deckers Creek in the Monongalia Glades, near the mouth of Laurel Run. Consideration: £500. Signed: Jesse Hanway, Rachael [mark] Hanway. Witnesses: Elihu Horton, Thomas [+] Doolittle, Henry [+] Criss. No acknowledgement recorded. Del: to Isaac H Williams, 25 May 1802. Recorded: OS 1:497.

10 May 1797. Francis DEAKINS and William DEAKINS Junr, Montgomery Co, MD, to James GOFF, Randolph Co. Quit claim for 205 acres in Randolph Co, on Cheat River, where Goff now dwells. Consideration: 20 shillings. Signed: Francis Deakins, Will Deakins Jur. Witnesses: Aens Campbell, Laurence ONeal [for Francis], Danl Reintzel, Geo French [for William]. Acknowledged by Francis Deakins, 13 May 1797; by William Deakins Junr, 8 June 1797. Certificate of Upton Beall, Clerk of Montgomery Co, MD. Del: to Jas J Goff, son of grantee, 2 December 1828. Recorded: OS 1:498-499.

12 February 1798. Philip and Luraina SHUTTLESWORTH to Samuel HUNT. 7½ acres, adjoining Tomes Run and the river road. Part of a 537 3/4 acre tract on which Shuttlesworth now lives. Consideration: $170. Signed: Philip Shuttlesworth, Lurana Shuttlesworth. Witnesses: none. Acknowledged in court. Del: to Joel Oxley, April 1800. Recorded: OS 1:500.

10 July 1797. Robert MINNIS to Morgan MORGAN. 400 acres on Plum Run, adjoining and above the lands and survey of Robert Campbell. Patented 11 May 1793.

Consideration: $100. Signed: Robt Minnis. Witnesses: none. Acknowledged in court. No delivery shown. Recorded: OS 1:501.

13 [30?] June 1798. Philip ROBERTS to Jesper WAYETT. 105 acres on Finches Run, part of a 400-acre tract sold to Roberts by John Webb, adjoining William Gray, [blank] Dawson. Consideration: £31.10, VA. Signed: Philip Roberts. Witnesses: William [W] Straight, John [+] Dragoe, Anne [A] Dragoe. No acknowledgement recorded. Del: to Jos Whisbey, 13 August 1802. Recorded: OS 1:502.

7 July 1798. George HOSKINSON and Benjamin and Nelly WILSON to Aaron POWELL. 807 acres on Laurel Run, a branch of Three Fork, adjoining Benjamin Brain, George Mordock. Part of a tract taken up by Hoskinson and Wilson. Consideration: £6.6, VA. Signed: George Hoskinson, Benjamin Wilson, Nelly Wilson. Witnesses: none. Acknowledged in court. No delivery shown. Recorded: OS 1:503.

5 January 1798. Jacob and Hannah SMITH to Daniel McCOLLUM. 100 acres adjoining McCollum's other land. No other adjoiners or place names mentioned. Consideration: £100, VA. Signed: Jacob Smith, Hannah Smith. Witnesses: Enoch Evans, Barthw Jenkins, James Jenkins. No acknowledgement recorded. No delivery shown. Recorded: OS 1:504.

10 June 1799. William and Sarah JOSEPH to Jeremiah JOSEPH. 50 acres, adjoining Elijah Burrows, Colo Evans, Nathan Joseph. Part of a 297-acre patent of 20 September 1785. Consideration: £100. Signed: William [+] Joseph, Sarah [X] Joseph. Witnesses: none. Acknowledged in court. Del: to J Joseph, 1804. Recorded: OS 1:505.

10 June 1799. William and Sarah JOSEPH to Nathan JOSEPH. 50 acres, adjoining Jeremiah Joseph, Lemuel Joseph. Part of a 297-acre patent of 20 September 1785. Consideration: £100, VA. Signed: William [X] Joseph, Sarah [X] Joseph. Witnesses: none. Acknowledged in court. Del: to Jeremiah Joseph, 1804. Recorded: OS 1:506.

11 June 1799. Francis (Jr) and Rachel BURREL and Catherine BURREL to George GRESMORE. 48 acres on Cobuns Creek, adjoining Philip Smell and Evan Morgan. Part of a 328-acre patent of 4 December 1784 to Francis Burrel Sr and conveyed by him to Francis Burrel Jr, 23 December 1797. Consideration: $160. Signed: Francis Burrel, Rachel [X] Burrel, Catherine [X] Burrel. Witnesses: none. Acknowledged in court. Receipt for $160. No delivery shown. Recorded: OS 1:507.

1 June 1799. Joseph and Ully WOLGAMOT to Tobias REAMS, Somerset Co, PA. 270 acres on Muddy Creek, adjoining David Morgan (deceased) and John Forsyth, the plantation on which Wolgamot now lives. Consideration: $420. Signed: Joseph Wolgamott, Ully [+] Wolgamott. Witnesses: John McClain, Edward Jones, Josanus Guber [sic! = *Johannes Huber*?]. Acknowledged by Ully Wolgamott before Edward Jones and John McClain, JP. Certificate 3 June 1799. No delivery shown. Recorded: OS 1:508-509.

28 June 1799. Christian HAGAMAN to Benjamin REEDER. Power of attorney to sue and recover of [blank] Thornton, Bucks Co, PA, who was appointed my guardian, and to recover all legacies and monies due me in PA. Signed: Christian Hagaman. Witnesses: J H Williams, Hugh McNeely. Recorded: OS 1:509.

10 June 1799. James and Mary Ann JENKINS to Charles MAGILL. 39 acres adjoining heirs of John Peirpoint, Robert Abercromby, Charles Magill, and Benjamin Jarrett. Part of a 200-acre patent of 1 May 1784 to Lewis Rodgers, conveyed by him to James Jenkins 26 July 1796. Resurveyed by order of court and repatented 27 December 1798. Consideration: $200. Signed: James Jenkins, Maryann [X] Jenkins. Witnesses: Faquire McCrea, Benj No Garrett, Barth Jenkins. Receipt for consideration money. No delivery shown. Recorded: OS 1:510.

10 March 1788. Thomas and Elizabeth HARDESTY to Samuel BYERS, all of Fayette Co, PA. 100 acres at Scotts Run, adjoining John Hamilton, Edward Evans. Part of a patent of 8 February 1784 to John Hamilton, conveyed by John and Martha Hamilton to Thomas Hardesty 12 December 1785. Consideration: £100, PA. Signed: Thomas [mark] Hardesty, Elizabeth [mark] Hardesty. Witnesses: Alexander Laughlin, John Skein. Acknowledged 13 March 1788 in Fayette Co, PA, by Thomas and Elizabeth Hardesty, before John Allen and Hugh Laughlin. Certificate of Ephraim Douglass, prothonotary, 24 June 1797. No delivery shown. Recorded: OS 1:511-512.

4 January 1797. David SCOTT and Clary BYRN. Articles of agreement. Scott is to maintain and educate Clary's young children and settle with them as they come of age. If he is the "longest liver," he is to return to the heirs unspecified Negroes and livestock (with their increase), as well as movable property. If Clary is the longest liver, she is to have 100 acres for life for her and her Negroes, with a good sugar camp thereon, and a comfortable framed house with two chimneys of brick or stone and furnished "in the best manner." 30 acres to be cleared and fenced, with 2 acres of meadow, adjoining

the Monongalia River and including the old orchard place at the lower end of the bottom, adjoining Savery's land on the river and up the mill run, the ferry and boat yard excepted. Clary renounces all other rights in Scott's estate. He is also to furnish her with corn, wheat, rye, and pork well salted. A codicil recites that use and benefit of Clary's land is to be used for cloathing and schooling the children, except for the part she has allowed to her son Charles Byrn. Scott to pay only so much as should come in to his hands of Samuel Byrn's estate. Scott to give bond and security to the executor when he receives the property of Clary's children. Signed: David Scott, Clary Byrn. Witnesses: Simon Cochran, John Magee, Stephen Gapen. Recorded: OS 1:513. [Evidently a marriage contract though not specifically identified as such.]

23 April 1798. Samuel and Rachel PETIT, Adams Co, Northwestern Territory, to Charles GALLAGHER, Mason Co, KY. 437 acres on Scotts Mill Run, adjoining Philip Lewis Senr, William Dawson, William Anderson. Surveyed 30 March 1785 and patented [blank]. Consideration: £140. Signed: Samuel Pettit, Rachel Pettit. Witnesses: none. Acknowledged in court, Mason Co, KY, 23 April 1798. Certificate of Thomas Marshall Jr, Clerk. Recorded: OS 1:514-515.

29 May 1799. Andrew ICE and John HENTHORN. Articles of agreement. Henthorn to lease a tract on the east side of Cheat River, known as Ices Ferry, for 5 years at annual rent of $113.33, due 1 March. $10 of this in cash, the rest in trade. If Henthorn makes any improvements on the tract, they are to be appraised and valued. Henthorn may not waste or sell timber without Ice's consent. Ice to regain the property on 1 April of the final year. Signed: Andrew [A] Ice, John Henthorn. Witnesses: F Warman, Joshua Warman. Recorded: OS 1:515.

4 December 1797. Mary ABBOTT and David CUSHMAN, Bracken Co, KY, to Hedgman TRIPLETT. 50 acres in Sandy Creek glades, adjoining Frazee's tract. Surveyed 18 March 1784. Consideration: £40. Signed: Mary [+] Abbott, David Cushman. Witnesses: Anderson Doniphan, John Morford, R S Thomas. Acknowledged in Bracken Co, KY, 4 December 1797. Certificate of Simon Walton, Clerk, 29 January 1798. Del: to H Triplett, 18 September 1801. Recorded: OS 1:516.

9 September 1799. William and Susannah JENKINS to Alexander RIGGS. 51 acres near the head of the east fork of Indian Creek, adjoining William Kennedy, William Jenkins. Part of a tract that Jenkins lives on.

Consideration: £50. Signed: William Jenkins, Susannah [mark] Jenkins. Witnesses: none. Acknowledged in court. Del: to Alex Riggs, 19 September 1814. Recorded: OS 1:517.

9 September 1799. James and Catherine ROBINSON to John WICKWARE, Harrison Co. 20 acres on the east side of Tygers Valley River, no adjoiners named. Part of a 100-acre patent of [blank]. Consideration: £5. Signed: Jas Robeson, Catherine [X] Robeson. Witnesses: none. Acknowledged in court. Del: to John Wickware, 2 August 1803. Recorded: OS 1:518.

20 April 1799. Martin and Margaret LOUDENSLAGER, Green Co, PA, to David HALL. Lot #30 in New Hampshier Town, part of a larger tract patented to John Stateler and conveyed by John and Eve Stateler to Loudenslager [blank] 1797. Includes 2s per annum quit rent to John Stateler. Consideration: $10. Signed: Martin Loudenslager, Margarett [X] Loudenslager. Witnesses: Abraham Miley, George Green Wood, John Downer. No acknowledgement recorded. No delivery shown. Recorded: OS 1:519.

28 May 1799. WILL of Margaret CUNNINGHAM. Daughter Susannah Pearce: 5s. Son Michael: 100 acres with a cabin, personalty (including Bible). Sons James and George: 400 acres, cattle, household furnishings, to be divided. Granddaughter Margarett Hersman: saddle. Granddaughters Eve and Margarett Hersman: wearing apparel. Executor: friend Hugh Sidwell. Signed: Margret [M] Cunningham. Witnesses: Tedey [?] Baker, Hugh Sidwell. No probate data. Recorded: OS 1:520. [Also recorded in Wills 1:292-293.]

13 August 1798. Jacob and Mary HOOVER, Fayette Co, PA, to John LANTZE, Green Co, PA. 126 3/4 acres, near the PA line on the north side of Dunker Creek, adjoining Nicholas Shins. Patented 15 June 1784. Consideration: £50, PA. Signed: Jacob Hoover, Mary [X] Hoover. Witnesses: none. Acknowledged in court. Del: to Jno Baldwin. Recorded: OS 1:521.

11 February 1799. Alexander and Margaret CLEG to John LANCE. 43 acres near the province line on the west side of Duncer Creek. No adjoiners named. Part of a 13 September 1788 patent. Consideration: £5. Signed: Alexander Cleg, Margret [mark] Cleg. Witnesses: Joseph Parrish, John Statelar, Richard Tennant. No acknowledgement recorded. Del: to Lance. Recorded: OS 1:522.

9 May 1799. Samuel JACOB, Annearundale Co, MD, to Mary BOYLE and James BOYLE, both of Annapolis, MD,

and Daniel BOYLE, Frederick Co, MD. 300 acres at Martins Run, adjoining Charles Donaldson. Consideration: £300, MD. Signed: Samuel Jacob. Witnesses: Saml [illegible], Nichs Brewer Junr. Acknowledged 9 May 1799 in Annapolis MD by Samuel Jacob, before Nicholas Carroll, mayor. Certificate of A Golden, Clerk. Recorded: OS 1:524-525. [Page 523 is blank.]

9 July 1798. Samuel HANWAY to William BIGGS. 195 acres at Muddy Creek, adjoining Enoch More and William Biggs. Patented 10 July 1784. Consideration: £30. Signed: Samuel Hanway. Witnesses: none. Acknowledged in court. No delivery shown. Recorded: OS 1:526-527.

11 February 1799. Dudley and Annarah EVANS to Robert BELL. 120 acres on Three Forks, adjoining Jabish Bell. Part of a 1700-acre patent of 23 August 1797. Consideration: $100. Signed: Dudley Evans, Ann Arah Evans. Witnesses: none. Acknowledged in court. No delivery shown. Recorded: OS 1:527.

9 July 1799. Samuel HANWAY to Joseph WEAVER. 160 acres, adjoining heirs of John Peirpoint, heirs of Lott Ridgeway, Jesse Bayles, Francis Tibbs, Nicholas Vandevort. Part of a 175-acre patent of 10 November 1791. Consideration: £100. Signed: Samuel Hanway. Witnesses: none. Acknowledged in court. Del: to J Weaver, April 1800. Recorded: OS 1:528.

9 July 1798. Dudley and Annarah EVANS to Thomas THOMAS. 172 acres on a drain of Big Sandy, and 168 acres adjoining Theophilus Phillips' heirs. [Both?] from a 23 August 1797 patent. Consideration: $344. Signed: Dudley Evans, Annarah Evans. Witnesses: none. Acknowledged in court. No delivery shown. Recorded: OS 1:529.

9 May 1800. Jeremiah JOSEPH's ear mark for cattle, sheep and hogs is entered. Recorded: OS 1:529.

13[?] August 1799. John and Elizabeth STUART to Andrew STERLING, Fayette Co, PA. 300 acres, known as Layton's land, adjoining Daniel Boyce. One moiety of a 400-acre settlement right, conveyed by Elias and Susannah Layton to John Stuart. Consideration: $500, VA. Signed: John [X] Stewart, Elisabeth [mark] Stewart. Witnesses: David Scott, Wm John. Acknowledged by Elisabeth Stuart. Certificate of David Scott and Wm John, 14 August 1799. Del: to Jonathan Harris, 26 August 1809, per order. Recorded: OS 1:530-531.

23 October 1797. Thomas POWEL, Bourbon Co, KY, by Blemus HAYDON, his attorney in fact, to John ORR, Fayette Co, PA. 139 acres on Sandy Creek, a branch of Tyger Valley River, adjoining William Augustus Smith and Theophilus Phillips. Consideration: £100, VA. Signed:

Blemus Haydon. Witnesses: Enoch Evans, F Warman, John Ramsey. No acknowledgement recorded. Del: to William DAVIS. Recorded: OS 1:532.

12 February 1798. John WIMP to Joseph FOX, Fayette Co, PA. 97 acres on Big Sandy Creek, adjoining Russel Potter. Part of a larger tract patented to John Judy. Consideration: £70, VA. Signed: John Wimp. Witnesses: none. Acknowledged in court. No delivery shown. Recorded: OS 1:533.

10 September 1798. John and Bashy SPRINGER to Uriah MORGAN. 100 acres on the west side of Monongalia River, adjoining Joseph Batten. Part of a larger tract patented 8 October 1789. Consideration: £60, specie. Signed: John Springer, Barsheba Springer. Witnesses: none. Acknowledged in court. Del: to Jas Hayes, 12 May 1802. Recorded: OS 1:534.

12 August 1799. Richard and Jane CAIN to Samuel CAIN. 200 acres on the right fork of Dunker Creek. No adjoiners named. Consideration: £200, VA. Signed: Richard Cain. [Jane does not sign.] Witnesses: Rawley Evans, Jona: Davis, J Evans Junr. No delivery shown. Recorded: OS 1:535.

10 June 1799. James and Maryann JENKINS to Saray Brook JENKINS, George JENKINS, Maryann JENKINS, and Josiah Bartholomew JENKINS, heirs of Josiah JENKINS, deceased. 248 acres on Cheet River, adjoining James Stafford. Moiety of a 496-acre tract purchased of Lewis Rogers and patented to James Jenkins 27 December 1798. Consideration: 1 shilling, VA. Signed: James Jenkins, Maryann [+] Jenkins. Witnesses: Benjn Norris Garrett, Charles Magell, Barth Jenkins. Acknowledged in court. Del: to Margrett Jenkins. Recorded: OS 1:536-537.

13 April 1799. Andrew and Elizabeth McKUNE to Jacob LOWERY, all of Dunbar Twp, Fayette Co, PA. 525 acres on Muddy waters of Cheat River. No adjoiners named. Surveyed 8 September 1787. Consideration: £200, PA. Signed: Andrew McKune, Elizabeth McKune. Witnesses: Henry Beason, Robert Patterson. Receipt for consideration money. Acknowledged before Jonathan Rowland and Robert Moore, 13 April 1799, in Fayette Co. Certificate of Ephraim Douglass, prothonotary, 4 November 1799. Recorded: 11 November 1799, OS 1:538-539.

13 December 1784. Thomas CLARE, Fayette Co, PA, to Bartholomew JENKINS. 400 acres on the dividing ridge between Booths and Coburns Creeks, no adjoiners named. Patented 20 September 1783. Consideration: £150, VA. Signed: Thomas Clare. Witnesses: none. Acknowledged in court. Del: to Josh Jenkins, 25 August 1800. Recorded:

OS 1:540.
8 July 1799. Thomas and Mary MILLER to Moses DOOLITTLE. 39 acres, adjoining Miller. Part of a larger tract patented [blank]. Consideration: £7.10. Signed: Thomas Millar, Mary Miller. Witnesses: none. Acknowledged in court. Del: to Moses Doolittle, 28 February 1807. Recorded: OS 1:541.

12 August 1799. Richard and Jean CAIN to James CAIN. 400 acres on Three Forks, no adjoiners named. Consideration: £500. Signed: Richard Cain, Jean [X] Cain. Witnesses: Rawley Evans, Jona: Davis, J Evans Jr. No acknowledgement recorded. No delivery shown. Recorded: OS 1:542.

8 July 1799. Richard and Jean CAIN to James CAIN. 303 acres on Cheat River, adjoining Thomas Mills, Richard Cain, Mason and Dickson's trail line, John McFarland. Consideration: £500. Signed: Richard Cain [Jean does not sign]. Witnesses: E Evans, F Warman, Thos Warman. No acknowledgement recorded. Del: to Richard Cain, 6 January 1810. Recorded: OS 1:543-544.

1 October 1798. Thomas and Olive MARTIN to Ann WATTON [who is referred to as "him" throughout the instrument]. 83 acres on Three Forks, adjoining an "oald line" said to be Owen Davies, and [blank] Jenkins. Part of an 8 February 1797 patent. Consideration: $83. Signed: Thomas Martin, Olive Martin. Witnesses [all to Thomas Martin's signature]: J H Williams, H Dering, Wm Tingle. Receipt for purchase money paid by Joseph Watton. No acknowldgement recorded. No delivery shown. Recorded: OS 1:544.

8 July 1799. Dudley and Annarah EVANS to Jacob JONES. 11 acres on Swamp Run, a branch of Sandy Creek, adjoining James Thomas. Part of a 23 August 1797 patent of 1700 acres. Consideration: $10. Signed: Dudley Evans, Annarah Evans. Witnesses: none. Acknowledged in court. Del: to Dudley Evans, 27 May 1803. Recorded: OS 1:545.

14 November 1799. Jacob NUZE to Joseph GRATE, hatter, Morgantown. Power of attorney to sue for and recover a 200-acre tract in Strawsburg Twp, York Co, PA, which is or was in possession of Peter Finkle [Tinkle?], merchant, of York Town, York Co, PA, and adjoining Thomas Earhart and Charles Deel. Signed: Jacob Nuze. Witnesses: J Williams, Jno Stealey. Recorded: OS 1:546.

1 April 1799. Charles and Sarah RAMSEY to William EVERLY. 100 acres adjoining Thomas Butlar, Joseph Butlar, Amos Roberts. Patented 18 January 1799. Consideration: $80. Signed: Charles [CR] Ramsey, Sarah [Z] Ramsey. Witnesses: Wm John, Lamuel John.

Acknowledged by Sarah Ramsey, before Wm John, Lamuel John. Certificate of 1 April 1799. No delivery shown. Recorded: OS 1:546-548.

1 June 1799. William McCLEERY to Bartholomew WICKART. 310 acres on both sides of Aarons Creek, where Wickert now lives, adjoining Michael Kerns (formerly James Russell), Peter Swisser, Augustine Wells. Patented 26 April [1799?]. Consideration: £310, VA. Signed: Wm McCleery. Witnesses: Nimrod Evans, Jona: Davis, Ezekiel Chaney. Acknowledged in court. Receipt for purchase money. No delivery shown. Recorded: OS 1:548-549.

13 March 1799. John HOYE, Montgomery Co, MD, to James PHILLIPS, Frederick Co, MD. 209 acres on Cheat River, at Woolf Pen Run, adjoining Wildy Taylor, Casey's survey, Joseph Butler's survey, [illegible] survey, Pringles [?] Run. Surveyed 11 September 1798 for Paul Hoye and assigned by him to John Hoye. Also, 600 [?] acres from a 300-acre [sic] survey, adjoining Thomas Laidley's survey, [blank] Casey, Thomas Butler's survey. Surveyed for Paul Hoye, 11 September 1798, and assigned by him to John Hoye. Consideration: $600. Signed: John Hoye. Witnesses: John Mountz Junr, Clement Smith, Lloyd Beall. Receipt for purchase money. Certificate of Lloyd Beall, mayor of George Town. No delivery shown. Recorded: OS 1:550-551.

10 February 1800. Nicholas and Martha VANDERVORT to Jonah VANDERVORT. 121 acres adjoining John Reed Junr, James Tibbs, et al. No place names mentioned. Consideration: £75, VA. Signed: Nicholas Vandervort, Martha Vandervort. Witnesses: none. Acknowledged in court. Del: to N Vandervort, 14 December 1807. Recorded: OS 1:552.

29 June 1799. William and Jenny TINGLE to William SLIDGER, Allegheny Co, MD. 616 acres at Booths Creek, adjoining William Robe Jr, David Sayre Jr, William Tingle, Millers Survey, Henry Banks, William Buckhannon, John Davis. Patented to Tingle and Thomas Miller, 20 December 1798. Consideration: $307. Signed: Wm Tingle, Jenny Tingle. Witnesses: Asa Dudley, Geo R Tingle, James Daugherty. No acknowledgement recorded. No delivery shown. Recorded: OS 1:553.

23 October 1797. Thomas POWELL, Burbon Co, KY, by Blemus HAYDON, his attorney in fact, to William DAVIS, Fayette Co, PA. 139 acres on Sandy Creek, a fork of Tyger Valley River, adjoining Theophilus Phillips and John Orr. Consideration: £98, VA. Signed: Blemus Haydon. Witnesses: Enoch Evans, F Warman, John Ramsey. No acknowledgement recorded. Del: to W Davis, 2 April 1800.

Recorded: OS 1:554.

11 October 1794. William and Mary DAWSON to James MORRIS, Washington Co, PA. 213½ acres on Scotts Mill Run, adjoining William Poole, part of a patent of [blank]. Consideration: £[blank]. Signed: William [W] Dawson, Mary [M] Dawson. Witnesses: none. Acknowledged in court. No delivery shown. Recorded: OS 1:555. Re-recording of burned instrument.

8 February 1790. Robert MINNIS to Michael OSWALT, Washington Co, MD. 200 acres near Big Papaw Creek, no adjoiners named. Part of a 400-acre patent to Minnis, of [date blank]. Consideration: £28, VA. Signed: Robt Minnis. Witnesses: none. Acknowledged in court. Del: to Michael Oswalt Junr. Recorded: OS 1:556.

14 October 1797. James LONG to James WILLIAMS. Contract. Long has sold to Williams 150 acres on Laurel Fork of Wickware, adjoining Edward Haymond, Thomas B Bennett, [blank] Coil, and Cuthbert Williams, as well as 4 "out lotts" and 4 "inn lotts," for $290. Payment schedule set. Williams to assume taxes from 1 May 1800 and to build a 16 x 20 house, with stone chimneys, on one of the inn lotts within 3 years, otherwise to forfeit. Long to make title for the land when obligations are met. Reversion provided for. Signed: James Long. Witnesses: J Williams, John Downer, Jona: Davis. Recorded: OS 1:557.

12 November 1799. Lewis and Christena CRISS to John HORNER, Green Co, PA. 400 acres on Sandy Creek, adjoining James Robnett. Patented [blank]. Consideration: £120, VA. Signed: Lewis [X] Criss, Christena [X] Criss. Witnesses: Asa Dudley, John W Dean, Alexr Hawthorn, J Williams. Acknowledged by Christena Criss, before Edward Jones and Asa Dudley, JPs. Certificate 12 November 1799. No delivery shown. Recorded: OS 1:558-559.

13 April 1799. Nathaniel and Ann HATFIELD to James CLARK. 200 acres on waters of Laurel, known as the sand spring. No adjoiners named. Patented 24 October 1792. Consideration: £200, VA. Signed: Nathaniel Hatfield, Ann Hatfield. Witnesses: George Roberts, John Fleming, Robert Henderson. No acknowledgement recorded. No delivery shown. Recorded: OS 1:559-560.

10 June 1799. William and Sarah JOSEPH to Lemuel JOSEPH. 100 acres, adjoining George Orson, Robert Hill, Col Evans, and Jeremiah Joseph. Moiety of a 279-acre patent of 20 September 1785. Consideration: £100. Signed: William [X] Joseph, Sarah [X] Joseph. Witnesses: none. Acknowledged in court. Del: to Perry J Jenkins,

Salt Lake City, UT, 25 April 1938. Recorded: OS 1:560-561.

10 June 1799. James and Mary Ann JENKINS to Benjamin Norriss JARRETT. 71 acres, adjoining Charles Magill, Josiah Jenkins, John Peirpoint's heirs. Part of a 496-acre patent of 27 December 1798. Consideration: $400. Signed: James Jenkins, Maryann [+] Jenkins. Witnesses: Barthw Jenkins, Charles Magill, Fauquire McCrea. No acknowledgement recorded. No delivery shown. Recorded: OS 1:561-562.

9 October 1798. James and Elisabeth HICKMAN, Frederick Co, to William HOLT. 100 acres on the right fork of Wickwares Creek and Haw Run, adjoining lands formerly belonging to James Bulland, part of a tract Edward Haymond now lives on. Conveyed by Haymond to James Hickman, 28 August 1796. Consideration: £40. Signed: James Hickman, Elizabeth [X] Hickman. Witnesses: Reynear Hall, Edward C Owen, John Haymond. No acknowledgement recorded. No delivery shown. Recorded: OS 1:562.

26 October 1797. Conrod HOGMIRE, Washington Co, MD, to Jacob TETER. 28 acres near Lot #103 in Salem (now Carmel) Town, adjoining Goff's tract, Deakens tract. Part of 1880 acres sold to Hogmire by Francis and William Deakins. Consideration: £42, MD. Signed: Conrod Hogmire. Witness: Wm Fitzhugh. Acknowledged by Conrod and Mary Hogmire, 26 October 1797, in Washington Co, MD. Receipt for consideration money. Certificate of Elie Williams, clerk, 1 November 1797. No delivery shown. Recorded: OS 1:563.

DEEDBOOK OS 2

11 September 1797. Richard and Phebe MERRIFIELD to James CURRANT. 600 acres on Three Fork and Wickware, no adjoiners named. Patented to Richard Merrifield. Consideration: £500. Signed: Richard Merrifield. Witnesses: none. Acknowledged in court, September 1797. Del: to James Currant, 13 April 1802. Recorded: OS 2:1.

13 April 1799. Nathaniel and Ann HATFIELD to James CLARK. 50 acres, no adjoiners or place names mentioned. Consideration: £100, VA. Signed: Nathaniel Hatfield, Ann Hatfield. Witnesses: Robert Henderson, Clement [+] hannon, Elizabeth Henderson. Acknowledged in court, September 1799. Del: to Alex Brandon. Recorded: OS 2:2.

14 February 1786. Henry CROLL to Francis WARMAN. 16 acres on the east side of Cheat River, adjoining Warman's other lands. Consideration: £3.15, VA. Signed: Henry Croll. Witnesses: none. Acknowledged in court. No delivery shown. Recorded: OS 2:3. Re-recording of burned instrument.

9 August 1790. John and Sarah PLUM to Morgan MORGAN. 200 acres on Pine Fork of Pricketts Creek, no adjoiners named. Moiety of a 400-acre tract patented 7 September 1789. Consideration: £60. Signed: John Plum, Sarah [mark] Plum. Witnesses: none. Acknowledged in court. Del: to Isaac Morgan pr Morgan Morgan's order. Recorded: October 1799, OS 2:4. Re-recording of burned instrument.

11 December 1796. Abraham WOTRING and David STEMPLE, executors of Godfrey STEMPLE, deceased, to Andrew FRIEND. 200 acres on Wolf Creek, no adjoiners named. Part of a 1000-acre tract conveyed to Stemple by Francis and William Deakins, surveyed November 1782. Consideration: £22.10, VA. Signed: Abraham Wotring, David Stemple. Witnesses: none. Acknowledged in court, 10 March 1798. No delivery shown. Recorded: OS 2:5.

10 June 1799. Jeremiah and Lettice TANAHILL to Christian SCRYER. 104 acres on Big Laurel Run, no adjoiners named. Consideration: £100.18.8½, VA. Signed: Jer Tannehill, Lettice [mark] Tanahill. Witnesses: none. Acknowledged in court, June 1799. No delivery shown. Recorded: OS 2:6.

30 June 1798. Philip ROBERTS to John HAYMOND. 108 acres on Finches Run, adjoining Thomas Dawson and Jasper Wyatte. Part of a 400-acre patent of 10 February 1787 to John Webb and conveyed by him to Roberts. Consideration: £64, VA. Signed: Philip Roberts. Witnesses: none. Acknowledged in court, July 1798. Del: to Calder

Haymond, 10 March 1802. Recorded: OS 2:7.

8 July 1799. Richard and Jane CAIN to Samuel CAIN. 300 acres on Cheat River, adjoining Thomas Mills, William Stuart, James Cleland. Consideration: £400. Signed: Richard Cain [Jane does not sign]. Witnesses: E Evans, F Warman, Thos Warman. Acknowledged by Richard Cain, July 1799. Del: to Richard Cain, 6 January 1810. Recorded: OS 2:8.

10 June 1799. James and Maryan JENKINS to Robert ABERCROMBY. 47 acres adjoining Charles Magill and the heirs of John Peirpoint. Part of a 496-acre tract purchased of Lewis Rodgers and patented to Jenkins 27 December 1798. Consideration: $200. VA. Signed: James Jenkins, Maryann [X] Jenkins. Witnesses: Charles Magill, Barthw Jenkins, Benj Nor Jarrett. Proved by witnesses, June 1799. Del: to R ACromby, 11 September 1804. Recorded: OS 2:9.

8 June 1799. James and Mary ROBNETT, Fayette Co, PA, to Jonathan BRANDON. 222 acres on Big Sandy, including Robnett's settlement, no adjoiners named. Patented 20 March 1784. Consideration: £110, VA. Signed: James Robnett, Mary [M] Robnett. Witnesses: Jesse Barnes, Jacob Harbough, Isaac Yancy. Acknowledged 8 June 1799 in Fayette Co, PA, before Jonathan Roland and Robert Moore, JP. Certificate of Ephraim Douglass, prothonotary, 8 June 1799. No delivery shown. Recorded: June 1799, OS 2:10.

8 October 1798. James and Mary McPECK to Martin WAGNER. 30 acres on Masons Run, a branch of Big Sandy, and part of a larger tract on which McPeck now lives. No adjoiners named. Consideration: $100. Signed: James McPeck, Mary [0] McPeck. Witnesses: Russel Potter, John McLain, Joseph McLain. Acknowledged by Mary McPeck before Russell Potter and John McLain, certificate 16 February 1799. Del: to A Brandon, 10 January 1807. Recorded: OS 2:11.

28 December 1796. Elisha and Mary BOYD, Berkley Co, to Lewis WOLF, residence not stated. 200 acres on Little Sandy, adjoining Thomas Berry and John Berry. Patented to Elisha Boyd, assignee of John Boyd [no date]. Consideration: $250. Signed: Elish Boyd, Mary Boyd. Witnesses: Jas A Faulkner, John Laufar [?], Ebenezer Sutton, John Drenker. Acknowledged 27 [sic] December 1796, before Berkeley Co court. Certificate of Mo Hunter, Clerk. No delivery shown. Recorded: OS 2:12-213.

24 November 1798. Francis and Phebe AYRES to Denis JEFFERIES, of PA. 64 3/4 acres in Crabs Orchard settlement, adjoining James Metheny, part of the tract

on which Ayres now lives. Consideration: £60, VA. Signed: Francis Ayers, Phebe [mark called for but blank] Ayres. Witnesses: Edward Jones, John Stiles, Joseph [J] Butler. Proved by witnesses, July and November 1799. Del: to Benjamin Trembly, 2 [or 12] May 1803. Recorded: OS 2:14.

25 November 1798. James and Mary METHENY to Dennis JEFFRES, no residence stated. 102 acres at Roaring Creek, adjoining Joseph Butler. Consideration: £75. Signed: James Metheny, Mary [mark] Metheny. Witnesses: Edward Jones, John Stiles, Joseph [J] Butler. Proved by witnesses, July and November 1799. Quitclaim of Joseph Butler, 24 November 1798, relinquishing any claim to 28 poles of the land conveyed by Metheny and adjoining his own property. Signed: Joseph [J] Butler. Del: to Benjamin Trembly, 12 May 1803. Recorded: OS 2:15.

11 February 1797. Neal and Nancey GELLESPIE, Washington Co, PA, to James GELLESPIE. 1½ acres, 10 poles on the east side of Cheat and north side of Morgans Run, adjoining Samuel Lewellin. Part of a 1 September 1783 patent to Lewellin. Consideration: £10. Signed: Neal Gellespie [Nancey does not sign]. Witnesses: F Warman, Eh Evans, John Fairfax. Proved by witnesses, 12 February 1798, April 1798. No delivery shown. Recorded: OS 2:16.

28 November 1796. Nicholas and Mary MARSTILLER, Randolph Co, to Christian WHITEHARE. Lot #45 in the town of Salem, including annual quitrent of one-half a silver dollar, due 1 July each year, to Francis Deakins, his heirs or assigns forever. Consideration: £16. Signed: Nicholas Marstiller, Mary Marstiller. Witnesses: none. Acknowledged in Randolph Co court, 28 November 1796. Del: to E B Tucker, 17 May 1954. Recorded: September 1798, OS 2:17.

24 September 1796. Adam GEIR, Berkley Co, to William ROARK. 100 acres on Indian Creek, adjoining Thomas Pindell (formerly James Cochran), John Stuart, Gilbert Butler, James Arnett, Andrew Arnett (the two latter from the same original tract as this parcel). Part of a 400-acre patent to Frederick Gaier and David Scott, 14 November 1792. Consideration: £50, VA. Signed: Adam Gayer. Witnesses: Dudley Evans, John Stealey, B Reeder. Proved by witnesses, 8 April 1799, 8 July 1799. No delivery shown. Recorded: OS 2:18.

8 July 1799. Thomas and Mary MILLER to William MILLER. 273 acres, near Mongalia River, adjoining Thomas Miller and William Gray. Part of a larger tract patented by Thomas. Consideration: $350. Signed: Thomas Miller,

Mary Miller. Witnesses: none. Acknowledged in court, 8 July 1800. Del: to grantee, 8 April 1822. Recorded: OS 2:19.

8 January 1799. John and Jane CASSADY to John STEALEY. 434 acres on Three Forks, adjoining Samuel Ruble and Benjamin Fields. Two surveys purchased from Reece Wolf, patented to Cassady 179[blank]. Consideration: £53, VA. Signed: John Cassadey, Jane [X] Cassadey. Witnesses: Thomas Martin, Wiliam Shaw, James Howell [all as to John Cassady]. Acknowledged by Jane Cassady, 9 September 1799. Del: to G Payne, Stealey's dir, 15 [illegible] 1803. Recorded: OS 2:20.

9 January 1798. James and Anne STEPHENSON, Berkley Co, to John P PLEASANTS, Baltimore MD. 1000 acres near the forks of Dunker Mill Run. Patented to David Gray, 16 September 1784, and sold by him to Stephenson, deed now of record in Morgan Town District Court. Consideration: £500, VA. Memo: 37 acres of the above claimed by a Mr Dudley of Morgan Town. If land is determined to be his, then it is not warranted by this deed. If Dudley does not get the land, Pleasants is to pay Stephenson an additional 10s, VA, per acre, for the 37 acres. If the tract in all exceeds 1000 acres, Pleasants is to pay for the surplus at 10s per acre; if it is less than 1000 acres, Stephenson to reimburse at the same rate. The purchase price includes Stephenson's bond to Pleasants for £325 MC [Maryland Currency?]. Signed: James Stephenson [Anne does not sign]. Witnesses: Robert Page, Thos Byrd, John Page. Acknowledged by James Stephenson, 5 [sic] January 1798, in Frederick Co. Certificate of Ja Keith, clerk. Reacknowledged by Stephenson, 3 September 1798, in Frederick Co, proven by witnesses John Peyton, Frederick Hurst, Henry Peyton. Del: to B Reeder, [illegible] November 1800 [this delivery appears in margin beside this deed but may be misplaced; cf the next entry]. Recorded: OS 2:21-22.

12 October 1803. Acknowledgement of Ann STEPHENSON to the preceding conveyance, before Magnus Tate Junr and A Waggener, JPs of Berkeley Co. Del: to Robert Pleasant, 17 September 1806. Recorded: unnumbered sheet interleaved between OS 2:21-22.

20 April 1799. John and Jane CASSADY to James HOWELL as tenant in common. $91\frac{1}{4}$ acres on a drain of Three Fork, no adjoiners named. Part of a patent to Henry Barnes, 8 June 1799 [sic], and conveyed by him to Cassady. Consideration: £15.19.6, VA. Signed: John Casaday, Jane [X] Casaday. Witnesses: Peter Grimm, Philip Moore, Benjamin Field. Receipt for consideration

money, witnessed by Thomas Martin, Peyton Byrn, Thomas Chipps Junr. Acknowledged in court, September 1799. Recorded: OS 2:22.

1 January 1800. Cornelius and Catherine LYNCH, Union Town, Fayette Co, PA, to Jonathan ROWLAND. Mortgage on 500 acres at Farrows Run, adjoining Charles Snodgrass, Samuel Musgrave, Gilbert Butler, and David Scott, and including a place known as Reeves improvement. Lynch owns 1100 acres in this location, including a settlement right and a treasury land office warrant entry, patented to him 5 October 1795. He may redeem the land by paying £118.14.7½ with interest, on or before 28 June 1800. Consideration: 5 shillings. Signed: Corns Lynch, Cathener [sic] Lynch, Jonathan Rowland. Witnesses: Jacob Hasbrough, James Richey, Thomas Rowland. Acknowledged in Fayette Co, PA, 27 March 1800, before Alexr Addison, JP. Receipt for 5s, consideration. Certificate of Ephraim Douglass, prothonotary, 7 May 1800. Del: to J Dent, 26 October 1800. Recorded: OS 2:23-24.

12 August 1799. Ezra and Elisabeth HORTON to George SNIDER. 94 acres in Dunker Bottom, no adjoiners named. Part of a 400-acre patent to James Morgan. Consideration: £225.12, VA. Signed: Ezra Horton, Elizabeth [+] Horton. Witnesses: Henry Dering Jr, Jno Stealey, Noah Linsley. Acknowledged January 1800. Del: to [illegible] Snider, June 1801. Recorded: OS 2:24.

28 July 1799. Bartholomew CLARK, Morgan Town, to Thomas WILSON. Mortgage on a lot in Morgan Town, on which Clark has built house in which he now lives. Purchased from Robert Minnis. $130 now due to Thomas Wilson. If not paid by 1 January 1800, Wilson may sell the lot to the highest bidder. Signed: Bar Clark. Witnesses: Asa Dudley, John Ebert, Augustus Werninger. Proved by witnesses, 8 September 1799, January 1800. Recorded: OS 2:25.

9 September 1799. Benjamin and Susannah BRAIN to Samuel GANDY. 4 acres, 35 poles, near the roadside, adjoining Gandy's other land. Consideration: £1.3.9. Signed: Benjamin Brain, Susanah Brain. Witnesses: none. Acknowledged in court, September 1799. Receipt for consideration money. No delivery shown. Recorded: OS 2:26.

9 September 1799. Thomas and Mary RUSSEL to Samuel GOODWIN. 35 acres adjoining William Russel, no place names mentioned. Part of a 4 July 1788 patent. Consideration: £15, specie. Signed: Thomas [mark] Russel, Mary [mark] Russel. Witnesses: none.

Acknowledged in court, September 1799. Del: to Saml Goodwin, 14 June 1806. Recorded: OS 2:27.

10 June 1799. Bartholomew and Rosanah WICKART to Ezekiel CHENEY. 75¼ acres, 12 poles on Aarons Creek, adjoining Michael Kerns Junr (formerly James Russell). Part of a 310-acre patent to William McCleery, 26 April [blank], and conveyed by him to Wickart 1 June 1799. Consideration: $301. Signed: Bartholomew [0] Wickart, Rosanah [C] Wickart. Witnesses: none. Acknowledged in court, June 1799. Receipt for consideration money. Del: to Ezl Cheney, [illegible] May 1801. Recorded: OS 2:28.

9 April 1799. Prudance POWEL, Moses and Rebecca POWEL, William and Elisabeth LINSEY, and Thomas POWEL, heirs of Richard POWEL, deceased, to Aaron POWEL. 200 acres on Deckers Creek, adjoining William Maneer, Aaron Powell, Moylan and Claiborne's survey, and John McCleland. Consideration: £60. Signed: Prudance [+] Powel, Moses Powel, Rebecca [+] Powel, William Linzey, Elizabeth [+] Linzey, Thomas [X] Powel. Witnesses: Alexr Hawthorn, Asa Dudley, Robert Ferrel. Acknowledged in court, September 1799. No delivery shown. Recorded: OS 2:29.

9 April 1799. Prudance POWEL, Moses and Rebecca POWEL, William and Elisabeth LINSEY, and Thomas POWEL, heirs of Richard POWEL, deceased, to Aaron POWEL. 200 acres on Deckers Creek, adjoining William Haymond. Consideration: £300. Signed: Prudance [+] Powel, Moses Powel, Rebecca [+] Powel, William Linzey, Elizabeth Linzey, Thomas [T] Powel. Witnesses: Alexr Hawthorn, Asa Dudley, Robert Ferrel. Acknowledged in court, September 1799. No delivery shown. Recorded: OS 2:30.

8 July 1799. James and Hannah MORGAN to David MORGAN. 400 acres on both sides of the road from Dunker Bottom to Yohogania Glades, near the east side of Briary Mountain. No adjoiners named. Patented to James [no date]. Consideration: £55, VA. Signed: James Morgan, Hannah Morgan. Witnesses: none. Acknowledged in court by James Morgan, September 1799. Del: to David Morgan, 17 October 1803. Recorded: OS 2:31.

7 December 1799. Richard CLAIBORNE to Benjamin REEDER. Bill of sale for a large assortment of household goods, table and kitchen ware, carpenter and farm tools and utensils, livestock, musical instruments, books, framed portraits, backgammon table, and 15 acres adjoining the 9th number of the big survey and lands of William McCleery and Daniel Fortney. Consideration: £344.10.7, VA. Signed: R Claiborne. Witnesses: Michael Kerns, David Farquer. No acknowledgement recorded. Del:

to B Reeder, 17 August 1800. Recorded: OS 2:32.

21 January 1800. Francis and Elizabeth HAMERSLY, Fairfax Co, to Benjamin REEDER. 3900 acres near the PA line, adjoining Michael Hillegas. Consideration: 5 shillings. Signed: F Hamersley, Elizabeth Hamersley. Witnesses: none. Acknowledged in Fairfax Co court, 21 January 1800. Certificate of G Deneale, Clerk. Del: to Ben Reeder, 24 May 1805. Recorded: 14 April 1800, OS 2:33.

11 February 1800. David (Sr) and Hannah SAYRE to David SAYRE, Junior. 195 acres on Booths Creek, adjoining William Robe, John Leaman, Theophilus Phillips. Patented to David Sr 13 August 1799. Consideration: £60, VA. Signed: David Sayre [Hannah does not sign]. Witnesses: none. Acknowledged in court, 10 [sic] February 1800. Del: to D Sayre, [illegible] September 1800. Recorded: OS 2:34.

26 February 1800. Francis DEAKINS, Montgomery Co, MD, to Leonard M DEAKINS, Prince Georges Co, MD. 200 acres on Yohogania River, between 9 and 10 miles north of the head of the north branch of Potomac, adjoining John T Goff's 241-acre survey, William Asbey's 300-acre survey. Patented [no date] to William Deakins Junr but title now vested in Francis. Consideration: £50.4.10. Signed: Francis Deakins. Witnesses: John Mitchell, Valentine Reintzel, Anthony Reintzel. Acknowledged in George Town, MD, 26 February 1800. Certificate of Daniel Reintzel, mayor. Del: to J Hoy, 22 November 1800. Recorded: January 1800, OS 2:35.

26 February 1800. Francis DEAKINS, Montgomery Co, MD, to Frederick HARSH, Washington Co, MD. 540 acres on the head waters of Yohogania River, adjoining 1260 acres of the same tract conveyed to Thomas Johnson. Conveyed to Harsh "some years since" by Francis Deakins and William Deakins Junr, the deed since burned. Consideration: $400. Signed: Francis Deakins. Witnesses: John Michell, Valentine Reintzel, Anthony Reintzel. Acknowledged in George Town, MD, 26 February 1800. Certificate of Daniel Reintzel, mayor. No delivery shown. Recorded: September 1800, OS 2:36.

14 April 1800. James and Mary ROBNETT, Fayette Co, PA, to George WOOLF. 400 acres on Beaver and Muddy Creeks, adjoining Lewis Criss and Martin Judy. Surveyed 30 April 1781. Consideration: $426.66. Signed: James Robinet, Mary [mark] Robinet. Witnesses: none. Acknowledged in court, April 1800. Del: to Alexr Brandon, 1800. Recorded: OS 2:37.

12 February 1799. John and Margaret WIMP, Fayette

Co, PA, to Thomas CHIPPS. 4 acres, 10 poles, adjoining the road to Ices Ferry, Thomas Pindell's cleared field, James Cochran and Zackquil Morgan. Patented to Thomas Pindell, 8 October 1790, and sold by to James Collins, who conveyed to Jeremiah Simpson, who sold to John Wimp. Consideration: £50, VA. Signed: John Wimp, Margaret [mark] Wimp. Witnesses: none. Acknowledged in court, 12 February 1799. Del: to Ths Chipps, 3 October 1800. Recorded: OS 2:38.

10 December 1799. William and Hannah CHIPPS to Jacob PINDEL. 400 acres on a drain of Papaw between Robinsons Run and the main fork. No adjoiners named. Patented to Hannah Scott, now Chipps, 2 October 1797 and including James Scott's 1776 settlement. Consideration: £300. Signed: William Chipps, Hannah [0] Chipps. Witnesses: none. Acknowledged in court, 10 December 1799. Del: to Jacob Pindell, 14 October 1800. Recorded: OS 2:39.

14 April 1798. Articles of agreement between Abraham MILEY and George MILEY. Abraham gives his son George 235 acres on Dunker Creek, where Abraham now resides. Also, livestock, carpenter and joiner tools, farm utensils. George is to pay all money now due or to become due on the land, and to maintain his father Abraham, mother Elizabeth, and brother John in "a good Decent genteel manner." If they are dissatisfied with his maintenance, George to pay them £20 each yearly, as long as they shall live. Signed: Abraham Miley, George Miley. Witnesses: John Willey, Sarah [mark] Da[??]. Del: to A Miley, 1800. Recorded: OS 2:40.

14 October 1799. John and Ann EVANS to Matthias DAVIS. 134 acres on Panther Lick Run, a branch of Papaw, adjoining Charles Harryman. Part of a 1000-acre patent of 26 December 1798. Signed: Jno Evans, Ann Evans. Witnesses: none. Acknowledged in court, 14 October 1800. No delivery shown. Recorded: OS 2:41.

11 February 1799. Philip SCRITCHFIELD, John SCRITCHFIELD, Arthur SCRITCHFIELD, Henry SCRITCHFIELD, Nathaniel HULL to George LAUNCE. 400 acres on Maricles Run, adjoining Phinehas Killums, Michael Hylegs third survey, and vacant lands. Surveyed by Phinehas Killums, assignee of Christian Cofman. Consideration: $400. Signed: John Crihfield, Arthur Crihfield, Henry Crihfield, Jean Crihfield, Natha Hull [Philip does not sign]. Witnesses: none. Acknowledged in court, February 1799. Del: to G Launce, 14 November [illegible]. Recorded: OS 2:42.

8 February 1800. Francis DEAKINS to John Thomas

MASON, attorney at law, both of George Town, Montgomery Co, MD. 1000 acres in two tracts. 529 acres between the heads of Yohogania and Cheat Rivers, 3 or 4 miles northwest of the town called Carmel. Surveyed for Francis and William Deakins, 7 July 1784. 471 acres adjoining the other tract, part of a survey of 7209 acres, no date shown. No adjoiners named. Consideration: 5 shillings. Signed: Francis Deakins. Witnesses: Valentine Reintzel, Joseph Mitchell, Daniel Reintzel. Acknowledged in George Town, MD. Certificate of Daniel Reintzel, mayor. Del: to J Hoy, 22 November 1800. Recorded: OS 2:43.

30 October 1799. Robert and Hannah FERREL to David SAYERS. 50 acres, near the Monongalia River, adjoining Jeremiah and John Wilson, Daniel Sayre. 14½ acres from a 966-acre patent of 6 February 1797, and 35½ acres from a 234-acre patent of 18 June 1798. Consideration: $300. Signed: Robert Ferrel, Hannah [+] Ferrel. Witnesses: Joseph Tricket, Daniel Sayre, Thomas Sayre. Proved by witnesses, 10 February 1800. Del: to D Sayre, 8 December 1800. Recorded: OS 2:44.

13 August 1792. William and Mary BUCKHANON to David SAYRE. 25 3/4 acres, 36½ rods, at Toms Run, adjoining other lands of Sayre and Buckhanon. Patented 2 December 1791. Consideration: £7.13, VA. Signed: Wm Buckhanon, Mary [mark] Buckhanon. Witnesses: none. Acknowledged in court, August 1792. Del: to Danl Sayre, 7 July 1801. Recorded: OS 2:45-46. Re-recording of a burned instrument.

9 June 1800. Henry and Sarah CORE, Fayette Co, PA, to Christopher MEAS, of MD. 50 acres, adjoining Caleb Hurley, Samuel Hurley. Part of a 225-acre patent to William Dawson. Consideration: $355. Signed: Henry Core, Sarah Core. Witnesses: none. Acknowledged in court, June 1800. Del: to J Dent, 4 December 1800. Recorded: OS 2:46-47.

14 October 1799. John and Ann EVANS to James TARNEY. 118 acres on a drain of Papaw Creek, adjoining Augusta Ballah, Charles Harryman, Mathias Davis, Robert Minnis. Part of a 1000-acre patent of 28 December 1798. Consideration: $177. Signed: John Evans, Ann Evans. Witnesses: none. Acknowledged in court, 14 October 1799. No delivery shown. Recorded: OS 2:47-48.

9 June 1800. James and Margaret MORRIS to John BARRICKMAN. 2 tracts. 213½ acres on Scotts Mill Run, adjoining William Postlewaith. Conveyed to Morris by William and Mary Dawson, 11 October 1794. 21½ acres on Scotts Mill Run, no adjoiners named. Conveyed to Morris

by John and Hannah Stag, 12 November 1798. Consideration: $500. Signed: James Morris, Margaret [M] Morris. Witnesses: none. Acknowledged in court, 9 June 1800. Del: to Henry Barrackman, 10 December 1804. Recorded: OS 2:48-49.

6 June 1800. Benjamin and Ann WHITSON to John ENGLAND. 15 acres on Sandy Creek, no adjoiners named. Part of 125 acres purchased by Whitson from Samuel Cobb. Consideration: £15, VA. Signed: B Whitson, Ann Whitson. Witnesses: none. Acknowledged in court, June 1800. No delivery shown. Recorded: OS 2:49.

14 October 1799. James SCOTT, high sheriff of Monongalia, to David SAYRE. 300 acres, adjoining Morgan Morgan Sr. Land formerly belonging to Godfrey Stonhill, sold by virtue of an execution against him on behalf of Dudley Evans. Sayre the highest bidder. Consideration: not shown. Signed: James Scott. Witnesses: none. Acknowledged in court, December 1799. No delivery shown. Recorded: OS 2:50.

8 April 1799. Joseph TRICKETT, attorney in fact for Thomas PEACOCK and Elijah CHAPMAN, addresses not given, to Ephraim SAYRE. 100 3/4 acres at Joes Run, adjoining Joseph Trickett. Part of a 400-acre patent, 4 July 1794. Consideration: £150, VA. Signed: Joseph Trickett. Witnesses: none. Acknowledged in court, April 1799. Del: to Danl Sayre, 7 July 1801. Recorded: OS 2:51.

10 February 1800. Anthony and Polly AMMON to Henry CORE, Fayette Co, PA. 50 acres adjoining Charles Hurley and Samuel Everley. Part of a 225-acre patent to William and Mary Dawson, in whose names Ammon was attorney in fact, and conveyed by them to him 12 December 1798. Consideration: £100, VA. Signed: Anthony Ammon, Polly Ammon. Witnesses: none. Acknowledged in court, February 1800. No delivery shown. Recorded: OS 2:52.

11 November 1799. Joseph and Sarah WISBEY to Ebenezer VANDIGRAFT, Fyatte Co, PA. $19\frac{1}{4}$ acres, 32 poles, on Gyses Run, the tract Wisbey now lives on, adjoining Anthony Hartley. Part of a 200-acre patent of 9 May 1796. Consideration: $75. Signed: Joseph [mark] Wisbey, Sarah [mark] Wisbey. Witnesses: Joseph Trickett, Davis Shockley, Nicholas Vandevort. Proved by witnesses, 10 February 1800. Del: to Vandegraft, 4 May 1807. Recorded: OS 2:53.

11 February 1800. David (Sr) and Hannah SAYRE to Benjamin SAYRE. 114 acres on Toms Run, adjoining William Robe and David Sayre. Part of 309-acre patent of 13 August 1799. Consideration: $100. Signed: David Sayre [Hannah does not sign]. Acknowledged in court by David

Sayre, 10 [sic] February 1800. Del: to Daniel Sayre, 20 November 1802. Recorded: OS 2:54.

8 September 1800. John (Sr) and Dorcus SNIDER to David SNIDER. 200 acres on Indian Creek, adjoining Charles Dawson, heirs of James Windsor, and John Snider Jr. Part of a 400-acre patent. Consideration: love and affection to their son. Signed: John [mark] Snider, Dorcus [mark] Snider. Witnesses: none. Acknowledged in court, September 1800. Del: to Jno Snider Junior. Recorded: OS 2:55.

9 December 1799. James and Tabitha HOARD to William JOHN. 5½ acres, no adjoiners or place names mentioned. Part of a 17 April 1784 patent. Consideration: $22. Signed: James Hoard, Tabitha [mark] Hoard. Witnesses: none. Acknowledged in court, 9 December 1799. Del: to Wm John, 27 November 1801. Recorded: OS 2:56.

26 July 1799. Thomas LAIDLEY to Isaac H WILLIAMS, trustee. Deed of trust. Laidley owes $100 to Benjamin Reeder. To secure this he entrusts a lot on Pleasant Street in Morgan Town, conveyed to him by Zackquill Morgan, 13 March 1786, and a bay horse. To be redeemed by 15 September 1799. Signed: Thomas Laidley. Witnesses: John Davis, Thomas Chipps, Hugh McNeely. Proved by witnesses, 9 December 1799. No delivery shown. Recorded: OS 2:57.

18 October 1799. Abraham and Mary SCISCO and Mary SCISCO Sr to William MILLER. 100 acres on Buffelow Lick Run, adjoining Matthew Fleming and John Grayham. Patented 16 April 1793 to Abraham Scisco Senr and left by his will to Abraham Junr. Consideration: £100. Signed: Mary [X] Cisco Jnr, Mary [X] Cisco Senr [Abraham does not sign]. Witnesses: Nathan Springer, Stephen Morgan, Abner Harp. Acknowledged by Mary Jnr and Mary Snr before Nathan Springer and Stephen Morgan, JPs, certificate 18 October 1799. Acknowledged by Abraham Cisco, 9 December 1799. Del: to William Miller, 19 October 1802. Recorded: OS 2:58-59.

18 October 1799. Mary SISCO and John and Letty SISCO to Mathew FLEMING. 100 acres on the east side of the Monongalia River, about 1½ miles from the mouth of Tyger Valley River. No adjoiners named. Part of a patent to Abraham Sisco, 16 April 1793. Consideration: £200, VA. Signed: John [+] Siscoe, Letice [+] Siscoe, Mary [+] Siscoe. Witnesses: Nathan Springer, Stephen Morgan, Abner Harp. Acknowledged by Mary and Lettice Sisco before Stephen Morgan and Nathan Springer, JPs, certificate 18 October 1799. Acknowledged by John Siscoe, in court 9 December 1799. Del: to Thomas

Fleming, 12 January 1803. Recorded: OS 2:60-61.

15 September 1798. George McDONNALD, Hampshire Co, to Valuntine KING. 185 acres on Laurel Run, adjoining Patrick Johnston. Surveyed for Adam Helmick and sold by him to George McDonnald. Consideration: $370. Signed: George [X] McDonnald. Witnesses: John J Jacob, James [X] Johnston, Robert Gassaway. Acknowledged [no date]. Del: to James King, 26 October 1813. Recorded: OS 2:62-63.

28 March 1798. Samuel and Magdalen COBB to John DOBBINS. 56 acres on Little Sandy Creek, no adjoiners named. Part of a resident right of 400 acres, patented to Thomas Berry (Jr) and assigned to Samuel Cobb. Consideration: $23. Signed: Samuel [S] Cobb, Magdalen [O] Cobb. Witnesses: Benjamin Whitson, Leonard Davisson, Enos More. Acknowledged in court, October 1798. No delivery shown. Recorded: OS 2:63.

4 April 1798. John and Catherine STILES to William WALLER. 200 acres, moiety of a 300-acre tract known as the Round Glade, adjoining James Conner. Patented to Balleshazzer Dragoo, 14 September 1785, and assigned by him to Stiles. Consideration: £160, VA. Signed: John Stiles, Catherine [mark] Stiles. Witnesses: Thomas Chipps, Edward Jones, Richard Stiles. Proved by witnesses, October 1798. No delivery shown. Recorded: OS 2:64.

8 April 1798. George and Hanah HOLLENBACK to Joshua HICKMAN. 16 acres on the east side of Monongahela River, including the mouth of Buffelow Lick Run, adjoining John McGee, Joshua Hickman, George Hollenbeck, Elias Perce. Part of a 61-acre patent, 29 July 1797. Consideration: £10. Signed: George Hollenback, Hannah Hollenback. Witnesses: Nathan Springer, Samuel Merifield, Abraham [+] Fransisco. Acknowledged in court, 8 April 1799. Del: to Joshua Hickman, 9 April 1805. Recorded: OS 2:65.

9 March 1798. John and Pheby SPENCER to Peirce BAILY, all of Loudoun Co. 5250 acres on west side of Cheat River, adjoining a 99,000 acre survey for Moyland and Claybourne, Spencer's second survey, and William McCleery's 47,000 acre survey. Consideration: £900, VA. Signed: John Spencer, Pheby Spencer. Witnesses: Israel Lacy, W A Rogers, Moses Dowdell. Receipt for consideration money. Acknowledged by Pheby Spencer in Loudoun Co. Certificate of William Ellzy and Israel Lacy, JPs, 9 March 1798. Del: to Pierce Bayly, 13 April 1803. Recorded: OS 2:66-67.

13 December 1800. Nathan and Lydia SPRINGER to Jacob TUSING, Frederick Co, MD. 500 acres on Flat Run, a branch of Buffaloe Creek, adjoining Henry Banks and

Lewellens Camp Run. Part of a 2000-acre patent of 28 July 1796 to Lydia Watson, executrix of Arthur Watson deceased and now Lydia Springer, wife of Nathan. Consideration: $750. Signed: Nathan Springer, Lydia [mark] Springer. Witnesses: Dudley Evans, James Morgan, John Springer. Acknowledged: proved by witnesses, 12 January 1801. Del: to Dudley Evans, 20 January 1801. Recorded: OS 2:68.

13 March 1798. Jonas SAMS to David MOORE and James MOORE, Essex Co, NY, and to John MORE and Josiah MOORE, Fayette Co, KY. 100 acres, the south side of a 400-acre tract patented to Jonas Sams 6 March 1795. Adjoining Isaac Powell and Thomas Hughes on the southwest, Ebenezer Vandergraft on the northwest, and Jonas Sams on the northeast. Consideration: £20. Signed: Jonas Sams. Witnesses: Thomas Chipps, Nathan Springer, Richard Merifield. Proved by witnesses, February 1799. Del: to John Moore, 4 March 1805. Recorded: OS 2:69-70.

11 February 1799. Thomas and Mary RUSSEL to Henry PARTMAS. 7 acres, along the PA line, part of a 4 July 1788 patent. Consideration: $72.50. Signed: Thomas Russel, Mary [C] Russel. Witnesses: none. Acknowledged in court, February 1799. Del: to H Partmus, 8 April 1805. Recorded: OS 2:70-71.

8 October 1798. Valentine and Mary SOWERHABER to James BROWN. 83 acres on the west side of Cheat, adjoining Moses Rice [also called Roice in the instrument], Andrew Johnston. Part of the survey on which John Green, deceased, formerly lived. Consideration: £83, VA. Signed: Valentine Sowerhebour, Mary [X] Sowerhebour. Witnesses: none. Acknowledged in court, 8 October 1798. No delivery shown. Recorded: OS 2:71.

11 February 1799. Joseph and Mary SAPP to Absalom WILLEY. 100 acres on Scotts Mill Run, adjoining Abraham Harding, William Willey, Caleb Hurley, John Davis, John Willey. Part of a tract taken up by William Dawson. Consideration: £100. Signed: Joseph [mark] Sapp, Sarah [+] Sapp. Witnesses: none. Acknowledged in court, 11 February 1799. No delivery shown. Recorded: OS 2:72.

26 May 1800. David SCOTT to Elizabeth SCOTT, Fayette Co, PA. Two tracts. 400 acres on the north side of Papaw, adjoining another survey of Scott's. 356 acres on the north side of Papaw. No adjoiners named. Both tracts patented 17 September 1784. Consideration: $1. Signed: David Scott. Witnesses: Wm G Payne, Daniel Merchand, Wm Martin. Acknowledged in court, October 1800. Del: to D Merchd [?], 18 May 1801. Recorded:

OS 2:73-74.
9 December 1800. Jacob and Mary BOWERS, late Mary PETERS, widow of Henry Peters, deceased, to Moses WILLIAMS. Henry Peters, former husband of Mary Bowers, owned a half lot on High Street in Morgantown, adjoining Hugh McNeely and Moses Williams. Mary conveys all her interest as relict and widdow. Consideration: £100, VA. Signed: Jacob [+] Bowers, Mary Bowers. Witnesses: none. Acknowledged in court, December 1800. No delivery shown. Recorded: OS 2:74.

20 October 1792. William and Hannah MORGAN to Thomas JOHNSON. 200 acres on the west side of Cheat, adjoining Wildey Taylor. Consideration: £20, VA. Signed: William Morgan, Hannah [+] Morgan. Witnesses: Thos Chipps, Thos Butler. No acknowledgement recorded. No delivery shown. Recorded: January, 1801, OS 2:75. Re-recording of burned instrument.

22 November 1800. John HORSE, Nelson Co, KY, to George NAST, Washington Co, MD. 310 acres, adjoining Francis and William Deekins. No place names mentioned. Consideration: £160, MD. Signed: John Horse "in dutch." Witness: George Scott, Senr. Acknowledged by John Horse, in Washington Co, MD, 22 November 1800. Receipt for consideration money. Certificate of J H Williams, clerk of Washington Co, MD. Del: to him, 25 November 1813. Recorded: January 1801, OS 2:76.

8 April 1799. Francis and Catherine WARMAN to Joshua WARMAN. 118 acres on the east side of Cheat River, adjoining William Stuart and lands surveyed for Barthw Jenkins, deceased. Consideration: £100. Signed: Francis Warman [Catherine's signature not recorded]. Witnesses: none. Acknowledged by Francis Warman, in court April 1799. Del: to Joshua Warman, 30 August 1801. Recorded: OS 2:77.

14 October 1799. Jacob and Jemima PRICKET to John JOLLIFFE. 127 acres on Prickets Creek, adjoining Nathan Springer, Elias Pearce, Edward Gutridge. Part of a 180-acre patent to Jacob Pricket, 28 June 1791. Consideration: $250. Signed: Jacob Prickett, Jemima [mark] Prickett. Witnesses: none. Acknowledged in court, 14 October 1799. Del: to J Jolliffe, 16 March 1801. Recorded: OS 2:78.

2 May 1794. Thomas GOFF, Clark Co, KY, by John T GOFF, his attorney in fact, to Abraham WOODRING. 567 acres on the head waters of Yohogania River, beginning at a place called Folleys Meadows and adjoining Adam Shaver and David Ridenhour. Part of a 13 October 1784 survey of 800 acres. Consideration: £150. Signed: John T

Goff. Witnesses: none. Acknowledged in court, 9 June 1794. Recorded: OS 2:79.

1 October 1794. Matthias RIDENOUR, Washington Co, MD, to Alexander BINGAMAN. 210 acres, adjoining [blank] Stemple. Part of a 500-acre tract conveyed by Francis and William Deakins to Matthias Ridenour deceased. Consideration: £180, MD. Signed: Matthias Ridenour. Witness: A Clagett, Adam Ott. Acknowledged by Matthias and Polly Ridenour, in Washington Co, MD, 8 October 1794. Receipt for consideration money. Certificate of Elie Williams, clerk. Del: to Alex Bingaman, 22 April 1801. Recorded: October 1794, OS 2:80-81.

14 March 1787. Francis and William DEAKINS, Montgomery Co, MD, to Godfrey STEMPLE, Washington Co, MD. 1000 acres adjoining Conrad Holston, between the headwaters of Yohogania and of Cheat. From two tracts surveyed in November 1782, of 1500 and 1000 acres. Consideration: £333.6.8, MD. Signed: Francis Deakins, Will Deakins Junr. Witnesses: Aens Campbell, Laurence ONeale. Acknowledged by William Deakins, 14 March 1787, before Campbell and ONeale, JPs; by Jean, wife of William Deakins, 21 March 1787, before Samuel W Magruder and Richard Thompson; by Eleanor, wife of Francis Deakins, 23 March 1787, before Campbell and ONeale. Certificate of Brooke Beall, clerk of Montgomery Co, MD, 21 March 1787. Receipt for consideration money. Del: to G Stemple, 22 April 1801. Recorded: OS 2:81-82.

27 March 1799. Christian WIREMAN, Fayette Co, PA, to Jacob ROHRER Sr, Washington Co, MD. 530 acres on Dunker Creek, adjoining Anthony Kirkhart. Part of a 1000-acre survey of 12 August 1791. Consideration: $537, MD. Signed: Christian Wireman, "Signed in Dutch." Witnesses: A Clagett, Jacob Schnebly. Acknowledged by Christian and Mary Wireman, 27 March 1799, in Washington Co, MD. Certificate of Elie Williams, Clerk, 29 April 1799. Del: to John Stealey, 9 October 1801. Recorded: OS 2:83-84.

11 June 1798. Nathaniel and Ann HATFIELD to Robert BUCHER. 100 acres on Sand Spring Run, adjoining Whiley Hatfield. Part of a 300-acre patent, 24 October 1792. Consideration: £40, VA. Signed: Nathaniel Hatfield, Ann [mark] Hatfield. Witnesses: none. Acknowledged in court, September 1798. Del: to R Bucher, 9 April 1801. Recorded: OS 2:84-85.

11 April 1801. Nathan and Lydia SPRINGER to John DUNN, Frederick Co. 312 acres on Flat Run, adjoining 500 acres of Jacob and Adam Tusing. Part of a 2000-acre patent to Lydia Watson, executrix of Arthur Watson, now

Lydia Springer, 28 July 1796. Consideration: $340. Signed: Nathan Springer, Lydia [X] Springer. Witnesses: Dudley Evans, James Coburn, Alexander McClelland. Proved by witnesses, 13 April 1801. Del: to J Dunn, 14 April 1801. Recorded: OS 2:86.

20 March 1801. Cornelius and Catherine LYNCH, Fayette Co, PA, to Henry COOKUS, Shephards Town, Berkley Co. 500 acres on Dunker Creek, adjoining a 1500-acre survey of Lynch. Patented 8 March 1798. Consideration: $500, PA. Signed: Cornelius Lynch, Catherine Lynch. Witnesses: Dudley Evans, William Hogue, Sam Swearingen, Alexr Hawthorn. Acknowledged by Catherine Lynch, in Fayette Co, PA, before Jonathan Rowland and Robert Moore, JPs, 23 March 1801. Proved by witnesses, 13 April 1801. Del: to A McClelland, 14 April 1801. Recorded: OS 2:87.

2 May 1794. Thomas GOFF, Clark Co, KY, by John T GOFF, his attorney in fact, to Adam SHAVER. 100 acres on the headwaters of Yohogania River, beginning at Foleys Meadows. No adjoiners named. Part of an 800-acre survey of 30 October 1784. Consideration: £30. Signed: John T Goff. Witnesses: none. Acknowledged in court, 9 June 1794, by John T Goff. No delivery shown. Recorded: OS 2:88. Re-recording of burned instrument.

24 March 1800. John and Ann POLLOCK, of the territory north west of the river Ohio, on waters of little Miami river, to James BOWLBY. 300 acres on Robesons Run, near the PA line. No adjoiners named. Part of a 400-acre patent of 20 September 1784. Consideration: $1350. Signed: John Pollock [Ann's signature not recorded]. Witnesses: Jona Davis, Amos Smith, George Smith, Alexr Hawthorn. Proved by witnesses, 9 February 1801. Del: to John Bolby, 24 July 1801. Recorded: OS 2:89.

23 February 1801. Isaac and Mary CAMP to Adam CAMP. 60 acres, 73 poles, adjoining Frederick Goyre, Jeremiah Hoskinson, Isaac Camp's spring run. Part of a 19 October 1784 survey. Consideration: £60. Signed: Isaac Camp [Mary's signature not recorded]. Witnesses: none. Acknowledged by Isaac Camp, in court, April 1801. Del: to A Camp, [illegible] June 1801. Recorded: OS 2:90.

25 September 1798. Whitely and Rhoda HATFIELD to James GILLESPIE. 400 acres, including Honsakers Glades. No adjoiners named. Consideration: $1400. Signed: Whitley Hatfield, Rhoda [+] Hatfield. Witnesses: E Evans, John Fowler, James Donaldson. Proved by witnesses, February 1799. Del: to James Gillespie, 8 June 1801. Recorded: OS 2:91.

8 April 1799. Nehemiah and Valeria HARP to Isaac POWEL. 250 acres adjoining Joseph Boultinghouse. Part of a 3 September 1788 patent for 350 acres, 100 acres of which has been sold to William Laycock. Consideration: $1800. Signed: Nehemiah Harp, Valeriah [V] Harp. Witnesses: none. Acknowledged in court, April 1799. Del: to Isaac Powell, June 1801. Recorded: OS 2:91-92.

10 December 1800. Bertrand and Catherine EWELL, Prince William Co, to Thomas EWING, Philadelphia, PA. 1000 acres on head of Scotts Mill Run and Dunker Creek, adjoining William Anderson's survey, Rudolf Snider. Surveyed 3 February 1786 for William Anderson's assignee, and patented to Alpheus Gustine, assignee of George Dent, assignee of Robert Minnis, assignee of William Anderson. Consideration: £600. Signed: Bertrand Ewell, Catherine B Ewell. Witnesses: Jonathan B Ewell, Jesse Ewell, Solomon Ewell Junr. Acknowledged by Catherine Barnes Ewell, in Prince William Co, before Jas Ewell Senr and Chs Ewell, JPs. Proved by witnesses in Prince William Co, 2 June 1801. Certificate of John Williams, clerk. Del: to Ewing, by post, 18 July 1802. Recorded: 13 July 1801, OS 2:93-94.

12 June 1786. William MOORE, Washington Co, MD, to Jonathan REESE, Georges Twp, Fayette Co, PA. Acreage not stated. Tract on the east side of Mongalia River, nearly opposite the falls. Patented to Joseph Boultinghouse, assignee of Jacob Hall, 20 October 1783, and sold by him to William Moore, 19 October 1784. Consideration: £100, VA. Signed: William Moore. Witnesses: Saml Hanway, John Hall. No acknowledgement recorded. No delivery shown. Recorded: July 1800, OS 2:95. Re-recording of burned instrument.

22 January 1800. James and Mary MATHENY to Aaron ROYSE. 65 acres on Roaring Creek, adjoining Joseph Butlar. Consideration: £50, VA. Signed: James Matheny, Mary [X] Matheny. Witnesses: Thos Smoot, Dennis Jeffers, James [X] Lemmon. Acknowledged in court, 14 April 1800. Del: to D Morgan, [illegible] March 1802. Recorded: OS 2:96.

22 January 1800. James and Mary METHENY to Aaron ROYCE. 186 acres, adjoining Joseph Butler. Tract on which James Matheny and James Lemon now live. Consideration: £200, VA. Signed: James Metheny, Mary [X] Metheny. Witnesses: Dennis Jefferiss, James [X] Leman. Acknowledged in court, 14 April 1800. Del: to D Morgan, 9 March 1802. Recorded: OS 2:97.

9 February 1800. William and Mary JOHN to James CURREY. 50 acres on Laurel Run, adjoining William John

on the north and east, John McFarland and Robert and John Davis on the south and west. Former lines to Owen Davis and David Scott. Part of a 135-acre patent of 17 August 1798. Consideration: $200. Signed: Wm John, Mary John. Witnesses: none. Acknowledged in court, February 1800. Del: to J Currie, August 1801. Recorded: OS 2:98.

14 April 1800. William and Elizabeth STUART to Alexander STUART, their son. 155 acres near the Mason and Dixon line and adjoining Daniel Stuart and "the school house place near the great road." Consideration: love and affection. Signed: William [X] Stuart, Elizabeth [mark] Stuart. Witnesses: none. Acknowledged in court, April 1800. Del: to Danl Stewart, 2 May 1803. Recorded: OS 2:99.

10 April 1801. William and Sarah ROBE to Robert ROBE. 163 acres on Booths Creek, inherited by William as heir at law of his son William Robe deceased. Adjoining William Robe's settlement entry, Josiah Wilson, Henry Tucker. Entered on a preemption warrant and patented in 1799 to William Robe deceased. Consideration: $10. Signed: William Robe, Sarah Robe. Witnesses: none. Acknowledged in court, April 1801. Del: to Robt Robe, September 1801. Recorded: OS 2:100.

13 April 1801. William and Sarah ROBE to David ROBE. 112 acres on Booths Creek, inherited by William as heir at law of his son William Robe deceased. Adjoining William Robe Sr, Capel Holland, Bartholomew Jenkins. Consideration: $10. Signed: William Robe, Sarah Robe. Witnesses: none. Acknowledged in court, 13 April 1801. Del: to D Robe, 20 February 1802. Recorded: OS 2:101.

13 April 1801. William and Sarah ROBE to David ROBE. 249 acres on Booths Creek, partly from 300 acres and partly from 186 acres patented in the name of William Robe deceased. Consideration: $10. Signed: William Robe, Sarah Robe. Witnesses: none. Acknowledged in court, 13 April 1801. Del: to D Robe, February 1802. Recorded: OS 2:102.

13 April 1801. William and Sarah ROBE to Robert ROBE. 231 acres on Booths Creek, partly from 300 acres and partly from 186 acres patented in the name of William Robe deceased. Consideration: $10. Witnesses: none. Acknowledged in court, 13 April 1801. Del: to Robert Robe, 3 September 1801. Recorded: OS 2:103.

14 October 1799. Henry and Mary TUCKER to Robert ROBE. 56 acres on Booths Creek, adjoining Tucker's former survey and William Robe. From a patent of 8 June 1790. Consideration: $106. Signed: Henry [+] Tucker, Mary [mark] Tucker. Witnesses: none. Acknowledged in

court, 14 October 1800. Del: to Robt Robe, 3 September 1801. Recorded: OS 2:104.

30 June 1798. Jacob (Sr) and Hannah JACOBS to Abraham GOOSMAN. 210 acres on Deckers Creek. No adjoiners named. Part of a 250-acre patent of 10 February 1787. Consideration: £150, VA. Signed: Jacob [J] Jacobs, Hannah Jacobs. Witnesses: Joseph Tricket, James Tibbs, Charles Magill. Acknowledged by Jacob Jacobs, 10 December 1798; by Hannah Jacobs, before Asa Dudley and Augusta Ballah, JPs, 10 January 1801. Del: to A Goosman, 18 April 1804. Recorded: OS 2:105-106.

12 August 1797. Alexander and Margaret CLEG to William THOMAS, son of William THOMAS and Elizabeth his [word apparently omitted]. 342 acres adjoining George Shin. Consideration: £50, VA. Signed: Alexander Cleg, Margaret [E] Cleg. Witnesses: Joseph Parrish, John Stateler, Richd Tennant. Acknowledged by Alexander Cleg, in court, 11 February 1799; by Margaret Cleg before John Dent and Edward Jones, JPs, 12 November 1798. Del: to Wm Thomas, 6 March 1805. Recorded: OS 2:107.

30 October 1799. Robert and Hannah FERREL to Daniel SAYRE. 225 acres on Joes Run, adjoining David Sayre, [blank] Shettlesworth, [blank] Wilson, Thomas Griggs. Part of a 6 February 1797 patent for 966 acres. Consideration: $333 1/3. Signed: Robert Ferrel, Hannah [+] Ferrel. Witnesses: Joseph Trickett, Thomas Sayre, David Sayre. Proved by witnesses, 10 February 1800. Del: to D Sayre, September 1801. Recorded: OS 2:108.

9 June 1800. Jacob and Hannah SMITH to Daniel McCOLLUM. 200 acres near the road from Morgan Town to Hagers Town. No adjoiners named. Part of 2068 acres patented to Charles Donaldson, 11 September 1789 [?] and conveyed by him to Jacob Smith. Consideration: $200, VA. Signed: Jacob Smith, Hannah [0] Smith. Witnesses: none. Acknowledged in court, June 1800. Del: to A Brandon, July 1801. Recorded: OS 2:109-110.

13 May 1800. John DOWNER to Alexander HAWTHORN, trustee. Deed of trust on 2 tracts at Dunkard Creek, totaling 800 acres, adjoining John Stateler, George Stateler, Randolfs [Rudolfs?] Run. Downer owes $100 to William McCleery, due on or before 1 September 1800. If not paid, Hawthorn may sell the land. Signed: John Downer. Witnesses: Jona Davis, John Davis, J Williams. Proved by witnesses, 10 December 1800. Recorded: OS 2:110-111.

14 July 1800. David and Eleanor DUNHAM to Joseph KRATZER. 174 acres. No adjoiners or place names mentioned. Part of the tract Dunham now lives on.

Consideration: $15. Signed: David Dunham, Elenor Dunham. Witnesses: Hugh McNeely, Rawley Evans, Joseph Davis, Nathan Springer, Stephen Morgan. Acknowledged by David Dunham in court, July 1800; by Eleanor Dunham before Nathan Springer and Stephen Morgan, JPs, date not shown. Del:to J Kratzer, August 1801. Recorded: OS 2:112.

18 September 1800. Clement BIDDLE, Esqr, Philadelphia PA, to Alexander SMITH, Alleghany Co, MD. Biddle has sold to Smith for $1333 1/3 his interest in lands once owned by Bartholomew Tarrison, conveyed by Tarrison's commissioners in bankruptcy to Francis and William Deakins. He now conveys that interest. Consideration: $1. Signed: Clement Biddle. Witnesses: J B Ozso [?], Thomas Biddle, Wm Coates. Acknowledged by Clement Biddle, 18 September 1800, in Philadelphia. Receipt for $1. Certificate of Robert Wharton, mayor of Philadelphia. No delivery shown. Recorded: 12 January 1801, OS 2:113-114.

11 February 1793. William and Mary HAYMOND, Harrison Co, to Alexander SMITH, Loudoun Co. 400 acres on Deckers Creek in the Monongalia Glades, adjoining Thomas Chipps' survey, Richard Powell. Consideration: $400. Signed: William Haymond, Mary Haymond. Witnesses: Watson Clark, John Ratcliff, Gentlemen Justices. Acknowledged by William Haymond, February 1793; by Mary Haymond before Ratcliff and Clark, no date. Del: to J Hoy, 17 August 1801. Recorded: 12 January 1801, OS 2:114-115. Re-recording of burned instrument.

8 September 1800. John (Senior) and Dorcas SNIDER to John SNIDER Junior. 200 acres on Indian Creek, adjoining David Snider's part of the survey, Jarred Evans, John Arnett. Part of a 400-acre patent. Consideration: love and affection. Signed: John [mark] Snider, Dorcus [mark] Snider. Witnesses: none. Acknowledged in court, 8 September 1800. Del: to John Snider Jr [no date]. Recorded: OS 2:116.

4 February 1801. Jonathan DAVIS to Thomas WILSON, trustee. Deed of trust on two tracts. 165 acres on the Monongalia River about six miles above Morgantown, adjoining Laben Perdue and George Balzer. 157 acres, moiety of a 314-acre survey, adjoining Peter Cook and Thomas Hellen [?]. Davis owes £246.7, VA, to Jacob Baker and Cornelius Comegys, of Philadelphia, payable on or before 5 February 1802. Signed: Jona Davis. Witnesses: John Stealey, Thos Graham, Hugh McNeely, Thomas Forster. Acknowledged in court, February 1801. Recorded: OS 2:117-118.

9 April 1799. Prudence POWELL, Moses and Rebecca

POWELL, William and Eliza LINSEY, and Thomas POWELL, heirs of Richard POWELL, deceased, to Aaron POWELL. 170 acres on Three Fork Creek. No adjoiners named. Consideration: £60. Signed: Prudence [+] Powell, Moses Powell, Rebeccah [+] Powell, William Linsey, Elizabeth [X] Linsey, Thomas [X] Powell. Witnesses: Alexr Hawthorn, Asa Dudley, Robert Ferrel. Acknowledged by Rebecca Powell and Elizabeth Linsey, before Asa Dudley and Robert Ferrel, 25 April 1799. Del: to Wm G Payne, October 1803. Recorded: OS 2:118-119.

8 April 1799. Simeon and Massey RIGGS to Reuben BUNNER. 30 acres, part of the tract on which Riggs now lives. Purchased by Riggs from Robison Lucas. Consideration: £100, VA. Signed: Simeon Riggs, Massey [X] Riggs. Witnesses: none. Acknowledged in court, April 1799. Del: to grantee, 28 October 1823. Recorded: OS 2:120.

8 June 1801. William and Ann WILLEY to Booz BURROWS. 100 acres, adjoining William Watkins, the tract on which Willey now lives. Consideration: £[blank]. Signed: William Willy, Ann [|] Willy. Witnesses: none. Acknowledged in court. Del: to John Willey **preacher** [sic], 2 April 1803. Recorded: OS 2:121.

14 September 1801. Elisha and Elizabeth CLAYTON to Jesse CHANEY [Chaney's residence not stated]. 190 acres on Indian Creek, no adjoiners named. Part of a 400-acre tract purchased by Clayton from Henry and Rebecca Dering and Isaac and Lucy Williams. Consideration: $800. Signed: Elish [sic] Clayton, Elizabeth Clayton. Witnesses: none. Acknowledged by Elisha Clayton in court, September 1801; by Elizabeth Clayton before John Dent and Wm Hamilton, JPs. No delivery shown. Recorded: OS 2:122.

13 April 1801. James RANDALL to William WEBSTER. 41½ acres on Robertsons Run, adjoining Christopher Raber. Purchased from Joel Smith. Consideration: $41.50. Signed: James Randall, Ann Randall. Witnesses: none. Acknowledged in court, April 1801. Del: to Wm Webster, 15 May 1802. Recorded: OS 2:123.

13 April 1801. Samuel and Caty HAZLET to Amos GLOVER. 200 acres in Sandy Creek glades, on a branch of Little Sandy Creek, adjoining John Mires, Samuel Worell, Thomas Cheny. Part of a grant to Joshua Worley and sold by him to Hazlet by a deed of 11 May 1781 [sic]. Consideration: £230, PA. Signed: Samuel Hazlet, Catherine [X] Hazlet. Witnesses: none. Acknowledged in court, April 1801. Del: to Alexr Brandon, September 1801. Recorded: OS 2:124.

8 April 1799. Joseph TRICKETT, attorney in fact for Thomas PEACOCK and Elijah CHAPMAN, late of Monongalia Co, to John CROTHERS. 20 acres on Joes Run, no adjoiners named. Part of a 400-acre patent to Peacock and Chapman, 4 July 1794. Consideration: £7, VA. Signed: [no signature]. Witnesses: none. Acknowledged in court, April 1799. Del: to John Carothers, 11 November 1805. Recorded: OS 2:125.

18 October 1800. John DOWNER to Jacob PINDELL, trustee. Deed of trust on 800 acres at Dunkard Creek. No adjoiners named. Downer is indebted to Thomas Chipps for $984.50. Pindell is trustee to sell the land, Downer to warrant title to whoever purchases. Land may be redeemed before 18 October 1801. Signed: John Downer. Witnesses: John Williams, Farquire McRay, Duncan F McRay, Thomas Chipps Jr, Wm G Payne. Proved by witnesses, July 1801. Del: to T Chipps, 30 September 1801. Recorded: OS 2:126-127.

14 July 1800. Henry WEAVER to Nicholas WEAVER. 114 acres, 14 poles on White Day Creek, adjoining Robinson Lucas' original survey and Morgan Morgan. Part of a 400-acre patent. Consideration: £64, VA. Signed: Henry [mark] Weaver. Witnesses: none. Acknowledged in court, July 1800. Del: to N Weaver, September 1802. Recorded: OS 2:128.

13 July 1801. Godfrey HOUR to Jacob BENNETT Senr, both of Harrison Co. 144 acres on Deckerds Creek, three miles from Morgantown. No adjoiners named. Consideration: £50, VA. Signed: Godfrey Hour. Witnesses: none. Acknowledged in court, July 1801. Del: to Jacob Bennett, 22 October 1802. Recorded: OS 2:129.

11 February 1801. James and Maryann JENKINS to Abraham GOOSMAN. 91 acres, 19 poles, adjoining Benjamin Jarrett and the heirs of John Peirpoint. Consideration: $748. Signed: James Jenkins, Maryann [X] Jenkins. Witnesses: Wm John, Lamuel John, Benj N Jarrett. Acknowledged by Maryann Jenkins before Lamuel John and Wm John, April 1801. Del: to A Goosman, 18 April 1804. Recorded: OS 2:130-131.

11 October 1801. John and Hannah BEVERLIN to Stephen MEREDITH. 50 acres at Lick Run in Dunker Bottom settlement. No adjoiners named. Part of a 400-acre patent to John Beverlin, assignee of Nathaniel Kidd. Consideration: $133.33. Signed: John Beverlin, Hannah [-] Beverlin. Witnesses: none. Acknowledged in court, October 1801. Del: to Davis Meredith, 8 December 1802. Recorded: OS 2:132.

11 October 1801. Joseph and Mary KRATSER to William

ANDERSON. 175 acres, no place names mentioned. Part of a survey that David Dunham also lives on, and conveyed by Dunham to Kratser. Consideration: [£? $?]200. Signed: Joseph Kratser, Mary Kratser. Witnesses: none. Acknowledged in court, October 1801. No delivery shown. Recorded: OS 2:133.

27 October 1799. Barney and Margaret HENEY to Booz BURROWS. 49 acres, no adjoiners or place names mentioned. Part of a 400-acre patent to John Golding, conveyed by him to Heney. Signed: Barney Heney, Margret [mark] Heney. Witnesses: Geo Greenwood, James Randall, John Lough. Acknowledged by Barney Heney, in court, April 1801; by Margaret Heney before George Greenwood and John W Dean, JPs, certificate of 9 June 1800. Del: to John Willey, preacher [sic], 2 April 1803. Recorded: OS 2:134-135.

8 August 1801. Abraham WOODRING to Francis DEAKINS. Release. Some years ago Francis Deakins and William Deakins conveyed to Woodring 269 acres. It was later found that 206½ acres lay within Thomas Goff's elder survey for 800 acres. The Deakins paid Goff $200 through John T Goff, Thomas' legal attorney and brother, and he conveyed Woodring 567 acres of the 800-acre survey, including the 206½ acres at issue. Woodring now releases Francis Deakins and the heirs of William Deakins deceased regarding the 206½ acres. Signed: Abraham Woodring, "signed in Dutch." Witnesses: John Stemple, Jacob Ridenhour, Jacob [+] Tetery. Proved by witnesses, October 1801. Del: to John Hoy, 15 June 1803. Recorded: OS 2:135.

8 August 1801. John T GOFF, attorney in fact for Thomas James GOFF, to David RIDENOUR, Randolph Co. 133 acres adjoining Woodring's bridge. Part of an 800-acre patent to Thomas J Goff. Consideration: $133. Signed: John T Goff. Witnesses: John Stemple, Jacob Ridenour, John [X] Fester. Proved by witnesses, October 1801. Del: to David Ridenour, March 1804. Recorded: OS 2:136.

8 August 1801. David RIDENOUR, Randolph Co, to Francis DEAKINS, George Town, DC. 3¼ acres between Woolf Creek and the waters of Yohogania. Part of a patent to Thomas Goff. Consideration: $16. Signed: David Ridenour. Witnesses: Jacob Ridenour, John Stemple, Jacob [+] Tetery. Proved by witnesses, October 1801. Del: to John Hoy, 15 June 1803. Recorded: OS 2:137.

8 August 1801. Francis DEAKINS, George Town, DC, to Abraham WOODRING, Jacob RIDENOUR, and Peter ECKHART, school trustees, and their successors. 100 acres, half a mile north of Mount Carmel, adjoining Jacob Tetery's

deed for 28 acres, Woolf Creek, and Abraham Woodring. Consideration: $1 and Deakins' will and desire to encourage morality, religion and education in the town called Mount Carmel. Land for the use and benefit of the school. Signed: Francis Deakins. Witnesses: Jacob [+] Tetery, John [X] Fester, John Stemple. Proved by witnesses, October 1801. No delivery shown. Recorded: OS 2:138.

8 August 1801. Francis DEAKINS, George Town, DC, to Jacob TETERY. 11 acres, 10 poles at Woolf Creek, adjoining Tetery's other lands. Part of a patent to Francis and William Deakins. Consideration: £10.15. Signed: Francis Deakins. Witnesses: Jacob Ridenour, John Stemple, John [X] Fester. Proved by witnesses, October 1801. Del: to Jacob Tetery, 15 September 1802. Recorded: OS 2:139.

8 August 1801. Francis DEAKINS, George Town, DC, to David RIDENOUR. Lot #61 in town of Mount Carmel. Consideration: $8, plus quit rent of $1 per year forever, payable on 4 July, for the use of the school. Signed: Francis Deakins. Witnesses: Jacob Ridenour, John Stemple, John [X] Fester. Proved by witnesses, October 1801. Recorded: OS 2:140.

9 February 1801. Benjamin and Ann WHITSON to William NEWLON, Harrison Co. 110 acres on Little Sandy Creek, adjoining Robert Brownfield and John England. Part of 125 acres sold to Whitson by Samuel and Magdalen Cobb. Consideration: £75. Signed: B Whitson, Ann Whitson. Witnesses: none. Acknowledged in court, February 1801. Del: to James Thomas, 13 September 1803. Recorded: OS 2:141.

28 March 1801. Gilbert and Huldey BUTLER to Bartholomew LOTT. 71 acres on Indian Creek, no adjoiners named. Part of a 20 December 1798 patent. Consideration: $142. Signed: Gilbert Butler, Huldey [H] Butler. Witnesses: John Dent, Wm Hamilton, Otho Henry. Proved by witnesses, April 1801. Acknowledged by Huldey Butler before John Dent and Wm Hamilton, 28 March 1801. No delivery shown. Recorded: OS 2:141-142.

8 August 1801. Francis DEAKINS, George Town, DC, to Jacob RIDENOUR. Lot #41 in Mount Carmel. Consideration: $8, plus quit rent of $1 per year for the use of the school. Signed: Francis Deakins. Witnesses: Jacob [X] Tetery, John [X] Fester, John Stemple. Proved by witnesses, October 1801. No delivery shown. Recorded: OS 2:143.

8 August 1801. Francis DEAKINS to John FESTER. Lot #49 in Mount Carmel. Consideration: $10, plus quit rent

of $1 per year for the use of the school. Signed: Francis Deakins. Witnesses: Jacob Ridenour, John Stemple, Jacob [X] Tetery. No acknowledgement recorded. No delivery shown. Recorded: OS 2:144. [cf below, OS 2:149]

8 August 1801. John HOYE, George Town, DC, to James GOFF Senr. Undivided half of 103 acres conveyed by Col Francis Deakins to John Hoye and Abraham Woodring. No adjoiners or place names mentioned. Consideration: $10. Signed: John Hoye. Witnesses: Jacob Tetery, John Stemple, John [+] Fester. Proved by witnesses, October 1801. Del: to Frederick Harsh, 8 September 1804[6?]. Recorded: OS 2:145.

8 August 1801. Francis DEAKINS, George Town, DC, to Elizabeth SHAVER [also SHABER in body of instrument]. Lot #50 in Mount Carmel. Consideration: $1, plus quit rent of $1 per year for the use of the school. Signed: Francis Deakins. Witnesses: Jacob Tetery, John Stemple, John [+] Fester. Proved by witnesses, October 1801. Del: to Christian Whitehair, 13 July 1807. Recorded: OS 2:145-146.

Undated. WILL of Francis WARMAN. [Preamble only, and the remainder of the page is blank. This instrument appears not to be otherwise recorded in Monongalia, though an attested clerk's copy was entered as evidence in a later lawsuit.] Recorded: [incompletely] OS 2:146.

27 April 1801. Nicholas and Mary MARSTILLER, Randolph Co, to Henry BISHOP, Frederick Co, MD. 152 acres on Salt Lick Creek, no adjoiners named. Consideration: $300. Signed: Nicholas Marstiller, Mary Marstiller. Acknowledged in Randolph Co, 27 April 1801. Del: to H Bishop, 13 June 1803. Recorded: 12 October 1801, OS 2:147.

13 April 1801. John HAVENER to James PARKER, both of Green Co, PA. 400 acres on Sandy Creek, adjoining James Robnett. Patented to Lewis Christ. Consideration: $600. Signed: John Havener. Witnesses: none. Acknowledged in court, October 1801. Del: to James Parker, September 1803. Recorded: OS 2:148.

8 August 1801. Francis DEAKINS, George Town, DC, to Johon [sic] FESTER. Lot #49 in Mount Carmel. Consideration: $10, plus quit rent of $1 per year for the use of the school. Signed: Francis Deakins. Witnesses: [name "signed in Dutch"], Jacob [+] Tetery, John Stemple. Proved by witnesses, October 1801. Del: to Christian Whitehair, 13 July 1807. Recorded: OS 2:149.

22 May 1801. William and Mary MENAR to Robert MOODY. 180 acres in the Monongalia Glades, adjoining [-]

McClelan, [-] Watson, [-] Manear, Moody's plantation land. Consideration: $500. Signed: William [+] Manear, Mary [+] Manear. Witnesses: Wm G Payne, George Zinn, Chas Byrn, Jas Coburn [all as to Wm Menear's signature]. Proved by witnesses, June 1801. By Mary Manear before Samuel Hanway and John Fairfax, JPs, 22 August 1801. Recorded: OS 2:150-151.

12 October 1801. Wm McCLEERY to Joseph LANE. Lot #98 in Morgantown. Consideration: $200. Signed: Wm McCleery. Witnesses: none. Acknowledged in court. Del: to Joseph Lane, 10 January 1804. Recorded: OS 2:151.

12 March 1800. Thomas FORSTER to Henry DERING, trustee. Deed of trust to secure $500 due to John Stealey. Large amount of personal property, including livestock, household furnishings, tools, metal. Signed: Thomas Forster. Witnesses: John Davis, Jona Davis. Acknowledged in court, July 1800. Del: to John Stealey, 14 January 1804. Recorded: OS 2:152.

[blank] 1801. Christopher and Margret TROY to John STEWART. 154 acres adjoining James Troy. Moiety of a tract patented to Simon Troy, 1 April 1784, and bequeathed to Christopher by Simon's last will and testament. Consideration: $595, VA. Signed: Christopher Troy, Marget [X] Troy. Witnesses: none. Acknowledged in court, February 1801. Del: to John Stewart, 8 [illegible] 1806. Recorded: OS 2:153-154.

2 October 1800. Joseph (Merchant) and Elizabeth SOMERVILLE, Clarksburg, Harrison Co, to Thomas SWAINE, Esqr, party of the second part, and William HODGSON, attorney in fact for the late firm of Robinson, Sanderson & Romey, Merchants, party of the third part. Swaine and Hodgson are both of Alexandria, territory of Columbia. Deed of trust. On 29 August 1800 execution was issued in Berkley Co, against the goods and chattels of Somerville as result of a suit filed by Robinson, Sanderson, & Romey. Somerville is indebted in the amount of £297.2.9, with interest from 4 April 1785, for a total of £530.19.10, VA. Hodgson, by his agent John McIver, has received £101.4.11 in dry goods and groceries and suspends immediate execution of the remainder, providing for a schedule of payments. Swaine, as trustee, receives 392 acres on Mud Lick, a branch of Tyger Valley. Land was patented 24 June 1791 to Isaac Morris, assignee of Daniel McFarland, and sold by Isaac and Ruth Morris to Joseph Somerville 2 October 1800. Swaine to sell the land if necessary. Signed: Joseph Sommerville, Elizabeth Somerville, John McIver, attorney in fact for Swaine and Hodgson. Witnesses: Daniel

Davisson, N Davisson, Wm Martin, Isaac Morris, John G Jackson. Acknowledged in Harrison Co court, 20 October 1800. Certificate of Benjamin Wilson, clerk. Del: to Smith for Hodgson, 1 November 1801. Recorded: 9 February 1801, OS 2:154-158.

6 August 1788. Thomas LAIDLEY to Samuel HANWAY and Francis BROOK, trustees. Deed of trust. Laidley is indebted to Reed & Ford in the sum of £1400, plus interest. To secure the debt, he entrusts to Hanway and Brook numerous tracts of land in Monongalia. Lots #30, 31, 33, 34, 35, 36, 43, 44, 94, 95, 96, and 97 in Morgantown. 300 acres in the Glades of Sandy Creek, commonly known as "the China place," and patented to Laidley. 300 acres in the Glades of Sandy Creek, adjoining William Spurgeon; tract originally patented to Thomas China. 100 acres on Cheat River below Lewis Rogers, conveyed to Laidley by William Jolliffe. Part of 200 acres, no location, surveyed for Henry Croll. 400 acres at Dunker Mill Run, surveyed for Thomas Laidley as assignee of Robert Ferrel, 10 December 1787. 400 acres, no location, surveyed for Thomas Laidley as assignee of William Lenham, 27 November 1787. 400 acres preemption survey at Dunker Mill Run, as assignee of Robert Ferrel, 10 December 1787. 200 acres preemption survey at Dunker Mill Run, 10 December 1787. 300 acres adjoining Scott's mill seat, located 22 December 1783. 700 acres in 2 locations on the head drains of Buffalo Creek, adjoining John Dent, located 23 January 1784. 400 acres on Buffalo Creek, adjoining Robert Campbell and Morgan Morgan, located 11 April 1786. Undivided one-third of 4075 acres on Mill Creek, surveyed for and patented to Sarah Province, assignee of Robert Bennet, Benjamin Archer, and Richard Lamaster. Lewis Rogers to convey said one-third to Laidley as soon as partition can be made. 300 acres on Booths Creek, adjoining Henry Tucker and Thomas Miller. 50 acres on the east side of the Monongalia River, 5 miles from Morgan Town. 400 acres on Papaw Creek, surveyed as assignee of William Owens. 400 acres at Dunker Mill Run, adjoining the last 4000 [sic] acres, located 20 December 1787. 750 acres on Papaw Creek, surveyed for Laidley; 400 acres of this a settlement right of David Scott. 1200 acres at Salt Lick, in three settlement rights, conveyed by William Robinson. 3000 acres on Buffalo, located 3 December 1781 for John Gray but surveyed for Laidley. 500 acres on the main road to Clarksburg, 10 miles from Morgantown, located 24 December 1786. 400 acres on the Monongalia River, 7 miles above Morgantown, located for John Hall and

surveyed for Laidley. 140 acres on Deckers Creek, 2 miles from Morgantown, patented to Jacob Youngman. 1000 acres on the head of Glady Creek, located 15 February 1784 for Laidley and Robert Cochran. 400 acres at the mouth of White Day, surveyed for Laidley as assignee of Jesse Parker. Lots #6, 15, 16, 56, and 57 in Morgantown. Lands may be sold at the end of 5 years. The 400 acres at White Day and the 5 town lots last named to be reserved from sale until the other land be sold. If to be sold, the land to be advertised in the *Virginia Gazette* and the Philadelphia paper for 6 weeks prior to sale. Signed: Thomas Laidley, Saml. Hanway, Francis Brooks. Witnesses: Zackl Morgan, Henry Dering Junr, John Downer. Proved by witnesses, August 1788. Del: to Ford, 14 November 1801. Recorded: 1801, OS 2:159-161. Re recording of burned instrument.

9 June 1800. Jacob RUBELL, heir at law of Samuel RUBELL deceased, and Mary RUBELL, widow of Samuel, to Joseph SMITH. 304 acres on Three Fork, adjoining Bazel Brater. Patented 25 August 1785 and including Samuel's 1775 improvement. Consideration: $300. Signed: Jacob Ruble, Mary [X] Ruble. Witnesses: none. Acknowledged in court, June 1800. No delivery shown. Recorded: OS 2:162-163.

14 April 1800. John and Catherine HAUT and Jacob and Magdalen HAUT (the latter couple of PA), to Peter TENNANT. Acreage not stated. Part of a 25 October 1792 patent for 324 acres, adjoining Hurry, Fortney, Leonard Metz. Consideration: $485. Signed: John [mark] Haut, Catherine [+] Haut, Jacob Haut, Magdaline [+] Haut. Witnesses: none. Acknowledged in court, April 1800. Del: to Peter Tenant, 6 September 1803. Recorded: OS 2:164.

9 June 1800. Levin and Esther OKEY to William JOHN. 112 acres on Cheat, below the mouth of Sandy Creek, adjoining Thomas Tanehill and Isaac Hayse. Tract on which Okey now lives, conveyed to him 12 February 1798 by Thomas and Martha Tanehill. Consideration: $333 1/3. Signed: Levin Okey, Esther [+] Okey. Witnesses: none. Acknowledged in court, June 1800. Del: to Wm John, 27 November 1801. Recorded: OS 2:165.

14 January 1799. William and Ruth PETTY JOHN to Mary BENNETT and George R TINGLE. Lot [# not shown] in Morgan Town, adjoining Tingle's lot, High Street, Spruce Street. Consideration: $40, VA. Signed: W PettyJohn, Ruth Petty John. Witnesses: none. Acknowledged by William Petty John in court, January 1799; by Ruth Petty John before Nathan Springer and William Haymond, 14 April 1800. Del: to Mary Bennett, 16 October 1804.

Recorded: OS 2:166-167.
14 April 1800. Dudley and Annarah EVANS to James THOMAS. 80 acres at the head drains of Swamp Run, adjoining Jacob Jones Senr, Josiah Wilson, and heirs of Theophilus Phillips. Part of a patent of 9 August 1799. Consideration: $160. Signed: Dudley Evans, Annarah Evans. Witnesses: none. Acknowledged in court, April 1800. No delivery shown. Recorded: OS 2:168.

23 September 1800. John and Ruth NIXON to James THOMAS. 411 acres on Little Sandy Creek, adjoining A Griffe, Edward Gutridge, Hilderbrand. Consideration: £200. Signed: John Nixon, Ruth [X] Nixon. Witnesses: John Kennedy, Jesse Hanway, William Myers, William Thomas. Acknowledged in court, October 1800. No delivery shown. Recorded: OS 2:169.

14 April 1800. Thomas and Joanna CHIPPS to Stephen WORKMAN. 260 acres, known as London's Glade. No adjoiners mentioned. Part of an 850-acre tract conveyed to Chipps by Bartholomew London, 11 October 1788. Consideration: £150, VA. Signed: Thos Chipps, Joanah Chipps. Witnesses: none. Acknowledged in court, April 1800. Del: to Isaac Armstrong. Recorded: OS 2:170.

28 March 1801. Gilbert and Huldy BUTLER to Sarah BARKER. 329 acres at Indian Creek, adjoining David Scott. Patented 20 December 1798. Consideration: $1096.66. Signed: Gilbert Butler, Hulday [mark] Butler. Witnesses: John Dent, Wm Hammilton, Oath Henry. Acknowledged by Hulday Butler before John Dent and Wm Hamilton, 28 March 1801. Proved by witnesses, 13 April 1801, 14 December 1801. Del: to John Dent. Recorded: OS 2:171-172.

12 August 1799. Asahel and Jane MARTIN, Fleming Co, KY, to William George WILSON, Mason Co, KY. 325 acres on the right fork of Buffalo, above Mahans Camp, no adjoiners named. Patented 31 October 1785. Consideration: £100. Signed: Ashahel Martin, Jane Martin. Witnesses: none. Acknowledged in Fleming Co, KY, 12 August 1799. Certificate of Joshua Stockton, Clerk of Fleming Co. Del: to John Minor, 12 May 1810. Recorded: September 1800, OS 2:173-174.

15 December 1801. Jonathan and Elizabeth ROBERTS to Thomas ANDERSON, Fayette Co, PA. 200 acres on a branch of Tygers Valley River, adjoining Jacob Prickett and William PettyJohn. Part of a 28 June 1791 patent to Jacob Prickett for 400 acres. Consideration: £80, VA. Signed: Jonathan Roberts, Elizabeth [X] Roberts. Witnesses: none. Acknowledged in court, 15 December 1801. Del: to Thos Anderson. Recorded: OS 2:174-175.

8 December 1800. John and Catharine YOST to Henry YOST. 240 acres on Little Indian Creek, adjoining Jacob Scott, Joseph Barker, John Lynch. Consideration: natural love and affection to their beloved son Henry. Signed: John [mark] Yost [Catharine does not sign]. Witnesses: none. Acknowledged in court, 8 December 1800. Del: to Henry Yost, 10 September 1805. Recorded: OS 2:175.

8 December 1800. James (Senr) and Mary WEST to John BUNNER. 400 acres on Tyger Valley waters, adjoining William Petty John. Patented 21 January 1784. Consideration: £400, VA. Signed: James [mark] West, Mary [0] West. Witnesses: none. Acknowledged in court, 8 December 1800. No delivery shown. Recorded: OS 2:176.

[blank] March 1797. William and Mary JOHN to Elender, William, and Nicholas WOOD. A deed was previously made to the grantees, conveying 410 acres adjoining the heirs of Jacob Strait, but was burned at the clerk's office. This instrument reconveys the property to Elender Wood during her natural life and to William and Nicholas in fee simple. Consideration: not stated but previous payment is acknowledged. Signed: William John, Mary John. Witnesses: none. Acknowledged in court, 13 October 1801. Del: to Jas Currie, 8 May 1802. Recorded: OS 2:177.

8 September 1800. Lewis and Nelly KEARNS to Samuel HANWAY. 64 acres, adjoining Anthony Carrel. Patented 8 June 1790. Consideration: $150. Signed: Lewis [0] Kerns, Elenor [X] Kerns. Witnesses: none. Acknowledged in court, 8 September 1800. Receipt for consideration money. Del: to John Hanway, 18 January 1835. Recorded: OS 2:178.

2 December 1801. John SAVARY, Millersburg, Bourbon Co, KY, now in Morgantown, to Enoch JONES. Two tracts on the Monongalia River. 400 acres, near the mouth of Robinsons Run. Patented to David Scott, heir of James Scott deceased, assignee of William Robinson, and conveyed by David and Rachel Scott to Savary, the deed later burned in the county clerk's office. 96 acres on both sides of Monongalia River, adjoining David Scott Jnr son of David, and David Scott Jnr heir at law of James. Surveyed for Savary 26 September 1800, the survey now at the register's office for issuance of patent. Savary conveys his title and interest to Jones. Consideration: £800, VA. Signed: J Savary. Witnesses: Augustus Werninger, Hugh McNeely, John Sanders, J G Laidley, Alexr Hawthorn. Proved by witnesses, 14 December 1801. Del: to Jones, January 1807. Recorded: OS 2:179-180.

13 July 1801. Samuel and Rachael SMITH to James FRAZER. 100 acres near Scotts Run, adjoining the county road and Jonathan Hoskinson's improvement. Consideration: $1, and in pursuance of a decree of Monongalia county court. Signed: Samuel Smith, Rachel Smith. Witnesses: George Hite, H Dering, Barney Haney. Acknowledged in court, July 1801. Del: to James Frazer, 19 February 1805. Recorded: OS 2:181.

8 April 1799. Henry and Mary TUCKER to Patrick KERNS. 244 acres at Booths Creek, near Little Laurel Run and adjoining Thomas Miller. Patented 20 April 1784. Consideration: £133.4, VA. Signed: Henry [+] Tucker, Mary [mark] Tucker. Witnesses: none. Acknowledged in court, 9 June 1800. Del: to Kerns. Recorded: OS 2:182.

29 May 1800. Robert and Hannah FERREL to Francis STANBURY. 184½ acres, 34 rods, adjoining David Sayers, John Sayre, other lands of Ferrel. Part of a 6 February 1797 patent for 966 acres. Consideration: $300. Signed: Robert Ferrel, Hannah [+] Ferrel. Witnesses: Daniel Sayre, Richard Smith, John Sayre. Proved by witnesses, 9 June 1800. Del: to him, 12 August 1811 by FPR. Recorded: OS 2:183.

12 April 1796. Godfrey and Leah WAGONER to Robert WOODS. 100 acres on Big Sandy, adjoining Martin Juda and other lands of Wagoner. Consideration: $100. Signed: Godfrey Wagoner, Leah Wagoner. Witnesses: Alexander Brandon, Jonathan Brandon, Joseph Brandon. Proved by witnesses, 12 September 1796. Del: to Woods, but Alexr Brandon assumes to pay recording fee. Recorded: OS 2:184.

30 June 1801. Samuel MARTIN, Hamilton Co, North Western Territory, yeoman, to Ephraim GUARD, Fayette Co, PA, yeoman. 100 acres on Sandy Creek, adjoining Thomas Coushman. Consideration: £80, PA. Signed: Samuel Martin. Witnesses: Michael [+] Andris, Jonas Smally, James Allison. Receipt for consideration money. Proved by witnesses, January 1802. No delivery shown. Recorded: OS 2:185.

16 June 1800. John and Elizabeth BERRY to John NIXON. 19 3/4 acres, 34 poles, on Little Sandy, adjoining Hilterbrand, Berry. Consideration: $40. Signed: John Berry, Elizabeth Berry. Witnesses: John Edwards, John Kennady, Jesse Hanway. Proved by witnesses, October 1800. No delivery shown. Recorded: OS 2:186.

13 July 1801. Andrew and Elizabeth JOHNSTON to James DEWIT. 50 acres on Cheat River, in the forks of Green's run. No adjoiners named. Part of a settlement

survey of John Green, deceased. Consideration: $125. Signed: Andrew Johnson, Elizabeth [/] Johnson. Witnesses: none. Acknowledged in court, July 1801. No delivery shown. Recorded: OS 2:187.

2 May 1801. Thomas CHINWORTH, Ross Co, Territory Northwest of River Ohio, to William MARTIN. Power of attorney to sell 231 acres at Scotts Mill Run, obtained by Chinworth in a suit against Thomas Lazzel and George Greenwood, Esqrs. Signed: Thomas Chinworth. Witnesses: none. Acknowledged in Ross Co, 2 May 1801, before Elias Langham and James Furgusson, JP. Certificate of Edward Tiffin, prothonotary. Recorded: September 1801, OS 2:188.

13 July 1801. Andrew and Elizabeth JOHNSTON to Thomas MONTGOMERY. 125.2 acres at Greens Run on Cheat River, adjoining James Brown. Part of a survey John Green held by settlement right. Consideration: $187.50. Signed: Andrew Johnston, Elizabeth [X] Johnston. Witnesses: none. Acknowledged in court, July 1801. Del: to Thos Montgomery, 21 January 1809. Recorded: OS 2:189.

6 April 1801. William and Elizabeth MARTIN to William, Simeon, and Jesse EVERLY. All right of Elizabeth Martin in the real and personal estate of Gasper Everly, deceased. Consideration: $100. Signed: William Martin, Elizabeth Martin. Witnesses: Lemuel John, David Scott. Acknowledged by William Martin in court, April 1801; by Elizabeth Martin before Lemuel John and David Scott, JPs, April 1801. No delivery shown. Recorded: OS 2:190.

14 April 1801. John and Prudence STEALY to Davis SHOCKLEY, Amos SMITH, John WILLEY, William HAMILTON, George SMITH, Calder HAYMOND, Lemuel JOSEPH, John COURTNEY, and George WILSON, trustees. Lot [# not shown] in Morgantown, adjoining lots of Dr Solomon Drown, Thomas Wilson. For the use of the Methodist Episcopal Church. Consideration: $5. Signed: John Stealey, Prudence [|] Stealy. Witnesses: none. Acknowledged by Prudence Stealey before Samuel Hanway and Benjamin Reeder, JPs, 6 June 1801. Receipt for consideration money. Del: to John Willey, 2 April 1803. Recorded: OS 2:191-193.

6 August 1800. James WILMARTH, Hagerstown MD, to Nicholas MEDERIA. 286 acres in Washington Co, Territory Northwest of the Ohio River, purchased 14 July 1799 from Isaac and James Miles. Consideration: $386. Signed: James Wilmoth. Witnesses: Wm G Payne, David Farquer, Faquire McCrea. Receipt for purchase money. Proved by witnesses, February 1801, October 1801. No delivery

shown. Recorded: OS 2:194.

[blank] September 1801. William and Mary JOHN to John LINN, Northwestern Territory. 100 acres on east side of Monongahela River, adjoining other lands of William John. Part of a 19 August 1794 patent for 150 acres. Consideration: $400. Signed: Wm John, Mary John. Witnesses: none. Acknowledged in court, October 1801. Del: to him, 14 March 1814. Recorded: OS 2:195.

26 April 1801. Benjamin ESTILL, Kentucky, to HENRY GRIM, trustee. Deed of trust. Estill owes $500 to Paul Grim. To secure the debt he entrusts to Henry Grim 250 acres in the Monongalia Glades, which he purchased of Henry Grim. Schedule of payment for the debt. Henry may advertise the land for sale in the *Winchester Gazette* 4 weeks after any of the payments be due and not paid. Signed: Benjamin Estill. Witnesses: Wm G Payne, George Zinn, Jesse Payne. Proved by witnesses, September 1801. Del: to Henry Grimm, 28 May 1802. Recorded: OS 2:186.

[blank] March 1801. Reece WOOLF to John STEALEY. Woolf sold 434 acres to John Casseday, who was not satisfied with the title and who gave bond to reconvey the same to Woolf. Casseday has now conveyed the land to John Stealey and Woolf releases all his claim to it. Signed: Reece Woolf. Witnesses: W Silliman, Thos Lord, John Stokeley. Acknowledged in Wood Co court, April 1801. Certificate of John Stokely, clerk of Wood Co. No delivery shown. Recorded: October 1801, OS 2:196.

13 July 1801. Thomas MONTGOMERY to Andrew JOHNSTON. Mortgage on 125 acres at Cheat River, part of the survey John Green, deceased, held by settlement right. Consideration: $187.50, with provision for redemption. Signed: Thoms Montgomery. Witnesses: none. Acknowledged in court, July 1801. No delivery shown. Recorded: OS 2:197.

11 June 1801. David SCOTT to Daniel MERCHAND. 500 acres, adjoining Samuel Lieuellen. Surveyed for Scott, assignee of Thomas Evans, assignee of William Hill, patented [blank]. Consideration: $500. Signed: David Scott. Witnesses: J Williams, Hugh McNeely, Wm Postle, James Daugherty. Acknowledged in court, 13 July 1801. Del: to Dr Daniel Merchand. Recorded: OS 2:198.

13 March 1801. William and Elizabeth ROARK to Charles BOYLES, Randolph Co. 180½ acres at Indian Creek, adjoining Charles Dawson and James Williamson. Patented to Richard Harrison and conveyed by him to Roark. Consideration: £180.10. Signed: William Roark, Elizabeth [+] Roark. Witnesses: J Evans, Alexr Hawthorn, Thos Wilson. Proved by witnesses, April 1801. Del: to Charles

Boyls, 20 August 1814. Recorded: OS 2:199.

8 July 1801. Edward and Sarah EVANS to Joseph NEAL. 180½ acres, adjoining other lands of Evans and Gasper Mike. Part of a larger tract conveyed to Evans by Jacob and Hannah Pindell. Consideration: £120. Signed: Edward [mark] Evans, Sarah [mark] Evans. Witnesses: none. Acknowledged in court, June 1801 [sic]. Del: to Joseph Neal, 20 August 1803. Recorded: OS 2:200.

8 June 1801. Fleming and Christena JONES to Davis MERYDITH. 150 acres at Papaw, near Robinsons Run, adjoining Jones' other land. Part of a 23 June 1785 patent to William McCleery for 400 acres. Consideration: $187.50. Signed: Fleming Jones, Christina Jones. Witnesses: none. Acknowledged in court, June 1801. Del: to Davis Merredith, 28 December 1802. Recorded: OS 2:201.

13 April 1801. Charles and Barbara SNODGRASS to Jacob FULK. 78 acres at Farows Run, part of a 19 October 1789 patent for 285 acres. No adjoiners named. Consideration: £125. Signed: Charles Snodgrass, Barbara Snotgrass. Witnesses: none. Acknowledged in court, April 1801. Del: to Mrs Foulk, 3 September 1804. Recorded: OS 2:202.

13 April 1801. Alexander and Margaret CLEG to James MORRIS. 49 acres at Dunkard Creek, near the PA line and adjoining John Lowe, John Hought, and Michael Barr's part of said land. Tract where Cleg formerly lived, part of a 279 acre patent. Consideration: £300. Signed: Alexander Cleg, Margaret [+] Cleg. Witnesses: none. No acknowledgement recorded. Del: to John Lance, 11 November 1805. Recorded: OS 2:203.

13 October 1799. Robert and Hannah FERRELL to Jeremiah and John WILSON. 111½ acres, 25 poles on the Monongalia River. 53 acres, 20 poles, from a patent of 284 acres, and 58¼ acres, 5 poles, from a patent of 966 acres. No adjoiners named. Consideration: $300. Signed: Robt Ferrell, Hannah [X] Ferrell. Witnesses: Joseph Trickett, Daniel Sayre, David Sayre. No acknowledgement recorded. Del: to Jeremiah Wilson, 14 April 1806. Recorded: OS 2:204.

26 August 1800. Thomas and Margaret PHILLIPS to Ephraim KOOKEN [?]. 50 acres on Big Sandy Creek. No adjoiners named. Consideration: $40. Signed: Thomas Phillips, Margaret [mark] Phillips. Witnesses: John Kennady, John England, Benjn Phillips, William Elerton. No acknowledgement recorded. No delivery shown. Recorded: OS 2:205.

3 May 1799. Michael FRANKS Jr and Jacob FRANKS,

executors of Michael FRANKS Sr, deceased, both of Fayette Co, PA, to Joshua JONES. 200 acres at Mill Fall Run, no adjoiners named. Part of a 2 June 1785 patent. Consideration: £30. Signed: Michael [+] Franks, Jacob [0] Franks. Witnesses: Jacob Franks Jr, David Stewart. Acknowledged in Fayette Co, PA, before Jonathan Rowland and Robert Moore, JPs, 12 October 1799. Certificate of Ephraim Douglass, prothonotary. Del: to J Franks, 2 April 1802. Recorded: OS 2:206.

3 May 1799. Michael FRANKS Jr and Jacob FRANKS, executors of Michael FRANKS Sr, deceased, to Jacob FRANKS Junr, all of Fayette Co, PA. 200 acres at Mill Fall Run, no adjoiners named. Part of a 2 June 1785 patent to Michael Franks, deceased. Consideration: £30. Witnesses: Joshua Jones, David Stewart. Signed: Michael [+] Franks, Jacob [0] Franks. Acknowledged in Fayette Co, PA, before Jonathan Rowland and Robert Moore, JPs, 12 October 1799. Certificate of Ephraim Douglass, prothonotary. Del: to J Franks, 2 April 1802. Recorded: OS 2:207.

15 March 1784. David PORTER to Thomas GIBSON and John JENKINS. 400 acres near Cheat River. No adjoiners named. Consideration: £70, VA. Signed: David Porter. Witnesses: none. Acknowledged in court, March 1784. No delivery shown. Recorded: OS 2:208. Re-recording of burned instrument.

8 September 1800. Samuel CAIN to Richard CAIN. 200 acres on righthand fork of Dunkert Creek, adjoining Asa Kellum. Consideration: £100, VA. Signed: Samuel Cain. Witnesses: none. Acknowledged in court, February 1801. Del: to Richard Cain, 6 January 1810. Recorded: OS 2:209.

9 June 1800. James CAIN to Richard CAIN. 300 acres on Cheat River, adjoining Thomas Miller, William Stewart, James Clelland, Mills. Consideration: £3000. Signed: James Cain. Witnesses: none. Acknowledged in court, June 1800. Del: to Richard Cain, 6 January 1810. Recorded: OS 2:210.

9 June 1800. Samuel CAIN to Richard CAIN. 303 acres on Cheat River, adjoining Thomas Mills, Mason and Nail, and John McFarland. Consideration: £300. Signed: Samuel Cain. Acknowledged in court, June 1800. Del: to Richard Cain, 6 January 1810. Recorded: OS 2:211.

1 March 1800. John GILLESPIE to Richard CAIN. Acquittance. Gillespie has previously instituted suits against Cain in Fayette Co, PA, and Monongalia Co. He will pay costs in Fayette Co and Cain will pay costs in Monongalia. Cain also gave bond to make title to

Gillespie for land in the Monongalia Glades. The bond being lost or mislaid, Gillespie releases on it. Consideration: 5 shillings. Signed: John Gillespie. Witnesses: John Davis, James Laidley. Proved by witnesses, April 1800, June 1800. Del: to Richard Cain, 6 January 1810. Recorded: OS 2:212.

12 January 1801. James CAIN to Charles STEWART. 210 acres on Papaw Creek, adjoining William Woods and the heirs of Jacob Streete. Part of an 18 September 1787 patent of 400 acres to William John. Consideration: £110. Signed: James Cain. Witnesses: none. Acknowledged in court, January 1801. Del: to C Stuart, 5 March 1808. Recorded: OS 2:213.

23 September 1799. Philip and Amelia CRITCHFIELD, John CRITCHFIELD, Arthur CRITCHFIELD, and Henry CRITCHFIELD, co-heirs of Arthur CRITCHFIELD, deceased, to William JOHN. 396 acres at the mouth of Three Lick Run on Dunkard Creek, adjoining Phinehas Killam and Daniel Barton. Originally patented to Christopher Rever, assignee of Ralph Hunt, assignee of Asa Killam, and conveyed by Rever to Arthur Critchfield, deceased, the deed acknowledged and recorded in Monongalia Co but afterward burned in the clerk's office. Proof of such deed established before the Commissioners appointed for that purpose. Consideration: £120. Signed: Philip Critchfield, Amelia Critchfield, John Critchfield, Arthur Critchfield, Henry Critchfield. Witnesses: John W Dean, John Seaman, George Cunningham. Proved by witnesses, October 1799 and April 1800. Del: to Wm John, 8 May 1802. Recorded: OS 2::214.

8 October 1798. Samuel and Catherine NIXON to Jacob NOOS. 2 parcels at Cobuns Creek, of 41 and 100 acres respectively, between lands surveyed for Joshua Jenkins and John McGee [Thomas McGee mentioned in metes and bounds]. Both tracts patented 2 December 1791 to Robert Bennet. Consideration: £150. Signed: Samuel Nixon, Catherine [4] Nixon. Witnesses: none. Acknowledged in court, October 1798. Del: to Jacob Noose, 8 February 1802. Recorded: OS 2:215-216.

1 December 1800. Thomas (Sr) and Rachel BERRY to Lewis WOLF. 54 acres on Little Sandy Creek, adjoining 200 acres Wolf purchased of a certain Elishua [?] Boyd. Part of the 200 acres that Berry lives on. Consideration: £25. Signed: Thomas Berry, Rachel Berry. Witnesses: B Whitson, Thomas Phillips, John England. Receipt for consideration money. Proved by witnesses, 8 December 1800. Acknowledged by Rachel Berry before Nathan Hall and Jesse Hanway, JPs, 24 December 1800. No

delivery shown. Recorded: OS 2:216-217.

8 July 1799. William and Elizabeth ROARK to Isaac Hite WILLIAMS, trustee. Deed of trust on 100 acres at Indian Creek, where Roark now lives and where his mill is situate, to secure payment of £295.5.3, balance of a note due to Dailey and Lemonier [?], Merchants, of Romney, Hamshire Co. If not paid by 1 July 1800, the land may be sold by Williams. Signed: William Roark. [Elizabeth does not sign.] Witnesses: Thos Wilson, Henry Dering, Noah Linsley. Proved by witnesses, December 1799/October 1802. Recorded: OS 2:218.

14 April 1800. Henry and Mary TUCKER to Jacob HOLLAND. 210 acres on Glady Creek, the upper end of 400 acres conveyed by Absalom Little to Henry Tucker. Consideration: $300. Signed: Henry [+] Tucker, Mary [+] Tucker. Witnesses: none. Acknowledged in court, April 1800. Del: to grantee, 8 March 1820. Recorded: OS 2:219.

20 November 1800. Asa DUDLEY to Thomas WILSON. 5½ acres on both sides of the [unnamed] run above John Stealey's stillhouse, adjoining Thomas Pindle survey, Thomas Laidley survey, and William Tingle. Patented to Dudley 12 September 1799. Consideration: $27.50. Signed: Asa Dudley. Witnesses: none. Acknowledged in court, December 1800. Del: to Thomas Wilson, 3 August 1803. Recorded: OS 2:220.

9 June 1801. Robert and Catherine WOODS to John LAP. 100 acres on Big Sandy, adjoining Godfrey Wagoner and Martin Juda. Part of a larger tract patented to Martin Juda. Consideration: $400. Signed: Robert Woods, Catherine [X] Woods. Witnesses: none. Acknowledged in court, October 1800. Del: to Alexr Brandon, 19 September 1803. Recorded: OS 2:221.

9 December 1799. David HANWAY, Harford Co, MD, by his attorney in fact, Jesse HANWAY, to Edward GUTRIDGE. 200 acres, no adjoiners or place names mentioned. Consideration: [blank]. Signed: Jesse Hanway. Witnesses: none. Acknowledged in court, December 1799. Del: to Edwd Gutridge, 8 September 1800. Recorded: OS 2:222.

13 April 1801. John and Hannah HAGEMAN to Samuel HAZLET. 200 acres on Little Sandy Creek, near Mill Run, Sang Hill, Pine Run, old bridge on Mill Run. Part of the survey on which Anthony Worley formerly lived, and where Hageman built his mill. Title obtained by a decree in chancery vs the heirs of Ezekiel Worley deceased. Consideration: £350, PA. Signed: Jno Hageman, Hannah Hageman. Witnesses: none. Acknowledged in court, April 1801. Del: to A Brandon, 7 April 1802. Recorded: OS 2:223.

6 September 1800. Aron POWELL to John and Molly FAIRFAX. 170 acres on both sides of Three Fork Creek; no adjoiners named. Consideration: £63.15. Signed: Aaron Powell. Witnesses: Jos Reed, John W Dean, Purnel Fowler. Proved by witnesses, September 1800. No delivery shown. Recorded: OS 2:224.

2 December 1800. Rees and Mary HASTINGS to Stephen McDAID. 10 acres along the road from Hastings' to Capt Chipps', adjoining Col William McCleery's part of Hastings' survey. Part of the tract Hastings lives on. Consideration: £30, VA. Signed: Reese Hastings, Mary [mark] Hastings. Witnesses: Henry Sidwell, Daniel MCarty, Hugh Sidwell. Proved by witnesses, December 1800. Del: to Hugh Sidwell, 7 April 1802. Recorded: OS 2:225.

9 June 1800. William and Phebe POSTLETHWAITE to Moses SNIDER. 23 acres, 15 poles, adjoining Lewis Karns. Consideration: $50. Signed: William Postle, Phebe Postle. Witnesses: none. Acknowledged in court, June 1800. Receipt for consideration money. No delivery shown. Recorded: OS 2:226.

11 April 1800. John FRANSISCO, Abraham FRANSISCO, William and Elizabeth McDONAL, Mary FRANSISCO, Hannah FRANSISCO, Rebeckah FRANSISCO, Absolon FRANSISCO, and Sarah FRANSISCO, heirs of Abraham FRANSISCO, deceased, to Robert GRAYHAM. During his lifetime Abraham sold to Robert 100 acres on Prickets Creek, adjoining William Miller, Elisha Broton, and Jeremiah Gallihue. Land is now conveyed by his heirs. Consideration: $80. Signed: John [+] Francisco, Abraham [+] Francisco, Wm McDonnald, Elizabeth McDonnald, Mary [+] Francisco. Witnesses: Wm Haymond, Nathan Springer, Levi Morgan, Morgan Morgan. Acknowledged by Elizabeth McDonnald, before Wm Haymond and Nathan Springer, JPs, 11 April 1800. A commission is directed to take acknowledgements of Lettice, wife of John Francisco; Molly, wife of Abraham Francisco, and of Mary, Hannah, Rebeccah, and Sarah Francisco, but no report is recorded. Del: to Mrs Buckhannon, 12 February 1808. Recorded: OS 2:227-228.

12 January 1801. David SCOTT to Nancy SCOTT, Fayette Co, PA. Two parcels: 400 acres on the Monongalia River, adjoining John Evans and William McCleery; 145 acres adjoining the other tract, John Evans, and John Ferry. Consideration: natural love and affection to his daughter, plus $1. Signed: David Scott. Witnesses: none. Acknowledged in court, January 1801. Del: to Doctor Daniel Marchand. Recorded: OS 2:229-230.

9 February 1801. Daniel and Sarah SAYRE to George

WILSON son of William WILSON. 196 acres on the west side of White Day Creek, adjoining Jeptha Wilkins. Part of 1000 acres patented to Richard Merifield and Rice Bullick, 11 April 1793, 300 acres of which was conveyed by Merifield to Sayre. Consideration: £98, VA. Signed: Daniel Sayre, Sarah Sayre. Witnesses: none. Acknowledged in court, February 1801. Del: to Arche Wilson, 15 February 1806. Recorded: OS 2:231.

9 October 1798. Philip and Lurany SHETTLESWORTH to Adam MELCHER. 5¼ acres, 8 rods, at the mouth of Toms Run. Part of a 16 May 1787 patent. Consideration: £25. Signed: Philip [X] Shettlesworth, Luranay [X] Shettlesworth. Witnesses: none. Acknowledged in court, 9 October 1798. Receipt for consideration money. Del: to Adam Melcher, 22 April 1803. Recorded: OS 2:232.

24 December 1799. Paul and Charity DEWIT to Thomas MAGEE. 58½ acres, 30 poles, adjoining Benjamin Brain. Part of a 5 October 1786 patent to Brain. Conveyed to Dewit by deed of 21 May 1796. Consideration: £36, VA. Signed: Paul Dewit, Charrety [+] Dewitt. Witnesses: Benjamin Brain, Levi Howel, Susanah Brain. Acknowledged in court, 10 February 1800. No delivery shown. Recorded: OS 2:233.

10 February 1800. James and Sarah HOWEL to William PATTON. 97 acres on a drain of Three Fork, no adjoiners named. Part of 319 acres patented to Henry Barnes and conveyed by him to John Casady. Consideration: $200. Signed: James Howel, Sarah [+] Howel. Witnesses: none. Acknowledged in court, February 1800. Del: to Wm Patton, 5 May 1804. Recorded: OS 2:234.

12 January 1801. Philip PINDELL to John COMBS. 57 acres at the head of Burchfields Run, adjoining Thomas Pindell. Consideration: natural love and affection to his daughter, wife of said Combs. Signed: Philip Pindell. Witnesses: Abraham Cox, David Scott, Jacob Pindell. Proved by witnesses, January 1801. Del: to John Combs, 6 August 1806. Recorded: OS 2:235.

1 November 1797. Elijah CHAPMAN and Thomas and Mary PEACOCK to Patrick LYNCH. Power of attorney to convey to Joseph Trickett 100 acres on Joes Run, adjoining Thomas Griggs, David Sayr Sr, "and Company." Signed: Elijah Chapman, Thomas Peacocke, Mary Peacocke. Proved by oaths of Joseph Trickett and Jedediah Sayre, April 1799. Recorded: OS 2:236.

1 November 1797. Elijah CHAPMAN and Thomas and Mary PEACOCK to Joseph TRICKETT. Power of attorney to convey lands to Patrick Lynch, Ephraim Sayre, John Crothers, and John Davis. Signed: Elijah Chapman, Thomas Peacocke,

Mary Peacocke. Witness: Jedediah Sayr. Acknowledged by Mary Peacock, April 1799. Proved by witness, April 1799. Recorded: OS 2:236.

12 January 1801. Stephen and Hannah MASTERS to Christian NINE. 170 acres on Salt Lick, adjoining Francis Deakins. Part of a 27 August 1797 patent and the tract on which Masters now lives. Consideration: $150. Signed: Stephen Masters, Hannah [mark] Masters. Witnesses: none. Acknowledged in court, January 1801. Del: to Christian Nine, 14 April 1806. Recorded: OS 2:237.

8 February 1800. Simion and Mascy RIGGS to Cyrus RIGGS. 40 acres on the west side of White Day Creek, adjoining Henry Weaver. Part of 400 acres patented to Robison Lucas, 9 July 1787, and conveyed by him to Riggs and wife, 13 October 1794. Consideration: £30. Witnesses: none. Acknowledged in court, February 1801. Del: to Cyrus Riggs, June 1802. Recorded: OS 2:238.

9 October 1798. Joel and Margaret SMITH [also written SMYTH in body of the instrument] to Robert HAMILTON. 43 acres on Robisons Run, adjoining John Thompson. Part of a 20 November 1783 patent. Consideration: £12.18. Signed: Joel Smith, Margaret [+] Smith. Witnesses: none. Acknowledged in court, 9 October 1798. No delivery shown. Recorded: OS 2:239.

12 January 1800. David SCOTT to Felix SCOTT, Harrison Co. 400 acres on Monongalia River, near Meadow Run. No adjoiners named. Patented 20 December 1786. Consideration: Love, good will, and natural affection to his son Felix. Signed: David Scott. Witness: James Laidley. Acknowledged in court, January 1801. Del: to Felix Scott, 31 August 1802. Recorded: OS 2:240.

8 April 1799. Elijah CHAPMAN and Thomas and Mary PEACOCK by Joseph TRICKETT, their attorney in fact, to Patrick LYNCH. 70 acres on Joes Run and White Day Creek, adjoining Joseph Trickett. Part of a 4 July 1794 patent for 400 acres. Consideration: £60. Signed: Joseph Trickett. Witnesses: none. Acknowledged in court, April 1799. No delivery shown. Recorded: OS 2:241.

13 July 1801. Richard and Elenor PRICE to Charles BOYLS, Randolph Co. 133 acres on Indian Creek, no adjoiners named. Part of a 400-acre patent. Consideration: $400. Signed: Richard Price, Elenor Price. Witnesses: none. Acknowledged in court, July 1801. No delivery shown. Recorded: OS 2:242.

20 October 1791. Owen and Lettice DAVIS, now of the District of KY, to John McFARLAND, Fayette Co, PA. 2 tracts on Wests Run, adjoining William John, Thomas

John, Carter's old line, and where Davis formerly lived. Patents of 391 and 124 acres, both 16 September 1784, totaling 515 acres [550 acres also called for in the instrument]. Consideration: £200, VA. Signed: Owen Davis [Lettice does not sign]. Witnesses: David Scott, Henry Dering Junr, Wm McCleery. Proved by witnesses, 14 November 1791. Acknowledged by Lettice Davis in Mason Co, KY, before George Stockton, John Willson, and Arthur Foxe, JPs, 25 September 1792. No delivery shown. Recorded: OS 2:243-244.

2 December 1800. Rees and Mary HASTINGS to Hugh SIDWELL. 78 acres at Wests Run, the moiety of a tract patented to Hastings and Sidwell, adjoining William McCleery, Stephen McDade, Thomas Chipps, and McFarland. Consideration: $600, VA. Signed: Rees Hastings, Mary [mark] Hastings. Witnesses: Daniel McCarty, Stephen McDade, Henry Sidwell. Acknowledged by Mary Hastings, 8 December 1800. Proved by witnesses as to Rees. No delivery shown. Recorded: OS 2:245.

24 January 1799. David BOYDSTONE and George BOYDSTONE, Greene Co, PA, two of the heirs of William BURROWS, late of Sussex Co, DE, to John W DEAN. Bond of indemnity. Dean had their power of attorney, 10 October 1798 and of record in Sussex Co, DE, regarding the estate of William Burrows deceased. William Martin was attorney for Booz and John Burrows, also heirs of William. Dean and Martin have sold claims in the estate to Ezekiel Riggs for £100. It now appearing that there is an alleged prior title to the real estate, the Boydstones agree to indemnify Dean should the sum be recovered against him. Signed: David Boydstone, George Boydstone. Witnesses: William Pride, John [X] Pride. Proved by witnesses, 12 March 1799. Recorded: OS 2:246.

13 January 1800. Charles and Rebeccah ROSE to James CAIN. 141 acres on Quarry Run, west of Pleasant Furnace and near the county road. No adjoiners named. Consideration: £50, VA. Signed: Charles Rose, Rebecah Rose. Witnesses: none. Acknowledged in court, 13 January 1800. Del: to James Cain, 28 February 1803. Recorded: OS 2:247.

13 March 1786. Zachll and Drusilla MORGAN to Thomas LAIDLEY. 1-acre lot [no # shown] in Morgantown. Near High Street, the meeting house lot, lots of Thomas Evans, David Bradford, Henry Banks. Includes quit rent of 6 shillings per annum to Morgan, his heirs and assigns. Consideration: £4.16. Signed: Zackl Morgan, Drusella Morgan. Witnesses: none. Acknowledged in court, March 1786. Del: to William N Jarrett, January 1806.

Recorded: 14 December 1801, OS 2:248. Re recording of burned instrument.

13 March 1786. Zackquill and Drusilla MORGAN to Thomas LAIDLEY. 3-acre lot [no # shown] in Morgantown, near High and Pleasant Streets, Deckers Creek, Kirk Alley. Includes quit rent of 18 shillings or $3 (Spanish) per annum. Consideration: £14. Signed: Zachqueall Morgan, Drusilla Morgan. Witnesses: none. Acknowledged in court, March 1786. Del: to Wm N Jarrett, 8 January 1807. Recorded: OS 2:249, 14 December 1801. Re-recording of burned instrument.

13 March 1786. Zachquill and Drusilla MORGAN to Thomas LAIDLEY. Lot in Morgantown [no # shown], near Front Street, the river, lots of Hugh McNeely and James Reed. Includes quit rent of 3 shillings per annum. Consideration: £2.8. Signed: Zachquill Morgan, Drusilla Morgan. Witnesses: none. Acknowledged in court, March 1786. Del: to Wm N Jarrett, 8 January 1807. Recorded: OS 2:250, 14 December 1801. Re-recording of burned instrument.

10 August 1785. Thomas CHENEY, Esqr, Harrison Co, to Thomas LAIDLEY. 297 acres adjoining Anthony Worley, Zebulon Hogue, Tomlinson, and Rattlesnake Glade. Surveyed 28 April 1781 and part of 400 acres patented 17 September 1783. Consideration: £110. Signed: Thos Cheney. Witnesses: Nichs Blake, Archd Menzies. Acknowledged in court, August 1785. Del: to Wm N Jarrett, 8 January 1807. Recorded: OS 2:251, 14 December 1801. Re-recording of burned instrument.

2 April 1802. Eli and Silvania JOSEPH and John and Bethena SIMPLER to Alexander McCLELAND, Springhill Twp, Fayette Co, PA. 185 acres on Cheat, adjoining Ignatious Butler. Patented to John Rams, 18 January 1792, and conveyed by him to Joseph Joseph, 8 February 1796. 135 acres left to Eli in the will of Joseph Joseph, and 50 acres bequeathed to John Simpler. Consideration: $725. Signed: Eli Joseph, Silvania [+] Joseph, John [+] Simpler, Bethena [+] Simpler. Witnesses: E Evans, Jos Warman, Barth Jenkins, E Horton. Acknowledged by John and Bethena Simpler in court, 13 April 1802; by Silvania Joseph before Enoch Evans and Lemuel John, JPs, 3 April 1802. Eli Joseph proved by witnesses, 13 April 1802. Del: to Alexr McCleland, 31 May 1802. Recorded: OS 2:252-253.

2 April 1802. Joshua and Ellen WALLS to Alexander McCLELAND, Fayette Co, PA. 100 acres on the east side of Cheat River. Conveyed to Walls by John and Elizabeth Leath, 12 February 1798. Consideration: $500. Signed:

Joshua Walls, Ellen [+] Walls. Witnesses: E Evans, Jos Warman, Barth Jenkins, E Horton. Acknowledged by Joshua Walls, in court, 13 April 1802; by Ellen Walls, 3 April 1802, before Enoch Evans and Lemuel John, JPs. Del: to Alexander McCleland, 31 May 1802. Recorded: OS 2:254-255.

13 March 1786. Zackquill and Drusilla MORGAN to Thomas LAIDLEY. Lot in Morgantown [no # shown], near Frunt Street, lots of Booz Burrows, John Peirpoint, Benjamin Laming [?]. Includes quit rent of 3s. Consideration: £2.8. Signed: Zackqll Morgan, Drusilla Morgan. Witnesses: none. No acknowledgement recorded. Del: to Wm N Jarrett, January 1807. Recorded: OS 2:256, 14 December 1801. Re-recording of burned instrument.

13 March 1786. Zackquill and Drusilla MORGAN to Thomas LAIDLEY. 1-acre lot in Morgantown [no # shown], near Front Street, Pleasant Street, David Bradford Esqr's lot. Includes 6s quit rent. Consideration: £4.16. Signed: Zackll Morgan, Drusilla Morgan. Witnesses: none. Acknowledged in court, March 1786. Del: to Wm N Jarrett, 8 January 1807. Recorded: OS 2:257, 14 December 1801. Re-recording of burned instrument.

13 March 1786. Zackquill and Drusilla MORGAN to Thomas LAIDLEY. 3-acre lot in Morgantown [no # shown], near Church lot, High Street, Deckers Creek, Front Street, Long Alley, and lot of Jacob Scott. Includes quit rent of 18 shillings. Consideration: £14.10. Signed: Zackll Morgan, Drusilla Morgan. Witnesses: none. Acknowledged in court, March 1786. Del: to Wm N Jarrett, 8 January 1807. Recorded: OS 2:258. Re-recording of burned instrument.

12 December 1785. Christian WIREMAN to Charles McMEEKIN, both of Bucks Co, PA. 250 acres at Deckers Creek, adjoining Richard Carson and Joseph Rodman. Consideration: £50. Signed: Christian Wireman, "signed in Dutch." Witnesses: none. Acknowledged in court, December 1785. Del: to John G Jackson, 15 May 1804. Recorded: OS 2:259, 13 April 1801. Re-recording of burned instrument.

23 November 1801. James and Nancy GILLESPIE to William HOGG, merchant, Fayette Co, PA. 400 acres, including Haunseckers Glades. No adjoiners mentioned. Land conveyed to Gillespie 25 September 1798 by Willey and Rhoda Hatfield. Consideration: $1221.17. Signed: James Gillespie, Nancy [+] Gillespie. Witnesses: Enoch Jenkins, Barth Jenkins, John Ramsey. Receipt for purchase money. By James in court, 14 December 1801. By Nancy before Enoch Evans and Nicholas Vandervort, JPs,

27 January 1802. Del: to Wm Hogg, 18 April 1802. Recorded: OS 2:260-261.

14 December 1801. Daniel and Sarah SAYRE to Patrick LYNCH. 120 acres adjoining Thomas Griggs, John Sayre, Richard Smith, Henry Weaver. Part of 833 acres patented to Robert Ferrel, 28 June 1796, and sold to Sayre on 17 May 1801 by Hugh McNeely, Commissioner, for money due the Commonwealth from Robert Ferrel, sheriff of Monongalia. Sayre limits warranty to claims of himself and wife. Consideration: $240, VA. Signed: Daniel Sayre, Sarah Sayre. Witnesses: none. Acknowledged in court, 14 December 1801. No delivery shown. Recorded: OS 2:262.

10 August 1801. George and Elizabeth NORTH, Fayette Co, PA, to Joshua OATLEY. 100 acres on Buffalo, adjoining Adam Ice, Anthony Mahon. Patented to John Ice deceased and conveyed by William and Margaret Ice to Aden Bayles, 11 January 1796, and by Bayles to North, 20 October 1797. Consideration: £50. Signed: George [+] North, Elizabeth [+] North. Witnesses: Jno Evans, Hugh McNeely, Tho [+] Doolittle, Moses Doolittle. Acknowledged by Elizabeth North, 10 August 1801, before Wm John and Thos Miller, JPs. Proved by witnesses, as to George North, 14 September 1801. Del: to Wm Bambridge, 6 September 1809. Recorded: OS 2:263-264.

11 June 1798. Asahel and Jane MARTIN, Fleming Co, KY, to David MARTIN, Harrison Co. Acreage not stated, on Buffalo Creek, adjoining James Morgan and formerly the right of David Gray. Consideration: £7.12. Signed: Asahel Martin. [Jane does not sign.] Witnesses: none. Acknowledged by Asahel Martin in Fleming Co, KY, 26 June 1798. Certificate of Joshua Stockton, clerk. No delivery shown. Recorded: OS 2:264-265.

1 April 1802. Moses and Susana DOOLITTLE and Major Dudley and Annarah EVANS to Alexander SUTHERLAND, merchant, Leesburg, Loudoun Co. 151 acres on Booths Creek, about a mile from the Monongalia River, adjoining Thomas Miller, Harry Tucker, William Wilson, James Wilson, and other lands of Evans and Doolittle. Part of a 16 August 1799 patent to Evans and Doolittle for 300 acres. Consideration: $500. Signed: Moses Doolittle, Susana Doolittle, Dudley Evans, Annarah Evans. Witnesses: Wm Tingle, Meshach Sexton, G Hite [all as to Moses Doolittle and Dudley Evans]. Acknowledged by Moses Doolittle, Dudley Evans and Annarah Evans in court, 13 April 1802; by Susanah Doolittle before Samuel Hanway and Benjamin Reeder, JPs, 28 May 1802. No delivery shown. Recorded: OS 2:266-267.

14 December 1801. David and Hannah SAYRE to John

SAYRE. 100 acres on the east side of Tygers Valley River, near the head of Flat Run. No adjoiners named. The southwest end of a 400-acre patent to David Sayres, 13 August 1799. Consideration: £20. Signed: David Sayre, Hannah [+] Sayre. Witnesses: none. Acknowledged in court, 14 December 1801. Del: to John Sayre, 27 March 1803. Recorded: OS 2:268.

25 December 1797. Robert and Sarah HARTNESS, Scott Co, KY, to John WILLETS. 400 acres on Sandy Creek adjoining David Davisson, including John Hartness' 1773 settlement. Consideration: £1000. Signed: Robert [mark] Hartness, Sarah Hartness. Witnesses: none. Acknowledged in Scott Co, KY, December 1797. Certificate of John Hawkins, clerk. Del: to Alexr Brandon, 30 May 1802. Recorded: OS 2:269.

12 October 1801. James and Mary TROY to Isaac MATHEW. 105 acres at Sims Run, a branch of Wests Run, adjoining Francis Tibbs. Part of a tract willed by Simon Troy to James Troy, his son. Consideration: £100. Signed: James Troy, Mary Troy. Witnesses: none. Acknowledged in court, October 1801. No delivery shown. Recorded: OS 2:270.

12 April 1802. Ephraim and Susannah GUARD to James LOWERY, all of Fayette Co, PA. 100 acres on Sandy Creek, adjoining Thomas Cooshman. Consideration: $300. Signed: Ephraim [X] Guard [Susannah does not sign]. Witnesses: none. Acknowledged by Ephraim Guard in court, April 1802. Commission directed to take Susannah's acknowledgement but none recorded here. Del: to Benjn Minton, pr order of James Lowery, 9 December 1802. Recorded: OS 2:271.

9 December 1800. John YOST to Henry YOST. Bill of sale for personal property, including livestock, beds and bedding, household furniture. Consideration: £60. Signed: John [0] Yost. Witnesses: none. Acknowledged in court December 1800. Del: to Henry Yost, 16 September 1805. Recorded: OS 2:272.

13 January 1800. William McCLEERY to Henry HAZLE. 147 acres adjoining Thomas Chaney, Zebulon Hogue, Richard Morris, heirs of Gabriel Greathouse. Patented 29 July 1797. Consideration: £20, VA. Signed: Wm McCleery. Witnesses: none. Acknowledged in court, January 1800. Del: to Russel Potter, July 1804. Recorded: OS 2:272.

14 March 1787. Francis and William DEAKINS, Montgomery Co, MD, to Jost HICKS, Washington Co, MD. 200 acres between the heads of Yohogania and Cheat Rivers. No adjoiners named. Part of a November 1782 survey for 1500 acres. Consideration: £66.13.4, MD. Signed: Francis

Deakins, Will Deakins Jnr. Witnesses: Aeneas Campbell, Laurance ONeal. Acknowledged by Francis and William Deakins, 14 March 1787 in Montgomery Co; by Jane Deakins, 21 March 1787; by Eleanor Deakins, 23 March 1787. Receipt for consideration money. Certificate of Brooke Beall, clerk of Montgomery Co. Del: to "lince" [?], 28 February 1815. Recorded: September 1799, OS 2:273. Re-recording of burned instrument.

14 September 1801. Anthony and Sarah MAHON to James CLELAND. 100 acres on Buffalow Creek, formerly property of John Ice deceased and inherited by William Ice, his heir at law. No adjoiners named. Consideration: £100, VA. Signed: Anthony [0] Mahon, Sarah [X] Mahon. Witnesses: none. Acknowledged in court, September 1801. Del: to James Cleland, 21 November 1806. Recorded: OS 2:274.

February 1802. Acknowledgement by James and Hannah WALKER of deed to Jeremiah KENDALL. [See below for instrument.] Recorded: OS 2:274.

13 April 1801. William and Elizabeth HOGUE to Simeon HURLEY. 30 acres on the head of Mcfarlands Run, part of a larger tract conveyed by John and Susanna Mcfarland to Hogue. No adjoiners named. Consideration: $120. Signed: William Hogue, Elizabeth Hogue. Witnesses: none. Acknowledged in court, April 1801. Del: to Simeon Hurley, 10 December 1805. Recorded: OS 2:275.

9 February 1802. James and Hannah WALKER to Jeremiah KENDALL. 265 acres on Papaw Creek, adjoining Samuel Musgrave and others. Patented 2 January 1799. Consideration: $400. Signed: James Walker, Hannah [X] Walker. Witnesses: none. Acknowledged see above, OS 2:274. Del: to Wm Kendal, 14 May 1803. Recorded: OS 2:275.

7 June 1800. George NEIGH, Washington Co, MD, and John KNOP, Shenandoah Co, executors of Daniel WENDERS, late of Washington Co, MD, to John DUELING, Washington Co, MD. 222 acres on Snowey Glade Creek, adjoining William Ashbey. Sale authorized by the 2 May 1795 will of Daniel Winders, deceased. Consideration: £100, MD. Signed: George Neigh, John Knop. Witnesses: Jacob Schnebly, Adam Ott. Acknowledged by George Neigh, 7 June 1800, in Washington Co, MD; by John Knop, 13 November 1800, in Washington Co, MD. Certificate of J H Williams, clerk of Washington Co. Del: to -- Mowerer, June 1806. Recorded: April 1801, OS 2:276.

6 June 1801. Hugh HOLMES, trustee, borough of Winchester, VA, to Edward McGUIRE Junr, residence not stated. Several tracts conveyed. 1200 acres on Cheat

River, adjoining [blank] Ramsey, John Davis, Daniel Terise [?], purchased by Major John B Armistead from Thomas Evans. One-fourth interest in a furnace on the said land, belonging to Armistead in common with Isaac H Williams, John Davis, and Henry Dering. 20,000 acres in Harrison Co between the Tyger Valley and West Fork Rivers, part of a 5 May 1797 patent to Armistead for 59,329 acres. Armistead had conveyed the property to Holmes in trust, 19 February 1799, to secure a debt to McGuire. Holmes has sold the property to McGuire for $1140, and Armistead subscribes as witness as a testimony of his approbation. Consideration: $1. Signed: Hh Holmes. Witnesses: Jno B Armistead, Josiah Watson Jr, Thomas Ball. Acknowledged 6 June 1801 in Winchester. Certificate of Henry Beatty, mayor. Del: to him, 14 June 1811. Recorded: OS 2:277.

18 February 1799. John B and Ann ARMISTEAD, residence not stated, to Hugh HOLMES, party of the third part, borough of Winchester. Edward McGUIRE Jr, party of the second part. Deed of trust on 1200 acres at Cheat River; one-fourth interest in a furnace on the said land; 20,000 acres in Harrison Co between the Tyger Valley and West Fork Rivers. Consideration: $5000. Signed: Jno B Armistead, Edward Mcguire Junr, Hh Holmes [Ann Armistead does not sign]. Witnesses: Wm Johnston, Thomas [X] Martin, Rebecka Holmes. On 6 October 1797 Armistead and William Johnston, his security, gave three bonds to Edward McGuire Jr, each for £496.1.10, due 6 April 1798, 6 October 1798, and 6 April 1799. McGuire has drawn an order on Armistead in favour of William Taylor, Baltimore MD, for £185.11.9, MD, and in favour of Thomas Cantwell for $550, and assigned the balance of the bond to Alexander Pit Buckhannon, attorney in fact for Andrew Buckhannon. Holmes shall advertise the land for sale at the courthouse in Morgantown and in the *Winchester Repository*. Signed: Jno B Armistead, Edward Mcguire Junr, Hh Holmes. Witnesses: Rebecca Holmes, Wm Johnston, Thomas [X] Martin. Acknowledged 6 June 1801, in Winchester. Certificate of Henry Beatty, mayor. Del: to him, 14 June 1811. Recorded: June 1801, OS 2:278-279.

4 November 1801. George and Mary ZINN to John FAIRFAX. $11\frac{1}{4}$ acres near the Monongalia Glades. No adjoiners named. Consideration: $45. Signed: George Zinn, Mary [+] Zinn. Witnesses: Peyton Byrn, Charles Byrn, John Zinn. Acknowledged in court, December 1801. Receipt for consideration money. No delivery shown. Recorded: OS 2:279.

12 October 1801. Joseph and Mary LANE to William

McCLEERY. 360 acres in two tracts. 200 acres patented to John Judy, 20 September 1785 and conveyed by him to Joseph Lane, 15 November 1791. 160 acres near the PA line and Little Sandy Creek, adjoining Russel Potter, patented to Lane 30 October 1793. The whole tract surveyed and re-patented to Lane 15 June 1801. Consideration: $360. Signed: Joseph Lane, Mary [X] Lane. Witnesses: none. Acknowledged in court, October 1801. Receipt for consideration money. Del: to Wm McCleery, 9 December 1808. Recorded: OS 2:280.

11 7th month ("commonly called July") 1801. William ANDERSON to Richard NUZUM. 120 acres at Burnt Cabin Run, adjoining James Nuzum, Jonathan Roberts, John Petty John. Consideration: $180. Signed: William Anderson. Witnesses: none. Acknowledged in court, July 1801. No delivery shown. Recorded: OS 2:281.

11 April 1801. Robert and Lydia BUTCHER to Robert HENDERSON, Fayette Co, PA. 100 acres at Sand Spring Run, adjoining Whitley Hatfield. Part of a 24 October 1792 patent for 300 acres. Consideration: £40, VA. Signed: Robert [+] Bucher, Lydia [X] Bucher. Witnesses: none. Acknowledged in court, April 1801. Recorded: OS 2:282.

13 April 1801. James and Alethia CLARK to Peter OSBURN. 200 acres at Laurel Run, known as the Sand Spring. No adjoiners named. Consideration: $575. Signed: James Clark, Alethia Clark. Witnesses: none. Acknowledged in court, April 1801. Del: to P Osburn, 7 May 1805. Recorded: OS 2:283.

2 November 1801. John T GOFF to Levi HOPKINS, Randolph Co. 67 acres, 95 poles, adjoining Peter Heckert. Consideration: $200. Signed: John T Goff. Witnesses: George Hite, Elihu Horton, John W Dean. Proved by witnesses, December 1801. Del: to Wild, 9 May 1803. Recorded: OS 2:284.

23 July 1801. Francis DEAKINS, Washington Co, District of Columbia, to Jonas HOGMIRE, Washington Co, MD. Several tracts at Sandy Creek, all originally surveyed for William Deakins Jr. 1000 acres, surveyed 20 October 1785. 1000 acres surveyed 15 October 1784. 594 acres surveyed 14 October 1785. 263 acres out of a 663-acre tract surveyed 12 October 1784. (The remaining 400 acres, on the west side of the tract, has been sold to the grandchildren of a certain Samuel Wulgamot.) These lands taken up by Francis Deakins, William Deakins Jr, and Jonas Hogmire in joint partnership about 1784 and 1785. On 13 April 1792 the three partners agreed to divide the land and the enumerated tracts fell to Hogmire's share. Francis and William made conveyance to

Hogmire 28 May 1792. The deed since being lost or burnt in the clerk's office of Monongalia and not now to be found, Francis reconveys the lands. Consideration: $1. Signed: Francis Deakins. Witnesses: Danl Reintzel, Thomas Corcoran, Nathan Walker. Acknowledged in District of Columbia, county of Washington, 23 July 1801. Certificate of Daniel Reintzel, mayor of George Town. Del: to John Stow, 8 March 1803. Recorded: December 1801, OS 2:285.

14 December 1801. David and Hannah SAYRE to Isaac REED. 22 3/4 acres, 36½ rods at Toms Run, adjoining Sayre's other land. Part of a tract sold by Simmons to William Buckhannon, 2 December 1791, and by Buckhannon to David Sayre, 13 August 1792. Consideration: £7.13, VA. Signed: David Sayre, Hannah [X] Sayre. Witnesses: none. Acknowledged in court, December 1801. Del: to Isaac Reed, 10 June 1804. Recorded: OS 2:286.

10 June 1801. Francis DEAKINS, George Town, Territory of Columbia, to Samuel SNOWDEN, Prince Georges Co, MD. 947 acres on the east side of Cheat, adjoining Daniel Severans. Part of a 4 May 1785 survey and 12 July 1787 patent to William Deakins Jr for 1227 acres. Consideration: $1246. Signed: Francis Deakins. Witness: Daniel Reintzel. Acknowledged by Francis, 10 June 1801, and by Elenor Deakins, 19 June 1801, in George Town, District of Columbia. Del: to Thos Clare, 24 January 1805. Recorded: December 1801, OS 2:287.

10 February 1800. Jonah and Jane VANDERVORT to Nicholas VANDERVORT. 11 acres, no adjoiners or place names mentioned. Consideration: £11, VA. Signed: Jonah Vandervort, Jane [X] Vandervort. Witnesses: none. Acknowledged in court, February 1800. Del: to Nichs Vandervort, 5 November 1802. Recorded: OS 2:288.

14 September 1801. James Smalwood and Susanna WILSON to Hugh MURPHEY. 58 acres, adjoining Bennets old improvement and William Robe. Consideration: £62 [52?], VA. Signed: James S Wilson, Susanna [X] Wilson. Witnesses: none. Acknowledged in court, September 1801. Del: to Hugh Murfey, 10 April 1804. Recorded: OS 2:289.

13 April 1801. Alexander and Margret CLEGG to John LAUNCE. 82 3/4 acres on Dunker Creek, near the PA line, adjoining Launce's other land. Part of the tract Clegg now lives on. Consideration: [blank]. Signed: Alexander Cleg, Margaret [+] Cleg. Witnesses: none. Acknowledged in court, April 1801. Del: to John Launce, 18 October 1805. Recorded: OS 2:290.

13 April 1801. John and Susannah MCFARLAND, Fayette Co, PA, to William HOGUE. 130 acres, no adjoiners or

place names mentioned. Part of a 5 April 1784 patent for 400 acres. Consideration: $460. Signed: John Mcfarland, Susannah Mcfarland. Witnesses: none. Acknowledged in court, April 1801. Del: to Sheilds, 8 May 1809. Recorded: OS 2:291.

14 June 1802. Cornelius and Catherine LYNCH, Union Town, Fayette Co, PA, to Samuel HOUGH, Leesburg, Loudoun Co. 500 acres on Dunker Creek, adjoining Thomas Laidley and William Bowers. Part of an 8 March 1798 patent for 1500 acres. Consideration: $506. Signed: Cornelius Lynch, Catherine Lynch. Witnesses: none. Acknowledged by Cornelius Lynch in court, June 1802; by Catherine Lynch before Jonathan Rowland and John Potter, JPs, in Fayette Co, PA, 17 June 1802. Del: to [blank] McCleland, 6 June 1802 [sic]. Recorded: OS 2:292-293.

14 June 1802. William and Anna WILSON and Thomas and Mary MILLER to George FOUKE, Alleghany Co, MD. 496 acres on Glady Fork of Three Fork Creek, adjoining William Wilson. Patented 5 February 1796. Consideration: £65, PA. Signed: Wm [mark] Wilson, Anna [-] Wilson, Thomas Miller, Mary Miller. Witnesses: James G Laidley, Wm Tingle, Thomas Wilson "as to TM", James Tibbs. Proved by witnesses, June 1802. Del: to George Fouke, 16 June 1802. Recorded: OS 2:294.

26 May 1802. John DAVIS, Morgantown, to George T ROSS, attorney in fact for Jacob KUHN, Corporation of Fredericksburg, VA. Two tracts: 400 acres on Muddy Creek, no adjoiners named; 400 acres in Blackburns Glades, purchased from two of the heirs of Charles Donaldson deceased. Consideration: $1350. Davis binds himself to convey a complete estate of inheritance in fee simple to Kuhn on 1 September next or else to repay the sum above stated. Signed: John Davis. Witnesses: H Dering, George S Dering, Stephen Root. Acknowledged in court, 15 June 1802. No delivery shown. Recorded: OS 2:295.

13 August 1796. David SCOTT to Stephen GAPEN, Green Co, PA. Title bond. Scott will convey to Gapen, before 1 June 1797 and under penalty of £200, 500 acres on Bigg Cove Run, a drain of Tygers Valley River in Randolph Co, VA, adjoining William Haddox and patented to Scott 24 June 1791. Signed: David Scott. Witnesses: James Scott, John Gallagher. Proved by James Scott, February 1802. Del: to S Gapen, 19 July 1802. Recorded: OS 2:296.

5 October 1800. William McCLEERY to Stephen GAPEN, Green Co, PA. Quitclaim deed. McCleery claims land on the west side of Monongalia River under the right of Zackquill Morgan deceased, while Gapen claims the same

land under right of David Scott. In conformity with the award of William John, Henry Dering, John Dent, Dudley Evans, and Lemuel John, arbitrators chosen by McCleery and Gapen, McCleery releases all the land that lies within the bounds of Scott's patent. Signed: Wm McCleery. Witnesses: John Dent, Thos Wilson, Simeon Everly. Proved by witnesses, October 1800. Del: to Stephen Gapen, 19 July 1802. Recorded: OS 2:296.

13 October 1794. Robeson and Mary LUCAS to Simeon RIGGS, Fayette Co, PA. 189½ acres, 11 poles on White Day Creek, adjoining John Bunner, Morgan Morgan Sr, and Henry Weaver, part of a 400 acre settlement right patented 9 July 1787. Consideration: £250, VA. Signed: Robinson Lucas, Mary [0] Lucas. No witnesses. Acknowledged in court, February 1801. Del: to Mrs Riggs, 11 November 1805. Recorded: OS 2:297.

31 March 1801. John and Unise PHILIPS, Fayette Co, PA, to James WILSON, Berkley Co. 200 acres on both sides of Booths Creek, patented to Theophilus Philips 20 November 1784 and conveyed to John by Ann Philips, executrix of Theophilus, 7 August 1790. Consideration: £200, PA. Signed: John Philips, Enise [--] Philips. Witnesses: James Laidley, Alex Hawthorn, Wm McCleery. Acknowledged by John Philips, April 1801, in court. Commission to D Scott and B Reeder to examine Eunice Philips, certificate 31 March 1801. Del: to James Wilson, 2 May 1803. Recorded: OS 2:298.

14 September 1801. Henry and Rebecca DERING and Isaac H and Lucy WILLIAMS to Elisha CLAYTON. 400 acres on Indian Creek, adjoining Henry Amos. Patented by Nathan Thomas and conveyed to John Ferguson by Thomas' attorney in fact, John Evans. Conveyed by Ferguson to Henry Dering and Fleming Jones, with Jones' moiety later conveyed by him to Williams. Consideration: $400. Signed: Henry Dering, Rebecca Dering, IH Williams, Lucy C Williams. No witnesses. Acknowledged in court, September 1801. Del: 15 November 1830. Recorded: OS 2:299.

13 April 1801. Hannah TROY, widow of Simon TROY, James and Mary TROY, William and Elenor BRUMEGEN, Christopher and Margaret TROY, Mary TROY, and Elizabeth TROY, all of Monongalia, and John and Jane TROY, Green Co, PA, to Abraham MILEY. 300 acres on Dunker Creek, adjoining the PA line and William Brumagen, patented 27 January 1787. Consideration: £300. Signed: Elizabeth [mark called for but not shown] Levingston, Christopher Troy, John Troy, Margrett [+] Troy, Mary [+] Troy [interlined "wife of James Troy who have [illegible

word"] Since this bargain"], Hannah [mark] Troy, Elenor [+] Brumegen, Mary [X] Troy, William Brumegen, James Troy, Tobias [mark] Livingstone. Witnesses: none listed, but Adam Brown and Richard Parish are named as proving the acknowledgement of Elizabeth Livingstone. Acknowledged by Elizabeth Livingstone, April 1801; by Mary Troy and Elenor Brumegen, June 1801; and by Margrett Troy, July 1801. Del: to Abm Mailey, 29 October 1802. Recorded: OS 2:300.

28 December 1799. Cornelius and Catherine LYNCH, Union Town, Fayette Co, PA, to James LONG, Brownsville, Fayette Co, PA. Mortgage on 400 acres at Three Forks Creek, surveyed 15 October 1785 and patented 9 March 1798. Lynch is indebted to Long in the sum of £83.4.8, payable 28 June 1800. Consideration: 5 shillings. Signed: Cornelious Lynch, Catherine Lynch, James Long. Witnesses: Jonathan Rowland, John Jenkins [?], William Allen. Receipt for consideration money. Acknowledged in Fayette Co, PA, before John Finley. Certificate of Ephraim Douglass, prothonotary. Del: to James Long, 15 December 1804. Recorded: OS 2:301-302.

8 January 1798. Jesse and Rachael HANWAY to John MELROSE. 34 acres, including a mill seat, on the main branch of Deckers Creek. No adjoiners named. Consideration: £10, VA. Signed: Jesse Hanway, Rachael [mark] Hanway. Witnesses: Elihu Horton, Thomas [+] Doolittle, Henry [+] Criss. Acknowledged in court, April 1798. Delivery not shown. Recorded: OS 2:302.

13 July 1801. Joseph and Elizabeth SOUTHWORTH to Robert WILSON. 150 acres on Little Sandy Creek, conveyed to Southworth by Jesse Hanway. No adjoiners named. Consideration: $100. Signed: Joseph Southworth, Elizabeth [+] Southworth. No witnesses. Acknowledged in court, July 1801. Delivery not shown. Recorded: OS 2:303.

26 July 1794. William and Susannah JENKINS to Christopher CALE. 198 acres on Cheat River, adjoining Thomas Jenkins, Thomas Gibson, John Jenkins. Consideration: £120. Signed: William Jenkins, Susannah Jenkins. Witnesses: John Jenkins, Thomas [mark] Jenkins. Acknowledged in court, October 1794. Re-recording of burned instrument. Del: to John Gibson, 11 November 1811. Recorded: OS 2:304.

14 March 1787. Francis DEAKINS and William DEAKINS, Montgomery Co, MD, to Abraham WOOTRING, Washington Co, MD. 269 acres on head of Yohogania River, surveyed 22 October 1783. No adjoiners named. Consideration: £89.13.4. Signed: Francis Deakins, William Deakins.

Witnesses: Aeneas Campbell, Laurance Oneal. Receipt for consideration money. Acknowledged by Francis and William Deakins, 14 March 1787, before Campbell and Oneal; by Jane Deakins, wife of William, 21 March 1787, before Samll Magruder and Richard Thompson; and by Elenor Deakins, wife of Francis, 23 March 1787 before Campbell and Oneal. Certificate of Brooke Beall, Clerk of Montgomery Co, MD. Re-recording of burned instrument. Recorded: OS 2:305.

12 October 1801. Alexander HAWTHORN to Edward DYER, heir at law of Peter DYER, deceased. On 23 March 1798 Moses and Elizabeth Methena conveyed 100 acres to Hawthorn. In March 1801 a decree of chancery orders Hawthorn to convey the land to Dyer and to warranty so much of it as is included in an 11 August 1785 survey for Edward Dyer of 206 acres. Consideration: $1. Signed: Alexr Hawthorn. No witnesses. Acknowledged in court, October 1801. Del: to Wm Tannihill, 14 April 1806. Recorded: OS 2:306.

25 April 1801. William WEBSTER to James WEBSTER. Bill of sale for goods, chattels, household stuff and implements, furniture, livestock, beds, and beddings, cooking utensils, copper still, "all the families wearing apparel except what they have on them," and other personalty, with one pewter plate delivered in the name of the whole. Consideration: $1. Signed: William Webster. Witnesses: Jonathan Harris, Joseph Severans, Joseph McLain. Acknowledged in court, May 1801. No delivery shown. Recorded: OS 2:307.

25 April 1801. William WEBSTER and James WEBSTER. Articles of agreement. James Webster will convey to William 150 acres, south east corner of the survey on which James lives. Consideration: $450, including $300 in property to be paid at the sealing, and $150 to be paid in three years in bar iron, pot mettle, or whiskey. On this payment James will make a conveyance to William for the land. Signed: James Webster, William Webster. Witnesses: Jonathan Harris, Joseph Severans, Joseph McLain. Acknowledged in court, May 1801. No delivery shown. Recorded: OS 2:308.

28 March 1801. Lucy LANHAM to William LANHAM. 218 acres on the east side of Monongalia River, part of a patent to James Wilson and conveyed by him to Lucy, 18 September 1797. No adjoiners named. Consideration: £100. Signed: Lucy [mark] Lanham. Witnesses: B Reeder, H Reeder, S Hanway. Receipt for consideration money. Proved by witnesses, June 1801. Del: to William Lanham, 22 February 1806. Recorded: OS 2:308.

17 October 1799. Samuel MARTIN, Mason Co, KY, to John SCOTT. 357 acres on a branch of Little Sandy Creek glades, adjoining Thomas Cooshman and David Frazey. Consideration: £456.5, PA. Signed: Samuel Martin. Witnesses: John Willits, Jonath Brandon, Jno Hageman. Proved by witnesses, January 1801. Del: "to him," 17 March 1811. Recorded: OS 2:309.

13 November 1801. John DOWNER to John T GOFF, Sheriff of Monongalia Co. All his remaining interest in 800 acres on Dunker Creek, now in trust to Jacob Pindell for raising consideration money in a deed of trust for the benefit of Thomas Chipps, now deceased, and under an act of Assembly for the relief of Downer on judgments against him by Jonathan Harriss, John Simeson, Thomas Hadden, and Thomas Wilson, assignees of John Duffey. Consideration: none stated. Signed: John Downer. Witnesses: Henry Dering, E Horton, Wm G Payne, John W Dean. Proved by witnesses, December 1801. No delivery shown. Recorded: OS 2:309.

9 December 1800. John and Ann SMITH to Robert FULLERTON. 200 acres adjoining Smith, heirs of Thomas Pindall, and Charles Snodgrass, part of a 400 acre patent. Consideration: £100, VA. Signed: John [+] Smith, Ann [+] Smith. Witnesses: none. Acknowledged in court, January 1801. Recorded: OS 2:310.

3 April 1802. James and Hannah MORGAN to George SNIDER. 20 acres in Dunkard Bottom settlement, adjoining Snider's other land. Part of a 400 acre patent. Consideration: £50. Signed: James Morgan [Hannah does not sign]. Witnesses: none. Acknowledged by James Morgan, April 1802. Del: to George Snider, 8 October 1803. Recorded: OS 2:311.

11 October 1796. James and Linny DONALDSON to William NEIGHBOURS. 36 acres, 35 poles, adjoining John Fouler, part of a 200 acre tract on which Donaldson now lives. Consideration: £23.7, VA. Signed: James Donaldson, Linny Donaldson. Witnesses: Jas Robinson, John Wimp, Jacob Smith. Interlineation acknowledged by Donaldson 23 May 1800, witnesses William N Jarrett, Enoch Jenkins. Acknowledged by James Donaldson, October

1800. No delivery shown. Recorded: OS 2:312.

12 April 1802. Patrick and Elizabeth LYNCH to Walter CAIN. 120 acres, adjoining Thomas Greggs, John Sayre, Richard Smith, Henry Weaver. Part of an 823 acre patent to Robert Ferrel, 28 June 1796, and sold 17 May 1801 at public auction to Sayre, who conveyed it to Lynch 14 December 1801. Consideration: $300. Signed: Patrick [P] Lynch, Elizabeth [&] Lynch. Witnesses: none. No acknowledgement recorded. No delivery shown. Recorded: OS 2:313.

15 February 1802. Alexander and Catherine McINTIRE, Crawford Co, PA, to William WILLEY Jr. 370 acres on Buffaloe Creek, adjoining Charles Martin and Robert Campbell. Patented to James Stafford, 9 February 1787, and conveyed by James and Lucretia Stafford to McIntire, 10 December 1790. Consideration: $800. Signed: Alexr McIntire, Catherine McIntire. Witnesses: William Moore, Edward Work. Receipt for consideration. Acknowledged 15 February 1802, Crawford Co, PA, before David Mead. Certificate of Thomas D Kennedy, prothonotary. Del: to Wm Willey, 9 April 1814. Recorded: OS 2:314-315.

9 April 1800. Jonas HOGMIRE, Washington Co, MD, to George WILES, Randolph Co. $212\frac{1}{4}$ acres near Yohogania River, adjoining John T Goff, Deakins tract, Harsh, and Johnson. Part of a larger patent. Consideration: $424.50. Signed: Jonas Hogmire. Witnesses: George Scott Senr, Willm Fitzhugh. Receipt for consideration. Acknowledged by Jonas and Susannah Hogmire in Washington Co, MD, 9 April 1800. Del: to G Wiles, 18 July 1809. Recorded: OS 2:315-316.

20 March 1802. John and Mary WICKWARE to John GIBBONS, Bedford Co, PA. 200 acres on third left hand fork of the right hand fork of Wickwares Creek. Consideration: $400. Signed: John Wickware, Mary Wickware. Witnesses: none. Acknowledged by John Wickware in court, April 1802. No delivery shown. Recorded: OS 2:317.

13 October 1800. William and Elisabeth TANEHILL to Archabold MOORE. 100 acres, no adjoiners or place names mentioned. Part of a tract patented 27 August 1783 by William Hamilton and bequeathed by his last will and testament to James Scott, who conveyed it to Tanehill 19 October 1795. Consideration: $200, VA. Signed: William Tanehill, Elisabeth [+] Tanehill. Witnesses: none. Acknowledged in court, October 1800. Del: to Wm Tannehill, 14 April 1806. Recorded: OS 2:318.

9 July 1800. John DAVIS to William McCLEERY. Bill of sale for Negro man Glasgow, Negro woman Nancy,

livestock, furniture, housewares. Consideration: $1200. Signed: John Davis. Witnesses: Faquer McCrea, Thomas [T] Evans, James Laidley. Acknowledged in court, July 1800. No delivery shown. Recorded: OS 2:319.

8 December 1800. John and Martha BUNNER to James WEST. 123 acres above the mouth of Parker Run, adjoining Henry Batten. Consideration: £200. Signed: John Bunner, Martha Bunner. Witnesses: none. Acknowledged in court, December 1800. No delivery shown. Recorded: OS 2:320.

9 June 1800. Robert MINNIS to Henry PETERS, late of Monongalia Co. Half lot [# not shown] in Morgantown, adjoining lots of Asa Dudley, Hugh McNeely, Moses Williams. Consideration [blank]. Signed: Robt Minnis. Witnesses: none. Acknowledged in court, June 1800. No delivery shown. Recorded: OS 2:321.

11 March 1800. Robert MINNIS to John DAUGHERTY, Burbon Co, KY, trustee. Deed of trust to secure a bond for £50 in castings, at 9d per lb, given by Minnis, Henry Dering, and William Anderson to Daugherty. 100 acres known as Plums Place, where John Plum now lives, on the state road from Morgantown to the Monongalia glades. Signed: Robt Minnis. Witnesses: Henry Dering, Ezra Horton, Zackl Morgan. Acknowledged in court, June 1800. Del: to E Horton, 15 February 1803. Recorded: OS 2:321.

9 September 1799. Sophia WILE, widow, John WILE, Jacob WILE, David WILE, and David HOOVER, heirs of William WILE deceased, to Henry WILE, all of Washington Co, MD. 238 acres on a ridge between Wolf Creek and Salt Lick Creek. No adjoiners named. Consideration: £133.17.6, MD. Signed: Sophia [mark] Wile, Jacob Wile, David Wile, David Hoover. Witnesses: A Clagget, Wm Lee. Acknowledged 9 September 1799 in Washington Co, MD. Acknowledged 26 February 1799 by Betsy Hoover, wife of David, same place. Certificate of Elie Williams, clerk. Del: to H Bisshop, 11 July 1803. Recorded: June 1800, OS 2:322.

14 July 1800. William ANDERSON to James NUZUM. 79 acres adjoining Constant Pettyjohn, widow of William Pettyjohn deceased, and Jonathan Roberts, conveyed to Anderson by Reuben Squires, 17 November 1796, and given at February 1797 court. Consideration: $108. Signed: William [mark called for but not shown] Anderson. Witnesses: none. Acknowledged in court, July 1800. No delivery shown. Recorded: OS 2:323.

14 April 1800. William and Elizabeth STEWART to Daniel STEWART. 245 acres near the Mason-Dixon Line, adjoining Stewart's home place, Alex Stewart, and the

schoolhouse place. Consideration: good will and affection. Signed: William [+] Stewart, Elizabeth [mark] Stewart. Witnesses: none. Acknowledged in court, April 1806. Del: to Danl Stewart, 2 May 1803. Recorded: OS 2:324.

14 October 1799. William & Phebe POSTLEWEIGHT to Henry BARRACKMAN. 101 acres on Rudolphs Run, adjoining Lewis Karnes. Part of a larger tract (287 acres) patented to Postleweight. Consideration: £101. Signed: William Postle, phebe Postle. Witnesses: none. Acknowledged in court, June 1800. Del: to H Barrackman, 10 December 1804. Recorded: OS 2:325.

19 April 1800. George and Elizabeth MARTIN to Jonathan BRYAN, Green Co, PA. 120 acres adjoining Spencer Martin and [blank] Tetrick, part of a 5 September 1799 patent. Consideration: $250. Signed: George Martin, Elizabeth [E] Martin. Witnesses: Levi Freeland, Clement [+] Davis, Henry [+] Davis. Proved by witnesses, December 1800. No delivery shown. Recorded: OS 2:326.

8 December 1800. Samuel and Rachael GANDY to Jonathan GANDY. 100 acres at Glady Run, adjoining Thomas Magee. Consideration: $100. Signed: Samuel Gandy, Rachael Gandy. Witnesses: none. Acknowledged by Samuel Gandy, December 1800. Del: to Saml Gandy, 20 August 1802. Recorded: OS 2:327.

14 April 1800. Valentine and Mary SOWERHABER to John SPURGIN and Lydia [surname not specified] his daughter [Lydia not named in preamble but mentioned repeatedly in body of the instrument]. 60.3 acres on the west side of Cheat River and south side of Buffelow Run, part of John Green's plantation. Consideration: [blank]. Signed: Valentine Sauerheber, Mary [X] Sauerheber. Witnesses: none. Acknowledged in court, April 1800. Del: to James E Beall, 15 February 1806. Recorded: OS 2:328.

17 June 1800. David and Elizabeth WATKINS, Hampshire Co, to John HAGEMAN. Power of attorney to convey to Benjamin Jefferies 200 acres, known as Rich Hill, adjoining Ezekiel Worley deceased and John Hageman, on the head of East Little Sandy Creek. Signed: David [X] Watkins, Elizabeth [X] Watkins. Witness: Jacob Slagle Thistle. Acknowledged in Allegany Co, MD. Certificate of John Lynn [Sym?], clerk of Allegany Co. No delivery shown. Recorded: October 1800, OS 2:329.

10 October 1800. David and Elizabeth WATKINS, by their attorney in fact, John HAGEMAN, to Benjamin JEFFERIES. 200 acres known as Rich Hill, adjoining Ezekiel Worley. Patented to Watkins 30 September 1797.

Consideration: $300. Signed: John Hageman. Witnesses: none. Acknowledged in court, October 1800. Del: to Alexr Brandon, 12 September 1802. Recorded: OS 2:330.

9 June 1800. Thomas and Catherine EVANS, Morgantown, to George WILSON Jr. 100 acres on a drain of Cheat River, adjoining James Coburn, Henry Banks, Alexander Addison. Part of a 19 April 1783 patent. Consideration: £40. Signed: Thomas [mark] Evans, Catherine [mark] Evans. Witnesses: none. Acknowledged in court, June 1800. No delivery shown. Recorded: OS 2:331.

21 November 1798. John (Sr) and Deborah PETTY JOHN to William BICE Sr. 102 acres on Tyger Valley River, adjoining John Springer, James Hartley, William Vincent. Part of a 21 August 1794 patent for 200 acres. Consideration: $100. Signed: John [+] PettyJohn, Deborah PettyJohn. Witnesses: Nathan Springer, Stephen Morgan [both as to Deborah]. Acknowledged by John PettyJohn, in court, November 1798. No delivery shown. Recorded: September 1800, OS 2:332.

14 April 1800. Levi and Marcy WALLS to John BURROWS, Elizabeth BURROWS, Catherine BURROWS, Ann BURROWS, and William BURROWS, heirs of Elijah BURROWS deceased. 100 acres on Little Laurel Run, adjoining Charles Scott and James Hamilton. Consideration: £45, VA. Signed: Levi Walls, Marcy [+] Walls. Witnesses: none. Receipt for 5 notes due from Elias Walls to the estate of Elijah Burrows, "and doubtful;" bond on William Adkins, assignee of Jonathan Walls, due the Burrows estate and doubtful, and an order on Henry Dering, amounting in total to £45. Acknowledged in court, April 1800. No delivery shown. Recorded: OS 2:333.

14 November 1797. Nathan and Clarisy THOMAS, Washington Co, MD, by John EVANS, their attorney in fact, to John FERGUSON. 400 acres on Indian Creek, adjoining Henry Amos, patented to Thomas. Consideration: $800. Signed: John Evans. Witnesses: none. Acknowledged by John Evans, November 1797. No delivery shown. Recorded: OS 2:334.

25 April 1797. Nathan and Claricy THOMAS to John EVANS Sr. Power of attorney to convey 400 acres on Indian Creek, now in possession of John Ferguson, for £150, MD, already received from Ferguson by Thomas. Signed: Nathan Thomas, Claricy Thomas. Witnesses: J Schnebly, Adam Ott. Acknowledged in Washington Co, MD. Certificate of Elie Williams. Recorded: November 1797, OS 2:335.

14 April 1800. Anthony and Mary CARREL to James

CARREL. 400 acres on Greens Run, a branch of Cheat River, adjoining [blank] Green. Anthony's settlement right, granted 15 May 1784. Consideration: $100. Signed: Anthony [A] Carroll, Mary [mark] Carroll. Witnesses: none. Acknowledged in court, April 1800. Del: to James Carrel, 10 October 1804. Recorded: OS 2:336.

1 November 1798. WILL of Charles MARTIN. Wife Mary: personalty. Negro woman Silvey to be freed after wife's decease [but her "increase" apparently to remain in slavery]. Eldest son Jesse: 400 acres, my river place, where he now lives, including the mouth of Crooked Run. Son George: 307 acres where he lives on Buffelow Creek, plus Negro man Aurthur [entailed to George's heirs]. Son William: Negro boy Litt. Son Spencer: 400 acres on Teaverbaugh, adjoining the tract he lives on. Daughter Elizabeth Randall: Negro girl Sall. Daughter Ann Harrison: Negro girl Peggy. Son Presley: 400 acres where I now live, plus Negro boy Abraham, Negro girl [not named], and the increase of Negro woman Silvey. Grandson Charles Martin, son of Jesse. Executors: wife Mary, son Presley, and Stephen Gapen of Dunker Creek. Signed: Charles Martin. Witnesses: Richard Patton, Simeon Everly, Thomas Patton, Stephen Gapen. No probate data. Recorded: OS 2:337. [Also recorded in Wills, 1:304-305.]

12 July 1800. Thomas and Mary SCOTT, North western Territory, to Ezekiel ASHCRAFT. 35 acres on the north side of Buffelow, part of a larger tract granted to William Ice. Consideration: £60, VA. Signed: Thomas Scott, Mary Scott. Witnesses: none. Acknowledged in court, July 1800. Del: to E Ashcraft, 2 November 1803. Recorded: OS 2:338.

18 February 1800. John WILSON to Jeremiah WILSON. 111¼ acres, 25 rods, on the Monongalia River, conveyed by Robert Ferrel to the said John and Jeremiah Wilson. Consideration: $150. Signed: John Wilson. Witnesses: none. Acknowledged in court, April 1800. Del: to Jeremiah Wilson, 14 April 1806. Recorded: OS 2:339.

16 September 1800. Asa DUDLEY to Benjamin REEDER. 7 acres, adjoining Thomas Pindell and Hill's line. Consideration: $40. Signed: Asa Dudley. Witnesses: none. Acknowledged in court, October 1800. Del: to B G Reeder, 3 November 1902. Recorded: OS 2:339.

9 June 1799. James and Linney DONALDSON to Jacob SMITH. 60 acres, adjoining William Neighbours, Joseph Sovereign. Consideration: one-sixth interest of Smith and wife Hannah in all the lands claimed by the heirs at law of Charles Donaldson deceased, Hannah being one of

the heirs. Signed: James [+] Donaldson, Linney [+] Donaldson. Witnesses: none. Acknowledged in court, June 1800. Del: to Jacob Smith, 29 November 1804. Recorded: OS 2:340.

16 September 1801. Commission to William Hamilton and John Dent to take the acknowledgement of Elizabeth Clayton, wife of Elisha, to a conveyance to John Chancy, and certificate of her acknowledgement. Recorded: OS 2:340-1,2 [slip pasted between pages 340 and 341].

14 October 1799. William and Phebey POSTLEWEIGHT to Lewis KERNS. 75 acres on Rudolph Run, a branch of Dunker Creek, adjoining Henry Barrackman's part of the same tract. Consideration: £75. Signed: William Postle, Phebe Postle. Witnesses: none. Acknowledged in court, June 1800. No delivery shown. Recorded: OS 2:341.

14 April 1800. Anthony and Mary CARROLL to William HALL. 67 acres, no adjoiners or place names mentioned. Part of a 3 September 1783 patent. Consideration: $50. Signed: Anthony [AC] Carroll, Mary [mark] Carroll. Witnesses: none. Acknowledged in court, April 1802. No delivery shown. Recorded: OS 2:342.

7 [9?] September 1800. James HAMILTON to John FLEMING. 150 acres at Laurel Run, adjoining Nathan Lowe [?] and others. Consideration: £100.19.9, VA. Signed: James [JH] Hamilton. Witnesses: none. Acknowledged in court, September 1800. Del: to J Fleming, 29 October 1806. Recorded: OS 2:343.

9 June 1800. James and Linny DONALDSON to Martin ABLE. 143 acres, 6 poles, on Morgans Run, between lands once claimed by Richard Falls and a survey for Samuel Canby, adjoining William Neighbours. Consideration: £120, VA. Signed: James [+] Donaldson, Linney [+] Donaldson. Witnesses: none. Acknowledged in court, June 1800. Del: to Martin Able, 14 January 1805. Recorded: OS 2:344.

26 March 1796. WILL of John RAMSEY. Son John: judgment in court obtained against Charles Donaldson, plus cart, plantation tools and utensils. Also, "should dispute arise due to distruction of the clerk's office," confirms sale to John of tract on Cheat River where John now lives. Daughter Rebecca Gibbony: Negro women Dinah, Flora, Leah, Mima. Grandson John Simpson: mulatto woman Luce and her increase, with exception. Grandson Joseph Simpson: Luce's first child. Luce and her increase never to be sold out of the family. Grandchildren Elizabeth, Rebecca, Andrew, and Ann Ramsey: personalty. Children of daughters Rebecca Gibeny, Mary Simpson, Hanah Haden. Son Andrew: legacy should he return to claim it. Witnesses:

F Warman, Jer Tannehill, Thos Warman. Codicil, 5 April 1796, witnessed by F Warman, Wm Norriss, Enoch Jinkins. Probated August 1796. Recorded: OS 2:345. [Also recorded in Wills, 1:300.]

28 February 1800. WILL of Thomas THOMSON. Wife Sarah: 43 acres where I live, to her and her heirs forever. Signed: Thomas [+] Thomson. Witnesses: Amos Smith, George Smyth, Elizabeth Lazzell. Probated April 1800. Recorded: OS 2:346. [Also recorded in Wills, 1:301, as "Thompson."]

1 November 1799. WILL of Fedellus FOSTER. Wife Catherine: lands for life, plus personalty. Daughter Rebecca Weaver: cash. Daughter Elizabeth Stewart: cash. Daughter Margaret Ortt: cash. Son John: cash. Daughter Catherine Stewart: cash. Grandchildren Catherine Ortt, Fedellus Ortt, Foster Stewart, Fedellus Stewart, Susannah Stewart consort to John Stewart. Lands to be sold after wife's death and proceeds to be divided among children. Executors: Samuel Evans, William Stewart (son-in-law). Signed: Fidellus [X] Foster. Witnesses: Samuel Evans, John Stewart. Probated June 1800. Recorded: OS 2:346. [Also recorded in Wills, 1:301-302.]

20 October 1796. WILL of John MORRIS, Campbell Co, KY, now residing at Georges Creek, PA. Son Joseph: 100 acres. Wife Elenor: cash, personalty. Son Morris: cash (to be paid in KY currency). Daughter Elenor: cash (KY currency). Sons Richard, James, Morris, John: cash from sale of other lands. Executor: son Joseph. Signed: John Morris. Witnesses: Job Bacorn, Saml Woodbridge, Dunham Martin. No probate data. Recorded: OS 2:347. [Also recorded in Wills, 1:302.]

[no date] WILL of Abraham LOWE. Wife Elizabeth: widow's thirds. Son James: Land, he to pay £20, VA, to my daughter Sarah within three years of my son David's becoming twenty-one years of age. Son David: Land, also to pay £20, VA, to Sarah. Executors: wife Elizabeth and Zackquill Morgan. Signed: Abraham [A] Lowe. Witnesses: James West, Zackll Morgan, William Scripps. Probated April 1798. Recorded: OS 2:347. [Also recorded in Wills, 1:303.]

12 August 1800. Woolery CONROD to Anthony WILLIAMS, a Negro man. Manumission from slavery. Signed: Woolery [mark] Conrad. Witnesses: none. Acknowledged in court, August 1800. Recorded: OS 2:348.

14 August 1801. Francis TIBBS Sr and Noah RIDGWAY. Agreement and deed of trust. Francis is appellant and George and Michael Cunningham appellees in a suit, and Noah has entered security for such costs as Francis may

be charged with. If at expiration or determination of the suit Francis should be charged with any costs or condemnations and fail to discharge them, by which failure Noah becomes liable, then Nicholas Vandervort, as trustee, is empowered to sell 100 acres adjoining Vandervort and John Pierpoint's heirs, upon which Francis now lives. Signed: Francis [mark] Tibbs, Noah Ridgway. Witnesses: James G Laidley, Ross Alley, James Pindell. Proved by witnesses, February 1802. Del: to Noah Ridgway, 12 April 1818. Recorded: OS 2:349.

14 February 1798. WILL of Elias SOULLARD. Son Benjamin: 5 shillings. Son Gabriel: all moveables; also, all land during his lifetime, with reversion to grandson Moses Soullard. Executors: son Gabriel, Mr John W McLain, Mr James Spurgin. Signed: Elias Soullard. Witnesses: Wm McLain, Joseph McLain, John W McLain. Proved by witnesses Joseph and John McLain, October 1798. Recorded: OS 2:350.

27 January 1796. WILL of Matthew KELLEY. Wife Jean: all effects and personal estate, for raising the smallest children [none named]. Signed: Matthew Kelley. Witnesses: Robt ACrumby, James Harrow, Charles Magill. Proved by witnesses Harrow and McGill, March 1796. Recorded: OS 2:350.

1 October 1796. James HENTHORN to John HENTHORN, both of Mason Co, KY. Power of attorney to sell tract on Big Sandy Creek, Harrison Co. Signed: James Henthorn. Witnesses: Reynolds Bennet, George Learden. Acknowledged 1 October 1796 in Mason Co, KY, before Robert Rankin, JP. Certificate of T Marshall Junr, county clerk. Recorded: OS 2:350.

17 April 1796. Charles VANHORN to Samuel EVERLY. 70 acres on Monongalia River, adjoining Casper Everly and John Collins. Patented to the said John Downer [sic], 30 August 1791. Consideration: £15, VA. Signed: Charles Vanhorn. Witnesses: Simeon Everly, James Hoard, John [0] Hutson. Proved by witnesses, April 1799. Del: to Saml Everly, 17 May 1804. Recorded: OS 2:351.

6 August 1796. James and Rachel POLLOCK, Hamilton Co, Territory of the US Northwest of the River Ohio, to Abraham FRANKS and Nicholas HELMICK. 108 acres at the PA line, adjoining Thomas Wade. Consideration: £150. Signed: James Pollock, Rachel [+] Pollock. Witnesses: Salla Shaw, Aaron Caldwell. Acknowledged 6 August 1796, Hamilton Co, Territory of the US, before Aaron Caldwell, JP. Certificate of John S Gans, Prothonotary of Hamilton Co. No delivery shown. Recorded: OS 2:352.

9 February 1801. Daniel and Sarah SAYRES to Jeptha

WILKINS. 100 acres on west side of White Day Creek, adjoining Morgan Morgan and Henry Weaver. Part of 1000 acre patent to Richard Merrefield and Rice Bullock, 11 April 1793, 300 acres of which was conveyed by Merrefield to Sayre. Consideration: £50, VA. Signed: Daniel Sayre, Saray Sayre. Witnesses: none. Acknowledged in court, February 1801. No delivery shown. Recorded: OS 2:353.

30 October 1799. Robert and Hannah FERREL to Joseph TRICKETT. 44 3/4 acres, 3 poles on Joes Run, part of a 966 acre patent to Ferrel, assignee of Nathaniel Reeves, 9 February 1797. Adjoining Daniel Sayres' black oak corner at the graveyard, Thomas Griggs, and Trickett's other land. Consideration: £10, VA. Signed: Robert Ferrel, Hannah [+] Ferrel. Witnesses: Daniel Sayre, Thomas Sayre, David Sayre. Proved by witnesses, February 1801. Del: to Jacob Holland Sr, 19 August 1807. Recorded: OS 2:354.

14 December 1801. Daniel and Sarah SAYRE to Archabald WILSON. 36 acres adjoining Robeson Lucas, Henry Weaver, and Richard Smith, part of 823 acres patented to Robert Ferrel, 28 June 1796, and sold by Hugh McNeely, coroner of Monongalia, to Sayre, 17 May 1801, for delinquency of the public revenue. Consideration: $72. Signed: Daniel Sayre, Sary Sayre. Witnesses: none. Acknowledged in court by Daniel Sayre, December 1801. Del: to J Wilkins, 3 July 1805[?]. Recorded: OS 2:355.

19 April 1799. Nathan LOWE, Allegany Co, MD, to Elijah BEALL, Montgomery Co, MD. Moiety of 177 acres patented to Nathan 20 April 1784, adjoining Samuel Tanehill and Jeremiah Tanehill. Consideration: 600 Spanish dollars. Signed: Nathan [+] Lowe. Witness: Murdoch Hanson Briscoe. Acknowledged 19 April 1799 before John Lynn, clerk, Allegany Co, MD. Del: to Jas Beall, 5 January 1804. Recorded: OS 2:356.

13 April 1801. Alexander and Margaret CLEG to Michael BAR. 73 acres on Dunker Creek, part of a larger patent, adjoining John Hott. Consideration: [blank]. Signed: Alexander Clegg, Margaret [+] Clegg. Witnesses: none. Acknowledged in court, April 1801. Del: to Saml Minor, 11 June 1805. Recorded: OS 2:357.

10 February 1800. Charles and Hannah MAGILL to Joseph JENKINS. 39 acres adjoining John Pierpoint, Robert Abbacrumba, Benjamin Jarrett, and Magill's other land. Consideration: $200. Signed: Charles Magill, Hannah Magill. Witnesses: none. Acknowledged in court, February 1800. Del: to Joseph Jenkins, 11 September

1802. Recorded: OS 2:358.

11 February 1799. Joel and Garthwright RIDGWAY to Rachael HANWAY, wife of Jesse HANWAY, and to Martha, Phebe, Sarah, Mary, Dorcas, and Lott RIDGWAY, part of the heirs of Lott RIDGWAY, deceased. Whereas Joel believes it was the intent of Lott Ridgway deceased that all his children should share equally of his estate in lands, and whereas a writing of 13 January 1785, said to have been signed in 1786, has been admitted to record as the last will of said Ridgway, it would appear that Lott bequeathed the land upon which he lived to said Joel, under certain conditions. Joel, wishing to establish equal justice upon his brothers and sisters, hereby conveys them 7/9 of an undivided 400 acre tract on the right bank of Cheat River, the same bequeathed to him in the will, subject to the dower &c mentioned in the will. Consideration: love and friendship, plus $1. Signed: Joel Ridgway, Garthwright Ridgway. Witnesses: none. Acknowledged in court, February 1799. No delivery shown. Recorded: OS 2:359. [Garthwright is the wife of Joel. Other records sometimes call her "Gertrude."]

1 February 1792. William and Isabella McCLEERY to Fleming JONES. 400 acres at the mouth of Robesons Run, a drain of Papaw, on both sides of the creek, patented to McCleery 25 October 1786. No adjoiners named. Consideration: £50, VA. Signed: Wm McCleery, Isabella McCleery. Witnesses: Henry Dering, Thos Pindell, Hugh McNeely, Jona Davis, as to Wm McCleery. Proved by witnesses Dering, McNeely, and Davis, February 1800. Delivered: to Fleming Jones, 12 August 1806. Recorded: OS 2:360.

9 February 1799. Asa DUDLEY, Morgans Town, to Alexander and Robert HENTHORN. House and lot [# not shown] in Morgans Town, near the lots of John Sullavan, James Daugherty, and Hugh McNeely, purchased by Dudley from Jemima Pindell. Consideration: $220. Signed: Asa Dudley. Witnesses: none. Acknowledged in court, February 1799. No delivery shown. Recorded: OS 2:361.

16 June 1800. Isaac and Mary Elizabeth ROBINS, Harrison Co, to Abicl GUSTIN [alternately spelled GUSTON throughout this and similar successive deeds]. 76 acres on Scotts Mill Run adjoining Coverdel Cole, Abel Gustin, Ashbel Gustin, Alpheous Gustin, part of a survey granted to David Gilkey. Consideration: [blank]. Signed: Isaac Robins, Mary Elizabeth [X] Robins. Witnesses: Jno Evans, John Dent, Geo Greenwood. Acknowledged by Mary Elizabeth Robins before John Dent and Geo Greenwood, JPs, 16 June 1800. Proved by witnesses Evans and Dent,

January 1801. Del: to Abel Gustin, 8 April 1805. Recorded: OS 2:362.

10 November 1788. Christopher and Catherine RAVER to Levi LINSLEY, Morris Co, NJ. 400 acres on the middle fork of the three forks of Dunker Creek, patented to Christopher Raver 7 June 1787. No adjoiners named. Consideration: £150, VA. Signed: Christopher [X] Raver, Catherine [M] Raver. Witnesses: F Warman, David Scott, John Evans. No acknowledgement recorded. Del: to Mr Linly, 6 December 1805. Recorded: April 1799, OS 2:363. Re-recording of burned instrument.

16 June 1800. Isaac and Mary Elizabeth ROBINS, Harrison Co, to Alpheus GUSTIN. 89 acres on Scotts Mill Run, adjoining Coverdel Cole, Ashbel Gustin, Abiel Gustin, Abel Gustin, part of a 310 acre patent. Consideration: £[blank]. Signed: Isaac Robins, Mary Elizabeth [X] Robins. Witnesses: J Evans, John Dent, Geo Greenwood. Acknowledged by Mary Elizabeth Robins, 16 June 1800, before John Dent and Geo Greenwood. Proved by witnesses Evans and Dent, January 1801. Del: to Asbel Gustin, 18 March 1805. Recorded:OS 2:364.

16 June 1800. Isaac and Mary Elizabeth ROBINS, no residence stated, to Ashbel GUSTON. 92 acres on Scotts Mill Run, adjoining Coverdel Cole, Alpheus Gustin, Abiel Gustin. Consideration: £[blank]. Signed: Isaac Robins, Mary Elizabeth [X] Robins. Witnesses: J Evans, John Dent, Geo Greenwood. Acknowledged by Mary Elizabeth Robins before John Dent and Geo Greenwood, 16 June 1800. Proved by witnesses Evans and Dent, January 1801. Del: to Ashbel Gustin, 18 March 1805. Recorded: OS 2:365.

16 June 1800. Isaac and Mary Elizabeth ROBINS, Harrison Co, to Abel GUSTON. 53 acres on Scotts Mill Run, adjoining Coverdel Cole, Alpheus Guston. Consideration: £[blank]. Witnesses: J Evans, John Dent, Geo Greenwood. Acknowledged by Mary Elizabeth Robins before John Dent and Geo Greenwood, 16 June 1800. Proved by witnesses Evans and Dent, January 1801. Del: to Abel Gustin, 7 September 1804. Recorded: OS 2:366.

8 April 1799. Thomas PEACOCK and Elijah CHAPMAN by Patrick LYNCH, their attorney in fact, to Joseph TRICKETT. 70 acres on the main branch of Joes Run, part of a certificate right of 400 acres granted to Peacock and Chapman, 4 April 1794. No adjoiners named. Consideration: £47, VA. Signed: no signature. Witnesses: none. Acknowledged in court, April 1799. No delivery shown. Recorded: OS 2:367.

8 October 1798. Baltzer and Nancy KRATZER to Thomas BIRD. 200 acres on Three Forks, part of a 25 October

1786 patent to Jeremiah Simpson, assignee of John Simpson. Jeremiah conveyed to Lewis Levy, who conveyed to John Bishop, who conveyed to Kratzer. No adjoiners named. Consideration: £110, VA. Signed: Samuel Postlethwait, attorney in fact for Baltzer Kratzer. Witnesses: none. Acknowledged in court by Samuel Postlethwait, February 1799. No delivery shown. Recorded: OS 2:368.

9 February 1801. Nicholas and Margrett WEAVER to Daniel JOHNSTON. 44¼ acres, 16 poles on the west side of White Day Creek, part of a 400 acre patent to Henry Weaver, 7 December 1793, and conveyed by Henry to Nicholas. Consideration: £70, VA. Signed: Nichlas Weaver, Margrett Weaver. Witnesses: none. Acknowledged in court, February 1803. Del: to Danl John·son, 10 December 1803. Recorded:OS 2:369.

8 August 1799. John and Mary GRAY, Berkeley Co, to George WATSON. 400 acres on Buffalow Creek, no adjoiners named. Patented [erased] 1784 to David Gray, assignee of John Mahon. David and Elizabeth Gray conveyed to James Stephenson of Berkeley Co, 9 October 1795; James and Ann Stephenson conveyed to John Gray, 26 November 1798. Consideration: £525, PA. Signed: John Gray, Mary Gray. Witnesses: Jacob Downar, Jasper Whestone, Daniel Hartley, Daniel Dimond. Receipt for consideration money. Acknowledged by John Gray, 17 June 1800; by Mary Gray in Berkeley Co, 14 October 1799, before George Cunningham and James Stephenson, JPs. Del: to John Watson, 22 October 1802. Recorded: December 1800, OS 2:370.

10 December 1798. Jonas and Sarah SAMS to Jacob MYERS, Fauquire Co. 300 acres on the head of Gices Run, adjoining William Robeson. Part of a 400 acre patent of 6 March 1795. Consideration: £150, VA. Signed: Jonas Sams, Sarah [mark] Sams. Witnesses: none. Acknowledged in court, December 1798. Del: to him, 3 September 1811. Recorded: OS 2:371.

26 July 1794. Conrad HOGMIRE, Washington Co, MD, to Nicholas MARSTILLER, Montgomery Co, MD. 3 lots in the town of Salem. Consideration: £66, plus $1 annual quit rent to Francis Deakins and 50¢ annual quit rent to Conrad Hogmire. Signed: Conrad Hogmire. Witnesses: Robert Hughes, A Clagett. Receipt for consideration money. Acknowledged before Robert Hughes and A Clagett, JPs. Certificate of Elie Williams, clerk of Washington Co, MD. No delivery shown. Recorded: OS 2:372. Re-recording of burned instrument.

13 October 1800. Godfrey and Leah WAGNER to James GUTHRIE. 100 acres adjoining John Sapp, Joseph Brandon,

and John Horader, part of a 200 acre tract. Consideration: £100. Signed: Godfrey Wagner, Leah Wagner. Witnesses: none. Acknowledged in court by Godfrey Wagner, October 1800. Commission ordered to take Leah's acknowledgement but no action recorded here. No delivery shown. Recorded: OS 2:373.

9 October 1798. Samuel and Magdaleen COBB to John KENNADY. 218 acres on Little Sandy Creek, adjoining Benjamin Whitson and John Dobins, part of a patent to Thomas Berry Jr dated [blank], and by him conveyed to Cobb on [blank]. Consideration: £200, VA. Signed: Samuel Cobb, Magdaleen Cobb. Witnesses: none. Acknowledged in court, October 1798. Del: to John Kennedy, 10 September 1804. Recorded: OS 2:374.

3 April 1799. John and Elizabeth DOBBINS to John KENNEDY. 56 acres on Little Sandy Creek, no adjoiners named. Consideration: $200. Signed: John [+] Dobbins, Elizabeth [0] Dobbins. Witnesses: Enos Moore, Robert Wilson, John England, Leonard Bowman. Proved by witnesses, April 1799. Del: to John Kennedy, 15 October 1804. Recorded: OS 2:375.

8 April 1799. Francis and Catherine WARMAN to Thomas WARMAN. 131 3/4 acres, 88 poles on the east side of Cheat River, adjoining John Ramsey, William Stuart, Henry Croll, and Lewis Rodgers. Consideration: £100. Signed: F Warman [Catherine does not sign]. Acknowledge by Francis Warman, no date. Del: to Thomas Warman, 3 April 1806. Recorded: April 1799, OS 2:375.

10 February 1800. Charles and Hannah MAGILL to John STAFFORD Jr. 400 acres on Buffelow Creek, patented to Magill 28 July 1796. No adjoiners named. Consideration: $120. Signed: Charles Magill, Hannah Magill. Witnesses: none. Acknowledged in court, February 1800. No delivery shown. Recorded: OS 2:376.

9 December 1799. James (Sr) and Mary WEST to James JEFFS. 70 acres, part of a 400 acre patent of 20 October 1786. No adjoiners or geographical features mentioned. Consideration: £100, VA. Signed: James [mark] West, Mary [mark] West. Witnesses: none. Acknowledged in court, December 1799. Del: to John Jeffs, 8 December 1803. Recorded OS 2:377.

28 December 1801. Hugh and Charlotte McCLELLAND, Union Twp, Fayette Co, PA, to Martha McCLELLAND, Joshua and Hannah REED, John and Jane PARR, Peter and Elizabeth STARKY, Alexander and Catherine McCLELLAND, John and Rachael McCLELLAND, Samuel and Elenor McCLELLAND, and Charles McCLELLAND. Grantees are all of Fayette Co, PA, except the Reeds, who are of Shelby Co, KY. John

McClelland, deceased, obtained 384 acres on waters of Dunkers Creek, adjoining Richard Achcraft, through a patent of 25 October 1786 on a certificate in right of settlement. McClelland was killed by Indians, leaving a widow Martha, and children Hugh (eldest son), Hannah, Jane, Elizabeth, Alexander, John, Samuel, and Charles. John also owned a tract at Redstone Creek, Fayette Co, PA, under the right of Richard Crooks, and another tract adjacent. The Crooks tract is in possession of Martha McClelland, the widow, and the adjoining tract held by Hugh McClelland, grantor. The remaining heirs (with the exception of Joshua and Hannah Reed) having made a quitclaim to Hugh regarding the tract upon which he lives, he now releases his claim to the Dunkers Creek tract and the Crooks tract. This release not to take effect until Joshua and Hannah Reed have executed a quitclaim upon the land where Hugh lives. Consideration: none stated. Signed: Hugh McClelland, Charlotte [+] McClelland. Witnesses: David Sutton, John Courtney. Acknowledged 26 December 1801 before Jonathan Roland and Robert Moore, JPs. Certificate of Ephraim Douglass, prothonotary. No delivery shown. Recorded: OS 2:378.

9 December 1799. John and Elizabeth MILLER to James WEST Jr. 184 acres, 30 rods on the east side of Monongalia River, adjoining David Morgan, part of a 400 acre patent of 2 July 1790. Consideration: £300, VA. Signed: John Miller, Elizabeth [mark] Miller. Witnesses: none. Acknowledged in court, December 1799. Del: to John Scott, 18 June 1805, per order from West. Recorded: OS 2:379.

8 April 1799. Thomas PEACOCK and Elijah CHAPMAN, late of Monongalia Co, by Joseph TRICKETT, their attorney in fact, to John HOUGHMAN. 60 acres on Joes Run, near the burnt cabin and adjoining Patrick Lynch and Joseph Trickett. Part of a 400 acre patent of 4 April 1794. Consideration: £60, VA. Signed: no signature. Witnesses: none. Acknowledged in court, April 1799. Del: to John Huffman, 1 July 1807. Recorded: OS 2:380.

11 October 1800. Samuel MERREFIELD to William McCLEERY. 181 acres on Prickets and Whiteday Creeks, adjoining John Spring. Tract patented to Robert Minnes and sold by him to Merrefield. Consideration: £50. Signed: Saml Merrefield. Witnesses: Thos McKinley, James Laidley, Ezekiel Chaney. Proved by witnesses, October 1801. Del: to Wm McClary, October 1805. Recorded: OS 2:381.

10 February 1801. John STUART to Christopher TROY.

Mortgage on 155 acres, adjoining James Troy, part of a larger tract patented to Simon Troy, deceased, and conveyed by Christopher and Margret Troy to Stuart. Troy holds Stuart's note for $435, payable in bar iron and castings to be delivered at the mouth of Georges Creek and at Morgantown. Note dated 4 December 1800 and payable 15 March 1805. Signed: John Stuart. Witnesses: none. Acknowledged in court, February 1801. No delivery shown. Recorded: OS 2:382.

[blank] 1801. Benjaman and Elenor WILSON to Daniel MICHAEL. 100 acres, adjoining John Barker, part of a patent of 12 May 1785. Consideration: [blank]. Signed: Benjaman Wilson, Elenor [+] Wilson. Witnesses: none. Acknowledged in court, December 1801. Del: to him, 14 April 1812. Recorded: OS 2:383.

14 September 1801. James and Dorothy DUNN to Joseph KRATZER. 56 acres on waters of Buffelow [illegible], south end of the tract Dunn now lives on, adjoining John Magee, William Miller, and John Carpenter. Consideration: $200. Signed: James [mark] Dunn, Dorothy Dunn. Witnesses: Nathan Springer, Stephen Morgan. Acknowledged by James Dunn in court, September 1801; by Dorothy Dunn, 6 March 1802, before Nathan Springer and Stephen Morgan, JPs. No delivery shown. Recorded: OS 2:384.

12 January 1801. Philip PINDELL to Levi PINDELL. 150 acres at the head of Burchfields Run, where Jemima Pindell, widow of Edward Pindell, now lives, part of the Philip Pindell Farm. No adjoiners named. Jemima Pindell's right to use of the property while she is unmarried or Levi Pindell under age. Should she die or remarry while Levi is underage, guardians to manage the property until his majority. Consideration: love and affection to his grandson Levi, plus $1. Signed: Philip Pindell. Witnesses: Abraham Cox, David Scott, Jacob Pindell. Acknowledged in court, January 1801. Del: to Levi Pindell, 10 June 1818. Recorded: OS 2:385.

9 February 1801. John and Hannah BEVERLIN to James Edmonston BEALL. 200 acres on Lick Run and Pringles Run, waters of Cheat River, adjoining Thomas Butler. Part of a 400 acre survey for Beverlin, assignee of Nathaniel Kidd. Consideration: £120. Signed: John Beverlin, Hannah Beverlin. Witnesses: none. Acknowledged in court, February 1801. Del: to J E Beall, 15 February 1806. Recorded: OS 2:386.

8 February 1802. Abraham and Mary BROWN, Christopher and Margrett BROWN, and Manus and Elizabeth BROWN, all of Fayette Co, PA, to Adam BROWN. 205 acres

at Dunker Creek, near the PA line, part of a 273 acre tract patented to George Hiley, 31 October 1785. No adjoiners named. Consideration: £100. Signed: Abraham [X] Brown, Mary [+] Brown, Christopher Brown, Margret Brown, Manis Brown, Elizabeth [X] Brown. Witnesses: none. Acknowledged in court, February 1802. Del: to Adam Brown, 8 August 1803. Recorded: OS 2:387.

14 April 1801. Abraham and Mary HILEY, Breckinridge Co, KY, to Adam BROWN. 34 acres, Abraham's full share of 273 acres patented to George Hiley, deceased, at Dunker Creek near the PA line. No adjoiners named. Consideration: £40, PA. Signed: Abm Hiley. Witnesses: none. Acknowledged in court by Abraham. Commission to take Mary's acknowledgement but no action recorded. Del: to Adam Brown, 8 August 1803. Recorded: OS 2:388.

[blank] 1801. John and Margret LIVINGSTON and Uz and Catherine MARSHALL to David PILES. $68\frac{1}{4}$ acres, part of a tract patented to George Hiley at Dunker Creek, adjoining Adam Brown. Consideration: [blank]. Signed: Hezekiah [W] Marshall, Catharine [+] Marshall [the Livingstons do not sign]. Witnesses: Richard Tenant, Adam Brown, John Statelar. Proved by witnesses as to Uz and Catherine Marshall, February 1802, and recorded as to them. Del: to D Piles, 2 October 1805. Recorded: OS 2:388.

8 February 1798. John and Sarah PLUM to Robert MINNIS. 200 acres on both sides of the road from Cobuns Fort to the Monongalia Glades, including the goose pen spring. No adjoiners named. Patented to Plum, 28 September 1797, assignee of Stafford Dixon, assignee of Adam OBryan, assignee of Nathan Allen, assignee of Jacob Noose, assignee of Henry Stafford. Consideration: $500. Signed: John Plum [Sarah does not sign]. Witnesses: Jeptha Curtis, John Melrose, Fredk Reed. Receipt for consideration money by Robert Minnis [sic]. Acknowledged October 1798. No delivery shown. Recorded: OS 2:389.

18 September 1800. Henry BANKS, Henrico Co, William W HENNING, no residence stated, and William B BANKS, no residence stated, by William G PAYNE, their attorney in fact, to Jesse PAYNE, Hanover Co. 4350 acres, agreeable to 31 surveys made for Henry Banks in March 1785. 25 surveys contain 150 acres each and the other 6 are for 100 acres each, all adjoining, on the west side of Cheat River adjoining Samuel Hanway and others. Consideration: $4350. Signed: William G Payne. Witnesses: B Reeder, Robert Ferrel, Jesse Martin, Wm Lanham, John Downer, Farquire MCrea. Proved by witnesses Reeder, Lanham, and MCrea, April 1801. No delivery

shown. Recorded: OS 2:390.

9 February 1801. John and Hannah BEVERLIN to James POST [PORT?]. 100 acres on waters of Cheat, adjoining Thomas Johnston. Part of the tract Beverlin now lives on, and including Post's improvements where he now lives. Consideration: £45, VA. Signed: John Beverlin, Hannah [mark] Beverlin. Witnesses: none. Acknowledged in court, February 1801. Del: to James Port [?], 15 February 1806. Recorded: OS 2:391.

29 June 1801. Martin and Mary HARDEN, Washington Co, KY, to William HAMILTON. 341 acres on the dividing ridge between Raccoon and Sandy Creeks, on both sides of the road to the Tyger Valley River. Patented to Harden 23 July 1788 and including his 1771 settlement. Consideration: $354. Signed: Martin Harden, Mary Harden. Witnesses: none. Acknowledged 29 June 1801 in Washington Co, KY. Certificate of John Reed, clerk, and Benjamin Hardin, presiding justice of quarter sessions. Del: to Wm Hamilton, 5 November 1802. Recorded: April 1802, OS 2:392.

8 December 1788. John and Nancy PEIRPOINT to Thomas BOYD. 166 acres adjoining Lewis Rodgers. Patented to Peirpoint 10 February 1787. Consideration: £60. Signed: John Peirpoint, Nancy [A] Peirpoint. Witnesses: none. Acknowledged in court, December 1788. Del: to Chas McGill, 2 October 1805. Recorded: September 1796, OS 2:393. Re-recording of burned instrument.

7 February 1792. Thomas BOYD, Mason Co, district of KY, to John DAVIS. Power of attorney to convey 166 acres to Charles Magill. Land patented to John Peirpoint and conveyed by him to Boyd. Signed: Thomas Boyd. Witnesses: none. Acknowledged 7 February 1792 before Alexander D Orr and Arthur Fox, JPs. Certificate of T Marshall Jr, CMC. Del: to Chs McGill, 2 October 1805. Recorded: September 1796, OS 2:393. Re-recording of burned instrument.

11 May 1792. Thomas BOYD, late of Monongalia Co, by John DAVIS, his attorney in fact, to Charles MAGILL. 166 acres adjoining Lewis Rodgers; patented in the name of John Peirpoint, 10 February 1787 and sold by him to Boyd, 8 December 1788. Consideration: £150, VA. Signed: John Davis. Witnesses: Wm McCleery, Henry Dering Junr, Thos Wilson. Receipt for consideration money. Del: to Charles McGill, 2 October 1805. Recorded: September 1796, OS 2:394. Re-recording of burned instrument.

18 March 1798. Robert and Catherine BENNET to Samuel NIXON. Two tracts, of 41 acres and 100 acres, on waters of Cobuns Creek, adjoining Joshua Jenkins, John

Magee, Thomas Magee, from a patent to Bennet of 2 December 1791. Consideration: £[obscured by mending tape]. Signed: Robert [B] Bennet, Catherine [mark] Bennet. Witnesses: Wm Tingle, Dudley Evans, Thomas Bennet. Proved by witnesses, October 1798. No delivery shown. Recorded: OS 2:395.

23 September 1800. James and Mary THOMAS to John NIXON. Mortgage on lands (acreage not given) at Sandy Creek, tract that Nixon now lives on. Thomas may pay Nixon £200 before 25 December 1805 and redeem the land. Signed: James [X] Thomas, Mary Thomas. Witnesses: William Myers, WIlliam Thomas, Jacob Miller, Jno Kennedy. No acknowledgement recorded. No delivery shown. Recorded: OS 2:396.

12 August 1794. Evan WATKINS, Washington Co, KY, by his attorney in fact William WATKINS, to Isaac ROBINS. 310 acres at Scotts Mill Run, adjoining Abraham Harding and lands formerly claimed by William Robeson deceased. Originally patented to David Gilkey, 26 January 1787, and sold by him to Watkins in a deed recorded February 1787. Consideration: £50, VA. Signed: William Watkins. Witnesses: Alexander Wade, John Wade, Benjamin Pearse. Receipt for consideration money. Acknowledged by Denuey [?] Watkins, wife of Evan, before Samuel Overton and John Grundy, JPs, Washington Co, KY, 3 January 1797. No delivery shown. Recorded: OS 2:397. Re-recording of burned instrument.

9 February 1802. William and Elizabeth HOGUE to William KENNEDY. 100 acres, adjoining Simeon Hurley. Part of a patent to John Mcfarland, 5 April 1784. Consideration: $600. Signed: William Hogue, Elizabeth ^ Hogue. Witnesses: none. Acknowledged in court, February 1802. Delivered: to grantor's son, 7 April 1818. Recorded: OS 2:398.

22 October 1801. William STIDGER, Alleghane Co, MD, to John STEPHENS. Title bond. Stidger will convey to Stephens 200 acres on Booths Creek, adjoining Thomas Miller, William Tingle, William Robe Jr, David Sayres Jr, Henry Banks, and William Buckhanon. Part of a larger tract conveyed by William and Jenny Tingle, 28 August 1799. The land is to be laid off at Stephens' expense and deed to be made when Stephens pays the balance of the purchase price, for which he has given 8 notes. Indemnity: $1000. Signed: Wm Stidger. Witnesses: J Evans Jr, Robert Hawthorn. Proved by witnesses, December 1801. Del: to Jno Stevens, June 1803. Recorded: OS 2:398.

no date, circa February 1793? Sarah SMITH, Fayette Co, PA, to Thomas and John COURTNEY. Articles of agreement. Sarah will let or lease a tract on Robesons Run, formerly owned by William Augustus Smith, with all its appurtenances, for 10 years, commencing 1 March 1793. The Courtneys are to clear and fence 40 acres of land, and to build a 20-foot square house and a 26-foot square barn, both with cabin roofs and puncheon floors. They are to plant 100 apple trees by 1 March 1798 and to keep them in proper order. The Courtneys to assume all taxes during the lease. Signed: Sarah Smith, John Courtney, Tho [L] Courtney. Witnesses: Amos Smith, Thomas [T] Lazzell, Thos Masterson. 5 December 1796. Assignment of the aforesaid lease to George Frazier. Signed: John Courtney, Thomas [mark] Courtney. Witnesses: Amos Smith, James Frazier. Proved by witnesses, April 1799. Del: to Thos Courtney, 6 August 1806. Recorded: OS 2:399.

  14 October 1799. James LONG, Fayette Co, PA, to Cuthbert WILLIAMS. Title bond. Long has sold Williams 150 acres on the Laurel Fork of Wickwares Creek, adjoining [blank] Coail [?], James Williams, as well as out and in lots in the town of Harmony. Payment schedule detailed, with final payments due in 1812. Williams to pay taxes on the land from March 1800 and to build a 16 by 20 foot house with stone chimney on the in lot within three years, else to forfeit the in lot. Procedure for reversion of land to Long if payments are not made per schedule. Indemnity: $450. Signed: James Long. Witnesses: J Williams, John Downer, Jona Davis. No acknowledgement recorded. No delivery shown. Recorded: OS 2:400.

  28 January 1801. Elisha and Nancy GRIFFETH [Nancy is alternatively Ann, and Griffeth alternatively Griffen through the instrument] to Thomas EVANS. 322 acres on Rubles Run, waters of Cheat River, patented 3 March 1785. No adjoiners named. Consideration: £300, VA. Signed: Elijah [sic] Griffeth, Ann [+] Griffeth. Witnesses: John Bills, John Chisler, John Evans. Acknowledged in court, February 1801. Del: to Thos Evans, 20 November 1807. Recorded: OS 2:401.

  13 September 1801. George and Mary WILSON to James MILLER. 200 acres on the east side of Tyger Valley River, adjoining John Wickware. Part of a 400 acre patent of 12 September 1799. Consideration: $100. Signed: George [>] Wilson [Mary does not sign]. Witnesses: none. Acknowledged in court by George Wilson, September 1801, and recorded as to him. Delivered: to Dudley Evans, Esq, 19 November 1818. Recorded: OS 2:402.

  12 January 1802. Joseph and Elizabeth REED to John

REED Jr. 200 acres adjoining Joseph Reed, Jonah Vandervort, and James Tibbs. Consideration: £100, PA. Signed: Joseph Reed, Elizabeth [X] Reed. Witnesses: none. Acknowledged in court, February 1802. No delivery shown. Recorded: OS 2:403.

    11 October 1798. Robert and Ann HAMILTON to Harry STEPHENS, Amos SMITH, John THOMPSON, John COURTNEY, William VEACH, Robert DAVIS, George BOYDSTON, and their successors, trustees for the Methodist Episcopal Church. Stephens and Boydston are residents of Green Co, PA; all other grantees of Monongalia. 1 acre, adjoining John Thompson, from a tract patented to William Smith 20 November 1783, devised by testament to Joel Smith, part of which was sold to Hamilton by Joel Smith. A church to be built for the use of members of the Methodist Episcopal church. Consideration: [blank]. Signed: Robert Hamilton, Ann [X] Hamilton. Witnesses: none. Acknowledged in court, October 1798. Del: to John Thompson, 13 November 1805. Recorded: OS 2:404-405.

    13 April 1799. Charles and Barbara SNODGRASS to William SNODGRASS Jr. 82 3/4 acres on Pharrows Run, adjoining William Snodgrass Sr, part of a 285 acre patent of 19 October 1789 to Charles Snodgrass. Consideration: $80. Signed: Charles Snodgrass, Barbara Snodgrass. Witnesses: none. Acknowledged in court, April 1801. Del: to David Hayhurst, 28 February 1804. Recorded: OS 2:405.

    7 October 1798. Robert and Ann HAMILTON to John THOMPSON. 1½ acres on Robensons Run, adjoining Thompson's and Hamilton's other lands. Part of a patent to William Smith, 20 November 1783. Consideration: $15. Signed: Robert Hamilton, Ann [X] Hamilton. Witnesses: none. Acknowledged in court, October 1798. Del: to John Thompson, 13 November 1805. Recorded: OS 2:406.

    April 1793 [? date has been written over]. John McGUIRE to William SCRIPPS. Power of attorney to convey to Dr Thomas Bond, of Alexandria, VA, one half of an undivided tract of 770 acres on the head of the right fork of Wickwares Creek, adjoining Richard Mansfield and others. Tract patented to Edward Gallagher, 1792; he conveyed to Dr Thomas Bond, who conveyed to McGuire and John Czigan as tenants in common. Bond is now willing to recant the sale and pay McGuire the sum he paid for his interest in the land. McGuire authorizes his attorney to receive the consideration and execute a release. Signed: John Maguire. Witnesses: Wm McCleery, Reece Wolf. Del: to Wm Scripps, 14 February 1807. Recorded: OS 2:406.

    2 October 1800. Isaac and Ruth MORRIS to Joseph

SUMMERVILLE, all of Harrison Co. 392 acres on Mud Lick Run, a branch of Tyger Valley River, patented to Morris, assignee of Daniel Mcfarland, 24 June 1791. No adjoiners named. Consideration: £100. Signed: Isaac Morris, Ruth Morris. Witnesses: Daniel Davisson, N Davisson, Wm Martin, John McIver. Acknowledged in Harrison Co, October 1801. Certificate of Benj Wilson, CHC. No delivery shown. Recorded: February 1801, OS 2:407.

8 February 1802. James and Mary THOMAS to Jeremiah LEACH. 145 acres on Sandy Creek, adjoining Michael Hilderbrand. 126 acres from a 3000 acre patent to David Hanway, 3 September 1788, part of which was conveyed by Hanway to John Nixon, 13 December 1796, and by Nixon to James Thomas, 23 September 1800; remaining 19 3/4 acres, 34 poles, patented to John Berry and conveyed by John and Elizabeth Berry to James Thomas, 16 June 1800. Consideration: $300. Signed: James [+] Thomas, Mary [+] Thomas. Witnesses: none. Acknowledged in court, February 1802. Del: to Leach, 8 August 1803. Recorded: OS 2:408.

10 February 1801. John DOWNER to Peter HINKINIAS. 79 acres at the PA line, adjoining John Stateler and James Marshall. Part of an 800 acre patent of 1 June 1796. Consideration: $100. Signed: John Downer. Witnesses: Thos Chipps, Thos Chipps Junr, Thos Laidley, J Williams. Receipt for consideration money. Acknowledged in court, July 1801. Del: to sd Hinkins, 3 October 1814. Recorded: OS 2:409.

8 February 1802. Charles and Barbara SNODGRASS to Christopher ERWIN. 181 acres on Snodgrass Run and Pappaw Creek, adjoining Adonijah Little, William Snodgrass, Thomas Wilson. Consideration: £100. Signed: Charles Snodgrass, Barbara Snodgrass. Witnesses: none. Acknowledged in court, February 1802. Del: to Christopher Erwin, 12 March 1804. Recorded: OS 2:409.

13 August 1801. Benjamin N and Elizabeth JARRETT to Caleb BENNETT. Undivided eighth part of 325 acres on the state road from Morgan Town to Winchester, part of a 400 acre tract patented to Joshua Jenkins, deceased, Elizabeth being one of his daughters and co-heirs. Other heirs are Drusey Jenkins, Joseph Jenkins, Mary Jenkins, Thomas Jenkins, Nancey Jenkins, Bartholomew Jenkins, and Elenor Jenkins. Consideration: $100, VA. Signed: Elizabeth [+] Jarrett, Benj N Jarrett. Witnesses: Duncan F McRea, Faquire McRea, Meshach Sexton. Acknowledged in court, February 1802. Del: to Jacob Holland, 12 March 1805. Recorded: OS 2:410.

29 October 1787. Benjamin and Sarah SUTTON to John BOYLE and George BAKER. Lot #83 in Morgans Town.

Consideration: £15. Includes annual quit rent of 5s 6d to Zackll Morgan, his heirs and assigns. Signed: Benj Sutton, Sarah Sutton. Witnesses: none. Acknowledged in court, October 1787. No delivery shown. Recorded: OS 2:411. Re-recording of burned instrument.

21 September 1801. John and Margret GRAYHAM to Rawley MARTIN. 76 acres on waters of Indian Creek, no adjoiners named. Part of a patent to Aaron Henry, 10 July 1787; sold by him to Richard Lemasters, 12 [illegible] 1792, by Richard to Isaac Lemasters, and by Isaac to John Grayham, 13 January 1797. Consideration: $400. Signed: John Grayham, Margret [X] Grayham. Witnesses: John Dent, Wm Hamilton, James Tarney. Acknowledged by Margret Grayham before John Dent and William Hamilton, JPs. Proved by witnesses, October 1801. Del: to Rawley Martin, 1 January 1809. Recorded:OS 2:412.

11 January 1801. David and Rachael FANSHER to James JEFFS. 300 acres on the south side of White Day Creek, which Fansher hath lived on a number of years, no adjoiners named. From a 1 November 1792 survey. Consideration: £300, VA. Signed: David Fanshier, Rachael Fanshier. Witnesses: none. Acknowledged in court, January 1801. Del: to John Jeffs, 8 December 1803. Recorded: OS 2:413.

7 January 1807. Aaron POWELL to Benjamin BRAIN. Tract of 94 3/4 acres, 28 poles on Three Forks Creek, adjoining George Murdock's survey. Consideration: $100. Signed: Aaron Powell. Witnesses: none. Acknowledged in court, January 1802. Del: to grantee, 14 July 1825. Recorded: OS 2:414.

20 July 1802. Moses WILLIAMS to Benjamin REEDER and William G PAYNE, trustees. Deed of trust. Jacob Foulk is indebted to William Lanham for $130: $40 due on or before 1 October next; $50 due on or before 1 April next; and $130 on or before 1 April twelvemonth. For value received, Williams assumes the debt and for security conveys to Foulk 200 acres on Bill Ices Run, a drain of Buffalo Creek, patented to Williams 5 September 1799. If Williams fails to satisfy Lanham, the trustees Reeder and Payne are empowered to advertise and sell the land. Signed: Moses Williams, Ruth [mark] Williams, Jacob Foulk. Witnesses: George Hite, John Hite, Faquer McCrea. Proved by witnesses, September 1802. Del: to Wm G Payne, 2 August 1803. Recorded: OS 2:414.

12 April 1802. Bartholomew and Susannah JENKINS to George BAKER. 76 acres, 15 poles adjoining Enoch Evans, John Ramsey, Enoch Jenkins, and heirs of Francis Warman,

conveyed by Warman to Jenkins, 22 November 1799. Consideration: $940. Signed: Barth Jenkins, Susanah Jenkins. Witnesses: none. Acknowledged in court, April 1802. Del: to George Baker, 22 September 1803. Recorded: OS 2:415.

1 March 1802. Thomas CHENWORTH [variously spelled throughout instrument] Jr, of [blank], by William MARTIN, his attorney in fact, to Thomas LAZZEL. 301 acres on Scotts Mill Run, no adjoiners named. Consideration: $301. Signed: William Martin. Acknowledged in court, April 1802. Del: to grantee, 20 May 1823. Recorded: OS 2:415.

8 March 1802. Philip ROBERTS to William HILLERY. 1?? acres on Finches Run, a branch of Buffalo Creek, adjoining John Haymond, Jesper Wyatt, Benjamin Brown, and John Brown. Part from a 400 acre patent to John Webb, conveyed by him to Roberts, and part from a 150 acre patent to Roberts. Consideration: £4, VA. Signed: Philip Roberts. Witnesses: Moses Williams, John Scott, Asa Dudley, Adam Camp. Proved by witnesses, April 1802. Del: to William Hillira, 6 August 1805. Recorded: OS 2:416.

14 June 1802. Isaac MATHEW to James DUNN. 105 3/4 acres adjoining Francis Tibbs, lands willed by Simon Troy to Christopher Troy, and Jonah Vandervort. Consideration: $405. Signed: Isaac Mathew. Witnesses: none. Acknowledged in court, June 1802. No delivery shown. Recorded: OS 2:417.

26 January 1802. David and Sarah HANWAY, Harford Co, MD, to Ann TAYLOR, Reuben GRIFFETH, Isaac GRIFFETH, Miriam RICHARDSON, Sophia GRIFFETH, Thomas Taylor GRIFFETH, Mary GRIFFETH, Rachel GRIFFETH, and Sarah GRIFFETH, all of Baltimore Co, MD. 412 acres on Sandy Creek, part of a 2000 acre survey granted to Hanway 3 September 1788. No adjoiners named. Consideration: £100. Signed: David Hanway, Sarah Hanway. Witness: Wm Smithson. Acknowledged in Harford Co, MD, 26 January 1802 before Wm Smithson, JP. Certificate of Henry Dorsey, clerk of Harford Co. Del: to Reuben Griffeths, 8 October 1802. Recorded: 14 June 1802, OS 2:418-[unnumbered second leaf].

15 June 1802. Enoch and Ann JONES to John SANDERS. 105 acres called the Long Bottom on Monongalia River near the mouth of Robesons Run. No adjoiners named. Conveyed to Jones by John Savary. Consideration: $700. Signed: Enoch Jones, Ann Jones. Witnesses: none. Acknowledged in court, September 1802. Del: to J Sanders, 3 July 1810. Recorded: OS 2:419.

11 October 1784. Zackquill and Drusella MORGAN to Henry BANKS, Gent, Henrico Co. Lot [# not shown] in Morgan Town. Consideration: £2.10, VA. Includes 3 shillings per annum quit rent to Morgan, his heirs and assigns. Signed: Zackll Morgan, Drusella Morgan. Witnesses: none. No acknowledgement recorded. No delivery shown. Recorded: January 1802, OS 2:420. Re-recording of burned instrument.

13 April 1802. John and Dorcus HAYMOND to Isaac RICE. 109¼ acres on Finches Run, adjoining Thomas Dawson, Jesper Wyatt, Philip Roberts. Consideration: $218. Signed: John Haymond, Dorcus Haymond. Witnesses: none. Acknowledged in court, April 1802. Del: to Isaac Rice, 15 October 1802. Recorded: OS 2:421.

6 September 1800. Thomas and Rebecca BUTLER to Jacob DRAPER. 128 acres on the east side of Cheat River in the forks of Buffalo Run. No adjoiners named. Part of a 400 acre patent [survey?] of 2 May 1781. Consideration: £5. Signed: Thos Butler [Rebecca does not sign]. Witnesses: none. Acknowledged in court. Del: to Isaac Draper, 2 April 1803. Recorded: OS 2:422.

17 May 1801. Hugh McNEELY, coroner, to David SAYRE. By virtue of a writ from the clerk of General Court of the commonwealth, McNeely has made sale of lands belonging to Robert Ferrel, sheriff of Monongalia Co, to settle a $361.96 deficiency in revenues. On May 1801 Sayre, as highest bidder, purchased a tract of 823 acres on waters of White Day, adjoining Ferrel's settlement survey, Thomas Gray, Thomas Peacock, and Robeson Lucas, and patented to Ferrel 28 June 1796. McNeely conveys only Ferrel's right, title and interest, and will not further warrantee the land. Consideration: $61.72½. Signed: Hugh McNeely. Witnesses: none. Receipt for consideration money, 17 May 1801. Acknowledged in court, July 1801. Del: to David Sayre, 20 [blank] 1802. Recorded: OS 2:423.

8 February 1802. William and Sarah BANBRIDGE to John STARN, Hampshire Co. 151 acres at the head of Little Creek and the head of a small branch of White Day Creek, adjoining Robert Bell. Part of a patent to Richard Merrefield. Consideration: $600. Signed: William [X] Banbrige, Sarah [+] Banbrige. Acknowledged in court, February 1802. Del: to Stern, 15 January 1807. Recorded: OS 2:424.

12 April 1802. Ezekiel and Hannah JONES, Bever Co, PA, to David REAMS. 500 acres on Muddy Creek, where John Stiles now lives. Consideration: $833.34. Signed: Joseph Severans, attorney for Ezekiel and Hannah Jones.

Witnesses: none. Acknowledged in court, April 1802. No delivery shown. Recorded: OS 2:425.

11 January 1802. Isaiah and Hannah HOSKINSON to Dudley EVANS. 150 acres on the west side of Monongalia River, adjoining Jordan Hall, David Scott, John Evans, James Thorn, Becket Wilson, and James Thompson. Patented to Hoskinson, 9 November 1791. Consideration: $850. Signed: Isaiah Hoskinson, Hannah Hoskinson. Witnesses: none. Acknowledged in court, April 1802. Del: to grantee, 14 December 1822. Recorded: OS 2:426.

12 April 1802. Dudley and AnnArah EVANS to Moses DOOLITTLE. 150 acres on the Monongalia River, adjoining Doolittle's other lands and William Gray. Patented to Doolittle and Evans as joint tenants, 16 August 1799. Consideration: $?£?100. Signed: Dudley Evans, AnnArah Evans. Witnesses: none. Acknowledged in court, April 1802. Del: to Doolittle, 28 October 1807. Recorded: OS 2:427.

12 April 1802. Samuel and Mary GRUBB to Sarah PLOM, wife of John PLOM, deceased, and the unspecified HEIRS of John PLOM. 200 acres on the head of Three Fork Creek, known as Grubbs Glade. No adjoiners named. Patented [blank]. Consideration: $100. Signed: Samuel [mark] Grubb, Mary [-] Grubb. Witnesses: none. Acknowledged in court, April 1802. Del: to Sarah Plum, 9 September 1805. Recorded: OS 2:427.

12 April 1802. Samuel and Elizabeth MUSGRAVE to David MUSGRAVE. 100 acres on a branch of the righthand fork of Papaw Creek, part of 394 acres patented to Samuel 13 October 1789. No adjoiners named. Consideration: £200, VA. Signed: Samuel Musgrave, Elizabeth [mark] Musgrave. Witnesses: none. Acknowledged in court, April 1802. Del: to David Musgrave, 16 September 1803. Recorded: OS 2:428.

15 June 1802. Waitman and Margret FURBEE to Nathan and Margret JOSEPH. 100 acres from a 400 acre tract conveyed to Furbee 21 January 1800 by Thomas and Polley Wilson. No adjoiners or place names mentioned. Consideration: $1. Signed: Waitman Furbee, Margret [M] Furbee. Witnesses: None. Acknowledged in court, June 1802. Del: to Nathan Joseph, 30 September 180[?]. Recorded: OS 2:429.

14 June 1802. Joseph and Elizabeth BUTLER to Benjamin TREMLEY. 104 acres at Roaring Creek, the eastern part of the survey Butler now lives upon. No adjoiners named. Consideration: $400. Signed: Joseph Butler, Elizabeth Butler. Witnesses: none. Acknowledged in court, June 1802. No delivery shown. Recorded:

OS 2:430.
14 June 1802. Jacob and Margratt FULK to Christopher IRWIN. 11 acres on Pharohs Run, part of an original patent to Charles Snodgrass. No adjoiners named. Consideration: £8.10. Signed: Jacob [X] Fulk, Margret [X] Fulk. Witnesses: none. Acknowledged in court, June 1802. Del: to Christopher Erwin, 4 March 1804. Recorded: OS 2:430.

[blank] June 1802. John and Margaret DENT to their daughter Elizabeth MARTIN, wife of Rawley. 100 acres at Scott's Run, patented to Dent 4 December 1785. No adjoiners named. Consideration: affection. Signed: John Dent, Margaret Dent. Witnesses: none. Acknowledged in court June 1802. Del: to Rawley Martin, 1 June 1809. Recorded: OS 2:431.

8 June 1799. Thomas LAIDLEY to Benjamin REEDER and Jonathan DAVIS, trustees. Deed of trust. Laidley owes $583 1/3 to Isaac H Williams. To secure payment he puts under trusteeship the following tracts: 800 acre survey on Buffalo Creek, assigned to Laidley by John Gray, heir of David Gray, and adjoining a settlement right sold by John Gray to [blank] Watson; a resident right of 400 acres on Buffalo Creek, granted to Owen Davis and assigned by him to Laidley; 825 acres between Toms Run and Joes Run, adjoining Abner Harper's then land, Laidley the assignee of Richard Merrifield, assignee of Robert Bullock, who entered the land 13 February 1782. Laidley obliges himself to have lands patented in the names of Reeder and Davis and to pay the costs thereof. Consideration: $1. Signed: Thos Laidley. Witnesses: Henry H Wilson, H Reeder, Jas Laidley. Proved by witnesses, February 1800. No delivery shown. Recorded: OS 2:432.

15 November 1802. Christiana CLOSTER to James MORRIS. Mortgage on 184 acres on the west side of Muddy Creek, adjoining George Sipolt, conveyed by Henry and Catherine Criss. James now has two notes of Christiana's, one for £50, dated 15 November 1801 and payable 15 November 1805, and another for £80, of the same date and payable 15 November 1808. If she makes the payments, this indenture to be null and void. Signed: Christiana [X] Closter. Witnesses: none. Acknowledged in court, April 1802. Del: to James Morris, 24 January 1807. Recorded: OS 2:433.

25 January 1802. Augustine FRIEND Sr, Gallipolis Twp, Washington Co, Territory of the United States North West of the River Ohio, to Augustine FRIEND Jr, his [?second] son. Power of attorney to deliver to James

Goff a deed for 97 acres on Cheat River, including the mouth of Buffelow Lick. Signed: Augustine [AF] Friend. Witnesses: ?? Leglerg [?], Robert Safford. Acknowledged before Robert Safford, JP. Certificate of Benj Ives Gilman, clerk of quarter sessions, Washington Co, Territory of the United States North West of the River Ohio, 8 February 1802. Recorded: OS 2:434.

13 April 1802. Augustine FRIEND, Washington Co, Territory of the US North West of the River Ohio, by Augustine FRIEND Jr, his attorney in fact, to James GOFF. 55 acres on the west side of Cheat River, including the mouth of Buffalo Run. No adjoiners named. Part of a 97 acre patent to Andrew Miller and conveyed by him to Augustine Friend. Consideration: $50. Signed: Augustine Friend. Witnesses: J Evans Jr, J G Laidley, Wm Tingle. Receipt for consideration money. Acknowledged in court, April 1802. Del: to Frederick Harsh, 8 September 1806. Recorded: OS 2:434.

12 April 1802. Enoch and Amelia EVANS to George BAKER. 6¼ acres adjoining Bartholomew Jenkins, part of the tract Evans now lives on. Consideration: $[illegible]½. Signed: E Evans, Amelia Evans. Witnesses: none. Acknowledged in court, April 1802. Del: to George Baker, 22 September 1803. Recorded: OS 2:445 [sic; pp 435-444 omitted in numbering].

8 March 1802. David SCOTT to Felix SCOTT. Bill of sale for Negro man Bill, Negro man Sam, brown mare, sorrel mare, gray mare and colt, six cows, all my grain and corn, one feather bed, all my [??] ware, household furniture. David to have full use of all property for his lifetime. Consideration: $1. Signed: David Scott. Witness: J G Laidley. Acknowledged in court, April 1802. Del: to Felix Scott, 9 October 1804. Recorded: OS 2:445.

8 March 1802. William (Jr) and Polly WILLEY to Matthew GEORGE. 159 acres on Scotts Mill Run, adjoining William Watkins and Booz Burrows. Part of a 400 acre patent to the aforesaid William Willey Senr [sic]. Consideration: $1200. Signed: William Willey, Polly Willey. Witnesses: Nathan Johnson, Thomas Fleming. Acknowledged in court, April 1802. Del: to Mathew George, 21 August 1807. Recorded: OS 2:446.

12 April 1802. Adley and Margaret RAY to Jacob WEAVER. 41½ acres on Booths Creek, adjoining Theophilus Philips and James Steel. Part of 185½ patent to Adley Ray, 7 April 1793. Consideration: £25, VA. Signed: Adley [A] Ray, Margaret [0] Ray. Witnesses: none. Acknowledged in court, April 1803. Del: to James Scul[?], 5 April 1806. Recorded: OS 2:446.

11 January 1802. James JEFFS to Henry DERING, trustee. Deed of trust to secure payment of numerous notes to David Sayre, variously payable in merchantable iron, casters, and saddles. Dering, as trustee, may sell a tract of 300 acres on the south side of White Day Creek, purchased by Jeffs from David Fancher, if payment not made. Signed: James Jeffs. Witnesses: none. Acknowledged in court, January 1802. David Sayre's full release, dated 11 June 1805 and recorded June 1805, follows the instrument. Del: to David Sayre, 11 June 1805. Recorded: OS 2:447.

9 February 1802. Jacob and Elizabeth NOOSE to James CONN. 54 1/8 acres, nine poles, on east side of Cheat River, adjoining James Stafford and Thomas Warman. Conveyed to Noose by Henry Croll. Consideration: $150. Signed: Jacob Noose, Elizabeth [mark] Noose. Witnesses: Thomas Warman, Henry Hamilton, Thomas Bennet. Acknowledged by Elizabeth Noose before Enoch Evans and Nicholas Vandervort, JPs, 13 September 1802. Proved by witnesses February 1802. Del: to Thos Warman, 20 August 1806. Recorded: OS 2:448.

12 April 1802. Dudley and AnnArah EVANS to Nathan HALL. Tract on Swamp Run, acreage not stated, adjoining Josiah Wilson, heirs of Theophilus Philips, and Thomas Thomas. Patented to Evans, 15 ?? 1801. Consideration: $125. Signed: Dudley Evans, Ann Arah Evans. Acknowledged in court, April 1802. Del: to N Hall, 9 April 1810. Recorded: OS 2:450 [p 449 omitted in numbering].

8 March 1802. Zepheniah and Elizabeth MARTIN, Washington Co, PA, to Eleazer BIGGS. 100 acres on Maracles Run, a branch of Dunker Creek, adjoining Jonathan Davis, Jeremiah Biggs, and Phinehas Killem. Part of a 1200 acre patent of 27 March 1789. Consideration: $100. Signed: Zepheniah Martin, Elizabeth Martin. Witnesses: Daniel Mcfarland, James Martin. Acknowledged in court, June 1802. No delivery shown. Recorded: OS 2:451.

8 March 1802. Zepheniah and Elizabeth MARTIN, Washington Co, PA, to Jonathan DAVIS. 100 acres on Maracles Run, a branch of Dunker Creek, adjoining Eleazer Biggs, Andrew Caston, Phinehas Killem. Part of a 1200 acre patent of 27 March 1789. Consideration: $100. Signed: Zepheniah Martin, Elizabeth Martin. Witnesses: Daniel Mcfarland, James Martin. Acknowledged in court, June 1802. Del: to Wm Jobs [illegible] 1805. Recorded: OS 2:451.

8 March 1802. Zepheniah and Elizabeth MARTIN, Washington Co, PA, to Jeremiah BIGGS. 100 acres on

Maracles Run, a branch of Dunker Creek, adjoining Eleazer Biggs, Phinehas Killem, and Andrew Casto. Part of a 1200 acre patent of 27 March 1789. Consideration: $100. Signed: Zepheniah Martin, Elizabeth Martin. Witnesses: Daniel Mcfarland, James Martin. Acknowledged in court, June 1802. Del: to John Launtz, ? April 1814. Recorded: OS 2:452.

    8 March 1802. Zepheniah and Elizabeth MARTIN, Washington Co, PA, to Andrew CASTO. 100 acres on Maracles Run, a branch of Dunker Creek, adjoining Noah Biggs, Phinehas Killem, Jonathan Davis, and Jeremiah Biggs. Part of a 1200 acre patent of 27 March 1789. Consideration: $100. Signed: Zepheniah Martin, Elizabeth Martin. Witnesses: Daniel Mcfarland, James Martin. Acknowledged in court, June 1802. Del: to Wm Jobs, 12 August 1806. Recorded: OS 2:452.

    8 March 1802. Zepheniah and Elizabeth MARTIN, Washington Co, PA, to Noah BIGGS. 100 acres on Maracles Run, a branch of Dunker Creek, adjoining Phinehas Killem and Andrew Casto. Part of a 1200 acre patent of 27 March 1789. Consideration: $100. Signed: Zepheniah Martin, Elizabeth Martin. Witnesses: Daniel Mcfarland, James Martin. Acknowledged in court, June 1802. Del: to Wm Jobs, 12 August 1806. Recorded: OS 2:453.

    27 March 1802. Ruth BUSSEY to Jesse BUSSEY. Half of 308 acres, with reference to a deed from Franks and Helmech. No place names or adjoiners mentioned. Consideration: none stated. Signed: Ruth Bussey. Witnesses: S Billingsley, Hezekiah Wade, Alexander Wade. Proved by witnesses, April 1802. Del: to Jesse Bussey, 7 March 1804. Recorded: OS 2:453.

    26 [blank] 1802. David and Sarah HANWAY, Harford Co, MD, to Jesse HANWAY. 84 acres on Sandy Creek, adjoining John Hardin Jr's survey and Michael Hilderbrand. Part of a 2000 acre survey granted to David, 3 September 1788. Consideration: £10. Signed: David Hanway, Sarah Hanway. Witness: Wm Smithson. Acknowledged before Wm Smithson, JP. Certificate of Henry Dorsey, Clerk of Harford Co, MD. Del: to John Hanway, 18 January 1835. Recorded: June 1802, OS 2:454.

    12 April 1802. Henry and Catherine CRISS to Christiana CLOSTER and Jacob CLOSTER. 185 acres, part from a conveyance by George and Mary Sipolt to Henry Criss, and the rest from a tract adjoining Henry's former survey. Consideration: £180. Signed: Henry Criss ["in dutch"], Catherine [X] Criss. Witnesses: Wm G Payne, John W Dean, John T Goff. Acknowledged in court, April 1802. Del: to Joseph Forman, 12 February 1805.

Recorded: OS 2:455.

2 June 1801. Ezekiel and Hannah JONES, Bever Co, PA, to Edward JONES. 133 acres on the west side of Muddy Creek, part of a 400 acre survey. No adjoiners named. Consideration: $100. Signed: Ezekiel Jones, Hannah Jones. Witnesses: Oliver Jones, Daniel Jones. Acknowledged before William Conner, JP, in Allegania Co, PA, 2 June 1801. Certificate of Tarleton Bates, prothonotary of Allegania Co, PA, 6 June 1801. No delivery shown. Recorded: April 1802, OS 2:456.

18 February 1802. Richard and Rachael STILES to David REAM, Summerset Co, PA. 100 acres on Muddy Creek, adjoining Ezekiel Jones and Jacob Minthorn. Consideration: $100. Signed: Richard Stiles, Rachael [X] Stiles. Witnesses: Edward Jones, John McLain, Tobias Ream. Acknowledged by Rachael Stiles before Edward Jones and John McLain, JPs, 18 February 1802. Proved by witnesses, April 1802. No delivery shown. Recorded: OS 2:457.

13 September 1801. Dudley and Ann Arah EVANS to Thomas LEWELLEN. 100 acres on Three Fork Creek and Swamp Run, adjoining Jabish Bell and James Thomas. Part of a 1700 acre patent of 23 August 1797. Consideration: $150. Signed: Dudley Evans, Ann Arah Evans. Witnesses: none. Acknowledged in court, April 1802. Del: to John Jones, 14 April 1806. Recorded: OS 2:458.

6 April 1802. John and Mary WICKWARE to Nathan HALL. 4 acres at Flat Run, adjoining Josiah Wilson. Part of a 200 acre patent to John Wickware, 5 September 1799. Consideration: $8. Signed: John Wickware, Mary Wickware. Witnesses: none. Acknowledged in court, April 1802. Del: to N Hall, 9 April 1810. Recorded: OS 2:459.

8 February 1802. Ezekiel and Hannah JONES, Allegheny Co, PA, to Major Joseph SEVERANS. Power of attorney to convey to David Ream a tract of 500 acres on Muddy Creek, now occupied and possessed by John Stiles. $833.34 payment due on the land. Signed: Ezekiel Jones, Hannah Jones. Witness: H Hohlet [? name appears to be in German script]. Acknowledged before Sampson Porsal [?] and William Conner, JPs, Alleghenia Co, PA. Certificate of Tarlton Bates, prothonotary of Alleghenia Co. No delivery shown. Recorded: April 1802, OS 2:459.

1 September 1802. George (Sr) and Ann WADE to George WADE Jr. 70 acres on Boidstones Run, a drain of Dunkard Creek, near the PA line. Part of a 21 November 1781 survey. No adjoiners named. Consideration: $100. Signed: George Wade, Ann [+] Wade. Witnesses: William Billingsley, Hezekiah Wade, Wenman Wade. Proved by

witnesses, October 1802. Del: to G Wade, 25 November 1802. Recorded: OS 2:460.

12 April 1802. Samuel and Elizabeth MUSGRAVE to Abraham HUFFMAN Jr. 100 acres on the righthand fork of Papaw Creek, the upper end of a tract patented to Samuel Musgrave 30 October 1789. No adjoiners named. Consideration: £100, VA. Signed: Samuel Musgrave, Elizabeth [X] Musgrave. Witnesses: none. Acknowledged in court, April 1802. Del: to Huffman, May 1806. Recorded: OS 2:461.

12 April 1802. Patrick and Elizabeth LYNCH to Daniel JOHNSTON. 77½ acres on the head of a branch of Joes Run, adjoining John Huffman and John Corothers. Part from a tract deeded to Lynch by Robert Ferrel, part from a tract deeded to Lynch by Thomas Griggs, and part from a tract deeded to Lynch by Joseph Trickett, attorney for Thomas Peacock and Elijah Chapman. Consideration: £50. Signed: Patrick [\] Lynch, Elizabeth [mark] Lynch. Witnesses: none. Acknowledged in court, April 1802. Del: to Danl Johnston, 10 December 1803. Recorded: OS 2:462.

9 February 1802. George GREENWOOD to James RANDALL, trustee. Deed of trust. 200 acres, where Greenwood now lives, adjoining George Smith, Amos Smith, and John Ramsey. The parcel was once sold by Thomas Lazzel to Simon Cochran, by Cochran to James Randall, and by Randall to Greenwood. With the land came an obligation to pay George Okell $152.25. Greenwood acknowledges that the payment is due 9 February 1803 and empowers Randall to sell the land to discharge the debt. Consideration: $1. Signed: George Greenwood. Witnesses: James Randall, Jesse Bussey, Alexander Wade. Acknowledged in court, April 1802. No delivery shown. Recorded: OS 2:463.

30 March 1802. James and Mary METHENY to Edward JONES. Mortgage. Jones possesses five notes of Metheny for $100 each, payable in cash, salt, bar iron, and castings, and due at yearly intervals. As security for the notes Metheny conveys 180 acres at Muddy Creek, consisting of two tracks. Jones lives on one tract and has possession of the other. Signed: James Metheny, Mary [mark] Metheny. Witnesses: John McLain, Russel Potter, William Johnston. Acknowledged by Mary Metheny before John McLain and Russel Potter, JPs, 30 March 1802; by James Metheny in court, October 1802. Del: to Saml Baker, executor of Edward Jones, 15 November 1807 [1817?]. Recorded: OS 2:464-465.

14 May 1802. William and Elizabeth ASHFORD to John MINTON, Fayette Co, PA. 277 acres on a drain of Cheat

River, adjoining James Conner and John Floyd. Patented to Peter Clutter, 6 June 1796. Consideration: $600. Signed: William Ashford, Elizabeth [+] Ashford. Witnesses: none. Acknowledged in court, June 1802. Del: to Benj Minton pr father's order, 9 December 1802. Recorded: OS 2:466.

1 December 1802. William and Jane TINGLE to Conrad SHAFFER Sr, William SHAFFER, and Conrad SHAFFER Jr, grantees all of Loudoun Co. 820 acres on White Day Creek, adjoining William Robe, Thomas Laidley, and William Tingle. From a patent to William Tingle and Thomas Miller, with Miller's part of the tract conveyed to Tingle by quitclaim deed. Consideration: $1640. Signed: Wm Tingle, Jane Tingle. Witnesses: Henry Dering, Robert C Scott, Mtt Hite, Alexr Hawthorn, Hugh McNeely. Acknowledged in court, 13 December 1802. Del: to Alexr McCleland, 15 December 1802. Recorded: OS 2:467.

1 November 1802. Dudley and Annarah EVANS to Henry WOLF, Loudoun Co. 800 acres on Three Fork Creek, adjoining lands of Dudley Evans, John Evans, James Cunant [?], Robert [??], [??] Bell, Thomas Lewellen, William Dragoo, and George Swank. Excepted is 100 acres already sold to John Jones. Consideration: $1400. Signed: Dudley Evans, Annarah Evans. Witnesses: Henry Dering, E Daugherty, Alexr Hawthorn, Mtt Hite, Hugh McNeely. Acknowledged in court, 13 December 1802. Del: to A McCleland, 15 December 1802. Recorded: OS 2:468.

1 November 1802. Dudley and Annarah EVANS to George SWANK, Loudoun Co. 200 acres on Three Fork Creek, adjoining William Dragoo and John Bradley. Part of a 23 August 1797 patent for 1700 acres. Consideration: $400. Signed: Dudley Evans, Annarah Evans. Witnesses: Henry Dering, Mtt Hite, E Daugherty, Alexr Hawthorn, Hugh McNeely. Acknowledged in court, 13 December 1802. Del: to A McCleland, 15 December 1802. Recorded: OS 2:469.

12 April 1802. Patrick KARN to Barney KERNS [surnames spelled variously through this and succeeding deeds]. 86 acres on Booths Creek, near Laurel Run; no adjoiners named. Part of a 2 April 1784 patent to Henry Tucker for 244 acres and conveyed by Tucker to Karn, 8 April 1799. Consideration: $133. Signed: Patrick [+] Kerns. Witnesses: none. Acknowledged in court, April 1802. No delivery shown. Recorded: OS 2:470.

12 April 1802. Patrick and Sary KERNES to Edward KERNS. 68 acres on Booths Creek, adjoining Thomas Miller. Part of a 2 April 1784 patent to Henry Tucker for 244 acres. Consideration: $133. Signed: Patrick Keran, Sarah Keran. Witnesses: none. Acknowledged by

Patrick and Sary [also Mary in acknowledgement], April 1802. Del: to John Kern, 28 December 1804. Recorded: OS 2:471.

12 April 1802. Patrick KERAN to John KERAN. 90 acres on Booths Creek, adjoining Thomas Miller. Part of a 2 April 1784 patent to Henry Tucker for 244 acres. Consideration: $133. Signed: Patrick Keran. Witnesses: none. Acknowledged in court, April 1802. Del: to John Kern, 28 December 1804. Recorded: OS 2:472.

24 March 1802. Hedgman TRIPLETT to Daniel SAYRE, trustee. Deed of trust. 1000 acres on Little Kenhaway River at the mouth of Nowls Creek; 2 tracts (1000 acres and 500 acres) at the head of Salt Lick Creek, a branch of Little Kenhaway; and 170 acres near Clarksburg, where Triplett now lives. Land to be sold 2 years from date if necessary to discharge a note from Hedgman Triplett, Benjamin Reeder, and Samuel Hanway to David Cooshman for £400, dated [blank], with interest from 1 November 1797. Signed: Hedgman Triplett. Witnesses: Wm G Payne, Thos McKinley, Jacob Pindell. Proved by witnesses, April 1802. Del: to Daniel Sayre, 10 March 1804. Recorded: OS 2:473.

14 April 1802. Sarah PLUM, widow of John PLUM deceased, to Samuel GRUBB. Quitclaim and release of dower on 70 acres near the Clarksburg road, part of a larger tract patented to John Plum 10 October 1786, and which Plum had sold during his lifetime to Samuel Grubb. Consideration: $2. Signed: Sarah [+] Plum. Witnesses: Robert Ferrel, John T Goff, Meshach Sexton. Acknowledged in court, April 1802. No delivery shown. Recorded: OS 2:474.

12 July 1802. Samuel HANWAY to James TATE. One equal third of 48 acres on Deckers Creek, adjoining Jacob Youngman. Consideration: $1666.67. Signed: Saml Hanway. Witnesses: none. Acknowledged in court, July 1802. Del: to James Tate, 10 February 1806. Recorded: OS 2:474.

12 July 1802. Samuel HANWAY to James TATE. One equal third of 496 acres at Deckers Creek, adjoining Joseph Wilson, John Reed, Beall, William McCleery, Goosman, and McIntire. Consideration: $1666.67. Signed: Saml Hanway. Witnesses: none. Acknowledged in court, July 1802. Del: to James Tate, 10 February 1806. Recorded: OS 2:475.

12 July 1802. Samuel HANWAY to John STEALEY. One equal third of 48 acres on Deckers Creek, adjoining Jacob Youngman. Consideration: $1666.67. Signed: Saml Hanway. Witnesses: none. Acknowledged in court, July

1802. Del: to John Stealey, 9 [??] 1804. Recorded: OS 2:476.

12 July 1802. Samuel HANWAY to John STEALEY. One equal third of 496 acres at Deckers Creek, adjoining Joseph Wilson, John Reed, et al. Consideration: $1666.67. Signed: Saml Hanway. Witnesses: none. Acknowledged in court, July 1802. Del: to John Stealey, 9 June 1804. Recorded: OS 2:476.

14 April 1792. James and Saborah COBUN, John and Sarah CONNOR, and Peter and Susannah HARNESS (latter couple of Hardy Co) to John BRUMAGE. 200 acres in Monongalia, no adjoiners or place names mentioned. Consideration: £100, VA. Signed: James Cobun, Saberah Cobun, John Conner, Sarah Conner, James Cobun attorney in fact for Peter Harness, Susannah Harness. Witnesses: none. Acknowledged in court, date not stated. No delivery shown. Recorded: October 1802, OS 2:477. Re-recording of burned instrument.

6 February 1802. William and Hester MARTIN to James BOOTH, all of Harrison Co. 312 acres on a lefthand drain that empties into Buffelow Creek, tract surveyed 29 July 1785. No adjoiners named. Consideration: $400. Signed: William [X] Martin [Hester does not sign]. Witnesses: Joseph Tucker, John Rogers, Jesse [X] Nixon. Proved by witnesses, September 1802. Del: to Zackll Morgan Jr, 22 March 1803. Recorded: OS 2:478.

13 September 1802. Charles and Barbary SNODGRASS to Jacob FULK. 12 acres adjoining other lands purchased from said Snodgrass. Consideration: £10. Signed: Charles Snodgrass, Barbara Snodgrass. Witnesses: none. Acknowledged in court, September 1802. Del: to Mr [Mrs?] Foulk, 3 September 1804. Recorded: OS 2:478.

12 July 1802. Michael FRITTS, Owen DARBY, and Abraham ELY to Samuel CLARK. 100 acres adjoining Mason's and Deakinses [?] land, from a tract conveyed to Fritts by John Sullevin, 18 November 1788. Consideration: £50, VA. Signed: Michael Fritts, Abraham Eley, Owen Darby. Witnesses: Wm G Payne, Abraham Miley, Meshach Sexton. Del: to Samuel Clark, 22 March 1805. Recorded: OS 2:479.

14 April 1802. Jesse MARTIN to William G PAYNE and Samuel HANWAY, trustees. Deed of trust to secure payment of $187.13 due to John T Goff. As security Martin conveys 800 acres on Indian Creek, from two separate patents of 22 August 1792. Land to be sold whenever Goff calls on the trustees to do so, with advertisement of the land both at the courthouse and in the *Winchester Gazette*. Signed: Jesse Martin, Wm G Payne, Saml Hanway. Witnesses: E Horton, Will N Jarrett, Thos McKinley, John

Taylor. Proved by witnesses (except Taylor), September 1802. No delivery shown. Recorded: OS 2:480.

13 September 1802. Samuel HANWAY and William and Sarah JOSEPH to John BAKER. 200 acres on West Run, adjoining William Joseph, Elijah Burrows, and John W Dean; 170 acres from a Hanway patent dated [blank], and 30 acres from a 20 September 1785 patent to William Joseph. Consideration: £300, VA. Signed: Saml Hanway, William [X] Joseph, Sarah [+] Joseph. Witnesses: none. Acknowledged in court, September 1802. Del: to John Baker, 18 June 1804. Recorded: OS 2:481.

12 July 1802. Joseph and Nancy WILSON to Samuel HANWAY. 48 acres at Deckers Creek, adjoining Jacob Youngman. Consideration: £48. Signed: Joseph Wilson, Ann S Wilson. Witnesses: none. Acknowledged in court, July 1802. No delivery shown. Recorded: OS 2:482.

23 March 1802. Philip ROBERTS to John BROWN. 35 acres at Finches Run, a branch of Buffelow, adjoining William Gray and William Hillery. Part of 150 acres patented to Roberts, [blank] 1799. Consideration: £35, VA. Signed: Philip Roberts. Witnesses: Wm Snodgrass, Fleming Jones, Wm [W] Straight. Acknowledged in court, June 1802. Del: to John Brown, 20 August 1806. Recorded: OS 2:482.

30 September 1802. Christopher and Mary IRWIN to Thomas KNIGHT. 64 acres on Papaw Creek, adjoining William Snodgrass, Adonijah Little, Thomas Wilson, and Albert Gallatin, Esq. Part of a 200 acre tract patented to Christopher. Consideration: £40.16. Signed: Christopher Erwin, Mary [+] Erwin. Witnesses: none. Acknowledged in court, September 1802. Del: to Thomas Knight, 11 April 1803. Recorded: OS 2:483.

8 July 1802. George Jacob BALTZEL to Daniel BALTZEL. Bill of sale. Copper still, milch cow, household furnishings, table ware, checkreel, spinning wheel, crout tubs, and other personal property, one pewter dish delivered in the name of the whole. Consideration: $120. Signed: Geo Jacob Baltzel. Witnesses: Ezekiel Cheney, "one other signed in Dutch." Acknowledged in court, September 1802. No delivery shown. Recorded: OS 2:484.

14 January 1802. Jacob PINDELL, trustee for Thomas CHIPPS, deceased, and for John DOWNER, to Joannah CHIPPS. Pindell sold 800 acres on Dunker Creek, formerly belonging to Downer, to fulfill a deed of trust, and Joanah Chipps being the highest bidder, Pindell conveys title to her. Consideration: $900. Signed: Jacob Pindell. Witnesses: Saml Hanway, Amos Roberts, Wm G

Payne. Acknowledged in court, June 1802. No delivery shown. Recorded: OS 2:484.

11 January 1802. James and Mary McPECK to Benjamin WOODS. 195 acres on the east side of Sandy Creek, adjoining Martin Wagner. Part of a 27 June 1796 patent to William McPeck, deceased, to whom James is heir at law. Consideration: $400. Signed: James McPeck, Mary McPeck. Witnesses: none. Acknowledged by Mary McPeck before Russel Potter and John McLain, JPs, 7 April 1802. Proved by witnesses Mathew Gay and Alexr Hawthorn [sic; no witnesses are indicated on instrument]. Del: to B Woods, 14 April 1806. Recorded: OS 2:485.

13 September 1802. Philip and Margrett MOORE to Daniel MARTIN. 75 acres on waters of Muddy Creek, adjoining Ephraim Metheny. Consideration: £75. Signed: Philip [X] Moore, Margret [-] Moore. Witnesses: none. Acknowledged in court, September 1802. Del: to Daniel Martin, 10 October 1803. Recorded: OS 2:486.

8 October 1787. John and Martha HAMILTON to John DENT. 92 acres on Scotts Mill Run, adjoining Edward Evans, Thomas Hardesty, and Aaron Henry. Part of a patent to Hamilton, 20 [blank] 1784. Consideration: £30, VA. Signed: John Hamilton, Martha Hamilton. Witnesses: none. Acknowledged in court, October 1787. Del: to John Dent, 7 July 1809. Recorded: October 1802, OS 2:487. Re-recording of burned instrument.

14 June 1802. Christopher and Mary ERWIN to Jacob FULK. 8½ acres adjoining Charles Snodgrass and Fulk's other land, Part of a patent for 200 acres. Consideration: £10.10. Signed: Christopher Erwin, Mary [mark] Erwin. Witnesses: none. Acknowledged in court, June 1802. Del: to Mr [Mrs?] Foulk, 2 September 1804. Recorded: OS 2:488.

26 April 1802. Wildey and Mary TAYLOR and John CLARK (latter of Montgomery Co, MD) to Daniel CONNER. 150 acres about two miles west of Cheat River. Land conveyed by Wildey Taylor to Raphel Whaten, 1792, and by him to John Clark. Consideration: £90. Signed: Wildey Taylor, Mary [X] Taylor, John Clark. Witnesses: John Beverlin, James Post, Robert [X] Beaty. Proved by witnesses Beverlin and Post, July 1802. No delivery shown. Recorded: OS 2:489.

10 June 1802. Evan and Cammelea MORGAN to Thomas MILLER, Henry HAMILTON, and William SCRIPPS. 1 acre on both sides of the Clarksburg road, part of the tract Morgan lives on, about 5 miles from Morgantown, for the use of the school and meeting house. Consideration: $1. Signed: Evan Morgan [Cammelea does not sign]. Witnesses:

none. Acknowledged by Evan Morgan, June 1802. Del: to H Hamilton, 14 April 1804. Recorded: OS 2:490.

11 October 1802. Jesse and Hannah BAYLES to John MOORE. 5 acres on the south side of Whites Run, adjoining heirs of Lott Ridgway. Part of a 240 acre patent to James Moore. Consideration: $5. Signed: Jesse Bayles, Hannah [+] Bayles. Witnesses: none. Acknowledged in court, October 1802. Del: to Ross Alley, 21 May 1804. Recorded: OS 2:490.

11 March 1801. James and Levina DUNWOODY, Fayette Co, PA, to James HUGGINS. 100 acres at Little Sandy Creek, adjoining John McLain and including the improvement on which Huggins now lives. Consideration: £100. Signed: James Dunwoody, Levina Dunwoody. Witnesses: James Webster, Joseph Severans, Robert Conner. Acknowledged by Levina Dunwoody before John McLain and Russel Potter, JPs, 19 June 1802. Proved by witnesses, October 1802. Del: to Wm Ayer, 15 September 1806. Recorded: OS 2:491.

2 June 1801. Ezekiel and Hannah JONES, Allegania Co, PA, to William JOHNSON. 266 acres on the west side of Muddy Creek, adjoining Edward Jones. Part of a patent for 400 acres. Consideration: £200. Signed: Ezekiel Jones, Hannah Jones. Witnesses: Oliver Jones, Daniel Jones. Acknowledged before Wm Conner, JP, 2 June 1801. Certificate of Tarleton Bates, prothonotary of Allegania Co, PA. Del: to Wm Johnston, 10 September 1804. Recorded: September 1802, OS 2:492.

[blank] 1800. William and Sarah SQUIRES, Fayette Co, PA, to Samuel DARBY. 1?8 acres, adjoining James McCollum, Samuel Clark, and Richard Stephens. Part of a 400 acre patent to Martin Judy. Consideration: £1??. Signed: Wm Squire, Sarah [+] Squire. Witnesses: Gabriel Fickle, Samuel Clark. Acknowledged before Alexander Addison, JP. Certificate of Ephraim Douglass, prothonotary, Fayette Co, PA. Del: to Alexr Brandon, 7 July 1804. Recorded: September 1802, OS 2:493-494.

28 September 1802. John GIBBON to Jacob FOLK. 9 acres adjoining Matthias Hite. Part of a tract formerly belonging to Thomas Laidley. No place names mentioned. Consideration: $300. Signed: John Gibbon. Witnesses: Wm Tingle, Alexr Hawthorn, J Williams. Acknowledged in court, October 1802. Del: to Jacob Foulk, 28 March 1804. Recorded: OS 2:494.

13 September 1802. John and Tasey BAKER to John TAYLOR. 25½ acres on the road from Morgantown to Martin's Ferry, from two separate surveys. One survey, 23½ acres, adjoining Alexander McIntire, William Lanham,

Thomas Wilson, John Evans, and John Stealey. Second survey, on opposite side of the road, adjoining Thomas Wilson and Alexander McIntire. Excepted are 4 acres sold to Alexander McIntire and 2 acres sold to Robert Lee. Consideration: $200. Signed: John Baker, Teacy Baker. Witnesses: Saml Hanway, Asa Dudley, Alexr Hawthorn. Acknowledged in court, September 1802. Del: "to him," 29 March 1816. Recorded: OS 2:495.

12 October 1802. Abner HARP to James JEFFS. $82\frac{1}{2}$ acres on the Monongalia river, no adjoiners named. Part of a 31 July 1800 patent for 400 acres. Consideration: $550. Signed: Abner Harp. Witnesses: none. Acknowledged in court, October 1802. Del: to John Jeffs, 8 December 1803. Recorded: OS 2:496.

[blank] 1800. William and Sarah SQUIRE, Fayette Co, PA, to Samuel CLARK. 175 acres adjoining Gabriel Fickle and Samuel Darby. Consideration: £90, VA. Signed: Wm Squier, Sarah [+] Squier. Witnesses: Gabriel Fickle, Daniel Demond. Acknowledged before Alexander Addison, JP. Certificate of Ephraim Douglass, prothonotary, Fayette Co, PA. Del: to Saml Clark, 22 March 1805. Recorded: September 1802, OS 2:497-498.

15 June 1802. William and Sarah SQUIRE, Fayette Co, PA, to Gabriel FICKLE. 50 acres on Big Sandy Creek, adjoining David Moore. Part of a survey patented to Martin Judy Jr. Consideration: $50. Signed: William Squire, Sarah [+] Squire. Witnesses: Samuel Clark, Daniel Demond. Acknowledged before Alexander Addison, JP. Certificate of Ephraim Douglass, prothonotary, Fayette Co, PA. Del: to Alexr Brandon, 12 April 1803. Recorded: September 1802, OS 2:498-499.

13 April 1802. John T GOFF, executor of Salathiel GOFF, deceased, to Thomas RINEHART, Randolph Co. The will of Salathiel Goff directed John to convey to James Goff one third of 1000 acres in Monongalia, now Randolph, Co, on the waters of Yohogania, adjoining James Goff's survey, Zarah Osborn, John Goff, and a survey for James and Salathiel Goff. Land patented to Salathiel Goff, 24 June 1785. James has since sold his right to Thomas Rinehart for $333 1/3, and John conveys to him. Signed: John T Goff. Witnesses: John W Dean, Wm G Payne, E Horton, Nicholas Madira. Proved by witnesses, July 1802. Del: "to Old Wild [sic]", 15 September 1803. Recorded: OS 2:500-501.

12 July 1802. Daniel CONNER to John CLARK, Montgomery Co, MD. Mortgage on 150 acres 2 miles west of Cheat River. Part of a 200 acre tract patented to Wildey Taylor. Daniel may redeem by paying £58 to Clark before

1 April 1803. Signed: Daniel [+] Conner. Witnesses: none. Acknowledged in court, July 1802. "Fully proven by the oath of James Beatty," April 1804 [sic]. Del: "to George Snider, 1 March 1805, Dunker bottom George [sic]." Recorded: OS 2:501.

12 October 1802. Abner and Jane HARPER [alternately HARP throughout instrument] to James COLLINS. 117½ acres on the east bank of the Monongalia River, adjoining Thomas B Kirkpatrick and James Jeffs. Consideration: $783.33, VA. Signed: Abner Harp, Jane [X] Harp. Witnesses: none. Acknowledged in court, October 1802. Del: "to him," 16 March 1805. Recorded: OS 2:502.

11 October 1802. Thomas and Cate DEWESE, Samuel and Sarah DEWESE, James and Eliz DEWESE, and Jethro DEWESE to Lewis DEWESE. 56 acres on the west side of Monongalia River, adjoining Jacob Pindall. Part of a survey granted to James Scott and conveyed to the heirs of Joshua Dewese by David Scott of James. Consideration: $400. Signed: Thos Dewees, Catherine Dewees, Samuel Dewees, Sarah Dewees, James Dewees, Elisabeth Dewees, Jethro Dewees. Witnesses: none. Acknowledged in court, October 1802. Del: to Lewis Deweese, 3 October 1804. Recorded: OS 2:503.

27 September 1802. John GIBBONS to Abel DAVIS. 200 acres on the third lefthand fork of the righthand fork of Wickwares Creek. No adjoiners named. Consideration: $400. Signed: John Gibbons. Witnesses: J Williams, John Scott, Wm Tingle. Acknowledged in court, October 1802. Del: to him, 3 January 1816. Recorded: OS 2:504.

11 October 1802. Thomas and Cate DEWESE, Lewis and Mary DEWESE, Samuel and Sarah DEWESE, James and Eliz DEWESE, and Jethro DEWESE to Jacob PINDELL. 66 acres on the west side of Monongalia River, no adjoiners named. Part of a survey granted to James Scott and conveyed to the heirs of Joshua Dewese by David Scott of Jonathan. Consideration: $400. Signed: Thos Dewees, Catherine Dewees, Lewis Dewees, Mary Dewees, Samuel Dewees, Sarah Dewees, James Dewees, Elizabeth Dewees, Jethro Dewees. Witnesses: none. Acknowledged in court, October 1802. Del: to Jacob Pindell, 24 January 1806. Recorded: OS 2:504.

11 October 1802. Lewis and Mary DEWESE, Samuel and Sarah DEWESE, James and Eliz DEWESE, and Jethro DEWESE to Thomas DEWESE. 56 acres on the west side of Monongalia River, no adjoiners named. Part of a survey granted to James Scott and conveyed to the heirs of Joshua Dewese by David Scott of Jonathan. Consideration: $400. Signed: Lewis Deweese, Mary Deweese, Samuel

Deweese, Sarah Deweese, James Deweese, Elizabeth Deweese, Jethro Deweese. Witnesses: none. Acknowledged in court, October 1802. No delivery shown. Recorded: OS 2:505.

12 October 1802. James and Hannah WALKER, Fayette Co, PA, to John SHUMAN Jr. 100 acres on Papaw Creek, no adjoiners named. Patented to James Walker, 2 January 1799. Consideration: £50, VA. Signed: James Walker, Hannah [K] Walker. Witnesses: none. Acknowledged in court, October 1802. Del: to John Shuman Jr, 25 August 1803. Recorded: OS 2:506.

11 October 1802. Caleb and Sarah FURBEE to Matthias FURBEE. 154 acres on Papaw Creek, adjoining John Furbee, part of a 400 acre patent. Consideration: love and affection to their son. Signed: Caleb Furbee [Sarah does not sign]. Witnesses: none. Acknowledged by Caleb Furbee, October 1802. No delivery shown. Recorded: OS 2:507

October 1802. Acknowledgement of Abel and Mary DAVIS to a conveyance to John GIBBONS. Recorded: OS 2:507.

27 September 1802. Abel and Mary DAVIS to John GIBINGS [also GIBBONS in body of instrument]. 9 acres adjoining a 6 acre out lot of Matthias Hite. Part of a 197 acre tract formerly belonging to Thomas Laidley. Consideration: $200. Signed: Abel [mark] Davis, Mary [X] Davis. Witnesses: J Williams, John Scott, Wm Tingle. Receipt for consideration money. Acknowledged: [see above]. No delivery shown. Recorded: OS 2:508.

14 December 1801. John and Sarah BUTLER to Nicholas CASEY. 240 acres on the east side of Cheat River, adjoining Henry Richards and P Richards. Originally granted to George Riddle, who conveyed to John Butler. Consideration: $400. Signed: John Butler, Sarah [+] Butler. Witnesses: John W Dean, James Scott, Elihu Horton, David Morgan, Robert [?], Joseph [J] Butler Sr. Acknowledged by John Butler, February 1802; by Sarah Butler, July 1802. Del: to Elijah Butler, 26 July 1806. Recorded: OS 2:509.

11 October 1802. Joseph and Catherine BARKER to Michael KERN. 205 acres on Indian Creek, no adjoiners named. Part of two tracts patented to Joseph Barker. Consideration: $2300. Signed: Joseph [mark] Barker, Catherine Barker. Witnesses: none. Acknowledged in court, October 1802. Del: to Michael Kern, 7 September 1803. Recorded: OS 2:510.

11 October 1802. Caleb and Sarah FURBEE to Andrew DAUGHERTY. 120 acres on Little Papaw, no adjoiners

named. Part of a 400 acre patent to Caleb Furbee. Consideration: love and affection. Signed: Caleb Furbee [Sarah does not sign]. Witnesses: none. Acknowledged by Caleb Furbee, in court, October 1802. Del: to A Daugherty, 9 April 1804. Recorded: OS 2:511.

11 December 1802. John and Susannah McFARLAND, Fayette Co, PA, to Daniel COX. 91½ acres, 32 poles, adjoining William Stewart. First patented to Thomas Miller, 1784, who conveyed to McFarland and to whom land was repatented 21 August 1798. Consideration: $183. Signed: John Mcfarland, Susannah Mcfarland. Witnesses: none. Acknowledged in court, December 1802. Del: to D Cox, 25 October 1803. Recorded: OS 2:512.

11 December 1802. Elijah HARRYMAN to Thomas WILSON, trustee. Deed of trust. To secure payment of $740.09 to Henry Heinsman HH & Co. he conveys in trust 100 acres on Guises Run, patented to Joseph Wisbey and conveyed by him to Elijah. Land may be sold after 1 March 1804. Signed: Elijah Harryman. Witnesses: Henry Dering, Alexr Hawthorn, Stephen Root. Acknowledged by Elijah Harryman, December 1802; continued for acknowledgement of Solome, his wife [her acknowledgement not recorded]. Del: to Thomas Wilson, 3 August 1803. Recorded: OS 2:513.

10 December 1802. Sarah BARKER to John SMITH. Tract of 145 3/4 acres on Indian Creek, no adjoiners named. Conveyed to Sarah by Gilbert Butler, 8 March 1801. Consideration: £109.5.9. Signed: Sarah [+] Barker. Witnesses: none. Acknowledged in court, December 1802. Del: to John Smith, 8 April 1805. Recorded: OS 2:514.

8 September 1802. James and Hannah RYNEER, Fayette Co, PA, to Simon HENDRICKSON, formerly of Fayette Co but now of Monongalia. 400 acres on Buffelow Run, waters of Yohogania, where Hendrickson now lives and Hezekiah Ryneer formerly lived. Surveyed 5 March 1790. No adjoiners named. Consideration: £400, PA. Signed: James [mark] Reinier, Hannah Reinier. Witnesses: Jesse Barnes, John McGrew, Hezekiah Reinier. Receipt for consideration money. Acknowledged by Hannah Ryneer in Fayette Co, PA, before Jonathan Rowland and Robert Moore. Proved by witnesses as to James Ryneer. Del: to Jesse Barnes, 9 June 1804. Recorded: OS 2:515.

13 December 1802. Jacob and Phebee NOOSE to George HITE. 34 acres adjoining and between James Coburn's former land, Matthias Hite, David Croll, Francis Burrell's former land (now Matthias and George Hite's). Patented to Jacob Noose, 5 March 1795. Consideration: $100. Signed: Jacob [mark] Noose, Phebee [mark] Noose. Witnesses: none. Acknowledged in court, December 1802.

Del: to grantee, 4 December 1816. Recorded: OS 2:516.

12 October 1802. Abner and Jane HARPER to Thomas Bell KIRKPATRICK. 200 acres on the bank of Monongalia River, adjoining James Jeffs and William Kirkpatrick. Patented to Harper, 26 February 1786. Consideration: $1333. Signed: Abner Harp, Jane [+] Harp. Witnesses: none. Acknowledged in court, October 1802. Del: to Thomas Kirkpatrick, [torn] June 1803. Recorded: OS 2:517.

15 December 1802. William McCLEERY to Thomas BROWN, Fauquire Co. 578 acres on Slacks Run, adjoining John Cox. Part from a conveyance by Joseph and Margaret Jenkins, and part from a 20 March 1797 conveyance by James and Maryann Jenkins. Consideration: $1100, which Brown has given in the form of bonds, John Fairfax his security. Signed: Wm McCleery. Witnesses: John Fairfax, Elizabeth Anderson, Thos Wilson. Acknowledged in court, January 1803. Del: to John Fairfax, 30 November 1805. Recorded: OS 2:518.

10 January 1803. David (Sr) and Hannah SAYRE to John NICKLIN Jr, Loudoun Co. 118 acres on Joes and Toms Runs, adjoining Thomas Sayre. From a 19 October 1789 patent to David and Daniel Sayre. Consideration: $708. Signed: David Sayre, Hannah Sayre. Witnesses: none. Acknowledged in court, January 1803. Del: to James Wilson, 11 July 1803. Recorded: OS 2:519.

10 January 1803. David (Sr) and Hannah SAYRE to John NICKLIN Jr, Loudoun Co. 50 acres on the river bank, adjoining Jeremiah and John Wilson and Daniel Sayre. 14½ acres from Robert Ferrel's 966 acre patent of 6 February 1797, and 35½ acres from Ferrel's 234 acre patent of 18 June 1798. Consideration: $166. Signed: David Sayre, Hannah Sayre. Witnesses: none. Acknowledged in court, January 1803. Del: to James Wilson, 11 July 1803. Recorded: OS 2:520.

11 January 1803. John NICKLIN Jr, Loudoun Co, to Daniel SAYRE, trustee. Deed of trust on 200 acres where David Sayre Sr and Thomas Sayre lived, lands deeded to Nicklin by David and Thomas Sayre, and on 50 acres adjoining the river, deeded by David and Hannah Sayre. Nicklin has given bond to David Sayre for $650 and to Thomas Sayre for $450, which are to be paid within 4 years or the land may be sold by Daniel Sayre. Signed: John Nicklin Jr. Witnesses: none. Acknowledged in court, January 1803. Del: to Daniel Sayre, 11 June 1805. Recorded: OS 2:521.

10 January 1803. Thomas and Martha SAYRE to John NICKLIN Jr, Loudoun Co. 84 acres on Joes and Toms Runs,

no adjoiners named. Part of a tract patented to David and Daniel Sayre, 19 October 1789. Consideration: $450. Signed: Thomas Sayre, Martha Sayre. Witnesses: none. Acknowledged in court, January 1803. Del: to James Wilson, 11 July 1803. Recorded: OS 2:521-522.

2 November 1802. John and Phebe SPENCER to John BAYLY, all of Loudoun Co. 600 acres on the west side of Cheat and south side of Pringles Run, adjoining Pierce Bayly's survey. Part of a 2000 acre patent of 17 April 1798. Consideration: £135, VA. Signed: John Spencer [Phebe does not sign]. Witnesses: W Bayly, George Bayly, Aris Buckner, Jas Lewin Gibbs, John Turley, Bartlett Leach, Wm Cooke. Receipt for consideration money. Proved by witnesses as to John Spencer in Loudoun Co, January 1803. Certificate of C Benns, CLC. Acknowledged by Phebe Spencer before Wm R Harrison and Chas Lewis, 4 October 1806. Del [deed]: to Wm Rodgers Junr, 30 June 1803. Del [Phebe Spencer's acknowledgement]: to W A Rogers, 10 April 1807. Recorded: OS 2:522-523.

11 April 1803. Charles and Ruth DAWSON to Michael KERNS. 195 acres on Indian Creek, adjoining Boyles. Patented to Richard Harrison and conveyed by him to Dawson, 4 May 1789. Consideration: £500. Signed: Charles [+] Dawson, Ruth [+] Dawson. Witnesses: Saml Hanway, Augustus Ballah, Thos Mckinley. Acknowledged by Charles Dawson, April 1803. Acknowledged by Ruth Dawson, 6 July 1803, in Dearborn Co, IN, before Barnett Hulick and Jabez Perceval, common pleas justices. No delivery shown. Recorded: OS 2:524-525.

28 March 1803. William and Margret VEACH to Barney HANEY. Power of attorney to convey to John Davis 106 acres adjoining Robert Davis and John Davis. Signed: William Veach, Peggy Veach. Witnesses: Geo Greenwood, George Smyth, Robert Davis. Recorded: April 1803, OS 2:526.

11 April 1803. William and Margret VEACH to John DAVIS. 106 acres adjoining John Davis and Robert Davis. Part of a 26 January 1787 patent to Joseph Neal. Consideration: $530. Signed: William Veach by Barney [+] Heney. Witnesses: none. Acknowledged by Heney, April 1803. Del: to John Davis, 11 June 1803. OS 2:526.

11 April 1803. Robert and Massey DAVIS to John DAVIS. 134½ acres adjoining Jesse Martin. No place names mentioned. Consideration: $179. Signed: Robert Davis, Maza Davis. Witnesses: none. Acknowledged in court, April 1803. Del: to John Davis, 11 June 1803. Recorded: OS 2:527.

14 February 1803. Daniel and Sarah SAYRE to Thomas

EWELL, Albemarle Co. 150 acres (excepting the graveyard) adjoining John Nicklin, Daniel Sayre, Jacob Holland. Part of a 19 October 1789 patent to David and Daniel Sayre. Consideration: $750. Signed: Daniel Sayre, Sarah [X] Sayre. Witnesses: none. Acknowledged in court, February 1803. Del: to Thomas Ewell, 11 July 1810. Recorded: OS 2:528.

12 April 1803. Samuel and Sarah WILSON, Fayette Co, PA, to Jacob LIVINGOOD, Greene Co, PA. 78 acres on Marrickles Run, no adjoiners named. Patented to James Miller, 22 March 1785, and conveyed to James and Aaron Mills, 15 September 1794, who conveyed to Samuel Wilson. Consideration: $160. Signed: Samuel Wilson, Sarah Wilson. Witnesses: John E Bills, Michael Core. Acknowledged in court, April 1803. Del: to Jacob Livingood, 24 June 1803. Recorded: OS 2:529.

26 April 1803. Benjamin STODDERT, George Town, DC, to Henry SCHROEDER, Baltimore, MD. 1000 acres, no adjoiners or place names mentioned. Patented to Stoddert, 10 September 1787. Consideration: $1. Signed: Ben Stoddert. Witnesses: Thomas G Slye, Walter Hunt, Clement Smith Hunt. Acknowledged before Daniel Reintzel, mayor of George Town. Del: to A Werninger, 14 July 1803. Recorded: 14 June 1803, OS 2:530.

11 April 1803. James BARNES to Uz BARNES. 100 acres on Plumb Run, part of a 28 August 1799 patent for 200 acres. No adjoiners named. Consideration: $1. Signed: James Barnes. Witnesses: none. Acknowledged in court, April 1803. Del: to Uz Barnes, 11 July 1803. Recorded: OS 2:531.

11 April 1803. Uz and Lydia BARNES to James BARNES. 326 acres on a branch of Buffaloe, at the Plumb Orchard, patented 1787. No adjoiners named. Consideration: $1. Signed: Uz Barnes, Lydia Barnes. Witnesses: none. Acknowledged in court, April 1803. Del: to Uz Barnes, 11 July 1803. Recorded: OS 2:532.

10 February 1803. Hugh and Polly McNEELY, Morgans Town, to Ralph BARKSHIRE. Half lot [# blank] in Morgans Town, on the west side of High Street, adjoining James Daugherty's lot (now occupied by Dr Enos Daugherty), and where Hugh formerly lived (now occupied by Barkshire and George Deibler). Consideration: $1200. Signed: Hugh McNeely, Polly McNeely. Witnesses: B Reeder, Wm Lanham, J Williams, Robt Minnis. Acknowledged in court, February 1803. Del: to Ralph Barkshire, 30 July 1803. Recorded: OS 2:533.

17 January 1803. David and Susanna NORRIS, Harrison Co, to John WICKWARE. 200 acres on Cherry Run, a branch

of Whiteday Creek, including Morgan's hunting camp. Patented 15 August 1799. No adjoiners named. Consideration: $400. Signed: David Norris, Susannah Norris. Witnesses: Meshach Sexton, David Hewes. Acknowledged in Harrison Co, 17 January 1803. Certificate of Ben Wilson, CHC. Del: to Wickware, 8 August 1803. Recorded: OS 2:534.

11 July 1803. Rhoda BACORN, widow and sole heir of Job BACORN, late of Fayette Co, PA, to John COLDREN, Enos COLDREN, Jesse COLDREN, and William COLDREN, heirs of Joseph COLDREN, deceased. 225 acres on waters of Big Sandy Creek, no adjoiners named. Consideration: £100 paid to Job Bacorn in his lifetime. Signed: Rhoda Bacorn. Witnesses: none. Acknowledged in court, July 1803. Del: to Col Brandon, 2 October 1804. Recorded: OS 2:535.

13 September 1803. John and Catherine McGEE to Isaac LAROWE, Loudoun Co. 400 acres on Bunners Run, no adjoiners named. Patented to Reuben Bunner and transferred by him to McGee. Consideration: £200, VA. Signed: John McGee, Catherine [+] McGee. Witnesses: none. Acknowledged in court, September 1803. Del: to John McGee, 3 October 1803. Recorded: OS 2:536.

[blank] 1803. Jacob and Hannah BENNETT, Harrison Co, assignee of George HOUR, to Lindsay BOGGESS. 144 acres between Deckers and Aarons Creeks on Laurel Hill. No adjoiners named. Consideration: £50, VA. Signed: Jacob Bennett, Hannah Bennett. Witnesses: Isaac Cox, James Killee, Moses Sutton Jr. Acknowledged in Harrison Co, April 1800. Certificate of Ben Wilson, CHC. Del: to L Boggess, 8 October 1803. Recorded: OS 2:537.

13 June 1803. Thomas and Rebecca BUTLER to George SNIDER. 50 acres on the bank of Cheat River in Dunker Bottom settlement, adjoining Reeder. Consideration: $50. Signed: Thomas Butler, Rebecca Butler. Witnesses: none. Acknowledged in court, June 1803. Del: to George Snider, April 1804. Recorded: OS 2:538.

[blank] 1803. Samuel and Martha EVANS to John WELTNER. 164 acres near Camp Run, adjoining Thomas Evans, William Stewart, and William John. Consideration: $1000. Signed: Samuel Evans, Martha Evans. Witnesses: Lemuel John, Wm John, James Knox. Acknowledged by Martha Evans before Wm John and Lemuel John, JPs, 3 May 1803. Proved by witnesses, September 1803. Del: to Danl Cox, 25 October 1803. Recorded: OS 2:539.

6 November 1801. John DAVIS to Samuel HANWAY and Benjamin REEDER, Esqs, trustee. Deed of trust on 200 acres near Cheat River, about 8 miles from Morgans Town,

purchased from John B Armistead and recorded in District Court; 140 acres adjoining the furnace tract, part of 200 acres surveyed 24 January 1785 for Henry Stephens, on both sides of the road from Ices Ferry to Sandy Creek (140 acres of the 200 acre survey was conveyed or would be conveyed to Davis by Jacob Fisher); 700 acres near or adjoining the furnace tract, on heads of different branches of Morgans Run, adjoining James Ross and Henry Stephens, and surveyed for Davis 24 October 1798; 1000 acres near or adjoining the furnace tract, adjoining Thomas Evans, on Quarry Run and Jenkins' Slab Camp tract, surveyed October 1798; 1000 acres on Laurel Run, near or adjoining the furnace tract and William Hamilton, surveyed 10 October 1798. To secure payment of $3276 with lawful interest of PA, due from Davis to Reid and Ford of Philadelphia; also, $2500 with lawful interest of VA, due to Standish Ford of Philadelphia for goods he is to have sent to Morgans Town. Signed: John Davis, Saml Hanway, B Reeder. Witnesses: Hugh McNeely, Alexr Hawthorn, J Williams. No acknowledgement recorded. Del: to Wm N Jarrett, 5 April 1804. Recorded: OS 2:540-542.

10 February 1801. Philip MOORE to Daniel MARTIN. 75 acres, part of a tract formerly owned by Bartholomew London. No place names or adjoiners mentioned. Consideration: £70. Signed: Philip [X] Moore, Margaret [|] Moore. Witnesses: none. Acknowledged in court, February 1801. Del: to Philip Moore, 12 September 1808. Recorded: OS 2:542.

18 August 1803. John and Isabella DAVIS to William N JARRETT. Lot #39 in Morgan Town, near Davis' brick house. Includes 75¢ quit rent annually to the legal representatives of Zackquill Morgan, deceased. Consideration: $227. Signed: John Davis [Isabella does not sign]. Witnesses: James Evans, J Evans, Meshach Sexton. Acknowledged by John Davis, September 1803. Order to take Isabella's acknowledgement, but no action recorded. No delivery shown. Recorded: OS 2:543.

4 February 1801. James (Esq) and Mary HANNAH, Newton, Bucks Co, PA, to Anthony KENNEDY, Bucks Co, PA. 1400 acres near the Ohio River, below the mouth of Little Kenhawa, adjoining William Tilton's survey. Patented 7 July 1788 to James Stark, assignee of Abraham Loyer [?], assignee of Thomas Atkins, assignee of John Hawkins. Stark endorsed said patent to Hannah, 15 April 1795, and has since executed a conveyance. Consideration: £173.17.5, PA. Signed: James Hanna, Mary Hanna. Witnesses: Francis Murray, Wm R Hannah, Js Hicks.

Receipt for consideration money. Acknowledged before Francis Murray, Associate Judge, 29 July 1801. Certificate of Matthew Lawler, Mayor of Philadelphia. Del: to Wm N Jarrett, 5 April 1804. Recorded: OS 2:544-545.

7 December 1803. Alexander and Barshabe McCLELAND, Fayette Co, PA, to Joseph LAMBERTH, Frederick Co, MD. 135 acres on Cheat River, part of a patent to Capt John Ramsey, 18 January 1792, for 185 acres. Ramsey conveyed to Joseph Joseph by deed 8 February 1796, and Joseph devised 135 acres to Eli Joseph and 50 acres to John Simpler. Eli and John conveyed their lands to McCleland, 2 April 1802, and he now conveys to Lamberth the 135 acres on the west side of the road. Consideration: $405. Signed: Alexander McCleland, Barshebe McCleland. Witnesses: William N Jarrett, Ralph Barkshire, Jacob Kyger, James Campbell. Acknowledged by Alexander McCleland, 12 December 1803. Commission to take Barshebe's acknowledgement, but no action recorded. Del: to Alexander McCleland, 12 December 1803. Recorded: OS 2:546-547.

13 September 1802. Thomas and Rebecca BUTLER to Edward ELLIOT. 100 acres on the south side of Roaring Creek, adjoining William Daugherty, part of Butler's pre-emption survey. Consideration: £100, VA. Signed: Thomas Butler, Rebecca Butler. Witnesses: none. Acknowledged in court, June 1803. Del: to David Morgan, 13 December 1803. Recorded: OS 2:548.

12 December 1803. Rhoda BACORN, devisee and administratrix of Job BACORN, deceased, late of Monongalia Co, to Neil PECK, Baltimore Co, MD. 600 acres on both sides of Sandy Creek, above land claimed by Benjamin Jennings. Patented to Jennings, 7 June 1788, and conveyed by him to Job Bacorn during Job's lifetime, 5 February 1802. Consideration: $100. Signed: Rhoda Bacorn. Witnesses: none. Acknowledged in court, 13 December 1803. Del: to John Stealey. Recorded: OS 2:549.

26 September 1803. Thomas JOHNSTON, now of Monongalia, to Philip SILLIG, Baltimore Co, MD. 200 acres on the west side of Cheat River, adjoining Wildy Taylor. Purchased by Johnston from William and Hannah Morgan, 13 October 1792. Consideration: $400. Signed: Thomas Johnston. Witnesses: Wm McCleery, Mathew Gay, Jno Stealey. Proved by witnesses, 12 December 1803. Del: to John Stealey. Recorded: OS 2:550.

28 July 1803. Jacob and Hannah PINDALL to Henry SCHROEDER, Commonwealth [sic] of MD. 165 acres on Monongalia River, adjoining Jonathan Davis. Another

tract of 35 acres on Monongalia River, no adjoiners named. Consideration: $300. Signed: Jacob Pindall, Hannah Pindall. Witnesses: Wm G Payne, Ezekiel Chaney, James Hurry. Acknowledged in court, 12 December 1803. Del: to John Stealey. Recorded: OS 2:551.

12 September 1803. John and Ann DAVIS to John ROAD [alternately RODES throughout instrument]. 100 acres on the river, near Laurel Run, adjoining Jesse Martin and Davis' other land. Consideration: $350. Signed: John Davis, Ann [+] Davis. Witnesses: none. Acknowledged in court, September 1803. Del: to John Roads, 12 March 1805. Recorded: OS 2:552.

9 February 1803. William McCLEERY to Benjamin WILSON Jr, Harrison Co, trustee. Deed of trust on Negro man slave James, sold to McCleery by Benjamin Wilson Sr, of Harrison Co. McCleery is indebted by his bond, 24 February 1800, to Benjamin Wilson Sr in the amount of $140.75. If not paid in 12 months, James to be sold by trustee. Signed: Wm McCleery, Ben Wilson Jr. Witnesses: A Wilson Jr, Michael [X] Roby, A Wilson 3rd. Proved by witnesses Roby, Archibald Wilson Jr and 3rd in Harrison Co, 21 February 1803. Certificate of Ben Wilson, CHC. Del: to Ben Wilson, September 1804. Recorded: 18 June 1803, OS 2:553.

6 September 1802. Michael and Catherine THORN to Samuel MINOR. 100 acres on Dunker Creek, part of a larger tract patented to John Statler, 17 June 1784. No adjoiners named. Consideration: $700, or £210, VA. Signed: Michael [M] Thorn, Catherine [U] Thorn. Witnesses: B Reeder, Saml Hanway, Thos Mckinley. Acknowledged by Catherine Thorn, 28 December 1802, before Samuel Hanway and B Reeder, JPs. Proved by witnesses, June 1803. Del: to Mr Minor, 8 December 1814. Recorded: OS 2:554.

12 November 1792. Enoch and Sarah JAMES, Harrison Co, to Sarah BOWERS, Franklin Co, PA. 250 acres on the West Fork, no adjoiners named. Part of a 1 May 1781 patent for 1000 acres. Consideration: £10. Signed: Enoch James, Sarah James. Witnesses: none. Acknowledged in court, November 1792. Del: to Ross, Esq, 14 September 1805. Recorded: June 1800, OS 2:555. Re-recording of burned instrument.

13 June 1803. James and Mary COLLINS to Sarah BARKER. 71 acres on Indian Creek, originally patented to Gilbert Butler. Later conveyed to Bartholomew Lott, who empowered Francis Collins to make conveyance to James Collins. Consideration: $333. Signed: James Collins, Mary [X] Collins. Witnesses: none. Acknowledged in

court, June 1803. Del: to Capt Dent, 12 January 1804. Recorded: OS 2:556.

11 July 1803. James and Mary WILLIAMSON to Abraham HOFFMAN. 33½ acres, no place names mentioned. Part of a 400 acre tract now the property of Charles Boyles, which was originally granted to Roger Parkes, who conveyed to Williamson by a deed burned in the clerk's office. Consideration: £40, VA. Signed: James Williamson, Mary [+] Williamson. Witnesses: Meshach Sexton, Adam Sriver, Peter Tennant. Acknowledged in court, July 1803. Del: to A Huffman, 12 May 1806. Recorded: OS 2: 557.

19 February 1803. William McCLEERY, Morgan Town, to Benjamin ROBINSON, Harrison Co, trustee. Deed of trust. McCleery and Benjamin Reeder are jointly bound to deliver property to satisfy an execution in the name of Edward Jackson for the use of the trustees of Randolph Academy and in the amount of $851. To secure the same, McCleery entrusts lots #28 and 29 in Morgan Town, conveyed by Zacquill and Drusilla Morgan to David Bradford, 10 August 1785, and by Bradford to McCleery, as well as livestock, household furnishings, tableware and dishes, Negro woman Liz, Negro girl child Beck, and Negro boy child Isaac (McCleery has a life estate in the Negroes), &c. McCleery is to pay on or before 1 October 1803, otherwise the property to be sold. Signed: Wm McCleery, Benjamin Wilson in behalf of Randolph Academy trustees, Benj Robinson. Witnesses: N Davisson, Prudence Davisson, Ben Wilson Jr. Credit for $26.13, Monongalia sheriff fees for forthcoming bond. Proved by witnesses in Harrison Co, September 1803. Certificate of B Wilson, CHC. Del: to Ben Wilson Jr, 20 September 1804. Recorded: September 1803, OS 2:558-559.

9 January 1804. Robert BROWNFIELD, Georges Twp, Fayette Co, PA, to Mary BROWNFIELD, single woman, Fayette Co, PA, and Rebecca McPHERSON, state of KY. 370 acres on Sandy Creek, no adjoiners named. Patented 9 July 1798. Consideration: £100, PA. Signed: Robert Brownfield. Witnesses: none. Acknowledged in court, January 1804. Del: to Mary Brownfield. Recorded: OS 2:560.

10 April 1803. John and Elizabeth STEWART to William BARRETT. 75 acres adjoining John Stewart, Simon Troy's heirs, Isaac Matthew. From 400 acres originally patented to Simon Troy. Consideration: $300, VA. Signed: John [4] Stewart, Elizabeth [X] Stewart. Witnesses: Isaac Matthew, Purnal Fowler. Acknowledged in court, April 1803. No delivery shown. Recorded: OS 2:561.

DEEDBOOK OS 3

7 June 1803. Jeremiah and Joanna WILSON to Robert FAWCET. 26 acres, part of 111½ acres on Joes Run and Monongahela River, conveyed to Wilson by Robert Ferrel. No adjoiners named. Consideration: $20. Signed: Jeremiah Wilson, Joanna Wilson. Witnesses: none. Acknowledged in court, July 1803. Del: to him, 25 June 1811. Recorded: OS 3:1.

12 July 1790. Philip and Lurena SHETTLESWORTH to Robert FERREL. 63 acres on west side of Toms Run, part of a 375-acre survey and grant dated [blank]. No adjoiners named. Consideration: £5. Signed: Philip [X] Shettlesworth, Luanna [X] Shettlesworth. Witnesses: none. Acknowledged in court. Del: to grantee's wife, 26 May 1819. Recorded: OS 3:2. Re-recording of burned instrument.

9 November 1803. William ANDERSON to Joseph BROMAGE. 175 acres, part of the survey David Dunham now lives upon. Conveyed by Dunham by poll deed to Joseph Kratzer, and conveyed by him to Anderson by deed of indenture, 11 October 1801. No adjoiners mentioned. Consideration: $500. Signed: William Anderson. Witnesses: Simon Kratzer, John [mark] Bromage, David Dunham. Acknowledged in court, December 1803. Del: to Joseph Brumage, 20 July 1804. Recorded: OS 3:3.

10 March 1803. Adam and Christena SHRIVER to Abraham SHRIVER. 180 acres by survey on Dunkard Creek, adjoining John Statler. Consideration: 20 bushels wheat, 10 bushels rye, 20 bushels corn, 300wt pork, 100wt beef annually for their subsistence; one pair men's shoes per annum to Adam, and two pair shoes to Christena, with all other necessary wearing apparel; two milch cows to be kept for use of Adam and Christina while both are alive but only one cow after decease of either party; a few sheep and a creature to ride upon for necessary occasions; one bushel of salt per annum; 25 pounds of good sugar per annum; Abraham to have their grinding done for them and brought to the house where they now reside, the house to be kept in good repair; and all due allowance to be rendered in time of sickness. Signed: Adam [mark] Shriver, Christiana [0] Shriver. Witnesses: Peter Henkins, John Statler, Adam Brown. No acknowledgement recorded. No delivery shown. Recorded: OS 3:4.

1 July 1803. Jesse PAYNE and William G PAYNE to Daniel FORTNEY Jr. 100 acres on the west side of Cheat River, adjoining Thomas Lankford and Payne's other land.

Consideration: $200. Signed: Jesse Payne, Rebecah Payne, Wm G Payne. Witnesses: Thos Fretwell, George Zinn, Moses Minnear (all as to Jesse and William G Payne). Acknowledged by William and Jesse Payne in court, July 1803. Commission to take acknowledgement of Rebecah, wife of Jesse Payne. Del: to Daniel Fortney, 9 March 1807. Recorded: OS 3:5.

1 July 1803. Jesse PAYNE and William G PAYNE to William MANEAR. 100 acres on the west side of Cheat River, adjoining Daniel Fortney and Payne's other land. Consideration: $200. Signed: Jesse Payne, Rebeccah Payne, Wm G Payne. Witnesses: Thos Fretwell, George Zinn, Moses Minnear [all as to Jesse and William G Payne]. No acknowledgement recorded. No delivery shown. Recorded: OS 3:6.

11 July 1803. Jesse and Rachael HANWAY to Lewis WOLF. 98 acres on waters of Sandy Creek, part of a patent of [blank], adjoining Thomas Berry's and Robert Brownfield's surveys. Consideration: $100. Signed: Jesse Hanway, Rachael Hanway. Witnesses: none. Acknowledged in court, July 1803. Del: to him, November 1810. Recorded: OS 3:7.

11 July 1803. Jesse and Rachael HANWAY to Noah, Elihu, and Joel RIDGWAY. Elihu and Joel the heirs of Joel Ridgway, deceased, who in his lifetime had made this purchase jointly with Noah Ridgway. One-ninth part of 400 acres at Whites Run, the part that fell to Hanway by his wife, who was a daughter and heir of Lott Ridgway deceased. Consideration: $200. Signed: Jesse Hanway, Rachael [mark] Hanway. Witnesses: none. Acknowledged in court, July 1803. Del: to Noah Ridgway, 3 January 1816. Recorded: OS 3:8.

14 June 1803. Thomas B and Mary KIRKPATRICK to James CLELAND. 200 acres on the bank of the Monongahela, part of a patent to Abner Harper, 26 February 1786, adjoining James Jeffs and William Kirkpatrick. Consideration: $1500. Signed: Thomas B Kirkpatrick, Mary Kirkpatrick. Witnesses: none. Acknowledged in court, June 1803. Del: to grantee's son John, 6 February 1823. Recorded: OS 3:9.

25 June 1803. James and Lucresa STAFFORD to Jane FRY. 9 acres, part of a 354 acre survey patented 5 April 1784, adjoining Thomas John's old survey and Joseph Jenkins. Consideration: one mare and saddle. Signed: James Stafford, Lucresa [mark] Stafford. Witnesses: Wm N Jarrett, Charles Magill, George S Dering. Acknowledged in court, September 1803. No delivery shown. Recorded: OS 3:10.

13 June 1803. Francis DEAKINS, George Town, DC, to John BISHOP and Christian BISHOP. 21 acres, adjoining land sold to the Bishops by Hogmire. Consideration: $30. Signed: Francis Deakins. Witness: Frederick Harsh. Acknowledged in court, June 1803. No delivery shown. Recorded: OS 3:11.

12 September 1803. Benjamin and Elenor WILSON to MOUNT TABER REGULAR BAPTIST CHURCH. 1 acre from the tract Benjamin now lives on, near the old state road at Scotts Run, for the use of the church. Consideration: good will. Signed: Benjamin [B] Wilson, Elenor [\] Wilson. Witnesses: Wm G Payne, Samuel Swearingen, Josiah [-] Wilson. Acknowledged in court, September 1803. Del: to John Dent, 7 July 1809. Recorded: OS 3:12.

21 March 1803. Jacob (Sr) and Dianah JONES to William JONES. 74 acres on waters of Swamp Run, part of 132 acres patented to Jacob Jones, 3 October 1797, adjoining Jacob's other land and heirs of Theophilus Philips. Consideration: $74. Signed: Jacob Jones, Dianah [mark not shown] Jones. Witnesses: Dudley Evans, Jacob Jones Junr, Nathan Hall. Acknowledged by Dianah Jones, 22 March 1803, before Dudley Evans and Nathan Hall, JPs. Proven by witnesses, April 1803. Del: to Wm Jones, 25 January 1804. Recorded: OS 3:13.

12 September 1803. James and Linney DONALDSON to Allen ROBNETT, York Co, PA. 200 acres known as Blackburn's Glade. No adjoiners mentioned. Consideration: a judgment obtained by Robnett vs Charles Donaldson, deceased, for $7?.43 debt and $72.59 damages, plus $2 cash. Signed: James [X] Donaldson, Linney [X] Donaldson. Witnesses: none. Acknowledged in court, April 1803 [sic]. Del: to Alex Brandon, 17 July 1804. Recorded: OS 3:14.

21 March 1803. Jacob (Sr) and Dinah JONES to Jacob JONES Jr. 58 acres on Swamps and Three Forks, part of a 132 acre patent of 3 October 1798, adjoining William Jones. Consideration: $58. Signed: Jacob [mark] Jones, Dinah Jones. Witnesses: Dudley Evans, Wm Jones, Nathan Hall. Acknowledged by Dinah Jones, 23 March 1803, before Dudley Evans and Nathan Hall, JPs. Proved by witnesses, April 1803. Del: to J Jones Jr, 9 April 1804. Recorded: OS 3:15.

21 March 1803. Jacob (Sr) and Dinah JONES to Solomon BURSON. 63 acres on Three Fork Creek, adjoining Jesse Sanders. Consideration: [blank]. Signed: Jacob [X] Jones, Dinah Jones. Witnesses: Dudley Evans, Jacob Jones Junr, Nathan Hall. Acknowledged by Dinah Jones, 23 March 1803, before Dudley Evans and Nathan Hall, JPs. Proved

by witnesses, April 1803. Del: to Samuel Jones, 14 April 1806. Recorded: OS 3:16.

15 June 1803. Francis DEAKINS, George Town, DC, to Jacob MISSELL, Frederick Co, MD, and Michael STONEBRAKER, Washington Co, MD. Three tracts on waters of Sandy Creek Glades. 88 acres adjoining Deakins' survey, William ??'s line, Hogmire's line, Martin Judie's line. 88½ acres adjoining Deakins' tract, Jonas Hogmire's survey, William ??'s line. 223½ acres adjoining Deakins' survey, Joseph Stewart's survey, for a total of 400 acres. Consideration: £100. Signed: Francis Deakins. Witnesses: none. Acknowledged in court, June 1803. Del: to Stonebraker, November 1810. Recorded: OS 3:17.

[blank] September 1803. Daniel and Anna McLEAN, Randolph Co, to Francis DEAKINS, George Town, DC. 2054 acres conveyed by Conrad Hogmire to John and Elizabeth Stough, and by Stough to McLean, adjoining Henry Hogmire and Daniel Hogmire. Consideration: $890. Signed: Daniel McLean, Anna McLean. Witnesses: none. Acknowledged in Randolph Co Court, 26 September 1803. Certificate of John Wilson, CRC. Del: to John Hoye, 20 June 1804. Recorded: October 1803, OS 3:18.

2 March 1803. Bartholomew and Mary LOTT to Francis COLLINS. Power of Attorney to convey to James Collins 71 acres on Indian Creek, formerly owned by Gilbert Butler and now by Lott. Signed: Bartholomew Lott, Mary [+] Lott. Witness: Asa Dudley. Acknowledged 2 March 1804 before Asa Dudley and Augustus Ballah, JPs. No delivery shown. Recorded: June 1803, OS 3:19.

26 July 1803. Joseph CAIN, Washington Co, PA, to James CAIN. Power of attorney to recover from estate of Joseph's deceased father Walter Cain all that was bequeathed to Joseph. Signed: Joseph Kain. Witnesses: Wm John, Lemuel John. Proved by witnesses, September 1804. Del: to James Cain, 28 April 1804. Recorded: OS 3:19.

14 June 1803. Samuel HANWAY to James HURREY. Lot [# not shown] in Morgan Town, between Front, Pleasant, and High Streets and another lot belonging to the heirs of Thomas Pindell. Consideration: $150. Signed: Samuel Hanway. Witnesses: none. Acknowledged in court, June 1803. Del: to him, 11 August 1807. Recorded: OS 3:20.

10 October 1803. Richard and Jenny CAIN to Anthony KIRKHART. 25 3/4 acres, part of the tract Richard now lives on. No adjoiners or place names mentioned. Kirkhart to have privilege of the water adjoining his line. Consideration: love and affection. Signed: Richard Cain, Jenny [+] Cain. Witnesses: none. Acknowledged in

court, October 1803. Del: to him, 19 May 1807. Recorded: OS 3:20.

[blank] 1803. John TROY, James and Mary TROY, Christopher and Margaret TROY, William and Elenor BRUMEGEN, Tobias and Elizabeth LEVINGSTON, and Mary TROY, heirs and legatees of Simon TROY, deceased, to Marsh Marine DEVALL. 48 acres on Wades Run, part of a patent to Simon Troy, deceased, and adjoining William Robe's survey. Consideration: $170. Signed: Christopher Troy, Margaret [X] Troy, James Troy, John Troy, Elenor Brumegen, Elizabeth Levenston, Mary Troy, William Brumegen, Tobias [mark] Leveston. Witnesses: Josiah Robe, James Weaver, Matthew Wilson, John Vandevort, Daniel Shean, Matthew Wilson [sic]. Proved by witnesses, October 1803. Del: to Duvall, 29 October 1805. Recorded: OS 3:21-22.

28 March 1803. Michael and Hannah HOY to Hugh MORGAN. Hannah, one of the five heirs of William Morgan, deceased, conveys all her right, claim, and title to the land estate of her father, which consists of 400 acres, minus 100 acres now pertaining to David Morgan, Esq; 100 acres; 66 acres; and 40 acres, all in Dunker Bottom settlement. Consideration: £70. Signed: Michael [X] Hoy, Hannah [X] Hoy. Witnesses: B Reeder, Henry Dering, John W Dean, N Vandervort. Acknowledged by Hannah Hoy, 2 April 1803, before B Reeder and N Vandervort, JPs. Del: to Hugh Morgan, 26 December 1807. Recorded: OS 3:22.

9 October 1803. David SCOTT Sr to Felix SCOTT. Negro man Sam, Negro boy William, sorrel mare, 3-year-old gray mare, and the crop of corn and hay on the plantation. Consideration: $1. Signed: David Scott. Witness: Wm G Payne. Acknowledged in court, October 1803. No delivery shown. Recorded: OS 3:23.

18 June 1802. WILL of William HURST. All property, real and personal, to wife Elizabeth, also named executrix. Signed: William [W] Hurst. Witnesses: Christian Whitehare, "two other names Signed in Dutch." Proven July 1802. Recorded: OS 3:23. [Also recorded in Wills, 1:307-308.]

3 August 1803. William and Catharine LANHAM, Morgan Town, to Lucy LANHAM. Lot #108 in Morgan Town. Includes 3 shillings quit rent to the heirs of Zackquell Morgan. Consideration: $333 1/3. Signed: Wm Lanham, Catharine Lanham. Witnesses: Wm G Payne, B Reeder, Meshach Sexton. Acknowledged in court by William Lanham, September 1803, and by Catharine Lanham, October 1803. No delivery shown. Recorded: OS 3:24.

20 July 1803. Joseph WILSON to his daughter

Elizabeth [also Eliza in the instrument] WILSON. Negro girl Amy, about five years old. Bill of sale not to take effect until the decease of Joseph Wilson. Consideration: Love and affection, $1. Signed: Joseph Wilson. Witnesses: Abner Ashton, Robert Abercromby. Acknowledged in court, September 1803. Del: to J F Wilson, 10 July 1807. Recorded: OS 3:24.

12 April 1803. James and Nancy GELLESPIE to John and Andrew OLIPHANT and Company, Fayette Co, PA. 354 acres on the east side of Cheat River, conveyed by Neal Gellespie to James, 11 February 1797. No adjoiners mentioned. Consideration: [deleted]. Signed: James Gellespie, Nancy Gellespie. Witnesses: Wm G Payne, Samuel Wilson, Russel Potter [all as to James Gellespie]. Commission to take Nancy's acknowledgement, not recorded here. Del: to Andrew Oliphant, 4 April 1808. Recorded: OS 3:25.

14 February 1803. Bengamen BRANE [wife Susannah is named only in final sentence of instrument] to Thomas MAGEE. 75 3/4 acres on Three Forks. No adjoiners mentioned. Consideration: $97.75. Signed: [erased]. Witnesses: Henry Dering, Alexr Hawthorn, Wm G Payne (all as to B Brain). Acknowledged by Benjamin and Susannah his wife, February 1803. Del: to Thomas McGee, 9 June 1806. Recorded: OS 3:26.

15 February 1803. Elijah PILES, executor of John Piles deceased, to John MOOR. 80 acres, adjoining Richard Cain. Consideration: $160 paid by Moor to John Piles during his lifetime. Signed: Elijah [X] Piles. Witnesses: Wm G Payne, John W Dean, Henry Dering. Proved by witnesses, February 1803. Del: to John Moore, 12 May 1806. Recorded: OS 3:27.

10 January 1804. William PATTON to Benjamin MATTHEWS. 97 acres on Three Forks, part of a 319 acre tract purchased by John Casady from Henry Barnes. No adjoiners mentioned. Consideration: $250. Signed: William Patten. Witnesses: Geo Cunningham, Hugh Pierce, Isaac Matthews. Acknowledged in court, January 1804. Del: to John Smith, per order from Matthews, 17 March 1813. Recorded: OS 3:28.

20 July 1803. Joseph WILSON to his daughter Partheny WILSON. Negro slave Jeffery, about nine years old. Bill of sale not to take effect until Joseph shall depart this life. Consideration: love and affection, $1. Signed: Joseph Wilson. Witnesses: Robert Abercromby, Abner Ashton. Acknowledged in court, September 1803. Del: to J F Wilson, 10 July 1807. Recorded: OS 3:28.

20 July 1803. Joseph and Ann S WILSON to their sons

John F WILSON and Samuel Griffith WILSON, as joint tenants. 200 acres on Deckers Creek, adjoining James Smallwood Wilson and Augustin Wells. Consideration: $1, love and affection. Signed: Joseph Wilson, Ann Skinner Wilson. Witnesses: Robert Abercromby, Abner Ashton. Acknowledged in court, September 1803. Del: to J F Wilson, 10 July 1807. Recorded: OS 3:29.

12 December 1803. Jesse and Hannah MARTIN to Ezekiel COX. 100 acres on Indian Creek, patented to Jesse Martin 22 August 1792, adjoining Abraham Cox. Consideration: $250. Signed: Jesse Martin, Hannah Martin. Witnesses: none. Acknowledged in court, December 1803. Del: to Cox, 27 December 1805. Recorded: OS 3:30.

12 September 1803. Samuel GANDY to Jonathan GANDY. 20½ acres, part of a tract conveyed to Samuel by Benjamin Brain and Thomas Magee. No adjoiners or place names mentioned. Consideration: $80. Signed: Samuel Gandy. Witnesses: none. Acknowledged in court. Del: to Samuel Gandy, 12 November 1807. Recorded: OS 3:31.

12 September 1803. Benjamin BRAIN and Thomas MAGEE [wives mentioned only in final sentence of instrument] to Samuel GANDY. 57½ acres, originally sold by Brain to Paul Dewit and by him to Magee. No adjoiners or place names mentioned. Consideration: $250. Signed: Benjamin Brain, Susannah Brain, Thomas Magee, Margaret Magee. Witnesses: none. Acknowledged in court, September 1803. Del: to his son, [illegible] Gandy, 12 December 1814. Recorded: OS 3:31.

30 August 1803. John and Anna DAVIS to George SMITH. 176 acres, adjoining Jesse Martin. No place names mentioned. Consideration: $430. Signed: John Davis, Anna [+] Davis. Witnesses: Caleb Furbee, Barney Haney, Robert Davis. Acknowledged in court, September 1803. Del: to Mr George Smith, 2 September 1812. Recorded: OS 3:32.

12 December 1803. Jesse and Hannah MARTIN to Zadock MORRIS. 176 acres at head of Dols Run, part of a 400 acre patent of 4 April 1792. Consideration: £47.10. Signed: Jesse Martin, Hannah Martin. Witnesses: none. Acknowledged in court, December 1803. Del: to Z Morris, 11 November 1805. Recorded: OS 3:32.

13 June 1803. Francis DEAKINS, George Town, DC, to Jacob TETRA. 3/4 acre adjoining Tetra's other land. No place names mentioned. Consideration: $7. Signed: Francis Deakins. Witness: Frederick Harsh. Acknowledged in court, June 1803. Del: to Jacob Teter, 9 April 1804. Recorded: OS 3:33.

12 December 1803. Samuel HANWAY to Henry PRIDE,

Jesse PRIDE, Burton PRIDE, and William PRIDE, heirs at law of William PRIDE, deceased. 122 acres adjoining Alexander Wade's heirs and Thomas Wade. Consideration: $213.50. Signed: Samuel Hanway. Acknowledged in court, December 1803. Del: to Noah Morris, 27 August 1807. Recorded: OS 3:33.

12 December 1803. Jesse and Hannah MARTIN to John WEST. 90 acres on the south side of Indian Creek, part of a 22 August 1794 patent, adjoining Isreal Thompson and Richard Harrison. Consideration: $180. Signed: Jesse Martin, Hannah Martin. Witnesses: none. Acknowledged: in court, December 1803. Del: to John West, 21 September 1805. Recorded: OS 3:34.

4 April 1803. William and Mary DAWSON, state of KY, by their attorney in fact Charles Dawson to Caleb HURLEY. 50 acres on head waters of Scotts Mill Run, part of a 225 acre patent, adjoining Samuel Everly and Christopher Meas. Consideration: £50. Signed: Charles [+] Dawson. Witnesses: Wm N Jarrett, David Scot, Thos McKinley. Proved by witnesses, June 1803. Del: to Caleb Hurley, 5 May 1806. Recorded: OS 3:35.

12 September 1803. Samuel and Sarah TANEHILL to James KING. 196 acres patented to Nathan Lane, 20 April 1784, and conveyed by him to Tanehill, near Laurel Run and adjoining James Hamilton, Robert Ewing, and Elijah Beale. Consideration: $296, VA. Signed: Samuel Tanehill, Sarah [+] Tanehill. Witnesses: none. Acknowledged in court, September 1803. Del: to James King, 26 February 1807. Recorded: OS 3:36.

4 April 1803. William and Mary DAWSON, state of KY, by Charles Dawson, their attorney in fact, to Christopher MEAS. 50 acres on head waters of Scotts Mill Run, adjoining Samuel Everly and Caleb Hurley. Consideration: £50. Signed: Charles [X] Dawson. Witnesses: William N Jarrett, David Scott, Thomas McKinley. Proved by witnesses, June 1803. Del: to Christopher Mease, 9 November 1804. Recorded: OS 3:37.

14 February 1803. Jeremiah and Sally TANEHILL to Francis COLLINS. 83 acres, part of the tract where Samuel Lewellen formerly lived, adjoining Charles Donaldson's former land and Widow Jenkins. Consideration: $400, VA. Signed: Jer Tanehill [Sally does not sign]. Witnesses: none. Acknowledged in court, February 1804. Del: to Robert Woods, 26 August 1806. Recorded: OS 3:38.

12 December 1803. Jesse and Hannah MARTIN to Levi MORRIS. 236 acres on Dolls Run, part of a 4 April 1792 patent, adjoining Zadock Morris. Consideration: £147.10.

Signed: Jesse Martin, Hannah Martin. Witnesses: none. Acknowledged in court, December 1803. Del: to Levi Morris, 5 November 1803. Recorded: OS 3:39.

9 June 1803. Thomas and Catherine EVANS to Caleb WISEMAN. 60 acres on both sides of Rush Run, on the west side of Cheat River, part of a patent to Thomas Evans, assignee of Thomas Perry, 3 October 1797, and adjoining William Stewart, Thomas Miller, and Thomas Laidley. Consideration: $60, VA. Signed: Thomas [mark not shown] Evans, Catherine [mark] Evans. Witnesses: none. Acknowledged in court, June 1803. Del: to Caleb Wiseman, 27 December 1806. Recorded: OS 3:40.

13 December 1802. Isaac and Elizabeth ["Betsy" in body of instrument] POWELL to John NUZUM. 113 acres on Tyger Valley River above the mouth of Lost Run, adjoining Nuzum's other land and John PettyJohn. Part of two patents to Thomas Wilson, 26 July 1798 (862 acres) and 22 January 1800 (400 acres), and conveyed by him to Powell. Consideration: $194. Signed: Isaac Powell, Elizabeth Powell. Witnesses: Ebenezer Vandegrift, Joseph Dickinson. Acknowledged in court by Isaac Powell, December 1802, and by Betsy Powell, February 1803. Del: to John Nuzum, 11 April 1805. Recorded: OS 3:41.

14 February 1802. James and Elizabeth JEFFS to John WATSON. 106 acres on Mods Run, a branch of Buffalo Creek. Half of a tract, the remainder of which is sold to Thomas Ice, agreeable to division between him and Watson. Adjoining lands of James Morgan. Consideration: $212. Signed: James Jeffs, Elizabeth Jeffs. Witnesses: none. Acknowledged in court, February 1803. Del: to him, 22 September 1810. Recorded: OS 3:42.

13 June 1803. Thomas and Rebecca BUTLER to Samuel POSTLETHWAIT. 100 acres on the east side of Cheat River at Buffalo Run near Dunker Bottom. Part of a 2 May 1781 survey and 1785 patent of 400 acres for Thomas Butler, assignee of James Butler. No adjoiners mentioned. Consideration: £100. Signed: Thos Butler, Rebecca Butler. Witnesses: none. Acknowledged in court, June 1802. Del: to him, 15 September 1807. Recorded: OS 3:43.

15 April 1803. Philip and Abba SHIVELY to Thomas MARTIN, Harrison Co. 262 acres on waters of Papaw Creek, patented to Eli Brumagen and conveyed to Shively. No adjoiners named. Consideration: $524. Signed: Philip Shively, Abba [+] Shively. Witnesses:none. Acknowledged in court, April 1803. Del: to Thos Martin, 11 April 1808. Recorded: OS 3:44.

14 September 1803. Thomas and Rebecca BUTLER to Peter MEREDITH [also MOORE in body of instrument]. 88

acres, 28 poles on waters of Cheat River, adjoining Robert Ballie[?], patented to Butler 4 April 1792. Consideration: £88. Signed: Thomas Butler, Rebecca Butler. Witnesses: none. Acknowledged in court, June 1803. Del: to Meredith, 9 April 1804. Recorded: OS 3:45.

13 October 1800. Sarah JOHNSTON, widow of Patrick, William and Mary JOHNSTON, and Abraham JOHNSTON, heirs of Patrick JOHNSTON, deceased, to David GALLOWAY, Fayette Co, PA. 185 acres on Laurel Run where said widow now lives, patented to Johnston 20 July 1784, adjoining Elias Layton and Adam Helmeck. Consideration: $500. Signed: Sarah [+] Johnston, William Johnston, Mary Johnson [sic], Abraham Johnson [sic]. Witnesses: J Evans, John McClain, Russell Potter. Galloway receipts $21.50 in satisfaction of 15 acres and some rods which fell to Elias Layton's land. Acknowledged by Mary Johnston, 2 October 1801, before Russell Potter and John McClain, JPs. Acknowledged in court, October 1800, by Sarah, William, and Abraham Johnston. Del: to David Galloway, 14 September 1808. Recorded: OS 3:46.

12 December 1803. Jesse and Hannah MARTIN to John DAWSON. 36 acres on Monongahela River, adjoining Ezekiel Cox, excepting a portion included in survey for Joshua Lowe. Consideration: $72. Signed: Jesse Martin, Hannah Martin. Witnesses: none. Acknowledged in court, December 1803. Del: to Joshua Low, 14 April [?] 1807. Recorded: OS 3:47.

11 February 1803. Ralph BARKSHIRE, Morgantown, to Hugh MC NEELY, Morgantown. Deed of trust to secure payment of $1200 due on a half lot in Morgantown, now in the possession of John Stealey and where McNeely formerly lived. Barkshire to pay on or before 1 April 1806. Signed: Ralph Barkshire. Witnesses: B Reeder, J Williams, Wm Lanham, Robt Minnis. Acknowledged in court, February 1803. No delivery shown. Recorded: OS 3:48.

12 December 1803. Jesse and Hannah MARTIN to Abraham COX. 135 acres on the north fork of Indian Creek, patented to Martin 22 April 1792, adjoining Jarard Evans. Consideration: $220. Signed: Jesse Martin, Hannah Martin. Witnesses: none. Acknowledged in court, December 1803. Del: to Abraham Cox, 7 July 1804. Recorded: OS 3:49.

9 December 1793. Charles GALLAGHER to Robert FAUSET. 205 acres on Glady Creek, part of a patent for 410 acres, 18 January 1792, adjoining Absolum Little, Thomas Laidly, David Hall. Consideration: £40, VA. Signed: Chas Gallagher. Acknowledged in court, December 1793. Del: to grantee, 26 May 1817. Recorded: June 1803,

OS 3:50. Re-recording of burned instrument.

[blank] April 1803. James and Catherine ROBESON to James COLLINS. 200 acres on Indian Creek, adjoining lands once surveyed for Rev William Worth, John Mcfarland, Gilbert Butler, and Zack Barker. Consideration: £55. Signed: James Robeson, Catherine Robeson. Witnesses: Henry Dering, Dudley Evans, J Evans Jr. No acknowledgement recorded. No delivery shown. Recorded: OS 3:51.

[blank] 1801. Wildey and Mary TAYLOR to Isaac DRAPER. 84 acres on Cheat River, part of a 500 acre survey where Wildey now lives, and including Draper's improvement where he now lives. No adjoiners mentioned. Consideration: $1. Signed: Wilday Taylor [Mary does not sign]. Witnesses: none. Acknowledged by Wilday Taylor in court, September 1801. Del: to Isaac Draper, 9 April 1804. Recorded: OS 3:52.

[blank] April 1803. Joshua and Nancy LEWMAN to James CLELAND. 31½ acres on Finches Run, adjoining other lands of Cleland. Consideration: $62. Signed: Joshua Lewman, Ann [|] Lewman. Witnesses: Dudley Evans, H Dering, J Evans Junr. Acknowledged in court, June 1803. Del: to James Cleland, 21 November 1806. Recorded: OS 3:53.

14 February 1802. James and Elizabeth JEFFS to Thomas ICE. 106 acres on Mods Run, a branch of Buffalo Creek, part of the tract where John Watson now lives, adjoining Watson and James Morgan. Consideration: $212. Signed: James Jeffs, Elizabeth Jeffs. Witnesses: none. Acknowledged in court, September 1803. Del: to Ice, 19 September 1807. Recorded: OS 3:54.

12 September 1803. William and Susannah HAMILTON to William K SMITH. 100 acres on the dividing ridge between Rackoon Creek and Sandy Creek, part of a patent originally granted to Martin Harden. Consideration: £100, VA. Signed: Wm Hamilton, Susannah [mark] Hamilton. Witnesses: none. Acknowledged in court, September 1803. Del: to W K Smith, 4 October 1804. Recorded: OS 3:55.

2 March 1803. Robert and Jane BELL to William MAGEE. 120 acres on Three Fork Creek, part of a 23 August 1797 patent to Dudley Evans for 1700 acres. No adjoiners named. Consideration: $180. Signed: Robert [X] Bell, Jane [blank] Bell. Witnesses: Dudley Evans, Jacob Jones Jr, Nathan Hall. Acknowledged by Jane Bell before Dudley Evans and Nathan Hall, JPs, 22 March 1803. Proved by witnesses, April 1803. No delivery shown. Recorded: OS 3:56.

13[?] June 1803. Samuel HANWAY and John DOWNER to

Henry SINE. 340 acres on Beaver Creek. No adjoiners named. Consideration: $100. Signed: Saml Hanway, John Downer. Witnesses: none. Acknowledged in court, June 1803. Del: to Alexr Brandon, 14 March 1804. Recorded: OS 3:57.

22 March 1803. Samuel MENEAR to Jacob JONES Sr. 5 acres on Swamp Run, part of a 23 August 1797 patent to Dudley Evans for 1700 acres; conveyed by Evans to Jabish Bell, 11 January 1799, and by Bell to Menear, 21 March 1803. Consideration: $12. Signed: Samuel Menear. Witnesses: Dudley Evans, Jacob Jones Jr, Nathan Hall. Proved by witnesses, April 1803. Del: to Wm Jones, 14 April 1806. Recorded: OS 3:58.

13 June 1803. Bartholomew LOTT, late of Monongalia, by his attorney in fact Francis COLLINS, to James COLLINS. 71 acres on Indian Creek, conveyed to Lott by Gilbert Butler and adjoining Butler's other land. Consideration: $340. Signed: Francis Collins. Witnesses: none. Acknowledged in court, June 1803. No delivery shown. Recorded: OS 3:59.

12 September 1803. William and Margaret WOOD to Thomas BARNES. 62 acres, part of the tract Wood now lives on. No place names or adjoiners mentioned. Consideration: $100. Signed: William Wood, Margaret Wood. Witnesses: none. Acknowledged in court, September 1803. Del: to Thomas Barnes, 9 April 1804. Recorded: OS 3:60.

11 April 1803. William and Mary DAWSON, KY, by their attorney in fact Charles DAWSON, to Samuel EVERLY. 175 acres on headwaters of Scotts Mill Run, part of a patent to William Dawson, adjoining Philip Lewis. Consideration: £50. Signed: Charles [X] Dawson. Witnesses: none. Acknowledged in court, April 1803. Del: to Saml Everley, 23 November 1804. Recorded: OS 3:61.

2 May 1803. John and Martha SEAMAN, Hamilton Co, OH, to Jonah SEAMAN and William SEAMAN [both addressed as Sr in body of instrument], Berkley Co. 200 acres, surveyed 14 May 1790, adjoining David Sayre and Aaron Garrett. Consideration: £200, PA. Signed: John Seaman, Martha [X] Seaman. Witnesses: John Armstrong, Tabetha Armstrong, Josiah Seaman. Acknowledged in Territory of the United States Northwest of River Ohio, alious State of the Ohio [sic], before John Armstrong, JP. Certificate of John S Gans, clerk of Hamilton Co, OH. Del: to Wm Reed, 1 March 1804. Recorded: OS 3:62.

12 April 1803. Samuel and Sarah WILSON, Fayette Co, PA, to William JOBES. 78 acres on righthand fork of Maricles Run, adjoining Irwin, lands formerly claimed by

Josiah Prickett, and Henry Dorrough. Part of a patent to James Mills, 22 March 1785, conveyed by him to James Mills and Aaron Mills, 15 September 1794, and by them to Wilson on [blank]. Consideration: $160. Signed: Samuel Wilson, Sarah Wilson. Witnesses: John E Bills, Michael Core. Acknowledged in court, April 1803. Del: to Wm Jobes, 12 August 1804. Recorded: OS 3:63.

7 May 1790. Conrad HOGMIRE, Washington Co, MD, to Abraham WOODRING and Francis DEAKINS, the latter of Montgomery Co, MD. Lot #56 in town of Salem, to be used for a schoolhouse. Consideration: For encouraging the education of youth of every Christian profession, plus 10s and annual quit rent of one peppercorn, due 1 March. Signed: Conrad Hogmire. Witnesses: Adam Shafer, David Stemple, George Stough. Proved by witnesses, November 1792. Del: to Christian Whitehair, 13 July 1807. Recorded: OS 3:64. [Evidently re-recording of a burned instrument but not identified as such.]

12 December 1803. Jesse and Rachel HANWAY, Noah and Jane RIDGWAY, John and Phebee MOORE, Martha RIDGWAY, Sarah RIDGWAY, Mary RIDGWAY, and Dorcus RIDGWAY to Elihu HORTON. 6 acres on the west side of Cheat River, adjoining Daniel Barnes and Jacob Scott's survey. Part of a patent to the heirs of Lott Ridgway. Consideration: $100. Signed: Jesse Hanway, Rachael Hanway, Noah Ridgway, Jane Ridgway, John Moore, Phebee Moore, Martha Ridgway, Sarah Ridgway, Mary Ridgway, and Darcus Ridgway. Witnesses: none. Acknowledged in court, December 1803 by all but John Moore; acknowledged by Moore, February 1804. Del: to Elihu Horton, 19 February 1805. Recorded: OS 3:65.

10 November 1803. William and Lurena NORRIS, Enoch and Charity JENKINS, and Bartholomew and Susanna JENKINS to Alexander McCLELAND, Springhill Twp, Fayette Co, PA. 102 acres on the great road from Ices ferry to Rubles mill, not more than a mile from Samuel Jackson's merchant mill on Cheat River, the same tract where Enoch now lives and part of the same survey on which Norris lives. Adjoining Widow Warman, Widow Jenkins, and James Donaldson. Consideration: $1500. Signed: Wm Norris, Lurena [X] Norris, Enoch Jenkins, Charity [+] Jenkins, Barth Jenkins, Susanna Jenkins. Witnesses: E Evans, Lemuel John, Samuel Jackson, William Nixon. Acknowledged by Lurena, Charity and Susanna before E Evans and L John, JPs, 11 November 1803. Proved by witnesses, 9 April 1804. Del: to McCleld. Recorded: OS 3:66-68.

9 April 1804. Alexander and Barshabe McCLELAND, Springhill Twp, Fayette Co, PA, to Justinea MABERRY

[addressed as "he" in body of instrument], Frederick Town, Frederick Co, MD. 100 acres on the east side of Cheat, "about one mile or rather more" below the mouth of Sandy Creek, and no more than a half mile from the riverbank. Conveyed by John Leach to Joshua Wells, 12 February 1798, and by Walls to McCleland, 10 April 1803. Joshua Collins lives on the tract and has enjoyment of all the crop of small grain he has sewed down, as well as flax and oats ground, agreeable to his bargain with McCleland. No adjoiners named. Consideration: $500. Signed: Alexander McCleland, Barshabe McCleland. Witnesses: none. Acknowledged by Alexander in court, 10 April 1804; by Barshabe before Robert Richey and Zadock Springer, JPs, in Fayette Co, PA, 11 June 1804. Del: to Alexr McCleland, 13 July 1804. Recorded: OS 3:69-70.

2 June 1804. Francis DEAKINS, George Town, DC, to Charles WALLACE and John MUIR, Annapolis Co, MD. 3155 acres in two tracts. 655 acres at Cheat River, adjoining 617 acres patented to William and Francis Deakins and conveyed to Wallace Johnston and Muir. 2500 acres near the MD boundary, patented 6 May 1796, adjoining a 6000 acre patent conveyed to Wallace Johnston and Muir. Deakins conveys the land by acreage and will provide other land in the neighborhood, of equal value, should any of this be lost to elder claims or the acreage as expressed be short. Consideration: $2140, the amount of their claims against the estate of William Deakins Jr, deceased. Signed: Francis Deakins. Witnesses: John Fairfax, Frederick Harsh, Jacob Ridenour. Proved by witnesses, June 1804. Del: to John Hoye, 20 June 1804. Recorded: OS 3:71.

2 June 1804. Francis DEAKINS, George Town, DC, to John HOYE, "of the United States of America." 771 acres on the west side of Cheat at Laurel Run, north of a chain of surveys made for Claiborne and Moyland, between those surveys and the river, near the path from where Jeremiah Simpson formerly lived to Ices Ferry, about 3 miles from Simpson's old farm. Tract patented to Francis and William Deakins. Consideration: $1. Signed: Francis Deakins. Witnesses: John Fairfax, Frederick Harsh, Jacob Ridenour. Proved by witnesses, June 1804. Del: to John Hay, 20 June 1804. Recorded: OS 3:72.

26 December 1803. William SLIDGER, Alleghaney Co, MD, to David SLIDGER, Baltimore, MD. 415 acres on Booths Creek, 9 miles from Morgantown, no adjoiners named. Part of a 615 acre patent to William Tingle and conveyed by him to Slidger, 200 acres of the tract having been sold to John Stephens. Consideration: $140. On 1 April 1801

David Slidger indorsed to William a note of hand from William Taylor of Baltimore for $140 and William gave title bond at that time. Title now conveyed. Signed: William Slidger. Witness: Edw J Coale. Acknowledged 26 December 1803 before James Calhoun, mayor of Baltimore. Del: to John Slidger, 16 July 1805. Recorded: OS 3:73.

1 October 1803. Francis DEAKINS, George Town, DC, to Israel COPE and James COPE, Baltimore, MD, as tenants in common. 100 acres, no adjoiners or place names mentioned. Consideration: $50. Signed: Francis Deakins. Witnesses: Zadok Lanham, Chas Irwin, Rich Thompson. Acknowledged before Daniel Reintzel, mayor of George Town, 10 October 1803. Del: to John Stealey, 23 June 1804. Recorded: OS 3:74.

[blank] 1804. Thomas and Catherine EVANS to Robert STEWART. 200 acres on Cheat River, adjoining William John, Lemuel John, and Thomas John, patented to Thomas Evans as assignee of Robert Gallaway, 6 April 1784. Consideration: £150, VA. Signed: Thomas [mark] Evans, Catherine [+] Evans. Witnesses: none. Acknowledged in court, June 1804. Del: to Robert Stewart, 2 July 1804. Recorded: OS 3:75.

9 April 1804. Hedgman and Molly TRIPLETT, state of VA, to Frederick SPAW, York Co, PA. 777 acres in three tracts. 400 acres at Little Sandy Creek, adjoining John Scott, conveyed by David Cushman, 3 November 1797. 327 acres adjoining Thomas Cushman, near the PA line. 50 acres adjoining John Scott. Consideration: £1000, VA. Signed: Hedgman Triplett, Molly Triplett. Witnesses: James Evans, Mathew Gay, Ralph Barkshire. Acknowledged by Hedgman Triplett, April 1804. Commission to William Martin and Charles Stilwell, Harrison Co JPs, to take Molly's acknowledgement, but not recorded here. No delivery shown. Recorded: OS 3:76-77.

13 September 1803. Jacob and Unice HAMPTON to John NUZUM. Deed of trust. Jacob owes Richard Nuzum $500, payable 4 August 1807, with interest from 4 August 1803. To secure payment, Jacob conveys to John Nuzum, trustee, 250 acres known as Forshays Levels on waters of Tyger Valley River, adjoining Sparks' survey. Part of 400 acres patented to Jacob, 11 September 1789. Signed: Jacob Hampton, Eunice Hampton, Richard Nuzum, John Nuzum. Witnesses: Nimrod Evans, W Tingle, Dudley Evans. Acknowledged by Eunice Hampton before Saml Hanway and Dudley Evans, JPs, 14 February 1804. Proved by witnesses, September 1803. Del: to Richd Nuzum, 10 April 1805. Recorded: OS 3:77-80.

13 February 1804. Thomas and Cathrine DEWEESE to

Robert MANLEY. 56 acres at Scotts Meadow Run, conveyed by David Scott to the heirs of Joshua Deweese. No adjoiners named. Consideration: $400. Signed: Thos Deweese, Catherine [X] Deweese. Witnesses: none. Acknowledged in court, February 1804. No delivery shown. Recorded: OS 3:81-82.

13 February 1804. William and Lurana NORRIS to George BAKER. 104 acres adjoining Enoch Jenkins and John Ramsey, part of a larger tract patented to William. Consideration: $300. Signed: Wm Norris [Lurana does not sign]. Witnesses: none. Acknowledged by William Norris, February 1804. Commission to take Lurana's acknowledgement but not recorded here. Del: to Geo Baker, 10 [?] 1806. Recorded: OS 3:82-83.

13 February 1803. Isaac and Sarah MORGAN to Joseph HARTLEY Jr. 123 acres on Morgan Run, a branch of Bufflow Creek, adjoining Jesse Martin. Patented to William Martin, 29 July 1785. Consideration: $[blank]. Signed: Isaac Morgan, Sarah Morgan. Witnesses: none. Acknowledged in court, February 1804. Del: to Jo Hartley, 27 March 1806. Recorded: OS 3:84.

14 February 1804. Edward ELLIOT to Benjamin AYERS. 100 acres on the south side of Roaring Creek adjoining William Daugherty, part of Thomas Butler's pre-emption survey. Consideration: $300, VA. Signed: Edward Elliot. Witnesses: none. Acknowledged in court, February 1804. Del: to Benjn Ayres, 17 June 1805. Recorded: OS 3:85.

[blank] February 1804. Noah and Jane RIDGWAY to John MOOR. One undivided ninth share in 400 acres surveyed to Lott Ridgway deceased, including a sawmill on the property. Consideration: £50, VA. Signed: Noah Ridgway, Jane Ridgway. Witnesses: none. Acknowledged in court, February 1804. No delivery shown. Recorded: OS 3:86-87.

[undated, cApril 1804?] SETTLEMENT of the ESTATE of George JENKINS with Benjamin REEDER, guardian of William Norris JENKINS, heir at law to George. George's estate consisted of an old horse worth $20, two cows, a few hogs, a bed, and a Negro woman Jane, who has had a child Bess born since the death of Jenkins. Per will and bequest, this property to Martha, the widow of Jenkins, for her lifetime. Martha has since remarried to Dennis Duval. Dennis, wishing to give ample justice to his stepson William N Jenkins, gives to him a horse worth $70, a saddle and bridle, and the Negro woman Jane, whom Dennis left in Nelson Co, KY, with his brother John Lewis Duval, in lieu of the other items belonging to George Jenkins' estate. William N Jenkins, who is above

20 years of age, and his grandfather William Norris, surety for the guardian, request this settlement to be allowed and that guardian be permitted to sell Jane in KY. William N to direct the sale if he is of age competent to judge but not to act. Signed: B Reeder, Dennis [X] Duval, Wm N Norris, Wm N Jenkins. Acknowledged in court, April 1804. Recorded: OS 3:87.

26 November 1803. Allen ROBINETT, Huntingdon Twp, Adams Co, PA, to Alexander BRANDON. Power of attorney to assign over to James Donaldson all of Allen's right, title, and interest in a judgment obtained against Charles Donaldson, deceased. Signed: Allen Robinett. Witnesses: John Delap, Joseph Hewitt. Acknowledged in Adams Co, PA, before William Help, JP, 26 November 1803. Certificate of W Scott, Judge of Common Pleas, and James Duncan, Prothonotary of Adams Co. No delivery shown. Recorded: OS 3:88-89.

9 April 1804. William and Elizabeth STEWART to Charles STEWART. 400 acres near Camp Run on Cheat River, adjoining Henry Crull and lands formerly claimed by Thomas Evans and Thomas Mills, and William Stewart's home and middle plantations. Consideration: love and affection for their son. Signed: William [X] Stewart. [Elizabeth does not sign.] Witnesses: none. Acknowledged in court by William Stewart, April 1804. Del: to Charles Stewart, 13 February 1809. Recorded: OS 3:89-90.

10 March 1804. Luke HARMONSON to John DIGMAN. 34 acres on Scotts Mill Run, adjoining James Buckhannon. Sold by Buckhannon to Thomas Bevan and now in Bevan's possession. Consideration: $200. Signed: Luke Harmonson. Witnesses: Ralph Barkshire, Davis Shockley, Jacob Kiger. Proved by witnesses, April 1804. Del: to John Digman, 15 May 1805. Recorded: OS 3:91-92.

21 March 1803. Jabish and Patty BELL to Samuel MENEAR. 100 acres on Swamp Run, adjoining heirs of Theophilus Philips, part of a 23 August 1797 patent to Dudley Evans for 1700 acres. Consideration: $200. Signed: Jabish [X] Bell, Martha Bell. Witnesses: Dudley Evans, Jacob Jones Jr, Nathan Hall. Acknowledged by Martha Bell before Dudley Evans and Nathan Hall, 22 March 1803. Proved by witnesses, April 1804. Del: to Wm Jones, 19 November 1807. Recorded: OS 3:92-94.

22 January 1804. WILL of Sarah ROBE. Daughters Mary Stewart and Sarah Sutton: $10 each. Sons David and Robert: $10 each. Granddaughter Sarah Stewart: cow. Granddaughter Sarah Robe: woman's saddle. Granddaughter Nancy Stewart: $20, clothing, other personalty. Son Josiah: all remaining property. Executor: son Josiah.

Signed: Sarah Robe. Witnesses: Paul Vandervourt, Marsh M Duvall. Proven April 1804. Recorded: OS 3:94-95. [Also recorded in Wills, 1:312.]

11 October 1803. Joseph BUTLER to Joseph SOVERNS. Power of attorney to transact all business in the Commonwealth of VA. Signed: Joseph [J] Butler. Witnesses: Wm G Payne, Saml Hanway. Proved by witnesses, April 1804. Recorded: OS 3:95.

8 March 1804. Edward and Sary HAYMOND to John HAYMOND Jr. 170 acres on Wickwares Creek, no adjoiners named. Part of a 1 August 1786 patent for 400 acres. Consideration: $300. Signed: Edward Haymond, Sarah Haymond. Witnesses: Jacob Jones Jr, William George, John Jones. Proved by witnesses, April 1804. Del: to John Haymond, 23 December 1805. Recorded: OS 3:96-97.

9 April 1804. William and Elizabeth STEWART to Charles STEWART. 4 acres, adjoining the schoolhouse place, Daniel Cox, and the home and middle places. No place names mentioned. Consideration: £[blank]. Signed: William [X] Stewart [Elizabeth does not sign]. Witnesses: none. Acknowledged by William Stewart, April 1804. Del: to Charles Stewart, 13 February 1805. Recorded: OS 3:97-98.

13 February 1804. Samuel HANWAY to Nicholas VANDERVORT. 7½ acres on the road from Morgan Town to Ices ferry, adjoining Vandervort's other land and Francis Tibbs. Consideration: £5, VA. Signed: Saml Hanway. Witnesses: none. Acknowledged in court, February 1804. Del: to N Vandervort, 18 September 1806. Recorded: OS 3:98-99.

21 March 1803. Samuel and Hannah MORTON to Jacob CHISLER. ¼ acre, 30 poles on bank of Big Sandy Creek. No adjoiners named. Consideration: $14.58. Signed: Samuel Morton, Hannah Morton. Witnesses: Alexr Brandon, John Gribble, Jonath Brandon. Acknowledged by Hannah Morton before Saml Hanway and John McClain, JPs, 12 September 1803. Proved by witnesses, September 1803. Del: to Chisler, 29 October 1805. Recorded: OS 3:100-102.

30 April 1804. John FORGUSON, Ohio Co, KY, by Nicholas BAKER, his attorney in fact, to William LANHAM. Unspecified acreage on Deckers Creek, tract which descended to John from his sister Peggy Ferguson, deceased. Baker operates under a power of attorney of 23 April 1803, and recorded in Breckinridge Co, KY. Consideration: $130. Signed: Nicholas Baker. Witnesses: none. Acknowledged by Baker in Breckinridge Co, KY, 30 April 1804. Certificate of Jo Allen, county clerk. Del: to Wm Lanham, 22 February 1805. Recorded: OS 3:102-103.

9 June 1804. Sias BILLINGSLEY to William BILLINGSLEY. 108 acres on Scotts Run, adjoining Christopher Raver and John Ramsey. Consideration: $50. Signed: Sias Billingsley. Witnesses: Geo Greenwood, Robt Minnis, Enoch Evans. Acknowledged in court, June 1804. Del: to J Dent, 19 November 1805. Recorded: OS 3:103-104.

23 April 1803. John FERGUSON to Nicholas BAKER. Power of attorney to convey a tract on Deckers Creek descended to Ferguson from his sister Peggy. Signed: John Ferguson. Acknowledged 23 April 1803 in Breckinridge Co, KY, before John Walker, JP. Certificate of Joseph Allen, county clerk. Del: to Wm Lanham, 22 February 1805. Recorded: OS 3:105.

2 April 1804. Matthias HITE to George HITE. One half of 243 acres on Cobuns Creek, purchased by Matthias and George from Francis Burrel Jr, 10 March 1800. No adjoiners named. Consideration: $500. Signed: Mtt Hite. Witnesses: Wm G Payne, Henry Dering, George S Dering. Proved by witnesses, June 1804. Del: to M Gay Esq, 4 December 1816. Recorded: OS 3:106.

9 June 1804. Samuel HANWAY to John STEALEY. One equal third of two tracts. 496 acres on Deckers Creek, adjoining Joseph Wilson, John Reed, Goosman, William McCleery, and McIntire. 48 acres adjoining Jacob Goosman. Consideration: $5000. Signed: Saml Hanway. Witnesses: none. Acknowledged in court, June 1804. Del: to him, 24 April 1812. Recorded: OS 3:107-108.

11 June 1804. Elisha and Elizabeth CLAYTON to Henry AMOS Jr. 94 acres, adjoining William Jenkins and Jesse Cherry. Part of a 400 acre tract where Amos now lives. Consideration: $237. Signed: Elisha Clayton, Elizabeth [X] Clayton. Witnesses: none. Acknowledged in court, June 1804. Del: to Henry Amos Jr, 30 January 1806. Recorded: OS 3:109.

10 May 1804. Thomas CHADWICK, Middleton, Washington Co, OH, to Noah ARNOLD, Marietia [sic], Washington Co, OH. Power of attorney to convey or to lease or rent $72\frac{1}{2}$ acres in Monongalia, purchased by Chadwick from John Stagg. Signed: Thomas Chadwick. Witnesses: Betsey Putnam, David Putnam. Acknowledged in Mariatta [sic], OH, before John Brough, JP, 10 May 1804. Certificate of Nathl Gates for Edward M Tupper, Washington Co clerk. No delivery shown. Recorded: OS 3:110-111.

9 July 1804. James and Catharine ROBINSON to James ARNETT Sr. 30 acres at Indian Creek, part of a larger tract adjoining James Arnett, heirs of John Stewart, and Gilbert Butler. Consideration: £15. Signed: Jas Robison,

Catharine Robinson. Witnesses: none. Acknowledged in court, July 1804. Del: to James Arnett, 12 May 1806. Recorded: OS 3:111-112.

8 August 1785. Jacob and Dianah JONES to Hugh McNEELY. 200 acres on Morgans Run, adjoining Richard Falls and John Scott. Patented to Jones, 22 March 1785. Consideration: £30, VA. Signed: Jacob Jones, Dianah [X] Jones. Witnesses: none. Acknowledged in court, August 1785. Del: to Mrs McNeely, 27 May 1805. Recorded: OS 3:113-114. Re-recording of burned instrument.

13 February 1786. Zackquill and Drusilla MORGAN to Hugh McNEELY. 34 acres adjoining Benjamin Jennings, Thos Laidley, Michael Karns. Part of a larger tract patented 7 April 1784. Consideration: £60, VA. Signed: Zackll Morgan, Drusella Morgan. Witnesses: none. Acknowledged in court, February 1786. Del: to Mrs McNeely, 27 May 1805. Recorded: OS 3:114-115. Re-recording of burned instrument.

13 February 1786. Zackquill and Drusilla MORGAN to Hugh McNEELY. Lots #89 and 106 in Morgan Town. Consideration: £10, VA. Signed: Zackll Morgan, Drusilla Morgan. Witnesses: none. Acknowledged in court, February 1786. Del: to Mrs McNeely, 27 May 1805. Recorded: OS 3:116-117. Re-recording of burned instrument.

11 June 1804. Elisha and Elizabeth CLAYTON to John W PATTERSON. 316 acres on Indian Creek, adjoining James Holtsclaw, formerly Gilbert Butler, William Stewart, John McFarland, Nathan Thomas, and John Stewart. Consideration: $395. Signed: Elisha Clayton, Elizabeth [X] Clayton. Witnesses: none. Acknowledged in court, July 1804. Del: to John W Patterson, 17 June[?] 1809. Recorded: OS 3:118.

9 July 180[blank]. James and Catharine ROBISON to John THOMPSON. 50 acres on Robisons Run, adjoining Grafton White, John Thompson, William Augustus Smith, Amos Smith, and Robert Hamilton. Consideration: £20, VA. Signed: Jas Robison, Catharine Robison. Witnesses: none. Acknowledged in court, July 1804. Del: to John Thompson, 20 January 1806. Recorded: OS 3:119.

9 July 1804. James and Catharine ROBISON to Robert FULLERTON. 62 acres on Indian Creek, adjoining Fullerton's other land, Andrew Arnett, John Smith, Cornelius Lynch, and former land of David Scott and Frederick Gire. Consideration: £40. Signed: Jas Robison, Catharine Robison. Witnesses: none. Acknowledged in court, July 1804. Del: to Mrs[?] Fullerton, September 1805. Recorded: OS 3:120.

9 July 1804. James and Catharine ROBISON to John

SMITH. 55 acres on Stone Cole Lick Run, a branch of Indian Creek, adjoining Gilbert Butler, Andrew Arnett, Robert Fullerton, and Cornelius Lynch. Consideration: £12. Signed: Jas Robison, Catharine Robison. Witnesses: none. Acknowledged in court, July 1804. Del: to John Smith, 10 October 1808. Recorded: OS 3:121.

9 July 1804. Samuel HANWAY to John DENT. 18½ acres, no place names or adjoiners mentioned. Consideration: [blank]. Signed: Saml Hanway. Witnesses: none. Acknowledged in court, July 1804. Del: to John Dent, 7 July 1809. Recorded: OS 3:122.

8 April 1793. Robert ERVIN to William BENSON. 98 acres at Beaver Creek. No adjoiners mentioned. Consideration: £20, VA. Signed: Robert [X] Ervin, Mary [X] Ervin [Mary is not named in the deed]. Witnesses: John Runyon, Jacob Wolf. Proved by witnesses, April 1794. Del: to Alexr Brandon, 10 October 1804. Recorded: OS 3:123-124. Re-recording of burned instrument.

21 August 1804. William N JARRETT to Benjamin HELLEN. Half of a lot in Morgantown [# not shown], on the east side of High Street, adjoining John Davis' brick house and where Nimrod Evans now lives. Consideration: $300. Quit rent of 25¢ per annum to heirs of Zackquill Morgan, deceased. Signed: William N Jarrett. Witnesses: Henry Dering, E Daugherty, Ralph Barkshire. Acknowledged in court, September 1804. Del: to Benjamin Hellen, December 1805. Recorded: OS 3:124-125.

9 April 1804. Luke and Easter HARMONSON to William POSTLETHWAIT. 103 acres on Scotts Mill Run, adjoining David Shockley's and William Hougue's parts of the same survey. From a 400 acre patent to Nune Howard. Consideration: [$£?]300. Signed: Luke Harmosno [sic], Easter Harmeson. Witnesses: none. Acknowledged in court, April 1804. Del: to grantee, 12 September 1818. Recorded: OS 3:125-126.

4 December 1802. William and Nancy HOULT, Harrison Co, to Edward HAYMOND. 100 acres on Wickwares Creek, where Haymond now lives. Conveyed by Haymond [?] to James Hickman, Frederick Co, and by him to Hoult. Consideration: $200. Signed: William Hoult, Nancy [mark] Hoult. Witnesses: Reynear Hall, James Morgan, James Miller. Proved by witnesses, January 1803. Del: to Edward Haymond, 15 May 1805. Recorded: OS 3:127.

19 March 1803. Aaron and Catherine POWELL to William Norris JENKINS. 136 acres, no place names mentioned. From a 476 acre patent, the remaining 340 acres of which has been sold to Thomas Fretwell.

Consideration: $300. Signed: Aaron Powell, Catherine [X] Powell. Witnesses: Wm G Payne, John W Dean, Elihu Horton. Acknowledged in court, April 1803. No delivery shown. Recorded: OS 3:128.

27 June 1802. Elihu HORTON to John WILSON. 50 acres, no adjoiners or place names mentioned. Consideration: £50. Signed: Elihu Horton. Witnesses: J Evans, Henry Dering, John Scott. Proved by witnesses, April 1803. Del: to John Wilson, 3 June 1809. Recorded: OS 3:129.

28 January 1804. John DAVIS to William N JARRETT. Deed of trust. To secure a debt of $200, with interest, due to Reed and Fordes store, Davis conveys the lot and building in Morgantown where he now lives. If the debt is not paid, the property to be sold. Signed: John Davis, Wm N Jarrett. Witnesses: Rolla Evans, Ben Williams, Mathew Gay. Proved by witnesses, September 1804 and [blank] 1805. Del: to Wm N Jarrett, 16 August 1806. Recorded: OS 3:130-131.

31 October 1804. John and Isabella DAVIS to James DAVIS, Lancaster Co, PA. 626¼ acres on Little Sandy Creek, adjoining Robert Sevear. Part of a 2000 acre survey. Consideration: $2000. Signed: John Davis [Isabella does not sign]. Witnesses: William N Jarrett, Wm McCleery, Nimrod Evans, Henry Dering. Proved by witnesses, December 1804. Del: by post, 5 January 1805. Recorded: OS 3:131-132.

14 January 1805. Thomas and Mary MILLER to P [full name not shown in this instrument] BERGDOLL and Jacob BERGDOLL, Washington Co, MD. 500 acres on Booths Creek, patented to Miller and William Tingle, 9 December 1798. Tingle's moiety conveyed to Miller, 18 May 1803. Adjoining William Robe Jr's survey, Tingle and Miller's other land. Consideration: $1000. Signed: Thomas Miller, Mary [|] Miller. Witnesses: J Evans Jr, Abraham Carver, E Daugherty. Acknowledged in court, January 1805. Del: to A McCleland, 5 July 1805. Recorded: OS 3:133-134.

14 January 1805. John (Jr) and Gilly C EVANS to Michael HOLLOMS, Washington Co, MD. 800 acres on Three Forks, adjoining Josiah Wilson, Dudley Evans, James Current, Valentine Merryweather, Col John Evans survey. Patented to John Evans, 11 July 1803. Consideration: $1600. Signed: J Evans Jr, Gilly C Evans. Witnesses: J Clark, Nimrod Evans, Jno Stealey. Acknowledged in court, January 1805. Del: to Alexr McCleland, 5 February 1805. Recorded: OS 3:135-136.

14 January 1805. John (Jr) and Gilly C EVANS to Philip STERN and John HOLLENGER, Washington Co, MD. No

acreage stated, on headwaters of Flat Run, a branch of Tygers Valley River, adjoining George Wilson, John Wickware, Dudley Evans, Theophilus Philips' heirs. Patented to Evans, 11 July 1803. Consideration: $800. Signed: J Evans Jr, Gilly C Evans. Witnesses: John Clark, Nimrod Evans, Jno Stealey. Acknowledged in court, January 1805. Del: to Alexr McCleland, 5 February 1805. Recorded: OS 3:137-138.

 14 January 1805. Alexander and Barshabe McCLELAND, Fayette Co, PA, to John YONG, Washington Co, MD. 50 acres on Cheat River, adjoining Joseph Lamberth and Ignatious Butler survey. Patented to John Ramsey. Consideration: $550. Signed: Alexander McCleland, Barshabe [X] McCleland. Witnesses: Jno Stealey, J Evans Jr, John Clark, Nimrod Evans. Acknowledged in court, January 1805. Del: to Alexr McCleland, 5 February 1805. Recorded: OS 3:139-140.

 14 January 1805. Alexander and Barsheba McCLELAND, Fayette Co, PA, to Henry BRAUCHMYER, Washington Co, MD. 102 acres in Cheat River neck, about a mile from the river, adjoining surveys of Warman, Jenkins, Norris, and Donaldson. Consideration: $1224. Signed: Alexander McCleland, Barshabe McCleland. Witnesses: Jno Stealey, J Evans Jr, John Clark, Nimrod Evans. Acknowledged in court, January 1805. Del: to A McCleland, 5 February 1805. Recorded: OS 3:141-142.

 14 January 1805. James and Ann CLELAND to Martin KEASAR, Washington Co, MD. 100 acres on Buffalo Creek, adjoining William Wood, John Webb, and Jacob Strait's heirs. Patented to Cleland, 15 August 1799. Consideration: $200. Signed: James Cleland, Ann Cleland. Witnesses: Jno Stealey, J Evans Jr, John Clark, Nimrod Evans. Acknowledged in court, January 1805. Del: to Alex McCleland, 5 February 1805. Recorded: OS 3:143-144.

 15 January 1805. John CLARK to Alexander McCLELAND, both of Fayette Co, PA. 182 acres on Sandy Creek, no adjoiners named. Patented to Theophilus Phillips, 17 May 1787. His will authorized his wife Ann to sell the land, and she conveyed to John Clark, 3 May 1796. Consideration: $750. Signed: John Clark. Witnesses: Jno Stealey, J Evans Jr, Nimrod Evans. Acknowledged in court, January 1805. Del: to Alexr McCleland, 5 February 1805. Recorded: OS 3:145-146.

 11 February 1805. Dudley and Annarah EVANS to Jacob MILLER, Washington Co, MD. 480 acres on the north side of Three Forks, adjoining Richard Merrifield's survey. Patented to Dudley, 7 October 1789. Consideration: $1000. Signed: Dudley Evans, Annarah Evans. Witnesses: H

Reeder, Wm Tingle, Abraham Carver. Acknowledged in court, February 1805. Del: to A McCleland, 5 February 1805. Recorded: OS 3:146-147.

21 April 1802. Jacob and Abigail MINTHORN to William JOHNSON. Power of attorney to convey to John Haston [?] 65 acres at Deep Hollow Run of Muddy Creek, and 50 acres to Samuel Crane, adjoining the land Crane now lives on, and to assign a plat of resurvey unto Crane for the tract on which he now lives. Signed: Jacob Minthorn, Abigail Minthorn. Witnesses: Samuel Crane, Elijah Gadd. Proved by witnesses, October 1804. Del: to Wm Johnson, Esq, 7 March 1805. Recorded: OS 3:149.

13 February 1804. William and Hannah CHIPPS to Edward EVANS. 53 acres on the Monongahela River, adjoining Edward Evans Sr, Edward Evans Jr, and Chipps' other lands. Consideration: $100. Signed: William Chipps, Hannah [0] Chipps. Witnesses: none. Acknowledged in court, February 1805. Del: to E Evans, 30 March 1805. Recorded: OS 3:150.

2 June 1804. Francis DEAKINS, George Town, DC, to Conrad HOLSTINE. 91 acres, no adjoiners or place names mentioned. From a 102 acre patent to William and Francis Deakins. Originally conveyed by Francis and William to Holstine, the deed later burned in the clerk's office. Consideration: $1. Signed: Francis Deakins. Witnesses: John Fairfax, Jacob Ridenour, Frederick Harsh. Proved by witnesses, June 1804. Del: to Holstine, 8 April 1805. Recorded: OS 3:151.

2 June 1804. David STEMPLE and Abraham WOODRING, executors of Godfrey STEMPLE, deceased, to Conrad HOLSTINE. 69 acres, no adjoiners or place names mentioned. Part of a 1000 acres conveyed to Godfrey by Francis and William Deakins in his lifetime; this portion from a 152 acre patent to the Deakins brothers. Conveyed by Godfrey in his lifetime to Holstine but the deed afterwards burned and the executors reconvey to make good the title. Consideration: $1. Signed: David Stemple, Abraham Woodring. Witnesses: John Fairfax, Jacob Ridenour, Frederick Harsh. Proved by witnesses, June 1804. Del: to C Holstine 8 April 1805. Recorded: OS 3:152.

2 June 1804. David and Margret RIDENOUR, Randolph Co, to Abraham WOODRING Jr. 150 [?] acres, part of 800 acres patented to Thomas Goff, adjoining Woodring's bridge and land conveyed to Ridenour by Francis Deakins. Consideration: $500. Signed: David Ridenour, Margret [+] Ridenour. Witnesses: John Fairfax, Frederick Harsh, Jacob Ridenour. Acknowledged by Margret Ridenour before

John Fairfax and Frederick Harsh, JPs, 11 June 1804. Proved by witnesses, June 1804. Del: to F Harsh, 9 April 1805. Recorded: OS 3:153-154.

2 June 1804. William and Sarah ASHBY, Allegany Co, MD, to Michael WILT. 190½ acres, no adjoiners or place names mentioned. Part of an 800 acre patent to Ashby. Consideration: $200. Signed: William Ashby, Sarah Ashby. Witnesses: John Fairfax, Frederick Harsh, Jacob Ridenour. Acknowledged by Sarah Ashby before John Fairfax and Frederick Harsh, JPs, 11 June 1804. Proved by witnesses, June 1804. Del: to Wilt, 17 May 1805. Recorded: OS 3:154-155.

15 March 1804. Jacob KUHN, Fredericksburg, Spotsylvania Co, to Thomas A TAYLOR, Chesterfield Co. Mortgage on four 1000 acre tracts near Salt Lick Creek, adjoining Stephen Masters, assignee of James Stall. Kuhn is to make annual payments per his bonds. Consideration: $2570. Signed: Jacob Kuhn. Witnesses: Wm Hernden, Wm Tisdale, Benjamin Ellis. Acknowledged in Fredericksburg, 22 October 1804. Certificate of N Chew, clerk. Del: to Wm G Payne, 24 May 1805. Recorded: OS 3:156-157.

8 October 1804. Thomas and Sarah MARTIN to James BRANT. 105 acres at the Ministers Run, adjoining Gallatine, where Martin now lives. Consideration: $420. Signed: Thomas Martin, Sarah [X] Martin. Witnesses: none. Acknowledged in court, October 1804. Del: to James Briant, 8 July 1805. Recorded: OS 3:158.

19 July 1804. Alexander HAWTHORN to Thomas WILSON. Deed of trust. Hawthorn owes $2000 to William Davison of Winchester, VA. To secure payment, he conveys in trust five parcels. 300 acres in the Dunkard Bottom settlement, adjoining James Port, conveyed to Hawthorn by William W Burris, part of a big survey. 50 acres in the forks of Laurel Run, a branch of Big Sandy Creek, conveyed by Moses and Elizabeth Matheny. 4 acres adjoining the northeast corner of Morgan Town, conveyed by Joseph and Mary Lane. A lot in Morgan Town, adjoining Widow Foster's residence, conveyed by John Doyle and wife. A lot on Water Street in Morgan Town, adjoining John Sullivan and opposite Nicholas Madera, conveyed by Asa Dudley. Payment to be made by 25 November 1804 or the lands sold. Signed: Alexr Hawthorn, W Davison, Thos Wilson. Witnesses: E Daugherty, W Tingle, John Chisler. Proved by witnesses, December 1804. No delivery shown. Recorded: OS 3:159-160.

1 April 1805. James DAUGHERTY to Enos DAUGHERTY, M.D. 200 acres in Wood, formerly Harrison, Co, on Stilwell Creek, patented to James Daugherty 11 September

1799. No adjoiners named. Consideration: $675, VA. Signed: James Daugherty. Acknowledged in court, April 1805. Del: to James Pindell, 28 May 1808 [?]. Recorded: OS 3:161.

9 February 1804. Benjamin and Eleanor REEDER to Thomas COURTNEY. 250 acres, adjoining David Scott, where Courtney now lives. Consideration: $365, VA. Signed: B Reeder, Eler Reeder. Acknowledged in court, February 1804. Del: to Thos Courtney, 22 August 1805. Recorded: OS 3:162.

24 January 1805. Thomas CLARE, Fayette Co, PA, to John SAVARY, Bourbon Co, KY. 400 acres at Lick Run and Cheat River, patented to Clare 25 January 1787 as assignee of John Salzer's settlement right. Consideration: 5s, PA. Signed: Thos Clare. Witnesses: E Evans, Rawley Evans, James Evans, Nimrod Evans. Proved by witnesses, February 1805. No delivery shown. Recorded: OS 3:163.

10 December 1804. Andrew and Mary DAUGHERTY to Gawen EDDY. 100 acres adjoining Peter Haught and Michael Myers. Patented to Daugherty 22 August 1797. Consideration: $100. Signed: Andrew Dehorthy [sic], Mary Dehorthy. Witnesses: none. Acknowledged in court, December 1805. Del: to Gawen Eddy, 6 June 1805. Recorded: OS 3:164.

13 October 1803. David and Hannah DUNHAM to Nicholas WEAVER. 32½ acres adjoining Simon Kratzer and Dunham's other land. Consideration: $150. Signed: David Dunham [Hannah does not sign]. Witnesses: none. Acknowledged in court by David, October 1803. Commission to take Hannah's acknowledgement, but not recorded here. Del: to N Weaver, 26 June 1805. Recorded: OS 3:165.

13 February 1804. James and Elizabeth BOOTH, Harrison Co, to Isaac MORGAN. 123 acres on Morgans Run, a branch of Buffaloe Creek, adjoining Jesse Martin. Patented to William Martin. Consideration: $[blank]. Signed: James Booth [Elizabeth does not sign]. Witnesses: Saml Swearingen, Michael Wilson, John Merrifield. Acknowledged by Elizabeth Booth in Harrison Co, before John Righter and Daniel Davisson, JPs, 10 November 1804. Proved by witnesses, June 1804. No delivery shown. Recorded: OS 3:166-167.

9 February 1804. Benjamin and Eleanor REEDER to John COURTNEY. 205 acres, adjoining John Ramsey and Thomas Lazzell, where Courtney now lives. Consideration: $364, VA. Signed: B Reeder, Elr Reeder. Witnesses: none. Acknowledged in court, February 1804. Del: to Courtney, 12 Sept [?] 1807. Recorded: OS 3:168.

10 October 1804. Jacob HARROW, Harrison Co, to James NEELY. 214 acres adjoining David Scott, David Watkins, William Watkins, Philip Shively, and Jacob Scott. Consideration: £100. Signed: Jacob Harrow. Witnesses: John Dent, George Brand, Rawley Martin. Proved by witnesses, December 1804 and April 1805. Del: to Joseph Neely, 2 January 1806. Recorded: OS 3:169.

14 July 1804. Francis DEAKINS, no address stated, executor of William DEAKINS Jr, to George OFFUTT, of KY. 150 acres on the west side of Cheat, a little above the Dunkard Bottom. No adjoiners named. Patented to John P Duvall, 1 August 1786, and conveyed by him to Francis and William Deakins, 21 November 1796. Consideration: $200, the amount of Offutt's claim against the estate of William Deakins. Signed: Francis Deakins. Witnesses: Danl Reintzel, Chas Wayman. Acknowledged in George Town, DC. Certificate of Daniel Reintzel, mayor. No delivery shown. Recorded: OS 3:170.

8 August 1801. Peter and [blank] FORTNEY to Jacob ZINN. 25 acres, adjoining Fortney's other land. Consideration: $50. Signed: Peter Fortney [unnamed wife does not sign]. Witnesses: George Zinn, John Zinn, William Zinn. Proved by witnesses, January 1802, December 1804. Del: to Jacob Zinn, 18 May 1808 [?]. Recorded: OS 3:171.

2 November 1802. Henry and Alsha HAWK, Hampshire Co, to Nicholas CASEY. 396 acres on waters of Yohogania, including Hawk's 1774 settlement claim, adjoining Gene [?] Beattie, Levi Beattie, George Beattie. Patented 1 October 1784. Consideration: £100, VA. Signed: Henry Hawk, Alsha Hawk. Witnesses: Peter Casey, Samuel Postlethwait, Wm Price. Commission to take acknowledgement of Alsha Hawk, but not recorded here. Proved by witnesses, October 1804. Del: to Elijah Butler, 2 July 1806. Recorded: OS 3:172-173.

2 April 1805. Philip and Mary DODDRIDGE, Washington Co, PA, to John EVANS. Power of attorney to convey two tracts in Monongalia and to relinquish Mary's dower in said land. 400 acres and 500 acres, both on Dunkard Creek, adjoining Phineas Killum and the PA state line, patented 10 October 1786, to be conveyed to Stephen Styles. Signed: Philip Doddridge, Mary [+] Doddridge. Witnesses: none. Acknowledged in Brooke Co, April 1805, before Geo Hammond and Francis McGuire, JPs. Del: to Stephen Stiles, 9 July 1805. Recorded: OS 3:174.

10 June 1805. Philip and Mary DODDRIDGE, Washington Co, PA, by John EVANS, their attorney in fact, to Stephen STYLES. 900 acres in two tracts on Dunkard

Creek, adjoining Phineas Killam. Patented to Philip Doddridge 10 October 1786. Consideration: $900. Signed: John Evans. Witnesses: none. Acknowledged in court, June 1805. Del: to Stephen Stiles, 9 July 1805. Recorded: OS 3:174-175.

10 June 1805. Jacob DONALDSON, address not stated, by James DONALDSON, his attorney in fact, to Henry MARTIN, Fayette Co, PA. 189 acres in Blackburns Glade on waters of Big Sandy, adjoining Daniel McCollum. Part of a tract divided by court order among the heirs of Charles Donaldson, deceased. Consideration: $189. Signed: James [X] Donaldson. Witnesses: none. Acknowledged in court, June 1805. Del: to Nichs Chisler, July 1805. Recorded: OS 3:176.

8 July 1805. John and Prudence STEALEY to Daniel LANCE, Allegheny Co, MD. 539 acres at Sandy Creek, conveyed by the heirs of Richard Morris and by Henry Hazle. No adjoiners named. Consideration: $2000. Signed: Jno Stealey, Prudence Stealey. Witnesses: none. Acknowledged in court, July 1805. Del: to John Stealey, 10 July 1805. Recorded: OS 3:177.

4 August 1803. Silas and Susanna LORD, city, county, and state of NY, to John STEALEY. Lot #84 in Morgan Town. Consideration: $500. Signed: Silas Lord, Susanna Lord. Witnesses: G C Verplanck, Benj Tucker Jr. Acknowledged in New York City, 6 August 1803. Certificate of Edward Livingston, mayor. Del: to him, 24 April 1812. Recorded: OS 3:178.

14 February 1802. Jacob and Elizabeth NOOS to John STEALEY. 300 acres on the south side of Deckers Creek, adjoining Anthony Carroll, William Barmejam's survey, Henry Crull, William McCleery. Consideration: $300. Signed: Jacob Nusz "signed in Dutch" [Elizabeth does not sign]. Witnesses: none. Acknowledged in court by Jacob Noos, February 1803. Del: to him, 24 April 1812. Recorded: June 1805, as to Jacob Noos, OS 3:179.

21 [?] August 1804. Benjamin HELLEN to Nimrod EVANS, trustee. Deed of trust. Hellen is indebted to William N Jarrett by four notes, three payable in Rorain [?] hats, the other for $20 [total amount of indebtedness not stated]. He conveys, in trust, his part of lot #39 in Morgan Town. Signed: Benjamin Hellen, Nimrod Evans. Witnesses: Henry Dering, E Daugherty, Ralph Barkshire. Acknowledged in court, February 1805. No delivery shown. Recorded: OS 3:180-181.

12 March 1805. Henry and Sarah HAZLE to John STEALEY. Acreage not stated, adjoining Thomas Cheney, Zebulon Hogue, Gabriel Gratehouse, and Richard Morris.

Consideration: $100. Signed: Henry Hazel, Sarah [mark] Hazle. Witnesses: Wm G Payne, Thos R Chipps, Jas Pindall (all as to Henry Hazle). Acknowledged by Sarah Hazle, 8 April 1805, before John McClain and J Clark, JPs. Proved by witness Chipps, July 1805. Del: to him, 24 April 1812. Recorded: OS 3:182-183.

10 September 1804. Charles and Jean STEWART to David PICKSLER. 7½ acres where Picksler now lives, near the great road from Morgan Town to Cheat River, adjoining Daniel Stewart. Part of a larger tract patented to Charles Stewart. Consideration: £60. Signed: Charles Stewart, Jean Stewart. Witnesses: none. Acknowledged in court, September 1804. Del: to Robert Henderson, 17 July 1805. Recorded: OS 3:184.

20 May 1804. Mary MORRISS, widow and relict of Richard MORRISS, Maurice MORRISS, Joseph and Rachel ROBINETT, Samuel and Catherine SPURGEN, and Andrew and Mary McCREERY, all of Bourbon Co, KY, heirs of Richard MORRISS deceased, to John STEALEY. Quit claim deed. Whereas Henry Hazle has obtained a decree in Monongalia court vs Richard Morriss, since deceased, for 547 acres on Sandy Creek, and Hazle has sold 400 acres thereof to Stealey, Morris' heirs now release the land to Stealey. 400 acres adjoining Thomas Cheney, Samuel Worrel Jr, E Frazee, and Daniel Gratehouse heirs. Consideration: 5s. Signed: Morris Moris, Joseph Robinett, Rachel Robinett, Samuel Spurgen, Catharine Spurgen, Andrew McCreery, Mary McCreery [Mary Morriss does not sign]. Witnesses: none. Acknowledged in Bourbon Co, KY, 20 August 1804, before Thomas Rule and Thomas Hughs, JPs. Certificates of William Garrard, clerk, and George Edwards, presiding justice. Del: to him, 24 April 1812. Recorded: OS 3:185-186.

9 April 1805. Elihu HORTON to Russel POTTER. Several parcels. 200 acres in the fork of Roaring Creek, adjoining the east side of Thomas Chipps' land; patented to Horton, 16 December 1799. 150 acres on the ridge between Roaring Creek and Drapers Run, including lands formerly claimed by London, and adjoining William Roberts; patented 14 December 1799. 1270 acres on the two main forks of Roaring Creek, adjoining Elihu Horton, William Hilton, and Henry Lewis; patented to John Davis and Elihu Horton, 20 November 1800, Davis' half having been conveyed to Horton since. Half of a 1500 acre tract on the main fork of Roaring Creek, adjoining William Hilton and an entry of John Davis and Elihu Horton; patented 19 August 1799 to Jonathan Davis and Elihu Horton. 6 acres on the bank of Cheat River, adjoining

Daniel Barnes. Consideration: $2000. Signed: E Horton. Witnesses: Wm G Payne, John Fairfax, Alexr Brandon. Acknowledged in court, April 1805. Del: to Russel Potter, 7 September 1805. Recorded: OS 3:187.

12 February 1805. Samuel and Rachel SMITH to John LIMING. 72 acres on Scotts Mill Run, adjoining William Dawson's lands that was. Consideration: $300. Signed: Samuel Smyth, Rachel Smyth. Witnesses: none. Acknowledged in court, February 1805. Del: to [?] Liming, 10 August 1805. Recorded: OS 3:188.

13 December 1804. Daniel and Isabella JOHNSON to Barney JOHNSON, state of PA. 44 acres on the west side of White Day Creek, adjoining Robison Lucas, part of 400 acres patented to Henry Weaver, 7 December 1793. Consideration: £70. Signed:Daniel [mark] Johnson, Isabella [X] Johnson. Witnesses: none. Acknowledged in court, December 1804. Del: to Danl Johnson, 2 September 1805. Recorded: OS 3:189.

10 December 1804. Nicholas and Margret WEAVER to Barney JOHNSON, state of PA. 69½ acres, 24 poles, at White Day Creek, from a 7 December 1793 patent. No adjoiners named. Consideration: $345. Signed: Nicholas [mark] Weaver, Margret [+] Weaver. Witnesses: none. Acknowledged in court, December 1804. Del: to D Johnson, 2 September 1805. Recorded: OS 3:190.

14 September 1789. John and Mary BURK to Godfrey GOOSMAN. 32 acres on Aarons Creek, adjoining Peter Switzer. Consideration: £20, VA. Signed: John Burk, Mary Burk. Witnesses: none. No acknowledgement recorded. Del: to G Goosman, 6 November 1805. Recorded: OS 3:191. Re-recording of burned instrument.

8 November 1793. Joseph and Margret TRICKETT to Godfrey GOOSMAN. 54 acres on Deckers Creek. No adjoiners named. Consideration: £56, VA. Signed: Joseph Trickett, Margrett [|] Trickett. Witnesses: none. Acknowledged in court, October 1793. Del: to G Goosman, 6 November 1805. Recorded: OS 3:192. Re-recording of burned instrument.

9 September 1805. Joseph PERSONETT, son of Joseph PERSONETT, deceased and of Queen Anne Co, MD, to James PARSONETT. Power of attorney to conduct business regarding Joseph's interest and claim in the estate of his deceased father Joseph. Signed: Joseph Parsonett. Witnesses: none. Acknowledged in court, 9 September 1805. Del: to Jo Parsonett, 12 September 1805. Recorded: OS 3:193.

5 August 1805. David and Elizabeth PIXLER to Rudolph SADLER, Fayette Co, PA. 7½ acres near the great road leading from Morgan Town to Cheat River, adjoining

Daniel Stewart and Charles Stewart. Tract conveyed to Pixler by Charles Stewart, 10 September 1804. Consideration: $200. Signed: David [+] Pixler, Elizabeth [X] Pixler. Witnesses: Nimrod Evans, Wm N Jarrett, N Bigelow (all as to David). Acknowledged by Elizabeth Pixler before Wm John, John W Dean, JPs, 12 August 1805; by David Pixler in court, September 1805. Del: to Sadler, 17 January 1806. Recorded: OS 3:194.

8 July 1805. Hugh and Mary MORGAN to Conrad SHEETZ. 80 3/4 acres on the west side of Cheat River, at Morgans Run, part of Hugh Morgan's settlement tract. Consideration: $200. Signed: Hugh Morgan, Mary [X] Morgan. Witnesses: none. Acknowledged by Hugh Morgan in court, July 1805; by Mary Morgan, 31 August 1805, before John Fairfax and David Morgan, JPs. Del: to Henry Sheets, 22 June 1818. Recorded: OS 3:195.

26 November 1803. Hugh and Massey MORGAN to Conrad SHEETS. Lots #24, 25, and 26 in the Ville called Kingwood. Consideration: $24. Signed: Hugh Morgan, Marcey [X] Morgan. Witnesses: Joseph Kelso, Thomas Montgomery, Jacob Draper. Acknowledged by Massey Morgan, 31 August 1805, before John Fairfax and David Morgan, JPs; by Hugh Morgan, April 1809. Del: to him, 18 April 1809. Recorded: OS 3:196.

26 March 1805. Joseph SCOTT, Marshal of the VA District, to Meshach SEXTON. 1500 acres on Dunkard Creek, delinquent for US direct tax in the name of Christian Wireman. Consideration: $1.50. Signed: Joseph Scott. Witnesses: J H Lynch, John G Smith, William McEner. Acknowledged at Richmond District Court, 1 April 1805, before J Robinson. No delivery shown. Recorded: OS 3:197.

[blank] 1798. Henry and Lydia BARNES to Elisha BRAUTON. 200 acres at Kratsers Run where Brauton now lives, adjoining Sisco and Gallahu. Part of 400 acres patented to Henry, 3 June 1899 [sic!]. Consideration: $100. Signed: Henry Barns, Lydia Barns. Witnesses: none. Acknowledged by Henry Barnes in court, January 1798; by Lydia Barnes, 23 August 1798, before Nathan Springer and Stephen Morgan, JPs. Del: to E Brauton, 28 October 1805. Recorded: OS 3:198-199.

9 January 1798. Henry and Lydia BARNES to Andrew FLEMING. 125 acres adjoining Nathan Fleming, Benjamin Veach, and John Wilson, and where John Fleming now lives. Part of John Beel's settlement right. Patented 10 May 1796. Consideration: $100. Signed: Henry Barns, Lydia Barns. Witnesses: Nathan Springer, Stephen Morgan. Acknowledged by Henry Barnes in court, January 1798; by

Lydia Barnes, 23 August 1798, before Nathan Springer and Stephen Morgan, JPs. No delivery shown. Recorded: OS 3:200.

21 September 1795. William GEORGE to Thomas COCHRAN, KY, Commonwealth of VA [sic]. 100 acres on Dents Run, adjoining Jacob Scott, James Neely, Booz Burris, and John Lough. Part of a 397 acre tract. Consideration: £50, VA. Signed: Thomas Cochran. Witnesses: John Dent, James Scott, Philip Shively. Proved by witnesses, October 1804 and September 1805. Del: to John Lough, 10 October 1805. Recorded: OS 3:201-202.

9 September 1805. Edward and Rachel KERNS to John ORSTON. 68 acres on Booths Creek, adjoining Thomas Miller. Part of 244 acres patented to Harry Tucker, 2 April 1784, conveyed by Tucker to Patrick Kerns, and by Patrick to Edward. Consideration: $90. Signed: Edward [X] Kerns, Rachel [+] Kerns. Witnesses: none. Acknowledged in court, September 1805. Del: to J Orton, 17 October 1805. Recorded: OS 3:202.

10 June 1805. Thomas and Sarah LAIDLEY to Thomas PINDELL. 106 acres on Buffaloe Creek. No adjoiners named. Consideration: $106. Signed: Thos Laidley, Sarah Laidley. Witnesses: none. Acknowledged in court, June 1805. Del: to Jacob Pindall, 5 September 1807. Recorded: OS 3:203.

10 June 1805. Thomas and Sarah LAIDLEY to William HICKENBOTTOM. 200 acres on Dunkard Mill Run. No adjoiners named. Consideration: $666 1/3. Signed: Thos Laidley, Sarah Laidley. Witnesses: none. Acknowledged in court, June 1805. Del: to Wm Willey, 14 September 1807. Recorded: OS 3:204.

8 April 1805. Joseph and Ann S WILSON to Fauquer McREA. All interest in 162 1/8 acres at Deckers Creek, willed by John Ferguson to his daughter Margret Ferguson, deceased, sister of Ann S Wilson. Consideration: $120. Signed: Joseph Wilson, Ann S Wilson. Witnesses: Duncan F McRa, Jas Scott, P Martin. Acknowledged in court, April 1805. Del: to D F McRea, 5 March 1810. Recorded: OS 3:205.

29 June 1805. Jesse PAYNE, Wm G PAYNE, and John PAYNE to Benjamin MATHEW. 160 acres adjoining Anderson. No place names mentioned. Consideration: none stated. Signed: Jesse Payne, Wm G Payne, John Payne. Witnesses: none. Acknowledged in court, July and September 1805. Del: to John Smith per order [blotted] Mathew, 17 March 1813. Recorded: OS 3:205.

11 June 1805. Asa KELLUM, Hardin Co, KY, to Peter

MYERS and Elias FLANAGAN, both of Green Co, PA. 100 acres at the head of Indian Run, a branch of Dunkard Creek. No adjoiners named. Patented to Asa, heir at law of Phineas Kellum, in whose name the entry and survey were made. Consideration: $60, VA. Signed: Asa Killam. Acknowledged in court, June 1805. Del: to Thomas Wilson, 22 October 1805. Recorded: OS 3:206.

30 March 1803. Robert WILSON to James THOMAS. 156 acres, 72 poles in Sandy Creek settlement, on both sides of Little Sandy Creek, adjoining John Kennedy. Consideration: $453. Signed: Robert Wilson. Witnesses: Thomas Thomas, Joshua Shahan, William [X] Thomas, Joseph Smith. Proved by witnesses, October 1804 and January 1805. No delivery shown. Recorded: OS 3:207.

[blank] 1803. Thomas and Margaret PHILIPS to Capt James THOMAS. 100 acres on Sandy Creek, adjoining Lewis Woolf and [??] Tiddball. Consideration: £75. Signed: Thomas Philips, Margret [X] Philips. Witnesses: Thomas Thomas, Joshua Shahan, William [X] Thomas, Joseph Smith. Proved by witnesses, October 1804 and January 1805. Del: to Jas Thomas, 9 November 1813. Recorded: OS 3:208.

[blank] June 1805. John and Ann WADE, Harrison Co, to James BAKER. 52½ acres adjoining Hezekiah Wade. Consideration: [blank], VA. Signed: John [J] Wade [Ann does not sign]. Witnesses: none. Acknowledged by John Wade in court, June 1805. No delivery shown. Recorded: OS 3:209.

1 January 1805. Jesse PAYNE to John IRVINE, Dudley EVANS, and Benjamin REEDER, trustees. Deed of trust to secure debt of $653.43, plus interest, due to John Peebles on or before 1 June next. Payne conveys 400 acres, including his dwelling house and improvement. Signed: Jesse Payne, John Erwin, Dudley Evans, B Reeder. Witnesses: N Davisson, John Snyder, Peter Hull, James Douglass, Christian Simon, John Davis. Acknowledged 2 April 1805 in Pendleton Co. Certificate of Z Dyer, clerk. Del: to Daniel [?], 27 June 1807, per order from B Reeder. Recorded: OS 3:209-210.

10 June 1803. Adam and Phebe ICE to John STREIGHT. Tract on Buffalo Creek, acreage not stated, adjoining Anthony Mahon. Part of a tract descended to William Ice as heir of John Ice, and conveyed by William to Adam. Consideration: $133.33. Signed: Adam [A] Ice [Phebe does not sign]. Witnesses: none. Acknowledged by Adam Ice in court, June 1805. Commission to take Phebe's acknowledgement but no action recorded. Del: to grantee, 22 March 1817. Recorded: OS 3:211.

29 August 1804. Thomas and Polly WILSON to James

TATE. 333 acres on Deckers Creek, adjoining Leonard Kimmel [?], Asahel Martin, William McCleery, and George Dorsey. Patented to Wilson, 21 January 1800. Consideration: $300. Signed: Thomas Wilson [Polly does not sign]. Witness: John W Campbell. Acknowledged by Thomas Wilson in court, September 1805. Commission to Dudley Evans to take Polly's acknowledgement, but no action recorded here. Del: to John Stealey, 19 December 1821. Recorded: OS 3:212.

20 February 1805. Robert and Ann HAMILTON, HubVille Twp, Trumbull Co, OH, to John THOMPSON. Two tracts. 18 acres on Robesons Run, adjoining William Morris, Gaston's heirs, and John McDougal; from a patent of 18 November 1802. 30 acres on Robesons Run, adjoining Thompson's old survey, Daniel Thompson, John McDougal, and William Morris; from a patent to William Smith, 20 September 1785, bequeathed by Smith to his son Joel, and conveyed by Joel to Robert Hamilton. Consideration: $166, VA. Signed: Robt Hamilton, Ann [X] Hamilton. Witnesses: Thos Wilson, Wm Lanham, James Thompson. Memo: 1¼ acres conveyed to Thompson by deed of record, and 1 acre conveyed to Thompson and others, Methodist church trustees, are not included in this conveyance. Proved by witnesses, June 1805; acknowledged by Ann Hamilton, 3 January 1806, before Caleb Baldwin and John P Bissell, JPs, Trumbull Co, OH. Del: to John Thompson, 20 January 1806. Recorded: OS 3:213-214.

9 March 1804. Christopher and Mary ERWIN to John FLOYD, Fayette Co, PA. 11½ acres on Pharoas Run, no adjoiners named. Part of a 90 acre tract sold by Charles Snodgrass to Jacob Foulk. Consideration: $57.50. Signed: Christofer Erwin, Mary Erwin ("written by B Reeder at her request at the time he [sic] relinquishment of dower was taken"). Witnesses: none. Acknowledged by Mary Erwin before Stephen Morgan, 27 August 1805. Proved by witnesses, September 1805. Del: to George Foulk, 27 January 1806. Recorded: OS 3:215.

17 March 1803. Thomas and Elizabeth PINDALL to Augustus BALLAH. 75 acres on Papaw Creek, adjoining Ballah's and Pindall's other lands and Richard Price. From a patent of 25 April 1789, the remainder of the land having been sold to Richard Price. Consideration: $50. Signed: Thomas [T] Pindall, Elizabeth [|] Pindall. Witnesses: none. Acknowledged by Thomas Pindall in court, June 1805. Commission to take Elizabeth's acknowledgement but no action recorded here. No delivery shown. Recorded: OS 3:216.

[blank] 1804. Simeon and Elizabeth ROYSE to William

JOHN. 143 acres on both sides of the road from Morgan Town to Mcfarland's ferry, adjoining John Mcfarland, James Stafford. From a 3 April 1784 patent to Thomas John for 304 acres, and conveyed by him to Simeon Royse, 15 March 1796. Consideration: $400. Signed: Simeon Royse, Eliza Royse. Witnesses: Saml Hanway, Wm Stevenson, Jacob Pindall. Acknowledged by Elizabeth Royse, 16 March 1804, before Samuel Hanway and B Reeder, JPs. Proved by witnesses, July 1804. Del: to Wm John, 12 February 1807. Recorded: OS 3:217.

[blank] 1798. Henry and Lydia BARNES to Jeremiah GALLAHUE. 200 acres on Kratzers Run, adjoining Siscoe, John Precket, Elias Pearse, Gallahue's other land, and Elisha Brauton. From a 3 June 1801 [sic] patent. Consideration: £25. Signed: Henry Barnes, Lydia Barnes. Witnesses: Nathan Springer, Stephen Morgan. Acknowledged by Henry Barnes in court, January 1798. Acknowledged by Lydia Barnes before Nathan Springer and Stephen Morgan, JPs, 23 August 1798. Del: to Henry Gallahue, [?] August 1806. Recorded: OS 3:218.

18 October 1802. Joseph and Elisabeth BUTLER to John KEMMERER, of PA. 462 acres adjoining Thomas Burchenal, William Trembley, Dennis Geffers, Aaron Rice, Amos Roberts, and John Chipps. Consideration: $1600. Signed: Joseph [J] Butler, Elizabeth [X] Butler. Witnesses: none. Acknowledged by Joseph Butler, October 1803. Acknowledged by Elizabeth Butler in Washington Co, OH, before Jesse Fulton, 27 September 1803. Reacknowledged by Elizabeth before Jesse Fulton and Seth Carhart, 28 February 1804. Del: to Benjn Trimbly, 13 April 1807. Recorded: OS 3:219-220.

[blank] June 1805. Articles of agreement between John STEALEY, James TATE, and John BRANT. Stealey and Tate have leased to Brant all their jointly owned land on the southeast side of Deckers Creek, as far as the mouth of Deer Hollow Run for the term of seven years, including mineral rights and the operation of an iron furnace there. Brant is to build a furnace within two years. Stealey and Tate agree to furnish $2000 in articles suitable for building the furnace and carrying on the business. Constructions to include a stack 27' square; casting house 37' x 50', 9' to the square; bellows house 27' square; bellows of 6' diameter; bridge house 20' wide and as long as necessary; frame coal house, weatherboarded, 40' wide, 60' long, 15' high; and a 30' wheel, all to be put under good shingle roofs and finished in a compleat and workmanlike manner. Brant to make as many pigs of iron at the customary

price on this side of the mountains and to sell them either for Barrison [?] or cash. Signed: Jno Stealey, James Tate, John Brant. Witnesses: David Moore, Thomas Lanham. Acknowledged, June 1805. Del: to John Brant, 30 November 1805. Recorded: OS 3:221.

10 June 1805. Samuel HANWAY and Rachel HANWAY, executors of Jesse HANWAY, deceased, to James DEMOSS. 124 acres on Three Forks, adjoining Jesse Snider. From a 22 March 1804 patent to Jesse Hanway for 248 acres. Consideration: $100. Signed: Saml Hanway, Rachel [mark] Hanway. Witnesses: none. Acknowledged in court, June 1805. Del: to grantee, 12 May 1823. Recorded: OS 3:222.

20 February 1805. Robert and Ann HAMILTON, Hu??ville Twp, Trumbull Co, OH, to John McDOUGAL. Two parcels. 45 acres on Robinsons Run, adjoining Grafton White and the heirs of Christ Garlow, from a patent to Hamilton of 18 November 1802. 20 acres on Robinsons Run, adjoining John Thompson and Graftin White. From a patent of 20 September 1785 to William Smith and by his will (of record in Monongalia) conveyed to his son Joel, who conveyed by deed to Hamilton. Consideration: $257. Signed: Robt Hamilton, Ann [X] Hamilton. Witnesses: Thos Wilson, Wm Lanham, James Thompson. Acknowledged by Ann Hamilton before John P Bissell and Caleb Baldwin, JPs, Trumbull Co, OH. Proved by witnesses, June 1805. Del: to John McDougall, 25 December 1805. Recorded: OS 3:223.

10 June 1805. Jesse and Margret BUSSEY to John BELL. 81 3/4 acres near the PA line, part of the tract Bussey now lives on. No adjoiners named. Consideration: $300. Signed: J Bussey, Margret Bussey. Witnesses: none. Acknowledged in court, June 1805. Del: to John Beall, 15 April 1807. Recorded: OS 3:224.

9 March 1804. Christopher and Mary ERWIN to John FLOYD, Fayette Co, PA. 103 acres on Papaw Creek, adjoining William Snodgrass, Gallaton, and Knight. Part of a 200 acre survey. Consideration: $515. Signed: Christefor Erwin, Mary Irwin ("written by B Reeder at her request when her relinquishment of dower was taken"). Witnesses: Thos McKinley, Wm Lanham, Jacob Foulk. Acknowledged by Mary Erwin before B Reeder and Stephen Morgan, JPs, 27 August 1805; by Christopher Erwin in court, September 1805. Del: to George Foulk, 27 January 1806. Recorded: OS 3:225.

8 March 1803. John and Catarine RAMSEY to Samuel JACKSON, Fayette Co, PA. 38 acres, 1 rood, and 30 perches on the east side of Cheat River, adjoining Ice. Part of a patent. Consideration: $1600. Signed: John Ramsey, Catherine [C] Ramsey. Witnesses: Joshua Warman,

Enoch Jenkins, Samuel Baker. Acknowledged in court, June 1805. No delivery shown. Recorded: OS 3:226-227.

18 February 1804. Joshua and Nancy WARMAN and Cathrine WARMAN to John RAMSEY. 118 acres on the east side of Cheat River, adjoining Barthw Jenkins deceased and William Stewart. Conveyed to Joshua by Francis Warman, 8 April 1799. Consideration: $650. Signed: Jos Warman, Nancy Warman, Catharine Warman. Witnesses: E Evans, N Vandervort, Samuel Jackson. Acknowledged by Nancy and Catherine Warman before E Evans and N Vandervort, JPs, 18 February 1804. Proved by witnesses, September 1804 and June 1805. Del: to John Ravenscraft, 10 April 1806. Recorded: OS 3:227-228.

10 June 1805. Jacob and Hannah SMITH to James DONALDSON. 233 acres on waters of Blackburns Glade. Patented to Charles Donaldson, 11 September 1789, and allotted to Smith's wife, one of Donaldson's heirs, October 1799. Consideration: $500. Signed: Jacob Smith [Hannah does not sign]. Acknowledged by Jacob Smith, June 1805. Commission to take Hannah's acknowledgement, but no action recorded here. Del: to J Donaldson, 10 November 1806. Recorded: OS 3:229.

25 March 1805. Samuel and Elizabeth MUSGRAVE to John DICKEN. 100 acres on a branch of the righthand fork of Papaw Creek, adjoining David Musgrave's part of the same tract. From a 13 October 1789 patent for 394 acres. Consideration: $400. Signed: Samuel Musgrave, Elizabeth Musgrave. Witnesses: B Reeder, Saml Hanway, Laban Perdew. Acknowledged by Elizabeth Musgrave before Samuel Hanway and B Reeder, JPs, 25 March 1805. Proved by witnesses, June 1805 and September 1805. Del: to D Musgrave, 11 May 1807. Recorded: OS 3:230-231.

8 August 1805. Davis and Elen SHOCKLEY to Henry BARRACKMAN. 185 acres on Scotts Mill Run, adjoining William Postleweight. Consideration: $1000. Signed: Davis Shockley, Elen [+] Shockley. Witnesses: Wm N Jarrett, Rawley Evans, Nichs Madera. Acknowledged by Davis Shockley, June 1805. Commission to take Elen's acknowledgement but no action recorded here. No delivery shown. Recorded: 3:231-232.

25 March 1805. Samuel and Elizabeth MUSGRAVE to James MUSGRAVE. 100 acres at Ministers Run, adjoining John Dicken. Part of a patent for 398 acres. Consideration: love and affection. Signed: Samuel Musgrave, Elizabeth Musgrave. Witnesses: Saml Hanway, B Reeder, Laban Perdew. Acknowledged by Elizabeth Musgrave before Samuel Hanway and B Reeder, JPs, 25 March 1805. Proved by witnesses, June 1805 and September

1805. Del: to James Musgrave, 30 June 1806. Recorded: OS 3:233-234.

12 March 1805. Joseph and Mary KRATZER to William MILLER and John CARPENTER. 56 acres, 33 poles on Sisco's Run, adjoining Carpenter and Miller's other land. Tract where James Dunn formerly lived, and conveyed by him to Kratzer. Consideration: $300. Signed: Joseph Kratzer, Mary [mark] Kratzer. Witnesses: Reynear Hall, Joshua Hickman, John [W] Gutteridge. Proved by witnesses, June 1805. Commission to take Mary's acknowledgement but no action recorded here. Del: to Carpenter, 14 August 1809. Recorded: OS 3:234.

9 September 1805. James and Mary COLLINS to Zachariah BARKER. 200 acres on Indian Creek, adjoining surveys made for Rev William Worth, John Mcfarland, Gilbert Butler, Zachariah Barker, and Thomas Laidley. Consideration: $200. Signed: James Collins, Mary [|] Collins. Witnesses: none. Acknowledged in court, September 1805. Del: to Zackariah Barker, 7 November 1806. Recorded: OS 3:235.

10 September 1805. Samuel and Ann WILLEY to Elizabeth WOLVERTON. All right and interest in 200 acres formerly owned by John Watts, deceased, Samuel Willey having intermarried with Ann Watts, one of his heirs. Consideration: $140. Signed: Samuel Willey, Anna Willey. Witnesses: none. Acknowledged in court, September 1805. Del: to Joseph Jenkins, 16 May 1808. Recorded: OS 3:236.

9 August 1805. James and Mary COLLINS to James JEFFS. 8½ acres on Monongalia River, part of Abner Harper's old survey, adjoining Jeffs' Harper Town Tract and Cleland. Consideration: $85. Signed: James Collins, Mary [|] Collins. Witnesses: none. Acknowledged in court, September 1805. No delivery shown. Recorded: OS 3:237.

18 September 1805. George JACKSON, Harrison Co, to John WAGNER. Lot in Morgan Town [# not stated], where Wagner now resides, adjoining Water Street, Middle Alley, and Thomas Doolittle's lot. Purchased by Jackson from Colonel Morgan. Consideration: $80. Signed: G Jackson. Witnesses: H Dering, J Campbell, Mathew Gay, John Payne. Proved by witnesses, October 1805. Del: to John Wagner, [?] January 1806. Recorded: OS 3:238.

18 July 1805. Alexander and Margret CLEG to Christian MADERA. Lots #11,12,13,14,15,16 in New Hampshire. Part of a tract patented to John Statler, 17 June 1784 and conveyed by him to Cleg, [?] July 1799. Includes yearly quit rent of $2. Consideration: $50. Signed: Alexander Cleg, Marget [+] Cleg. Witnesses: Thos

Sidgwick, Richard Tennent, Alexander Tenant. Acknowledged by Alexander Cleg, October 1805. Commission to take Margret's acknowledgement, but no action recorded here. Del: to him, 28 July 1809. Recorded: OS 3:239.

10 December 1804. Caleb and Sarah FURBEE to Andrew DAUGHERTY. 12½ acres on Little Papaw Creek, adjoining Daugherty's other lands. Consideration: £12.10, VA. Signed: Caleb [X] Furbee [Sarah does not sign]. Witnesses: none. Acknowledged by Caleb Furbee, December 1804, and recorded as to him. Del: to A Daugherty, 14 April 1806. Recorded: OS 3:240.

10 September 1804. John and Mary KENNEDY to William SHAW. 61 acres on Little Sandy Creek, no adjoiners named. Consideration: $250. Signed: John Kennedy, Mary Kennedy. Acknowledged in court, September 1804. Del: to him, 11 April 1814. Recorded: OS 3:241.

19 November 1803. John SCOTT to Thomas WILSON. Deed of trust on 300 acres, conveyed to Scott by Samuel Martin, where Scott now lives, to secure a debt of $125 and costs to William Cochran, Samuel Meeker, and Alexander Cochran, of Baltimore, MD, doing business as Cochran, Meeker, and Co. The debt to be paid or the land sold by 1 May 1804. Signed: Jno Scott. Witnesses: Nim Evans, J Evans, John Dent. Proved by witnesses, July 1804 and September 1804. Del: to Thos Wilson, 28 January 1806. Recorded: OS 3:242.

8 July 1805. James and Rodah HAMILTON to George BOWMAN. 137 acres at Hazel Run, adjoining Elias Seaton and Charles Donaldson. Consideration: $100. Signed: James [JH] Hamilton, Rodah Hamilton. Witnesses: none. Acknowledged by James Hamilton, July 1805; by Rodah Hamilton before James Clark and John McLain, JPs, 24 January 1806. No delivery shown. Recorded: OS 3:243.

10 June 1805. James and Lydia BOWLSBY to John BELL. 18¼ acres adjoining Carlisle and Jesse Bussey. No place names mentioned. Consideration: £18. Signed: James Bowlby [Lydia does not sign]. Witnesses: none. Acknowledged by James Bowlby, June 1805. Commission to take Lydia's acknowledgement, but no action recorded here. Del: to John Beall, 15 April 1807. Recorded: OS 3:244.

8 April 1805. James THOMAS to Hugh EVANS. 267 acres on Sandy Creek, adjoining Jeremiah Leach and Michael Hilterbrand. Patented to a certain Hanway, conveyed by him to John Nixon, and by Nixon conveyed to James Thomas. Consideration: $1000, VA. Signed: James Thomas. Witnesses: Alexander McCleland, Nimrod Evans, Sam Evans,

Jacob Miller. Acknowledged in court, April 1805. Del: to Hugh Evans, 9 September 1820. Recorded: OS 3:245.

14 March 1805. James DUNN, of OH, by Henry DUNN, his attorney in fact, to Joshua HICKMAN. 68 acres on Buffalo Lick Run, adjoining John Megee, William Miller, and John Carpenter. Consideration: $450. Signed: Henry Dunn. Witnesses: Wm Haymond, James Morgan, Jacob Polsley. Acknowledged by Henry Dunn. Del: to J Hickman, 28 March 1807. Recorded: OS 3:246.

20 June 1803. James and Elizabeth BOOTH, Harrison Co, to Jesse MARTIN. 200 acres on Buffalo Creek, adjoining Isaac Morgan. Part of a 312 acre survey. Consideration: $200. Signed: James Booth, Elizabeth Booth. Witnesses: none. Acknowledged in Harrison Co, June 1804. Certificate of B Wilson, CHC. Del: to him, 6 June 1812[?]. Recorded: OS 3:247.

10 September 1804. Jacob and Catharine SCOTT to Thomas WARE. 204 acres where Ware now lives. No adjoiners or place names mentioned. Consideration: $600. Signed: Jacob Scott, Catharine [S] Scott. Witnesses: none. Acknowledged in court, September 1804. Del: to Thomas Ware, 22 May 1807. Recorded: OS 3:248.

8 October 1804. Jacob RUBLE to Daniel ANDERSON. 45 acres adjoining Samuel Ruble. No place names mentioned. Consideration: $300. Signed: Jacob Ruble. Witnesses: Wm G Payne, Joseph [X] Personett, William [X] Stewart. Acknowledged in court, October 1804. Del: to Danl Anderson, 12 September 180?. Recorded: OS 3:248.

10 September 1804. Charles and Jean STEWART to Caleb WISEMAN. 28 acres on Cheat River where Wiseman now lives. Part of a 400 acre tract. Consideration: $196, VA. Signed: Charles Stewart, Jen Stewart. Witnesses: none. Acknowledged in court, September 1804. Del: to Caleb Wiseman, 29 December 1806. Recorded: OS 3:249.

29 March 1805. Meshach SEXTON, Fayette Co, PA, to Asher LEWIS, Harrison Co. 200 acres, formerly belonging to Richard Petty John and sold to Sexton for nonpayment of the direct tax. No place names or adjoiners mentioned. Consideration: $400. Signed: Meshach Sexton. Witnesses: Geo C Arnold, John Prunty, David Hewes. Proved by witnesses in Harrison Co, June 1805. Certificate of B Wilson, CHC. Del: to grantee's son Chas Lewis, 21 May 1821. Recorded: OS 3:250.

10 September 1804. Abel and Sophia GUSTIN to James BAKER. 53 acres on Scotts Mill Run, adjoining Coverdill Cole and Alpheus Gustine. Consideration: [blank]. Signed: Abel Gustin, Sophia [mark] Gustin. Witnesses: none. Acknowledged in court, September 1804. No delivery

shown. Recorded: OS 3:251.

6 July 1805. John and Sarah PETTYJOHN to John JOHNSON. 650 acres on the east side of Tyger Valley River, adjoining John Baines and Mathew Hines. From a tract patented to John Pettyjohn and from another tract, patented to William Pettyjohn and conveyed by him to John. Consideration: $3250. Signed: John Petty John [Sarah does not sign]. Witnesses: Wm Haymond Jr, Joshua Hickman, Jessee Mellett. Acknowledged by John Pettyjohn, December 1805; by Sarah before Robert Ferrell and Morgan Morgan, JPs, 29 March 1806. No delivery shown. Recorded: OS 3:252.

1 March 1805. Philip and Keziah SILLIG to Thomas RUCKLE, all of Baltimore, MD. 200 acres on the west side of Cheat River, near Lick Run, no adjoiners named. Conveyed to Philip by Thomas Johnson, 26 September 1803. Consideration: $400. Signed: Philip Sillig, Keziah Sillig. Witnesses: Edwd J Crale, Nathl Lock. Receipt for consideration money. Acknowledged before the mayor of Baltimore, 1 March 1805. Certificate of Thorowg [sic] Smith, Mayor. Del: to Joseph Kelso, 15 February 1806. Recorded: OS 3:253.

1 February 1806. Thomas and Polly WILSON to Caleb TARLTON, Franklin Co, PA. 200 acres on the east side, near the great road from Morgantown to Clarksburg, adjoining David Sayre and Arin Garrett. Patented to Wilson, 5 July 1798. Consideration: $400. Signed: Thos Wilson, Polly Wilson. Witnesses: J W Campbell, James Evans, Wm N Jarrett. Acknowledged in court, February 1806. Del: to Caleb Tarlton, 6 March 1806. Recorded: OS 3:254-255.

1 January 1806. Thomas and Polly WILSON to John SHRIBER, Washington Co, MD. 450 acres on Glady Creek and Tygers Valley, no adjoiners named. Part of 1000 acres surveyed for David Gray and Samuel Hanway and patented to Thomas Wilson, 21 January 1800. Consideration: $900. Signed: Thos Wilson, Polly Wilson. Witnesses: J W Campbell, James Evans, Wm N Jarrett. Acknowledged in court, February 1806. Del: to McCleland. Recorded: OS 3:255-256.

1 February 1806. Thomas and Polly WILSON to John BASHORE, Franklin Co, PA. 300 acres on White Day Creek, adjoining William Robison, Richard Merrifield, Bambridge, John Stern, Morgan Morgan, James Morgan, and William Tetrick. Part of a 2200 acre tract. Consideration: $600. Signed: Thos Wilson, Polly Wilson. Witnesses: J W Campbell, James Evans, Wm N Jarrett. Acknowledged in court, February 1806. Del: to John

1 February 1806. Thomas and Polly WILSON to Christian KING, Franklin Co, PA. 347 acres on White Day Creek, adjoining Morgan Morgan, David Bullock, and James Morgan. Part of a 2200 acre survey, patented 17 June 1798. Consideration: $694. Signed: Thos Wilson, Polly Wilson. Witnesses: J W Campbell, James Evans, Wm N Jarrett. Acknowledged in court, February 1806. Del: to C King, 6 March 1806. Recorded: OS 3:258-259.

1 February 1806. Davis and Elen SHOCKLEY to Barten BEEN and Robert HOOEY, Washington Co, MD. 389 acres on the great road from Morgan Town to the head of Dunker Creek, adjoining Philip Leas [alternately Lewis], William Dawson, Christopher Meas, Thomas Dawson, Thomas Wilson, Rudolph Snyder, and Samuel Hanway. Part of a 12 February 1805 patent. Consideration: $1778. Signed: Davis Shockley, Elen Shockley. Witnesses: James Evans, Thos Wilson, Nimrod Evans. Acknowledged in court, February 1806. Del: to Barton Been, 7 March 1806. Recorded: OS 3:260-261.

1 February 1806. Thomas and Polly WILSON to Philip WAGGONER, Frederick WAGGONER, and Jacob WAGGONER, Franklin Co, PA. 500 acres on Glady Creek and Tigers Valley. Part of 1000 acres surveyed for David Gray and Samuel Hanway and patented to Wilson, 21 January 1800. Consideration: $1000. Signed: Thos Wilson, Polly Wilson. Witnesses: J W Campbell, James Evans, Wm N Jarrett. Acknowledged in court, February 1806. Del: to Wagner, 4 April 1806. Recorded: OS 3:261-262.

1 February 1806. Thomas and Polly WILSON to John TOMS, Franklin Co, PA. 130 acres on Coburns Creek, adjoining Jesse Hanway, Henry Banks, Israel Thompson, Standish Forde, and William Bones. Consideration: $260. Signed: Thos Wilson, Polly Wilson. Witnesses: J W Campbell, James Evans, Wm N Jarrett. Acknowledged in court, February 1806. Del: to McCleland. Recorded: OS 3:263.

8 October 1804. Jacob and Abigal MINTHORN, Hamilton Co, OH, by William JOHNSON, their attorney in fact, to William WALLER. 90 acres on the west side of Muddy Creek. No adjoiners named. Consideration: £32, VA. Signed: William Johnson. Witnesses: none. Acknowledged in court, October 1804. Del: to Wm Waller, 14 March 1806. Recorded: OS 3:264.

1 February 1806. Thomas and Polly WILSON to Abraham BAKER, Franklin Co, PA. 583 acres on White Day Creek, adjoining David Bullock and William Robison. Part of a 17 June 1798 patent for 2000 acres. Consideration: $1166. Signed: Thos Wilson, Polly Wilson. Witnesses: J W

$1166. Signed: Thos Wilson, Polly Wilson. Witnesses: J W Campbell, James Evans, Wm N Jarrett. Acknowledged in court, February 1806. Del: to Abraham Baker, 2 May 1806. Recorded: OS 3:265.

20 October 1804. Elihu HORTON to Noah RIDGWAY. Bill of sale for personal property, including Negro boy Isaac, Negro girl Rachel, livestock, household furnishings, and tableware. Consideration: $2000. Signed: Elihu Horton. Witnesses: B Reeder, Wm G Payne, John Scott. Proved by witnesses, June 1805. No delivery shown. Recorded: OS 3:266.

1 February 1806. Thomas and Polly WILSON to John HEFFNER, Franklin Co, PA. 200 acres on the bank of Monongalia River, adjoining David Scott, William John, and Robert Davis. Patented 17 January 1800. Consideration: $500. Signed: Thos Wilson, Polly Wilson. Witnesses: J W Campbell, James Evans, Wm N Jarrett. Acknowledged in court, February 1806. Del: to J Heffner, 12 April 1806. Recorded: OS 3:266-267.

10 February 1806. Thomas and Polly WILSON to Daniel STOVER, Franklin Co, PA. 300 acres on Sandy Creek, adjoining Charles Donaldson, Jacob Nuez, and Daniel Moore. Patented 9 March 1801. Consideration: $600. Signed: Thos Wilson, Polly Wilson. Witnesses: J W Campbell, James Evans, Wm N Jarrett. Acknowledged in court, February 1806. Del: to Daniel Stover, 4 April 1806. Recorded: OS 3:267-268.

11 March 1806. Daniel JONES to Negro girl LEAH. Manumission of slave. Jones owns Leah for the term of her life. Desirous of moving to PA and unwilling to dispose of her by sale in VA, he manumits, liberates, and sets her free, on condition she remain with him until the age of 28. Signed: Daniel Jones. Witnesses: none. Acknowledged in court, March 1806. No delivery shown. Recorded: OS 3:269.

8 October 1804. Josiah and Charity PRICKETT to Isaiah PRICKETT. 77½ acres, no adjoiners or place names mentioned. From a patent for 373 acres. Consideration: $300. Signed: Josiah Prickett, Charity [-] Prickett. Witnesses: none. Acknowledged in court, October 1804. Del: to Isaiah Prickett, 14 April 1806. Recorded: OS 3:269.

9 December 1805. William N and Mary JARRETT, Mary being the executrix of Hugh McNeely, deceased, to Samuel JACKSON, Fayette Co, PA. 224 acres known as the Jones place, adjoining Charles Donaldson and Joseph Swearengen. Consideration: $224. Signed: Wm N Jarrett, Mary Jarrett. Witnesses: none. Acknowledged in court,

January 1806. No delivery shown. Recorded: OS 3:270.

1 February 1806. Thomas and Polly WILSON to John SHULL, Franklin Co, PA. 78 acres on Big Sandy Creek, adjoining Robert Thornton, Daniel Macolm, and John Gribble. Consideration: $156. Signed: Thos Wilson, Polly Wilson. Witnesses: J W Campbell, James Evans, Wm N Jarrett. Acknowledged in court, February 1806. Del: to J Shull, 12 April 1806. Recorded: OS 3:271.

1 February 1806. Thomas and Polly WILSON to John WINGER, Fayette Co, PA. 42 acres on Big Hazle Run, adjoining William Taunehill, Joseph Downing, Charles Donaldson, and Abraham Faw[?]. Patented 17 January 1800. Consideration: $136. Signed: Thos Wilson, Polly Wilson. Witnesses: J W Campbell, James Evans, Wm N Jarrett. Acknowledged in court, February 1806. Del: to John Winger, 12 April 1806. Recorded: OS 3:272.

1 February 1806. George and Mary WILSON to David TOMS. 100 acres on the east side of Tygers Valley River, the main fork of the Monongalia River, adjoining lands surveyed for James Miller. From a 12 September 1799 patent. Consideration: $300. Signed: George [X] Wilson, Mary [+] Wilson. Witnesses: George Roberts, Wm N Jarrett, Benj N Jarrett. Del: to David Toms, 2 May 1806. Recorded: OS 3:273.

1 February 1806. George and Elizabeth ROBERTS, Fayette Co, PA, to John WINGER, Franklin Co, PA. 238 acres on Hazle Run, adjoining Joseph Martin. Patented to Joseph Downing, 20 April 1784. Consideration: $1066. Signed: George Roberts, Elizabeth Roberts. Witnesses: Wm N Jarrett, James Evans, M Evans. Acknowledged by George Roberts in court, February 1806; by Elizabeth in Fayette Co, PA, before Robert Richey and Zadock Springer, JPs, 26 February 1806. Del: to Winger, 12 April 1806. Recorded: OS 3:274-275.

1 February 1806. Alexander and Barshabe McCLELAND, Fayette Co, PA, to David SIMPSON, Franklin Co, PA. 182 acres on Sandy Creek, near a buffalo lick. Patented to Theophilus Phillips, 16 May 1787. Consideration: $546. Signed: Alexander McCleland, Barshabe McCleland. Witnesses: none. Acknowledged by Alexander McCleland in court, February 1806; by Barshabe in Fayette Co, PA, before Robert Richey and Zadock Springer, JPs, 26 February 1806. Del: to D Simpson. Recorded: OS 3:276-277.

8 October 1804. Benjamin and Sarah LEGGETT, Moses and Nancy MUSGRAVE, Frederick and Catherine SUMMERS, and Elizabeth HAMILTON to Thomas HAMILTON. 160 acres at Scotts Meadow Run, no adjoiners named. Part of

a tract patented to John Hamilton. Consideration: $300. Signed: Benjamin Leggett, Sarah [|] Leggett, Moses Musgrave, Nancy [X] Musgrave, Frederick [0] Summers, Cathrine [/] Summers, Elizabeth [X] Hamilton. Witnesses: none. Acknowledged in court, October 1804. Del: to Thos Hamilton, 14 April 1806. Recorded: OS 3:278.

4 February 1805. John and Elizabeth FESTER to William JAMES. Lots #49 and 50 in the town of Mount Carmel, laid out by Francis Deakins, now deceased. Includes $1 annual quitrent on each lot. Consideration: $80. Signed: John Fester, Eliz [+] Fester. Witnesses: Frederick Harsh, Elijah Butler. Acknowledged in court, September 1805. Del: to Wm James, 12 September 1809. Recorded: OS 3:279.

2 June 1804. David and Margret RIDENOUR to Jacob RIDENOUR. 77 acres on waters of Woolf Creek, between 210 acres conveyed to Alexander Bingamon and other lands of Jacob Ridenour. The remainder of 210 acres willed to David by Matthias Ridenour. David has conveyed the rest of the land to Francis Deakins or Abraham Wootring Jr. Consideration: $100. Signed: David Ridenhour, Margret [X] Ridenour. Witnesses: John Fairfax, Frederick Harsh, Conrad Holste. Acknowledged by Margret before John Fairfax and Frederick Harsh, JPs. Proved by witnesses, June 1804. Del: to Jacob Ridenour, 20 May 1806. Recorded: OS 3:279-280.

[blank] 1805. Thomas and Mariah RINEHART to Jacob RIDENOUR. 16 3/4 acres, no adjoiners or place names mentioned. Part of 315 acres conveyed to Rinehart by William Deakins Jr. Consideration: $51. Signed: Thomas [+] Rinehart, Maryann [sic] [+] Rinehart. Witnesses: none. Acknowledged in court, October 1805. Del: to Jacob Ridenour, 20 May 1806. Recorded: OS 3:281.

23 November 1805. Mary STEPHENS to her son EVAN STEPHENS, both of Warren Co, OH. Power of attorney. Mary is daughter and heir of Joseph DAVIS, deceased, late of VA, and entitled to receive a share of his estate, including real property. Evan is to recover of the administrators the share due to Mary. Signed: Mary [mark] Stephens. Witness: James Davis. Acknowledged in Warren Co, OH, before James Davis, JP, 25 November 1805. Certificate of David Sutton, clerk of Warren Co, OH. Del: to Jordan Hall, 26 April 1806. Recorded: OS 3:282.

10 December 1805. Mary STEPHENS, Warren Co, OH, by Evan STEPHENS, her attorney in fact, to Jordan HALL. 66 2/3 acres on Tygers Valley River, from a 400 acre tract patented to Joseph Davis, the portion claimed by Mary as her right of dower [sic]. Consideration: $111.

Signed: Evin Stephens. Witnesses: J W Campbell, N Evans, John Kimel. Acknowledged in court, December 1805. Del: to Jordan Hall, 26 April 1806. Recorded: OS 3:283.

8 June 1805. George GOULD to James WALLS. Mortgage on personal property, including bed and furnishings, shoemaker tools, table wares, washtub, shotgun. Gould may redeem by paying $20. Signed: George Gould. Witnesses: Ezekiel Cheney, Robert Boggess. Acknowledged in court, June 1805. Del: to James Walls, 18 June 1806. Recorded: OS 3:283-284.

8 October 1804. Jacob and Magdalen HAUGHT and John and Catharine HAUGHT to Samuel VARNER, Green Co, PA. 155 acres, no adjoiners or place names mentioned. Part of a larger tract patented to Jacob and John, 5 October 1792. Consideration: $310. Signed: Jacob Haught, Magdalen [+] Haught, John [mark] Haught, Catharine [X] Haught. Witnesses: none. Acknowledged in court, October 1804. Del: to Saml Varner, 24 February 1818. Recorded: OS 3:284.

22 November 1804. Theophilus MINOR, administrator with the will annexed of Theophilus PHILLIPS, late of Fayette Co, PA, to Absalom KNOTTS. Tract on Sandy Creek, adjoining Phillips' settlement right. Patented 1 June 1782 for 1000 acres. Consideration: $150, VA. Signed: T Minor. Witnesses: G R Tingle, Henry H Wilson, Thos Wilson. Proved by witnesses, December 1804. Del: to A Knotts, 9 November [sic] 1804. Recorded: OS 3:285.

22 November 1804. Francis BARNET, Elinor MINOR, Joana WILLIAMS, Mary WALDER, Elizabeth PHILLIPS, Sarah PHILLIPS, John PHILLIPS, Theophilus PHILLIPS, and Pamilla PHILLIPS, children and heirs of Theophilus PHILLIPS, deceased, of Fayette Co, PA, by Theophilus MINOR, administrator with the will annexed, to Joshua GOFF. 400 acres on the lower side of Bigg Sandy Creek, no adjoiners named. Patented to the grantees as heirs of Theophilus Phillips, 6 September 1799, and sold per directions in his will. Consideration: $200, VA. Signed: T Minor. Witnesses: G R Tingle, Henry H Wilson, Thos Wilson. Proved by witnesses, December 1804. Del: to Byram Gough, 14 April 1829. Recorded: OS 3:286.

17 September 1804. Joseph REED to Isaac POWELL. Deed of trust to secure payment of $110 on or before 1 November 1804. Entrusted property consists of 150 acres on Three Forks Creek, patented 24 June 1802, and every particle of Reed's movable property, livestock, hay, grain, flax, household furniture, farm tools, &c. Signed: Joseph Reed. Witnesses: Jonathan Roberts, Johannah Wilson, Marcy Wilson. Acknowledged in court,

February 1806. Del: to Isaac Powell, 17 September 1806. Recorded: OS 3:287.

9 October 1804. David SCOTT to Felix SCOTT. Deed of gift for sorrel horse, 20 steers, all my corn and hay. Consideration: $1, good will and affection to his son. Signed: David Scott. Witnesses: none. Acknowledged in court, October 1804. No delivery shown. Recorded: OS 3:287.

11 February 1805. Hannah STANLEY, widow and executrix of John STANLEY, deceased, and Henry SNIDER, father and guardian of John Stanley SNIDER, great-grandson of said John STANLEY, to Lindsay BOGGESS. Lease of 14 years, commencing 1 April 1805, on a plantation bequeathed by John Stanley to Hannah his wife for her lifetime, with reversion to John Stanley Snider. Land from two tracts on which all the parties now reside. If Hannah should die before expiration of the lease, Snider will allow Boggess to hold the property for the full term. Boggess is to pay to Hannah $15 rent per year, and the same sum to Snider if she should die. Seven years' rent is due on 1 April next, if he can spare so much, or more if he can spare so much, the whole rent to be paid in property. Boggess to seed half the cleared land in the fall of the last year and to cut and carry off the crop when he goes. Signed: Hannah [X] Snider, Execx, Henry [X] Snider, guardn, Lindsay Boggess. Acknowledged in court, February 1805. Del: to L Boggess, 22 April 1807. Recorded: OS 3:288.

13 July 1805. Thomas and Mariah RINEHART to Frederick HARSH. $108\frac{1}{4}$ acres where Harsh now lives, part of a larger tract sold to Rinehart by William Deakins Jr. Consideration: £360, MD. Signed: Thomas [+] Rinehart, Maryann [sic] [+] Rinehart. Witnesses: none. Acknowledged in court, October 1805. Del: To F Harsh, 5 February 1807. Recorded: OS 3:289.

9 October 1805. Thomas and Mariah RINEHART to George RINEHART, Allegany Co, MD. 150 acres, adjoining Frederick Harsh, the same tract where Thomas formerly lived. Part of a tract sold to Thomas by William Deakins Jr. Consideration: "several good causes and considerations." Signed: Thomas [+] Rinehart, Maryann [+] Rinehart. Witnesses: none. Acknowledged in court, October 1805. Del: to him, 16 August 1811. Recorded: OS 3:290.

9 January 1806. John and Barbary FIKE, Allegania Co, MD, to Thomas BURCHINAL. 150 acres at Butlers Mill Run, where Burchinal now lives. Consideration: $100. Signed: John Fike, Barbary [0] Fike. Witnesses: Wm

Barbary Fike before William Johnson and John McLain, JPs, 10 February 1806. Proved by witnesses, April 1806. Del: to Thos Burchinal, 11 March 1807. Recorded: OS 3:291.

10 September 1804. John and Mary KENNEDY to Stephen MYERS. 213 acres on Little Sandy Creek, adjoining Inatious [sic] Anderson. Patented to Thomas Berry Jr, conveyed by him to Samuel Cobb, and by Cobb to John Kennedy, 9 October 1798. Consideration: $200, VA. Signed: John Kennedy, Mary Kennedy. Witnesses: none. Acknowledged in court, September 1804. Del: to S Myers, 13 April [?] 1807. Recorded: OS 3:292.

15 October 1805. Meshach SEXTON to John TRIMBLE, both of Fayette Co, PA. Two tracts. 165 acres on Big Yohogania, formerly owned by Ann Clark and sold to Sexton for non-payment of the direct tax. Part of a larger tract of 785 acres. 130 acres on Sandy Creek, formerly owned by Benjamin Wade and sold to Sexton for non-payment of the direct tax. Both tracts conveyed to Sexton by Joseph Scott, marshal of the VA District, 26 March 1805. Consideration: $100. Signed: Meshach Sexton. Witnesses: none. Acknowledged in court, October 1805. No delivery shown. Recorded: OS 3:293.

27 June 1802. Elihu HORTON to Henry H WILSON. 50 acres, agreeable to a patent hereto annexed [but not recorded here], the metes and bounds to be determined later. No place names or adjoiners mentioned. Consideration: £50. Signed: Elihu Horton. Witnesses: J Evans, Henry Dering, John Scott. Proved by witnesses, April 1803. Del: to Henry H Wilson, 24 January 1809. Recorded: OS 3:293.

15 October 1804. William and Sarah NEWLON, Harrison Co, to William MYERS. 110 acres on Little Sandy Creek, adjoining Robert Brown and John England. Conveyed to Newlon by Benjamin and Ann Whitson. Consideration: £75. Signed: William Newlon, Sarah Newlon. Witnesses: none. Acknowledged in Harrison Co, September 1805. Certificate of B Wilson, CHC. Del: to William Myers, 15 July 1806. Recorded: OS 3:294.

8 April 1805. William and Hannah CHIPPS to Teterick DUCKMAN ["Toothman" interlined in a modern hand]. 301½ acres, no adjoiners or place names mentioned. Consideration: £300, VA. Signed: William Chipps, Hannah Chipps. Witnesses: Nimrod Evans, Jas Pindall, Forbes Britton. Acknowledged by William Chipps, December 1805; by Hannah before Robert Ferrel and William Hamilton, JPs, 11 February 1806. Del: to Tetrick Duckman, 4 June 1806. Recorded: OS 3:295.

1806. Recorded: OS 3:295.

10 June 1805. Samuel DAVIS, attorney at law, of Kent Co, MD, but now of Baltimore, to George W BLAIKISTON, merchant, Baltimore, MD. Two tracts. Unspecified acreage on the east side of Monongahela River, near Pricketts Creek, adjoining Nathan Springer and lands formerly belonging to William Robinson. Patented to Thomas Armet [?], 27 April 1787, and conveyed by him to Davis, 11 July 1803, as recorded in Deeds, Book C, page 156. Another tract in the same location, near White Day Creek, patented to Joshua Selsby, 27 April 1787, and conveyed by him to Davis, 11 July 1803, as recorded in Deeds, Book C, page 153. Consideration: $800. Signed: Sam Davis. Witnesses: Wm G Cochran, Wm Hollins, Henry Hollins. Acknowledged before Thorowg Smith, mayor of Baltimore, 10 June 1805. Certificate of Tho Worrell, clerk of Kent Co, MD. Del: to Edward Conley, 12 June 1806. Recorded: OS 3:296-297.

1 November 1804. William WILLEY Sr to Elizabeth WILLEY, his daughter, and Mary WILLEY alias GRIFFITH, his granddaughter. 141 acres, adjoining William Wadkins at Scotts Mill Run. Patented to David Watkins, 1 December 1804. The remainder of 400 acres he purchased of David Watkins (159 acres previously conveyed to William Willey Jr, and 100 acres to Booz Burrows). Willey reserves lifetime use of the land and conveys to daughter Elizabeth for her lifetime, with reversion in fee simple to granddaughter Mary. Consideration: $1, love, good will, and affection. Signed: William Willey. Witnesses: Henry Dering, Rawley Evans, John W Dean. Proved by witnesses, June 1805 and June 1806. Del: to E Willey, 22 October 1806. Recorded: OS 3:298-299.

9 June 1806. David HENDRIXON to Thomas BIRCH. 100 acres adjoining Mason and Deakins. Conveyed by Samuel and Mary Clark, 14 May 1805. Consideration: $200. Signed: David Hendrickson. Acknowledged in court, June 1806. Del: to [illegible], 4 July 1809. Recorded: OS 3:300.

11 April 1803. Zachariah and Ann BARKER to John GLASSCOCK. 100 acres on Indian Creek, adjoining John Mcfarland, William Worth, and Barker's other land. Consideration: $300. Signed: Zachariah Barker, Ann [+] Barker. Witnesses: none. Acknowledged in court, April 1803. No delivery shown. Recorded: OS 3:300.

15 April 1806. James and Lucresa STAFFORD to William BAMBRIDGE. Two tracts. 95 acres on Little Creek, conveyed to Stafford by Alexander McIntire, 13 June 1795. 105 acres on the east fork of Little Creek,

adjoining Morgan Morgan, Rice Bullock, and Mary Fields. Patented 14 October 1796. Consideration: $200. Signed: James Stafford, Lucresa Stafford. Witnesses: none. Acknowledged in court, June 1806. Del: to grantee, 9 March 1816. Recorded: OS 3:301.

21 April 1802. Joshua and Barbara OATLEY to William BAMBRIDGE. 100 acres on Buffalo Creek, adjoining Adam Ice. Part of a larger tract granted to John Ice, deceased, of which William Ice became heir at law, and which was conveyed to Aden Bayles, 11 January 1796. Consideration: £98. Signed: Joshua [0] Oatley, Barbary [0] Oatley. Witnesses: Hugh McNeely, Thomas Foster, Elihu Horton. Acknowledged by Barbary, 21 April 1802, before Michael Kerns and B Reeder, JPs. Proved by witnesses June 1805. Del: to William Bambridge, 6 September 1809. Recorded: OS 3:301-302.

8 July 1805. Nester and Katy HARDIN, Randolph Co, to Samuel HANWAY, Jesse HANWAY, and John HANWAY, co-heirs of Jesse HANWAY, deceased. 340 acres on Little Sandy Creek, waters of Tygers Valley River. No adjoiners named. Purchased by Jesse in his lifetime and willed to his three sons. Consideration: £340, previously paid. Signed:Nester Hardin, Katy Hardin. Witnesses: none. Acknowledged in court, July 1805. No delivery shown. Recorded: OS 3:303.

16 May 1805. Enoch LEWIS, Tyrone Twp, Cumberland Co, PA, to John BASNETT. Undivided one-fourth interest in 207 acres on Scotts Mill Run, adjoining Willey and Caleb Hurley, where Catherine Marles and Basnett now live. Land formerly belonged to Philip Lewis, who died intestate. Consideration: $80. Signed: Enoch Lewis.Witnesses: Philip Lewis, Wilson McClure. Receipt for consideration money. Acknowledged in Cumberland Co, PA, before Samuel Laird, JP, 20 May 1805. Certificate of Willm Lyon, prothonotary. Del: to John Basnett, 2 February 1809. Recorded: OS 3:304.

8 October 1804. David and Hannah WRIGHT to John BASNETT. One-fourth interest in 207 acres on Scotts Mill Run, adjoining David Watkins and Doll Snyder. Patented to Philip Lewis, 16 December 1784, and including his 1774 settlement. Philip died intestate, leaving four heirs, one of them Rachel Lewis, who married John Williams, "who by absence are dead in law," Hannah being the daughter and heir of Rachel Lewis Williams. Consideration: $100, VA. Signed: David [mark] Wright, Hannah [mark] Wright. Witnesses: none. Acknowledged in court, October 1804. Del: to John Basnett, 2 February 1809. Recorded: OS 3:305.

11 April 1806. William and Mary MYERS to James KNOTTS. 366 acres on the head of Glade Run, adjoining Robert Knotts, Dudley Evans, A??? Knotts. Patented 27 July 1802. Consideration: $732. Signed: William [W] Myers [Mary does not sign]. Witness: Joseph Smith. Acknowledged by William Myers, April 1806. Commission to take Mary's acknowledgement, but no action recorded here. Del: to James Knotts, 24 April 1808. Recorded: OS 3:3:306.

10 February 1806. Jacob and Jemima PRICKET and James and Dorethy MORGAN to Morgan MORGAN Jr. 88 acres on Pricketts Creek, adjoining James Morgan and Jacob Prickett. Consideration: $1. Signed: Jacob Prickett, Jemima [mark] Pricket, James Morgan, Dorothy [+] Morgan. Witnesses: none. Acknowledged in court, February 1806. Del: to Morgan Morgan, 24 January 1807. Recorded: OS 3:307.

29 March 1802. Jacob FOULK to Moses WILLIAMS. Release. Williams gave Foulk a deed of trust on 20 July 1802 to secure payments to William Lanham. Lanham is satisfied, and Foulk releases the deed of trust. Signed: Jacob Foulk. Witnesses: Thos Laidley, Zackquill Morgan, Jas Pindall. Acknowledged in court, January 1806. Recorded: OS 3:307.

27 August 1805. James THOMAS to James DAILEY, Hampshire Co. Bill of sale for personal property, including horses, wagon and gears, cattle, sheep, hogs, hay, wheat, rye, 27 acres of corn, beds and furniture, farm tools. Consideration: $2000. Signed: James [X] Thomas. Witnesses: Jos Smith, Aaron Chance, William [X] Thomas. Acknowledged in court, October 1805. Del: to James Dailey, 22 September 1806. Recorded: OS 3:308.

14 October 1805. Lewis and Elizabeth SNELL to Godfrey GOOSMAN. Elizabeth, formerly the widow of Christopher Goosman, relinquishes to his father Godfrey all her claim to Christopher's estate, real or personal. Consideration: none stated. Signed: Lewis [X] Snell, Elizabeth [+] Snell, formerly Elizabeth Goosman. Witnesses: Edw W Boswell, Augustus Werninger, James Wells. Proved by witnesses, December 1805 and February 1806. Del: to Lewis Smell [sic], 12 July 1838. Recorded: OS 3:308.

11 February 1806. Benjamin and Eleanor REEDER to Thomas CLAGG and Thomas CLAGG Jr. 200 acres on Dunker Creek, where Humes now lives. No adjoiners named. Part of a 3900 acre tract. Consideration: $1. Signed: B Reeder, El Reeder. Witnesses: none. Acknowledged by Benjamin, February 1805, and recorded as to him. Del: to

grantee, 8 December 1819. Recorded: OS 3:309.

1 March 1806. Jonathan and Betsy GANDY to Samuel GANDY. 20½ acres, adjoining Samuel Gandy. Consideration: $50. Signed: Jonathan Gandy, Betsy Gandy. Witnesses: John [X] Moore, Levy Gandy, Mary Gandy. Acknowledged in court, April 1806. Del: to him, 29 October 1812. Recorded: OS 3:309.

1 April 1806. William and Mary McGEE to William GEORGE. 120 acres on Three Forks, adjoining Jabish Bell. Part of 1700 acres patented to Dudley Evans, 28 August 1797. Consideration: $360. Signed: William McGee, Mary McGee. Witnesses: B Reeder, John W Dean, Henry Dering. Acknowledged by Mary before B Reeder and John W Dean, JPs, 1 April 1806. Proved by witnesses, April 1806. Del: to Wm George, 15 February 1809. Recorded: OS 3:310.

15 January 1806. William GEORGE to Joseph LOUGH. 100 acres at Dents Run, adjoining Jacob Scott, James Neely, Booz Burrows, and John Lough. Part of a larger tract of 397 acres. Consideration: $400, VA. Signed: William George, Ann George. Witnesses: Nimrod Evans, John Payne, Davis Shockley, Wm G Payne (all as to William George). Acknowledged by Ann George before Thomas Miller and Augustus Ballah, JPs, 15 January 1806. Proved by witnesses, February 1806. Del: to John Lough, 12 January 1810. Recorded: OS 3:311-312.

10 September 1804. Charles and Jean STEWART to Casper OTT. 9 3/4 acres adjoining Daniel Cox and Samuel Harman. Part of 400 acres patented to Charles Stewart. Consideration: £39.15. Signed: Charles Stewart, Jen Stewart. Witnesses: none. Acknowledged in court, September 1804. Del: to Casper Ott, 9 September 1809. Recorded: OS 3:312.

11 September 1806. William and Margret DARLING to Benjamin LEADY. 162 acres on the west side of Cheat River, adjoining James Morgan, John Daugherty, and John Green. Consideration: £225, VA. Signed: William Darling [Margret does not sign]. Witnesses: none. Acknowledged by William Darling, February 1806; by Margaret Darling, September 1806. Del: to Wm Haning, 16 July 1806. Recorded: OS 3:313.

22 March 1806. Thomas R CHIPPS, Morgan Town, to Nimrod EVANS. Bill of sale for Negro woman Sarah, Negro girl Betty, Negro boy Charles, Negro girl Nelly, purchased by Thomas from Hannah Chipps. Also for sorrel horse purchased by Thomas from Alexander Hawthorn, plus cattle and household furnishings. Consideration: $500. Signed: Thos R Chipps. Witnesses: Jacob Foulk, James Evans, Davis Shockley. Acknowledged in court, July 1806.

No delivery shown. Recorded: OS 3:314.

15 July 1806. William and Mary MYERS to Henry WALTER, Fayette Co, PA. 110 acres on Little Sandy Creek, adjoining Robert Brownfield and John England. Conveyed by Benjamin and Ann Whitson to William Newlon, and by Newlon to William Myers. Consideration: $150. Signed: William [mark] Myers [Mary does not sign]. Witnesses: none. Acknowledged by William Myers, July 1806. Commission to take Mary's acknowledgement but no action recorded here. Del: to H Walter, 27 February 1807. Recorded: OS 3:315.

11 February 180[blank]. Christopher and Sharlott MEAS to Abraham WISECUP. 50 acres on Scotts Mill Run, adjoining Caleb Hurley and Samuel Everly. Conveyed to Christopher Meas 4 April 1803 by Charles Dawson, attorney in fact for William and Mary Dawson. Consideration: $400. Signed: Christopher Meas, Sharlott [mark] Meas. Witnesses: none. Acknowledged in court, February 1805. No delivery shown. Recorded: OS 3:316.

11 December 1802. Hugh DUNN to John SNIDER. Bill of sale for personal property, including horse, cows, sheep, hogs, rye, wheat, Indian corn, flax, tableware, household furnishings. Consideration: $200. Signed: Hugh Dun. Witnesses: John Garlow, Amos Snider. Acknowledged in court, February 1806. No delivery shown. Recorded: OS 3:316.

10 September 1804. Charles and Jean STEWART to Samuel HARMAN. Lot #1 in Middle Town [location of town not indicated]. Consideration: £10. Signed: Charles Stewart, Jen Stewart. Witnesses: none. Acknowledged in court, September 1804. Del: to Samuel Harman, 10 September 1806 [1808?]. Recorded: OS 3:317.

14 March 1805. James DUNN, OH, by Henry DUNN, his attorney in fact, to James MORGAN. 93 acres on Buffalow Lick Run, adjoining Joshua Hickman, Jeremiah Gallahew, and John Carpenter. Consideration: $800. Signed: Henry Dunn. Witnesses: Jacob Palsley, Joshua Hickman, Wm Haymond Jr. Proved by witnesses, April 1805. Del: to James Morgan, 1 April 1807. Recorded: OS 3:317.

10 September 1804. Benjamin and Eleanor REEDER to John CALFFLESH. 89 acres adjoining John Dragoo, Jacob Strait, William Gray, Jasper Wait, and James Cleland. From a patent of 12 September 1799. Consideration: $200. Signed: B Reeder, Elenor Reeder. Witnesses: none. Acknowledged in court, September 1804. No delivery shown. Recorded: OS 3:318.

11 September 1797. Richard and Phebe MERIFIELD to David SAYRE Jr. 200 acres on the middle fork of Booths

Creek, about three miles from the river, adjoining John Phillips. Consideration: £50. Signed: Richard Merifield [Phebe does not sign]. Witnesses: none. Acknowledged in court by Richard, July 1797 [sic]; acknowledged by Phebe, September 1806. Del: to Ben Sayre, 15 May 1807. Recorded: OS 3:319.

1 September 1806. James and Mary ARNOLD, Harrison Co, to John HAGNEAR, Baltimore Co, MD. 300 acres on Buffalow Lick Creek, one mile from Cheat River, no adjoiners named. Patented 14 November 1801. Consideration: $500. Signed: James Arnold, Mary Arnold. Acknowledged in Harrison Co, September 1806. Certificate of B Wilson, CHC. Del: to James Arnold, 20 September 1806. Recorded: OS 3:320.

8 September 1806. William and Margret DARLING to Moses ROYSE. 400 acres on the west side of Cheat River at a knob called Bufalow Knob, adjoining James Morgan, John Green, and John Daugherty. Patented to William Darling in 1785 as assignee of Jeremiah Gray. Consideration: $2000. Signed: William Darling, Mary [0] Darling. [Incompletely recorded; see below, OS 3:369.] Recorded: OS 3:321.

13 August 1806. John HOYE, of the USA, to Thomas MORGAN and David MORGAN, Fayette Co, PA. 400 acres on Muddy Creek, formerly belonging to the heirs of David Morgan and deeded to Hoye by the marshal on 14 June 1805 for non-payment of the direct tax. Consideration: $1. Signed: John Hoye. Witnesses: William N Jarrett, John Davis, Zackquill Morgan, Jacob Kiger, Nimrod Evans, John Stealey. Proved by witnesses, September 1806. No delivery shown. Recorded: OS 3:322.

9 October 1798. John and Mary KENNEDY to Samuel COBB. 500 acres on the north side of Elk River in Kanaway Co, adjoining survey for Ann Raines. Part of 1000 acres patented to John Davidson, 1786. Consideration: £200, VA. Signed: John Kennedy, Mary Kennedy. Acknowledged in court, October 1798. No delivery shown. Recorded: OS 3:323.

9 June 1806. Richard and Elizabeth SMITH to Asher LEWIS, Harrison Co. Lots #8 and 15 in the town of Smithfield. Consideration: $100. Signed: Richard Smith, Elizabeth Smith. Witnesses: none. Acknowledged in court, June 1806. Del: to him, 29 December 1813. Recorded: OS 3:324.

10 June 1806. Robert and Hannah FARRELL to Walter CAIN. 200 acres adjoining Henry Weaver, John Sayre, James Gray, and Richard Smith. From an 823 acre survey. Consideration: $500. Signed: Robert Ferrell, Hannah

[mark] Ferrell. Witnesses: none. Acknowledged by Robert Ferrell, June 1806; acknowledged by Hannah, September 1806. Del: to Walter Cain, 10 July 1809. Recorded: OS 3:325.

20 February 1806. Jacob and Hannah PINDEL, John and Hannah CHIPPS, William and Hannah CHIPPS, Simeon and Elizabeth ROYSE, Thomas R and Rachel CHIPPS, and Amos CHIPPS to Benjamin MIDDLETON. 112 acres, adjoining Stephen Workman. Patented to Bartholomew London, 10 October 1786, and sold by him to Thomas Chipps. Consideration: $120. Signed: Jacob Pindell, Hannah Pindell, William Chipps, Hannah Chipps, Rachel Chipps [other grantors named do not sign]. Witnesses: none. Acknowledged by the signers, February 1806. Del: to B Middleton, 13 April 1807. Recorded: OS 3:326-327.

9 September 1805. Daniel and Mary CONNER to George SNIDER. 150 acres on the west side of Cheat, about 2 miles from the river, no adjoiners named. Part of a 500 acre survey conveyed by Wildy and Mary Taylor to Raphel Wathan in 1792, the record supposed to be burnt; conveyed by Wathan to John Clark, and by Clark and the Taylors to Daniel Conner in 1802. Consideration: $450. Signed: Daniel Conner, Mary Conner. Witnesses: none. Acknowledged in court, September 1805. No delivery shown. Recorded: OS 3:327.

11 June 1805. Thomas and Sarah LAIDLEY to John GRUB. 133½ acres on King Cabin Run, no adjoiners named. Consideration: $394.50. Signed: Thomas Laidley, Sarah Laidley. Witnesses: none. Acknowledged in court, June 1805. Del: to him, 4 March 1811. Recorded: OS 3:328.

9 December 1805. Elisha and Elisabeth BRAUTON to John MILLER. 200 acres on Kratzers Run, adjoining Sisco and Gallyhew. Conveyed to Brauton by Henry Barnes in 1798. Consideration: $265. Signed: Elisha Brauton, Elizabeth [X] Brauton. Witnesses: none. Acknowledged in court, December 1805. No delivery shown. Recorded: OS 3:329-330.

12 October 1805. Amos and Susannah PETTY JOHN to William LINN. 175 acres adjoining Henry Tucker and Abraham Pettyjohn. Patented to William Pettyjohn, 25 January 1782. Consideration: £170, VA. Signed: Amos Petty John, Susannah [+] Pettyjohn. Witnesses: none. Acknowledged in court, December 1805. Del: to John Lynn, 8 March 1805. Recorded: OS 3:330-332.

9 December 1805. Elisabeth LYNCH and Daniel and Isabella JOHNSTON to James GRAY. 107 acres, no place names or adjoiners mentioned. Part of 3 tracts formerly purchased by Patrick Lynch from Robert Ferrel, Thomas

Greggs, and Thomas Peacock. Consideration: $535. Signed: Elizabeth [+] Lynch, Daniel [+] Johnston, Isabella [X] Johnston. Acknowledged in court, December 1805. Del: to James Gray, 11 March 1807. Recorded: OS 3:332-333.

8 November 1805. Jonathan and Rebeckah HARRIS to Jonathan SMITH. 100 acres on Severns Run, where Harris now lives, near the bridge on Crab Orchard road. Part of a larger tract. Consideration: £100, VA. Signed: Jonathan Harris [Rebeckah does not sign]. Acknowledged by Jonathan Harris, December 1805 [large blank space, evidently intended for commission and acknowledgement of Mrs Harris]. Del: to Griffith Powel by order of Smith, 22 June 1812. Recorded: OS 3:334.

9 September 1805. Daniel and Iba JOHNSON to William STITTS and Edward STITTS. 77½ acres adjoining John Huffman and John Corothers. Part of tracts conveyed to Patrick Lynch by Thomas Greggs, Joseph Trickett as attorney for Thomas Peacock and Elijah Chapman, and Robert Ferrel, and conveyed by Patrick and Elisabeth Lynch to Daniel Johnson. Consideration: $310. Signed: Daniel [+] Johnson, Isabella [+] Johnson. Witnesses: none. Acknowledged in court, December 1805. Del: to E Stitts, 8 February 1810. Recorded: OS 3:335-336.

15 October 1805. James THOMAS to Thomas MEEKS. 32 acres adjoining William Jones, Jacob Jones, and Thomas' other land. Consideration: $80. Signed: James [X] Thomas. Witnesses: none. Acknowledged in court, October 1805. Del: to Jacob Means, 1 June 1835. Recorded: OS 3:337-338.

14 March 1805. Lawrence SNIDER to Jacob NOOZ Jr. Mortgage on personal property, including horse, steers, cattle, hogs, crosscut saw and all other tools, beds, household furnishings, &c. Snider is to repay £150 within 6 years. Signed: Lawrence Snider, Jacob Nooz. Witnesses: Samuel Crane, John Dawson. 23 July 1806. Jacob NOOZ to Abraham WOODROW. Assignment of the aforesaid mortgage. Signed: Jacob Nooz. Witness: Nimrod Evans. Acknowledged in court, October 1806. No delivery shown. Recorded: OS 3:338. [Followed by a lengthy blank space.]

2 October 1805. James WILSON to John GILLISPIE, Armstrong Co, PA. Mortgage on tract where Wilson now lives, purchased from John and Eunice Philips by deed, 21 March 1801. Wilson owes Gillispie $263.91, with interest, due by several notes. Sum to be paid by 1 November 1806 or the land to be sold. Signed: James Wilson. Witnesses: Wm C Payne, H Dering, John Payne. Proved by witnesses, October 1805. Del: to Gillespie, 13

November 1806. Recorded: OS 3:339.

15 October 1805. William N JARRETT and Nimrod EVANS to Benjamin HELLEN. Release. Hellen made a deed of trust to Evans, for the use of Jarrett, to secure a payment and mentioning a lot in Morgan Town. Hellen, having paid the full amount mentioned in the deed of trust, is now released from it. Signed: William N Jarrett, Nimrod Evans. Witnesses: none. Acknowledged in court, October 1805. No delivery shown. Recorded: OS 3:340.

6 April 1805. Andrew and Sarah MILLER to Jacob MILLER. 100 acres on Swamp Run, no adjoiners named. Part of 400 acres patented to Theophilus Philips, 1 September 1782. Consideration: £50. Signed: Andrew Miller [Sarah does not sign]. Witnesses: Absolum Knots Sr, James Thomas, Samuel Evans, Hugh Evans, Joh Smith. Acknowledged by Andrew, October 1805, and recorded as to him. No delivery shown. Recorded: OS 3:341-342.

10 December 1805. Thomas and Polly WILSON to Leonard KIMBLE. 44¼ acres on the left side of Laurel Hill, near Deckers Creek, adjoining Guseman and Shaver. Patented to Wilson 21 January 1800. Consideration: $22.12½, VA. Signed: Thomas Wilson, Polly Wilson. Witnesses: J W Campbell, John Kemiel. Acknowledged by Thomas, December 1805, and recorded as to him. Del: to Jno Kemble, 2 November 1807. Recorded: OS 3:342-343.

14 October 1805. James and Margret CURRENT to John CURRANT. 300 acres on Three Forks, no adjoiners named. Consideration: £100, VA. Signed: James [X] Currant [Margret does not sign]. Witnesses: none. Acknowledged by James, October 1805, and recorded as to him. Del: to him, 31 May 1815. Recorded: OS 3:344-345.

27 February 1805. John DOWNER to Peter HENKINS. 29 acres on Dunkard Creek, adjoining James Marshell and William Lemaster. Consideration: $20, VA. Signed: John Downer. Witnesses: Alexander Clegg, Robert Cunningham. Acknowledged in court, October 1805. Del: to Peter Henkins, 10 October 1808. Recorded: OS 3:345-346.

10 December 1805. Hedgman and Molly TRIPLETT to Jacob GILMORE. 165 acres on the headwaters of Sandy Creek, near the MD line, adjoining Frederick Spahr Jr, Widow Burkham, and Ephraim Frazee. Consideration: $300, VA. Signed: Hedgman Triplett, Molly Triplett. Witnesses: none. Acknowledged in court, December 1805. Del: to John ???, 11 April 18??. Recorded: OS 3:346-347.

11 October 1805. James and Margret CURRANT to James CURRANT Jr. 300 acres on Threefork Creek, adjoining John Current. Consideration: £100, VA. Signed: James [X] Current [Margret does not sign]. Witnesses: none.

Acknowledged in court by James, October 1805, and recorded as to him. Del: to him, 10 April 1809. Recorded: OS 3:347-348.

14 October 1805. John DOWNER to John HEADLEE, Green Co, PA. Tract, acreage not stated, on Dunkard Creek, adjoining Adam Brown, Headlee's other land, and Martin Varner. Consideration: $20, VA. Signed: John Downer. Witnesses: none. Acknowledged in court, October 1805. Del: to Jno Headlee, 17 October 1807. Recorded: OS 3:349.

14 October 1805. Edward (Sr) and Sarah EVANS to William CHIPPS. 116½ acres adjoining Edward Evans Jr. Part of a 400 acre patent. Consideration: $200, VA. Signed: Edward Evans Senr, Sarah Evans. Witnesses: none. Acknowledged in court, October 1805. Del: to Thomas R Chipps, 9 September 1807. Recorded: OS 3:350.

7 February 1804. Joseph and Jane TIDBALL, Corporation of Winchester, Frederick Co, to Archabald WATTS, Hampshire Co. 2666 acres between Big and Little Sandy Creeks, adjoining Robert Brownfield, James Arnold, William McCleery's large survey, Aaron Ogden, John Harden, John Berry, and Thomas Berry. Patented 3 October 1794. Consideration: £500, VA. Signed: Joseph Tidball, Jane Tidball. Witnesses: Thomas A Tidball, Josiah Tidball, Alexr F Lanham. Acknowledged by Jane in Frederick Co, before W Davison and Thos Stribling, JPs. Proved by witnesses in Frederick Co, February 1804. No delivery shown. Recorded: OS 3:351-353.

14 October 1805. Meshack SEXTON, Fayette Co, PA, to Enos DAUGHERTY. 245 acres on a branch of the Valley River, no adjoiners mentioned. Part of 445 acres taxed in the name of William Vincent and sold for non-payment of the direct tax by Alexander Hawthorn, collector of the direct tax. Conveyed to Sexton by Joseph Scott, marshal of the VA District, 26 March 1805. Consideration: $245, VA. Signed: Meshack Sexton. Witnesses: none. Acknowledged in court, October 1805. Del: to Enos Daugherty, 21 November 1808. Recorded: OS 3:353-354.

[no date] George and [wife's name called for but blank] BEATY, heir at law of Levy BEATY deceased, late of Hampshire Co, to Nicholas CASEY. 276 acres on Snowey Creek, adjoining a tract formerly belonging to Henry Hawk and now property of Nicholas Casey. Patented to Levy Beaty, 20 March 1785. Consideration: [blank]. Signed: Geo Batty. Witnesses: Wm Buffington, Wm Nayler, Samuel Nuzum, And Woodrow. Acknowledged by George in Hampshire Co, 16 September 1805. Certificate of Andrew

CHC. Del: to E Butler, 2 October 1807. Recorded: OS 3:354-356.

19 November 1805. The heirs and legal representatives of Colonel Zackwell MORGAN, deceased [none of the heirs are named in this instrument], by Jacob SCOTT, their attorney, to Frederick GEBLER. Lot #125 in Morgan Town. Subject to 25¢ ground rent annually. Consideration: $7. Signed: Jacob Scott. Witnesses: Nimrod Evans, James Evans, Mathew Gay, John W Campbell, Thomas Laidley, E Horton. Acknowledged in court, December 1805. Del: to R Barkshire, 6 August 1832. Recorded: OS 3:357-358.

11 December 1805. Thomas and Polly WILSON to Thomas KNIGHT Jr. 50 acres on the west side of Monongalia River, on Pawpa Creek and Woods Run, adjoining William Knight. Part of 400 acres patented to Wilson, 21 January 1800. Consideration: $100, VA. Signed: Thomas Wilson, Polly Wilson. Witnesses: none. Acknowledged in court, December 1805. Del: to Thos Knight, 25 October 1806. Recorded: OS 3:358-359.

[blank] 1805. James PINDALL, Jemima PINDALL, Rachael PINDALL, Forbes and Elizabeth BRITTON, heirs of Thomas PINDALL, deceased, to Moses BEARD. 162 acres on Flaggy Meadow Run, adjoining John Dawson, John Combs, and Edward Pindall's heirs. Consideration: £50, VA. Signed: James Pindall, Forbes Britton, Eliza Britton [other named grantors do not sign]. Witnesses: Edward [X] Evans, John [X] Dawson, Benjamin [X] Jenkins, Thomas R Chipps, Daniel Cox. Acknowledged in court by Forbes and Elizabeth, December 1805. Proved by witnesses as to James. Del: to M Beard, 14 June 1809. Recorded: OS 3:359-360.

11 December 1805. Thomas and Polly WILSON to William KNIGHT. 50 acres on the west side of Monongahela River, on Popaw Creek and Woods Run, adjoining Thomas Knight. Part of 400 acres patented to Wilson, 21 January 1800. Consideration: $100. Signed: Thomas Wilson, Polly Wilson. Witnesses: none. Acknowledged in court, December 1805. Del: to Wm Knight, 6 February 1818. Recorded: OS 3:360-361.

7 September 1805. Moses and Sarah CURRY to Moses CURRY Jr, Alleghany Co, PA. 335 acres on Sandy Creek, no adjoiners named. Part of 800 acres patented to Thomas Moore, 25 April 1784, and conveyed by him to John Kelly, 5 May 1791. Kelly conveyed to John Richy, 6 September 1793, and John and Jane Richy conveyed to Curry, 10 November 1802, for £200, PA. Consideration: $300. Signed: Moses Curry, Sarah Curry. Witnesses:

Nimrod Evans, Robert Ferrel, John W Dean. Acknowledged by Sarah before Robert Ferrel and John W Dean, JPs, 11 December 1805. Del: to Moses Curry, 24 October 1809. Recorded: OS 3:361-363.

11 July 1791. Albert GALITAN [sic], Fayette Co, PA, to Thomas MASON, Washington Co, PA. Release. On 3 March 1790 a patent was issued to Albert Galitan, assignee of Thomas Mason, assignee of Dennis Springer, for 376 acres south of the lands of Jacob Jacobs. Galitan held the tract in trust for Mason and now releases the trust. Consideration: 5s. Signed: Albert Galitin. Witnesses: John Davis, Saml Hanway, William MCleery. 10 December 1805. Release. Mason has sold this tract to Leonard Kimble. It has since been learned that this tract and a Thomas Wilson patent overlap one another. Kimble and Wilson have come to terms, and Kimble releases any land within this patent that is also claimed by Wilson. Signed: Leonard Kimble. Witnesses: J W Campbell, John Kemel. Acknowledged by Leonard, December 1805. No delivery shown. Recorded: OS 3:364.

3 December 1804. William McCLEERY to George DOSSEY. 400 acres on Deckers Creek, near Deep Hollow Run. No adjoiners named. Consideration: $150, VA. Signed: William McClerry. Witnesses: J Evans, Robt Boggess, H Dering. Acknowledged in court, December 1804. Del: to George Dorsey, 19 December 1807. Recorded: OS 3:365-366.

9 December 1805. Zackariah and Ann BARKER to Nathan CANFIELD. 15 acres on Big Indian Creek, adjoining John Mcfarland. Consideration: $200, VA. Signed: Zachariah Barker [Ann does not sign]. Witnesses: none. Acknowledged by Zachariah, December 1805, and recorded as to him. Del: to N Canfield, 28 November 1806. Recorded: OS 3:366.

9 December 1805. Charles and Hannah MAGILL to Robert ABERCRUMBY. 8 acres in the forks of Pairpoints Run, adjoining Levi Rogers and near the old mill house. Purchased by Magill from Thomas Boyd. Consideration: $500, VA. Signed: Charles Magill, Hannah Magill. Acknowledged in court, December 1805. Del: to Mrs Abercrumby, 14 October 1808. Recorded: OS 3:367-368.

[undated] John DOWNER to Jacob SCOTT. Letter of release. In 1786 Colonel Zackquell Morgan and Drusilla sold two lots to Downer. Downer sold one of them to Baldwin Weaver and has since been informed that Weaver sold to Gebler, who now lives on it. Gebler has the original deed from Morgan to Downer. Downer requests Scott to make Gebler a deed for the said lot. Signed: John Downer. Witnesses: Thos Wilson, Polly Wilson, John

W Campbell, Frederick Gibler. Proved by witnesses, December 1805. No delivery shown. Recorded: OS 3:368.

8 September 1806. William and Margret DARLING to Moses ROYSE. 400 acres on the west side of Cheat River, at Buffalo Nob, adjoining James Morgan, John Green, and John Daugherty. Consideration: $2000. Signed: William Darling, Margret [mark] Darling. Witnesses: none. Acknowledged in court, September 1806. Del: to Moses Royce, 12 May 1809. Recorded: OS 3:369.

12 October 1805. George and Charlotte PECKENPAUGH to Joseph SUTTON. 145 acres on one of the heads of Scotts Mill Run, adjoining William Dawson, Luke Harmenson, and James Buckannon. Consideration: $400. Signed: George [X] Peckenpaugh, Charlottee [sic] [X] Peckenpaugh. Witnesses: none. Acknowledged in court, October 1805. Del: to Joseph Sutton, 2 September 1808. Recorded: OS 3:370.

14 April 1805. Samuel and Mary CLARK to John FICKLE. 165 acres adjoining Gabriel Fickle, Terah Doran, and Samuel Darley. Part from a 1 September 1801 conveyance to Clark by William and Sarah Squire, and part from a 21 December 1798 patent for 41 acres. Consideration: £130. Signed: Samuel Clark, Mary Clark. Witnesses: Alexr Brandon, John Cwey[?], Terah Doran, James Clark. Acknowledged by Mary before James Clark and John McLain, JPs, 14 May 1805. Proved by witnesses, October 1805 and December 1805. Del: to J Fickle, 13 April 1807. Recorded: OS 3:371-372.

9 October 1798. John and Mary KENNEDY to Samuel COBB. 500 acres on the north side of Elk River, adjoining a survey of Ann Raines. Part of 1000 acres patented to John Davis, 29 August 1786. Consideration: £200, VA. Signed: John Kennedy, Mary Kennedy. Witnesses: none. Acknowledged in court, October 1798. No delivery shown. Recorded: OS 3:373.

4 April 1805. Jonathan DAVIS, Wilkinson Co, MS Territory, to Luke TIERNAN, Baltimore, MD. Two tracts. 6 acres near the north end of Morgan Town, adjoining Pindall's heirs. Conveyed to Davis by Thomas and Sarah Laidley. Undivided moiety of a 1505 acre patent of 19 August 1799 on Roaring Creek, adjoining William Daugherty and Joseph Butler Jr. Consideration: $500. Signed: Jonathan Davis. Witnesses: none. Acknowledged in Natchez, MS Territory, 26 October 1805. Certificate of Samuel Brooks, mayor. Del: to John Stealey, 25 September 1809. Recorded: OS 3:374-375.

25 November 1803. WILL of Clement MERL. Wife Catharine: all property for her life (1/3 if she

remarry), with reversion to daughter Catharine (to take 2/3 immediately if and when her mother should remarry). Executrix: wife Catharine. Signed: Clement Merl. Witnesses: John Dent, Thomas Cordray, Margret Dent. Proved by witnesses, December 1804. Recorded: OS 3:375-376. [Also recorded in Wills 1:311-312.]

8 October 1804. Uriah and Sarah MORGAN to Josiah PRICKETT. 100 acres on the west side of Monongahela River, adjoining heirs of Joseph Batton and John Martain. Part of John Springer's survey. Consideration: $300. Signed: Uriah Morgan, Sarah Morgan. Witnesses: none. Acknowledged in court, October 1804. Del: to Josiah Prickett, 12 January 1807. Recorded: OS 3:376-377.

2 [?] October 1804. James DUNN to his son Henry DUNN. Power of attorney. James is about to remove from Monongalia Co and names Henry his attorney to sell property and collect debts. Signed: James [X] Dunn. Witnesses: Morgan Morgan, Jacob Polsley, James Morgan. Proved by witnesses, April 1805. Del: to James Morgan, 1 April 1807. Recorded: OS 3:377.

8 October 1804. Jacob and Abigal MINTHORN, Hambleton Co, OH, by William JOHNSON, their attorney in fact, to John HASTON, Fayette Co, PA. 61½ acres on the east side of Muddy Creek, no adjoiners named. Part of a 2000 acre survey. Consideration: $60. Signed: Wm Johnson. Witnesses: none. Acknowledged in court by Johnson, October 1804. Del: to him, 13 June 1812. Recorded: OS 3:378.

31 August 1802. Jesse MARTIN to David SWANK. Mortgage on 400 acres on the west side of Monongalia River. Patented to Charles Martin, 20 April 1784, and conveyed by his will to Jesse Martin. Jesse may redeem by paying £65, PA, to Swank on or before 1 May 1804. Swank to pay rent according to their former contract, which remains in force until 1 March 1804. Swank gives Martin an order on Joshua Jones for £65. If Jones protests, this writing is to be returned to Martin. Signed: Jesse Martin. Witnesses: H Reeder, Peter [mark] Swank. Memo by Jesse Martin, 11 July 1803, reacknowledging the mortgage, and witnessed by Abraham [+] Mayfield, Ames Mayfield, and John [X] Swank. Proved by witnesses, September 1803. Del: to Presley Martin, 1 September 1812. Recorded: OS 3:379.

15 February 1803. John and Ann EVANS to their son Nimrod EVANS. 1000 acres on Robinson Run, a branch of Popaw Creek, adjoining William McCleery and heirs of James Scott. Patented 24 June 1791. Consideration: 1

silver dollar, natural love and affection. Signed: John Evans [Ann does not sign]. Witnesses: none. Acknowledged by John Evans, February 1803, and recorded as to himself. No delivery shown. Recorded: OS 3:380.

22 October 1804. John W DEAN to William G PAYNE, trustee. Deed of trust. Dean owes $250 to Henry Dering, to be paid on or before 20 October 1806. To secure the debt, Dean entrusts 2 sorrel horses, a pair of oxen, milch cows, beds, rifle guns, chest, loom, kettles, tables, and other personal property. Signed: John W Dean, Henry Dering, Wm G Payne. Witnesses: James Pindall, Robert Hawthorn. Proved by witnesses, January 1805 and February 1805. No delivery shown. Recorded: OS 3:381.

13 April 1803. Thomas TANEHILL to John GRIBLE. 97 acres on Sandy Creek and Cheat River, no adjoiners named, the south end of a survey. Consideration: $300. Signed: Thos Tonnehill. Witnesses: Sammuel Baker, Uriah Joseph, John Soyers, Philip [X] Shuman. Proved by witnesses, September 1804 and October 1804. Del: to John Gribble Jr, 6 July 1808. Recorded: OS 3:382.

8 December 1806. Peyton BYRN, Harrison Co, to William SMITH, executor of John SMITH, late of Prince William Co. 200 acres on the west side of Cheat River, adjoining Thomas Butler and Robert Bettill[?]. Part of 400 acres patented to Byrn. Consideration: £88. Signed: Peyton Byrn. Witnesses: none. Acknowledged in court, December 1806. Del: to Wm Smith, 10 December 1806. Recorded: OS 3:383.

13 June 1804. John DOWNER to Thomas SEDGWICK. 112 acres at the mouth of Rudolph Run, adjoining Michael Statler, Peter Henkins, John Statler, and the PA line. Consideration: $110, VA. Signed: John Downer. Witnesses: Wm G Payne, Wm N Jarrett, Fauquer [X] McCrea. Acknowledged in court, September 1804. No delivery shown. Recorded: OS 3:384.

19 May 1806. Margaret HERFORT, Frederick Co, to her daughter Nancy WOODROW, wife of Abraham WOODROW, of Morgan Town. Deed of gift. Negro woman Rachel, 21 years old, and her children Clary, 4 years old, and Reuben, 2 years old, with all the increase of the females. Nancy to have said Negroes for her lifetime, and after her death they are to descend to her children or to such persons as she may direct and appoint under a writing or a last will and testament. Signed: Margret Herfort. Witnesses: Obed Waite, John Bell, William Peper. Proved by witnesses at court of hustings for the corporation of Winchester, 30 May 1806. Certificate of Thomas McKeean,

clerk. Del: to A Woodrow, 29 September 1807. Recorded: OS 3:384-385.

11 November 1806. Robert and Issabella PATTON to James BELL. 291 acres on Deckers Creek, adjoining William Watson, James Coburn, and Frances Patton. Consideration: $1000, VA. Signed: Robert Patton, Issabella [X] Patton. Witnesses: Wm G Payne, Henry Dering, Marmaduke Evans. Acknowledged in court, December 1806. Del: to James Beall, 18 December 1806. Recorded: OS 3:385-386.

8 December 1806. James McGEE to Archabald ANDERSON. 312 acres on Three Forks, adjoining Benjamin Brain and Anderson's survey. Conveyed by Thomas McGee to James McGee. Consideration: $800. Signed: James McGee. Witness: James Evans. Acknowledged in court, December 1806. Del: to him, 3 August 1811. Recorded: OS 3:386-387.

11 June 1805. Jacob and Catharine SCOTT to Elisha CLAYTON. 400 acres on Indian Creek, adjoining Gilbert Butler, John Mcfarland, William Stewart, Nathan Thomas, and heirs of John Stewart. Minus 40 acres of the original, taken by prior claim of Stewart. Consideration: $400. Signed: Jacob Scott, Catherine [X] Scott. Witnesses: none. Acknowledged in court, July 1804. Del: to grantee, 23 May 1815. Recorded: OS 3:387-388.

8 October 1804. Josiah and Charity PRICKETT to Uriah MORGAN. 100 acres, no adjoiners or place names mentioned. Part of a 373 acre patent. Consideration: $300. Signed: Josiah Prickett, Charity [+] Prickett. Witnesses: none. Acknowledged in court, October 1804. Del: to him, 9 March 1812. Recorded: OS 3:89.

9 January 1804. Philip and [wife called for but not named] SHIVELY to William SHAHAN. 25 acres, adjoining William Hamilton. Patented to Barnett Haney and conveyed by him to Shively. Consideration: £[blank], VA. Signed: Philip Shively. Witnesses: none. Acknowledged by Philip, January 1804, and recorded as to him. Receipt for consideration money. No delivery shown. Recorded: OS 3:390.

10 May 1800. Jacob and Leticia WILSON to William WILSON, all of Berkeley Co. John Wilson, father of Jacob and William, died intestate and seized of 4 tracts in Monongalia Co: 430 acres adjoining Robert Minnis, James Morrison, and Thomas Davis. 327 acres, no adjoiners named. 122 acres adjoining John Simpson and Philip Doddridge. 121 acres adjoining Jesse Bayles. Jacob conveys all his interest, amounting to 1/3, of the

tracts described. [Text is ambiguous but Michael Wilson, evidently another son of John Wilson, is mentioned in passing.] Consideration: £105. Signed: Jacob Wilson, Leticia Wilson. Witnesses: Wm Lang, J Brown, D Thomas. Receipt for consideration money. Acknowledged in Berkeley Co, 23 September 1800. Certificate of J Bedinger, CBC. Del: to John P Wilson, July 1810. Recorded: OS 3:391-393.

13 April 1795. David and Rachael SCOTT to Andrew ARNET. 200 acres on Indian Creek, adjoining James Arnet and Thomas Pindel. From a patent to Scott and Frederick Gire. Consideration: £100. Signed: David Scott, Rachael Scott. Witnesses: John Dent, Joseph Cox, John Collins. Receipt for consideration money. Acknowledged in court, April 1795. No delivery shown. Recorded: OS 3:393-394. Re-recording of burned instrument.

12 February 1805. John and Ann EVANS to Dudley EVANS. 183 acres on the west side of Monongalia River, where Dudley now lives, adjoining Henry Stephens and John Ferry. Consideration: $1. Signed: J Evans, Ann Evans. Witnesses: none. Acknowledged by John, February 1805, and recorded as to him. Del: to grantee, 14 November 1821. Recorded: OS 3:394-395.

3 November 1804. Isaac and Rebecca VENMETER, Hampshire Co, to Abraham VENMETER, Hardy Co. Two tracts: 156 acres on Snowey Glade Creek, no adjoiners named, surveyed 26 April 1785. 126 acres on Snowy Glade Creek, surveyed 30 October 1784 and part of Isaac's 400 acre tract. No adjoiners named. Consideration: $300. Signed: Isaac Venmeter, Rebecca [*] Venmeter. Witnesses: Andrew Woodrow, Edward Dyer, Samuel McGuire, James Darley. Acknowledged in Hampshire Co, 17 December 1804. Certificate of Andrew Woodrow, CHC. No delivery shown. Recorded: OS 3:395-396.

3 November 1804. Isaac and Rebecca VENMETER, Hampshire Co, to Abraham VENMETER, Hardy Co. 400 acres on waters of Yohogania, including Isaac's 1774 improvement. No adjoiners named. Consideration: $150. Signed: Isaac Venmeter, Rebecca [R] Venmeter. Witnesses: And Woodrow, James Dailey, Samuel Mcguire, Edward Dyer. Acknowledged in Hampshire Co, 17 December 1804. Certificate of Andrew Woodrow, CHC. No delivery shown. Recorded: OS 3:396-397.

[blank] December 1804. Thomas and Ann RUSSEL to William RUSSEL. 120 acres at Crooked Run, near the PA line, no adjoiners named. Part of 345 acres patented to Thomas, 4 July 1788. Consideration: $1. Signed: Thomas Russel, Ann Russel. Witnesses: Wm McCleery, Mathew Gay,

James West. Acknowledged in court, December 1804. Del: to Wm Russel, 13 April 1807. Recorded: OS 3:398-399.

8 April 1805. Thomas and Ann RUSSEL to James TARNEY, of PA. 55 acres adjoining William Russel, Samuel Gooding, and John Mckinely. Patented to Thomas Russel, 4 July 1788. Consideration: $220.72. Signed: Thomas Russel, Ann [X] Russel. Witnesses: none. Acknowledged in court, April 1805. Del: to James Tearney, 9 February 1807. Recorded: OS 3:399-401.

8 April 1805. Elihu and Catherine HORTON to Alexander BRANDON. 250 acres on LIttle Sandy Creek, adjoining Richard Brandon. Surveyed 7 June 1785. Consideration: $250. Signed: Elihu Horton, Catherine Horton. Witnesses: none. Acknowledged in court, April 1805. No delivery shown. Recorded: OS 3:401-402.

[blank] April 1805. Henry and Cloe SYNE to Leonard CUPP. 94 acres on Beaver and Little Sandy Creeks, where Leonard now lives. Part of a larger tract conveyed to Henry by Samuel Hanway. Consideration: $[blank]. Signed: Henry [+] Syne, Clary[?] [+] Synes. Witnesses: none. Acknowledged in court, April 1805. Del: to Leonard Cupp, 12 September 1808[?]. Recorded: OS 3:402-403.

6 April 1805. Absalom and Nancy KNOTS to John RUNNER, Frederick Co, MD. 50 acres on Sandy Creek, no adjoiners named. From patents of 21 July 1800 and 5 April 1803. Consideration: $100, VA. Signed: Absalom [+] Knotts, Nancy [+] Knotts. Witnesses: none. Acknowledged in court, April 1805. No delivery shown. Recorded: OS 3:404.

26 March 1805. Joseph SCOTT, Marshal of the VA District, to Meshack SEXTON. 500 acres, no place names or adjoiners mentioned, assessed in the name of Jacob BOWEN and sold for non-payment of $2.17 direct tax. Signed: Joseph Scott. Witnesses: J H Lynch Jr, John G Smith, William McEnry. Acknowledged in Richmond, VA, 1 April 1805. Certificate of J Robinson, CDC. No delivery shown. Recorded: OS 3:405-406.

26 March 1805. Joseph SCOTT, Marshal of the VA District, to Meshack SEXTON. 782 acres, assessed in the name of Ann CLARK and sold for non-payment of $1.31 direct tax. 185 acres of the land, located on Big Youghioghany, is conveyed. Signed: Joseph Scott. Witnesses: J H Lynch Jr, John G Smith, John McEnna[?]. Acknowledged in Richmond District Court, 1 April 1805. Certificate of J Robenson, CDC. No delivery shown. Recorded: OS 3:407-408.

26 March 1805. Joseph SCOTT, Marshal of the VA District, to Meshack SEXTON. 130 acres, no place names

or adjoiners mentioned, assessed in the name of Benjamin WOODS and sold for non-payment of $1.13 direct tax. Signed: Joseph Scott. Witnesses: J H Lynch, John G Smith, William McEnry[?]. Acknowledged in Richmond District Court, 1 April 1805. Certificate of J Robinson, CDC. No delivery shown. Recorded: OS 3:411-412.

5 September 1806. James BARKER to James BOWLBY. 52 acres adjoining Hezekiah Wade and James Pollock, land formerly belonging to James and John Pollock. Consideration: [blank]. Signed: James Barker, Mary Barker [wife is not mentioned in body of instrument]. Witnesses: none. Acknowledged in court, September 1806. Del: to James Bowlby, 11 April 1808. Recorded: OS 3:413.

14 April 1806. Robert and Jane GRAHAM, Jefferson Co, OH, to John CARPENTER. 92 acres on waters of Monongalia, where Carpenter now lives, adjoining William Miller, John Graham, Elisha Brotton, and Jeremiah Galihew. Part of a patent to Abraham Sisco, deceased, and conveyed to Graham by his heirs. Consideration:$300. Signed: Robert [+] Graham, Jane [+] Graham. Witnesses: none. Del: to J Carpenter, 14 August 1809. Recorded: OS 3:414.

9 April 1806. John and Margret DENT to John Evans DENT. 225 acres on Booths Creek, adjoining Capel Holland and Robe. Consideration: love, good will and natural affection. Signed: John Dent [Margret does not sign]. Witnesses: none. Acknowledged by John Dent in court, April 1806, and recorded as to him. No delivery shown. Recorded: OS 3:415.

9 April 1803. Nathan and Rachael MATHENY to John MATHENY. 50 acres adjoining Nathan Matheny. No place names mentioned. Consideration: £30. Signed: Nathan [X] Matheny, Rachel [X] Matheny. Witnesses: none. Acknowledged by Nathan Matheny in court, April 1803, and recorded as to him. Acknowledged by Rachel Matheny before William Johnson and Amos Roberts, JPs, 19 September 1806. Del: to the [word missing], 2 September 1808. Recorded: OS 3:416.

[blank] April 1806. Robert and Jane GRAHAM, Jefferson Co, OH, to Jeremiah GALLYHEW. Parcel adjoining Gallyhew's other land. Consideration: £8, VA. Signed: Robert [+] Graham, Jane [+] Graham. Witnesses: none. Acknowledged in court, April 1806. Recorded: OS 3:417.

11 June 1806. William and Margit BIGGS to William BUCKALEW. 100 acres adjoining Jacob Smith. Part of a 195 acre patent to Biggs, 9 July 1798. Consideration: $283.33, VA. Signed: William Biggs, Margret [X] Biggs. Witnesses: none. Acknowledged by William Biggs, June

1806; acknowledged by Margret Biggs before John McLain and Amos Roberts, JPs, 14 September 1806. Del: to him, 10 April 1809. Recorded: OS 3:417-418.

15 April 1805. John and Easter STAFFORD to James STAFFORD. 400 acres on Buffalo Creek, no adjoiners named. Patented to Charles Magill, 28 July 1796. Consideration: $120. Signed: John Stafford, Easter [+] Stafford. Acknowledged in court, April 1806. No delivery shown. Recorded: OS 3:419.

15 April 1806. Andrew KIRK PATRICK by Samuel BROWN, his attorney in fact, Fayette Co, PA, to Rodger HUNT. 100 acres, no adjoiners or place names mentioned. Patented to Andrew Kirk Patrick for 600 acres, 19 November 1801. Consideration: $200, VA. Signed: Samuel Brown. Witnesses: none. Acknowledged by Brown in court, April 1806. No delivery shown. Recorded: OS 3:420.

24 May 1806. Jacob (Sr) and Elisabeth NUSE to Alexander HAWTHORN and Robert HAWTHORN. 300 acres at Aarons Creek, where the Hawthorns now live, all adjoining but from several separate tracts: 22 acres formerly owned by David Croll and conveyed to Jacob Nuse 9 July 1798. 40 acres purchased from Joshua Jenkins. 88 acres from a patent to Nuse, 20 March 1800. 150 acres from a patent of 200 acres to Nuse, 18 April 1788. Consideration: $3000, VA. Signed: Jacob Nuse, Elisabeth [+] Nuse. Witnesses: Wm G Payne, Henry Dering, B Reeder. Acknowledged in court, July 1806. Del: to Mr Alexander Hathorn, 5 January 1813. Recorded: OS 3:420-421.

14 July 1806. Articles of agreement between Alpheus WICKWARE and Mary WICKWARE, widow of John WICKWARE, deceased. Peter Johnson and William Lake have been chosen as referees to determine what portion of John Wickware's estate his widow shall take as sufficient compensation for relinquishment of her dower rights in his real estate. Alpheus is to pay Mary £200, plus 1/3 of the corn and small grain now sowing, half of the flax and hemp, plus the garden vegetables. A note for £20 on Aaron McDonald is assigned to her as part of the payment, and she is to take the remainder in property at the cash valuation set by the appraisers. She will give up the premises on or before 1 April next and relinquish all claims whatever to dower. Signed: Peter Johnson, William Lake, Alpheus Wickware, Mary [X] Wickware. Acknowledged in court, July 1806. Del: to Saml Wickware, 20 February 1818. Recorded: OS 3:421-422.

1 April 1806. William PETTY JOHN to George LAKE, Harrison Co. 109 acres on Glady Creek, part of a settlement right belonging to the heirs of William Petty

John deceased. No adjoiners named. Consideration: $300. Signed: William Petty John. Witnesses: William Lake Jr, Robert Henderson, Barney [0] Byrnes, Nathan Hall. Proved by witnesses, April 1806. Del: to George Lake, 24 August 1807. Recorded: OS 3:422-423.

11 July 1806. Alpheus WICKWARE, Warren Co, KY, heir at law to John WICKWARE, deceased, to Noah FORD. 400 acres on the east side of Tigervalley River, adjoining George Wilson. Surveyed4 October 1794 for John Wickware, assignee of Josiah Wilson. Consideration: $180. Signed: Alpheus Wickware. Witnesses: Peter Johnston, [name erased], John Nuzum. Acknowledged in court, July 1806. No delivery shown. Recorded: OS 3:424.

9 August 1805. John HOYE, George Town, DC, to Ketty BRANNAN and Absalom BRANNAN. 331 acres on Snowey Glade Creek, adjoining Smith. Conveyed to Hoye by John Hooker. Consideration: $1. Signed: John Hoye. Witnesses: Nimrod Evans, R Barkshire, James Evans. Proved by witnesses, September 1806. Del: to grantee, 22 August 1806 [sic]. Recorded: OS 3:425.

10 May 1806. Henry and Abigal BARRAKMAN to Michael KOR. 164 acres, part of 2 tracts, adjoining Lewis Kerns, Samuel Davis, William Lamaster, Joseph Hunt, David Piles, Hanway and Ford, and Randolph [sic] Snider. Consideration: $640, VA. Signed: Henry [+] Barrakman, Abigal [+] Barrakman. Witnesses: Samuel Minor, Moses Snider, Christopher Core. Acknowledged in court, September 1806. Del: to M Core, 26 January 1808. Recorded: OS 3:426-427.

9 June 1806. Thomas and Margret McGEE to James McGEE. 312 acres on Threefork, adjoining Benjamin Brain. Part from a tract patented to Francis Woolf, deceased, 14 October 1787; from him to Reese Woolf, and from him to Thomas McGee; the rest from a tract deeded by Benjamin Brain. Consideration: $400. Signed: Thomas McGee, Margret [X] McGee. Witnesses: none. Acknowledged in court, June 1806. No delivery shown. Recorded: OS 3:427-428.

8 September 1806. David (Jr) and Sarah SAYRE, Mason Co, [VA?] to James WEST Jr. 200 acres purchased from Richard Maryfield. No adjoiners or place names mentioned. Consideration: $600. Signed: David Sayre, Sarah [S] Sayre. Witnesses: none. Acknowledged in court, September 1806. Del: to George Fimple, per order from West, 3 February 1807. Recorded: OS 3:428.

27 May 1805. Premarital agreement between William N JARRETT, Mary alias Polly McNEELY, and Ralph BARKSHIRE and Thomas WILSON. Hugh McNeely's will, dated 8 February

1804, bequeathed his entire estate, real and personal, to his wife Polly McNeely. She intends to remarry to William N Jarrett. If the marriage takes place, Jarrett and his heirs, assigns, executors, &c, are to take no part or have any interest in law or equity in a house and lot in Morgan Town where Polly now lives and which was part of her former husband's estate. This will remain for her sole and separate use and benefit. Barkshire and Wilson to act as trustees for the property, but she reserves the right to dispose of it by will or other writing. Signed: William N Jarrett, Mary McNeely, Ralph Barkshire, Thomas Wilson. Witnesses: Sarah Barkshire, Nancy Kiger, Fielding Kiger. Proved by witnesses, December 1805, February 1806. No delivery shown. Recorded: OS 3:429-431.

13 March 1806. John and Phebe MORE to Zacquell PAIRPOINT. 70 acres, no adjoiners or place names mentioned. Lot #6 of the division among Lott Ridgeway's heirs, the portion that fell to Noah Ridgeway's share. Consideration: $200. Signed: John More, Phebe[+] More. Witnesses: B Reeder, John W Dean, Noah Ridgway. Acknowledged by Phebe More before B Reeder and John W Dean, JPs, 13 March 1806. Proved by witnesses, September 1806. Del: to James Watson, 12 June 1810. Recorded: OS 3:431-432.

13 October 1806. Jacob and Hannah PINDALL, John and Hannah CHIPPS, William and Hannah CHIPPS, Simian and Elisabeth RICE, Thomas R and Rachel CHIPPS, and Amos CHIPPS to Peter WILLHAM [alternately WILLHLEM]. 238 acres at Roaring Creek, adjoining Cunningham and John Chipps. From a 375 acre patent to Thomas Chipps, 1 May 1784. Consideration: $200, VA. Signed: William Chipps, Elizabeth Rice, Thomas R Chipps, Rachael Chipps, Amos Chipps, Jacob Pindall, Hannah Pindall, John Chipps, Simeon Rice, Hannah [+] Chipps, Hannah [+] Chipps. Witnesses: Zacquell Morgan, Nicholas Madera, Philip Pindall, Charles Byrn, James Evans. Acknowledged in court by Thomas R, Amos, Elisabeth Royse, Rachel, Hannah, and Hannah Chipps, October 1806; by William, John, Jacob Pindall, and Simeon Royse, January 1808; by Hannah Pindall, February 1808. Del: to grantee's son, 31 March 1828. Recorded: OS 3:432-433.

9 June 1806. Robert (Sr) and Hannah FERREL to James JEFFS. 3 acres, 1 rood, 10 perches on White Day, adjoining Smithfield Town, James G Watson, Richard Smith, Assa [?] Harris. Consideration: $49. Signed: Robert Ferrel, Hannah [+] Ferrel. Witnesses: none. Acknowledged in court, June 1806. Del: to him, 17

February 1809. Recorded: OS 3:434.

13 March 1806. John and Phebe MORE to Catherine RIDGEWAY. 44 acres, no adjoiners or place names mentioned. Lot #4 in the division of Lott Ridgeway's real estate, the portion that fell to Phebe More. Consideration: $120. Signed: John More, Phebe [+] More. Witnesses: B Reeder, John W Dean, Noah Ridgeway. Acknowledged by Phebe More before B Reeder and John W Dean, JPs, 18 March 1806. Proved by witnesses, September 1806. Del: to grantee, 13 October 1823. Recorded: OS 3:435.

[blank] April 1806. Henry and Abigal BARRAKMAN to Samuel DAVIS. 60 acres adjoining Joseph Hunt, Michael Kor, and William Anderson. Consideration: $60, VA. Signed: Henry [+] Barrakman, Abigal [+] Barrakman. Witnesses: none. Acknowledged in court, September 1806. Del: to Mrs Davis, 21 December 1807. Recorded: OS 3:436.

21 December 1805. John (Sr) and Hannah BRUMAGE to David DUNHAM. 60 acres adjoining William Haymond, from the survey that John Brumage Sr and John Brumage Jr live on. Patented to Arthur Trader, 2 December 1785, and conveyed by him to John Brumage Sr, 14 April 1794. Consideration: $200. Signed: John [+] Brumage [Hannah does not sign]. Witnesses: Wm Haymond, Jacob Pawlsley, Henry Barns. Acknowledged in court by John Brumage, April 1806. Commission to take Hannah's acknowledgement but no action recorded here. Del: to David Dunham, 9 February 1807. Recorded: OS 3:437.

[blank] 1806. Henry and Abigal BARRAKMAN to James HENDERSON. 50 acres adjoining Joseph Hunt and Samuel Davis. Consideration: $50, VA. Signed: Henry [+] Barrakman, Abigal [+] Barrakman. Witnesses: none. Acknowledged in court, September 1806. Del: to James Henderson, 11 April 1808. Recorded: OS 3:438.

15 June 1806. Thomas GLENN, late of Jefferson Co, to James HITE, Jefferson Co. 200 acres on Bingaman, including the Stone Coal Lick, below lands entered for Thomas Rutherford and adjoining Jacob Reisch [?]. Consideration: $500. Signed: Thomas Glenn. Witnesses: John Abell, Daniel Morgan, John Baker, B Stephenson. Proved by witnesses in Jefferson Co. Certificate of Geo Hite, CJC. No delivery shown. Recorded: OS 3:438-439.

14 July 1806. Barnabas and Elizabeth JOHNSON [alternately JOHNSTON in body of instrument] to Jepthah WILKINS. 5 acres on the west side of Johnson's land, adjoining Wilkins' other land. Part of 2 small tracts conveyed by Nicholas Weaver and wife and by Daniel Johnston and wife, originally from a 400 acre survey

granted to Henry Weaver 7 December 1793. Consideration: $25. Signed: Barnabas Johnson, Elizabeth Johnson. Witnesses: none. Acknowledged in court, July 1806. Del: to Wilkins, 12 December 1807. Recorded: OS 3:440.

10 February 1806. John BARKER to James BARKER. 103 acres, 34 perches at Dents Mill Run, adjoining Nancy Martin and Aaron Henry. Consideration: £5, VA. Signed: John [+] Barker. Witnesses: none. Acknowledged in court, February 1806. Del: to Jas Barker, 25 January 1808. Recorded: OS 3:441.

24 June 1805. Jacob FOULK to William TINGLE. Deed of trust. On 31 December 1803 Foulk entered 2 obligations to David Bayles, with Elihu Horton as security, by which Foulk was to provide Bayles with $600 in crockery ware, payable 1 October 1804, and a further $600 in crockery ware, payable 1 March 1805. At that time Foulk gave to William Tingle a deed of trust on land he had purchased from Bayles. Bayles and Foulk agree to defer the payments to 1 March 1806, at that time to be made in full. To secure the obligation, Foulk now conveys in trust to Tingle the house and lot in Morgan Town where he has his potter's kiln. Signed: Jacob Foulk, David Bayles, W Tingle. Witnesses: J[oseph] Campbell, Abner Grant, John Thompson. Proved by witnesses, January 1806. No delivery shown. Recorded: OS 3:442-443.

13 March 1806. John and Phebe MORE to Ross ALLEY. 89 acres on the south side of Whites Run, adjoining lands belonging to the heirs of Lott Ridgeway. Part of 240 acres patented to James More. Consideration: $200. Signed: John Moore, Phebe [+] Moore. Witnesses: B Reeder, J Evans, John W Dean. Acknowledged by Phebe More, 13 March 1806, before B Reeder and John W Dean, JPs. Proved by witnesses, July 1806. No delivery shown. Recorded: OS 3:443-444.

14 July 1806. Thomas and Sarah MARTIN to John CUNNINGHAM. 66 acres on Little Popaw, no adjoiners named. Part of the tract where Martin lives. Consideration: $165. Signed: Thomas Martin, Sarah Martin. Witnesses: none. Acknowledged in court, July 1806. Del: to John Cunningham, 20 June 1807. Recorded: OS 3:445.

8 April 1805. Christeen CLUSTER and Jacob CLUSTER [not identified as husband and wife] to Peter EVERLY. 185 acres, no place names mentioned. From a parcel conveyed by George and Mary Sipolt to Henry Criss, and by Henry and Catherine Criss to Christina Cluster and Jacob Cluster, and also from a parcel patented to Henry

Criss. Consideration: £188. Signed: Jacob Cluster ["signed in Dutch"], Christian [+] Cluster. Witnesses: none. Acknowledged in court, April 1805. No delivery shown. Recorded: OS 3:446.

26 March 1804. Letters of administration on the estate of John HARDIN, deceased, late of Fayette Co, PA, to Cato Hardin (Zadock Springer, one of the nominated executors, having renounced). Signed: Alexander McClean.

13 May 1803. WILL of John HARDIN, Fayette Co, PA. Wife Issabella: whatever the law allows her. Sons John and Absalom Hardin: Bauld Hill tract, 400 acres, in Springhill Twp, Fayette Co, PA, minus 50 acres otherwise bequeathed; also, 400 acres called Middle Cove in Randolph Co. Son Henry and illegitimate son John: 359 acres in Harrison Co. Daughter Mariam: 300 acres out of a pre-emption in Hardins Cove, to be taken at the end known as Rich Gap. Daughter Mary Ann: 5s. Isabella and Elizabeth, daughters of Mary Ann: 208 acres on Threefork Creek, Monongalia Co. Daughter Molthea[?]: 5s. Son Hector: 5s. Son Nester: 100 acres from the preemption at Hardins Cove, he having received 400 acres previously. Daughter Alice: 50 acres of Bauld Hill, adjoining the great road. Sons George and Cato: 290 acres where they now live. Grandson Henry and granddaughters Mathilda and Mary Ann, children of son Hector: 600 acres in Hardins Cove, if so much remains of the pre-emption there. Mills and conveniencies of water works, with 12 acres from the tract I live on, to be sold and money divided among the children (those who received 5s in the will to take nothing of this division). Executors: son Cato and Zadock Springer. Signed: John Hardin. Witnesses: John Smith, Lott Abraham, John Gans. Proved by witnesses, 3 June 1803, in Fayette Co, PA.

13 June 1803. Francis MITCHEL enters a caveat against the alleged will of John Hardin.

16 March 1804. Certificate of Abraham Douglas, prothonotary of Fayette Co, PA, that in a suit, Zadock Springer and Cato Hardin, Executors of John Hardin, vs Francis Mitchell, verdict had been given for the plaintifs. Preceding documents recorded: OS 3:447-449. [Also recorded in Wills, 1:308-311.]

8 April 1805. James and Mary THOMAS to Reuben JACO. 156 acres at Sandy Creek, adjoining John Kenedy. Tract conveyed to Thomas by Robert Wilson. Consideration: $1000, VA. Signed: James [+] Thomas [Mary does not sign]. Witnesses: Nimrod Evans, Jacob MIller, Hugh Evans, Samuel Evans. Acknowledged in court by James Thomas, April 1805, and recorded as to him. No delivery

shown. Recorded: OS 3:449.

[blank] 1806. John and Lucrecia TAYLOR to John STOCKWELL. 120 acres on Sandy Creek, a branch of Tegers Valley River, adjoining George Keller[?] and Thomas Berry. Patented to Taylor, 26 February 1805. Consideration: $150, VA. Signed: John Taylor, Lucrecia Taylor. Witnesses: none. Acknowledged in court, April 1806. Del: to J Stockwell, 21 August 1809. Recorded: OS 3:450.

23 July 1806. Charles DAWSON, Dearbourn Co, IN, to Parthena WINDSOR, William WINDSOR, Jemima WINDSOR, Blanche WINDSOR, and Moan[? but sic] WINDSOR, legal heirs of James WINDSOR, deceased. 54 acres on Little Indian Creek, no adjoiners named. Consideration: $160. Signed: Charles Dawson. Witnesses: Nimrod Evans, Wm N Jarrett, R Barkshire. Proved by witnesses, September 1806. Del: to Wm Winsor, 27 August 1808. Recorded: OS 3:451.

10 March 1806. John and [wife mentioned but not named] PETTY JOHN to George BARNS. 400 acres on a branch of Teger Valley River below Gladey Creek, no adjoiners named. Patented 11 December 1795. Consideration: $640, VA. Signed: John [H] Petty John. Witnesses: Rawley Martin, Geo R Tingle, Ezekiel Chaney. Proved by witnesses, April 1806. Del: to G Barnes, 18 February 1807. Recorded: OS 3:452.

14 July 1806. Jacob and Elizabeth NOOSE to Abraham WOODROW and Simeon WOODROW. 2 tracts, one of 40 and the other of 100 acres, on Coburns Creek, between the surveys of Joshua Jenkins and John McGee, adjoining Joshua Jenkins, Thomas McGee, and McCrea. Both tracts patented to Robert Bennett, 2 December 1791, conveyed by him to Samuel Nixon, 18 March 1798, and conveyed by Nixon to Jacob Noose, 8 October 1798. Consideration: $600. Signed: Jacob [+] Noose, Elizabeth [X] Noose. Witnesses: none. Acknowledged in court, July 1806. Del: to Simeon Woodrow, 23 November 1811. Recorded: OS 3:453.

15 April 1806. George and Margaret BARNS to John A BARKSHIRE. 62 3/4 acres on Scotts Meadow Run, adjoining Jacob Pindall, John Bran, and William Smith. Part of a larger tract patented to John Hamilton, from him to Samuel Byers, from him to Barns. Consideration: $500. Signed: George Barns, Margret Barns. Witnesses: Jacob Kiger, R Barkshire, Augustus Ballah. Acknowledged in court, April 1806. Del: to grantee, 31 May 1817. Recorded: OS 3:454.

14 July 1806. James and Catharine ROBINSON to Adam MINEAR. 100 acres on Tiger Valley River, adjoining John

Wickware, opposite where Minear now lives. Consideration: $150. Signed: James [+] Robinson, Catherine [+] Robinson. Witnesses: none. Acknowledged in court, July 1806. No delivery shown. Recorded: OS 3:455.

14 July 1806. James and Sarah MUSGRAVE to William MORRIS. 94½ acres on Pappa Creek, no adjoiners named. Part of 395 acres patented to Samuel Musgrave, 13 October 1789, and conveyed by him to James Musgrave, 25 March 1805. Consideration: $115. Signed: James Musgrave, Sarah [+] Musgrave. Witnesses: none. Acknowledged in court, July 1806. Del: to Wm Morris, 24 September 180[?]. Recorded: OS 3:456.

15 April 1806. David and Ann CROLL to Jacob NUSE. 17½ acres near Joseph Trickett. No place names mentioned. Consideration: £17.10, VA. Signed: David Croll, Ann Croll. Witnesses: none. Acknowledged in court, April 1806. No delivery shown. Recorded: OS 3:457.

29 December 1805. Jacob and Elizabeth NUSE to Joseph JANES [Jones?]. 59½ acres, no place names mentioned, including a tenement now in possession of Samuel Rolston. Part of 2 tracts, one patented to Nuse, the other to Joshua Jenkins, latter tract conveyed by decree of Monongalia County court and by a deed from Jenkins' heirs. Consideration: $225, VA. Signed: Jacob [X] Nuse, Elizabeth [+] Nuse. Witnesses: Thomas Byrn, Charles Byrn, George Zinn, Nimrod Evans, Wm G Payne. Acknowledged by Elizabeth Nuse before N Vandervort and Thomas Miller, JPs, 27 January 1806. Proved by witnesses, February 1806. Del: to Janes, 5 June 1807. Recorded: OS 3:458-459.

12 July 1806. Alpheus WICKWARE, Warren Co, KY, heir at law of John WICKWARE, to Aaron McDONALD [alternately McDANIEL throughout instrument]. 99 acres on the east side of Tegervalley River, opposite Minear. Consideration: $130. Signed: Alpheus Wickware. Witnesses: none. Acknowledged in court, July 1806. Del: to Mathew Robison, 27 May 1806. Recorded: OS 3:460.

8 July 1806. Jacob PINDALL to Amos ROBERTS. Lien on black woman Rose, black girls Els and Suck, black boy Charles, waggon and oxen, cows, horse creatures, and hay in the meadow at the crab orchard of Pindall's land. Roberts has 2 notes of Pindall, for £100 each, and the property is invested "to mak payment for them two obligations without any further suit at law." The property to be valued by 2 disinterested parties and to be conveyed to Roberts "all or as much thereof as will satisfy the debt with Damages." Consideration: $200.

Signed: Jacob Pindall. Witnesses: none. Acknowledged in court, July 1806. No delivery shown. Recorded: OS 3:461.

14 July 1806. Thomas and Sarah LAIDLEY to Amos CHIPPS. The Sepulchre Lot [# not given] in Morgan Town, between High Street and Water Street, opposite Frederick Gibler's tanyard. Includes 3s annual quit rent. Consideration: $300. Signed: Thomas Laidley, Sarah Laidley. Witnesses: none. Acknowledged in court, July 1806. Del: to Chipps, 31 October 1807. Recorded: OS 3:462.

14 July 1806. Amos ROBERTS to William WALLER. 140 acres on waters of Cheat[?] River, no adjoiners named. Part of a 290 acre survey. Consideration: $400. Signed: Amos Roberts. Witnesses: none. Acknowledged in court, July 1806. Del: to him, 15 September 1807. Recorded: OS 3:463.

14 July 1806. Henry and Nancy WEAVER to Adam FAST. 201 acres on Whiteday Creek, no adjoiners named. Consideration: $772.50. Signed: Henry Weaver, Nancy [+] Weaver. Witnesses: none. Acknowledged in court, July 1806. Del: to Fast, 24 March 1807. Recorded: OS 3:464.

14 July 1806. Jonathan and Elizabeth GANDY to John MORE. 100 acres at Gladey Run, near the Clarksburgh road. Conveyed by Samuel Gandy to Jonathan Gandy. Consideration: $300. Signed: Jonathan Gandy, Elizabeth Gandy. Witnesses: none. Acknowledged in court, July 1806. No delivery shown. Recorded: OS 3:465.

15 April 1806. James and Lucrecia STAFFORD to John STEALY. 150 acres on Laurel Run, adjoining and below Stafford's mill place, adjoining William Tonnehill. Part of a preemption warrant issued 18 December1784. Consideration: none stated. Signed: James Stafford, Lucrecia Stafford. Witnesses: none. Acknowledged in court, April 1806. Del: to grantee, 10 December 1821. Recorded: OS 3:466.

8 September 1806. Edward GUTRIDGE to John S BARNS. 200 acres on Sandy Creek, a branch of Tiger Valley River. No adjoiners named. Consideration: $300, VA. Signed: Edward Gutridge. Witnesses: none. Acknowledged in court, September 1806. Del: to J S Barns, 3 June 1809. Recorded: OS 3:467.

1 April 1805. Joseph (Jr) and Mary SEVERNS to William MICHAELS. 118 acres on Little Sandy Creek, adjoining James Dunwoody, the same survey that Severns has lived on for several years past. Consideration: £118, VA. Signed: Joseph Severns, Mary [+] Severns. Witnesses: James Webster, John McLain, Joseph Severns. Acknowledged by Mary Severns before John McLain and J

Clark, JPs, 23 October 1805. Proved by witnesses, January 1806. Del: to him, 10 April 1809. Recorded: OS 3:468-469.

8 September 1806. George and Henrietta Isabella GREENWOOD to Elizabeth CLARK. 100 acres at Aarons Creek, adjoining George Dossey and Peter Swisher. Part of a tract conveyed to Greenwood by David Croll. Consideration: $500. Signed: George Greenwood, Henrietta Issabella Greenwood. Witnesses: none. Acknowledged in court, September 1806. Del: to Shackelford, 30 December 1807. Recorded: OS 3:470.

16 May 1806. Dr Daniel and Elizabeth MERCHANT, Fayette Co, PA, to Henry DERING. Several adjoining tracts on the east bank of the Monongalia River, 111 acres adjoining and below the mouth of Falling Run, adjoining B Reeder. 2 acres adjoining, with reference to conveyance by Richard Lee to McIntire. 50' of land from the high water mark, from the mouth of Falling Run to Henry Dering's line, conveyed by Benjamin Reeder to Alexander McIntire. Total, 150 acres. Consideration: $2000. Signed: Daniel Merchant [Elizabeth does not sign]. Witnesses: J Evans, Thos Wilson, Nimrod Evans, Samuel Hanway. Proved by witnesses as to Daniel Merchant, [blank] 1806. Del: to G S Dering, 14 November [blank]. Recorded: OS 3:471.

8 September 1800. Joseph and Elizabeth SOUTHWORTH to Samuel MERIDITH. Tract on Sandy Creek, acreage not stated, no adjoiners named. Part of 2000 acres patented to David Hanway, 3 September 1788, and conveyed by him to Southworth the same date. Consideration: $50. Signed: Joseph Southworth, Elisabeth Southworth. Witnesses: none. Acknowledged in court, September 1806. Del: to L Manear[?], 13 April 1807. Recorded: OS 3:472.

[undated, c1802/3?] Sarah SMITH, Fayette Co, PA, to Thomas LAZZEL. Lease on 375 acres where George Fraizier now lives. Lazzel to take possession 1 March 1803 and to retain land until the heirs of William Augustus Smith shall be of legal age. If ejected earlier, Sarah will make Lazzel a clear title to 400 acres where he now lives. Consideration: none stated. Signed: Sarah Smith, Thomas [mark] Lazzell. Witnesses: George Smith Sr, Amos Smith, George Smith Jr. Acknowledged by both parties, 1 April 1806. Witnesses: George Smith, William Goodwin. Proved by witnesses, September 1806. Del: to Thos Lazzel, 5 June 1809. Recorded: OS 3:473.

12 February 1806. Jacob and Hannah PINDALL to William CHIPPS. 400 acres on a creek between Robinson Run and the main fork, including Scott's 1776

settlement. No adjoiners named. Pindall warrants only so much title as William and Hannah Chipps had conveyed to him in this property. Consideration: $1000. Signed: Jacob Pindall, Hannah Pindall. Witness: Thomas Chipps. Acknowledged in court, February 1806. No delivery shown. Recorded: OS 3:473-474.

10 February 1806. Jacob and Nancy PINDALL to Benjamin HAMILTON. 54 3/4 acres on the west side, adjoining John Evans' survey. Patented to James Scott and conveyed by David Scott of James to the heirs of Joshua Deweese. Consideration: $300. Signed: Jacob [+] Pindall, Nancy [+] Pindall. Witnesses: none. Acknowledged in court, February 1806. Del: to him, 13 November 1809. Recorded: OS 3:474-475.

20 October 1804. Gerrard CLARY, Alleghany Co, MD, to James McALESTER, Hampshire Co. 2 tracts. 400 acres in Sandy Creek Glades, between Little Sandy and Beaver Creeks, adjoining lands John Willack[?] conveyed to Richard Swan, from a patent to Anthony Worley Jr. Conveyed to Clary by Thomas Baker. 125 acres on Buffalo Run and Beaver Creek, no adjoiners named. Conveyed to Clary by Enoch Hand[?]. Consideration: £500, MD. Signed: Gerrard Clary. Witnesses: Rodger Perry, Saml Hughes Jr. Acknowledged in Allegany Co, MD, 15 October 1804. Certificate of John Lynn, clerk. Del: "to Alexander King grantor J McAlister [sic]," 4 September 1809. Recorded: OS 3:475-477.

2 September 1805. Herman GREATHOUSE to Thomas EVANS. Bill of sale for one young horse, one red cow, one red and white cow. Consideration: $50 for horse, $12 each for the cattle. Signed: Harman Greathouse. Witnesses: John Waggoner, Josiah [+] Hoskinson. Acknowledged in court, January 1806. No delivery shown. Recorded: OS 3:477.

29 March 1805. Elijah PILES, one of the heirs and executors of John PILES, deceased, to Nemiah [alternately Nehemiah] SQUIRES. 100 acres adjoining a Big survey, Cain, and Daniel Fortney. Consideration: $100, VA. Signed: Elijah [+] Piles. Witnesses: Wm G Payne, Thomas Payne, Samuel Prunty. Acknowledged in court, April 1805. Del: to Squires, 12 December 1809. Recorded: OS 3:478.

14 September 1806. John EVANS to James EVANS and Marmaduke EVANS. 2 tracts. 971 acres on Papa Creek, patented 13 August 1786 and adjoining a settlement survey. 400 acres adjoining a preemption survey. To be divided equally by quality and quantity. Consideration: natural love and affection, plus $1. Signed: J Evans.

Witnesses: none. Acknowledged in court, April 1806. No delivery shown. Recorded: OS 3:479.

10 September 1793. David and Judith SCOTT to Stephen GAPPEN, Washington Co, PA. 438 acres on the west side, nearly opposite Morgan Town, adjoining James Scott, Jacob Scott, and Thomas Pindall. From patents of 17 December 1774 [sic] and 24 June 1791. Consideration: 5s, VA. Witnesses: none. Acknowledged by Judith Scott before John Dent and Thomas Chipps, September 1793. Del: to Stephen Gapen, 31 January 1807. Recorded: OS 3:480-481. Re-recording of burned instrument.

14 July 1806. Charles and Priscilla CONWAY, late widow of Jonathan REES, and Barnabas and Elisabeth SMITH, Elisabeth formerly REES, daughter and heir of Jonathan REES, all of Fayette Co, PA, to John CARTER. Conveyance of Priscilla's dower right and Elisabeth's undivided third in 400 acres on the east bank of Monongalia River, formerly belonging to Jonathan Rees, deceased, and conveyed to him by William Moore, 12 June 1786. No adjoiners named. Consideration: $1000. Signed: Charles Conway, Pricilla [+] Conway, Barnabas Smith, Elisabeth Smith. Witnesses: J Evans, Nimrod Evans, Thos Wilson. Acknowledged by Priscilla and Elizabeth before Wm N Jarrett and Jno Stealey, JPs, 11 August 1806. Proved by witnesses, September 1806. Del: to him, 13 October 1812. Recorded: OS 3:481-483.

8 September 1806. John and Sarah MORE to Amos[?] GANDY. 55 acres adjoining Samuel Gandy. No place names mentioned. Consideration: $200. Signed: John Moore, Sarah Moore. Witnesses: none. Acknowledged in court, September 1806. Del: to [illegible], April 1831[?]. Recorded: OS 3:483-484.

9 April 1806. John and Margret DENT to Dudley ["Evans" written and erased] DENT. 225 acres on Booths Creek, adjoining John Evans, Dent, Robe, and others. Consideration: love, good will, and affection. Signed: John Dent [Margret does not sign]. Witnesses: none. Acknowledged in court, April 1806, by John Dent, and recorded as to himself. Del: to D Dent, 23 March 1807. Recorded: OS 3:484.

14 April 1806. Jordan and Nancy HALL to Dudley EVANS. 150 acres on the west bank of Monongalia River, adjoining Allen Hall and Evans' other land. Patented to Jordan Hall, 2 January 1807. Consideration: $800. Signed: Jordan Hall, Nancy Hall. Witnesses: none. Acknowledged in court, April 1806. Del: to grantee, 16 December 1822. Recorded: OS 3:485.

14 January 1806. James and Elisabeth JEFFS to John JEFFS, of PA. 91 acres on the east side of Monongalia River, no adjoiners named. Part of a larger tract patented to Abner Harper, 13 April 1800. Consideration: $900. Signed: James Jeffs, Elisabeth Jeffs. Witnesses: none. Acknowledged in court, April 1806. Del: to him, 21 October 1807. Recorded: OS 3:486.

8 September 1806. Jacob and Sarah WEAVER to James STEEL. 41+ acres on Booths Creek, adjoining Theophilus Philips and Steel's other land. Consideration: $160, VA. Signed: Jacob Weaver, Sarah [+] Weaver. Witnesses: none. Acknowledged in court, September 1806. Del: to Jas Steel Jr, 5 September 1808. Recorded: OS 3:487.

27 August 1805. James HARTLEY [LAMASTER originally written and deled, HARTLEY interlined above it] to Henry BARNS. 100 acres on Gises Run, at the west end of the tract where Anthony Hartley lives. Conveyed by Anthony to James, 9 October 1797. Consideration: $140. Signed: James Hartley. Witnesses: Wm G Payne, Henry Dering, Davis Shockley, J Campbell, John Scott. Proved by witnesses, January 1806. Del: to Henry Barns, 9 November 1808. Recorded: OS 3:488.

10 June 1806. James McGEE to Henry DERING. Deed of trust. McGee has given 2 bonds to John Evans, payable 9 October 1807 and 9 October 1808, amounts not stated. To secure the debt he entrusts 312 acres on Threefork Creek, adjoining Benjamin Brain. The land to be sold in 2 years and 4 months, if the debt not satisfied. Signed: Jas McGee, Henry Dering. Witnesses: Nimrod Evans, James Evans, Thos R Chipps. Proved by witnesses, September 1806. No delivery shown. Recorded: OS 3:488-489.

13 July 1806. Henry DERING to Michael KERNS Jr. One half of a tract on the east side, conveyed to Dering by Daniel Merchand. Kerns has built a compleat water gristmill on the property, at his own expense. Dering is to pay half the expenditures on the building, millhouse, dam, and abutments. Should he fail to pay, Kerns is to complete the works and receive all rents and profits after the mill ["she"] is in full operation, and until Dering shall make the required payments. Signed: Henry Dering, Michael Kerns. Witnesses: none. Acknowledged in court, July 1806. No delivery shown. Recorded: OS 3:490-491.

19 April 1806. Elisabeth LYNCH and Daniel and Issabella JOHNSTON to John NICHOLAS. 40 acres adjoining David Sayre Jr, James Steele, Philip Shacklesworth, and land where Nicholas now lives. From a 28 July 1800 patent to Patrick Lynch. Consideration: $50. Signed:

Elis [sic] [+] Lynch, Danl [+] Johnson, Issabella [mark called for but blank] Johnson. Witnesses: B Reeder, Samuel Hanway, Jacob Foulk. Proved by witnesses as to Elisabeth Lynch and Daniel Johnson, no date. Del: to him, 27 March 1815. Recorded: OS 3:491.

8 September 1806. William and Mary MYRES to Jacob WEVELY and Frederick WEVELY, Fyatte Co, PA. 110 acres on Glade Run, a branch of Sandy Creek, adjoining George and Michael Noze. Part of 600 acres patented to Samuel Hanway. Consideration: $250. Signed: William [+] Myers [Mary does not sign]. Witnesses: none. Acknowledged in court by William Myers, September 1806. Order to take Mary's acknowledgement but no action recorded here. Del: to Henry Walter, 27 February 1807. Recorded: OS 3:492.

8 September 1806. William and Mary MYRES to George NOOZ and Michael NOOZ. 148 acres on Glade Run, a branch of Sandy Creek, adjoining James Hotts[?], Absalom Hotz, and Jacob Wively. Part of 600 acres patented to Samuel Hanway. Consideration: $200. Signed: William [+] Myres [Mary does not sign]. Acknowledged in court by William Myers, September 1806. Order to take Mary's acknowledgement but no action recorded here. Del: to H Walter, 27 February 1807. Recorded: OS 3:493.

8 September 1806. William and Margret DARLING to Hugh KELSO. 106 acres on the west bank of Cheat River, no adjoiners named. Patented to William Darling in 1804. Consideration: $367. Signed: William Darling, Margret [+] Darling. Acknowledged in court, September 1806. Del: to him, 15 February 1815. Recorded: OS 3:494.

19 August 1806. John HOYE, George Town, DC, to John SMITH. 450 acres on Snowey Glade Creek, adjoining lands conveyed to Ashby and to Branham. From a tract conveyed to Hoye by John Hooker. Consideration: $1, plus a note of James Goff assigned to Hoye, amount not stated. Signed: John Hoye. Witnesses: Frederick Harsh, Jacob Smith, Henry [+] Smith. Proved by witnesses, 10 June 1808. Del: to John Smith, 10 June 1808. Recorded: OS 3:495.

14 April 1806. John RUNYON, Champaign Co, OH, to James CLARK. 300 acres on Muddy Creek, adjoining William Biggs, former land of Lewis Criss, and George Woolf. Consideration: $200. Signed: John Runyon. Acknowledged in court, April 1806. Del: to Jas Clark, 12 June 1806. Recorded: OS 3:496.

11 April 1805. Hugh and Mary MORGAN to John ROBERTS, Washington Co, PA. Lots #1,2, and 3 in Kingwood, adjoining Jacob Foulk and Coonrod Sheetz. From a 400 acre patent of 20 April 1784. Consideration: $22,

VA. Signed: Hugh Morgan, Mary [+] Morgan. Witnesses: Wm Herring, George Peters, Abraham Fullen. Acknowledged in court, October 1805, by Hugh Morgan; by Messia [sic] Morgan before David Morgan and James E Beall, JPs, 10 January 1807. Del: to Roberts, 6 May 1807. Recorded: OS 3:497.

12 October 1805. Hugh and Mary MORGAN to Abraham S FULLEN. Lots #6,7,8,9,10 in Kingwood. From a 400 acre patent for 20 April 1784. Consideration: $24. Signed: Hugh Morgan, Mary [+] Morgan. Witnesses: Wm Herrin, Michael [+] Floyd, Jacob Funk. Acknowledged in court, October 1805, by Hugh Morgan; by Messia [sic] Morgan before David Morgan and James E Beall, JPs, 10 January 1807. Del: to A P[?] Fullen, 14 April 1807. Recorded: OS 3:498.

8 September 1806. John and Elisabeth MATHENY to Samuel MARRAIN[?]. 50 acres, no adjoiners or place names mentioned. Conveyed to John by Nathan and Rachel Matheny. Consideration: £50, VA. Signed: John [+] Matheny, Elisabeth [+] Matheny. Acknowledged in court, September 1806. Del: to Saml Marain[?], 10 August 1807. Recorded: OS 3:499.

7 May 1806. Margret McGINLEY, Moyamening Twp, Philadelphia Co, PA, widow of John McGINLEY (blacksmith), Isaac (tailor) and Mary DAVIS, Southwark, Philadelphia Co, PA (Mary a daughter of John McGINLEY deceased), Martha OWENS, Pasyank Twp, Philadelphia Co, PA, Samuel (shoe seller) and Christiana MEEKER, Philadelphia Co, PA (Christiana a daughter of John McGINLEY deceased), William McGINLEY, Pasyank Twp, Philadelphia Co, PA, Christian (yeoman) and Ann STUTLER, Lemerick Twp, Montgomery Co, PA (Ann a daughter of John McGINLEY deceased), Samuel McGINLEY (cordwainer), Philadelphia, PA, and Joseph [illegible initial] McGINLEY, Moyamening Twp, Philadelphia Co, PA, to Robert M WILSON, Southwark, Philadelphia Co, PA. 100 acres adjoining Thomas Russell, no place names mentioned. Part of 345 acres patented to Russell, 4 July 1788, and conveyed by Thomas and Mary Russell to John McGinley in his lifetime, 12 April 1790. Consideration: $400. Signed: Margret McGinley, Isaac Davis, Mary Davis, Martha Owins, Samuel Meeker, Christiana Meeker, William McGinley [other grantors named do not sign]. Witnesses: Samuel Mcferran, Samuel [+] Thomas, Wm McIlhenny Jr, James Tarney. Receipt for consideration money, signed by Margret McGinley only. Acknowledged by signatory parties in Philadelphia, PA, 7 October 1808. Certificate of John Inskip, mayor. Proved by witness Samuel Thomas in court,

July 1806. Del: to Joseph Peckinpaugh, 8 June 1807. Recorded: OS 3:499-501.

23 July 1806. John E BILLS, late of Morgan Town, to Ruth E BILLS, his wife, and John SULLIVAN, her trustee and next friend. Articles of separation. Ruth is to keep, maintain, and support the children until they are of an age to support themselves, and to "breed them up in habits of morality & Industry." Any property now owned or later acquired by Ruth is to be vested in Sullivan as trustee, and no property of hers may be subject to payment of debts contracted by John E Bills. She relinquishes claim to any estate hereafter acquired by John, who agrees not to interrupt or disturb her or their children without permission. Signed: John E Bills, John [+] Sullivan. Witnesses: W Tingle, Geo R Tingle. Proved by witnesses, January 1807. No delivery shown. Recorded: OS 3:501-502.

4 September 1797. Commission to Bourbon Co, KY, to take the acknowledgement of Mary SIMPSON. 12 November 1798. Acknowledgement of Mary SIMPSON, wife of Jeremiah SIMPSON, to a 15 June 1797 conveyance to James Edmonstone BEALL and James BEALL, for 389½ acres, before Peter Flemmon and James Bryan, JPs. Del: to J E Beall, 10 February 1807. Recorded: OS 3:502.

12 April 1790. Thomas and Mary RUSSELL to John McGINLEY. 100 acres adjoining Thomas Russell's other land. Consideration: £5, natural affection and love [no relationship stated]. Signed: Thomas Russell, Mary [+] Russell. Witnesses: Thomas Laidley, James Daugherty. Acknowledged 12 April 1790 before [unsigned], JPs. Proved by witnesses, April 1790. Del: to Joseph Peckenpaugh, 8 June 1807. Recorded: OS 3:502-503. Re-recording of burned instrument.

15 April 1806. David and Ann CROLL to George GREENWOOD. 293 acres on Aarons Creek, adjoining George Dossey, Peter Swisher, Joshua Jenkins, Hawthorns, and the heirs of Stanley. Consideration: $1500, VA. Signed: David Croll, Ann [+] Croll. Witnesses: Robert Boggess, Amesiah Davisson. Acknowledged in court, April 1806. Del: to G Greenwood, 21 May 1808. Recorded: OS 3:504.

8 September 1806. Evan and Elisabeth JENKINS to John MATHENY. 75 acres on Big Sandy, opposite the falls. Part of a tract patented to Jenkins, 2 December 1791. 100 acres of the land sold to Daniel Hill, the rest divided and sold to John Matheny and his brother Nathan. Refers to division line made by Jenkins and John Matheny, previous to Nathan's purchase, and in the presence of William Stuart. Consideration: $500, VA.

Signed: Evan [+] Jenkins, Elisabeth [+] Jenkins. Witnesses: none. Acknowledged in court, September 1806. Del: [blotted, illegible]. Recorded: OS 3:505.

13 September 1806. Jeremiah and Sarah WARREN to Samuel M WILLIAMS, all of Rockingham Co. 187 acres on Daughertys Run, no adjoiners named. Patented to Warren 27 May 1793. Consideration: $187. Signed: Jeremiah Warren, Sarah [+] Warren. Witnesses: none. Acknowledged in Rockingham Co, December 1805 [sic]. Certificate of S McWilliams, CRC. No delivery shown. Recorded: OS 3:506.

[blank] 1807. Richard and Elisabeth SMITH to James JEFFS. Lots #14 and 26 in the town of Smithfield on waters of White Day. Consideration: $72. Signed: Richard Smith, Elisabeth Smith. Witnesses: none. Acknowledged in court, January 1806 [sic]. No delivery shown. Recorded: OS 3:507.

4 February 1805. WILL of John HIRADER. Wife Mary: one third of movables. Two youngest sons, Daniel and John: rest of movables. Daniel to take the property at settling of the estate, and to pay half the value to John when he arrive at 21. Value to be paid in trade, such as horses, cattle, and grain, at common market price. Land to be divided between Daniel and John, with John to have the mill and Daniel to have his grinding free. Daniel also required to give 2 days' work per year cleaning the race. If the widow and sons disagree, Daniel is to provide her with a comfortable house during her widowhood. If she remarry and afterward be left without a home, she is to be provided for as if she had not remarried. Executor to deed 50 acres to Henry Coleman. Executors: Andrew Every, Russell Potter, son Daniel Hirader. Signed: John Hirader. Witnesses: John Gass, Henry Haufman, Levi Potter, Samuel Martin, Levi Potter [sic]. Proved by witnesses, January 1807. Recorded: OS 3:508. [Also recorded in Wills, 1:310-311.]

13 December 1806. Martin WAGNER, Fairfield Twp, Butler Co, OH, to Alexander BRANDON. Power of attorney to convey 30 acres to James Guthrie, land purchased by Wagner from James McPeck. Signed: Martin Wagner. Witnesses: Isaac Stanley, George Wagner. Acknowledged in Butler Co, OH, before Isaac Stanley, JP. Certificate of John Riely, clerk. Recorded: OS 3:509.

13 January 1807. Martin WAGNER, Butler Co, OH, by Alexander BRANDON, his attorney in fact, to James GUTHRIE. 30 acres on Masons Run, a branch of Big Sandy Creek, adjoining Benjamin Woods. Conveyed to Wagner by James McPeck. Consideration: $35. Signed: Alexander Brandon. Witnesses: none. Acknowledged in court, January

1807. Del: to Jesse M Willetts, 6 April 1821. Recorded: OS 3:510.

18 May 1806. Jesse MARTIN to Phebe MARTIN, his daughter. Bill of sale for 2 horses, yoke of oxen, waggon and gears, and 8 head of cattle. Consideration: $115 paid by Robert Scott and David Scott. Signed: Jesse Martin. Witnesses: Scott Martin, Govey Triplett. Proved by witnesses, January 1807. No delivery shown. Recorded: OS 3:511.

20 August 1805. WILL of Paul SHERIDAN. All real and personal property to wife Anna, during her life or widowhood. $50 to her sons William and John Welch. Remainder of property to son Jacob Sheridan. Executor: wife Anna. Signed: Paul Sheridan. Witnesses: Christian Whitehair, Henry Weil, Henry Lantz. Proved by witnesses, January 1807. Recorded: OS 3:511. [Not recorded in Wills.]

27 October 1806. Isaac PRICE to George WILSON. 130 acres on Little Pawpaw, adjoining Laidley and Stokeley, Philip Pierce, and Col John Evans. Consideration: $162. Signed: Isaac Price. Witnesses: Abraham Woodrow, Isaac Price, Benjamin [+] Wilson. Proved by witnesses, January 1807. Del: to Alexr Eddy, per order, 14 September 1821. Recorded: OS 3:512.

18 February 1806. Robert and Margret STERRET to Lester DICKENSON, all of Mckean Twp, Erie Co, PA. 1000 acres on Statlers and Days Runs, branches of Dunkard Creek, adjoining Michael More and Richard Tenant. Patented to Robert Sterret, assignee of John Downer, assignee of Charles Broughton, assignee of William Roberts. Consideration: $500, PA. Signed: Robert Sterett, Margret [+] Sterrett. Witnesses: John Cochran, Sarah Cochran. Receipt for consideration money. Acknowledged in Erie Co, PA, before John Cochran, JP. Certificate of James E Herren, prothonotary. Del: to Lester Dickenson, 1 [December?] 1808. Recorded: OS 3:513-514.

13 January 1807. Thomas and Hannahella [sic] LAZELL to Enoch EVANS, Greene Co, PA. 255 acres on Robinsons Run and Scotts Mill Run, adjoining Abraham Comingys, William Bodley, John Cartney, and John Ramsey. Part from a tract patented to Lazzel, 4 January 1800, and the rest from a tract patented to Thomas Chinowith, whose attorney in fact, William Martin, conveyed to Lazzell 1 March 1802. Consideration: $700. Signed: Thomas [+] Lazzell, Hannahella [+] Lazzell. Witnesses: Geo Greenwood, Robert Boggess, James Royce. Receipt for consideration money. Acknowledged in court, January

1807. Del: to E Evans, 30 September 1809. Recorded: OS 3:514-515.

10 January 1807. George and Henrietta Issabella GREENWOOD to John GOODWIN. Tract on Sandy Creek, acreage not stated, no adjoiners named. Consideration: $200, VA. Signed: George Greenwood, Henrietta Issabella Greenwood. Witnesses: E Daugherty, Jacob Pindell, Pattrick[?] Ream. Acknowledged in court, January 1807. Del: to him, 5 September 1814. Recorded: OS 3:515-516.

30 August 1806. James and Eleanor PORT to John COZAD. 100 acres, no place names or adjoiners mentioned. Consideration: $400. Signed: James Port, Eleanor [+] Port. Witnesses: David Morgan, Anthony Cozad, James E Beall. Acknowledged by James Port in court, January 1807; by Eleanor before David Morgan and James E Beall, JPs, 30 August 1806. Del: to his father, 20 April 1808. Recorded: OS 3:516-517.

13 November 1806. John and Jemima FUNK to James DEWEES. 60 acres adjoining Henry Flayer [?]. Consideration: £50. Signed: John Funk, Jemima Funk. Witnesses: Nathan Matthew, William Watson, Edward Mathew. Receipt for consideration money. Proved by witnesses, January 1807. No delivery shown. Recorded: OS 3:518.

30 August 1806. John COZAD to James PORT. Mortgage on 100 acres which Port sold to Cozad, to secure payment of $266.67 balance due. One fifth the sum to be paid 27 October 1807, and annually from that date. Signed: John Cozad. Witnesses: David Morgan, Anthony Cozad, James E Beall. Acknowledged in court, January 1807. Del: to him, 4 June 1807. Recorded: OS 3:519.

15 January 1807. Amos CHIPPS to John COOPER. One-fifth interest in 75 acres on the west side, adjoining Noah Ridgway, descended to Amos from his father Thomas Chipps. Consideration: $90. Signed: Amos Chipps. Witnesses: none. Acknowledged in court, January 1807. Del: to him, 15 September 1812. Recorded: OS 3:519.

12 January 1807. Jacob SCHISLER to Benjamin TRIMBLY. ¼ acre, 30 poles on Big Sandy Creek, no adjoiners named. Part of a tract conveyed to Jacob by Samuel Morton, 21 March 1803. Consideration: $300. Signed: Jacob Schisler. Witnesses: none. Acknowledged in court, January 1807. Del: to B Trimbly, 13 April 1807. Recorded: OS 3:520.

12 January 1807. Catherine SHEHAN to Robert BUCHER. 25 acres adjoining William Hamilton. Part of a tract patented to Barnet Haney, conveyed by him to Philip Shiveley, and conveyed by Shiveley to Catherine Shehan.

Consideration: $75. Signed: Catherine [+] Shehan. Witnesses: none. Acknowledged in court, January 1807. Del: to R Butcher, 30 April 1808. Recorded: OS 3:521.

9 April 1799. William and Margarett SMILEY to Robert STERRETT, all of Fayette Co, PA. 1000 acres on Statlers and Days Run, branches of Dunkard Creek, adjoining Michael More and Richard Tenant. Patented to William Smiley, assignee of John Downer, assignee of Charles Broughton, assignee of William Roberts. Consideration: £150, PA. Signed: William Smiley, Margret [+] Smiley. Witnesses: Morris Morris, Robert Morris. Receipt for consideration money. Acknowledged in Fayette Co, PA, before Jonathan Rowland and Robert Moore, JPs, 9 April 1799. Certificate of Ephraim Douglass, prothonotary. Del: to Lester Dickenson, 1 [?] 180[8?]. Recorded: OS 3:521-523.

8 October 1804. William and Ann STEPHENSON, Morgan MORGAN, Levy MORGAN, James MORGAN, Uriah MORGAN, Zadock MORGAN, Zacquell MORGAN, Horatio MORGAN, and James and Temperance COCHRAN to Jacob SCOTT. Power of attorney to receive rents, issues and other profits due to the heirs of Col Zack Morgan, agreeable to the deeds, and to recover all town lots which may have descended to the heirs. Signed: William Stephenson, Ann [+] Stephenson, Morgan Morgan, Levi Morgan, Uriah Morgan, Horatio Morgan, Zacquill Morgan, James Cochran, Temperance Cochran, James Morgan, Zadock Morgan. Witnesses: Nimrod Evans, J Kerns (both as to Zadock), Marmaduke Evans. Acknowledged by all parties except Zadock Morgan, October 1804; his acknowledgement proved by witnesses, June 1805. No delivery shown. Recorded: OS 3:523-524.

10 September 1806. Robert and Catherine STUART to William JOHN, John McFARLAND, and Samuel BOWEN, members and agents of the Babtists [sic] church in the forks of Cheat. 1 acre adjoining William John and Robert Stewart. Part of a patent to Thomas Evans, assignee of Galloway, 6 June 1784, and conveyed by Thomas and Catherine Evans to Robert Stuart and John S[???], June court 1804. Consideration: $5. Signed: Robert [+] Stewart, Catherine [+] Stewart. Witnesses: none. Acknowledged in court, September 1805 [sic]. No delivery shown. Recorded: OS 3:524.

14 [illegible] 180[illegible]. Isaac DEARDORF, Monaughan Twp, York Co, PA, and George ROBINETTE, Huntington Twp, Adams Co, PA, executors of Jacob DEARDORF, deceased, of Huntington Twp, Adams Co, PA, to Samuel DEARDORF, Huntington Twp, Adams Co, PA, son of the said deceased. Jacob owned 250 acres in the forks of

Sandy Creek (known as the Five Fork and Sanghill Fork), including the Maple Flats, patented 4 October 1789. His will, dated 9 January 1798, bequeathed this tract to his son Samuel and requested the executors to make him a title for it. Consideration: 5s, PA. Signed: Isaac Deardorf, Geo Robinette. Witnesses: Christian Hoert[?], Jacob Jones. Receipt for consideration money. Acknowledged in Adams Co, PA, 31 May 1804. Certificate of James Duncan, prothonotary. Del: 13 June [year blank] to [illegible]. Recorded: OS 3:525-526.

14 April 1806. Thomas and Sarah WARMAN and Catherine WARMAN to John RAMSEY. 130 3/4 acres, 21 poles, on the east side of Cheat River, adjoining Ramsey's other land, William Stewart, Henry Croll, and Lewis Rogers. Consideration: $800. Signed: Thos Warman, Sarah Warman, Catherine Warman. Witnesses: Enoch Evans, Lemuel John, Andrew Ramsey. Acknowledged by Sarah and Catherine Warman 16 April 1806, before Enoch Evans and Lemuel John, JPs. Proved by witnesses, June 1806. No delivery shown. Recorded: OS 3:527-528.

25 October 1805. Samuel BEVIER[?] to William THOMAS. Bill of sale for personal property, including horse, cattle, grain, still and its vessels, household furnishings, farm tools, a waggon load of potters ware, and a silver watch delivered in the name of the whole. Consideration: $250 in hand or secured to be paid. Signed: Saml Pevire[?]. Witnesses: Joseph Smith, James Thomas, John [+] McClain. Proved by witnesses, June 1806. No delivery shown. Recorded: OS 3:528.

21 February 1805. William STEPHENSON to Joseph WEAVER, for the use of Ann STEPHENSON, wife of William. All of William's right, title, and interest in property that Ann held by dower as the widow of John Pairpoint, including the tract where he lives, 2 lots in Morgan Town willed to Ann by Pairpoint, livestock, farm utensils, household furnishings, and Negro woman Tamer. As long as he and Ann live together, the property may be subject to just debts of William Stephenson now owing. Consideration: $1000. Signed: William Stephenson. Witnesses: Samuel Hanway, Nicholas Vandervort, John Pairpoint. Proved by witnesses, June 1805. Del: to Mrs[?] Stevenson, 30 August 1805. Recorded: OS 3:529.

14 April 1806. John and Catherine RAMSEY to John RAVENSCRAFT. 118 acres, 19 poles on the east side of Cheat River, adjoining Bartholomew Jenkins and William Stewart. Tract conveyed to Ramsey by Joshua Warman, 18 February 1804. Consideration: $650. Signed: John Ramsey, Catherine Ramsey. Witnesses: Nimrod Evans, James Henry,

Rawley Martin, Enoch Evans, Lemuel John. Acknowledged by Catherine Ramsey before Enoch Evans and Lemuel John, 16 April 1806. Proved by witnesses, June 1806. Del: to Enoch Evans, 26 April 1830. Recorded: OS 3:530-531.

14 May 1806. Rebecca WEST to William SMITH. Bill of sale for personal property, including feather bed, bed clothes, bedstead, table, chest, and spinning wheel. Consideration: $100. Signed: Rebecca [+] West. Witnesses: George Debler, Thomas [+] Evans. Acknowledged in court, October 1806. No delivery shown. Recorded: OS 3:532.

8 September 1806. James and Elisabeth BOOTHE, Harrison Co, to James JEFFS. 300 acres on Plum Run, adjoining Jacob Holland. Part of 400 acres patented to Richard PettyJohn, 23 March 1799. Consideration: $400. Signed: James Booth [Elisabeth does not sign]. Witnesses: none. Acknowledged in court by James Booth, October 1806. Order to take Elisabeth's acknowledgement but no action recorded here. Del: to James Jeffs, [?] February 1807. Recorded: OS 3:532.

13 October 1806. Jonathan and Catherine KERNS to William HART. 60 acres at Indian Creek, adjoining John Linch, Abraham Huffman, William Stewart, Zachariah Barker, and William Jenkins. Part of a tract conveyed to Linch by Zachariah Barker. Consideration: $120. Signed: Jonathan [+] Kerns, Catherine [+] Kerns. Witnesses: none. Acknowledged in court, October 1806. Del: to William Hart, 6 August 1807. Recorded: OS 3:533.

9 June 1806. Thompson and Elisabeth PHIDDY to Elisabeth STEWART. 7 acres adjoining John Glasscock, Henry Shoeman, and John Mcfarling. Part of 47 acres conveyed to Thompson Pheady by Zachariah Barker. Consideration: $20. Signed: Thompson Phiddy, Elisabeth [+] Fiddy. Witnesses: none. Acknowledged in court, June 1806. No delivery shown. Recorded: OS 3:534.

17 April 1806. Jeremiah and Johannah WILSON to Henry WEAVER. 100 acres, no adjoiners or place names mentioned. Part of a tract sold by Nehemiah Harper to William Laycock, and by Laycock to Gabriel and Jessey Wilson. Consideration: $500, VA. Signed: Jeremiah Wilson, Johannah Wilson. Witnesses: James G Watson, Jas Jeffs, Thomas West. Acknowledged in court, June 1806. Del: to him, 26 May 1812. Recorded: OS 3:535.

6 June 1806. Samuel HASLET to James GUTHRIE. 180 acres on Piny Run, adjoining John Myers, Samuel Worall, Haslet's other land, and the mill place. Consideration: $8. Witnesses: none. Acknowledged in court, June 1806. Del: to grantee, 8 August 1821. Recorded: OS 3:536.

13 October 1806. Charles and Hannah MAGILL to Samuel HANNAN. 78 acres on the west bank of Cheat River, adjoining Lewis Rogers' former land, Thomas Laidley, Thomas Evans, Lemuel John, and William Stuart. Patented to Magill, assignee of Joshua Noland, 23 August 1797. Consideration: $300, VA. Signed: Charles Magill, Hannah Magill. Witnesses: none. Acknowledged in court, October 1806. Del: to Saml Hanway, 10 September 1808. Recorded: OS 3:537.

6 December 1805. Alexander and Margret CLEGG and Samuel and Susanah MINOR to John JOHNSON. Two tracts. 80 acres on Dunkard Creek, adjoining Michael Barr, James Morris, the PA line, Cleg's other land, Samuel Hanway, Ford & Dering, and John Baldin. 32 acres adjoining the other tract, near the PA line. Consideration: $300. Signed: Samuel Minor, Susanah Minor, Allexander Clegg, Margret Clegg. Witnesses: William Jobes, Michael Core. Acknowledged by Susanah and Margret before William Jobes and Michael Core, JPs, no date; by Samuel and Alexander in court, October 1806. Del: to John Lanse, 10 March 1807. Recorded: OS 3:538-539.

13 October 1806. James and Elisabeth BOOTHE, Harrison Co, to Jacob PRICKETT. 60 acres on Plum Run, adjoining Henry Tucker, part of a 400 acre survey. Consideration: $60. Signed: James Boothe [Elisabeth does not sign]. Witnesses: none. Acknowledged by James Boothe in court, October 1806. Order to take Elisabeth's acknowledgement but no action recorded here. Del: to him, 15 September 1807. Recorded: OS 3:539-540.

10 February 1806. Frederick and Nancy GIRE to James ARNET Sr. 100 acres on Big Indian Creek, adjoining Gilbert Butler and John Stewart's heirs. Part of 400 acres patented to Gire and David Scott. Consideration: $200. Signed: Frederick Gire [Nancy does not sign]. Witnesses: none. Acknowledged by Frederick in court, June 1806, and recorded as to himself. Del: to Danl Arnet, 5 May 1807. Recorded: OS 3:540.

4 September 1806. Commission to Morgan Morgan and Jacob Pawlsley to take the acknowledgement of Hannah Brumage to a conveyance of 25 December 1805 from John and Hannah Brumage to David Dunham. 6 September 1806. Acknowledgement of Hannah Brumage to the conveyance. Recorded: OS 3:541.

15 October 1805. John and Nancy LYNCH to Jonathan KEARNS. 60 acres on Indian Creek, adjoining Lynch's other land, Abraham Huffman, William Stewart, and Zachariah Barker. From a larger tract conveyed to Lynch by Zachariah Barker. Consideration: $120. Signed: John

Lynch, Nancy [+] Lynch. Witnesses: none. Acknowledged in court, October 1805. Del: to Wm Hart, 8 August 1807. Recorded: OS 3:541-542.

13 January 1807. Jonathan ROWLAND, Esq, Borough of Union Town, Fayette Co, PA, to William WILLIAMS, Washington Co, MD. 100 acres on Farrows Run, adjoining James Walker and lands sold to George Young. Part of an 1100 survey adjoining Charles Snodgrass and including a place known as Reeves Improvement. Tract patented to Cornelius Lynch of Union Town, 9 March 1798. Order for resurvey granted in Monongalia Court, May 1801, and tract resurveyed by Col Dudley Evans, assistant to Col Samuel Hanway, on 22 March 1802 for 1195 acres. On 12 June 1804 Lynch conveyed the property in trust to Jonathan Rowland, Esq, and James Morris, Esq, for the benefit of his creditors and under provisions of the Act of Insolvency in the state of PA. Lynch has made a further conveyance to Rowland, dated 24 Inst [sic], the better to warranty title. This tract part of lot #5 in the draft of resurvey taken by William N Jarrett. Consideration: $250. Signed: Jonathan Rowland. Witnesses: John Stealey, Nimrod Evans, Jos Shinn, J Evans Jr, William N Jarrett. Acknowledged in court, February 1807. Del: to William Williams, 11 February 1807. Recorded: OS 3:542-544.

20 January 1807. Jonathan ROWLAND, Esq, Borough of Union Town, Fayette Co, PA, to Thomas MERRIDETH, Washington Co, MD. 169 acres at Farrows Run, adjoining Philip Shively and Adam Trougan [?]. [Same history of title as preceding tract.] Consideration: $422.50. Signed: Jonathan Rowland. Witnesses: John Stealey, Nimrod Evans, Henry Dering, Jos Shinn, J Evans Jr, William N Jarrett. Acknowledged in court, February 1807. Del: to T Merideth, 11 February 1807. Recorded: OS 3:544-545.

14 July 1806. Selee SAYRE and James and Elisabeth JEFFS to Henry WEAVER. 3 acres, 1 rood, and 10 perches on White Day Creek, adjoining Smithfield Town, Asa Harris, James G Watson, and Richard Smith. Consideration: $75. Signed: Selee Sayre, James Jeffs, Elisabeth Jeffs. Witnesses: none. Acknowledged in court by Selee Sayre and James Jeffs, July 1806; by Elisabeth Jeffs, September 1806. Del: to him, February 1811. Recorded: OS 3:546.

7 June 1806. Samuel HASLET to John MYRES. 20 acres on Piny Run, adjoining Myres' other land. Consideration: $10. Signed: Samuel Haslet. Witnesses: none. Acknowledged in court, June 1806. Del: to A Brandon, 22

July 1807. Recorded: OS 3:547.
19 March 1806. Henry HAZLE, late of Monongalia, to Samuel HASLET. 200 acres on Piny Run, adjoining the mill place now held by Haslet. Consideration: $100. Signed: Henry Hazle. Witnesses: Russel Potter, Levi Potter, James Spurgin, James Guthrie, John Mayor, Samuel Willets, [blank, erased] Hendrixon. Proved by witnesses [including Solomon Hendrixon], June 1806. Del: to A Brandon, 15 [illegible] 1809. Recorded: OS 3:547-548.

9 June 1806. James (Sr) and Mary WEST to John MERRILL. 123½ acres on the west side, above the mouth of Parker Run and adjoining Henry Batton. Consideration: $600, VA. Signed: James West, Mary [+] West. Witnesses: none. Acknowledged in court, June 1806. Del: 2 November 1819 [recipient not named]. Recorded: OS 3:548-549.

9 June 1806. Dudley and Annarah EVANS to John BRADLEY, William BRADLEY, and John BRYAN, equal devisees of John BRADLEY, deceased. 287 acres on Sandy Creek, adjoining William Dragoo and George Swank. Part of 1700 acres patented to Dudley Evans, 23 August 1797. Consideration: $500. Signed: Dudley Evans, Annarah Evans. Witnesses: none. Acknowledged in court, June 1806. Del: to Bradley, 9 March 1818. Recorded: OS 3:549.

9 June 1806. James (Jr) and Jane WEST to James JEFFS. 76 acres on the west side of Monongalia River. No adjoiners named. Consideration: $600. Signed: James West, Jane West. Witnesses: none. Acknowledged in court, June 1806. Del: to him, 27 February 1809. Recorded: OS 3:550.

11 June 1804. Zachariah and Nancy BARKER to Abraham HUFFMAN. 113½ acres on Indian Creek, adjoining John Lynch, heirs of John Stewart, Huffman's other land, John Kearns, and Boyles. Part of a 300 acre patent. Consideration: £56, VA. Signed: Zachariah Barker, Ann [+] Barker. Witnesses: none. Acknowledged in court by Zachariah, June 1804, and recorded as to him; acknowledged by Ann, June 1806. Del: to Ab Huffman, 18 May 1808. Recorded: OS 3:551.

9 June 1806. Richard and Elisabeth SMITH to Timothy WARDEN. Lot #16 in the town of Smithfield. Consideration: $25. Signed: Richard Smith, Elisabeth Smith. Witnesses: none. Acknowledged in court, June 1806. Del: to T Warden, 11 September 180[?]. Recorded: OS 3:552.

9 June 1806. Richard and Elisabeth SMITH to Abraham OWENS. Lots #1 and 13 in the town of Smithfield. Consideration: $52. Signed: Richard Smith, Elisabeth Smith. Witnesses: none. Acknowledged in court, June

1806. Del: to Abraham Owen, 12 January 1809. Recorded: OS 3:553.

16 January 1806. Timothy SMITH, Redstone Twp, Fayette Co, PA, to Richard SMITH. 50 acres on White Day Creek, no adjoiners named. Part of Peter Parker's 400 acre settlement right, patented to him 9 July 1787, 143 acres, 31 poles of which was conveyed by Parker to Timothy Smith, the deed burnt in Col Evans' office. Consideration: $500. Signed: Timothy Smith. Witnesses: John Cooper, Charles Byrn, Thomas McKinley. Proved by witnesses, June 1806. Del: to him, 27 April 1813. Recorded: OS 3:554.

2 February 1807. William and Esther McCLERRY to Ebenezer STEEL, Washington Co, MD. 181 acres on White Day and Pricketts Creeks, adjoining John Springer's survey. Patented to Robert Minnis, 11 May 1793, and conveyed by him to Samuel Merryfield, 11 September 1797, and by Merryfield to McClerry, 11 October 1800. Consideration: $362. Signed: William McClerry, Esther McClerry. Witnesses: J Campbell, Enoch Evans, Robert Hawthorn, Mathew Gay. Acknowledged in court, February 1807. No delivery shown. Recorded: OS 3:555-556.

2 February 1807. Col David SCOTT to Ludwick ENSAMINGER, Washington Co, MD. 100 acres on the Flat Run, adjoining Philip and John Wient's and Jacob Rivers' parts of the tract. From a 6 June 1796 patent to Scott of 700 acres, adjoining Arthur Watson's survey. Consideration: $200. Signed: David Scott. Witnesses: David Scott, Noah Ridgway, Nimrod Evans, Wm N Jarrett. Proved by witnesses, February 1807. Del: to L Ensminger, 9 March 1807. Recorded: OS 3:556-557.

2 January 1807. Col David SCOTT to Jacob PECK, Washington Co, MD. 150 acres on the Flat Run, adjoining Jacob River's, Philip and John Went's, and Ludwick Ensaming's parts of the tract. From a 6 June 1796 patent to Scott for 700 acres, adjoining Arthur Watson's and Henry Banks' surveys. Consideration: $300. Signed: David Scott. Witnesses: Nimrod Evans, William N Jarrett, James Evans, David Scott, Noah Ridgway. Proved by witnesses, February 1807. Del: to Peck, 9 March 1807. Recorded: OS 3:558-559.

2 February 1807. Col David SCOTT to Philip WIENT and John WIENT, Washington Co, MD. 100 acres on the Flat Run, adjoining Jacob Peck's and Ludwick Ensaminger's parts of the same tract. From a 6 June 1796 patent to Scott for 700 acres, adjoining Arthur Watson's survey. Consideration: $200. Signed: David Scott. Witnesses: Nimrod Evans, William N Jarrett, James Evans, David

Scott, Noah Ridgway. Proved by witnesses, February 1807.
Del: to P & J Wents, 9 March 1807. Recorded: OS 3:559-561.

2 February 1807. Col David SCOTT to Henry SHOOP, Washington Co, MD. 100 acres on the Flat Run, adjoining Jacob Rivers. From a 6 June 1796 patent to Scott for 700 acres, adjoining Arthur Watson's survey. Consideration: $200. Signed: David Scott. Witnesses: Nimrod Evans, Wm N Jarrett, James Evans, David Scott, Noah Ridgway. Proved by witnesses, February 1807. Del: to Henry Shoop, 18 March 1807. Recorded: OS 3:561-562.

20 January 1807. Jonathan ROWLAND, Esq, Borough of Union Town, Fayette Co, PA, to George YOUNG, Washington Co, MD. 181 acres on Farrows Run, no adjoiners named. [For history of title, see OS 3:542-543.] From tract #4 on the plat of resurvey. Consideration: $543. Signed: Jonathan Rowland. Witnesses: John Stealey, Nimrod Evans, Henry Dering, Jos Shinn, J Evans Jr, Wm N Jarrett. Proved by witnesses, February 1807. Del: to G Young, 26 February 1807. Recorded: OS 3:563-564.

10 January 1807. Jonathan ROWLAND, Esq, Borough of Union Town, Fayette Co, PA, to Benjamin KUGAL, Washington Co, MD. 200 acres on Farrows Run, adjoining lands sold to George Young, John Coss, Benjamin Ridenour, and John Bowser. [For history of title, see OS 3:542-543.] Consideration: $500. Signed: Jonathan Rowland. Witnesses: John Stealey, Henry Dering, Jos Shinn, J Evans Jr, William N Jarrett, Nimrod Evans. Proved by witnesses, February 1807. Del: to Ben Kugle, 26 February 1807. Recorded: OS 3:565-566.

3 February 1807. Col David SCOTT to Jacob RIVER, Washington Co, MD. 250 acres on the Flat Run, adjoining Henry Shoop's part of the same tract. From a 6 June 1796 patent for 700 acres, adjoining Arthur Watson's survey. Consideration: $500. Signed: David Scott. Witnesses: Nimrod Evans, Wm N Jarrett, James Evans, David Scott, Noah Ridgway. Proved by witnesses, February 1807. No delivery shown. Recorded: OS 3:567-568.

7 February 1807. Mary DONALDSON and Susannah DONALDSON to John SHARK, Washington Co, MD. 305 acres on Blackburns Glade Run, adjoining James Spurgin and the heirs of John Judy, on both sides of the great road. Part of 2268 acres patented to Charles Donaldson, 11 September 1789, and divided among his heirs after his death. Consideration: $1075. Signed: Mary [+] Donaldson, Susannah [+] Donaldson. Witnesses: Thomas Jenkins, Enoch Evans, John Jarrett, Benj N Jarrett. Proved by witnesses, February 1807. Del: to John Shark, 19 April

1807. Recorded: OS 3:568-570.

13 January 1807. Jonathan ROWLAND, Esq, Borough of Union Town, Fayette Co, PA, to John COSS, Washington Co, MD. 200 acres on Farrows Run, adjoining Benjamin Ridenour, Benjamin Kugal, Robert Fullerton, and Charles Snodgrass. [For history of title, see OS 3:542-543.] Part of division #2 on the plat of resurvey. Consideration: $500. Signed: Jonathan Rowland. Witnesses: John Stealey, Nimrod Evans, Henry Dering, Jos Shinn, J Evans Jr, Wm N Jarrett. Proved by witnesses, February 1807. Del: to John Coss, 26 February 1807. Recorded: OS 3:571-572.

[illegible] January 1807. Jonathan ROWLAND, Esq, Borough of Union Town, Fayette Co, PA, to Benjamin REDENOUR, Washington Co, MD. 192½ acres on Farrows Run, adjoining Thomas Merrideth, John Bowser, and John Coss. [For history of title, see OS 3:542-543.] From division #2 on the plat of resurvey. Consideration: $577.50. Signed: Jonathan Rowland. Witnesses: John Stealey, Nimrod Evans, Henry Dering, Jos Shinn, J Evans Jr, Wm N Jarrett. Proved by witnesses, February 1807. Del: to B Redenour, 26 February 1807. Recorded: OS 3:572-574.

4 November 1805. John and Martha ERWING to Samuel JACKSON, all of Fayette Co, PA. 83 acres on Morgans Run, on the east side of Cheat River, adjoining Jacob Jones. Consideration: $83. Signed: John Erwing, Martha [+] Erwing. Witnesses: Enoch Evans, Benj N Jarrett, John Jarrett. Acknowledged by Martha Erwing in Fayette Co, PA, before Andrew Oliphant and Robert Ritchie, 17 October 1806. Proved by witnesses, February 1806. No delivery shown. Recorded: OS 3:574-575.

30 January 1807. Jonathan ROWLAND, Esq, Borough of Union Town, Fayette Co, PA, to John BOWSER, Washington Co, MD. 159 acres on Farrows Run, adjoining Benjamin Kugal, Benjamin Redenour, and Thomas Meredith. [For history of title, see OS 3:542-543.] Consideration: $397.50. Signed: Jonathan Rowland. Witnesses: Jno Stealey, Nimrod Evans, Henry Dering, Joseph Shinn, J Evans Jr, Wm N Jarrett. Proved by witnesses, February 1807. Del: to John Bowser, 26 February 1807. Recorded: OS 3:576-577.

[blank] December [year blank]. Joseph McDOUGAL to Richard McDUGAL and Polly McDUGAL. Deed of gift, conveying horses, waggon with chains and harness, cattle, sheep, hoggs, beds and bedclothes, household furnishings, cooking and table ware, farm tools, bar iron, wheat, corn, rye, flax, and all the notes and bonds Joseph owns. Consideration: Love and affection to

his son and daughter, plus $1. Signed: Joseph McDougal. Witnesses: David Scott Jr, James McVicker, Thomas Warman, Joseph McDugal. Acknowledged in court, February 1807. Del: to Joseph McDougall, 2 March 1807. Recorded: OS 3:577.

9 February 1807. David and Hannah DUNHAM to Joseph BRUMAGH. 60 acres, no adjoiners or place names mentioned. It is understood that about 3/4 acre is lost to an older right. Consideration: $400, VA. Signed: David Dunham, Hannah [+] Dunham. Witnesses: Jacob Polsley, John Nuzum. Acknowledged by David Dunham in court, February 1807; by Hannah Dunham before Jacob Polsley and John Nuzum, JPs, 16 February 1807. Del: to [illegible] Hall, 8 February 1810. Recorded: OS 3:578-579.

18 August 1806. George BEATY, Hampshire Co, to Nicholas CASEY. 350 acres on Youghegania, adjoining Henry Hawk and Levi Beaty. Patented to George Beaty, 20 March 1785. Consideration: £75. Signed: George Beaty. Witnesses: Wm Naylor, William Buffington, Samuel McGuire. Acknowledged in Hampshire Co, 16 September 1805 [sic]. Certificate of Andrew Woodrow, CHC. Del: to E Butler, 2 October 1807. Recorded: OS 3:579.

9 February 1807. Lewis and Mary DEWEESE to James BARKER. 86 acres on the west side of Monongalia River, no adjoiners named. Part of a survey granted to James Scott deceased and deeded to the heirs of Joshua Deweese deceased by David Scott son of James. Consideration: $550. Signed: Lewis Deweese, Mary Deweese. Witnesses: none. Acknowledged by Lewis Deweese in court, February 1807; by Mary Deweese before B Reeder and Wm N Jarrett, JPs, 20 March 1807. Del: to Jas Barker, 25 January 1808. Recorded: OS 3:580-581.

11 September 1806. William and Linny NEIGHBOURS to Jesse EVANS, Fayette Co, PA. 67 acres adjoining John Fowler, James Donaldson, Samuel Jackson, Jacob Smith, and Martin Able. Consideration: $400. Signed: William Neighbours, Linny [+] Neighbours. Witnesses: Wm N Jarrett, Martin Abel, Arthur Trader (all as to Linny), Thomas Adamson. Acknowledgement unfinished. No delivery shown. Recorded: OS 3:581.

9 February 1807. Forbes and Elisabeth BRITTON to Benjamin HAMILTON. 40 acres on the west side of Monongalia River, where Hamilton now lives. Originally granted to George Weaver. Consideration: $130. Signed: Forbes Britton, Elisabeth Britton. Witnesses: none. Acknowledged in court, February 1807. Del: to him, November 1809. Recorded: OS 3:582.

7 February 1807. James and Sarah McLAUCHLIN, George HOOK, Nancy MORRISON, Ann MORRISON, Jane MORRISON, and James MORRISON, heirs and legatees of James MORRISON deceased, Oultuta [?] Co, Orleans Territory, to John BATES and James BATES, Jefferson Co, KY. 400 acres on the dividing ridge between the Westfork and Buffaloe Creek, above the head of the lefthand fork of Joes Run. No adjoiners named. Consideration: $500. Signed: James McLauchlin, Sally McLauchlin (by James Morrison, their attorney in fact), George Hook, Nancy Morrison, Ann Morris, Jane Morrison (by James Morrison, their attorney in fact), James Morrison. Witnesses: none. Acknowledged in Jefferson Co, KY, 14 February 1807 by George Hook and James Morrison, before George Wilson and J Gwathmey, JPs. Certificate of Worden Pope, Clerk of Jefferson Co, and Frederick Edwards, presiding justice. No delivery shown. Recorded: OS 3:583.

14 May 1805. Samuel and Mary CLARK to Terah DORAN. 50 acres adjoining Thomas Morris and Gabriel Fickle. Part of the tract from land conveyed to Clark by William Squier, and part from a 40 acre patent to Clark, 21 December 1798. Consideration: $100, VA. Signed: Samuel Clark, Mary Clark. Witnesses: John Curry, John Fickle, Alexr Brandon, David Hendrickson. Acknowledged by Mary Clark before James Clark and John McClane, JPs, 14 May 1805. Proved by witnesses, September and October 1805. Del: to A Brandon, 22 July 1807. Recorded: OS 3:584-585.

17 February 1803. WILL of John T GOFF. His old farm in MD and tract "Addition" (excepting 100 acres sold to John Watts) to be sold and money used to pay debts. Wife Monica: dwelling plantation, the Mill Farm, during her life and for the support of the unmarried children who are willing to stay with her. Second son, John S Goff: land where he now lives, on the River Rhine [sic]. Eldest son, James C Goff: land where he lives. Jacob, Adam, Philip, Susanah, and Gustus, heirs of daughter Marsa Hull [sic]: to have the tract where Yost Heck now lives, adjoining land sold to George Wild, and no more of my estate than this. Daughters Hannah and Ludee [?]: remainder of 2000 acres south of the big road. Daughter Joanah: remainder of 2000 acres north of the big road. Daughter Allalujah's heirs: $300 to be paid in 10 annual installments. Grandsons John and James Goff, sons of Alexander: land where their father now lives (Alexander to have no right of inheritance). Grandsons John B, John T, and John A Goff: the Mill Farm at the death of their grandmother. Daughter Tamer [?]: 250 acres on Teters Creek in Randolph Co, purchased from William Harsh.

Neighbor John Watts not to be oppressed or harmed in paying what he owes, but to pay how and when he is able, "working on the farm to support my Relic." Signed: John T Goff. Witnesses: James More, Henry Smith, George G Goff, Levi Hopkins. [Apparent codicil, though not identified as such, directs that all unappropriated lands be sold to pay debts, with any remaining cash divided among the legatees.] Proved by witnesses, April 1803. Recorded: OS 3:586-587. [Also recorded in Wills, 1:305-307.]

26 November 1806. John HARMAN to Anthony WOODS. Bill of sale for 1 horse, 2 cows, 8 sheep. Consideration: $35. Signed: John Harman. Witnesses: William Woods, Barney Haney. Acknowledged in court, June 1807. No delivery shown. Recorded: OS 3:588.

26 June 1790. WILL of Jesse BAYLES. Sons William and Jesse: plantation where I now live, to be equally divided among them. William to have the river end and Jesse the upper part. If either wishes to sell, the other to have first preference. Son David: 200 acres on the right hand fork of Binnomun, "which he is to clear and 200 for me from our land office." Son Adin: "my part" of said tract, he to pay £6 to his sister Peggy. Daughters Mary Ieyce, Betsey Ieyce, Peggy Bayles, and Phebe Bayles: 400 acres at Tyger Valleyfork, the land to be divided and Peggy to have first choice. Land at head of Muddy Creek to be sold. William and Jesse's land to be rented at the best price while they are underage and the profits applied to their schooling. Widow Moore not to be disturbed during her lifetime, but she may not put anyone else on the property. Executors: Capt Warman, John Ramsey, and Andrew Ieyce. Signed: Jesse Bayles. Witnesses: Andrew Ice, William Laws, Thomas Boyd. Proved by witness Andrew Ice, April 1807, the others being dead or removed. Recorded: OS 3:588. [Also recorded in Wills, 1:307.]

14 June 1804. Thomas CHADWICK (no residence stated), by Noah ARNOLD, his attorney in fact, to Samuel SMITH. 72 acres on Scotts Mill Run, adjoining William Dawson. Consideration: $400. Signed: "Thomas [X] Shadock, attorney in fact for Noah Arnold [sic; text of instrument indicates Chadwick is the grantor]." Witnesses: Wm G Payne, John E Bills, Wm N Jarrett. Acknowledgement unfinished. No delivery shown. Recorded: OS 3:589.

9 June 1807. Francis TIBBS Sr to Samuel JACKSON, Fayette Co, PA. 6 3/4 acres on an island in Cheat River, the first island below Ices Ferry. Surveyed 16 February

1798 and patented 23 July 1800. Consideration: $50, VA. Signed: Francis [mark] Tibbs Sen. Witnesses: none. Acknowledged in court, June 1807. No delivery shown. Recorded: OS 3:589-590.

8 April 1807. Benjamin and Drusilla HELLEN to Abraham WOODROW and Simeon WOODROW. Lot #3 in Morgan Town, between the brick house formerly owned by John Davis and Isaac Hite Williams' frame house. Consideration: £330, VA. Signed: Benjamin Hellen, Drusilla Hellen. Witnesses: B Reeder, Wm N Jarrett, Charles Byrn. Acknowledged by Drusilla Hellen before B Reeder and Wm N Jarrett, JPs, 8 April 1807. Proved by witnesses, June 1807. Del: to Simeon Woodrow, 23 November 1811. Recorded: OS 3:590-591.

17 March 1807. William and Elisabeth RUSSEL to Joseph PECKENPAW, Green Co, PA. 88 acres on the head of Crooked Run, near the state line, where Russel now lives. Part of a tract taken up by Thomas Russel and conveyed by him to William. Consideration: $528. Signed: William Russel, Elisabeth [+] Russel. Witnesses: Henry Fortney, James Tearney, Peter Peckenpaw. Acknowledged in court, June 1807. Del: to R M Wilson, 2 September 1808. Recorded: OS 3:592-593.

5 June 1807. Jacob SMITH to Frederick SMITH. 171 acres at the head of Craborchard Run, adjoining Ezekiel Jones, Wells, and Biggs. Consideration: $700. Signed: Jacob Smith. Witnesses: none. Acknowledged in court, June 1807. Del: to F Smith, 14 December 1807. Recorded: OS 3:593.

22 September 1806. Simon TROY and Benjamin TROY, sons of John TROY, to Michael CORE. 260 acres on Dunkard Creek, no adjoiners named. Patented to Simon Troy, assignee of John Godfrey, 10 February 1787, and willed by Simon Troy to Simon and Benjamin. Consideration: $2000. Signed: Simon Troy, Benjamin Troy. Witnesses: Adam Brown, John Statler, William Tenant. Proved by witnesses, February and June 1807. Del: to M Core, 26 January 1808. Recorded: OS 3:594.

20 December 1806. David (Sr) and Hannah SAYRE, now of Gallia Co, OH, to Dr John NICKLIN, late of Louden Co. 118 acres between Joes and Toms Runs, adjoining Thomas Sayre and Thomas Ewell. Part of a tract patented to David and Daniel Sayre in joint tenancy, 19 October 1789. Originally conveyed to Nicklin 10 January 1803, but the description not sufficiently accurate, this new conveyance is made. Consideration: $708, VA. Signed: David Sayre, Hannah [+] Sayre. Witnesses: Wm N Jarrett, Nimrod Evans (both as to David), Henry Dering.

Acknowledged by Hannah Sayre before John Stealey and Wm N Jarrett, JPs, 20 December 1806. Proved by witnesses, June 1807. Del: to J Nicklin, 22 July 1808. Recorded: OS 3:595-596.

9 June 1807. Philip ROBERTS to Benjamin BROWN. 56 acres on Finches Run, a branch of Buffaloe Creek, adjoining William Hillary, John Brown, William Gray, and Jasper Wyatt. Part of 150 acres patented to Philip Roberts, 1799. Consideration: £50, VA. Signed: Philip Roberts. Witnesses: none. Acknowledged in court, June 1807. Del: to Brown, 18 July 1807. Recorded: OS 3:596-597.

28 May 1807. Rhoda BACORN, Fayette Co, PA, devisee and legal representative of Job BACORN, deceased, to Philip BARBROWER. 371 acres on Sandy Creek, adjoining Frederick Spader, New Mexico, Alexander Sommerville, Amos Spencer, and John Scott. Consideration: $1000, VA. Signed: Rhoda Bacorn. Witnesses: E Daugherty, Hedgman Triplett, Wm McCleery. Proved by witnesses, June 1807. Del: to H Triplett, 18 July 1807. Recorded: OS 3:597-598.

DEEDBOOK OS 4

9 June 1807. Robert MINNIS to Samuel HANWAY. 5 acres on the bank of Monongalia River, adjoining Zacquell Morgan. From a 151 acre patent to James Cochran, assignee of Zacquell Morgan. Consideration: $300, VA. Signed: Robt Minnis. Witnesses: none. Acknowledged in court, June 1807. Del: to him, 31 March 1813. Recorded: OS 4:1.

14 April 1806. Leonard M DEAKINS and John HOYE, executors and devisees of Francis DEAKINS, deceased, no address given, to Joseph HUSTON, Esq, of PA. Two tracts on the state road from Morgan Town to Thomas Stewart's, at Snowey Glade Creek. 400 acres surveyed 18 October 1784 and 50 acres surveyed 9 April 1785. About the year 1790 Francis Deakins, deceased, and Augustine Friend agreed to purchase the 2 tracts from George Ashby. Deakins advanced the purchase money and Ashby conveyed to Deakins and Friend. Friend, wishing to live on the land, purchased Deakins' interest via a note, promising to refund the balance due to Deakins, and Deakins gave his bond to convey title. Friend did not repay the money but did transfer Deakins' title bond to M Davis. By various assignments the bond is now in the possession of Huston, who gave his note to fulfill the payment still due for Deakins' half interest in the land. This now complied with, the executors transfer title to Huston, noting that Deakins never owned more than an undivided half of the land and they convey no more than this to Huston. Consideration: none stated. Signed: L M Deakins, John Hoye. Witness: Danl Rantzel. Acknowledged in George Town, DC, 14 April 1806. Certificate of Daniel Reintzel, mayor. Del: to Jo Huston, June 1807. Recorded: OS 4:1-2.

30 March 1807. Enoch and Amelia EVANS to Dudley EVANS. Power of attorney to lease or sell 400 acres on Cove Lick Run of Middle Island Creek. Signed: Enoch Evans, Amelia Evans. Witnesses: Jacob Kyger, G R Tingle, J Evans, Fields Martin. Proved by witnesses, June 1807. Del: to Dudley Evans, 16 September 1838. Recorded: OS 4:3.

13 March 1807. Enoch and Amelia EVANS to Nimrod EVANS. Power of attorney to lease or sell 100 acres on the east side of Cheat River. Enoch and Amelia are also entitled under the will of Bartholomew Jenkins to 200 acres where Jenkins' widow now lives, as well as 1/3 of Negroes Toney, Nancy, Rachel, and Rachel's increase, and to 1/3 of any personal property remaining at Widow Jenkins' death, subject to the terms of the will. Nimrod

281

may lease or sell this property, the purchaser to take possession at the death of Widow Jenkins. Signed: Enoch Evans, Amelia Evans. Witnesses: Ja Kyger, G R Tingle, J Evans, Fields Martin. Proved by witnesses, June 1807. Del: to Nimrod Evans, 11 April 1825. Recorded: OS 4:3-4.

10 January 1803. David and Hannah SAYRE to John NICKLIN Jr, Louden Co. 50 acres on the bank of Monongalia River, adjoining Daniel Sayre and John and Jeremiah Wilson. 14½ acres from Robert Ferrel's 966 acre patent, 6 February 1797; 35½ acres from Ferrel's 234 acre patent, 18 June 1798. Consideration: $166. Signed: David Sayre, Hannah Sayre. Witnesses: none. Receipt for consideration money. 30 December 1806 relinquishment by John Nicklin. The land has been recovered of Nicklin by Robert Moody; Sayre has repaid the consideration money; and Nicklin relinquishes all claim to the land under the foregoing deed. Witnesses: Tho Wilson, H Dering, Nimrod Evans. Proved by witnesses, June 1807, and recorded with note that instrument has previously been recorded. Del: to J Nicklin, 22 July 1808. Recorded: OS 4:4-5.

8 June 1807. Forbes and Elizabeth BRITTON to Henry DERING, Morgan Town. Lot #13 in Morgan Town, conveyed by Zacquill and Drusilla Morgan to Thomas Pindall, 13 December 1784, and descended to Elizabeth Britton, one of Pindall's heirs, under partition decree made at District Court in Stauntown [sic]. Includes annual quit rent of 50¢ to the heirs of Zacquill Morgan, deceased. Consideration: $250, VA. Signed: Forbes Britton, Elizabeth Britton. Witnesses: none. Acknowledged in court, June 1807. No delivery shown. Recorded: OS 4:5-6.

13 April 1807. Fauquier and Susana McREA to Duncan F McREA. 140 acres adjoining William PettyJohn, Jacob Jones, Absalom Little, and Zacquill Morgan. Consideration: $1. Signed: Fauquir McRea, Susanna McRea. Witnesses: Thomas McKinley, John Taylor, Anthony Evans. Acknowledged in court, June 1807. Del: to D F McRea, 19 December 1807. Recorded: OS 4:6.

9 February 1807. Joseph and Rebecca BRUMAGE to David DUNHAM. 175 acres adjoining Dunham's other land. Purchased by Brumage from William Anderson. No place names mentioned. Consideration: $350, VA. Signed: Joseph Brumage, Rebecca Brumage. Witnesses: Jacob Pawlsley, John Nuzum. Acknowledged in court by Joseph Brumage, February 1807; by Rebecca before Jacob Pawsley and John Nuzum, JPs, 10 February 1807. Del: to D Dunham, 22 June 1809. Recorded: OS 4:6-7.

21 May 1807. Philip and Elizabeth HILL to Thomas LITTLE, Harrison Co, and Elijah HAWKINS. 85 acres on

Tiger Valley River, opposite Hill's Mill. Includes saw mill and a small island in the river between the land and Hill's mill and ferry. Patented to Stockley Little, 17 June 1799. Consideration: $200. Signed: Philip Hill [Elizabeth does not sign]. Witnesses: Philip Rutherford, Jacob Hill, Abraham Hill, Andrew Bettz, John Wilkins. Proved by witnesses, June 1807, and recorded as to Philip Hill. No delivery shown. Recorded: OS 4:8.

8 June 1807. Andrew KIRKPATTRICK, OH, by Samuel BOWEN, his attorney in fact, to Jacob SMITH. 125 acres at Muddy Creek, adjoining land sold to James Cain and Leonard Cup. Part of a 600 acre patent of 19 November 1801. Consideration: $300, VA. Signed: Samuel Bowen. Witnesses: none. Acknowledged in court, June 1807. Del: to J Smith, 13 July 1808. Recorded: OS 4:8-9.

8 June 1807. Frederick and Barbara WAGONER, Franklin Co, PA, to Thomas WILSON. All their part in 550 acres near Tyger Valley Falls, sold by Thomas and Polly Wilson to Philip, Frederick, and Jacob Wagoner, 21 January 1800. Consideration: $1000, VA. Signed: Frederick Wagoner, Barbara [X] Wagoner. Witnesses: Philip Wagoner, Jacob Simerson, Susannah Simerson. Proved by witnesses, June 1807, and recorded as to Frederick Wagoner. No delivery shown. Recorded: OS 4:9.

8 June 1807. Andrew KIRKPATTRICK, OH, by Samuel BOWEN, his attorney in fact, to Frederick WILHELMA. 198 acres on Muddy Creek, adjoining James Cain. Part of a 600 acre patent of 19 November 1801. Consideration: $200. Signed: Samuel Bowen. Witnesses: none. Acknowledged in court, June 1807. Del: to Frederick Smith, per verbal order, [illegible] 1809. Recorded: OS 4:10.

12 April 1802. Andrew and Elisabeth KIRK PATTRICK, by Samuel BOWEN, their attorney in fact, to Frederick WILHELMA. 90 acres, no place names or adjoiners mentioned. Consideration: $[blank]. Signed: Samuel Bowen. Witnesses: none. Acknowledged in court, April 1802. On motion of Frederick Wilhelma, a commission ordered to take the acknowledgement of Elisabeth Kirk Pattrick, but no action recorded here. Del: to J Erwin, 11 April 1809. Recorded: OS 4:10-11.

[blank] 1807. Nicholas MADERIA to Victoria ADAMSON. House where she now lives, adjoining the north end of Maderia's house on the west side of Water Street in Morgan Town. Conveyance is for the term of her her natural life and may not be disposed of to any other person by sale, lease, or any other means. Consideration: $1, natural love and affection. Signed:

Nicholas Maderia. Witnesses: none. Acknowledged in court, April 1807. No delivery shown. Recorded: OS 4:11.

21 December 1796. Mary BEALL to John PETER, both of Frederick Co, MD. One half of 1000 acres on Sand Creek, in Sandy Creek Glades, adjoining Thomas Cheney and John Morris. Patented to William Hilton and John Orr, 7 August 1767, and later resurveyed in the same names. Consideration: 5s, MD. Signed: Mary Beall. Witnesses: Geo Murdock, Geo Baer Jr. Acknowledged in Frederick Co, MD, before Geo Murdock and Geo Baer Jr, JPs. Certificate of Wm Ritchie, CFC. No delivery shown. Recorded: OS 4:12 (recorded June 1807).

14 April 1807. James CAIN to John GILLISPIE, Fayette Co, PA. 400 acres on Deckers Creek and Threefork Creek, adjoining Joseph Cox. Includes a settlement right of 1776, patented to Richard Cain, 2 December 1791, and conveyed by Richard and Jane Cain to James Cain, 12 August 1799. Consideration: $1666 2/3, VA. Signed: James Cain. Witnesses: none. Acknowledged in court, April 1807. Del: to Gillespie, 5 March 1808. Recorded: OS 4:13.

14 April 1807. John and Elisabeth STEWART to Owen HAWKER. 79 acres adjoining William Barrett and Isaac Matthew. Part of a larger tract patented to Simon Troy, 1 April 1784, and left to Christopher Troy in Simon's last will and testament. Consideration: $350, VA. Signed: John Stuart, Elisabeth [mark] Stuart. Witnesses: none. Acknowledged in court, April 1807. Del: to Joseph F Weaver, 24 January 1867. Recorded: OS 4:14.

14 February 1807. George and Jenny STUART, Fayette Co, PA, to Peter DRAGOO. 128 acres on Buffaloe Creek, no adjoiners named. Part of 400 acres patented to William Gray, 16 September 1784; by him conveyed to John Glen, 5 May 1785; by him conveyed to Hugh Maxwell; and by him conveyed to Stuart "by deed of this date." Consideration: $200, VA. Signed: George Stuart, Jane [+] Stuart. Witnesses: none. Acknowledged in court, April 1807. Del: to Dragoo, February 1818. Recorded: OS 4:15.

29 September 1806. James and Mary THOMAS to John SHIOR [?], Fayette Co, PA. 50 acres on Big Sandy, adjoining Robert Brownfield. Patented to John England, 26 November 180[?], and conveyed by him to Thomas. Consideration: $200. Signed: James [X] Thomas [Mary does not sign]. Witnesses: none. Acknowledged in court, April 1807, by James Thomas, and recorded as to him. Del: to him, 8 April 1811. Recorded: OS 4:15-16.

15 September 1791. George GILLESPIE, by Thomas CLARE, his attorney in fact, to John GILLESPIE, all of

Fayette Co, PA. 400 acres on Scotts Meadow Run, west side of Monongalia River, adjoining Isaac Kemp and David Scott. Consideration: £100. Signed: Thomas Clare, Witnesses: John Doyle, Baldn Weaver, John Davis. Proved by witnesses, November 1791. No delivery shown. Presented for re-recording, September 1796. Recorded: OS 4:16-17. Re-recording of burned instrument.

8 April 1805. Henry and Barbary FORTNEY to Richard TENANT. 353 acres on Jakes Run, waters of Dunkard Creek, adjoining Tenant's other land. Patented to Henry Fortney, 11 April 1793. Consideration: $550. Signed: Henry Fortney [Barbary does not sign]. Witnesses: Nimrod Evans, James Evans, John Payne. Proved by witnesses, June 1805/June 1807. Acknowledged by Barbara Fortney before B Reeder and Jno W Dean, JPs, 13 May 1805. Del: to his son, 10 August 1807. Recorded: OS 4:17-18.

4 April 1807. James EVANS to Nimrod EVANS. Undivided half of 2 tracts conveyed to James and Marmaduke Evans by John Evans Sr, 14 September 1806. One tract of 971 acres, the other 400 acres. No place names or adjoiners mentioned. As there appears to be an interference on one of the surveys [unspecified], James conveys only title to such land as may be found clear of dispute. If Nimrod succeeds in the title, then James warrants the entire tract as described. Consideration: £100, VA. Signed: James Evans. Witnesses: Rawley Evans, Jacob Kyger, Marmaduke Evans, James McGee. Proved by witnesses, June 1807. Del: to grantee, 25 June 1821. Recorded: OS 4:18-19.

21 May 1807. Charles and Barbara SNODGRASS to William SNODGRASS Jr, Joseph SNODGRASS, and Elisha SNODGRASS. Two tracts. 142 acres at Pharoas Run, adjoining Henry Batten and James Longwell. Part of (acreage unspecified) a 230 acre tract. Consideration: £10, VA. Signed: Charles Snodgrass, Barbara [X] Snodgrass. Witnesses: none. Acknowledged in court, June 1807. Del: to Wm Snodgrass, September 1810. Recorded: OS 4:19-20.

8 June 1807. Samuel SMITH, by Joseph HARRISON, his attorney in fact, to John WELLS. 260 acres, no adjoiners or place names mentioned. Part of a 400 acre tract conveyed by John Gillespie to Samuel Smith, 19 June 1797. 100 acres of said tract sold to James Frazier and 40 acres sold to Daniel Knox. Consideration: $1200, VA. Signed: Joseph Harrison. Witnesses: none. Acknowledged in court, June 1807. Del: to Ricd Wells, [illegible] March 1809. Recorded: OS 4:20.

8 June 1807. John and Mary RAMSEY to Abraham

COMEGYS. 52½ acres on Scotts Mill Run, adjoining Comegys' other land. Patented to Ramsey, 1 December 1784. Consideration: $222. Signed: John [+] Ramsey, Mary [+] Ramsey. Witnesses: none. Acknowledged in court, June 1807. Del: to [illegible], 30 August 1805 Recorded: OS 4:21.

28 March 1807. Philip WAGGONER and Jacob WAGGONER to Thomas WILSON. Their part of 550 acres near Tyger Valley falls, no adjoiners named. Tract conveyed by Thomas and Polly Wilson to Philip Waggoner, Jacob Waggoner, and Frederick Waggoner, 21 July 1800. Consideration: $1000, VA. Signed: Philip [+] Wagoner, Jacob Wagoner. Witnesses: James Thompson, George W Thompson, J W Campbell. Proved by witnesses, April 1807/June 1807. No delivery shown. Recorded: OS 4:22.

14 April 1807. James and Jane WEST to James JEFFS. 87 acres on the west bank of Monongalia River, adjoining Zacquill Morgan, Stephen Morgan, and Jeffs' other land. Consideration: $500, VA. Signed: James West, Jane West. Acknowledged in court, June 1807. Del: to him, 17 February 1809. Recorded: OS 4:22-23.

23 March 1807. Samuel SMITH to Joseph HARRISON. Power of attorney, authorizing Harrison to make conveyance to John WELLS, late of the state of MD, for a tract on Scotts Meadow Run, adjoining and below Isaac Camp. Signed: Samuel Smith. Witnesses: Richard Harrison, William Everly. Proved by witnesses, June 1807. Recorded: OS 4:23.

4 April 1807. John EVANS to James EVANS. Deed of gift. Negro girl Ellenor, 11 years old next November and now in the possession of Enoch Evans, with all her increase. She is a slave for life if not otherwise directed by law hereafter to be done. Consideration: $1, natural love and affection. Signed: J Evans. Witnesses: none. Acknowledged in court, June 1807. Del: to [no name], 23 June 1821. Recorded: OS 4:23.

8 April 1806. William PETTY JOHN and John POOR to William HAYMOND Jr. Their part of 100 acres on Monongalia River, adjoining Jordan Hall, Arthur Trader, and Haymond's other land. Patented to William Petty John, 16 December 1799, and willed by him to William Petty John, John Poor, and John Petty John. Consideration: $1. Signed: William Petty John, John Poor. Witnesses: Jordan Hall, Jno Johnson, Arthur Miller, Henry Barnes. Proved by witnesses, April 1806/June 1807. Del: to Haymond, 21 October 1807. Recorded: OS 4:24.

10 April 1807. Leonard M DEAKINS and John HOYE,

executors and devisees of Francis DEAKINS, deceased, who was the executor and devisee of William DEAKINS Jr, all of George Town, DC, to Alexander SMITH, Aleghany Co, MD. 250 acres on the west side of Cheat River, adjoining a tract conveyed to George Offutt by Francis Deakins, executor and devisee of William Deakins Jr. Smith had purchased 3000 acres from Francis and William Deakins, lot #1 of Claiborne's Chain of Surveys on the west side of Cheat, near Dunkard Bottom, and part of it has been lost to George Galaspie's earlier survey, Consideration: $1, and the loss Smith has had in the tract previously sold to him. Signed: L M Deakins, John Hoye. Witnesses: Daniel Reintzel. Acknowledged in George Town, DC. Certificate of Danl Reintzel, mayor. Smith receipts the deed. Del: to A Smith, 30 March 1818. Recorded: OS 4:24-25.

8 June 1807. Fauquer and Susanna McREA to Abraham WOODROW and Simon WOODROW, all of Morgan Town. 20 acres on Cobuns Creek, adjoining lands formerly of Joseph Trickett and now of Woodrow. Part of 200 acres surveyed for Solomon Hogue. Consideration: $150, VA. Signed: Fauquer McRea, Susanna McRea. Witnesses: none. Acknowledged in court, June 1807. Del: to Abm Woodrow, 10 September 1811. Recorded: OS 4:26.

8 June 1807. John and Mary RAMSEY to William RAMSEY. 51 3/4 acres adjoining John Ramsey Sr and Christopher Raver. Consideration: $32. Signed: John [+] Ramsey, Mary [+] Ramsey. Witnesses: none. Acknowledged in court, June 1807. Del: to Wm Ramsey, February 1808. Recorded: OS 4:27.

5 June 1807. Jacob SMITH to Isaac EWING. 100 acres on the east side of the county road from Cheat River to Muddy Creek, adjoining Andrew KirkPattrick and Thomas Chipps. Consideration: $300. Signed: Jacob Smith. Witnesses: none. Acknowledged in court, June 1807. Del: to J Smith, 8 July 1808. Recorded: OS 4:27.

8 April 1807. Isaac and Elisabeth POWELL to John JEFFS, Fayette Co, PA. 250 acres adjoining Joseph Boltinghouse. Part of a 350 acre patent to Nehemiah Harp, 3 September 1788. The other 100 acres, south end of the tract, was sold by Harp to William Laycock. Consideration: $1850. Signed: Isaac Powell, Elisabeth Powell. Witnesses: none. Acknowledged in court, June 1807. Del: to him, 21 October 1807. Recorded: OS 4:28.

13 February 1786. Zacquell and Drusilla MORGAN to Thomas PINDALL. Lot # [blank] in Morgan Town. Consideration: £3, VA. Signed: Zacquil Morgan, Drusilla Morgan. Witnesses: none. Acknowledged in court, February

1786. No delivery shown. Recorded: OS 4:29. Re-recording of burned instrument.

10 October 1791. George and Mary TETRICK to Henry TETRICK. 500 acres on the right hand branch of Tevebaughs Run, including a small lick. No adjoiners named. Consideration: £39. Signed: George Tetrick, Mary Tetrick. Witnesses: none. Receipt for consideration money. Acknowledged in court, November 1791. Produced for re-recording, September 1796. No delivery shown. Recorded: OS 4:30. Re-recording of burned instrument.

3 August 1796. Boaz BURROWS [generally spelled BURRESS in body of instrument], Harden Co, KY, to Daniel FERRY, Nelson Co, KY. Power of attorney to claim and receive all due to Boaz from his deceased father John Burress, to convey Boaz' interest in 400 acres, and if necessary to commence and prosecute in law or equity to compel performance of bond and the conditions of his father's last will and testament. Boaz' parents, John (deceased) and Elisabeth (whom he supposes is yet alive) had given him a title bond for 400 acres on West Run, about 2½ miles from Morgan Town. After the death of John Burress the bond was recorded in the office of Col John Evans, then clerk, or was lodged with him to be recorded "but said office being Since burnt Refferance Cannot be thereunto had." James Johnson and Jesse Martin were witnesses to the bond. Signed: Boaz Burress. Acknowledged in Nelson Co, KY, 4 August 1796, before James Slaughter and Wm Rogers, JPs. Certificate of Ben Grayson, Clerk of Nelson Co. Produced for recording, August 1798. No delivery shown. Recorded: OS 4:31.

24 January 1807. Richard and Jane CAIN, James CAIN, and Samuel and Rebecca CAIN (latter couple of Mulenburg Co, KY) to John GILLESPIE, Fayette Co, PA. 134 acres on Quarry Run, west of Pleasant Furnace, near a powder mill. No adjoiners named. Land conveyed to Richard Cain on 13 January 1800 by Charles Rose and wife, excepting 6 acres and powder mill. Deed made in compliance with a decree of the High Court of Chancery at Stanton, 25 January 1806, in a case where John Gillespie was plaintiff and Richard, James, and Samuel Cain and John Davis were defendants. Consideration: $666 2/3, VA. Signed: Richard Cain, Jane [+] Cain, James Cain, Samuel Cain, Rebecka [+] Cain. Witnesses: none. Acknowledged by Samuel and Rebecka Cain in Muhlenberg Co, KY, 24 January 1807, before Thos Irwin and John Graddys, JPs. Certificates of Charles Fox Wing, Clerk of Muhlenberg Co, and Lewis Kinchaloe, presiding justice. Acknowledged in court by other grantors, April 1807. Del: to

Gillespie, 5 March 1808. Recorded: OS 4:32-33.

14 February 1807. Hugh MAXWELL, Berkley Co, to George STUART, Fayette Co, PA. 400 acres on Buffaloe Creek and Dragoos Run, adjoining Jno Webb. Patented to William Gray, 16 September 1784; conveyed by him to John Glenn, of Berkley Co, 5 May 1785; and by Glenn to Maxwell, 20 September 1785. Consideration: $600, VA. Signed: Hugh Maxwell. Witnesses: Thos Wilson, Robert Boggess, John Cooper. Proved by witnesses, April 1807. Del: to John Prickett [illegible] of George Stuart, 16 March 1813. Recorded: OS 4:33.

23 October 1805. Theophilus MINOR, administrator with the will annexed of Ann PHILIPS, who was executrix of Theophilus PHILIPS, deceased, addresses not stated, to George ZINN and George GANTZ. 400 acres on Threefork Creek, adjoining Samuel Rebble[?] and John Simpson, including a 1776 improvement. Consideration: $400, VA. Signed: T Minor. Witnesses: Wm G Payne, Henry Dering, Duncan F McRea, George Jacob Baltzel. Proved by witnesses, February 1807/April 1807. Del: to him, 11 May 1809. Recorded: OS 4:34.

13 April 1807. Stephen MYRES to Isaac MARKUS. 213 acres on Little Sandy Creek, adjoining Ignatious Anderson. Consideration: £200, VA. Signed: Stephen Myres. Witnesses: none. Acknowledged in court, April 1807. Del: to him, 13 April 1815. Recorded: OS 4:34-35.

4 September 1806. Alpheus and Sally WICKWARE, Barren Co, KY, to William ELLIS. 100 acres on the east side of Tyger Valley River, adjoining a survey for John and Alpheus Wickware. Consideration: $300. Signed: Alpheus Wickware, Sally Wickware. Witnesses: Peter Johnston, Stephen Poe, Daniel Grimsley. Proved by witnesses, April 1807. Del: to Wm Ellis, 20 November 1807. Recorded: OS 4:35.

16 March 1807. James and Mary THOMAS to Henry WATTERS. 40 acres on Little Sandy Creek, no adjoiners named. Part of a patent to Thomas Berry Jr and part of a patent to John Ingland [or a patent to Berry *and* Ingland?]. Conveyed by John Berry to Samuel Cob, by Cob to Benjamin Whitson, and by Whitson to James Thomas. Consideration: $100. Signed: James [+] Thomas [Mary does not sign]. Witnesses: Thomas Martin, Isaac [+] Markus, Stephen [+] Myres, William Patton, William [+] Myres. Acknowledged in court by James, April 1807, and recorded as to himself. Del: to John Miller pr order, 1 October 1808. Recorded: OS 4:36.

11 February 1806. James TATE to John STEALY. One equal third of 496 acres on Deckers Creek, adjoining

Joseph Wilson, John Reed, Goosman, William McClerry, and McIntire. Consideration: $1666.67. Signed: James Tate. Witnesses: Thomas Wilson, Jo Shinn, Jacob Stealey. Proved by witnesses, June 1806. Del: to him, 24 April 1812. Recorded: OS 4:36-37.

15 August 1798. Booz BURROGHS, Harden Co, KY, by Daniel FERRY, his attorney in fact, to John BURROGHS, Elisabeth BURROGHS, Catherine BURROGHS, Ann BURROGHS, Charles BURROGHS, and William BURROGHS, surviving children of Elisha BURROGHS deceased. Booz Burroghs' interest in a tract on West Run for which John Burroghs, deceased, had given title bond to Booz but which, by his last will and testament, was bequeathed instead to Elisha. Consideration: Booz' legacy from his father's estate, plus $1 paid by John Wilson Dean and John Evans Jr, Elijah Burroghs' executors. Signed: Daniel Ferry. Witnesses: none. Acknowledged in court, August 1798. No delivery shown. Recorded: OS 4:37.

10 March 1784. Zacquell and Drucilla MORGAN to Thomas PINDALL. Lot #5 in Morgan Town. Consideration: £2, VA. Signed: Zacquill Morgan, Drucilla Morgan. Witnesses: none. Acknowledged in court, May 1784. Presented for re-recording, June 1805. No delivery shown. Recorded: OS 4:38. Re-recording of burned instrument.

10 March 1784. Zacquell and Drucilla MORGAN to Thomas PINDALL. Lot #3 in Morgan Town. Consideration: £2, VA. Signed: Zacquill Morgan, Drucilla Morgan. Witnesses: none. Acknowledged in court, May 1784. Presented for re-recording, June 1805. No delivery shown. Recorded: OS 4:39. Re-recording of burned instrument.

8 January 1803. Jacob DONALDSON to James DONALDSON. Power of attorney to convey Jacob's part of a tract on Sandy Creek, known as Blackburns Glade, to Henry Watters of Fayette Co, PA. Signed: Jacob Donaldson. Witnesses: E Evans, George Norriss. Proved by witnesses, September 1803/June 1805. No delivery shown. Recorded: OS 4:40.

[undated] John and Sarah THOMPSON to Daniel THOMPSON. 50½ acres on Robinsons Run, no adjoiners named. Consideration: $300. Signed: John Thompson, Sarah [+] Thompson. Witnesses: none. Acknowledged in court, February 1807. Del: to Danl Thompson, 10 April 1809. Recorded: OS 4:40.

28 July 1806. Charles and Mary POWELL, Nicholas Co, KY, to Capel HOLLAND. 200 acres, no adjoiners or place names mentioned. Patented to Isaac Harrow, 22 November 1794, and descended to Mary Powell as his heir

at law. Consideration: $500, VA. Signed: Charles Powell, Mary [+] Powell. Witnesses: none. Acknowledged in Nicholas Co, KY, 28 July 1806. Certificate of Joseph Morgan, Clerk of Nicholas Co. Del: to C Holland, 26 March 1808. Recorded: OS 4:41.

29 March 1806. Joseph WILSON to John F WILSON. Deed of gift, conveying all of Joseph's goods and chattels, including unspecified lands and tenements, Negroes Watt, Jeff, Anne, Lewis, and Diner, horses, cattle, sheep, hogs, beds, bedding, kitchen and household furniture, farming utensils, and small grain in the ground. John F is to find and keep Joseph and his family, as long as Joseph liveth. Consideration: $1, natural love and affection for his son. Signed: Joseph Wilson. Witnesses: D F McRea, James Beall, James Elliott. Acknowledged in court, October, 1806. Del: to John F Wilson, 10 July 1807. Recorded: OS 4:42.

28 April 1806. Verlinder BEALL, widow of Zephaniah BEALL, Montgomery Co, MD, to Alexander F LANHAM. Undivided 1/6 interest in 160 acres on Deckers Creek, formerly owned by John Ferguson, deceased. Consideration: $120. Signed: Verlinder Beall. Witnesses: Sabra Beall, Robert Beall, Deborah Beall. Acknowledged in Montgomery Co, MD, 6 May 1806, before John Thomas and John Adamson, JPs. Certificate of Upton Beall, Clerk of Montgomery Co. Del: to him, 26 July 1807. Recorded: OS 4:42-43.

10 April 1786. George and Hannah HOLLENBAUGH to Thomas PINDALL. Lot # [blank] in Morgan Town, adjoining Samuel Hanway and the lot purchased for the public buildings. Includes annual quit rent of 3s, payable to Zacquell Morgan and his heirs. Consideration: £100, VA. Signed: George Hollenbaugh, Hannah Hollenbaugh. Witnesses: none. Acknowledged in court, April 1786. Produced for re-recording, June 1805. No delivery shown. Recorded: OS 4:44.

9 February 1807. John and Mary BARKER to James ARNETT. 72 acres, 115 poles on the west side of Monongalia River, on Scotts Meadow Run. No adjoiners named. Consideration: $130, VA. Signed: John [mark] Barker [Mary does not sign]. Witnesses: none. Acknowledged in court by John Barker, February 1807, and recorded as to him. Del: to Jas Arnett, 14 May 1808. Recorded: OS 4:45.

24 January 1807. Cornelius LYNCH to Jonathan ROWLAND, Esq, both of borough of Union Town, Fayette Co, PA. 1100 acres, including a place known as Reeves Improvement, on Farrows Run, adjoining Charles

Snodgrass. 95 acres of surplus land within the boundaries was added by a resurvey, 22 March 1802, by Dudley Evans, assistant to Samuel Hanway. Consideration: $675. Signed: Cornelius Lynch. Witnesses: Thomas Mason, Richd Wm Lane, John Kennedy. Acknowledged in Union Town, PA, 24 January 1807. Certificate of Reuben Bailey, chief magistrate. Del: to A McCleland, 24 October 1807. Recorded: OS 4:46.

10 March 1784. Zacquill and Drusilla MORGAN to Thomas PINDALL. Lot #12 in Morgan Town. Consideration: £2, VA. Signed: Zacquill Morgan, Drusilla Morgan. Witnesses: none. Acknowledged in court, May 1784. No delivery shown. Recorded: OS 4:47. Re-recording of burned instrument.

13 December 1784. Zacquill and Drusilla MORGAN to Thomas PINDALL. Lot #13 in unspecified town. Consideration: £3, VA. Signed: Zacquell Morgan, Drusilla Morgan. Witnesses: none. Acknowledged in court, January 1785. No delivery shown. Recorded: OS 4:48. Re-recording of burned instrument.

13 December 1784. Zacquill and Drusilla MORGAN to Thomas PINDALL. Lot #12 in unspecified town. Consideration: £3, VA. Signed: Zacquill Morgan, Drusilla Morgan. Witnesses: none. Acknowledged in court, January 1785. No delivery shown. Recorded: OS 4:49. Re-recording of burned instrument. [Text differs from instrument on page 47, above, though both appear to convey the same town lot.]

18 March 1805. James PINDALL, one of the heirs of Thomas PINDALL, to John CHISLER. One undivided fourth of a lot in Morgan Town, between Pleasant and Water Streets, adjoining a lot claimed by Thomas Laidley. Deed made in consequence of a sale of the lot by Thomas Pindall to James Reed, who transferred to assignees, who transferred to Chisler. Consideration: [blank], VA. Signed: James Pindall. Witnesses: Nimrod Evans, Henry Dering, William Tingle, Wm G Payne. Proved by witnesses, September 1805. Del: to grantee, 20 August 1818. Recorded: OS 4:50.

11 February 1806. James TATE to John STEALEY. 48 acres on Deckers Creek, adjoining Jacob Youngman. Consideration: $1666.67. Signed: James Tate. Witnesses: Thomas Wilson, Jos Shinn, Jacob Stealey. Proved by witnesses, June 1806. Del: to grantee, 19 December 1821. Recorded: OS 4:50-51.

9 February 1806. Andrew KIRK PATTRICK by his attorney in fact, Samuel BOWEN, to James CAIN. 214 acres at Little Woolf Glade, adjoining Wilhelm, Leonard Cup,

and Smith. Part of 600 acres patented 27 September 1785. Consideration: £200, VA. Signed: Samuel Bowen. Witnesses: none. Acknowledged in court, February 1807. Del: to Andrew Kirkhart, administrator of James Cain, 10 October 1814. Recorded: OS 4:51-52.

18 August 1803. Henry DILLMAN, Washington Co, MD, to Jacob LOWRY, Michael LOWRY, John LOWRY, Mary DEVILY wife of Martin DEVILY, Judith PHILSON wife of Robert PHILSON, and Susannah FLETCHER wife of John FLETCHER, sons and daughters of Michael LOWRY of Sommerset Co, PA. 100 acres, no adjoiners or place names mentioned. From a tract sold to Dillman by Francis Deakins and William Deakins Jr, 4 February 1797, part of a 1094 acre patent. Consideration: £100, MD. Signed: Henry Delman. Witness: William Clagett. Acknowledged in Washington Co, MD, 18 August 1803, before William Clagett, chief justice, and Robert Hughes, assistant justice. Certificate of Otho H Williams, Clerk, Washington Co court. Del: to [blank], 13 July 1807. Recorded: OS 4:52-54.

28 March 1807. WILL of Josiah PRICKETT. Wife Charity: one third of homeplace during her life, and one third of personal estate. Son Josiah: $4. Son John: 100 acres where he formerly lived, lot in Pleasantville, and $4. Daughters Susanna Carberry, Ann Dragoo, Sarah Morgan, Dorothy Morgan, Lydia Ross, and Drusilla Jolliff: $4 each. Son Job: 173 acres where I now live and remainder of moveables after debts, funeral expenses, and legacies are paid. Executors: wife Charity and John Hall Sr. Signed: Josiah Prickett. Witnesses: Calder Haymond, James S Fleming, Rynear Hall. Proved by witnesses, July 1807. Recorded: OS 4:54. [Also recorded in Wills 1:330-331.]

25 December 1805. James and Rhoda MANN to Cornelius KING. 200 acres adjoining Jesse Payne. Consideration: $500. Signed: James Mann, Rhoda Mann. Witnesses: Thomas Fretwell, James A Walton. Acknowledged in court, July 1807. No delivery shown. Recorded: OS 4:55.

19 February 1807. James and Rheuamma PINDALL, Harrison Co, to John COOPER. Lot in Morgan Town, now occupied by Davis Shockley, adjoining Benjamin Reeder, Col Samuel Hanway, Fauquer McRea, and the courthouse lot. Consideration: $1100. Signed: James Pindall, Rheuamma Pindall. Witnesses: Arch B Wilson, Thomas Tate, B Wilson Jr. Acknowledged by Ruammah Pindall before Daniel Morris and Alex Britton, JPs, 17 February 1817 [sic]. Del: to Jno Cooper, 25 March 1808. Recorded: OS 4:55-56.

14 July 1807. Fauquer and Susanna McREA to William LANHAM. 80¼ acres on Deckers Creek, formerly property of John Furguson. Consideration: $1, VA. Signed: Fauquer McRea, Susanna McRea. Witnesses: B Reeder, S Morgan, D F McRea, Benjamin Hison. Acknowledged in court by Fauquer McRea, July 1807; by Susanna McRea before Stephen Morgan and Benjamin Reeder, JPs, 14 July 1807. Del: to Wm Lanham, 25 May 1808. Recorded: OS 4:56-57.

13 July 1807. Thomas and Polly WILSON to George HITE. Lot [# not shown] in Morgan Town where Hite now lives, conveyed to Thomas Wilson by Joseph Wilson. Excepts such rents and incumbrances on said lot as it was conveyed to Thomas. Consideration: $727. Signed: Thos Wilson, Polly Wilson. Witnesses: none. Acknowledged in court, July 1807. No delivery shown. Recorded: OS 4:57-58.

1 April 1806. Richard and Mary PETTYJOHN to James BOOTH, all of Harrison Co. 360 acres on a "lefthand drain of Tagers Value cauld Plum Run," adjoining Major Power and Jacob Holland. Patented 23 March 1799. Consideration: $500. Signed: Richard Petty John [Mary does not sign]. Witnesses: John Wood, Horatio Morgan, Wm Hayhurst Jr. Proved by witnesses, October 1806, June 1807. No delivery shown. Recorded: OS 4:58.

14 April 1806. John and Sarah PETTYJOHN to Matthew HINES, Harrison Co. 200 acres on the east side of Tyger Valley River. From two different surveys, one of 400 acres, conveyed by William Pettyjohn, deceased, to John Pettyjohn, and another of 1000 acres patented to John Pettyjohn 1 May 1785. No adjoiners named. Consideration: $800. Signed: John Pettyjohn, Sarah Pettyjohn. Witnesses: Samuel Hanway, William McClerry, Thomas Laidley. Proved by witnesses, September 1806, July 1807. Commission to Jacob Pawlsey and [blank] to take Sarah's acknowledgement. Unsigned acknowledgement certificate, 14 April 1806. "NB the Commission returned with this deed is only part recorded being alltogether unteligible [sic]." No delivery shown. Recorded: OS 4:59-60.

14 July 180[blank]. William and Catharine LANHAM to Fauquer McREA. 100 3/4 acres on Aarons and Deckers Creeks, formerly property of John Ferguson, adjoining Henry Dering, Kerns, and Lanham's other land. Consideration: 1¢, VA. Signed: Wm Lanham, Catherine Lanham. Witnesses: B Reeder, S Morgan, D F McRea, Benjamin Hixon. Acknowledged in court by William Lanham, July 1807; by Catherine Lanham before S Morgan and B Reeder, JPs, 14 July 1807. Del: to grantee, 27 May 1822. Recorded: OS 4:60-61.

20 May 1805. WILL of Samuel MORTON. Son Benjamin: £45. Three children of deceased son Thomas Morton: £45, to be divided among them, payable at age 21. Son William Morton: £200, his choice of horse creatures after Samuel's widow takes her choice, plus blacksmith tools now in the shop, gears, and plow irons. Daughter Hannah: £45, to be used by executors for her advantage and benefit. Daughter Elisabeth, wife of Samuel Willetts: £20, she having been advanced £25 previously. Daughter Sarah, wife of John Foreman: the same. Daughter Ann, wife of Absalom Brandon: £30, she having been advanced £15 previously. Daughter Susanna, wife of William Neil: £35, she having been advanced £10 previously. Daughters Mary, Rebecca, Phebe, and Edith Morton: £45 each. All legacies to be paid in PA currency. Wife Hannah: silver watch and first choice of 2 horse creatures. Remainder of estate, except as noted above, to be sold and legacies to be paid from the proceeds. Any remaining property to wife Hannah. No securities to be taken for executors and no inventory or sale bill to be made. Executors: wife Hannah, son William, and son-in-law John Foreman. Signed: Samuel Morton. Witnesses: Alexander Brandon, Jesse Penrose, Joseph Fickle. Proved by witnesses, June 1805. Recorded: OS 4:62-63. [Also recorded in Wills 1:312-313.]

16 August 1799. WILL of William PETTYJOHN. Wife Ruth: plantation where I live during her life, with Negro woman Darcus, beds and furniture, a horse and saddle, cow, and house furniture, all for life. Darcus to be free after wife's death. Grandsons William and John, sons of William Pettyjohn deceased, and John Poor: home plantation at wife's death, plus 300 acres on Punking Run, adjoining where I now live; 450 acres in Harrison Co, at the forks of the road adjoining William Tucker, to be equally divided among the three. Mary Randolph, wife of David: 50 acres where she now lives, to be conveyed by executors. David Little: 50 acres where he lives. Son John, daughter Mary (wife of William Haymond), and all grandchildren now born: remainder of estate, real and personal. [Added after the main text] Amos Petty John, son of William: my riding horse. Executors: son John Pettyjohn and son-in-law William Haymond, of Harrison Co. Signed: W Pettyjohn. Witnesses: Jordan Hall, William Haymond Jr, Thomas Little. Proved by witnesses, October 1799. Recorded: OS 4:63. [Also recorded in Wills 1:313-314.]

21 June 1801. WILL of John STANLEY. Wife Hannah: one third of estate during her lifetime. William Deaver:

one Spanish mill dollar. Amealia and Henry Snider: one Spanish mill dollar. "Little friend John Stanley Snider": two thirds of estate, plus reversion of the portion willed to widow for her lifetime. James Stanley: $1. Executors: Henry Hamilton, Thomas Miller. Signed: John [X] Stanley. Witnesses: Joseph Reed, Caleb Bennet, Jacob [+] Noose. Proved by witnesses, July 1801. Recorded: OS 4:64. [Also recorded in Wills 1:314-315.]

17 April 1802. WILL of Thomas BERRY. Wife Rachel: plantation where I live, during her lifetime. After her death, to be divided among children as per: 121 acres to sons Curtis and John, John to have the part adjoining Little Sandy Creek. Curtis to pay youngest son Nathan £13.8, and John to pay him £6.12 when Nathan comes of age. If the 200 acres on Little Sandy that Berry claims, adjoining James Sullivan, can be obtained, Nathan is to have 100 acres of it and Curtis and John need not pay him the £20 called for above. The remainder of the tract, if obtained, to be divided among four daughters, Margret Berry, Sarah Berry, Elisabeth Berry, and Rachel Berry. [sum blank] to be paid to sons Samuel, Thomas, Joseph, and John by Robert Bromfield, assistant executor, who is also to pay the daughters $2 each when convenient. Signed: Thomas Berry. Witnesses: Lewis Woolf, George Keller, Jno Kennedy. Proved by witnesses, June 1802. Recorded: OS 4:64-65. [Also recorded in Wills 1:315.]

[undated] WILL of Casper EVERLY. Son Simeon: 150 acres where he lives. Son Samuel: 50 acres between Simeon's land and the river. William Everly: 50 acres. Jesse Everly: 150 acres. William and Jesse to divide 300 acres [sic]. Household furniture and livestock to widow for her lifetime. Not signed. Witnesses: none. December 1800: "This Writing which is supposed to be the last will and testament of Casper Everly was produced in Court and Severall witnesses being there upon Severally Sworn and Examined upon hearing whose testimony the opinion of the Court was that the same be be [sic] recorded." Recorded: OS 4:65. [Also recorded in Wills 1:316.]

16 May 1805. WILL of Jonathan MATTHEW. Two oldest children, Rachel and William: one cow or the price of a cow. The rest to be equally divided among the children, but not until the youngest is of age. "the boys should try to make out to pay for the land first and my wife to wile she lives single have a good living of the place but if she marries to go so." Signed: Jonathan Matthew. Witnesses: None named. Proved, October 1805, by John

Snider, a subscribing witness [sic]. Recorded: OS 4:65. [Also recorded in Wills, 1:316.]

10 January 1785. WILL of Lott RIDGWAY. Wife Catherine: house, furniture, and one third of lands for life, as well as all profits of the plantation until second son Joel comes of age, for the use of the younger children. Eldest son Noah: £5, he having been left lands by his grandfather Josiah Ridgway in Barkley Co. Second son Joel: two thirds of the plantation where I now live, at wife's second marriage, and all at her decease, if she remains a widow until he comes of age. Six daughters: £10 each. Executors: friends Jacob and Henry Beason, Fayette Co, PA. Not signed. Witnesses: None named. "This Will was Rot in the year 85 & Was not Signed till the year 86." Proved November 1796 by Nicholas Vandevort, Jonah Vandevort, and David Hayhurst, who believe it to be Ridgway's handwriting. Recorded: OS 4:66. [Also recorded in Wills, 1:316-317.]

26 January 1798. WILL of Leonard TITZARD. Wife Chashey: whole estate during her life, afterwards to be divided among 8 children Sarah, Lenah, Susannah, Rachel, Catherine, Hanner, Marah, Isaack. Daughter Elisabeth Souther: 5s. Executor: wife Chashey. Signed: Leonard [+] Titzard. Witnesses: John Fairfax, William Watson, Robert Patton. Proved by witnesses, June 1801. Recorded: OS 4:66-67. [Also recorded in Wills, 1:317.]

14 September 1790. WILL of Abraham SCISCO. Sons John and Abraham: plantation where I now live, 200 acres, to be equally divided in quantity. Abraham to have the improved portion and John the upper part adjoining John Vandruff and William Fancher. Son John: rifle gun. Son Abraham: cow. Wife Mary: bed, furniture, wheel. Remainder of estate to be divided among children Elisabeth, Mary, Hannah, Rebecca, Absolam, and Sarah. Executor: wife Mary. Signed: Abraham [+] Sisco. Witnesses: W Pettyjohn, W Pettyjohn, Desire [+, his mark] Fanche. Proved April 1799 by William Petty John, who attests that William Petty John Jr and Desire Fancher also witnessed, the one dead and the other removed. Recorded: OS 4:67. [Also recorded in Wills, 1:317-318.]

20 January 1807. WILL of William WILSON. Wife Rebecca: what the law will allow her, and no more. Son Stephen, son George, daughter Barsha, daughter Linny, daughter Rebecca, daughter Harriet, son Josiah, son Abraham, daughter Ruth Livina, and daughter Nancy: 5s each. Daughter Ellenor: all land and remainder of movable estate, brother Josiah to make her a deed for

the land as soon as he can. Signed: William [+] Wilson. Witnesses: John Linch, James Barker. Proved by witnesses, February 1807. Recorded: OS 4:68. [Also recorded in Wills, 1:318.]

8 September 1800. WILL of John PILES. Oldest son Elijah: Negro woman Milly and her child Daniel. Son David: Negro man Spencer, and the improved part of the land where I now live, 130 acres, plus 100 acres on Threefork. Son Hunter: 180 acres where he now lives, including his improvement. Son Elijah: 300 acres on Three Fork. Remainder of estate to be divided among sons Elijah, David, and Hunter, who are also named executors. Signed: John [+] Piles. Witnesses: John Fairfax, Elias Rice. Proved by witnesses, January 1801. Recorded: OS 4:68. [Also recorded in Wills, 1:319.]

24 November 1804. WILL of James DAUGHERTY, Morgan Town. Son Enos: lot where I live, on Main Street, adjoining John Stealey's tanyard lot (now the property of William Tingle), plus "all other legacies and bequests." Signed: James Daugherty. Witnesses: Nimrod Evans, J[oseph] Campbell, F Britton. Proved by witnesses, December 1805. Recorded: OS 4:69. [Also recorded in Wills, 1:319.]

26 6mo 1802. WILL of James CONNER. Wife: use of plantation during her widowhood, as well as 3 cows, a yoke of oxen, mare and colt, household goods, farming utensils, sheep and hogs. Daughter [not named] and her husband, Richard Foreman: tract where they live. Daughter Elisabeth and her husband, John Hott [Holt?]: cow and calf. Son John: 100 acres from the southeast corner of the tract I live on. Daughter [not named] and her husband Abraham Workman: my part of an undivided tract between me and Joseph Foreman, Abram to pay £20 in salt, iron, and grain. Son Daniel: 100 acres, northeast corner of the tract I live on. Son James: 100 acres, southwest corner of the tract I live on. Son Robert: 100 acres, northwest corner of the tract I live on. Rest of livestock to be sold and the proceeds divided among the younger girls. "As there is something a coming to me about my fathers Estate," he allows this, with the £20 due from Abram Workman, to be used for schooling and support of the younger children. Executors: son-in-law Richard Foreman, son John, and testator's wife. Trustee: brother, William Conner. Signed: James [+] Conner. Witnesses: James Webster, Joseph Severns, William Workman. Proved by witnesses, September 1802. Recorded: OS 4:69. [Also recorded in Wills, 1:320.]

26 April 1803. WILL of Alexander WADE. Place I now

live on to remain in wife's hands as long as she remains a widow. Children to be raised there till the two youngest boys, Elisha and Hosea, come of age, and then all to have an equal share. Oldest boys, Aaron, Elijah, Alexander, and Thomas: to have shares out of the land up the river. A mare, colt, and cow to be charged to George, or taken out of his share. Elijah: a mare. Price of Mary's saddle to be taken out of her share. Executors: Aaron and his mother. Signed: Alexander Wade. Witnesses: William Billingsly, Jesse Bussey, Sias Billingsly. Proved by witnesses, June 1803. Recorded: OS 4:70. [Also recorded in Wills, 1:320-321.]

[not dated] WILL of Philip PINDALL. Son Jacob: 687 acres on Buffaloe, divides [Davys?] run and Dunker Mill Run. Wife Rachel: plantation on the head of Burchfield where Long Jacob Pindall lives, for her life, if she survives me. At her death, this plantation and all land not otherwise conveyed to son-in-law John Combes. Grandson Jacob Pindall, son of Thomas and Judah: surveying instruments. Thomas McFarland, son of John and Susannah: watch. Philip Combes, son of John and Rachel: rifle gun. Beds and other small property to wife, if she survives, during her life. Not signed. Witnesses: none named. "Produced in court January 1804 and ordered to be recorded." Recorded: OS 4:70. [Also recorded in Wills, 1:321.]

6 November 1797. WILL of Abner HARP. Wife: one third of land during her life. Son Richard: 200 acres to be equally divided by Stephen Morgan, son of David. Daughters Elisabeth, Catherine, Mary, and Martha: 50 acres each. If Mary or Martha die underage, their share to be equally divided among the children living. Son Richard: [word missing] named Prince and a cow. Daughters Elisabeth and Catherine: a cow each. Daughters Mary and Martha: a spring heifer calf each. James West Sr to divide whatever personal estate remains, and the heirs to abide by his division. Executors: Stephen Morgan and John Sayre. Signed: Abner [+] Harp. Witnesses: Thomas Knight, James Little, Nehemiah Harp. Proved by witnesses, April 1804. Recorded: OS 4:71. [Also recorded in Wills, 1:321-322.]

19 May 1800. WILL of Alpheus GUSTIN. Son Abel: land southeast of the big run running through the place. Son Ashbel: tract where Benjamin Pearce formerly lived. Son Abiel: land between Ashbel and Abel. Wife Mary: saddle, bridle, rest of lands while she remains widow, until youngest sons Ammoniah and Ammia [?] come of age. If she marries, land to be used by executors for benefit of the

two youngest children. Daughters Maple Pearce, Mary Steward: £5, VA, each. Daughter Margret Gustin: £30, VA, and a cow she claims, if she stays and lives with her mother till she comes of age. Son Alpheus: £5, VA. Grandchild Mary Pearce: £5, VA, if she stays with testator's widow until she comes of age. Executors: Ashbel Gustin and James [illegible]. Signed: Alpheus Gustin. Witnesses: Coverdale Cole, Samuel [+] Davis, Hannah [+] Davis. Proved by witnesses Samuel and Hannah Davis, September 1800. Recorded: OS 4:72. [Also recorded in Wills, 1:322-323.]

13 January 1805. WILL of John GARDNER. Friend Thomas Powell: horse, best saddle, cow, household goods, and all my outstanding debts. Apprentice Levi Hendrixon: mare, saddle, wearing apparel. Friend Jacob Tinney: silver watch. Friend William Franklin: half of 250 acre plantation about two miles from the Illinois town, Thompson Co, the rest of the land to be sold and proceeds given to the poor. Negro woman Nancy manumitted. Executor: Thomas Powell. Signed: John [+] Gardner. Witnesses: James Spurgen, Thomas Powell. Proved by witnesses, February 1805. Recorded: OS 4:73. [Also recorded in Wills, 1:323-324.]

29 March 1799. WILL of Simon TROY. Sons James and Christopher: lands surveyed for them. The portion of tract I kept for myself to be sold. Wife Hannah and her daughters Mary and Elisabeth: plantation I now live on, with livestock and household furniture, as long as my wife shall live. Daughter Elisabeth: Negro girl Rachel, £100, VA, an equal part of the livestock and household goods, excepting wife's bed. If Mary and Elisabeth live with their mother till she dies, all the moveables to be divided among them. If either decides to move away, she is to have one third of the moveables. Daughter Mary: Negro girl Jain and the home plantation, after wife's death, for life, with reversion to John Troy's two sons, Benjamin and Simon. Daughter Eleanor: £30, VA, personal property, and land surveyed for her on Dunkard Creek. Land is for lifetime only, with reversion to her firstborn son John Bromigan. All remaining estate to wife and her two daughters Mary and Elisabeth. Signed: Simon Troy. Witness: Abraham Miley. Proved by witness, July 1799. Recorded: OS 4:73. [Also recorded in Wills, 1:324.]

3 March 1801. WILL of William ROBE. Wife Sarah: tract where I now live, west of Surats [sic] Run, and where Marsh Duvall lives, with full power to dispose of the same. Undisturbed use of the lower room in the new

building on the tract; her choice of two beds and bedding; as much of the household furniture as she chooses; and her choice of a horse and two cows. Son Josiah: to provide support, provisions, and firewood to Sarah, and to pay her £50 when she requests it. Sons David and Robert: remainder of lands, excepting the plantation where I live and 15 acres adjoining it. Robert to have the place where he lives, and David to have no improvements made by Robert. Son David: half of grain now in my stackyard, he to assist in thrashing and cleaning. Son Josiah: tract where I live, except the portion left to wife, as well as a 15 acre survey adjoining. If wife dies intestate, Josiah to have the land bequeathed to her, as well as all other livestock, household furnishings, farming tools, and personal property not otherwise bequeathed. Daughters Mary Stuart and Sarah Sutton: a Bible each, to be purchased by executors. Executors: sons Robert and Josiah. Signed: William Robe. Witnesses: William McClerry, Alexr Hawthorn, Ezekiel Chaney. Proved by witnesses, April 1803. Recorded: OS 4:74. [Also recorded in Wills, 1:325.]

20 June 1807. Leonard M DEAKINS and John HOYE, executors and devisees of Francis DEAKINS, deceased, who was executor and devisee of William DEAKINS, deceased, all of George Town, DC, to Patrick MURDOCH, Alleghania Co, MD. 1800 acres on Woolf Creek, a branch of Cheat River, adjoining Stemple, Conrad Holstine, Martin Stemple, Bishop, and John Litchfield. From 14,050 acre and 400 acre tracts belonging to Francis and William Deakins. Consideration: $1, plus certain soldier's lots in Alleghania Co, sold for the direct tax and assigned to Murdoch. Signed: L Deakins, John Hoye. Witness: Danl Reintzel. Acknowledged in George Town, DC, 20 June 1807. Certificate of Daniel Reintzel, mayor. Del: to E Butler, 29 October 1807. Recorded: OS 4:75-76.

13 February 1797. Martin and Ann MYRES to Christian WIREMAN, all of Union Town, Fayatte Co, PA. 100 acres adjoining Jacob Judy, David Moore, and Martin Judy's settlement survey. Patented to Myres, assignee of Martin Judy, assignee of John Judy's heirs. Consideration: $200, PA. Signed: Martin Myres, Ann [+] Myres. Witnesses: Solomon Hickman, Cornelius Lynch. Receipt for consideration money. Acknowledged before Jonathan Rowland, JP, in Fayette Co, PA, 13 February 1797. Del: to Thos Gillings by mail, 24 September 1807. Recorded: OS 4:77-78.

4 August 1807. Richard LAUGHFORD to Thomas

GETTINGS, both of Montgomery Co, MD. 100 acres adjoining David Moore, Jacob Judy, and Judy's settlement survey. Patented to Martin Myres, who conveyed to Christian Wireman, who conveyed to Laughford, 21 July 1797. Consideration: $300. Signed: Richard Laughford. Witnesses: Wal B Beall, Thomas Simpson. Receipt for consideration money. Acknowledged in Montgomery Co, MD, 4 August 1807 before Wal B Beall and Thomas Simpson, JPs. Certificate of Upton Beall, Clerk. Recorded: OS 4:78-81.

14 September 1807. Tobias and Catherine REAMS to Benjamin SHAW. 139 acres, no adjoiners or place names mentioned. Tract conveyed to Reams by Joseph Vulgamott. Consideration: $500, VA. Signed: Tobias Reams, Catherine Reams. Witnesses: none. Acknowledged in court, September 1807. Del: to Alexander Brandon, 15 November 1808. Recorded: OS 4:81-82.

23 November 1807. Joseph and Amelia BRANDON, Bourben Co, KY, to Robert WOODS. 200 acres on Big Sandy, no adjoiners named. Part of Martin Judy's big survey. Consideration: £200, PA. Signed: Joseph Brandon, Amelia Brandon. Witnesses: J Clark, Alexander Brandon, Jonathan Brandon. Acknowledged by Amelia Brandon in Bourboun Co, KY, 29 January 1806 [sic], before William Mitchell and Robert Scott, JPs. Certificates of William Gerrard Jr, clerk, and William Mitchell, presiding justice. [Commission to take Amelia's acknowledgement is dated 26 October 1805 and refers to deed of 23 November 1805.] Proved by witnesses A Brandon and J Clark, April 1806. Del: to R Woods, 23 May 1808. Recorded: OS 4:82-84.

[blank] September 1807. Matthew and Elisabeth GEORGE to James KELLY. 77 acres, 8 perches, adjoining Booz Burress and William Willey Sr. Part of a tract sold to Matthew by William (Sr) and Polly Willey, 8 March 1802. Consideration: $348.97½. Signed: Matthew George, Elisabeth George. Witnesses: none. Acknowledged in court, September 1807. Del: to him, 5 September 1807. Recorded: OS 4:85-86.

4 September 1807. Jesse PAYNE to Henry DERING. Deed of trust. Payne owes $1087.59 to William Lowrey & Co, payable 25 December next, one half in bar iron @ $150 per ton and half in pot metal castings @ $90 per ton. To secure payment, Payne conveys to Dering Negro slaves Vachel, Will, and Maria, a waggon and gears, and 8 head of horses. Signed: Jesse Payne, William Lowrey, Henry Dering. Witnesses: William Tingle, Nicholas B Madera. Proved by witnesses, September 1807. Del: to Wm Lowry, 29 February 1808. Recorded: OS 4:86-87.

6 April 1807. Russel and Rhoda POTTER to Daniel LANTZ, Alleghania Co, MD. 182 acres on Little and Big Sandy Creek, adjoining John Judy and Martin Judy. Consideration: $432. Signed: Russel Potter, Rhoda [+] Potter. Witnesses: John Willets, Jonathan Brandon, Nicholas Frankhouser, Daniel McCullum. Proved by witnesses, July and September 1807. Del: to D Lantz, 28 November 1807. Recorded: OS 4:88.

14 September 1807. David SCOTT to George PECKENPAW. 100 acres on Scotts Mill Run, adjoining Philip Shiveley and Thomas McKinley. Part of the mill farm. Consideration: $300. Signed: David Scott. Witnesses: none. Acknowledged in court, September 1807. Del: to him, 14 March 1814. Recorded: OS 4:89.

19 February 1805. Jonas HOGMIRE, Washington Co, MD, to Nicholas FRANKHOUSER. 594 acres on Little Sandy Creek, adjoining William Springer and William Deakins. Surveyed for William Deakins, 14 October 1784. Consideration: £300, MD. Signed: Jonas Hogmire. Witnesses: William Clagett, Robert Houghes. Acknowledged in Washington Co, MD, before William Clagett, chief judge, 19 February 1805. Certificate of O H Williams, clerk of Washington Co. Del: to A Brandon, 10 August 1808. Recorded: OS 4:90-92.

4 March 1807. David SCOTT, son of David, to Enoch JONES. Deed of trust. Scott owes [blank] to Isaac Ogden, by notes due 1 November 1809 and [blank] 1807. To secure the debt he conveys 100 acres of the Mill Tract, formerly owned by Col David Scott, including cleared land lately occupied by Robert Means and now by James Reed. If the debt is not paid, the land to be sold, after being advertised for 4 weeks in the *Monongalia Gazette*, published at Morgan Town. Signed: David Scott, Isaac Ogden, Enoch Jones. Witnesses: John Sanders, Enoch Jones, Joseph Dunlap. Acknowledged in court, September 1807. No delivery shown. Recorded: OS 4:92-93.

14 September 1807. John and Elisabeth HOULT to John HOULT Jr. 130 acres on Parkers Run, no adjoiners named. Part of a larger tract patented 12 October 1791. Consideration: love, good will and affection. Signed: John Hoult, Elisabeth Hoult. Witnesses: none. Acknowledged in court, September 1807. Del: to E Holt, 22 December 1807. Recorded: OS 4:94.

14 September 1807. John and Elisabeth HOULT to John JOLLIFF. 67 acres on the river, adjoining Raphael Hoult and Hollenback. Part of a larger tract patented 10 October 1786. Consideration: love, affection, and good will. Signed: John Hoult, Elisabeth Hoult. Witnesses:

none. Acknowledged in court, September 1807. Del: to John Jolliff, 5 June 1808. Recorded: OS 4:95.

14 September 1807. John and Elisabeth HOULT to Elijah HOULT. 58 acres on Monongalia River, adjoining Josiah Prickett. Part of a larger tract patented 25 October 1786. Consideration: love, affection, and good will. Signed: John Hoult, Elisabeth Hoult. Witnesses: none. Acknowledged in court, September 1807. Del: to Elijah Holt, 22 December 1807. Recorded: OS 4:96.

14 September 1807. John and Elisabeth HOULT to Elisha HOULT. 75 acres near Monongalia River, adjoining John Jolliff and Raphael Hoult. Part of two tracts: a 25 October 1786 patent for 400 acres and a 10 October 1786 patent for 150 acres. Consideration: love, affection, and good will. Signed: John Hoult, Elisabeth Hoult. Witnesses: none. Acknowledged in court, September 1807. Del: to John Jolliffe, 4 June 1808. Recorded: OS 4:97.

14 September 1807. John and Elisabeth HOULT to Joseph HOULT. 132 acres on Parkers Run, where Joseph now lives. No adjoiners named. Part of a 12 October 1791 patent. Consideration: love, good will, and affection. Signed: John Hoult, Elisabeth Hoult. Witnesses: none. Acknowledged in court, September 1807. Del: to John Jolliff, 4 June 1808. Recorded: OS 4:98.

14 September 1807. John and Elisabeth HOULT to Raphael HOULT. 92 acres on Monongalia River, adjoining John Joliff and Elisha Hoult. Part of two tracts: a 25 October 1786 patent for 400 acres, and a 10 October 1786 patent for 150 acres. Consideration: love, good will, and affection. Signed: John Hoult, Elisabeth Hoult. Witnesses: none. Acknowledged in court, September 1807. Del: to Jno Hoult, 24 February 1809. Recorded: OS 4:99.

12 November 1806. James and Hannah MORGAN to John FAIRFAX. 416 acres, in two parcels. A 408 acre tract on the west side of Cheat, at Buffaloe Run, adjoining John Green (minus 116 acres previously sold to George Snider). 270 acres at Cheat River, adjoining the former tract (minus 146 acres previously sold to Samuel Taylor). Consideration: $2000. Signed: James Morgan, Hannah Morgan. Witnesses: W G Payne, John W Dean, Ross Alley. Acknowledged by Hannah Morgan before David Morgan and James E Beall, JPs, 21 September 1807. Proved by witnesses, April 1807, June 1808, January 1814 [Thomas P Ray indicated as witness in these memos but not named as such in the instrument]. Del: to Col Bucker Fairfax, 19 September 1866. Recorded: OS 4:100-101.

13 September 1807. Simeon and Elisabeth ROYSE to John CHIPPS. 220 acres adjoining William John, John

McFarland, Thomas Evans, and James Stafford. Part of 304 acres patented to Thomas John. Consideration: $500, VA. Signed: Simeon Royse [Elisabeth does not sign]. Witnesses: none. Acknowledged in court by Simeon, September 1807, and recorded as to him. Del: to John Chipps, 15 November 1808. Recorded: OS 4:102.

7 April 1807. Lewis and Eleanor KERNS to William RUSSEL. 75 acres on Dunkard Creek, adjoining Henry Barrackman's part of the same tract, Consideration: $500, VA. Signed: Lewis [0] Kerns, Eleanor [+] Kerns. Witnesses: Rawley Scott, George Debler, Mosses Snyder. Acknowledged in court, September 1807. Del: to W Russel, 23 September 1809. Recorded: OS 4:103.

14 September 1807. John and Barsheba SPRINGER to [unspecified] CREDITORS of Richard MERRYFIELD, deceased. Barsheba, one of the heirs and legal representatives of Richard, relinquishes all claim to his real or personal estate as she and her husband do not wish to be liable for Richard's debts. Signed: John Springer, Barsheba Springer. Witnesses: William G Payne, William McClerry, Matthew Gay. Acknowledged in court, September 1807. Del: to John Springer, pr T Wilson, 27 September 1813. Recorded: OS 4:104.

14 September 1807. John BARRACKMAN to James MORRIS. Release. On 11 October 1794 William and Mary Dawson sold to James Morris 213½ acres on Scott's Mill Run. Morris also held 21½ acres adjoining, purchased from John and Hannah Stag, 12 November 1798. On [blank] 179[blank] Morris conveyed 100 acres of this land to William Veek. On 1 April 1800 Morris gave bond to convey to John Barrackman the balance of the tract, supposed to be 150 acres. Deed was made 9 June 1800, but the description of the tract erroneously included the whole of the two former tracts, thereby making it appear that Morris had also sold to Barrackman the 100 acres previously conveyed to Veek. This was never meant or intended. John Barrackman Sr, never having learned of the error, conveyed the land to his son John Barrackman Jr on 6 January 1801 and has since departed this life. John Barrackman Jr now releases all claim under the deed to the 100 acres conveyed to Veek. Consideration: $1. Signed: John Barrackman. Witnesses: none. Acknowledged in court, September 1807. Del: to him, 11 April 1814. Recorded: OS 4:104-105.

14 September 1807. George and Margret BARNS to Richard NUZUM. 400 acres on a branch of Tyger Valley River below Glady Creek, near a place known as the Levels. No adjoiners named. Patented 8 September 1794.

Consideration: $600, VA. Signed: George Barnes, Margret Barnes. Witnesses: none. Acknowledged in court, September 1807. Del: to Richd Nuzum, 6 June 1809. Recorded: OS 4:105-106.

19 February 1807. William and Elizabeth RUSSEL to Thomas RUSSEL Sr. 50 acres adjoining corner of the land where George Zinn now lives. Consideration: $1. Signed: William Russel [Elizabeth does not sign]. Witnesses: Allen Martin, Henry Fortney, George Zinn. Proved by witnesses, April and September 1807. Del: to Thos Russell wife, 25 February 1810. Recorded: OS 4:106-107.

11 September 1807. Simon and Hannah KRATZER to Jacob LYMAN. 261 acres adjoining William Robinson, Edward Huss [?], and Kratzer's other land. Consideration: $750, VA. Signed: Simon Kratzer, Hannah Kratzer. Witnesses: none. Acknowledged in court, September 1807. Del: to Jacob Lyman, 5 August 1808. Recorded: OS 4:108.

12 March 1804. Tobias and Catherine REAMS to Jacob FETHER, formerly of Somerset Co, PA. 75 acres on Muddy Creek, part of the plantation where Reams now lives. No adjoiners named. Consideration: $111. Signed: Tobias Reams, Catherine Reams. Witnesses: B Reeder, David Scott, E Horton, John Pew. Acknowledged in court by Tobias Reams, September 1807; by Catherine before David Scott and B Reeder, JPs, 13 March 1804. No delivery shown. Recorded: OS 4:109-110.

24 April 1806. Samuel and Elisabeth WEST (formerly BURROWS, daughter of Elijah BURROWS, deceased) to James McVICKER. 50 acres, an undivided moiety of 100 acres, adjoining John W Dean, John Baker, John Burress, Charles Burress, and William Burress. A tract bequeathed to Elisabeth and Catherine Burrows by their father Elijah Burrows, to be equally divided but partition not yet made. Consideration: $200. Signed: Samuel West, Elisabeth [+] West. Witnesses: B Reeder, Jas Scott, Thomas Laidley, John West. Acknowledged by Elisabeth West before B Reeder and Jas Scott, JPs, 24 April 1806; written acknowledgement by Samuel West, 30 June 1807, witnessed by Nimrod Evans, Marmaduke Evans, and James McGee. No delivery shown. Recorded: OS 4:110-112.

16 April 1806. Allen and Rachel ROBINETT to Isaac SADLER, all of Huntingdon Twp, Adams Co, PA. 200 acres known as Blackburns Glade. No adjoiners named. Consideration: £100, PA. Signed: Allen Robinett, Rachel Robinett. Witnesses: A Robinett, Jas Robinett, John Cooper. Receipt for consideration money. Acknowledged 10 April 1806 before John Fukle [?], JP. Del: to Isaac

Sadler, 13 September 180[?]. Recorded: OS 4:112-113.

14 September 1807. Thomas and Olive MARTIN to Isaac MATTHEW. 201 3/4 acres at Threefork, on the great road to Clarksburg, adjoining Thomas Martin's and John Wilson's surveys. Patented to Martin, 20 July 1804. Consideration: $258. Signed: Thomas Martin, Olive Martin. Witnesses: none. Receipt for consideration money. Acknowledged in court, September 1807. Del: to him, 19 March 1814. Recorded: OS 4:114.

21 September 1807. Jacob RIVER, Washington Co, MD, to Alexander McCLELAND, Springhill Twp, Fayette Co, PA. 250 acres at Flat Run, on the state road from Morgan Town to the mouth of Fishing Creek, adjoining Henry Shoop. Part of 700 acres patented to Col David Scott, Esq, 6 June 1796, and conveyed by him to River, 2 February 1807. Consideration: $500. Signed: Jacob River. Witness: Jno Buckhannon. Acknowledged in Washington Co, MD, 22 September 1807, before Jno Buckhannon. Certificate of Jno Buckhannon, chief judge, 5th judicial district, and O H Williams, clerk. Del: to A McCleland, 24 October 1807. Recorded: OS 4:115-117.

5 September 1807. B REEDER and David SCOTT to William TINGLE. Request to execute deed of release. Col David Scott has satisfied us for the claim of Dennis Springer against him, and to secure which Scott had given a deed of trust on 700 acres at Flat Run. Signed: B Reeder, David Scott. Witnesses: Wm N Jarrett, Nimrod Evans, Ralph Barkshire, Augustus Werninger. Recorded: OS 4:117.

5 September 1807. William TINGLE, trustee, to Ludwick ENSAMINGER, Jacob PECK, Philip and John WIENT, Henry SHOOP, and Jacob RIVER, all of Washington Co, MD. On 24 July 1804 Col David Scott gave deed of trust on 700 acres and 300 acres, for the use of Benjamin Reeder and David Scott 2nd. If Reeder and Scott should be made liable re: an injunction obtained by Col David Scott in District Court of Chancery at Stanton vs Dennis Springer, then the land to be sold to indemnify them. All claims satisfied, and the land having been sold by Scott to the grantees on 2 February 1807, Tingle releases title to them. Consideration: $1. Signed: Wm Tingle. Witnesses: Wm N Jarrett, Nimrod Evans, Ralph Barkshire, Augustus Werninger. Proved by witnesses, October 1807. Del: to McCleland, 24 October 1807, Recorded: OS 4:117-118.

12 October 1807. Christian and Susanah SCRYER to John STEALEY, Esq, Morgan Town. 104 acres on Big Laurel Run, no adjoiners named. Patented to Jeremiah Tonnehill,

10 October 1786, and conveyed by him to Stealey [sic]. Consideration: £100. Signed: Christian Scryer, Susanah [+] Scryer. Acknowledged in court, October 1807. Del: to grantee, 19 December 1821. Recorded: OS 4:119.

30 March 1807. Russel and Rhoda POTTER to Abraham and Simeon WOODROW. 6 acres adjoining James Moore. Conveys the interest sold by some (but not all) of the heirs of Lott Ridgway to Elihu Horton, who conveyed the same to Potter. Consideration: $250, VA. Signed: Russel Potter [Rhoda does not sign]. Witnesses: William G Payne, Charles Byrn, Paul Vigus (all as to Russel Potter). Proved by witnesses, October 1807. No delivery shown. Recorded: OS 4:120.

14 September 1807. Thomas and Agness FRETWELL to John BRANDT. 1340 acres on the state road from Morgan Town to the Dunkard Bottom, adjoining Benjamin Reeder, Alexander Smith, William Manear, Ann Holly, and near the schoolhouse. Consideration: $360, VA. Signed: Thomas Fretwell, Agness Fretwell. Witnesses: Jesse Payne, James Beason, John White. Receipt for consideration money. Proved by witnesses, October 1807. Acknowledged by Agness Fretwell before Wm N Jarrett and John Stealey, JPs, 10 March 1808. Del: to J Brant, 12 August 1808. Recorded: OS 4:121-122.

12 October 1807. Robert DAVIS Sr to his son Robert DAVIS Jr. 51½ acres at Robinsons Run, adjoining John Davis and Barnet Heney. Consideration: love and affection. Signed: Robert Davis. Witnesses: R Barkshire, Zackquill Morgan, Jacob Kyger. Acknowledged in court, October 1807. Del: to Polly Davis, 13 May 1809. Recorded: OS 4:122-123.

11 October 1807. Samuel and Sarah RICHIE, Green Co, PA, to Amos GANDY. 75 acres on Little Sandy Creek, adjoining Elijah Nicholas and former land of Theophilus Philips. Consideration: $120. Signed: Samuel Richie, Sarah Richie. Witnesses: none. Acknowledged in court, October 1807. Del: to him, 11 December 1815. Recorded: OS 4:123-124.

12 October 1807. Thomas and Sarah LAIDLEY to John DOUGHMAN. 121½ acres on Dunker Mill Run, adjoining James Fleming. Part of a 2800 acre patent. Consideration: $386, VA. Signed: Thos Laidley, Sarah Laidley. Witnesses: none. Acknowledged in court, October 1807. Del: to William Windsor, 3 March 1807. Recorded: OS 4:124.

12 January 1807. Grafton and Elisabeth WHITE to John CLARK. 45 3/4 acres on Scotts and Robinsons Mill Runs, known as Mount Pleasant. No adjoiners named.

Consideration: $170.50, VA. Signed: Grafton [+] White, Elisabeth [+] White. Witnesses: none. Acknowledged in court, October 1807. Del: to Isaac Ogdon, 12 March 1810. Recorded: OS 4:125.

12 October 1807. Eliazer and Sarah BIGGS to Andrew CASTOW. 100 acres on Marical Run, adjoining Jonathan Davis, Phinehas Kellum, and Jeremiah Biggs. Consideration: $200. Signed: Elieazer Biggs, Sarah [+] Biggs. Witnesses: none. Acknowledged in court, October, 1807. Del: to Mrs[?] Wm Jones, 9 December 1811, by order of Casto. Recorded: OS 4:126.

12 October 1807. Thomas and Sarah LAIDLEY to John McDOUGAL. 150 acres on middle fork of Dunker Mill Run, a branch of Bufaloe Creek, adjoining Pitzer and Jacob Pindall. Consideration: $600, VA. Signed: Thomas Laidley, Sarah Laidley. Witnesses: none. Acknowledged in court, October 1807. Del: to J McDougal, 18 [?] December 1807. Recorded: OS 4:127.

12 October 1807. Morgan and Drusilla MORGAN to William WILSON the third. 60 acres on Pine Fork of Prickets Creek, no adjoiners named. Patented to John Plom and Isreal [sic] Pricket, 17 September 1789, and sold to Morgan 9 August 1790. Consideration: $20. Signed: Morgan Morgan, Drusilla [X] Morgan. Witnesses: none. Acknowledged in court, October 1807. Del: to Wm Wilson the 3rd, 16 August 1809. Recorded: OS 4:128.

1 March 1805. Thomas LAIDLEY to James SCOTT, late sheriff of Monongalia. Laidley promises to pay $160 with interest from the time Scott sold Laidley's lot in Morgan Town, for revenue due to the commonwealth. If payment is not made in 15 months, Laidley will confirm and release the sale made by Scott. Signed: Thomas Laidley. Witnesses: W G Payne, Jas Pindall, Duncan F McRea. Proved by witnesses, October 1805, October 1806, October 1807. No delivery shown. Recorded: OS 4:129.

12 October 1807. John and Margret McDOUGAL to Thomas LAIDLEY. Two tracts. 45½ acres adjoining Grafton White, part of an 18 November 1802 patent to Robert Hamilton. 20 acres adjoining Grafton White and John Thompson, part of a 20 September 1785 patent to William Smith. Consideration: $275, VA. Signed: John McDougal, Margret McDougal. Witnesses: none. Acknowledged in court, October 1807. Del: to him, 13 October 1812. Recorded: OS 4:129-130.

[blank] 17[blank]. Thomas and Iszabella COURTNEY to John CLARK. 43 3/4 acres on Scotts and Robinsons Runs, known as Mount Pleasant, adjoining Enoch Jones. Consideration: $130, Va. Signed: Thomas [+] Courtney,

Isabelle [+] Courtney. Witnesses: none. Acknowledged in court, October 1807. Del: to Isaac Ogdon, 12 March 1810. Recorded: OS 4:130-131.

30 March 1807. Acknowledgement of Amelia EVANS, wife of Enoch EVANS, to powers of attorney, same date, issued to Dudley EVANS and Nimrod EVANS, empowering them to sell lands in Ohio and Monongalia Co. Given before Russel Potter and Nicholas Vandavort. Recorded: OS 4:131-132.

28 November 1807. Jacob and Eunice HAMPTON to John SCHRIVER, Washington Co, MD. 2 tracts on the east side of Tyger Valley River. 300 acres, no adjoiners named, part of a 9 September 1789 patent for 400 acres. 130 acres, patented to Thomas Wilson, 22 January 1800. Consideration: $3000. Signed: Jacob Hampton, Eunice Hampton. Witnesses: M Evans, Joseph Lowry, James McGee. Acknowledged in court by Eunice Hampton, December 1807, and proved by witnesses. Del: to Jacob Hampton, 12 June [Janr?] 1809. Recorded: OS 4:132-133.

14 December 1807. James and Elisabeth JEFFS to William KINCADE, of PA. 300 acres on Whiteday Creek, no adjoiners named. Patented to Jeffs [date blank]. Consideration: $500, VA. Signed: James Jeffs, Elizabeth Jeffs. Witnesses: none. Acknowledged in court by James Jeffs, December 1807, and by Elisabeth, October 1808. Del: to Wm Kincaid, 31 August 1808. Recorded: OS 4:134.

15 December 1807. William HART to Joshua HART. 60 acres, adjoining John Linch, Abraham Huffman, William Stuart, Zackariah Barker, William Jenkins, and James Leeson. Part of a tract conveyed by Zachariah Barker to John Linch. Consideration: $140, VA. Signed: William Hart. Witnesses: none. Acknowledged in court, December 1807. Del: to Jas Hart, 27 June 1808. Recorded: OS 4:135.

7 November 1807. WILL of John RAVENSCROFT, Cheat Neck. Wife Elisabeth: one third of all estate. Personal estate to be sold, his debts collected, and money used to support the family and educate children John, Catherine, and Samuel (youngest). Executor: John Ramsey of Cheat Neck. Signed: John Ravenscroft. Witnesses: Andrew Ramsey, Edward Pritchard, William Cracraft. Proved by witnesses, December 1807. Recorded: OS 4:136. [Also recorded in Wills, 1:332.]

9 September 1785. Zacquill and Drusilla MORGAN to James DAUGHERTY. 2 lots in Morgan Town [#s not shown], adjoining Hugh McNeely. Consideration: £6, VA. Signed: Zacquell Morgan, Drusilla Morgan. Witnesses: Jas Trumble, Joseph Cox. Acknowledged in court, August 1785.

No delivery shown. Recorded: OS 4:137-138. Re-recording of burned instrument.

14 December 1807. Morgan and Drusilla MORGAN to William BAMBRIDGE. 132 acres on Little Creek, no adjoiners named. Part of 361 acres patented 30 September 1785. Consideration: $400. Signed: Morgan Morgan, Drusilla [X] Morgan. Witnesses: none. Acknowledged in court, December 1807. Del: to him, 25 April 1812. Recorded: OS 4:138.

23 May 1807. WILL of Elias PEARSE. Wife Amy: household furniture and livestock, at her disposal, and one third of lands during her life. Son Isaac: remainder of lands, 2 horses, farming tools; he to pay daughters Elisabeth Hill $20, Elenor Hawkins $10, Drusilla Pearse $80, and Sarah Pearse $80. Remainder of estate to be divided among youngest daughters Drusilla and Sarah Pearse. Executors: wife Amy and Joshua Hickman. Signed: Elias [+] Pearse. Witnesses: Rynear Hall, John Haymond, Mary [+] Haymond. Proved by witnesses, December 1807. Recorded: OS 4:139. [Also recorded in Wills, 1:331-332.]

15 September 1807. William and Sarah WALLER to Samuel CLUTTER. 11½ acres on Muddy Creek, no adjoiners named. From a 200 acre survey. Consideration: $60. Signed: William Waller, Sarah Waller. Witnesses: John Fairfax, Booz Burrows, James McGee, Nimrod Evans. Acknowledged by Sarah Waller before John Fairfax and Booz Burrows, 15 September 1807. Proved by witnesses, December 1807. Del: to him, 19 August 1809. Recorded: OS 4:140-141.

18 November 1806. Frederick and Nancy GIBLER and Samuel HANWAY to John STEALEY, Morgan Town. 2 parcels. Lot #125 in Morgan Town, adjoining Hanway's meadow lot on Water Street. Conveyed to Gibler by the heirs of Zacquill Morgan. 31½ poles on Front Street, adjoining Gibler's other land. Conveyed to Gibler by Samuel Hanway. Consideration: $500, VA. Signed: Frederick Gibler, Nancy [+] Gibler, Samuel Hanway. Witnesses: James Evans, John Taylor, George Hickman, Thomas [+] Doolittle. Proved by witnesses, June and December 1807. Del: to Cornelius Barkshire, 13 January 1815. Recorded: OS 4:141-142.

10 December 1807. Thomas WILSON, trustee of George HOLLENBACK, late of Monongalia Co, to Clark HOLLENBACK. Tract on the east side of Monongalia River, conveyed by George Hollenback to Wilson to secure a payment due to John M Price. Clark was purchaser under trustee's sale. Wilson makes no warranty of title beyond that given by George in his deed of trust. Consideration: $406.01.

Signed: Thomas Wilson. Witnesses: Rawley Scott, James McGee, Alexander Hawthorn. Acknowledged in court, December 1807. Del: to Clark Holliback, 19 August 1809. Recorded: OS 4:143.

    2 November 1807. Dudley EVANS and Thomas WILSON, special commissioners, to Nimrod EVANS. 539 acres at Sandy Creek, no adjoiners named. Tract was originally conveyed by John Stealey and wife to Daniel Lantz, 8 July 1805 and is sold under decree in Stanton District Chancery Court, 20 July 1807, in the case of John Stealey vs Daniel Lantz, after having been advertised for 6 weeks in the *Monongalia Gazette*. No warranty of title is made by the commissioners. Consideration: $800. Signed: Dudley Evans, Thomas Wilson. Witnesses: J Evans Jr, J Evans, Joseph Lowry. Receipt for consideration money ($757, after deduction of $40 commissioners' fees and $3 for advertising costs) signed by John Stealey. Acknowledged in court, December 1807. Del: to grantee, 25 June 1821. Recorded: OS 4:143-145.

    16 May 180[6??? overwritten]. Asa and Hannah DUDLEY to John COOPER. 3 acres on Falling Run, adjoining Thomas Pindall, John Stealey, Thomas Wilson, and Benjamin Reeder. Part of a 17 acre patent. Consideration: $20, VA. Signed: Asa Dudley [Hannah does not sign]. Witnesses: Nimrod Evans, G Hite, Daniel Baltzel, Rawley Evans, Booz Burrows, G B Hoskinson. Proved by witnesses as to Asa Dudley, December 1807. Commission ordered to take Hannah's acknowledgement but not recorded here. Del: to [illegible, due to binding tape], 15 September 1812. Recorded: OS 4:145-146.

    11 January 1808. Martin and Margarett ABEL to John FELLER, Shanedoah Co. 240 acres on Sandy Creek, adjoining James Spurgen and John Judy. Part of 2868 acres patented to Charles Donaldson, 11 September 1789, and divided among his heirs by decree of Monongalia court. This portion fell to Martin Abel by his intermarriage into the Donaldson family. Consideration: $600. Signed: Martin [+] Abel, Margaret [+] Abel. Witnesses: Felix Scott, James McGee, Jno Evans. Acknowledged in court, January 1808. Del: to Alex McCleland. Recorded: OS 4:146-148.

    1 December 1807. James MORRISON, Esq, formerly of Union Town, Fayatte Co, PA, and now of Shanedoah Co, to Benjamin KUGAL, John BOWSER, John COSS Jr, William WILLIAMS, Thomas MARADETH, George YOUNG, and Benjamin RIDENOUR, all of Washington Co, MD. Release on 1201½ acres at Farrows Run, on the west side of Monongalia River, adjoining Charles Snodgrass. Land was patented to

Cornelius Lynch, 9 March 1798, and afterwards resurveyed. On 12 June 1804 Lynch conveyed all his property real and personal to Morrison and Jonathan Rowland, Esq, in trust for the benefit of his creditors, under the PA statute regarding insolvent debtors. On 24 January 1807 Lynch made a further conveyance of the land to Rowland, who conveyed to the parties named above on 2 February 1807. Morrison now releases his claim to the land. Consideration: $7 ($1 per tract). Signed: James Morrison. Witnesses: Henry Huff, Jacob [illegible], Esas Casle [?]. Acknowledged in Shanedoah Co, 7 December 1807. Certificate of P [?] Williams, CSC. Del: to A McCleland. Recorded: OS 4:148-151.

11 January 1808. Alexander and Barshaba McCLELAND, Fayatte Co, PA, to John BECKET, Barkley Co. 100 acres on the east side of Tigers Valley River, the main fork of the Monongalia River, adjoining James Miller. From a 12 September 1799 patent to George Wilson for 400 acres. Wilson conveyed this parcel to David Jones, 1 February 1806, and Jones conveyed to McCleland. Consideration: $300. Signed: Alexander McCleland, Barshaba McCleland. Acknowledged in court, January 1808. Del: to A McCleland. Recorded: OS 4:151-153.

11 January 1808. James and Verlinda DONALDSON to Peter BLACK, Shanadoah Co. 233 acres on Sandy Creek, adjoining James Spurgen and John Judy. Patented to Charles Donaldson, 11 September 1789. Consideration: $460. Signed: James [+] Donaldson, Verlinda [+] Donaldson. Witnesses: James McGee, Felix Scott, Jno Evans. Acknowledged in court, January 1808. Del: to A McCleland. Recorded: OS 4:153-155.

[?] January 1808. Thomas and Sarah LAIDLEY to Mrs Rebeckah DERING, widow of Henry DERING deceased, and George Small DERING, Maria EVANS (formerly Dering), Harriot DERING, Young DERING, Sophia DERING, Musser DERING, John DERING, and Augustus DERING, children and heirs of Henry DERING deceased. 2 tracts. 5 acres on the road from Morgan Town to Ices Ferry, adjoining John Stealey. 5 acres adjoining Benjamin Reeder. Grantors convey to Rebeckah her dower rights in the property, with full title in fee simple to the children. Consideration: $1000, VA, paid by Henry in his lifetime. Signed: Thomas Laidley, Sarah Laidley. Witnesses: none. Acknowledged in court, January 1808, by Thomas Laidley. Order to take Sarah's acknowledgement but not recorded here. No delivery shown. Recorded: OS 4:156-157.

[blank] January 1808. Nathan and Peggy JOSEPH to John EVANS Jr. 50 acres adjoining Baker, Jeremiah

William Joseph. Consideration: $400, VA. Signed: Nathan Joseph, Margaret Joseph. Witnesses: none. Acknowledged in court, January 1808. No delivery shown. Recorded: OS 4:158.

31 December 1807. Arthur TRADER to Thomas EVANS, Morgan Town. Mortgage on personal property. Trader owes Evans $1200, due on or before 31 December next. To secure the debt he conveys livestock, household furnishings, looms and tackling, farm tools, cart and gears, and 2 stacks of grain. Signed: Arthur Trader. Witnesses: Michael [+] McCarta, John [+] Trader. Proved by witnesses, January 1808. No delivery shown. Recorded: OS 4:159-160.

4 December 1807. Josiah and Isabella HOSKINSON to Nicholas CHISLER. Lot #8 in Morgan Town, between #7 owned by Ralph Barkshire and #9 owned by Col John Evans. Conveyed by Col Nicholas Shisler [sic] to Isabella Evans, now Hoskinson, 11 October 1784. Consideration: $150, VA. Signed: Josiah [+] Hoskinson, Isabella [+] Hoskinson. Witnesses: Dudley Evans, Zacquill Morgan, R Barkshire. Acknowledged by Isabella before Dudley Evans and R Barkshire, JPs, 4 December 1807. Proved by witnesses, January 1808. No delivery shown. Recorded: OS 4:160-162.

8 February 1808. George and Jenny STUART to John PRICKET. 270 acres adjoining John Webb. From a 400 acre tract conveyed to Stuart by [blank] Maxwell. 127½ acres of the tract previously conveyed by Stuart to [blank] Dragoo. Consideration: $1, VA. Signed: George Stuart [Jenny does not sign]. Witnesses: none. Acknowledged in court by George Stuart, February 1808, and recorded as to him. Commission, addressed to [blank] Co, MD, to take Jenny's acknowledgement [although the Stuarts are described as residents of Monongalia in the instrument]. Note by Nimrod Evans on the reverse of the commission: "The commission sent to Delaware [sic] of which the within is a copy was returned to my office with no indorsement on it but the names of the persons subscribed to the deed, who are I suspect justices of the peace and knew not that it was necessary to certify their act on the back of the commission and merly [sic] signed it as witnesses." Del: to John Prickett, 12 March 1810. Recorded: OS 4:162-163.

9 September 1806. Samuel and Sarah TONNEHILL to William TONNEHILL, Turkeyfoot Twp, Sommerset Co, PA. 122 acres on Laurel Run, adjoining James King. From a patent to Nathan Low, 328 acres. Low conveyed 196 acres to Sarah Tonnehill, 11 October 1784. Consideration: £144.

Sarah Tonnehill, 11 October 1784. Consideration: £144. Signed: Samuel Tonnehill, Sarah [+] Tonnehill. Witnesses: Wm Johnson, James Clark, Thos Burchenal. Acknowledged by Sarah before William Johnson and James Clark, JPs, 28 January 1807. Proved by witnesses, April 1807 and February 1808. Del: to [illegible] Bayles, 23 March 1808. Recorded: OS 4:164-166.

8 February 1807. John and Ann EVANS to Thomas McGEE. 400 acres on Threefork [and Raccoon] Creek, a branch of Tyger Valley River, no adjoiners named. Patented to John Evans, 30 August 1785. Consideration: $800, VA. Signed: J Evans, Ann Evans. [In a PS below the deed, Evans warrants title no further than the patent issued to him had done.] Witnesses: none. Acknowledged by Ann Evans before Wm N Jarrett and Jno Stealey, JPs, 9 February 1808; by John Evans in court, February 1808. Del: to Thos McGee, 11 July 1809. Recorded: OS 4:166-168.

8 February 1808. James and Alethia CLARK to Benjamin JONES, Fayatte Co, PA. 200 acres at Sandy Creek and Laurel Run, adjoining Jeremiah Tanyhill and Nathan Low. Consideration: $1200, VA. Signed: James Clark, Alethia Clark. Witnesses: none. Acknowledged by James Clark in court, February 1808; by Alethia before Amos Roberts and Wm Johnson, JPs, 9 February 1808. Del: to Jesse Evans, 4 April 1808. Recorded: OS 4:168-170.

15 March 1808. Alexander and Barsheba McCLELAND, Fayett Co, PA, to Benjamin TOUCHSTONE, Frederick Co. 400 acres at Flat Run, on the west side of Monongalia River, adjoining Henry Shoop, Philip and John Wient, Jacob River, Ludwick Ensaminger, and Arthur Watson's survey. Part of 700 acres patented to Col David Scott, 6 June 1796. Scott conveyed 250 acres to Jacob River and 150 to Jacob Peck, among others, and McCleland now conveys the tracts deeded to River and Peck. Consideration: $800. Signed: Alexander McCleland, Barshaba McCleland. Witnesses: R Barkshire, N Vandavort, Nimrod Evans, William N Jarrett, John Evans. Acknowledged by Barshaba in Fyette Co, PA, before Zadock Springer and Robert Richey, JPs, 23 March 1808; by Alexander in court, April 1808. No delivery shown. Recorded: OS 4:170-173.

15 March 1808. Joseph BUTLER, Muskingum Co, OH, by Joseph SEVERINS, his attorney in fact, to Enoch CALVERT, Jesse CALVERT, and Samuel JACKSON, all of Frederick Co. 760 acres on the east side of Cheat River, at Joes Run and some of the drains of Buffellow Run, adjoining Joseph Butler's settlement right. Patented 20 September 1785. 39 acres of the tract previously conveyed by

Consideration: $1520. Signed: Joseph Severins. Witnesses: W N Jarrett, N Vandevort, R Barkshire. Acknowledged in court, 11 April 1808. Del: to A McCleland, 4 May 1808. Recorded: OS 4:173-175.

14 March 1808. David SCOTT to Dr Daniel MARCHAND, Fayatte Co, PA. Power of attorney to receive from Joseph Kerr, Chillicothe, OH, patent for half of 2000 acres in the state of OH, due to Scott from the state of VA for services rendered the United States, and to convey the said land to Zadock Walker, merchant of Union Town, upon receiving adequate payment for it. Signed: David Scott. Witnesses: John Scott, Jacob Stealey, D Scott 3rd. Acknowledged in court, April 1808. Del: 20 April 1808. Recorded: OS 4:176.

18 November 1807. Robert MINNIS, Harrison Co, to Jacob FOULK. 1000 acres on Threefork, adjoining Francis and Edward [sic] Dekinses' line. Part of 2000 acres patented [blank]. Consideration: $1, VA. Signed: Robert Minnis. Witnesses: Rawley Scott, John Cooper, Mathew Gay. Proved by witnesses, April 1808. Del: to Foulk, 31 August 1809. Recorded: OS 4:177.

14 March 1808. Samuel and Susannah VARNER to Peter TENANT. 155 acres on Jacobs Run, no adjoiners named. Part of a larger tract patented to John and Jacob Haught, 20 October 1792. Consideration: [£?$?]400, VA. Signed: Samuel Varner, Susannah [X] Varner. Witnesses: none. Acknowledged in court, April 1808. Del: to Peter Tenant, 24 February 1810. Recorded: OS 4:178-179.

11 April 1808. Harry MARTIN, no address stated, by his attorney in fact, John EVANS Jr, to Joseph SAPP. 97 acres on Scotts Mill and Murphey Run, adjoining Henry Purviance and John Ramsey. Patented to Harry Martin [blank]. Consideration: $150. Signed: John Evans. Acknowledged in court, April 1808. Del: to him, 7 June 1811. Recorded: OS 4:179-180.

11 April 1808. Nathan and Elizabeth CANFIELD to Jonathan ARNETT. 98 acres on Indian Creek, adjoining John Patterson, James McMullen, and Sarah Barker. Consideration: $2094. Signed: Nathan Canfield, Elizabeth [X] Canfield. Witnesses: none. Acknowledged in court, April 1808. Del: to Jona Arnett, 13 June 1808. Recorded: OS 4:180.

11 April 1808. Abraham and Magdalena WISECOP to Caleb HURLEY. 62 acres, adjoining Hurley's other lands, Samuel Everley, and John Liming. Consideration: $200, VA. Signed: Abraham Wisecup, Magdalene Wisecup. Witnesses: none. Acknowledged in court, April 1808. Del: to him, 8 May 1809. Recorded: OS 4:181.

to him, 8 May 1809. Recorded: OS 4:181.

26 March 1808. Alpheus WICKWARE, heir of John WICKWARE, deceased, by his attorney in fact, Samuel WICKWARE, Barren Co, KY, to William N JARRETT, Esq. 200 acres on waters of White Day, including Morgan's hunting camp on Cherry Run. Patented to David Norris, 15 August 1799, and conveyed by David and Susannah Norris to John Wickware, 17 January 1803. Consideration: $800. Signed: Samuel Wickware. Witnesses: Nimrod Evans, E Daugherty, R Barkshire, M Evans, Jas Wagner. Receipt for consideration money. Acknowledged in court, April, 1808. Del: to Wm N Jarrett, 16 September 1809. Recorded: OS 4:182-183.

11 April 1808. John W and Sarah PATTERSON to Nathan CANFIELD. 131 acres at Indian Creek, adjoining Charles [torn]. Consideration: $162. Signed: John W Patterson, Sarah Patterson. Witnesses: none. Acknowledged in court, April 1808. Del: to W T Willey, per order, 12 April 1855. Recorded: OS 4:183-184.

10 December 1807. Clark HOLLENBACK, Muskingum Co, OH, to Rynear HALL. 61 acres on the east side, minus 13½ acres previously sold to Joshua Hickman, adjoining Elias Pierce. Conveyed by George and Hannah Hollenback to Thomas Wilson by deed of trust. Consideration: $406.01. Signed: Clark Hollenback. Witnesses: James McGee, Ozburn Hilleary, Rolley Scott. Proved by witnesses, December 1807, April 1808. Del: to R Hall, 12 October 1808. Recorded: OS 4:184-185.

11 April 1808. John and Elizabeth BRANT to Peter BURNES, Hamshire Co. 1340 acres on the state road from Morgan Town to Dunkard Bottom, near the Monongalia Glades, adjoining Benjamin Reeder, Alexander Smith, William Mannear, and Amos Holly. Consideration: $5000, VA. Signed: John Brant, Elizabeth Brant. Witnesses: none. Acknowledged in court, April 1808. Del: to J Brant, 9 March 1809. Recorded: OS 4:186-187.

26 March 1808. William N (heir at law to George JENKINS, deceased) and Priscilla JENKINS to William NORRIS. Parcel, size not known, adjoining where Norris now lives and where George Baker now lives. Consideration: $250. Signed: William N Jenkins, Pressilla Jenkins. Witnesses: B Reeder, Dudley Evans, James McGee, William N Jarrett. Receipt for consideration money. Acknowledged by Pressilla Jenkins before B Reeder and William N Jarrett, JPs, 26 March 1808; by William N Jenkins in court, April 1808. No delivery shown. Recorded: OS 4:187-188.

11 April 1808. John and Mary BELL to William WHITE.

100 acres on Dunkard Creek near the PA line. No adjoiners named. Consideration: $200, VA. Signed: John [B] Bell, Mary [X] Bell. Witnesses: Nimrod Evans, French S Ray, D Evans, William N Jarrett. Acknowledged by Mary Bell before D Evans and William N Jarrett, JPs, 11 April 1808. Proved by witnesses, April 1808. Del: to him, 8 May 1809. Recorded: OS 4:189-190.

4 March 1805. Richard and Mary PETTYJOHN to Henry TUCKER. 130 acres on Glady Creek, no adjoiners named. Patented to William Pettyjohn Jr, deceased, 25 January 1782. Consideration: $300. Signed: Richard Pettyjohn, Mary Pettyjohn. Witnesses: Morgan Morgan, Stephen Morgan, John Springer. Acknowledged by Mary Pettyjohn in Harrison Co, 6 September 1805, before Daniel Davisson and Spencer Martin, JPs. Proved by witnesses, September 1805, September 1806, April 1808. Del: to him, 10 July 1815. Recorded: OS 4:191-193.

26 March 1808. William N and Prissilla JENKINS to Samuel JACKSON. 2 tracts. 200 acres near Ices Ferry on Cheat River, adjoining William Norris and James Donaldson. Patented 7 October 1789 and descended to William from his father George Jenkins deceased. 200 acres near the Monongalia Glades, adjoining Henry Banks, John Mc[Cleland?], and Clackburn [?]. Patented to William [blank]. Consideration: $532, VA. Signed: William N Jenkins, Presella Jenkins. Witnesses: Benjamin Reeder, Dudley Evans, James McGee, William N Jarrett. Acknowledged by Priscilla before B Reeder and William N Jarrett, 26 March 1808; by William N Jenkins in court, April 1808. No delivery shown. Recorded: OS 4:194-195.

16 November 1807. William and Eliza MORE, George Twp, Fayette Co, PA, to Joseph FICKLE. 108½ acres at Hazel Run, adjoining Charles Dollison. Part of a tract patented to David More, 15 June 1785, including his 1775 settlement. David was later resident of Cumberland Twp, Adams Co, PA. His will, dated 17 June 1803, devised to his son Joseph 100 acres of this tract for life, with reversion to Joseph's oldest son living at his death. The remainder of the land was devised in 3 equal shares, one of which fell to William, grantor. Consideration: $270. Signed: William More, Eliza More. Witnesses: William Tanehill, Thomas Hadden. Receipt for consideration money. Acknowledged before Samuel Roberts, president of court, Fayette Co, PA, 6 November 1807. Certificate of Ephraim Douglass, prothonotary. No delivery shown. Recorded: OS 4:195-197.

[blank] 1808. Samuel and Catherine BASNET to Joseph MORGAN. 10 3/4 acres, 4 poles, adjoining Basnett's other

land, William Martin, and George Martin. Part of a tract patented to Robert Crow, conveyed by him to John Johnson, and by Johnson to Basnett. Consideration: $33, VA. Signed: Samuel Basnett, Catherine Basnett. Acknowledged in court, April 1808. Del: to Joseph Morgan, 14 March 1809. Recorded: OS 4:197-198.

14 March 1808. Benjamin and Elenor REEDER to Abner MESSENGER. Lot [# not shown] in Morgan Town, between Water Street and the Monongalia River. Half the lot previously sold to Nicholas Main [?]. Abner occupies the other half, formerly occupied by John Scott. Consideration: $400, VA. Signed: B Reeder [Elenor does not sign]. Witnesses: John W Thompson, Nicholas P Maderia, James Miller. Acknowledged in court by Benjamin Reeder, April 1808. Commission to take Elenor's acknowledgement, but no action recorded here. Del: to Abner Messenger, 15 May 1809. Recorded: OS 4:199-200.

12 April 1808. William and Elizabeth STEWART to John TAYLOR. Lot [# not shown] in Morgan Town, adjoining High Street, John Pierpoint's heirs, and Zacquill Morgan's heirs. Consideration: $300, VA. Signed: William [X] Stewart [Elizabeth does not sign]. Witnesses: none. Acknowledged in court by William Stewart, April 1808, and recorded as to him. No delivery shown. Recorded: OS 4:200-201.

11 April 1808. Jacob and Margaret POLSLEY to John TONCRY. 8 acres on the east side of Monongalia River. No adjoiners or place names mentioned. Consideration: $100. Signed: Jacob Polsley, Margaret Polsley. Witnesses: none. Acknowledged in court by Jacob Polsley, April 1808; by Margaret before Morgan Morgan and John Nuzum, JPs, 30 July 1808. Del: to him, 25 November 1808. Recorded: OS 4:201-203.

[blank] March 1807. Benjamin and Sarah THORN to Henry COROTHERS. 125 acres on Booths Creek, adjoining Thomas Evans. Part of 500 acres patented to William Bohannon and John Downard, 19 September 1799. Consideration: $500. Signed: Benjamin Thorn, Sarah Thorn. Witnesses: Zack Morgan, Stephen Morgan, Davi [sic] Lowe. Acknowledged by Sarah before Morgan Morgan and Stephen Morgan, JPs, 22 April 1807. Proved by witnesses, July 1807 and April 1808. Del: to him, 26 July 1809. Recorded: OS 4:203-205.

23 July 1804. Philip and Elizabeth SMYTH [SMAUGS originally written and deleted], Somerset Co, PA, to Timothy GARD, Fayette Co, PA. 400 acres at Buffaloe Creek, adjoining Rutherford. Patented to Henry Smyth, assignee of Job Bacorn, 26 October 1792, and conveyed by

Henry and Mary Smyth to Philip Smyth, 21 September 1795. Consideration: £100. Signed: Philip Smyth, Elizabeth [+] Smyth. Witnesses: Jacob Hartzell and [illegible, apparently an attempt to imitate a witness signature in German script]. Receipt for consideration money. Acknowledged in Somerset Co, PA, 28 July 1804, before Jacob Hartzell, JP. Certificate of Otho Shrader, prothonotary. Del: to him, 3 April 1814. Recorded: OS 4:205-207.

27 March 1808. John and Catherine RAMSEY to Samuel JACKSON, Fayette Co, PA. 100 acres on the east side of Cheat River, adjoining William Micael and Henry Crall. Consideration: $50, VA. Signed: John Ramsey, Catherine [mark] Ramsey. Witnesses: E Daugherty, John Staley, N Vandevort, William Cracraft. Acknowledged by Catherine Ramsey before N Vandevort and John Staley, JPs, 30 March 1808. Proved by witnesses, April 1808. No delivery shown. Recorded: OS 4:207-209.

11 April 1808. Richard and Mary BRANDON and Alexander BRANDON to George ROBINSON, Somerset Co, PA. 100 acres on Big and Little Sandy Creeks, adjoining Robert Foreman. Part of 2 tracts on which Richard and Alexander now live. Consideration: $400. Signed: Richard Brandon, Mary Brandon, Alexr Brandon. Witnesses: none. Acknowledged in court, April 1808. Del: to A Bannon, 5 November 1809. Recorded: OS 4:209-211.

14 December 1801. William and Sarah SQUIER, Fayette Co, PA, to John GRIBBLE. 131½ acres on the west side of Big Sandy Creek, adjoining Samuel Morton and Adam Brown, where Gribble now lives. Consideration: $140. Signed: William Squires, Sarah [X] Squires. Witnesses: Samuel Ritchey, Isaac Sutton. Acknowledged in Fayette Co, PA, before R Richey, JP, 14 December 1801. Certificate of Ephraim Douglass, Prothonotary. Also acknowledged in Warren Co, OH, before Francis Dunlavy, president of Common Pleas Court, 20 January 1801. Certificate of David Sutton [?], clerk. Del: to John Gribble, 26 July 1808. Recorded: OS 4:211-213.

24 October 1805. David EVANS, yeoman, Newbriton Twp, Bucks Co, PA, to Jesse EVANS, yeoman, Springhill Twp, Fayett Co, PA. 1000 acres adjoining Samuel Canby, Samuel Ruble, and Arthur Trader. Conveyed to David by William Worth, Pitsgrove, Salem Co, NJ, 12 April 1794, and of record in Monongalia. Consideration: $1000. Signed: David Evans. Witnesses: Benjamin Stephens, John Griffith. Receipt for consideration money. Acknowledged in Bucks Co, PA, before Matthias Hutchinson, associate judge of Common Pleas, 22 May 1807. Certificate of Wm

Hart, recorder. Del: to Jesse Evans, 8 June 1808. Recorded: OS 4:213-215.

[blank] 1807. John and Hannah CHIPPS, William and Hannah CHIPPS, Thomas R and Rachel CHIPPS, Amos CHIPPS, Jacob and Hannah PINDALL, and Simeon and Elizabeth ROYSE, children and legal heirs of Thomas CHIPPS, deceased, to John RODEHEFFER, Shanandore Co. 191 acres on Crab Orchard Run, no adjoiners named. Consideration: $ [blank]. Signed: Jacob Pindall, Hannah Pindall, John Chipps, Hannah Chipps, Simeon Royse, Elizabeth Royse, Hannah Chipps, William Chipps, Thomas R Chipps, Rachel Chipps, Amos Chipps. Witnesses: William John, Lemuel John, G R Tingle. Acknowledged in court, January 1808, by Jacob Pindall, Simeon Royse, William Chipps, and John Chipps; February 1808, by Amos Chipps, Hannah Chipps, Hannah Pindall, and Hannah Chipps; by Rachel Chipps before William John and Lemuel John, JPs, 8 February 1808; and by Elizabeth Royse before William and Lemuel John, 26 April 1808. Thomas R Chipps proved by witnesses, June 1808. Del: to Amos Chipps, 15 June 1808. Recorded: OS 4:215-217.

24 September 1807. Benjamin REEDER to James SCOTT. Deed of trust. $531.49 is due to John Wilson Dean from the heirs of James Johnston, deceased. Of this, Reeder has paid $300, 1 April 1802, and a further $33 1/3 to William G Payne and John Coalter for defending a suit in chancery at Staunton, Shinn's Heir vs James Johnston's heirs, John Wilson Dean et al. To secure the remainder of the debt, Reeder conveys 400 acres, adjoining George Zinn, sold to him by John Simpson. If balance not paid in 9 months, the property to be advertised in the *Monongalia Gazette* and sold to the highest bidder. Valentine Johnston, Ohio Co, is administrator of James Johnston deceased. Signed: B Reeder, Valentine Johnson. Witnesses: Wm G Payne, George R Tingle, Zackquil Morgan. Proved by witnesses, April and June 1808. Del: to Mrs Dean, 5 July 1809. Recorded: OS 4:217-218.

13 June 1808. James and Ellice BROWN to Jeremiah HOSKINSON. 9 acres, 54 poles on the west side of River Monongalia, no adjoiners named. Patented to Brown [blank]. Consideration: $100, VA. Signed: James Brown, Alice [0] Brown. Acknowledged in court, June 1808. Del: to him, 1 May 1809. Recorded: OS 4:218-219.

[blank] September 1807. Jacob (Sr) and Margret FOULK to Thomas FLOYD. 134 acres, adjoining Charles and William Snodgrass, in 4 tracts: 78 acres, no adjoiners or place names mentioned. 8½ acres conveyed to Foulk by Christopher Erwin, 14 June 1802. 36 acres adjoining

Edward Hamilton and Downer and Dent. 12 acres conveyed by Charles Snodgrass, 13 September 1802. Consideration: $500. Signed: Jacob [X] Foulk [Margret does not sign]. Witnesses: William Snodgrass, Charles Snodgrass, David Hayhurst. Proved by witnesses William Snodgrass and David Hayhurst, June 1808, who also proved Charles Snodgrass, since deceased, the third witness. Del: to John Watson, September 1810. Recorded: OS 4:219-220.

12 April 1808. Nathan and Elizabeth CANFIELD to William MICHAEL. 48 acres on Indian Creek, adjoining Jonathan Arnett and the heirs of John Stewart. Consideration: $120. Signed: Nathan Canfield [Elizabeth does not sign]. Witnesses: Jonathan Arnett, Henry Michael, Thomas Jenkins. Proved by witnesses, June 1808, as to Nathan Canfield and recorded as to him. Del: to him, 16 June 1817. Recorded: OS 4:220.

2 May 1808. John and Hannah ARCHER to William MAXSON. 124 acres on Little Sandy Creek, no adjoiners named. Consideration: £125. Signed: John Archer, Hannah [X] Archer. Witnesses: Amos Robbarts, William Johnson, Alexander Brandon. Acknowledged by Hannah Archer before Amos Roberts and Wm Johnson, JPs, 12 May 1808. Proved by witnesses, June 1808. Del: to him, 10 April 1809. Recorded: OS 4:220-221.

6 June 180[blank]. Steven and Deborah STILES to William STILES. 450 acres, no adjoiners or place names mentioned. Patented to Philip Doldridge [sic], 10 October 1785[6?], and conveyed by him to Steven, 16 June 1805[6?]. Consideration: $800, VA. Signed: Stephen Stiles [Deborah does not sign]. Witnesses: none. Acknowledged in court by Stephen Stiles, June 1808; by Deborah Stiles before Saml Minor and Booz Burrows, JPs, 6 June 1808. Del: to him, 1 April 1811. Recorded: OS 4:222-223.

23 August 1806. Stiven and wife [not named] STILES to John COX. 500 acres near the state line, no adjoiners or place names mentioned. Patented to Philip Doldridge [sic], 17[blank], and conveyed by him to Stiles, 13 August 1806. Consideration: [blank], VA. Signed: Stephen Stiles, Deborah Stiles. Witnesses: Samuel Minor, Wm Jobes, James Evans, Wm G Payne, Marmaduke Evans, Henry Dering, Nimrod Evans. Acknowledged in court by Stephen Stiles, June 1806; by Deborah Stiles before William Jobes and Samuel Minor, JPs, 22 August 1806. Del: to John Cox, 12 December 1808. Recorded: OS 4:223-224.

4 July 1807. Michael and Catherine KOR to Richard TENANT Jr. 200 acres adjoining John Haught. Patented 23 July 1796. Consideration: $200, VA. Signed: Michael

Kore, Catherine [X] Kore. Witnesses: none. Acknowledged in court, June 1808. Del: to him, 29 April 1810. Recorded: OS 4:224-225.

16 March 1808. Amos [Moses entered and deleted, throughout instrument] and Rachel GANDAY to Levy GANDAY. 55 acres adjoining Samuel Gandy and John More. Part of a tract conveyed by Jonathan Ganday to John More, and by More to Amos Ganday. Consideration: $150. Signed: Amos Gandy, Rachael Gandy. Witnesses: Jonathan Gandy, John [+] More. Acknowledged in court, June 1808. Del: to Levi Gandy, 6 November 1809. Recorded: OS 4:225.

14 April 1808. Benjamin and Nancy MORTON to Thomas WILSON. Deed of trust. Benjamin Woods has 5 of Morton's notes for $50 each. To secure these, Morton conveys 165 acres at Big Sandy Creek, adjoining James Guthrie, conveyed by James and Mary McPeck to Woods. If not paid, the land to be advertised in *Monongalia Gazette* or some other convenient circulating paper and then to be sold. Signed: Bengamin Morton, Nancy Morton, Thomas Wilson. Witnesses: Amos Robbarts, William Johnson, Alexander Brandon. Acknowledged by Nancy Morton before Amos Roberts and William Johnson, JPs, 14 April 1808. Proved by witnesses, June 1808. Del: to Wood, 20 September 1813. Recorded: OS 4:226-227.

14 April 1808. Benjamin and Jane WOODS to Benjamin MORTON. 165 acres on the east side of Big Sandy Creek, adjoining James Guthrie. Conveyed by James and Mary McPeck to Woods. Consideration: $500. Signed: Benjamin Woods, Jane Woods. Witnesses: Amos Roberts, William Johnson, Alexander Brandon. Acknowledged by Jane Woods before Amos Roberts and William Johnson, JPs, 14 April 1808. Proved by witnesses, June 1808. Del: to Willetts, 15 May 1809. Recorded: OS 4:228-229.

8 June 1808. Joshua HICKMAN, state of VA, to Able WILLIAMS. 68 acres on Buffellow Lick Run, adjoining John Carpenter, William Miller, and John Miller. Consideration: $1. Signed: Joshua Hickman. Witnesses: none. Acknowledged in court, June 1808. No delivery shown. Recorded: OS 4:229-230.

11 June 1804. John CHIPPS, William CHIPPS, Thomas R CHIPPS, Amos CHIPPS, Jacob and Hannah PINDALL, and Simeon and Elizabeth RICE, heirs and legal representatives of Thomas Chipps deceased, to Jacob SMITH. 207 acres, adjoining John Stiles. Consideration: $300, VA. Signed: Hannah Pandall, Simeon Roys, Elizabeth Roys, John Chipps, William Chipps, Thomas R Chipps, Amos Chipps, Jacob Pindall. Relinquishment of dower in the property by Joannah Chipps, widow and relict of Thomas,

12 June 1804. Witnesses: none. Acknowledged in court, June 1804, by Thomas R Chipps, John Chipps, William Chipps, Joannah Chipps, and Elizabeth Royse; July 1804 by Amos Chipps, Jacob and Hannah Pindall; June 1808 by Simeon Royse. Del: to Alexander Brandon, 2 April 1811. Recorded: OS 4:230-231.

13 June 1808. Benjamin and Phebe BROWN to Peter GARDNER. 56 acres on Finches Run, a branch of Buffellow Creek, adjoining William Hillery, John Brown, William Gray, and Jasper Wyatt. Part of 150 acres patented to Philip Roberts in 1799. Consideration: $150. Signed: Benjn Brown, Phebe Brown. Witnesses: none. Acknowledged in court, June 1808. Del: to him, 7 September 1813. Recorded: OS 4:231-232.

10 June 1806. John (Jr) and Gilley C EVANS to Elenor ICE, heir at law of Abraham ICE, deceased. 160 acres on Buffellow Creek, no adjoiners named. The same tract held by Abraham when he died intestate. On 13 December 1801 Alexander Hawthorn, Collector, sold the land to John Evans Jr, as it was delinquent $1.10 on the direct tax. The time for redemption having passed, Joseph Scott, marshal of the VA District, made a deed to Evans on 18 December 1805, the deed of record in District Court. Consideration: $10. Signed: John Evans Junr, Gilly C Evans. Witnesses: none. Acknowledged in court by John Evans, June 1808; by Gilly C Evans before R Barkshire and Wm N Jarrett, JPs, 13 June 1808. Del: to Conway, Elenor's husband, 13 October 1809. Recorded: OS 4:233-234.

15 March 1804. William (Jr) and Elizabeth SNODGRASS to David HAYHURST. 82 3/4 acres on Pharows Run, adjoining William Snodgrass. Part of 285 acres patented 19 October 1749 [sic!]. Consideration: $300. Signed: Wm Snodgrass, Elizabeth [X] Snodgrass. Witnesses: Stephen Morgan, Charles Snodgrass, Asa Hall, William Snodgrass Senr, Asa Dudley. Acknowledged by Elizabeth Snodgrass before Stephen Morgan and Asa Dudley, JPs, 15 March 1804. Proved by witnesses, September 1804 and June 1808. Del: to him, 16 May 1811. Recorded: OS 4:234-236.

15 June 1808. John and Ann DRAGOO to John BROWN Sr. 77½ acres on Finches Run, a branch of Buffellow Creek, where Brown now lives. No adjoiners named. Part of a 400 acre tract. Dragoo warrants and defends title only against himself and his heirs. Consideration: $267. Signed: John [X] Dragoo, Ann [X] Dragoo. Witnesses: none. Acknowledged in court, June 1808. Del: to Brown, 9 April 1810. Recorded: OS 4:236-237.

13 June 1808. George R and Sarah TINGLE to Philip I

SHEETS. Lot [# not shown] in Morgantown, adjoining Mary Bennett (now occupied by Zackquill Morgan), opposite William Lanham's [?] house, and Thomas Laidley. Consideration: $100, VA. Signed: George R Tingle, Sarah Tingle. Witnesses: none. Acknowledged in court, June 1808. Del: to P I Sheets, 13 August 1808. Recorded: OS 4:237-238.

2 November 1807. Daniel and Peggy LANCE, Alegheny Co, MD, to John STEALEY. Tract, acreage not stated, in the Monongalia Glades, previously conveyed by John and Prudence Stealey to Lance, 17 May 1803. Consideration: $800, VA. Signed: Daniel Lance [Peggy does not sign]. Witnesses: Wm Tingle, James McGee, Wm N Jarrett. Proved by witnesses, June 1808. Del: to grantee, 10 December 1821. Recorded: OS 4:238-239.

6 January 1801. Leonard TITSWORTH to Joseph SOUTHWORTH. 130 acres adjoining Isaac H Williams. Consideration: $1, love, good will and affection to his son-in-law. Signed: Leonard Titsworth. Witnesses: Wm G Payne, Jesse Payne, Zachariah Toler, David Mathers. Proved by witnesses, July 1801, June 1808. Del: to him, [illegible] July 1809. Recorded: OS 4:239-240.

12 September 1805. John WILLEY, William HAMILTON, George SMITH, Samuel JOSEPH, John COURTNEY, Calder HAYMOND, and George WILSON, trustees to the Methodist Episcopal Church, to John STEALY. 158¼ poles adjoining lot formerly owned by Dr Solomon Drown [?], now Thomas Wilson's residence. Tract formerly conveyed by John and Prudence Stealy, 14 April 1801, to Davis Shockley, Amos Smith, John Willey, William Hamilton, George Smith, Calder Haymond, Samuel Joseph, John Courtney, and George Wilson, trustees. Having failed to comply with the terms and stipulations agreed, and finding more to the advantage of the church, trustees now reconvey. Consideration: $1, VA. Signed: Wm Hamilton, George Smyth, Lemuel [sic] Joseph, John Courtney, George [//] Wilson, C Haymond, John Willey. Witnesses: N Evans, J Myers, E Daugherty, Marmaduke Evans, Jo Shinn. Proved by witnesses, June 1808. Del: to grantee, 19 December 1821. Recorded: OS 4:240-241.

9 December 1806. Jesse and Rebeckah PAYNE to James DEWEES. 100 acres at Dillens Creek, near the state line, adjoining Henry Floy. Consideration: £100. Signed: Jesse Payne, Rebeckah Payne. Witnesses: none. Acknowledged in court by Jesse Payne, January 1807. No delivery shown. Recorded: OS 4:241-242.

3 November 1807. Absalom and Nancy KNOTTS to Joseph HILL. 33 3/4 acres on the east side of Sandy Creek,

adjoining Robert Knotts, Evans, and Edward Knotts. Patented to Absalom, 21 July 1800. Consideration: $300, VA. Signed: Absalom [X] Knotts, Nancy [V] Knotts. Witnesses: Wm Sisler, Jacob Huts, William Dragoo, Wm N Jarrett, Nimrod Evans, Lemuel John. Acknowledged by Nancy Knotts before Wm N Jarrett and Lemuel John, JPs, 9 November 1807. Proved by witnesses, June 1808. Del: to grantee, 1 March 1817. Recorded: OS 4:242-244.

10 August 1807. Samuel and Ruth MARVIN to William SHAW. 50 acres on Cheat River, adjoining Nathan Matheny and Joseph Matheny. Tract conveyed to Samuel Marvin by John Matheny. Consideration: £50, VA. Signed: Samuel Marvin, Ruth Marvin. Witnesses: B Reeder, Nathan Matheny, Wm G Payne. Acknowledged by Ruth Marvin before James Clark and Amos Robbarts, JPs, 22 August 1807. Proved by witnesses, February and June 1808. Del: to him, 11 September 1809. Recorded: OS 4:244-245.

18 April 1808. Joseph and Mary SMITH, Harrison Co, to Thomas BARTLETT. 305 acres adjoining Bazel Prater, of which Bartlett is already in possession. Tract conveyed to Smith by Samuel Ruble. Consideration: $1000. Signed: Joseph Smith, Mary Smith. Witnesses: none. Acknowledged in Harrison Co court, April 1808. Certificate of Ben Wilson, CHC. No delivery shown. Recorded: OS 4:245-246.

16 September 1807. Aaron TICHENAL to Nimrod EVANS. Deed of trust. Tichenal is to pay Thomas Clare $75 on or before 15 September 1809. To secure the debt he conveys 195 acres on the headwaters of James Ferrys [?] Run, adjoining Edward Evans. Tract was patented to Thomas Clare, Fayette Co, PA, and conveyed by him on this date to Tichenal. Signed: Aaron Tichenal, Thomas Clare. Witnesses: James McGee, Marmaduke Evans, John C Payne. Proved by witnesses, June 1808. Del: to Aron Tichenal, 4 October 1814. Recorded: OS 4:246-248.

16 September 1807. Thomas CLARE, Fayett Co, PA, to Aaron TEACHINAL. Tract, acreage unspecified, adjoining Edward Evans (now Jacob Pindall). "It is suggested" that William Chipps' survey may interfere with a portion of the land. It is agreed that Clare is not bound to make up deficiencies vs this or other conflicting titles to the land. Consideration: $200, VA. Signed: Thomas Clare. Witnesses: Marmaduke Evans, James McGee, Nimrod Evans. Acknowledged in court, June 1808. Del: to him, 14 July 1812. Recorded: OS 4:248-249.

7 December 1807. Allen and Nancy HALL, Muskingum Co, OH, to James SCOTT. 208 acres on the Monongalia River, adjoining James Thomas. Part of a tract patented to Jordan Hall, 2 January 1807, and conveyed by him to

Allen Hall, 17 May 1799 [sic]. Consideration: $1000, VA. Signed: Allen Hall, Nancy [mark] Hall. Witnesses: Nimrod Evans, James McGee, Geo S Dering, M Evans. Proved by witnesses, June 1808. No delivery shown. Recorded: OS 4:249-250.

13 March 1802. Edward and Jane JONES to James MATHENY, Hampshire Co. 183 acres, in two tracts, on Muddy Creek, including the place where Edward now lives and also his sugar camp. Consideration: $800. Signed: Edward Jones, Jane Jones. Witnesses: John McLain, Russel Potter, William Johnson. Acknowledged by Jane Jones before John McLain and Russel Potter, JPs, 30 March 1802. Proved by witnesses, June 1808. Del: to A Brandon, April 1810. Recorded: OS 4:250-252.

16 May 1808. James and Mary WATSON, formerly Mary RIDGWAY, Fayett Co, PA, to John WATSON. 55 acres on the west side of Cheat River, about 5 miles from Morgantown. No adjoiners named. Part of 400 acres owned by Lott Ridgway at the time of his death. On 22 September 1805 James Tibbs, John Ramsey, and Hugh Sidwell, commissioners, divided the land among Ridgway's heirs by order of court. Consideration: $500. Signed: James Watson, Mary [X] Watson. Witnesses: Nimrod Evans, James McGee, French Gray, Wm N Jarrett, John Stealey. Acknowledged by Mary Watson before Wm N Jarrett and John Stealey, JPs, 11 May 1808. Proved by witnesses, June 1808. Del: to grantee's widow, 26 August 1820. Recorded: OS 4:252-254.

14 June 1808. Josiah WILSON to William GEORGE. 100 acres adjoining George Wilson and John Wickware. Patented 12 September 1799. Consideration: $1000. Signed: Josiah Wilson. Witnesses: none. Acknowledged in court, June 1808. Del: to him, 10 June 1811. Recorded: OS 4:254-255.

13 March 1808. John Evans and Rebecca DENT to Moses DOOLITTLE. 225 acres on Booths Creek, adjoining Capel Holland and Robe. Consideration: $500. Signed: John Evans Dent, Rebecah Dent. Witnesses: Nimrod Evans, James McGee, Marmaduke Evans, Wm N Jarrett. Acknowledged by Rebecah Dent, 25 March 1808, before Wm N Jarrett and Dudley Evans, JPs. Proved by witnesses, June 1808. Del: to D Evans, 16 January 1810. Recorded: OS 4:255-257.

15 September 1807. John and Phebe JUDY, Green Co, OH, to Daniel LANCE, Alligania Co, MD. 170 acres at Sandy Creek, adjoining Daniel Hirader and Volentine [illegible]. 5 acres laid out for use of the meeting house excepted from the conveyance. Consideration: $1050. Signed: John Judy, Phebe [+] Judy. Witnesses:

OH, before Andrew Read and Wm McFarland, JPs, 15 September 1807. Certificate of John Paul, clerk, and Francis Dunlavy, presiding judge. Del: to D Launce by A Werninger, 8 August 1809. Recorded: OS 4:257-259.

21 May 1803. Hugh McNEELY, Morgan Town, to Thomas WILSON. Deed of trust. Hugh owes $3407.54 to William DAVISON of Winchester, VA. To secure $1703.77, due by 21 May 1807, Hugh conveys 34 acres, adjoining Thomas Laidley, Michael Kerns, and Benjamin Jennings, purchased from Zachariah Morgan, and 4 slaves: Negro man Tom, his wife Rachel, her child (boy of 4 years, not named), and Negro man Stephen. Signed: Hugh McNeely, Wm Davison, Thomas Wilson. Witnesses: Jacob Kiger, Polly Wilson, Alexander Hawthorn. Acknowledged in writing by Hugh McNeely, 20 August 1804. Proved by witnesses, December 1804, January 1805, June 1808. Del: to Thos Wilson, 5 July 1809. Recorded: OS 4:259-262.

4 May 1808. Jacob (Jr) and Elizabeth FOULK to David YOUNG, Fayett Co, PA. 108 acres at Quarry Run and Woolf Pen Ridge, on the bank of Cheat River, part of the tract where Charles Rose now lives. Conveyed by Joshua Lowe to David Bales, and by David and Sarah Bales to Jacob Foulk Jr, 31 December 1803. Consideration: $1000. Signed: Jacob Foulk, Elizabeth [X] Foulk. Witnesses: D F McRea, French S Gray, Nimrod Evans. Acknowledged in court, June 1808. Del: to D Young, [illegible] November 1808. Recorded: OS 4:262-263.

5 July 1808. Leonard M DEAKINS and John HOY, executors and devisees of Francis DEAKINS, who was the executor and devisee of William DEAKINS, all of George Town, DC, to Daniel FORTNEY. 110 acres on the west side of Cheat River, near the Monongalia Glades, no adjoiners named. Part of #4 in Richard Claiborne's chain of surveys. Consideration: $165. Signed: Leonard M Deakins, John Hoye. Acknowledged in George Town, DC, 5 July 1808. Certificate of Thomas Corcoran, mayor. Del: to Daniel Fortney, 8 August 1808. Recorded: OS 4:264.

10 April 1801. John SAVARY, Millersburg, Burbon Co, KY, to Thomas CLARE, New Geneva, Fayette Co, PA. Power of attorney to sell 400 acres on the Monongalia River, below Morgan Town, which Savary purchased of David Scott. Signed: J Savary. Witnesses: James Barry, J R [illegible]. Acknowledged in Philadelphia, PA, [blank] April 1801. Certificate of Jno Inskeepe, mayor. Certificate of Alexander McClain, recorder of Fayett Co, PA. Del: Sent to him by D Marchd, February 1811. Recorded: OS 4:265-266.

14 March 1807. George HOLLENBACK to Thomas WILSON. Deed of trust. Hollenback had given a note to Matthias Hollenback, 26 September 1795, for £204.15.5. Matthias endorsed the note to John M Price, Philadelphia, PA, who obtained judgment for it in District Court. "George is now in jail being delivered up by his Special Bail in said suit." To secure payment ($546.08 plus interest), George conveys 2 tracts: 200 acres on the east side of Monongalia River, conveyed to him by Thomas and Judath Pindall, 10 June 1793 (excepting 50 acres previously sold to Samuel Burrows), and 61 acres on the east side of Monongalia River, patented to George (alias Hollenbaugh) 27 July 1797. Payment to be made by 6 August 1807 or the land to be sold. Signed: George Hollenback, Thomas Wilson [also as attorney for John M Price], Hannah Hollenback. Witnesses: Wm Lowry, Wm G Payne, Enos Daugherty. Acknowledged by Hannah Hollenback before B Reeder and Wm N Jarrett, JPs, 2 September 1809. Proved by witnesses, October and December 1807. No delivery shown. Recorded: OS 4:266-270.

12 April 1808. Thomas WILSON, attorney in fact and trustee for Jonathan DAVIS, late of Monongalia Co, to Henry PRATT, in trust for the heirs of Thomas ALLEBAM [?] and Samuel HARVEY, assignees of Jacob BAKER and Cornelius COMEGYS, all of Philadelphia, PA. 2 tracts: 165 acres on the Monongalia River, about 6 miles above Morgan Town, adjoining Laban Perdue and George Baltzel. 157 acres adjoining Peter Cook and Thomas Statton, part of a 314 acre survey. Tracts were conveyed by Jonathan Davis, 4 February 1801, to secure payment of $658.25 due to Baker and Comegys. Pratt was highest bidder, at $59. Wilson is bound in no way for the title or accountable for the money bid for the same. Consideration: $59. Signed: Thomas Wilson. Witnesses: none. Acknowledged in court, July 1808. Del: to T Wilson, 17 December 1808. Recorded: OS 4:271-272.

27 June 1808. William C PAYNE and John PAYNE to William LOWERY and Joseph LOWERY. 141 acres adjoining James Coburn, Jesse Payne, William C Payne, and John Payne. Consideration: $700.65. Signed: William G Payne, John Payne. Witnesses: Mathew G[ay], C Bark[shire], Wm N Ja[rrett; names obscured by large inkblot]. Acknowledged in court, July 1808. Del: to Joseph Lowery, 10 October 1808. Recorded: OS 4:272-273.

23 November 1807. Jesse PAYNE to his children, John PAYNE, Polly C PAYNE, Susanah G PAYNE, Elizabeth PAYNE, Francis PAYNE, Rhody PAYNE, William PAYNE, and Annah PAYNE. Bill of sale. Negroes Chaney, Young Betel [?],

Nancy, Peggy, little William, Mariah, Sarah and Caty, Susannah, Selah, and Isaac, as well as beds, furniture, desk, and cupboard. Consideration: £500. Signed: Jesse Payne. Witnesses: John Payne, Jesse Patton, Thomas Payne. Proved by witnesses, June 1808. Del: to John C Payne, 4 October 1809. Recorded: OS 4:273.

23 November 1807. Jesse PAYNE to his son John C PAYNE. Bill of sale. Negro boy Alexander. Consideration: $400. Signed: Jesse Payne. Witnesses: John Payne, Jesse Patton, Thomas Payne. Proved by witnesses, June 1808. Del: to J C Payne, 4 October 1809. Recorded: OS 4:274.

12 September 1808. Samuel and Rebecah LEMLEY and Joseph and Mary SUTTON to Christopher CORE. Two parcels of 40 acres each on Doll Snider's Run, part of more than 300 acres owned by Rudolph Snider at his decease, Rebecah and Mary being his daughters. Consideration: $200 to Sutton and $80 to Lemley. Signed: Samuel Lemley, Rebeckah [X] Lemley, Joseph [+] Sutton, Mary [X] Sutton. Witnesses: Wm G Payne, Rawley Scott, Mathew Gay. Acknowledged in court, September 1808. Del: to Core, 31 [sic] September 1809. Recorded: OS 4:274-275.

9 July 1802. Edmund (Gentleman) and Amelia MILNE to Elizabeth PRINGLE, widow and administratrix of John PRINGLE, merchant, all of Philadelphia city and Co, PA. On 10 May 1787 or 1788 Milne conveyed to John Pringle, for £50, 2 tracts: 1000 acres on Slate Creek, adjoining Richard Renshaw's entry, surveyed 10 June 1784. 1000 acres on a branch of Walkers Creek, adjoining Dr Benjamin Say's entry, surveyed 13 June 1784. Tracts were patented 1 June 1787. Pringle is now dead and the deed is lost or mislaid. Milne has been requested to make a reconveyance and confirm the sale. Consideration: 5s. Signed: [not signed]. Witnesses: Robt H Rose. Acknowledged in Philadelphia, PA, 31 March 1803. Certificate of Mathew Lawler, mayor. Del: to E Pringle, at Germantown, PA, by mail. Recorded: OS 4:275-277.

15 August 1808. Dr Amos CHIPPS to Augustus WERNINGER, Morgan Town. Lot [# not shown] in Morgan Town, opposite the northward side of the courthouse lot. Consideration: $1640, VA. Signed: Amos Chipps. Witnesses: Wm G Payne, R Barkshire, John Stealey, Rawley Scott. Proved by witnesses, September 1808. Del: to A Werninger, 6 December 1808. Recorded: OS 4:277-278.

5 March 1808. Eligah HAWKINS to William HILL. Undivided half interest in 85 acres on the Tiger Valley River, opposite Hills Ferry and including a sawmill, which Eligah owns jointly with Philip Hill. Consideration: $260. Signed: Eligehe [X] Hawkins.

Witnesses: Philip Hill, John [X] Hobbs, Jacob Hill. Acknowledged in court, September 1808. Del: to Wm Hill, 15 November 1808. Recorded: OS 4:278-279.

13 April 1808. Thomas and Polly WILSON to Levi FREELAND. 100 acres on Dunkard Mill Run and its lefthand branch, adjoining lands sold to Furbee and since conveyed to Nathan Joseph. Part of 400 acres patented 21 January 1800, from the south end of the tract. Consideration: $200, VA. Signed: Thomas Wilson, Polly Wilson. Witnesses: Rawley Scott, Wm N Jarrett, Nimrod Evans. Acknowledged in court by Thomas Wilson, September 1808; by Polly Wilson before William N Jarrett and R Barkshire, JPs, 11 January 1809. Del: to Levi Freeland, 11 January 1809. Recorded: OS 4:279-280.

14 September 1807. Jacob and Hannah PINDLE, John and Hannah CHIPPS, William and Hannah CHIPPS, Simeon and Elizabeth ROYSE, and Amos CHIPPS to Thomas R CHIPPS. Lot [# not shown] in Morgantown, opposite the northward side of the courthouse lot. Consideration: $2000, VA. Signed: Jacob Pindle, Hannah Pindle, John Chipps, Hannah Chipps, Simeon Royse, Elizabeth Royse, Amos Chipps. Witnesses: D Evans, Wm N Jarrett, E Daugherty [all as to William Chipps]. Acknowledged by Elizabeth Royse and Hannah Chipps (wife of William) before Dudley Evans and Wm N Jarrett, 10 August 1808. Proved by witnesses, September 1808. Del: to A Werninger, 6 December 1808. Recorded: OS 4:281-283.

12 September 1808. Mathew and Elizabeth GEORGE to Booz BASNET. 15 acres, no adjoiners or place names mentioned. Consideration: $150, VA. Signed: Mathew George, Elizabeth George. Witnesses: none. Acknowledged in court, September 1808. Del: to him, November 1810. Recorded: OS 4:283-284.

15 December 1807. Alpheus WICKWARE, Baran Co, KY, to Samuel WICKWARE, Barren Co, KY. Power of attorney to sell 350 acres on Tiger Valley River, patented in the name of John Wickware; 200 acres adjoining the Swamps, patented in the name of John Wickware; and 200 acres on Whiteday Creek, patented in the name of David Norris. Signed: Alpheus Wickware. Witnesses: none. Acknowledged in Baran Co, KY, 16 December 1807. Certificates of William Logan, clerk, and Thomas Dickinson, JP. Del: to Saml Wickware, 24 May 1809. Recorded: OS 4:284-285.

16 July 1804. Thomas MARTIN to Thomas WILSON. Deed of trust. Martin owes $127 to Simeon Beall or his attorney Thomas Wilson, payable by 1 August 1805. To secure the debt he conveys undivided half of $536\frac{1}{4}$ acres adjoining John Casaty and David Anderson. Patented to

John Fairfax, Esq [date blank]. Signed: Thomas Martin. Witnesses: Wm Tingle, Jas Pindle, James Campbell. Acknowledged in court, September 1808. Del: to Jacob Weaver pr order of Thos Wilson, July 1809. Recorded: OS 4:285-286.

12 May 1808. William and Martha HILL to Richard HARRIS, Harrison Co. 6¼ acres on Tyger Valley River, no adjoiners mentioned. Part of 85 acres patented to Stokeley Little, 16 December 1799. Consideration: $18. Signed: William Hill, Martha [X] Hill. Witnesses: Daniel Davisson Jr, Thomas Hobbs, D Harris, Thomas Little. Acknowledged by Martha Hill before Morgan Morgan and John Nuzum, JPs, 20 May 1808; by William Hill in court, September 1808. Del: to Harris, 26 May 1810. Recorded: OS 4:286-287.

12 September 1808. George and Mary GRESMER to James HAMILTON. 50 acres adjoining Joseph Trickett, Zebulon Hogge, Standish Ford, and Thomas Clare. Consideration: $50. Signed: George [X] Gresmore, Mary [X] Gresmore. Witnesses: none. Acknowledged in court, September 1808. Del: to James Hamilton, 9 February 1810. Recorded: OS 4:288-289.

12 September 1808. Alpheus WICKWARE, heir at law to John WICKWARE, deceased, by his attorney in fact, Samuel WICKWARE, Baran Co, KY, to William N JARRETT, Esq. 200 acres on the east side of Tyger Valley River, adjoining George Wilson, Josiah Wilson, and J Thomas' Swamp settlement. Excepting 4 acres conveyed by John Wickware to Nathan Hall. Patented to John Wickware 5 September 1799. Consideration: $800. Signed: Samuel Wickware. Witnesses: none. Acknowledged in court, September 1808. Del: to Wm N Jarrett, 16 September 1809. Recorded: OS 4:289-290.

17 March 1808. Francis and Ann COLLINS to William STAFFORD. 300 acres on the east side of Cheat River, near Sandy Creek, adjoining Thomas Gibson. Conveyed by Stacy Garwood to Francis Collins, [illegible] December 1805. Consideration: $200, VA. Signed: Francis Collins [Ann does not sign]. Witnesses: Nimrod Evans, Zackquil Morgan, Noah Ridgway, Robert Ferrel, Lemuel John. Acknowledged in court by Francis Collins, September 1808. Del: to him, 11 April 1814. Recorded: OS 4:290-291.

13 September 1808. Joseph and Sarah SAPP to James TUCKER. 67 acres, 16 perches, no adjoiners or place names mentioned. Consideration: $201. Signed: Joseph [X] Sapp, Sarah [-] Sapp. Witnesses: none. Acknowledged in court, September 1808. Del: to Robert Courtney, 16

August 1811. Recorded: OS 4:291-292.

8 August 1808. Abraham and Hannah HUFFMAN to their son Isaac HUFFMAN. 2 tracts. 113½ acres on Charleys Run adjoining John Lynch, John Kerns, Boyles, and John Stewart's heirs. 33¼ acres, no adjoiners or place names mentioned. Consideration: love and affection. Signed: Abraham Huffman [Hannah does not sign]. Witnesses: Jno Wagner, Nimrod Evans, French Gray, George S Dering. Acknowledged in court, September 1808. Del: to A Huffman, 31 May 1810. Recorded: OS 4:292-293.

11 April 1808. Abiel and Mary GUSTIN to George BELL. 76 acres on Scotts Mill Run, adjoining Ashbel Gustin and James Baker. Part of 310 acres patented to David Gilkey. Consideration: £40. Signed: Abiel Gustin, Mary [G] Gustin. Witnesses: Nimrod Evans, French Gray, N Vandevort. Acknowledged by Mary Gustin before Dudley Evans and Wm N Jarrett, JPs, 11 April 1808. Proved by witnesses, September 1808. Del: to G Bell, 16 September 1809. Recorded: OS 4:293-294.

21 June 1808. Davis WEAVER to Abraham HESS. 100 acres on Big Sandy Creek, adjoining Charles Donaldson. Patented 17 February 1797. Consideration: $100, VA. Signed: Davis Weaver. Witnesses: B Reeder, George Cunningham, William Chipps, Fielding Kiger, James Deasly [?]. Proved by witnesses, September 1808. Del: to A Hess, 24 January 1810. Recorded: OS 4:295.

5 8mo 1808. WILL of John SMITH. Wife Sarah: improved part of tract I live on, at Elk Run, to just below the fulling mill, adjoining a tract purchased of John Willets. Oldest son Joseph: tract on which Aran now lives. Son Samuel: 200 acres at the north end of the tract I live on, he to take the improved part at his mother's death. Son Aran: 200 acres on the creek below lands of Robert Harkness. Son Jonas: 200 acres adjoining the south end of Robert Harkness' land and Peter Cook. Daughters Mary, Phebe, Ann, Sarah: $60 each, to be paid from sale of remaining lands. Samuel to pay 2 of the girls' legacies, as his land is better improved than the others. Legacies to be paid in no more than 5 years. If necessary, other sons to make up the balance of legacies. Son Joseph: new wagon. Wife: choice of horse, 2 cows, plow and gears, bed, bedding, case of drawers. Rest of movable property to be sold and the money divided between sons Aaran and Jonas. Executors: wife Sarah and 2 oldest sons [not specified]. Signed: John Smith. Witnesses: Robert Foreman, Joseph Wood, John Willits. Proved by witnesses, September 1808. Recorded: OS 4:295-296. [Also recorded in Wills, 1:333.]

21 July 1808. WILL of James CLARK. Wife Elenor: all estate during her life. Eldest son John Clark: $40. Son James: $40. Son Samuel: $40. Daughter Mary: $70, bed, furniture. Isabella McGrew [no relationship stated]: $10. Grandson John Corey: $10. Mary Kirkpatrick [no relationship stated]: $10 in property when plantation is sold after wife's death. Youngest sons Robert and Isaac: remainder of property. Executors: son Robert and James McGrew. Witnesses: none. Signed: [not signed]. Proved in court, September 1808. "This writing purporting to be the last will and testament of James Clark Senior deceased was produced in court and Samuel Moore Jane Moore and Margrett Curry being sworn as witnesses thereto and the Court being satisfied from their testimony that the same is the last will and testament of the same James Clark though through weakness of body the said James Clark was unable to sign said Will it therefore ordered that the same be recorded." Recorded: OS 4:297. [Also recorded in Wills, 1:326.]

26 August 1808. John and Sarah DIGMAN to Joseph SUTTON. 34 acres at Scotts Mill Run, adjoining James Buckhannan. Part of 400 acres formerly belonging to Buckhannan, who sold to Thomas Bevins, and of which Sutton is now in possession. Consideration: $200. Signed: John [J] Digman, Sarah [X] Digman. Witnesses: James Kelly, John Turkeyhiser, John Barrackman. Proved by witnesses, September 1808. Commission to take Sarah's acknowledgement, no action recorded here. Del: to Mary Sutton, 30 August 1809. Recorded: OS 4:298-299.

9 June 1808. WILL of Thomas EVANS. Wife Katherine: all property during her widowhood. If she and son Richard W Evans think proper, Thomas' 2 tracts to be sold. When property divided among his 11 children, the following to be noted: Richard W has received $133 1/3, to be deducted from his share; John has received $133 1/3; James has received $100; Isabella Hoskinson has received $133 1/3; Thomas has received $40; Evan no deduction; David has received $40; Peggy Hammond has received $30; Benjan, Caty, and Polly to have no deduction made. "I have a particular aversion to law suits and wish to prevent my Estate from falling into the hands of Lawyers." If any disputes arise about division, 3 honest and sensible men of the neighbourhood to referee. "My desire is that my children shall not go to law with each other." Signed: Thomas [mark] Evans. Witnesses: Robert Cary, Reuben Chalfont, Jno Wagner. Proved by witnesses, September 1808. Recorded: OS 4:299-300. [Also recorded in Wills, 1:326-327.]

10 October 1808. Michael and Barbara BARR to Peter HINCKINS. 23 acres adjoining Alexander Clegg and Hinckins' and Barr's other lands. Consideration: $100, VA. Signed: Michael [X] Barr, Barbara [X] Barr. Witnesses: none. Acknowledged in court, October 1808. No delivery shown. Recorded: OS 4:300-301.

10 October 1808. Michael and Barbara BARR to John JONSTON. 73 acres at Dunkard Creek, adjoining Alexander Clegg and John Hott. Patented to Alexander Clegg and conveyed to John Jonston [sic] 13 April 1801. Consideration: $500. Signed: Michael [X] Barr, Barbara [X] Barr. Witnesses: none. Acknowledged in court, October 1808. No delivery shown. Recorded: OS 4:301-302.

10 October 1808. John and Catherine JONSTON to Michael BARR. 100 acres at Dunkard Creek, adjoining Samuel Minor. Part of a tract patented to John Statler, 7 February 1787, and conveyed to Jonston 13 March 1796. Consideration: $500, VA. Signed: Catherine Jonston [John does not sign]. Witnesses: none. Acknowledged in court, October 1808. Del: to Michl Barr, 10 [illegible] 1811. Recorded: OS 4:302-303.

10 October 1808. William and Elizabeth RUSSEL to James BRITTON. 19 3/4 acres on Crooked Run, part of 88 acres owned and claimed by Josep [sic] Pickenpaw. Consideration: $120, VA. Signed: William Russel, Elizabeth [X] Russel. Witnesses: John Fortney, Joseph Lowry, Saml Lowry. Acknowledged in court, October 1808. Del: to Go Peckenpaw, 9 April 1810. Recorded: OS 4:303-304.

11 October 1808. Jacob and Hannah PINDELL to Laban PERDEW. 121½ acres on the river, no adjoiners named. Patented 25 October 1787. Consideration: [blank]. Signed: Jacob Pindell, Hannah Pindell. Witnesses: none. Acknowledged in court, October 1808. No delivery shown. Recorded: OS 4:304-305.

25 August 1808. Philip MAINES and Nicholas MAINES, Bever Co, PA, to John COOPER. Power of attorney to sell a tract on Sanday Creek, known as the Crab Orchard settlement, formerly property of John Mains. Signed: Phillip Main, Nicholas Main. Witnesses: Robert Ferrel, Jacob Yoha, A Woodrow. Proved by witnesses, October 1808. Del: to John Cooper, 13 Dm [?] 1808. Recorded: OS 4:305-306.

[no date] WILL of Joseph KELSO. Wife Elizabeth: all property while she remains single. At her death to be divided among the children. Wife's sons Edward and John Bennett to share equally with my own, if they stay with their mother and help raise the family till they are 21

years old. If they leave, to have no share. Eldest son William: silver knee buckles, he having been deeded a tract already. Signed: Joseph Kelso. Witnesses: Alexander Arthur, Ann Arthur. Proved by witnesses, October 1808. Recorded: OS 4:308. [Also recorded in Wills, 1:327-328.]

4 August 1808. WILL of Simeon RIGGS. Wife Mercy: 1/3 of estate during her lifetime. Daughters Sarah Pick [?], Rhoda Grier, Phebe Daugherty, Catherine Thomas and Nancy Thomas: 2/3 of personal estate or the money from sale of my perishable estate. Son Cyrus: $10. Land to be sold after wife's death and money divided among sons Joseph, Isaac, and Aaron. Cyrus' legacy to be paid from this money also. Executor: friend Dr John Nicklin and my son Isaac. Signed: Simeon Riggs. Witnesses: Henry Ferrel, Adam Fast, Adam Fast Jr. Codicil, with same witnesses, giving sorrel mare, bridle and saddle to son Aaron. Proved by witnesses, October 1808. Recorded: OS 4:306-307. [Also recorded in Wills, 1:328.]

22 May 1801. WILL of Jacob SCOTT. Wife Catherine: homeplace during her life. Negro woman Charlott, Negro boys James and Harry during her widowhood, with household goods, furniture, farm tools, &c, my rifle gun excepted. Son James: land where he now lives, called the meadow ground, and my rifle gun. Daughter Phebe: the Barker place, plus balance due from Elisha Claten on a note for $200, payable next Christmas. Son Morgan: the part of my homeplace where Widow Watson lives (reference to old schoolhouse and Indian grave in the description); also a tract called the Dering place. If the land that I am at law with Parish about is lost, Morgan to have half the Dering place. Son Joseph: rest of the home place after wife's death, as well as the tract that I am at law with Parish about. If it be lost, to have half the Dering place. Son Morgan: Negro boy Harry and Negro girl Cassay. Son Joseph: Negro boy James and Negro woman Charlott. If any of the Negroes die before they are inherited, the remainder to be equally divided between Morgan and Joseph. Executors: wife Catherine and son-in-law Benjamin Hamilton. Signed: Jacob Scott. Witnesses: William Hamilton, Joseph Morgan, John Lough. Codicil: if either Morgan or Joseph dies before coming of age, the survivor to have all of the home tract. Proved by witnesses, October 1808. Recorded: OS 4:308-309. [Also recorded in Wills, 1:329.]

14 July 1808. William and Mary BARNES and Abbigail BARNES to Abram BARNES. 70 acres on Tygers Valley River, adjoining Mathew House [?], William Barns, and John

Johnson. Consideration: $200. Signed: William [-] Barnes, Mary Barnes, Abigail [X] Barnes. Witnesses: Jorden Hall, Jacob Polsley, John Fanshear. Proved by witnesses, October 1808. Del: to Abm Barnes, 16 September 1811. Recorded: OS 4:309-310.

8 December 1808. Thomas and Sarah LAIDLEY to Rawley SCOTT. Deed of trust. Joseph Allen has entered security for Laidley on a forthcoming bond in favour of Philip I Sheets, to amount of $10.57. John Sullivan entered security for Laidley on appeal from a judgement of John Stealey, Esq, to amount of $18.33, with interest from 1 June 1794. Allen also entered security for Sullivan in another matter. If Allen becomes liable, Scott, the trustee, may sell Laidley's property. To secure the debt, Laidley conveys 289 acres adjoining Robinson Lucus and Robert Ferrel, patented to William Austin 2 June 1800 and conveyed by him to Laidley, and 200 acres patented to Austin 2 February 1803 and conveyed by him to Laidley. Signed: Thos Laidley, Sarah Laidley, Rawley Scott. Witnesses: C Barkshire, S Wickware, W Tingle. Acknowledged in court by Scott and Laidley, December 1808. Commission to take Sarah's acknowledgement but no action recorded here. Del: to Rawley Scott [blank] December 1808. Recorded: OS 4:310-312.

13 October 1808. William and Elizabeth STEWART to their grandson William STEWART. 177½ acres on Stewarts Run, no adjoiners named. From a patent of 4 June 1783. Consideration: love, goodwill, and affection. Signed: William [X] Stewart [Elizabeth does not sign this or any of the following conveyances]. Witnesses: William N Jarrett, Ralph Barkshire, Thos McKinley [all as to William Stewart only]. Proved by witnesses, December 1808, and recorded as to him. Del: to him, 7 May 1809. Recorded: OS 4:313.

13 October 1808. William and Elizabeth STEWART to Agness STEWART. 88 acres, 60 poles at Stewarts Run, no adjoiners named. From patents of 4 June 1783 and 15 September 1784. Consideration: $100. Signed: William [X] Stewart. Witnesses: William N Jarrett, Ralph Barkshire, Thos McKinley. Proved by witnesses, December 1808, and recorded as to him. Del: to David Stewart, 2 January 1810. Recorded: OS 4:314-315.

13 October 1808. William and Elizabeth STEWART to David STEWART. 124 acres at Stewarts Run, no adjoiners named. The upper end of a 15 September 1784 patent. Consideration: $100. Signed: William [X] Stewart. Witnesses: William N Jarrett, Ralph Barkshire, Thos McKinley. Proved by witnesses, December 1808, and

recorded as to him. Del: to him, same time. Recorded: OS 4:315-316.

13 October 1808. William and Elizabeth STEWART to Thomas CORDRY. 42 acres at Stewarts Run, no adjoiners named. From a 4 June 1783 patent. Consideration: $100. Signed: William [X] Stewart. Witnesses: William N Jarrett, Ralph Barkshire, Thos McKinley. Proved by witnesses, December 1808, and recorded as to him. Del: to him, same time. Recorded: OS 4:316-317.

13 October 1808. William and Elizabeth STEWART to Mary STEWART. 100 acres on Stewarts Run, no adjoiners named. From a 4 June 1783 patent. Consideration: $100. Signed: William [X] Stewart. Witnesses: William N Jarrett, Ralph Barkshire, Thos McKinley. Proved by witnesses, December 1808, and recorded as to him. Del: to him, same time. Recorded: OS 4:318-319.

13 October 1808. William and Elizabeth STEWART to Samuel STEWART. 115 acres on Stewarts Run, adjoining David Stewart. From a 15 September 1784 patent. Consideration: $100. Signed: William [X] Stewart. Witnesses: William N Jarrett, Ralph Barkshire, Thos McKinley. Proved by witnesses, December 1808, and recorded as to him. Del: to him, same time. Recorded: OS 4:319-320.

13 October 1808. William and Elizabeth STEWART to Elizabeth STEWART. 83 acres on Stewarts Run, adjoining Samuel Stewart. Part of a 15 September 1784 patent. Consideration: $100. Signed: William [X] Stewart. Witnesses: William N Jarrett, Ralph Barkshire, Thos McKinley. Proved by witnesses, December 1808, and recorded as to him.Del: to him, same time. Recorded: OS 4:320-321.

17 November 1808. John and Prudence STEALEY to Rawley SCOTT. Lot in Morgan Town [# not shown], adjoining the shop built by Silas Lord and the lot that Stealey lives on. Conveyed by Silas Lord to Stealey, 4 August 1803. Consideration: $1. Signed: John Stealey [Prudence does not sign]. Witnesses: E Daugherty, Alexr Hawthorn, Nimrod Evans. Acknowledged in court by John Stealey, December 1808. Order to take Prudence's acknowledgement but no action recorded here. Del: to Rawley Scott [blank] December 1808. Recorded: OS 4:322-323.

10 November 1808. John and Hannah SMITH to Peter HECKART. 100 acres adjoining Justus Heck on the road leading to the Horse Shoe. Part of a tract willed by John T Goff to his daughter Hannah. Consideration: $300. Signed: John Smith "wrote in Dutch", Hannah [X] Smith.

Witnesses: John Wagner, Marmaduke Evans, French S Gray, Wm N Jarrett, R Barkshire. Acknowledged by Hannah Smith before Wm N Jarrett and Ralph Barkshire, JPs, 14 November 1808. Proved by witnesses, December 1808. Del: to Mr Christian Whitehair, 13 May 1811. Recorded: OS 4:324-325.

19 October 1808. William and Hannah CHIPPS to Abraham HESS. 108½ acres at Poppaw Creek, adjoining Flemmin Jones. Part of a larger tract patented to Hannah Scott. Consideration: $215. Signed: William Chipps, Hannah Chipps. Witnesses: Nimrod Evans, R Barkshire, Amos Chipps, D Evans, C Barkshire. Acknowledged by Hannah Chipps before D Evans and R Barkshire, JPs, 19 October 1808. Proved by witnesses, December 1808. Del: 24 January 1810. Recorded: OS 4:326-327.

26 October 1808. William and Hannah CHIPPS to Hugh SIDWELL. 28 acres at Wests Run, adjoining William McCleery and on the road from Sidwell's house to Martin's Ferry. Part of a tract conveyed by William Orson to Thomas Chipps, 30 June 1795, and of record in District Court deedbook 1, page 168. Consideration: $251. Signed: William Chipps, Hannah Chipps. Witnesses: B Reeder, Wm N Jarrett, C Barkshire, John Chipps. Acknowledged by Hannah Chipps before B Reeder and William N Jarrett, JPs, 26 October 1808. Proved by witnesses, December 1808. Del: to grantee, 29 April 1829. Recorded: OS 4:328-330.

12 December 1808. John and Christina HARTMAN to Henry MILLER. 200 acres on Muddy Creek, no adjoiners named. Consideration: $900. Signed: John Hartman "wrote in Dutch", Christine [X] Hartman. Witnesses: none. Acknowledged by Christenah Hartman before David Morgan and Amos Robbarts, JPs, 3 December 1808; by John Hartman in court, December 1808. Del: to Henry Miller, 28 August 1809 [instrument is also noted as del: to Ralph Barkshire agent (illegible) 1810, perhaps erroneously]. Recorded: OS 4:330-332.

2 December 1808. Bartholomew and Rosina WICKART to Abraham GUSEMAN. 235 acres east of Aarons Creek, adjoining James Russel (now Michael Kerns) and Peter Swisher. From a 310 acre tract conveyed to Wickart by William McCleery, 1 June 1799. 75 acres of the tract has been sold to Ezekiel Cheney and even though the metes and bounds include this parcel, it is understood to be excepted from the conveyance. Consideration: [$?£?]1100, VA. Signed: Bartholomew Wickart "wrote in Dutch", Rosina [X] Wickart. Witnesses: none. Acknowledged in court, December 1808. Del: to him, 20 April 1810. Recorded:

OS 4:332-333.
2 December 1808. Abraham GUSEMAN to Bartholomew WICKART. Mortgage on 235 acres at Aarons Creek, conveyed to Guseman this day by Bartholomew and Rosina Wickart. Payment schedule, with discounts for early payment. Signed: Abraham Guseman "wrote in Dutch." Witnesses: William N Jarrett, S Wickware, R Barkshire. Acknowledged in court, December 1808. No delivery shown. Recorded: OS 4:333-334.

17 October 1808. Enoch and Elizabeth MORE, Harrison Co, to John BIGGS. 190 acres on Muddy Creek, adjoining Samuel Hanway. Consideration: $500. Signed: Enoch [X] More, Elizabeth [X] More. Witnesses: Demcy C Carroll, Solomon Jarvis, Joseph Davisson Jr. Acknowledged in Harrison Co, October 1808. Certificate of Ben Wilson, CHC. Del: to him, 31 December 1810. Recorded: OS 4:334-335.

2 November 1808. William FRETWELL, Albemarle Co, to William TINGLE. Power of attorney to receive from Agnes Fretwell, administratrix of Thomas Fretwell, deceased, any money due to William. Signed: William Fretwell. Witnesses: James A Watton. Proved by witness, December 1808. Del: to Wm Tingle, 7 September 1809. Recorded: OS 4:335.

[blank] December 1808. John DAVIS, Green Co, OH, to William N JARRETT, Morgan Town. Power of attorney to sell house and lot on the east side of Spruce Street in Morgan Town. Previously conveyed to Jarrett in trust to secure $200 for use of John Reed and Standish Ford, Reed the surviving member of the partnership. Signed: John Davis. Witnesses: C Barkshire, Job Kyger, Zackquil Morgan. Proved by witnesses, December 1808. Del: to Mr Geo McNeely, 14 January 1817. Recorded: OS 4:336.

29 October 1807. Absalom and Sarah MORRIS to Joseph MORGAN. Undivided half of 200 acres on Buffelloe Creek, no adjoiners named. Conveyed by George and Elizabeth Martin to Absalom Morris and Thomas Burchinal, 1 June 1797. Consideration: $200, VA. Signed: Absalom Morris, Sarah Morris. Witnesses: Wm John, Lemuel John, Wm Morris. Acknowledged by Sarah Morris before William John and Lemuel John, JPs, 30 October 1807. Proved by witnesses, January 1809. Del: to him, 13 April 1813. Recorded: OS 4:337-338.

10 December 1808. Thomas BRITTON to Catherine WARMAN. Negro woman Lucy, 16 years old, plus beds and furniture, livestock, and all other property, to be held in trust and for the benefit of Nancy Britton, Thomas' wife, and her heirs. Consideration: $1. Signed: Thomas

Britton Jr, Catherine [X] Warman. Witnesses: Enoch Warman, Bartholomew Warman, Margaret Warman. Proved by witnesses, January 1809. Del: to [blank], 13 February 1809, per order from Thos Wilson. Recorded: OS 4:338-339.

14 September 1807. Basil and Joanna LUCAS, Harrison Co, to Thomas R CHIPPS. Release of dower on a lot in Morgan Town, conveyed by Jacob and Hannah Pindall, John and Hannah Chipps, William and Hannah Chipps, Simeon and Elizabeth Royse, and Amos Chipps to Thomas R Chipps, 14 September 1807. Joanna is the widow of Thomas Chipps deceased, and Basil her present husband. Consideration: none stated. Signed: Basil Lucas, Joanna Lucas. Witnesses: B Wilson, Elias Stillwell, M Armstrong. Acknowledged in Harrison Co, before Elias Stillwell and Ben Wilson Jr, JPs, 5 August 1808. Proved by witnesses in Harrison Co, August 1808. Del: to Augustus Werninger, 20 April 1809. Recorded: OS 4:339-340.

14 November 1808. John REED, merchant, Philadelphia, PA, to William N JARRETT, Morgan Town. Power of attorney. On 12 December 1807 John and Rachel Reed conveyed to Joseph Ball and William Page, merchants, Philadelphia, PA, all estate belonging to John as surviving partner of Standish Ford deceased. On 7 May 1808 Ball and Page gave John Reed their power of attorney to recover all debts due under the second schedule in the previous conveyance. Reed now appoints William N Jarrett as attorney in the same capacity. Signed: John Reed. Witnesses: R Barkshire, Jno Stealey, Jacob Kyger. Proved by witnesses, December 1808. Del: to James McGee for WNJ, 1 November 1810. Recorded: OS 4:340-342.

11 April 1800. John FRANCISCO, Abraham FRANCISCO, William and Elizabeth McDONNAL, Hannah FRANCISCO, Rebekah FRANCISCO, Absalom FRANCISCO, and Sarah FRANCISCO, heirs at law to Abraham FRANCISCO, deceased, to David GRAHAM, Ebenezer GRAHAM, and Robert GRAHAM, heirs of John GRAHAM, deceased. 100 acres on Pricketts Creek, adjoining Elisha Bratton, Robert Graham, and William Miller, and including the place where David Graham now lives. Part of a 400 acre tract. Consideration: $80. Signed: John [X] Fransisco, Abraham [X] Fransisco, Wm [X] McDonnal, Elizabeth [X] McDonnal, Mary [+] Fransisco [remainder of named grantors do not sign]. Witnesses: Wm Haymond, Nathan Springer, Levi Morgan, Morgan Morgan. Acknowledged by Elizabeth McDonald before William Haymond and Nathan Springer, JPs, 11 April 1800. Proved by witnesses, April 1800,

January 1809. Del: to David Graham, 18 April 1810. Recorded: OS 4:342-344.

8 February 1808. James and Alethia CLARK to Samuel JACKSON. 50 acres on the maine road from Ices ferry to the said spring [sic]. No adjoiners named. Consideration: $200. Signed: James Clark [Alethia does not sign]. Witnesses: none. Acknowledged by James Clark in court, February 1808; by Alethia Clark before Amos Roberts and Mr Wm Johnson, JPs, 19 February 1808. No delivery shown. Recorded: OS 4:345-346.

20 December 1808. William and Drusella HILLIRA to Israel FREE. 102 acres on Finches Run, a branch of Buffellow Creek, adjoining John Webb's former land, John Haymond, Jasper Weatt, Benjamin Brown, and John Brown. Part of 2 tracts: 400 acres patented to John Webb and conveyed by him to the said Roberts [sic], and 150 acres patented to the said Roberts. Consideration: $403.33. Signed: William [H] Hillery, Drucella [X] Hillery. Witnesses: none. Acknowledged in court, February 1809. Del: to B Brown, 7 January 1810. "Fee pd in ½ bushel salt at $3 per bushel." Recorded: OS 4:346-347.

12 December 1808. Roger PARKS to Joseph MERREL. Lots #11 and 12, town of Pleasantville. Consideration: $50, VA. Signed: Roger [R] Parks. Witnesses: none. Acknowledged in court, February 1809. Del: to Joseph Merrill, 6 May 1809. Recorded: OS 4:347.

31 October 1808. Benjamin and Elinor REEDER to Grafton WHITE, no addresses stated. 1055 acres on Dunker Creek, near the PA line, adjoining Alexander Clegg. Consideration: $500, VA. Signed: B Reeder, Eler Reeder. Witnesses: none. Proved by witnesses Samuel Hanway and Alexander Hawthorn, January 1809 [sic]. Acknowledged by Benjamin Reeder in court, February 1809; by Elenor Reeder before Jas Scott and Booz Burris, JPs, 29 July 1809. Del: to G White, 15 June 1810. Recorded: OS 4:348-349.

14 October 1805. David SCOTT to Felix SCOTT, his son. All estate in my home plantation, previously conveyed to Felix with reservation of lifetime rights. David reserves the present crop and the small grain. Consideration: $1, and Felix's agreement to pay Robert Scott $300, @ $100 per year. Signed: David Scott. Witnesses: Wm G Payne, David Scott Junr, Noah Ridgway. Proved by witnesses, October 1805, February 1809. No delivery shown. Recorded: OS 4:349.

13 February 1809. William and Allender BRUMINGHAM and John and Nancy BRUMINGHAM, Allender and Nancy being heirs of Simon TROY, deceased, to Samuel LEMLEY, Green

Co, PA. Unspecified acreage adjoining Samuel Hanway's survey, the state line, and Absalom Willey. Consideration: $725, VA. Signed: William [0] Brumingham, Elenor [|] Brumingham, John [+] Brumingham, Nancy [+] Brumingham. Witnesses: none. Acknowledged in court, February 1809. Del: to Saml Lemley, 5 June 1809. Recorded OS 4:350.

13 February 1809. Samuel HANWAY and Rachel HANWAY, executors of Jesse HANWAY, deceased, to Michael HELDERBRAND. 9½ acres, no adjoiners named. Patented to John Harden Jr, and conveyed by Nester Harden, his son and legal [word missing] to Jesse Hanway. Consideration: $10, in compliance with the directions of Jesse in his lifetime. Signed: Samuel Hanway, Rachel [X] Hanway. Witnesses: none. Acknowledged in court, February 1809. Del: to him, 12 June 1809. Recorded: OS 4:351.

15 September 1808. William and Ester McCLEERY to Mathew GAY. 110 acres on Fall Lick Creek, east side of Cheat River, no adjoiners named. Patented to McCleery, 6 June 1788. Consideration: $1, VA. Signed: William McCleery, Esther McCleery. Witnesses: none. Acknowledged in court, February 1809. Del: to Wm Reid, 8 April 1811. Recorded: OS 4:352.

13 February 1809. Joseph REED to John REED Sr and William REED. Mortgage. On [blank] 179[blank] John Reed, at the request of Joseph, became his surety for [sum blank] owed to William Hanna, now deceased, of Berkely Co. Joseph failed to pay Hanna during his lifetime, and his executors brought suit in Monongalia District Court to collect the debt and have obtained judgment for $180.68 1/3. Joseph has appealed the judgment to District Chancery Court in Staunton, and has obtained an injunction against Hanna's executors. William Reed is his security on the injunction bond. In case the judgment is confirmed, and in order to save harmless John and William Reed, Joseph conveys 200 acres at Deckers Creek, adjoining John Reed Jr, on which he now lives. If the judgment is confirmed and Joseph satisfies it, with no loss to John or William, the conveyance to be null and void. Signed: Joseph Reed. Witnesses: Rawley Scott, Hedgman Triplett, Nimrod Evans, Zackquil Morgan. Proved by witnesses, February 1809. No delivery shown. Recorded: OS 4:352-354.

12 February 1809. William and Ann GEORGE to Christian HARDING, Frederick Co, MD. 120 acres on Threefork Creek, adjoining Jabish Bell. Part of 1700 acres patented to Dudley Evans, 23 August 1799. Consideration: $290. Signed: William George, Ann [-]

George. Witnesses: none. Acknowledged in court, February 1809. Del: to D Musgrave, 15 March 1822. Recorded: OS 4:354.

20 June 1808. Frederick and Margrett STAIR to John LIGHT, all of Berkley Co. 204 acres, 4 miles from Cheat River, adjoining George Ashby. A tract conveyed by Conrad Hogmire to Frederick Stair and Abraham Stair, and of record at Morgan Town. Consideration: $245.54. Signed: Frederick Starr "wrote in Dutch", Margarett [X] Starr. Witnesses: Robt Wilson, John Albertes, Moses Collins. Proved by witnesses in Berkeley Co, 27 June 1808. Certificate of A D Hunter, CBC. Del: to Wm Summerville (who sent the deed here), 4 April 1812. Recorded: OS 4:355-356.

16 January 1809. Isaac PRICKETT, Adams Co, OH, to Henry DUNN, no address stated. Power of attorney to sell 200 acres on Buffellow Lick Run, adjoining John McGee, Robert Graham, and Elias Pearce. Tract surveyed in Isaac's name "through a mistake in the surveyor in saying Isaac Pricket heir of Isaiah Instead of John Prickett heir of Isaiah." Signed: Isaac [mark] Prickett. Witnesses: Bernard Thompson, James Thomson. Acknowledged in Clermont Co, OH, before Bernard Thompson, JP, 16 January 1809. Certificate of Roger W Waring, Clerk. No delivery shown. Recorded: OS 4:356-357.

9 September 1808. WILL of William LINN. Four first children, now in KY or elsewhere: $1. Wife Isabelle: one third of estate, real and personal. Four youngest children, Ann, Sally, Hughey, and Gibson, with 3 older children Jno, William, and Samuel: equal share of the remainder. Son William: to have his own mare, beyond his quoto [sic]. Four youngest children to be raised and educated under their mother's inspection. Executors: William Poor and son John Linn. Signed: William Linn. Witnesses: Gardner Leonard, Robert Henderson, Henry [X] Tucker. Proved by witnesses, February 1809. Recorded: OS 4:357-358. [Also recorded in Wills, 1:330.]

21 September 1808. Enoch and Amelia EVANS, formerly of Monongalia [no current address stated] to Nimrod EVANS. 304 acres at Cheat Neck, adjoining Francis Warman, William Norris, James Donaldson, and Samuel Lewellen. Patented to Bartholomew Jenkins, 1 November 1782, and devised by his will to his daughter Amelia, who has since intermarried with Enoch Evans, but not to take effect until the death of Mary Jenkins, his widow, and Amelia's mother. Consideration: $3000. Signed: Enoch Evans, Amelia Evans. Witnesses: Rawley Scott, French S Gray, John Evans Jr. Acknowledged by Amelia Evans in

Cape Girardeau District [territory not identified here] before Robert Blair and Geo Henderson, JPs, 16 December 1808. Proved by witnesses, March 1809. Recorded: OS 4:358-360.

14 March 1809. George and Mary GRISMER to John WAGNER. 48 acres adjoining Philip Smell and Evan Morgan. From a 4 December 1784 patent to Francis Burrell, assignee of Henry Hains. Conveyed by Francis Burrell Sr to Francis Burrell Jr, 28 December 1797, and by Francis (Jr) and Rachel Burrell and Katherine Burrell to George Grismer, 11 June 1799. Consideration: $400. Signed: George Gresmore, Mary [+] Gresmore. Witnesses: none. Acknowledged in court, March 1809. Del: to John Wagner, 12 March 1810. Recorded: OS 4:360-361.

22 September 1808. John DOWNER to Jacob FOULK. 375 acres at Booths Creek, adjoining David Sayre Jr and Thomas Evans. Part of 500 acres patented to Downer and William Buckhannon [blank] 1808. Consideration: $300. Signed: John Downer. Witnesses: A Woodrow, Thomas McKinley, John Chipps. Proved by witnesses, May 1809. Del: to him, 2 November 1814. Recorded: OS 4:364-365.

9 March 1809. Enos and Jane DAUGHERTY to Augustus WARNINGER. Lot #86 in Morgan Town. Consideration: $700. Signed: E Daugherty, Jane Daugherty. Witnesses: Nimrod Evans, Jno Stealey, Amaziah Davisson, Wm N Jarrett. Acknowledged by Enos in court, March 1809; by Jane before Wm N Jarrett and R Barkshire, JPs, 24 March 1809. Del: to A Warninger, 20 April 1809. Recorded: OS 4:362-364.

6 March 1809. John RAMSEY, Cheat Neck, executor of John RAVENSCROFT, deceased, and Elizabeth RAVENSCROFT, widow and relict of John, to Samuel WILSON. Lease of 14 years, to commence 1 April next, on the farm now in Elizabeth Ravenscroft's occupation. Rent is $55 per year, payable in merchantable bar iron or pot mettle castings, wheat, rye, or corn, to be delivered at Samuel Jackson's mill in Cheat Neck. Wilson to be credited $20 on the first year's rental for putting the fences in order. Signed: John Ramsey, Elizabeth Ravenscroft, Samuel [X] Wilson. Witnesses: Wm Tingle, Jno Wagner, Thos Wilson. Proved by witnesses, March 1809. No delivery shown. Recorded: OS 4:364-365.

17 October 1808. Peter and Catherine BREWER, Hampshire Co, to John BRANDT. 1340 acres on the state road from Morgan Town to Dunkard Bottom, adjoining the Monongalia Glades, Benjamin Reeder, William Mannear, Amos Holly, and Alexander Smith. Consideration: $5000. Signed: Peter Brewer, Catherine [+] Brewer. Witnesses:

Basel Athy, David Harry, George Athy, John Harry. Acknowledged by Peter Brewer, 18 October 1808, in Hampshire Co. Certificate of And Woodrow, CHC. Acknowledged by Catherine in Hampshire Co before Beal Dimmit and Frederick Buzzard, JPs, 8 December 1808. Del: to John Brant, 28 March 1809. Recorded: OS 4:365-367.

 28 September 1808. John and Hannah GRIBBLE to William WEBSTER, Fayette Co, PA. 109 1/10 acres at Big Sandy Creek, no adjoiners named. Conveyed to Gribble by William Squire. Consideration: $1400, VA. Signed: John Gribble, Hannah [#] Gribble. Witnesses: Amos Robbarts, Wm Johnson, Alex Brandon. Acknowledged by Hannah before Amos Roberts and William Johnson, JPs, 29 September 1808. Proved by witnesses, January 1809. Acknowledged in court by John Gribble, March 1809. No delivery shown. Recorded: OS 4:367-369.

 20 September 1808. John and Hannah GRIBBLE to Robert THOMPSON. 94 acres on Big Sandy Creek, no adjoiners named. Conveyed to Gribble by William Squires. Consideration: $120. Signed: John Gribble, Hannah Gribble. Witnesses: Amos Robbarts, Wm John, Alex Brandon. Acknowledged by Hannah before Amos Robbarts and Wm Johnson, JPs, 29 September 1808. Proved by witnesses, January 1809. Acknowledged in court by John Gribble, March 1809. Del: to him, 14 September 1812. Recorded: OS 4:369-371.

 8 March 1809. David and Elizabeth SCOTT, Harrison Co, to Robert SCOTT. Lot [# not shown] in Morgan Town, on the south side of Walnut Street. Conveyed by Zackquil Morgan to David Scott, and by him to his daughter Nancy, who married George Metcalf. By operation of laws the lot has reverted to David. Consideration: $1, VA, and consanguinity. Signed: David Scott, Elizabeth Scott. Witnesses: Felix Scott, Dudley E Dent, John Shively. Acknowledged in court, April 1809. No delivery shown. Recorded: OS 4:371.

 27 February 1809. David SCOTT to Felix SCOTT. Power of attorney to sue, demand, and receive debts, damages, interest and costs due from Stephen Gappen, of PA. Under colour of a bill of sale, conveying certain Negroes and other property, Gappen used fraudulent power in converting the same to his own use. Felix to reserve the first half of any proceeds for his own use, the remainder to David. Signed: David Scott. Witnesses: John Dent, Margaret Dent, Nimrod Dent. Acknowledged in court, April 1809. No delivery shown. Recorded: OS 4:372-373.

 [blank] April 1809. Jacob and Mary FETTERS to John ANNON [?]. 75 acres, no adjoiners or place names

mentioned. Part of a tract conveyed to Joseph Volgamut to Tobias Reems, and by Reems to Jacob Fetters. Consideration: $150, VA. Signed: Jacob Fetters, Mary Fetters. Witnesses: none. Acknowledged in court, April 1809. Del: to him, 12 August 1811. Recorded: OS 4:373-374.

6 April 1809. John and Lucretia TAYLOR to Abraham HALE. Lot [# not shown] in Morgan Town, adjoining High Street, John Pairpoint's heirs, and Zackquil Morgan's heirs. Conveyed to Taylor by Wm and Elizabeth Stewart, 12 April 1808. Consideration: $1, VA. Signed: John Taylor, Lucretia Taylor. Witnesses: none. Acknowledged in court, April 1809. Del: to A Hale, 7 October 1809. Recorded: OS 4:374-375.

[blank] April 1809. Morgan MORGAN to his son Isaac MORGAN. 130 acres on Little Creek, adjoining Bambridge. Part of 350 acres patented 2 October 1786. Apple orchard is reserved for Morgan and his wife Drusilla during their natural lives, as is the upper meadow, now in possession of William Bambridge. Consideration: $100. Signed: Morgan Morgan. Witnesses: none. Acknowledged in court, April 1809. Del: to him, 10 June 1811. Recorded: OS 4:375-376.

18 March 1809. Jonathan HARRIS to John HARRIS. 300 acres on Big Sandy Creek, adjoining Evan Jenkins and Abraham Harris. Consideration: £100, VA. Signed: Jonathan Harris. Witnesses: John Jenkins, Jonathan Smith. Acknowledged in court, April 1809 by Jonathan and Rebecca Harris [Rebecca is not mentioned in body of instrument]. Del: to Jonath Harris, 12 August 1811. Recorded: OS 4:376-377.

18 March 1809. Jonathan and Rebecca HARRIS to William HARRIS. 100 acres on Great Sandy, adjoining Jonathan Smith. Consideration: £100. Signed: Jonathan Harris, Rebecca Harris. Witnesses: John Jenkins, Jonathan Smith. Acknowledged in court, April 1809. Del: to Severan, [illegible] March 1816, Recorded: OS 4:377-378.

1 July 1807. George DEIBLER and John SULLIVAN to Augustus WERNINGER. Bond, under penalty of $200. Deibler and Sullivan will provide Werninger with workmanlike saddle work, to the value of $89.78 at customary Morgantown prices, and to pay in saddle work for the materials furnished, within 6 months. Signed: George Deibler, Jno [+] Sullivan. Witnesses: Henry Dering, Charles Byrn. No acknowledgement recorded. Del: to Thos Sweringen, 21 April 1809. Recorded: OS 4:378.

18 March 1809. Jonathan and Rebecca HARRIS to

Abraham HARRIS. 100 acres on Big Sandy and Severns Run, no adjoiners named. Consideration: £100, VA. Signed: Jonathan Harris [Rebecca does not sign]. Witnesses: John Jenkins, Jonathan Smith. Acknowledged in court, April 1809, by Jonathan and Rebecca. No delivery shown. Recorded: OS 4:379.

10 April 1809. John and Mary Ann WELLS to Richard WELLS. 156 acres on Scotts Meadow Run, no adjoiners named. Part of 400 acres patented to George Gallespie, and conveyed by his heir at law John Gallaspie to Samuel Smith, who conveyed to John Wells. Consideration: $800. Signed: John Wells [Mary Ann does not sign]. Witnesses: none. Acknowledged in court, April 1809, by John Wells. Del: to him, 19 November 1810. Recorded: OS 4:380.

11 January 1808. Joseph and Ann Skinner WILSON and John F and Janey WILSON to Benjamin DOOLITTLE. 2 tracts. 100 acres on the Monongalia River, adjoining James Wilson and Philip Shettlesworth. Patented to Joseph Wilson, 25 February 1797. 50 3/4 acres adjoining Josiah Wilson and Philip Shettlesworth. Patented to Joseph Wilson, 28 July 1800. These lands previously conveyed by Joseph to John F Wilson. Consideration: $1000, VA. Signed: Joseph Wilson, Ann S Wilson, John F Wilson, Jane Wilson. Witnesses: John Harman, Samuel G Wilson. Acknowledged in court by John F Wilson and Ann Wilson, January 1808; by Joseph Wilson and Jane Wilson, April 1809. Del: to B Wilson, 17 October 1809. Recorded: OS 4:381-382.

2 May 1808. James and Mary GUTHRIE to Henry RUMBLEY [also RUMBLE in body of instrument]. 200 acres on Little Sandy, no adjoiners named. Consideration: $300. Signed: James Guthrie, Mary [X] Guthrie. Witnesses: Amos Roberts, Wm Johnson, Alexr Brandon. Acknowledged by Mary Guthrie before Amos Roberts and Wm Johnson, 2 May 1808. Proved by witnesses, October 1808. Acknowledged in court by James, April 1809. Del: to Alexr Stewart, August 1812, fee paid by him. Recorded: OS 4:382-384.

4 May 1809. Christopher RAVER to Christopher RAVER and William RAVER, "laid to him by Margaret Sister which he owns to be his own sons [sic]." Bond to convey title to lands previously laid off for William and Christopher. They shall not sell or make away with the lands they now live on till their youngest child comes of age. Signed: Christopher Raver "wrote in Dutch." Witnesses: Wm Billinsley, George Peckinpaugh. Christopher and William Raver agree to keep their father in a reasonable way as long as he lives. Signed: Christopher Raver, William Raver. Proved by witnesses,

May 1809. Del: to them, August 1810. Recorded: OS 4:385.

12 April 1809. Joseph and Elizabeth JEANS to Henry RUNNER. 42 acres on the state road, no adjoiners or place names mentioned. Consideration: $300. Signed: Joseph Janes, Elizabeth Janes. Witnesses: none. Acknowledged in court, May 1809. Del: to him, 28 March 1815. Recorded: OS 4:385-386.

8 May 1809. George and Catherine SHINN to John W DEAN. 333 acres on West Run, adjoining William Joseph, John Jonston, Elijah Burrows, John Burroos[sic], David Scott, and Samuel Hanway. Consideration: $800. Signed: George Shinn, Caty Shinn. Witnesses: none. Acknowledged in court, May 1809. Del: to Isaac Dean, son of the grantee, 27 October 1814. Recorded: OS 4:386-387.

19 September 1808. John WELLS to Richard WELLS. Bill of sale for "all my personal estate," including horses, cows, sheep, hogs, horse cart and gears, farm utensils, and various household furnishings. Consideration: $126. Signed: John Wells. Witnesses: D Evans, Hedgman Triplett. Proved by witnesses, May 1809. Del: to him, 19 November 1810. Recorded: OS 4:387.

15 April 1809. William N JARRETT to Dr Enos DAUGHERTY, both of Morgan Town. Lots #54 and 55 on the east side of Spruce Street. Tracts were conveyed on 28 January 1804 by John Davis, under deed of trust to secure $200 owed to John Reed and Standish Ford, merchants of Philadelphia, PA, but the trust had never been carried into effect. Ford is now deceased, and his surviving partner Reed has conveyed to Joseph Ball and William Page, merchants of Philadelphia, all the goods, lands, effects, &c of Reed and Ford in the USA. Page and Ball empowered Reed to collect all debts owing to the former partnership, and Reed has further empowered Jarrett to do the same, hence this sale. Consideration: $500. Signed: William N Jarrett. Witnesses: Nimrod Evans, M Evans, R Barkshire. Acknowledged in court, May 1809. Del: to Mr Enis Daugherty, May 1811. Recorded: OS 4:388-389.

15 April 1809. Samuel HANWAY and William G PAYNE to [presumably Dr Enos DAUGHERTY, although instrument does not specifically say so]. Release. On 4 September 1805 John Davis conveyed all his estate in lands and lots in Morgantown and in Monongalia, Harrison, Ohio, Brook, and Wood Co to the grantors, in trust to be divided among his creditors. One house and lot in Morgantown and an unimproved adjoining lot were encumbered by a previous deed of trust to secure $279 [sic] due to Reed and Ford. William N Jarrett, as trustee, has sold these lots. Due

to a scarcity of money and to avoid a sacrifice, Jarrett did not make a public sale for ready money but instead sold privately to Dr Enos Daugherty, for $500. Of this sum, $221 is payable to Hanway and Payne in bar iron, for the use of Davis' just creditors in proportion to their claims. They release title under the conveyance to them. Consideration: none stated. Signed: Samuel Hanway, Wm G Payne. Witnesses: R Barkshire, Joseph Laury, Fielding Kyger. Acknowledged in court, May 1809. No delivery shown. Recorded: OS 4:390.

10 April 1809. Philip and Mary PEARCE, Fayett Co, PA, to Dudley EVANS. 176 acres on Little Papaw, including Pearce's 1775 settlement. No adjoiners named. Consideration: $440. Signed: Philip Pearce [Mary does not sign]. Witnesses: Wm G Pane, French S Gray, Richard Wells. Proved by witnesses, May 1809. Del: to him, 20 September [?] 1813. Recorded: OS 4:390-391.

[blank] April 1809. Morgan MORGAN to his son James MORGAN. 200 acres on Pine Fork of Pricketts Creek, no adjoiners named. Moiety of a 400 acre patent to John Plum and Isaac Pricket, 7 September 1789, and conveyed to Morgan by Plum in 1790. Excepting 60 acres on the south side of the tract conveyed to William Wilson. Consideration: $20. Signed: Morgan Morgan. Witnesses: B Reeder, French S Gray, Rawley Martin. Proved by witnesses, May 1809. Del: to his son, 2 September 1845. Recorded: OS 4:391-392.

18 March 1809. Josiah and Jane ROBE to James Smallwood WILSON. 30 acres on Deckers Creek, no adjoiners named. Part of a tract patented to William Robe, deceased. Consideration: $115. Signed: Josiah Robe, Jane Robe. Witnesses: B Reeder, Wm N Jarrett, Jas McVicker. Receipt for consideration money. Acknowledged by Jane Robe before B Reeder and Wm N Jarrett, JPs, 18 March 1809. Proved by witnesses, 8/10 May 1809. Del: to James S Wilson, 7 July 1809. Recorded: OS 4:392-393.

10 April 1809. William PETTY JOHN and John PETTY JOHN, both of Highland Co, OH, by their attorney [not named in instrument], and John and Martha POWERS to Mathew FLEMING Sr. 192 acres east of Monongalia River, near the mouth of Punking Run, adjoining Jordan Hall and Arthur Trader. Patented to William Petty John, deceased, 1 March 1785. Conveyance to take effect after the death of Ruth Little, now wife of James Little. Consideration: $300. Signed: William Haymond, John Powers, Jno Evans [sic; his involvement not specified; Martha Powers does not sign]. Witnesses: George S Dering, French S Gray, Robt Hawthorn, Nimrod Evans. Proved by witnesses, May

1809. Del: to Wm [?] Fleming, 20 July 1811. Recorded: OS 4:394.

10 April 1809. William PETTY JOHN and John PETTY JOHN, both of Highland Co, OH, by their attorney in fact, William HAYMOND Jr, and John and Martha POWER to John BONNER. 60 acres on the side of Tygers Valey River, adjoining Petty John and Jordan Hall. Part of a tract patented to William Petty John, deceased, and willed by him to William and John Petty John and John Power. Consideration: $60. Signed: Wm Haymond, John Power, Jno Evans [as above]. Witnesses: French S Gray, George S Dering, Robt Hawthorn, Nimrod Evans. Proved by witnesses, May 1809. Del: to him, 7 December 1815. Recorded: OS 4:395.

10 April 1809. Caleb and Sarah FURBEY to George FURBAY. 268 acres on Pappaa Creek, adjoining Andrew Daugherty and Augustus Ballah. Part of a 400 acre patent. Consideration: $300. Signed: Caleb Furbee [Sarah does not sign]. Witnesses: French S Gray, Nimrod Evans, Thos Wilson. Proved by witnesses, May 1809. Del: to him, 30 December 1809. Recorded: OS 4:396.

8 May 1809. John and Mary Ann WELLS to Thomas WELLS. 100 acres adjoining Richard Wells, David Scott, H B Wilson, Daniel Knox, and Hoskinson's improvement. Part of a larger tract conveyed by John Gallaspie to Samuel Smith, 19 June 1797, and by Smith to Wells. Consideration: $400. Signed: John Wells [Mary Ann does not sign]. Witnesses: none. Acknowledged in court by John Wells, May 1809, and recorded as to him. Del: to R Wells, 9 November 1810. Recorded: OS 4:397.

24 March 1809. William and Hannah CHIPPS to Thomas R CHIPPS. Moiety of 171 acres, 110 perches on West [word missing], adjoining William Chipps and McFarland. Part of a tract conveyed by William Orson to Thomas R Chipps, 30 June 1795, recorded in District Court Deedbook 1, page 168. Consideration: $1000, VA. Signed: William Chipps, Hannah [0] Chipps. Witnesses: Wm N Jarrett, D Evans, James McVicker. Acknowledged by Hannah Chipps before Wm N Jarrett and D Evans, JPs, 24 March 1809. Proved by witness McVicker, May 1809. No delivery shown. Recorded: OS 4:398-399.

8 April 1809. John and Catherine RAMSEY to Samuel JACKSON, Washington Twp, Fayette Co, PA. 2 tracts: 388 acres on Cheat River, adjoining Francis Warman's heirs and William Norris. Surveyed 6 November 1806 upon a grant of 1 May 1784 [sic]. Half of 273 acres on Cheat River, adjoining James Moore. Patented to John Ramsey and James Shaw, 9 May 1796. Consideration: $1000, VA.

Signed: John Ramsey, Catherine Ramsey. Witnesses: R Barkshire, Wm N Jarrett, Thos Wilson. Memo notes that 38 acres, 35 perches of the tract was previously conveyed to Jackson by deed of 8 March 1803 and admitted to record in June 1805. Signed: Saml Jackson. Witnesses: Wm N Jarrett, Thos Wilson. Acknowledged by Catherine Ramsey before R Barkshire and Wm N Jarrett, JPs, 6 April 1809. Proved by witnesses, May 1809. No delivery shown. Recorded: OS 4:400-401.

14 April 1809. Nicholas CASEY to James PARSONS, Hampshire Co. 4 tracts: 400 acres at Dunker Bottom on Cheat River, adjoining Thomas Butler and including his [whose?] actual settlement made in 1766. Tract conveyed by Andrew and Eve Ramsey to Casey, 7 May 1795, recorded in District Court. 100 acres on the east side of Cheat, adjoining Henry Richards, James Morgan, and Thomas Butler. Conveyed by Andrew and Eve Ramsey to Casey, 2 May 1795, recorded in District Court. 100 acres on the east side of Cheat, adjoining Henry Richards, Joseph Butler, and Thomas Butler. Conveyed by Andrew and Eve Ramsey [date blank], recorded in District Court. 240 acres on the east side of Cheat, adjoining Henry Richards. Patented to George Riddle and conveyed by him to John Butler, and by John and Sarah Butler to Casey, 14 December 1801, recorded in county court. Consideration: $12,000. Signed: Nicholas Casey. Witnesses: none. Acknowledged in Hampshire Co, 17 April 1809. Certificate of Andrew Woodrow, CHC. Del: to him, September 1810. Recorded: OS 4:402-404.

6 February 1809. William PETTY JOHN and John PETTY JOHN, both of Highland Co, OH, to William HAYMOND Jr. Power of attorney to sell 3 tracts: 200 acres on Monongalia and Tygers Valey Rivers, including the parcel where Griffeth now lives. An adjoining tract where John Bonner lives. Tract on Glady Creek assigned to John Petty John in the division of his father's land. Signed: William Petty John, John [+] Petty John. Witnesses: none. Acknowledged in Highland Co, OH, before George Caley, JP, 6 February 1809. Certificate of Allen Trumble, CHC, and Richard Evans, associate judge. No delivery shown. Recorded: OS 4:404-405.

8 May 1809. Sias BILLINGSLY to Francis BILLINGSLY. 154 acres on Scotts Mill Run, adjoining Christopher Raver. Part of a 400 acre patent. Consideration: $100, VA. Signed: Sias Billingsly. Witnesses: none. Acknowledged in court, May 1809. Del: 8 May 1832. Recorded: OS 4:406.

6 April 1809. John and Eve BENNETT to Lewis WOOLF.

131 acres adjoining Joshua Jenkins' heirs, Jacob Noose, Farquer McCrea, and Hawthorn. Conveyed to Bennett by Jacob and Elizabeth Noose, 17 May 1799. Consideration: $400, VA. Signed: John Bennett, Elizabeth [|] Bennett. Witnesses: Nimrod Evans, French S Gray, B Reeder, all as to Bennett. Acknowledged by Elizabeth Bennett before R Barkshire and B Reeder, JPs, 6 April 1809. Proved by witnesses, May 1809. Del: to him, November 1810. Recorded: OS 4:407-408.

16 January 1809. Isaac PRICKETT, OH, to James MORGAN. 93 acres on Buffaloe Lick Run, adjoining Joshua Hickman, Jeremiah Gallihue, John Carpenter. Consideration: $1. Signed: Isaac [mark] Prickett, by Henry Dunn, his attorney [sic], Polly [m] Prickett. Witnesses: Bernard Thompson, James Thompson. Acknowledged by Polly Prickett in Adams Co, OH, before William Lacock and John Linsey, JPS. Certificate of Joseph Dartwiler, clerk of common pleas court. No delivery shown. Recorded: OS 4:409-410.

21 March 1809. Francis and Ann COLLINS to John DOWNER. 83 acres adjoining Samuel Luellen, Widow Jenkins, and Charles Donaldson, tract where Samuel Luellen used to live. Consideration: $382, VA. Signed: Francis Collins, Ann Collins. Witnesses: John Jackson, John Watson, Owen Hawker. Acknowledged in court, June 1809. Del: to him, April 1810. Recorded: OS 4:411.

13 June 1809. Joseph and Elizabeth ALLEN to Leonard CUP Jr. 75 acres adjoining Jacob Pindel. Part of a 157½ acre survey. Consideration: $100. Signed: Joseph Allen, Elizabeth [+] Allen. Witnesses: none. Acknowledged in court, June 1809. Del: to Leonard Cup Jr, 3 October 1811. Recorded: OS 4:412.

19 April 1809. Rebecca WILSON, widow of William WILSON deceased, to Benjamin WILSON. Release of all her dower in the real estate of William Wilson, deceased. Consideration: $110. Signed: Rebecca Wilson. Witnesses: B Reeder, Thos McKinley, Davis Shockley. Proved by witnesses, June 1809. No delivery shown. Recorded: OS 4:413.

13 April 1809. Russel POTTER, Butler Co, OH, to Nimrod EVANS. Power of attorney to recover various notes on A and S Woodrow and Elihu Horton. Signed: Russel Potter. Witnesses: Levi Potter. Acknowledged in Butler Co, OH, April 1809. Certificate of John Reily, clerk. Del: to attorney, 25 June 1821. Recorded: OS 4:413-414.

24 March 1809. William and Hannah CHIPPS to James McVICKER. 143 acres, 110 perches at Wests Run, adjoining Thomas R Chipps, heirs of Thomas Pindall, William

McCleery, and Hugh Sidwell. Part of a tract conveyed by William Orson and wife to Thomas Chipps, 13 June 1795, recorded in District Court deedbook 1, page 168. Consideration: $1000. Signed: William Chipps, Hannah Chipps. Witnesses: Wm N Jarrett, M Evans, Wm Tingle, Z Morgan. Acknowledged by Hannah Chipps before R Barkshire and Wm N Jarrett, JPs, 24 March 1809. Proved by witnesses, April and June 1809. Del: to grantee, 13 August 1821. Recorded: OS 4:414-416.

16 November 1808. Henry and [blank throughout instrument] MILEY, Fayett Co, PA, to George RICH. 100 acres on Dunkard Creek, no adjoiners named. Conveyed to Henry by Abraham and Elizabeth Miley, 14 December 1801. Consideration: [blank]. Signed: Henry Miley, Ruth Miley. Witnesses: William Roun[remainder illegible, partly erased], David Porter. Acknowledged in Fayette Co, PA, 23 November 1808. Certificates of Sam Roberts, president of common pleas court, and Ephraim Douglass, prothonotary. Del: to him, 24 May 1813. Recorded: OS 4:416-418.

23 July 1808. Robert SCOTT to William N JARRETT. Deed of trust. By his note, Scott owes $194 to Nimrod Evans, payable in 6 months. To secure payment he conveys 100 acres adjoining Thomas Wilson and William Burrows. Tract conveyed by David Scott the elder. Description refers to division line between Robert Scott and heirs of Elijah Burrows. Note to be paid by 22 February 1809. Signed: Robert Scott, Nimrod Evans, Wm N Jarrett. Witnesses: John Stealey, M Evans, French S Gray. Proved by witnesses, June 1809. Del: 25 June 1821. Recorded: OS 4:418-420.

29 August 1807. Isaac PRICKET, OH, to Joshua HICKMAN. 68 acres on Buffellow Lick Run, adjoining John Megee, William Miller and John Carpenter, and James Morgan. Consideration: $1. Signed: Isaac [+] Prickett, Polly [m] Prickett. Witnesses: Bernard Thompson, James Thompson. Acknowledged in Clermont Co, OH, before Bernard Thompson, JP. Certificate of Roger W Waring, clerk. Del: to J Hickman, 13 February 1810. Recorded: OS 4:420-421.

21 September 1808. Henry HIGHSHEW to Stephen MORGAN, sheriff of Monongalia Co. One equal half of 273 acres on Cheat River, adjoining Charles Scott. Tract conveyed to Henry and David Highshew by James and Margaret Brumagin, as recorded in District Court. Purpose of the conveyance is for Henry to be discharged as an insolvent debtor and to settle an execution in favour of James Walls against Henry, as far as it will

go. Consideration: of the premises above. Signed: Henry [H] Highshew. Witnesses: R Barkshire, M Evans, Wm G Payne. Proved by witnesses, June 1809. No delivery shown. Recorded: OS 4:421.

19 November 1808. John C PAYNE, deputy sheriff of Stephen MORGAN, sheriff of Monongalia Co, to James WALLS. Half of 273 acres on Cheat, adjoining Charles Scott, or whatever right Henry Highshew actually has in the property. Land is sold as conveyed to the sheriff by Highshew and warrants no other right than what Highshew had in the property when he gave his schedule as an insolvent debtor. Consideration: $87.54. Signed: John C Payne. Witnesses: Rawley Scott, B Reeder, Mathew Gay. Acknowledged in court, June 1809. Del: to James Walls, 2 May 1810. Recorded: OS 4:421-422.

12 June 1809. William and Hannah CHIPPS to Jacob PINDALL. 61 acres adjoining Thomas Chipps, Amos Roberts, and William Jarvis. Consideration: $300, VA. Signed: William Chipps, Hannah Chipps. Witnesses: none. Acknowledged in court, June 1809. Del: to Jacob Pindall, 28 October 1822 [?]. Recorded: OS 4:422.

12 June 1809. Thomas and Isabel MORGAN and David MORGAN, all of Fayett Co, PA, to Isaac BARB. 250 acres on Beaver and Little Sandy Creeks, known as Morgan's glade. No adjoiners named. Consideration: £100. Signed: Thomas Morgan, Isabel [X] Morgan, David Morgan. Witnesses: none. Acknowledged in court, June 1809. Del: to him, 14 August 1810. Recorded: OS 4:423.

15 December 1801. Abraham and Elizabeth MILEY to Henry MILEY, Fayette Co, PA. 100 acres at Dunkard Creek, on the PA line. No adjoiners named. Part of a patent to Simon Troy, 27 January 1787. Consideration: £100. Signed: Abraham Miley, Elizabeth Miley "wrote in dutch." Acknowledged in court by Abraham, December 1801; by Elizabeth, June 1809. No delivery shown. Recorded: OS 4:423-424.

6 July 1809. Meshach and Hannah SEXTON to Peter MYRES, all of Green Co, PA. 1560 acres on the left hand fork of the three forks of Dunkard Creek, no adjoiners named. Part of a tract deeded to Sexton by the marshal of the state of VA, 26 March 1805. Consideration: $1500. Signed: Meshach Sexton, Hannah Sexton. Witnesses: William Dakan, Chesman Drake, Bengamine Allton, William Young. Proved by witnesses, June 1809, and recorded as to Meshach. Del: to Peter Myres, 22 September 1809. Recorded: OS 4:424-425.

1 June 1809. Meshach and Hannah SEXTON to William DAKIN, all of Green Co, PA. 230 acres on the left hand

fork of the three forks of Dunkard Creek, adjoining Peter Myres. Part of a tract deeded to Sexton by the mareschal of the state of VA, 26 March 1805. Consideration: $230. Signed: Meshach Sexton, Hannah Sexton. Witnesses: Peter Myres, Benjamin Allton, William Young, Chesman Drake. Proved by witnesses, June 1809, and recorded as to Meshach. Del: to Jas Morgan, November 1811. Recorded: OS 4:426.

1 June 1809. Meshach and Hannah SEXTON to William DAKIN, all of Green Co, PA. 370 acres on Merrical Run, a branch of Dunkard Creek, adjoining Benjamine Allton. Part of a tract deeded to Sexton by the mareschal of the state of VA, 26 March 1805. Consideration: $370. Signed: Meshach Sexton, Hannah Sexton. Witnesses: Peter Myres, Benjamin Allton, William Young, Chesman Drake. Proved by witnesses, June 1809, and recorded as to Meshach. Del: to Jas Morgan, November 1811. Recorded: OS 4:426-427.

1 June 1809. Meshach and Hannah SEXTON to Benjamine ALLTON, all of Green Co, PA. 350 acres on Maracle Run, a branch of Dunkard Creek, no adjoiners named. Part of a tract deeded to Sexton by the mareschal of the state of VA, 26 March 1805. Consideration: $100. Signed: Meshach Sexton, Hannah Sexton. Witnesses: Peter Myres, Chesman Drake, William Dakin, William Young. Proved by witnesses, June 1809, and recorded as to Meshach. Del: to B Allton, 24 August 1809. Recorded: OS 4:427-428.

1 June 1809. Meshach and Hannah SEXTON to William YOUNG, all of Green Co, PA. 100 acres on Maracle Run, a branch of Dunkard Creek, adjoining Joseph Thomas. Part of a tract deeded to Sexton by the mareschal of the state of VA, 26 March 1805. Consideration: $100. Signed: Meshach Sexton, Hannah Sexton. Witnesses: Peter Myres, Benjamin Allton, William Dakin, Chesman Drake. Proved by witnesses, June 1809, and recorded as to Meshach. Del: to [erased], 1809. Recorded: OS 4:428-429.

1 June 1809. Meshach and Hannah SEXTON to Chesman DRAKE, all of Green Co, PA. 96 acres on Maracle Run, a branch of Dunkard Creek, no adjoiners named. Part of a tract deeded to Sexton by the mareschal of the state of VA, 26 March 1805. Consideration: $100. Signed: Meshach Sexton, Hannah Sexton. Witnesses: Peter Myres, Benjamine Allton, William Young, William Dakin. NB: the metes and bounds, as given in the deed, interfere about 4 3/4 acres with William Dakin but it is understood that Dakin holds the interfering land. Proved by witnesses, June 1809, and recorded as to Meshach. Del: to Joshua Coob, 21 March 1810. Recorded: OS 4:429-430.

30 March 1809. Meshach and Hannah SEXTON to Edward

MERCER and James MORGAN, all of Green Co, PA. 200 acres on Marracles Run, a branch of Dunkard Creek, adjoining Alexander Clegg. From a tract sold for nonpayment of the direct tax and deeded to Meshach by Joseph Scott, US Martial for the District of VA, 1805. Consideration: $200. Signed: Meshach Sexton, Hannah Sexton. Witnesses: William Dakin, Chesman Drake, William Young. Proved by witnesses, June 1809, and recorded as to Meshach. Del: to J Morgan, 15 August 1810. Recorded: OS 4:430-431.

[blank] 1809. Mathias FURBAY to John ARNETT. 154 acres on Big Sappa [sic] Creek, adjoining John Furbay. Consideration: $700. Signed: Mathias [M] Furbey. Witnesses: none. Acknowledged in court, June 1809. Del: to Wm G Payne his atto, 13 January 1814. Recorded: OS 4:431-432.

4 January 1809. Robert WOODS to Amos GLOVER and Henry WOODS. Bill of sale for all his livestock, farming utensils, household furniture. NB: Woods has already sold and delivered hay, wheat, and rye. Consideration: $130. Signed: Robert Woods. Witnesses: Alexander Brandon, James Guthrie. Proved by witnesses, June 1809. No delivery shown. Recorded: OS 4:432.

19 November 1808. William G PAYNE to John PAYNE. Trustee's deed. 200 acres on the west side of Cheat River, conveyed by Cornelius and Orpha King to William G Payne, trustee for James Mann (who has since assigned his right to John Roberts). Reference is made to deeds from Jesse Payne to James Mann, James Mann to Cornelius King, and King's deed of trust to William G Payne. Title is warranted against King or those claiming under him only. Consideration: $66 (@ 33¢ per acre). Signed: William G Payne. Witnesses: A Woodrow, Joseph Allen, French S Gray. Acknowledged in court, June 1809. Del: to Jno Payne, 11 April 1810. Recorded: OS 4:432-433.

20 October 1808. Peter FORTNEY Sr to Henry FORTNEY and Peter FORTNEY Jr. 335 acres on the middle fork of Three Forks. No adjoiners named. Consideration: $1000. Signed: Peter Fortney. Witnesses: David [+] Grim, John Fortney, Henry [^] Fortney. Proved by witnesses, June 1809. No delivery shown. Recorded: OS 4:433-434.

12 June 1809. Caleb and Sarah FURBEY to James ARNETT. 116 acres on Little Papaw, adjoining Richard Price, Augustus Ballah, and Daniel Musgrave's and Matthias Furbey's parts of the original 400 acre tract. Consideration: $300. Signed: Caleb Furbee, Sarah Furbee. Witnesses: none. Acknowledged in court, June 1809. Del: to himselfe, 4 April 1810. Recorded: OS 4:434.

[blank] 1809. Isaac and Elizabeth POWELL to Joseph

POWELL. 100 acres on Tyger Valey River, opposite the mouth of Lost Run, adjoining Jacob Hampton. Part of 2 tracts patented to Thomas Wilson: 862 acres patented 26 July 1798 and 400 acres patented 22 January 1800. Consideration: $500, VA. Signed: Isaac Powell, Elizabeth Powell. Witnesses: none. Acknowledged in court, June 1809. Del: to Joseph Powell, 12 October 1809. Recorded: OS 4:435.

[blank] 1809. Isaac and Elizabeth POWELL to Jacob VANDEGRAPP, Whashinton [sic] Co, PA. 100 acres adjoining Richard Nuzum, John Nuzum, and Jacob Hampton. Part of 2 tracts patented to Thomas Wilson: 862 acres patented 26 July 1798 and 400 acres patented 22 January 1800. Consideration: $200, VA. Signed: Isaac Powell, Elizabeth Powell. Witnesses: none. Acknowledged in court, June 1809. Del: to Wm Fosset, 14 September 1809. Recorded: OS 4:435-436.

13 February 1809. George and Mary WILSON to Thomas WELLS. 65 3/4 acres, 34 perches on Monongalia River and Coburns Creek, adjoining George Dorsey, Moses Doolittle Sr, and Arthur Wilson. Consideration: $200. Signed: George [mark] Wilson, Mary [+] Wilson. Witnesses: none. Acknowledged in court, June 1809. Del: to Thos Wells, 18 July 1810. Recorded: OS 4:436-437.

[blank] 1809. Caleb and Sarah FURBEY to David MUSGRAVE. 119 acres on Little Pappaw, adjoining Matthias Furbey and Richard Price. Part of a 400 acre patent. Consideration: $150, VA. Signed: Caleb Furbee, Sarah Furbee. Witnesses: none. Acknowledged in court, June 1809. No delivery shown. Recorded: OS 4:437-438.

12 June 1809. George and Leddy WILSON to Archibald WILSON. 57 acres adjoining Jeptha Wilkinson. Part of a patent to Rice Bullock and Richard Merryfield, 11 April 1793. Consideration: $100. Signed: George Wilson, Lidia Wilson. Witnesses: none. Acknowledged in court, June 1809. Del: to Arch Wilson, 9 April 1810. Recorded: OS 4:439.

16 January 1809. Levi LYNN, Washington Co, MD, to James WEBSTER. 400 acres on Big Beaver Dam Run, adjoining Joseph Severens. Consideration: £175. Signed: Levi Lynn. Witnesses: William Yates, John Hunter, John Oliver. Receipt for consideration money. Acknowledged by Levi Lynn and Mary his wife in Washington Co, MD, before William Yates and John Hunter, JPs, 16 January 1809. Certificate of O H Williams, clerk of Washington Co, OH [sic!]. Del: to him, July 1810. Recorded: OS 4:439-440.

20 June 1809. George and Mary ZINN to Jacob ZINN. 50 acres, no adjoiners or place names mentioned.

Consideration: $50. Signed: George Zinn [Mary does not sign]. Witnesses: Charles Byrn, Thomas Brown, George Ashby. Proved by witnesses, June 1809, and recorded as to George Zinn. Del: to Jacob Zinn, 30 May 1811. Recorded: OS 4:441-442.

10 April 1809. John and Jane LOUGH to John LOUGH Jr. 100 acres on Scotts Run, adjoining Joseph Lough and John Lough Sr. Part of a tract patented to John Cochran, 27 June 1791. Consideration: $20, VA. Signed: John Lough [Jane does not sign]. Witnesses: N Evans, French S Gray, Rawley Evans. Acknowledged by Jane Lough before B Reeder and John Stealey, JPs, 10 April 1809. Proved by witnesses, July 1809. Del: to himselfe [sic], 2 January 1810. Recorded: OS 4:442-443.

22 March 1808. Jacob FOULK to Abner MESSENGER. On [date blank] of this instant, Abner purchased the house and half lot where he now lives in Morgan Town, on Water Street adjoining Nicholas B Madira. Title to said lot had been in Benjamin Reeder, Esq, who made a deed to Messenger. Foulk has received full compensation from Messenger, who entertains doubt of the validity of Reeder's deed. Therefore, Foulk warrants the title. If Messenger is evicted or dispossessed, Foulk will repay him the $400 involved. Signed: Jacob Foulk. Witnesses: William Tingle, A Woodrow, Asa Harris, R Evans, William Tingle [sic], John Shisler. Proved by witnesses, March and July 1809. No delivery shown. Recorded: OS 4:443-444.

31 July 1809. Lester DICKINSON, formerly of Erie Co, PA, to John PHILLIPS, Greene Co, PA. 1000 acres on Statlers and Days Runs, branches of Dunkard Creek, adjoining Richard Tennant Sr and Michael Moore. Conveyed by Robert and Margaret Sterrett to Dickinson, 18 February 1806. Consideration: $3000. Signed: Lester Dickinson. Witnesses: Nimrod Evans, French S Gray, John Payne. Proved by witnesses, August 1809. No delivery shown. Recorded: OS 4:444-445.

8 March 1809. Alpheus WICKWARE by his attorney in fact, Samuel WICKWARE, both of Barren Co, KY, to John STEALEY of Monongalia and Jesse EVANS of Fayette Co, PA. 359 acres on Tyger Valey River and Wickwares Creek, no adjoiners named. Patented to John Wickware on a settlement certificate, 1 September 1783. Consideration: $800. Signed: Samuel Wickware. Witnesses: Wm Tingle, Rawley Scott, Fielding Kiger. Proved by witnesses, August 1809. Del: to grantee, 19 December 1821. Recorded: OS 4:445-446.

13 July 1809. Jacob and Elizabeth FOULK to John

STEALEY. Lot [# not shown] at the mouth of Deckers Creek, purchased by Foulk from Thomas and Catherine Evans in 180[blank]. Consideration: $50. Signed: Jacob Foulk [Elizabeth does not sign]. Witnesses: Rawley Scott, S Woodrow, Jacob Stealey 2nd, Moses Doolittle. Acknowledged in court by Jacob Foulk, August 1809, and recorded as to him. Del: to grantee, 19 December 1821. Recorded: OS 4:446-447.

13 July 1809. Leonard M DEAKINS and John HOY, executors and devisees of Francis DEAKINS, deceased, to George JOHNSON, all of George Town, DC. On 28 September 1802 Francis Deakins conveyed to John Bowie, Montgomery Co, MD, Lots #1, 2, 13, 14, 25, and 26 in the town of Mt Carmel. Bowie neglected to have the deed recorded within the time prescribed by VA law, and it became defective. On 18 November 1806 Bowie sold the lots to John Hoy. Consideration: $1, and the premises. Signed: L M Deakins, John Hoye. Witness: Thomas Corcoran. Acknowledged in George Town, DC, 13 July 1809. Certificate of Thomas Corcoran, mayor. Del: to John Hoy, 11 June 1811. Recorded: OS 4:447-449.

21 October 1809. Alpheus WICKWARE [by his attorney in fact, Samuel WICKWARE, though the instrument does not so specify], Barren Co, KY, to William McDANIEL. 150 acres on the east side of Tiger Valey River, adjoining lands surveyed for John Wickware, David Sayre, and Robinson. Consideration: $80. Signed: Samuel Wickware. Witnesses: E Daugherty, Mathew Gay, C Barkshire, Zackquil Morgan. Proved by witnesses, August 1809. Del: to him, 11 June 1811. Recorded: OS 4:449.

15 August 1809. John and Prudence STEALEY to Daniel LANTZ, Alleganey Co, MD. 1224 acres adjoining Thomas Chaney, Samuel Worrel Sr, David Frazee, and Ephraim Frazee, and consisting of 2 original patents to Richard Maurice and another to John Stealey [dates blank]. Consideration: $5000, VA. Signed: John Stealey, Prudence [mark called for but not shown] Stealey. Witnesses: none. Acknowledged in court, August 1809. Del: "sent to D Lance by A Warninger" 28 August 1809. Recorded: OS 4:450-451.

27 July 1808. Leonard M DEAKINS and John HOY, executors and devisees of Francis DEAKINS, deceased, who was executor and devisee of William DEAKINS, deceased, all of George Town, DC, to Samuel WARD and Elizabeth FRIEND, Alleganey Co, MD. 130 acres on the west side and near the head of Spring Run, a branch of Buffellow Run, on the north side of Netley [?] Ridge, no adjoiners named. Patented to William Deakins, 21 August 1787.

Gabriel Friend did contract with Francis and William Deakins in their lifetime to locate certain VA land warrants, for which he was to receive a certain portion of the lands. At Friend's request, this tract was conveyed to W Ward. The deed was later destroyed or lost, and Friend has requested the executors to reconvey the tract to Samuel Ward and Elizabeth Friend, who he states to be the legal heirs of the said Ward. Consideration: $1. Grantors are not liable for the title or for any loss. Signed: L M Deakins, John Hoye. Witnesses: none. Acknowledged in George Town, DC, 27 July 1808. Certificate of Thos Corcoran, mayor. Del: to J Severns, 13 November 1810. Recorded: OS 4:451-452.

14 July 1809. George JOHNSON, Washington Co, DC [sic], to John HOYE, of the USA. Lots #1, 2, 13, 14, 25, and 26 in Mt Carmel. Conveyed to him by Leonard M Deakins and John Hoye, 13 July 1809. Consideration: $1. Grantor is not liable for the title, as he conveys only the title he derived from previous grantors. Signed: Geo Johnson. Witness: Thos Corcoran. Acknowledged in George Town, DC, 14 July 1809. Certificate of Thos Corcoran, mayor. Del: to John Hoy, 11 June 1811. Recorded: OS 4:452-453.

13 July 1809. Jacob FOULK to John STEALEY. Right of way bond. Jacob and Elizabeth Foulk have conveyed to John Stealey a lot [# not shown] at the mouth of Deckers Creek, for the express purpose of building a warehouse. On inspection, there is not sufficient room for a yard. Therefore Foulk conveys part of another lot for a yard to the premises. If he thinks proper, Zackquill Morgan may move the house presently on the lot a distance of 3 feet (no more than 4 feet) onto the "priviledged ground." Consideration: none stated. Signed: Jacob Foulk. Witnesses: Rawley Scott, Jacob Stealey, S Woodrow. Acknowledged in court, August 1809. Del: to grantee, 19 December 1821. Recorded: OS 4:453-454.

17 March 1806. Charles and Martha BENNET to Polly BILLINGSLEY, wife of Francis BILLINGSLEY. 100 acres on both sides of Coburns Creek, adjoining Philip Smell. Part of a tract conveyed by Thomas McGee in 17[blank]. Consideration: $350. Signed: Charles [C] Bennet, Martha [X] Bennet. Witnesses: B Reeder, Augustus Werninger, Thomas Miller. Acknowledged by Martha before B Reeder and Thos Miller, JPs, 17 March 1806. Proved by witnesses, June 1808 and August 1809. Del: to Jas Randall, 7 October 1812. Recorded: OS 4:454-456.

27 April 1809. William and Grace SCRIPS to Henry HAMELTON. 70 acres on the road from Morgan Town to

Clarks Burg, no adjoiners named. Patented to Scripps, assignee of John Plum, 26 July 1796. Consideration: $300. Signed: W Scripps, Grace Scripps. Witnesses: Archibald Hamilton, John Jolliffe, James Hamilton. Acknowledged in court, August 1809. Del: to him, 15 October 1810. Recorded: OS 4:456-457.

27 April 1809. James MORGAN to John MILLER. Mortgage on 2 tracts: 50 acres purchased from Jacob Pricket Jr, and 120 acres conveyed by Jacob Prickett Sr, by his attorney in fact James Prickett. Morgan has sold Miller 115 acres and the present conveyance is to secure that he will support title of that parcel. If Miller is not dispossessed of the land, this deed to be of no effect. Signed: James Morgan. Witnesses: William Hays, Thos Knight, William G Payne. Proved by witnesses, August 1809. Del: to Miller, 31 August 1810. Recorded: OS 4:457.

5 April 1809. Joseph and Jane WISBY to Philip WAGNER. 30 acres adjoining Elijah Hereman. Part of a divided tract conveyed by Joseph Wisby Sr to his heirs and part of a tract conveyed by Abraham Wells to Joseph Wisby Jr. Consideration: $157. Signed: Joseph Wisby, Jane [X] Wisby. Witnesses: Jacob Polsley, John Nuzum, Joseph Foreman. Acknowledged by Jane Wisby before John Nuzum and Jacob Polsley, JPs, 5 April 1809; by Joseph Wisby in court, August 1809. Del: to Jacob Wagner pr order, 13 September 1810. Recorded: OS 4:457-459.

14 August 1809. Thomas and Isabella MORGAN, Fayette Co, PA, to Jacob THOMAS. 225 acres on Muddy Creek, no adjoiners named. Consideration: $100. Signed: Thomas Morgan, Isabella [X] Morgan. Witnesses: none. Acknowledged in court, August 1809. Del: to Isaac Barb, 14 August 1810. Recorded: OS 4:459-460.

14 August 1809. Jeremiah and Jemima BIGGS to William JONES. 100 acres on Mericls Run, a branch of Dunkard Creek, adjoining Eliazer Biggs, Pinehas Kellam, and Andrew Casto. Patented to Zephaniah Martin, 27 March 1789, and conveyed by Zephaniah and Elizabeth Martin to Jeremiah Biggs, 8 March 1802. Consideration: $100, VA. Signed: Jeremiah Biggs, Jamima Biggs. Witnesses: none. Acknowledged in court, August, 1809. No delivery shown. Recorded: OS 4:460.

26 June 1809. James and Sarah DUNN to David GALLAWAY. 105 acres adjoining Francis Tibbs, Christopher Troy, and Jona Vandevort. Part of a tract patented to Simon Troy in 178[blank], and devised by him to his son James, who conveyed to Isaac Mathew, 12 October 1801, and by him to James Dunn, 14 June 1802. Consideration:

$405, VA. Signed: James Dunn, Sarah Dunn. Witnesses: R Barkshire, Wm N Jarrett, French S Gray. Acknowledged by Sarah Dunn before Wm N Jarrett and R Barkshire, JPs, 26 June 1809. Proved by witnesses, August 1809. Del: to him, 12 August 1813. Recorded: OS 4:461-462.

12 July 1809. Simon REEDER to John Abraham GUSEMAN. Part of a lot [# not shown] in Morgan Town, adjoining Col Hanway, the Publick ground, and the porch at John Cooper's house. Conveyed by Thomas Pindall to Benjamin Reeder and by Benjamin to Simon. Consideration: $400. Signed: Simon Reeder. Witnesses: Nicholas B Medera, A Woodrow, George Jacob Baltzel. Acknowledged in court, August 1809. Del: to him, 19 March 1811. Recorded: OS 4:462-464.

[blank] August 1809. William and Jane TINGLE to Enos DAUGHERTY, all of Morgan Town. Lot [# not shown] in Morgan Town, on the north side, adjoining the 5-acre lot of Henry Dering's heirs and Tingle's other lot. Conveyed by Robert Minnis to Samuel Hanway, 9 June 1807, and by Hanway to Tingle, 15 July 1809. Consideration: $1. Signed: Wm Tingle [Jane does not sign]. Witnesses: none. Acknowledged in court by William Tingle, August 1809, and recorded as to him. No delivery shown. Recorded: OS 4:464.

9 January 1809. Thomas and Olive MARTIN to Mary BENNETT. 200 acres on Threefork Creek, no adjoiners named. Part of Martin's 1200 acre survey. Consideration: $[blank], VA. Signed: Thomas Martin [Olive does not sign]. Witnesses: Wm Tingle as to Thos Martin, C Barkshire, Mathew Gay, R Barkshire. Proved by witnesses, August 1809. Del: to her, 10 April 1815. Recorded: OS 4:465.

18 April 1809. James and Mary TARNEY to Joseph PECKENPAUGH. 55 acres, 29 poles, adjoining William Russel, Samuel Gooding, and John McKinley. Part of 345 acres patented to Thomas Russel, 4 July 1788, and conveyed to James Tarney, 8 April 1805. Consideration: $300, VA. Signed: James Tarney, Mary [+] Tarney. Witnesses: French S Gray, R Barkshire, Wm N Jarrett. Acknowledged by Mary Tarney before R Barkshire and Wm N Jarrett, JPs, 18 April 1809. Proved by witnesses, August 1809. Del: to him, 7 July 1815. Recorded: OS 4:466-467.

24 March 1809. Thomas R and Rachel CHIPPS to William CHIPPS. Moiety of 101 acres, 110 perches on Wests Run, adjoining Thomas' other land. Conveyed by William Orson to Thomas, 30 June 1795, recorded in District Court deedbook 1, page 168. Consideration: $1000, VA. Signed: Thomas R [X] Chipps, Rachel Chipps.

Witnesses: Wm N Jarrett, Jacob Pindall, D Evans. Acknowledged by Rachel before Wm N Jarrett and D Evans, JPs, 24 March 1809. Proved by witnesses, April and August 1809. No delivery shown. Recorded: OS 4:467-469.

28 April 1809. WILL of William WATSON. Wife Jany: house for her lifetime and thirds of the property. Son Jacob: homeplace at death of wife, as well as the tools now on the property. Son William: place he lives on. Son David: tract at the end of the hill near the glade, where he formerly lived. Son John: equal share in the land but to take none of the improvements. The boys to pay the girls $80 each in good trade, at the end of 3 years. Granddaughter Nansy: $80 when she comes of age; also to have her schooling. Executors: son David and wife Jeany. Signed: William Watson. Witnesses: Jonathan Cobun, James A Watton, Jer Tannehill. Proved by witnesses, June and August 1809. Recorded: OS 4:469. [Also recorded in Wills, 1:334.]

9 June 1809. John and Polly SCOTT, Springfield Twp, Hammilton Co, OH, to William N JARRETT. 93 acres at Muddy Creek, adjoining John Runyon, David Morgan, and William Biggs. Patented to John Scott, 27 February 1805. Consideration: $300. Signed: John Scott, Mary Scott. Witnesses: William Laury, Zephh Hart, RS [?] Thomas. Acknowledged in Warren Co, OH, 23 June 1810. Certificate of David Sutton, Clerk of Common Pleas. Del: to Wm N Jarrett, 16 September 1809. Recorded: OS 4:470-471.

12 September 1809. William BUCKHANNON to Isaac REED. 30 acres, 51 poles, no adjoiners or place names mentioned. Part from the tract that Buckhannon lives on, and part from a patent of 2 December 1791. Consideration: $121.25. Signed: Wm Buckhannon. Witnesses: none. Acknowledged in court, September 1809. Del: to Isaac Reed, 1 April 1811. Recorded: OS 4:471-472.

12 September 1808 [sic]. William BUCKHANNON to Isaac REED. 109 acres adjoining Dr John Nicklin and Buckhannon's other lands. Consideration: $40. Signed: William Buckhannon. Witnesses: none. Acknowledged in court, September 1809. Del: to Isaac Reed, 1 April 1811. Recorded: OS 4:472-473.

12 September 1809. William BUCKHANNON to Benjamin HARTLEY. 69½ acres, 80 poles near Booths Creek. No adjoiners named. Part of a patent to Buckhannon and John Downard. Consideration: $174. Signed: William Buckhannon. Witnesses: none. Acknowledged in court, September 1809. Del: to him, 25 April 1811. Recorded: OS 4:473.

24 March 1809. James and Anny CURRY to Lewis JOHN. 50 acres at the falls of Laurel Run, adjoining William John and John McFarland. Part of 135 acres patented to William John, 17 August 1798, and conveyed by him to James Curry, 9 February 1800. Consideration: $150. Signed: James [+] Curry, Anny [X] Curry. Witnesses: James Adare, Owen John, Wm John. Proved by witnesses, September 1809, and recorded as to him. Del: to him, 4 February 1811. Recorded: OS 4:474.

11 September 1809. Cyus and Hannah BILLINGSLEY to Cyus BILLINGSLEY Jr. 110 acres on Scotts Mill Run, adjoining Christopher Raver. Part of a patent to Nicholas Horner. Consideration: $1. Signed: Cyus [X] Billingsley [Hannah does not sign]. Witnesses: none. Acknowledged by Cyus in court, September 1809, and recorded as to him. Del: to him, 12 December 1811. Recorded: OS 4:475.

12 September 1809. Corverdill and Sophia COLE to William COLE. 100 acres, no adjoiners or place names mentioned. Part of a larger tract patented to Abraham Hardin and conveyed by him [date blank] to Cole. Consideration: $500, VA. Signed: Corverdill Cole, Sophia [X] Cole. Witnesses: William Laury, Joseph Lowry, Hynson Cole. Acknowledged in court, September 1809. Del: to him, 22 August 1812. Recorded: OS 4:475-476.

15 April 1809. Jane MELEY, wife of George MELEY deceased, to Sarah DIEL [or DEIL]. All her dower interest in the plantation where she lives. Consideration: none stated. Signed: Jane [V] Meley. Witnesses: George Boydston Jr, David Boydston, Easther Boydston, George Boydston Sr. Proved by witnesses, September 1809. Del: to Davis Shockley, 4 December 1809. Recorded: OS 4:476-477.

9 September 1809. Corverdill and Sophia COLE to Hyson [Hynson in body of instrument] COLE. 113 acres, no adjoiners or place names mentioned. Part of a tract patented to Abraham Hardin, 6 December 1781, and conveyed by him to Cole, 14 March 1796. Consideration: $500, VA. Signed: Corverdill Cole, Sophia [X] Cole. Witnesses: Joseph Laury, Wm Laury, Wm Cole. Acknowledged in court, September 1809. Del: 15 November 1830. Recorded: OS 4:477-478.

12 September 1809. Corverdill and Sophia COLE to Joseph COLE. 100 acres, no place names or adjoiners mentioned. Part of 302 acres patented to John Shively 8 July 1788. Consideration: $500, VA. Signed: Corverdill Cole, Sophia [X] Cole. Witnesses: Joseph Laury, Wm Laury, Hynson Cole. Acknowledged in court, September

1809. Del: 15 November 1830. Recorded: OS 4:478-479.

12 September 1809. Corverdill and Sophia COLE to John DAVIS. 113 acres at the Mill Run, adjoining Philip Shively. Consideration: $500, VA. Signed: Corverdill Cole, Sophia [X] Cole. Witnesses: Joseph Laury, Wm Laury, Hynson Cole. Acknowledged in court, September 1809. No delivery shown. Recorded: OS 4:479-480.

11 September 1809. George SNIDER Sr to John HANTZEL. 200 acres, no adjoiners or place names mentioned. From a 400 acre patent of 8 October 1789. Consideration: $300, VA. Signed: George Snider. Witnesses: none. Acknowledged in court, September 1809. Del: to him, 16 May 1810. Recorded: OS 4:480.

26 May 1809. John and Elizabeth BRANT to Thomas PRITCHARD Jr. 1340 acres on the state road from Morgan Town to Dunkard Bottom, adjoining the Monongalia glades, Benjamin Reeder, Alexander Smith, William Manear, and Amos Holly. Consideration: $5000. Signed: John Brant "wrote in Dutch" [Elizabeth does not sign]. Witnesses: French S Gray as to him, Saml Lowry, Nimrod Evans, Jacob Foulk. Proved by witnesses, September 1809, and recorded as to him. Del: to him, 12 July 1814. Recorded: OS 4:481-482.

11 September 1809. Henry and Abigale BARRACKMAN to William POSTLEWAIT. 100 acres adjoining Postlewait's home place. Conveyed to Barrackman by Davis Shockley, 8 April 1805. Consideration: $1000, VA. Signed: Henry [X] Barrackman, Abigale [X] Barrackman. Witnesses: none. Acknowledged in court, September 1809. Del: to grantee, 12 September 1818. Recorded: OS 4:482-483.

11 September 1809. Wenman and Sala WADE to James DUNN. 146 acres, no adjoiners or place names mentioned. Part of 374 acres patented to Wade [date blank]. Consideration: $300. Signed: Wenman [X] Wade, Salah [X] Wade. Witnesses: none. Acknowledged in court, September 1809. No delivery shown. Recorded: OS 4:483-484.

22 December 1804. Elisabeth ROGERS, OH, executrix and sole heir of Lewis Rogers, deceased, to James STAFFORD. 240 acres on both sides of Cheat River, adjoining Henry Crull and Lemuel John, where Stafford now lives. Excepting about 3/4 acre which seems to be a small interference by Joshua Jenkins' heirs. Consideration: £300, VA. Signed: Elisabeth Rogers. Witnesses: Wm John, Lemuel John, Owen John. Proved by witnesses, January 1805 and September 1809. Del: to him, 23 August 1811. Recorded: OS 4:484-485.

29 October 1807. Absalom and Sarah MORRIS to Joseph MORGAN, no addresses stated. Undivided half of 200 acres

on Buffellow Creek, no adjoiners mentioned. Conveyed by George and Elizabeth Martin to Absalom Morris and Thomas Burchenal, 23 May 1797. Consideration: $200, VA. Signed: Absalom Morris, Sarah Morris. Witnesses: Wm John, Lemuel John, William Morris. Acknowledged by Sarah Morris before Wm John and Lemuel John, 30 October 1807. Del: to him, 13 April 1813. Recorded: OS 4:486-487.

26 November 1808. James and Kiziah GRADY (late MORGAN, daughter of William MORGAN, deceased) to William ROYSE, Adams Co, OH. One equal fifth of 3 tracts owned by William Morgan, deceased: 40 acres in Dunkard Bottom, patented 15 May 1784; 400 acres patented 1 September 1783 (minus 100 acres of this tract conveyed to David Morgan); 140 acres patented 22 November 1793. Consideration: $200. Signed: James Grady, Kiziah Grady. Witnesses: David Morgan, Thomas Montgomery, Moses Royse. Acknowledged by Kiziah before David Morgan and Wm Johnson, JPs, 27 November 1806; by James in court, September 1809. No delivery shown. Recorded: OS 4:487-489.

26 March 1805. Joseph SCOTT, marshall of the VA district, to Meshach SEXTON, no addresses stated. 190 acres from a 364 acre tract taxed in the name of James McLaw and sold for nonpayment of the direct tax. Consideration: 39¢. Signed: Joseph Scott. Witnesses: J H Lynch Jr, John G Smith, William McEnry. Acknowledged in Richmond District Court, 1 April 1805. Certificate of A J Robinson. Del: to Wm Jobes, 3 March 1812 pr order filed. Recorded: OS 4:489-491.

11 September 1809. Rhoda BACORN, Fayette Co, PA, devisee and legal representative of Job BACORN deceased, to Philip BEARBROW. 2 tracts: 14 3/4 acres, 13 square perches, adjoining Bearbrow's other land, Frederick Spair, the PA line, and lots of Coddington and Summerville. 5 acres, 25 square perches west of Coddington's lot and south of the PA line. Consideration: $79.95. Signed: Rhoda Bacorn. Witnesses: none. Acknowledged in court, September 1809. Del: to him, 8 April 1811. Recorded: OS 4:492-493.

18 September 1807. John PREPLES [sic], Montgomery Co, KY, to Abraham SHOBE, Hardy Co. Power of attorney to have sold a tract conveyed in trust by Jesse Payne. Signed: Jno Peebels. Witnesses: D Trimble, Jno Pugh. Acknowledged in Montgomery Co, KY, before Jeremiah Davis and Will Orear, JPs. Certificate of Micajah Harrison, Clerk. Del: to him, 14 October 1809. Recorded: OS 4:493-494.

28 May 1808. WILL of Baulser SHUMAN [sic]. Daughter

Suzannah Garlow, late Suzannah Lott, and her husband Andrew have $293 of my money. She to pay my daughter Christinah and her husband Zachariah Rhodes $60 ($30 in cash and $30 in country produce) by 25 December next. Son John Shuman: to have $100 ($50 by 25 May 1809, the rest by 25 May 1810). Remainder of money, $133, to Suzannah. Executor: Richard Harrison. Signed: Baulser [X] Shumaker [sic]. Witnesses: Richard Harrison, Nancy Harrison. Proved by witnesses, September 1809. Fee paid by Joseph Harrison. Recorded: OS 4:494-495. [Also recorded in Wills, 1:333-334, as "Shumaker".]

15 April 1809. Nicholas CASEY to James PARSONS, Hampshire Co. [this conveyance appears to be identical to that recorded at OS 4:402-404, except for the acknowledgement. Acreage, title, and consideration are the same]. Signed: Nicholas Casey. Witnesses: James Bailey, William Throckmorton, David Parsons. Acknowledged in court, October 1809. Del: to him, September 1810. Recorded: OS 4:495-498.

7 October 1809. Thomas and Drusella FLOYD to John SNODGRASS. 32½ acres on Pharos Run, adjoining William Snodgrass and heirs of Charles Snodgrass. Part of a tract conveyed to Floyd by Jacob Foulk. Consideration: $50. Signed: Thomas Floyd, Drusillah Floyd. Witnesses: none. Acknowledged in court, October 1809. Del: to John Watson, September 1810. Recorded: OS 4:499.

26 June 1809. Leonard M DEAKINS and John HOY, executors and devisees of Francis DEAKINS, who was executor and devisee of William DEAKINS, all of George Town, DC, to Martin STEMPLE. 50 acres in the forks of Woolf Creek, on the ridge on which the road runs from Concord [sic] Holestine's to the mouth of Woolf Creek, adjoining Jasper Cope's 100 acres and Conrod Hostine. Part of 300 acres patented to Francis and William Deakins, 3 May 1796. Consideration: $5. Signed: L M Deakins, John Hoye. Witness: Thos Corcoran. Acknowledged in George Town, DC, 26 June 1809. Certificate of Thos Corcoran, mayor. Del: to F Harsh, 3 September 1810. Recorded: OS 4:500-501.

[blank] 1809. Frederick and Catherine [mentioned late in body of instrument] HARSH to Daniel WOOTRING. 104 acres at the head of Yochaganey River, no adjoiners named. Part of 540 acres conveyed by Francis Deakins, 26 February 1800. Consideration: $200. Signed: Frederick Harsh, Catherine [+] Harsh. Witnesses: none. Acknowledged in court, October 1809. Del: to F Harsh, 3 September 1810. Recorded: OS 4:501-502.

9 October 1809. Elizabeth STRAIGHT, widow, to Peter

STRAIT. 65 acres, one third of a 195 acre tract at Finches Run, adjoining John Dragoo. Consideration: $100. Signed: Elizabeth [0] Strait. Witnesses: none. Acknowledged in court, October, 1809. Del: to him, 2 September 1812. Recorded: OS 4:502-503.

9 October 1809. Zaquil and Sinah MORGAN to Joshua THORN. 105 acres adjoining Abraham Low and John Springer. Part of 200 acres patented 19 November 1801. Consideration: £100, VA. Signed: Zackquill Morgan, Sinah [X] Morgan. Witnesses: none. Acknowledged in court, October 1809. Del: to grantee, 6 May 1822. Recorded: OS 4:503-504.

20 March 1809. William PRICE to John SNIDER and Michael BOYLES. Bill of sale for horses, waggons and gears, cows, pigs, beds, tables, household furnishings, tableware, corn, bacon, farming tools, &c. Consideration: $800 grantor owes to grantees. Signed: Wm Price. Witnesses: Samuel Taylor, David Miller. Proved by witnesses, October 1809. Del: to Mr John Snider, 2 September 1813. Recorded: OS 4:504-505.

22 May 1809. Charity PRICKETT to her son-in-law John DRAGOO. All her goods and chattels, including cattle, horses, sheep, hogs, furniture, tableware, "and some other necessarys to tedious to mention." Consideration: love, good will, and affection. Signed: Charity [+] Prickett. Witnesses: Thomas Knight, William Knight. Acknowledged in court, November 1809. Del: to Peter Dragoo, 30 December 1809. Recorded: OS 4:505.

13 November 1809. Henry and Prissella FORTNEY and Peter FORTNEY Jr to Jacob ZINN. 19 acres adjoining Peter Fortney Sr and Dodridge. Consideration: $300. Signed: Henry Fortney, Peter [+] Fortney [Prissella does not sign]. Witnesses: none. Acknowledged in court by Henry and Peter, November 1809, and recorded as to them. Del: to grantee, 16 September 1822. Recorded: OS 4:506.

7 December 1809. William and Mary ANDERSON, Henderson Co, KY, to David MORGAN. The one-fifth share which may fall to William and Mary in a division of the lands of William Morgan, deceased, Mary being one of his heirs. Tracts: 300 acres on Cheat River, opposite Dunkard Bottom, patented 1 September 1783, including William's survey settlement as assignee of James Morgan. 66 acres patented 29 May 1791. 143 acres patented 22 November 1793. 40 acres patented 15 May 1784. Consideration: $200. Signed: Wm Anderson [Mary does not sign]. Witnesses: none. Acknowledged by William Anderson, December 1809; by Mary Anderson in Henderson Co, KY, 9 August 1810, before Jas Latham and Jos Hoy,

JPs. Certificate of Ambrose Barbour, clerk, and John Waggoner, presiding justice. Del: to Morgan, 12 December 1809. Recorded: OS 4:507-509.

3 October 1809. Hugh and Mercy MORGAN to John S ROBERTS, no address stated. 200 acres adjoining Morgan's settlement survey. Patented 3 June 1786. Consideration: $850. Signed: Hugh Morgan [Mercy does not sign]. Witnesses: none. Receipt for consideration money. Acknowledged in court by Hugh Morgan, December 1809, and recorded as to him. Del: to him, 14 July 1815. Recorded: OS 4:510-511.

15 January 1805. Richard and Jane CAIN to Henry MILLER, Green Co, PA. 150 acres on the righthand fork of Dunkard Creek, adjoining William John and near an Indian grave. Part of a 1794 patent. Consideration: $60. Signed: Richard Cain, Jane [+] Cain. Witnesses: Henry Dering, John W Dean, Thos R Chipps. Proved by witnesses, June 1805. Acknowledged in court by Richard Cain, December 1809, and recorded as to him. Del: to him, April 1810. Recorded: OS 4:512-513.

28 September 1809. William WALKER to Nicholas B MEDERA. Bill of sale. Cow, beds, chairs, tableware, blacksmith's tools. Consideration: $20. Signed: William [X] Walker. Witnesses: John A Guseman, French S Gray. Proved by witnesses, December 1809. No delivery shown. Recorded: OS 4:513-514.

[blank] 1809. Larkin and Jane PAIRPOINT and Zackquil and Darkess PAIRPOINT to Joseph WEAVER. 37 acres, 3 rods, 9½ perches adjoining Lewis Rogers survey (conveyed to James Jenkins and now held by Robert Abercromby), Zackquil's other land, and Weaver's other land. Part of 100 acres patented to John Pairpoint, assignee of Samuel Hanway, assignee of Colder Haymond, which was surveyed 12 April 1785 and willed by John to his sons Larkin and Zackquill. Consideration: [blank]. Signed: Larken Pairpoint, Jane [X] Pairpoint, Zackquill Pairpoint, Darky Pairpoint. Witnesses: none. Acknowledged in court, December 1809. Del: to him, 7 July 1810. Recorded: OS 4:514-516.

26 September 1808. James MANN to William GRAHAM, Green Co, PA. Mortgage on Negro boy Anderson. Mann has received $40 as a loan from Graham and owes him $100 due next Christmas, and $100 due at Christmas come a year, with interest. If he repays by 25 December 1809 he may redeem Anderson. Signed: James Mann. Witnesses: Wm G Payne, Wm N Jarrett. Proved by witness Jarrett, December 1809. Del: to him. Recorded: OS 4:516-517.

9 December 1809. John GEFFS, Fayette Co, PA, to

Isaac POWELL. 250 acres adjoining Joseph Boltinghouse. Part of a tract patented to Nehemiah Harp, 3 September 1788, for 350 acres, minus 100 acres sold by Harp to William Laycock. Consideration: $840. Signed: John Geffs. Witnesses: none. Acknowledged in court, December 1809. Del: to Mr Isaac Powell, 30 April 1811. Recorded: OS 4:517-519.

20 December 1809. Unspecified HEIRS of Theophilus PHILIPS, deceased, no address stated, to James WILSON. On 1 March 1802 John Philips, late of Fayette Co, PA, conveyed to James 200 acres on Booths Creek, which was his property. By some means the grant was made in the name of Theophilus Philips, who died intestate regarding this tract. Legal title has descended to his heirs, who release title to Wilson. Consideration: $1. Signed: Permelia Philips, Theophilus Philips, John Philips, Sally [+] Philips. Witnesses: Daniel Cox, Daniel Stewart, Samuel Bowen. Proved by witnesses, January 1810. Del: to James Wilson, 4 April 1812. Recorded: OS 4:519.

[blank] January 1810. William and Anna GRAY to Henry COROTHERS. 104 acres on the Monongalia River, no adjoiners named. Part of a survey granted to Henry Robinson and conveyed by him to Gray. Consideration: $200. Signed: William Gray, Anna Gray. Acknowledged in court, January 1810. Del: to H Corothers, 15 January 1810. Recorded: OS 4:520-521.

8 January 1810. Henry and Sarah COROTHERS to James JEFFS. Tract, acreage not stated, at Booths Creek, adjoining Thomas Evans. Part of 500 acres patented to William Bohannon and John Downard, 19 September 1791, and conveyed to Corothers [blank] March 1807. Consideration: $700. Signed: Henry Corothers, Sarah Corothers. Witnesses: none. Acknowledged in court, January 1810. No delivery shown. Recorded: OS 4:521-522.

21 August 1809. James SCOTT, trustee for Benjamin REEDER and Valentine JOHNSON, to John W DEAN. Sale under deed of trust. On 24 September 1807 Benjamin Reeder conveyed to Scott in trust 400 acres to secure payment due to Dean, who is highest bidder for the property. Consideration: $580. Scott warrants title only so far as the deed of trust gives him a right to do so. Signed: Jas Scott. Witnesses: George S Dering, Scott Martin, B F Reeder, Wm G Payne. Acknowledged in court, January 1810. Del: to Isaac Dean, 30 August 1831. Recorded: OS 4:522-523.

7 August 1809. Benjamin and Rachel POWELL, Dearbourn Co, IN, to Andrew WAYT, Washington Co, PA. 150

acres on Tyger Valley River, adjoining David Dunham and Thomas Huse. Part of 400 acres patented 27 July 1796 to Jacob Hampton, assignee of James Mills, assignee of Simon Hendrexson, and conveyed to Powell. Consideration: $400. Signed: Benjamin Powell, Rachel Powell. Witnesses: J Hamilton, James Dice. Receipt for consideration money. Acknowledged before B Chambers and Jabez Percival, JPs, in Dearbourn Co, IN territory, 7 August 1809. Certificate of Saml C Vance, clerk of Common Pleas. Del: to John Gregg, 12 August 1816. Recorded: OS 4:523-525.

2 October 1809. Daniel and Margaret HILL, Wood Co, to James LEMMONS. 100 acres on Big Sandy Creek, no adjoiners mentioned. Consideration: £100, VA. Signed: Daniel Hill, Margret Hill. Witnesses: none. Acknowledged in Wood Co, October 1809. Certificate of James H Neal, CWC. Del: to James Metheny, 3 June 1811. Recorded: OS 4:526-527.

28 September 1809. Abraham WOODROW and Simeon WOODROW, Morgan Town, to Benjamin REEDER. Deed of trust. The Woodrows owe $1362 to Jacob Foulk, payable within 3 years. To secure the debt they convey in trust a lot on Main Street in Morgan Town, purchased from Benjamin Hellen; cows, hogs, beds, furniture, horses, other personal property, and Negro man Nelson; 141 acres on Cobuns Creek, purchased from Jacob Nuse; and 14 acres on Cheat River nearly opposite Ices Ferry, purchased from Russel Potter, who purchased from the heirs of Lott Ridgway. Properties to be sold if the debt is not paid. Signed: A Woodrow, S Woodrow. Witnesses: John A Guseman, Abram Owens, Henry H Wilson. Proved by witnesses, November 1809 and January 1810. Del: to Jacob Foulk, 26 May 1813. Recorded: OS 4:528-529.

31 August 1809. Jacob FOULK to Francis GILLMEYER Jr, attorney in fact for Francis GILLMEYER and John ZIMMER, the grantees of Baltimore, MD. Deed of trust. Foulk owes $1371.17 to Gillmeyer and Zimmer, payable on or before 31 August 1812. To secure the debt he conveys in trust 1000 acres adjoining Francis and Edward [sic] Deakins. Land to be sold if the debt is not paid. Signed: Jacob Foulk, Francis Gellmeyer. Witnesses: Wm G Payne, Thos McKinley, James Hurry. Proved by witnesses, January 1810. Del: to Mr Gilmeyer, 28 August 1812. Recorded: OS 4:529-531.

15 November 1809. Benjamin REEDER, trustee for Jesse PAYNE, to Abraham SHOBE, Hardy Co. On 1 January 1805 Jesse Payne conveyed to John Ervin, Dudley Evans, and Benjamin Reeder a 400 acre tract, to secure $653.43 due to John Peebles. The land has been sold at Peebles'

request in his power of attorney to Shobe, and Shobe is the highest bidder for the tract, adjoining James Coburn, Alexander Addison, and William and John Payne. Consideration: $400. Signed: Benjamin Reeder. Witnesses: Thos Wilson, French S Gray, Paul Vigers [?]. Proved by witnesses, January 1810. Del: to Jesse Shobe, 2 February 1811. Recorded: OS 4:531-532.

12 April 1809. James (Sr) and Sarah THOMPSON to unspecified HEIRS of James THOMPSON Jr. 32 acres, 21 perches, adjoining Camp, Dudley Evans, and Becket Wilson. Consideration: $1, VA. Signed: James Thompson. Witnesses: B Reeder, John Dent, James Hurry, Joseph Lowry. Proved by witnesses, January 1810 [which identifies this as a deed to John W Thompson and others, heirs of James Thompson Jr but no individual heirs are named in the instrument]. Del: to J W Thompson, 30 August 1811. Recorded: OS 4:532-533.

12 April 1809. James (Sr) and Sarah THOMPSON to their son Andrew THOMPSON. 53 acres adjoining Isaac Van Camp and James' other lands. Consideration: love and affection. Signed: James Thompson [Sarah does not sign]. Witnesses: B Reeder, John Dent, James Hurry, Joseph Lowry. Proved by witnesses, January 1810. Del: to him, 8 October 1810. Recorded: OS 4:533-534.

12 July 1809. Felix SCOTT to Enoch JONES. Deed of trust. Daniel Marchand has entered appearance and special bail for David Scott Sr at the suit of Stephen Gapen in Fayette Co, PA. Felix conveys 260 or 270 acres at the mouth of Scotts Meadow Run, conveyed to him by David Scott, 26 May 1800. When the judgment is rendered, the land is to be sold to reimburse Marchand for such expenses and costs as he can receipt. Signed: Felix Scott. Witness: Wm Gregg. Acknowledged in Fayette Co, PA, 12 June 1809, before Jonathan Rowland and James Lindsay, JPs. Certificate of Richard William Lane, prothonotary. No delivery shown. Recorded: OS 4:535-536.

8 February 1809. Mathias FURBEE, Williamson Co, TN, to John SAMPLE & Co. Deed of trust. Mathias owes Sample $737.78, payable by 1 May 1809. To secure the debt he conveys 154 acres on the east side of Little Papaw, adjoining James Robertson. Tract originally patented to Charles Perryman. Land to be sold if payment not made. Signed: Mathias [X] Furbee. Witnesses: David [Danl?] Montgomery, Thos V Benton, Wm Huline [?]. Acknowledged in Williamson Co, TN, before John Overton, JP, 12 February 1809. Certificate of Nicholas P Hardaman, clerk, and David McEwen, presiding justice. Del: to Thos Wilson, 24 May 1813. Recorded: OS 4:537-539.

15 November 1809. Amos CHIPPS to Fielding KIGER. Lot [# not shown] in Morgan Town, at High Street and Bumbo Lane, adjoining William Lanham. Conveyed by George R and Sarah Tingle to Augustus Werninger, 15 August 1808, and by Augustus and Mathilda Werninger to Amos Chipps, 15 August 1808. Consideration: $500, VA. Signed: Amos Chipps. Witnesses: Wm N Jarrett, N Evans, Thos Wilson. Proved by witnesses, January 1810. Del: to grantee, 17 June 1822. Recorded: OS 4:539-540.

5 November 1809. Robert SUTER to Kennedy OWEN, both of Baltimore, MD. 1008 acres, no adjoiners or place names mentioned. From a survey for Richard Clabourn, who assigned to Bartholomew Tarrison, for whom the tract was patented. Richard Ralston and James Vanuxsen, trustees for Tarrison, conveyed lots #1 and 5 of Clabourn's chain of surveys to Francis and William Deakins, 10 May 1796; they conveyed to Alexander Smith, 12 September 1798. Clement Biddle also conveyed to Smith, 18 September 1800. On 23 April 1804 Alexander and Volenda Smith, Allegany Co, MD, conveyed this tract (lot #2, a part of lot #1 as purchased by the Deakins) to Robert Suter. Consideration: $833.41. Signed: R Suter. Witnesses: Ovid Johnson, John Hargrove. Acknowledged in Baltimore, MD, 1 November 1809. Certificate of Edward Johnson, mayor. Del: to --ger, 10 [--] 1811 [data lost under binding tape]. Recorded: OS 4:540-543.

25 September 1809. George G and Joanna GOFF, Randolph Co, to John STINEBAUGH. 120 acres adjoining the Horse Shoe road, Hannah and George G Goff, and Levi Hopkins. Part of a tract willed by John T Goff to his daughter Joanna. Consideration: $328. Signed: George G Goff, Joanna Goff. Witnesses: none. Acknowledged in Randolph Co, November 1810. Certificate of John Wilson, CRC. Del: to him, 24 November 1815. Recorded: OS 4:544-545.

6 February 1810. Thomas WILSON, Commissioner, to John ZEAGAN. 233 acres adjoining Zeagan's other land. This tract sold as result of decree of court in the case of Zeagan vs Edward Gallagher and others, with Zeagan the highest bidder. Consideration: $10. Wilson is not liable for any fault in the title. Signed: Thos Wilson. Witnesses: none. Acknowledged in court, February 1810. Del: to Zeagan, 26 June 1810. Recorded: OS 4:546-547.

12 February 1810. Samuel and Hannah DAVIS to Holley JOHNSON. 60 acres adjoining Joseph Hunt and William Anderson. Conveyed by Henry Barrackman and wife to Davis, [blank] April 1806. Consideration: $500, VA. Signed: Samuel [X] Davis, Hannah [X] Davis. Witnesses:

none. Acknowledged in court, February 1810. Del: to him, 9 February 1811. Recorded: OS 4:547-548.

APPENDIX:

OTHER EARLY MONONGALIA LAND TRANSFERS

Despite the loss of pre-1796 records, many missing conveyances can be identified. The surviving Monongalia Land Books begin in 1788, and although they appear to be somewhat incomplete for the earliest years, numerous sales of land are mentioned in the assessments. Occasionally a partial date for the conveyance is also shown. The notes are most detailed for the section of Monongalia that later became Preston Co, WV, which lost all of its own early records to an 1869 courthouse fire.

The original Land Books were filmed at the WV State Auditor's Office, in Charleston, by the Genealogical Society of Utah. My notes were made from this microfilm copy, Family History Library film 0549701. The originals are in very poor condition and the film (a negative print) is not always clearly legible. I have identified the lists by year and by assessor. Arrangement is alphabetical, by initial of surname, keyed to the name of the *grantee*. All conveyance notes legible to me through 1796 are listed below. (Not all of the annual Land Books include memos of conveyances, and the following is *not* an inventory of surviving Land Books for Monongalia.)

1788, assessor not identified

Thomas Craft to Joseph Agnew. 400 acres. 1784.
David Davisson to Joseph Agnew. 140 [?] acres. no date.
David Frazee to Job Bacorn. 400 acres. 1787.
Zebulon Hogue to Jonathan Casebeer. 400 acres. 1786 [1784?]
Samuel Luellen to James Cleland. Acreage illegible. 1787.
William Deakens to Henry Dise. 602 acres. 1787.
Samuel Worl to Hezekiah Davisson. 400 acres. 1787.
Francis & Will Deakins to Christian and Jacob Derick. 373 acres. 1787.
Thomas Chaney to Squire Frazee. 200 acres. 1786.
David Frazee to Ephraim Frazee. 343 acres. 1786.
Samuel Hess to Joseph Hunt. 293 acres. 1786.
Francis & Wm Deakins to Conrad Hogmire. 823 acres. 1787.
Francis & William Deakins to Philip Hess. 108 [?] acres. 1787.

Francis & Will Deakins to Jost Hecke. 211 acres. 1787.
David Carter [?] to John Jenkins and Thomas Gibson. 100 acres. 1784.
Charles Donaldson to Ezekiel Jones. 300 acres. 1785.
Thomas Chaney to Thomas Laidley. 297 acres. 1785.
Jacob Cozad to Samuel Lewellen. 103 acres. 1787.
John Daugherty to Jacob Minthorn. 133 acres. 1787.
James Spurgen to Samuel Morton. 400 acres. October 1788.
Samuel Luellen to Thomas Neely. 306 acres. 1787.
Samuel Luellen to Thomas Neely. 135 [?] acres. March 1788.
James Luellen to Daniel Neely. 133 acres. March 1788.
John Murphy to John Ramsey. 348 acres. May 1788.
Jacob Counts to John Runnion. 211 acres. April 1788.
Francis & Wm Deakins to Henry Startsman. 500 acres. 1787.
Francis & Will Deakins to Godfrey Stemple. 400 acres. 1787.
Francis and Will Deakins to Ludwick Stull. 150 acres. 1787.
Joseph Robbinet to Richard Stephens. 382 acres. 1787.
John J Judy to Richard Stephens. 400 acres. October 1788.
Nathan Lowe to Sarah Tannahille. 96 acres. 1784.
John Lefevere to Arthur Trader. 400 acres. 1784.
Thomas Chaney to Joseph Tomlinstone. 103 acres. 1785.
Francis & Will Deakins to Peter Troxel. 164 acres. 1787.
Henry Crull to Francis Warman. 16 acres. 1786.
Francis & William Deakins to Daniel Winans. Acreage illegible. 1787.
Francis & William Deakins to Abraham Wolumper [?]. 269 acres. 1787.
Francis & William Deakins to William Wiles. 162 acres. 1787.
Samuel Wood to John [illegible]. 333 acres. 1787.

1789, Thomas Chipps' District

William Norris to George Baker, 63 acres. August 1789.
John LuAlen to John Fowler. 96 acres. November 1789.
William Norris to Enoch Jenkins. 120 acres. 1789.

William McCleery to Andrew McKewn. 525 acres. 1789.
William Spurgen to Andrew McKewn. 174 acres. April 1789.
John LuAlen to William Neighbours. 40 acres. November 1789.
Francis & William Deakins to John, Joshua, and John Wallace and John Mires. 4328 acres. March 1789.
David Morgan to Jacob Wolf. 328 acres. March 1789.

1790, James Cochran's District

William Roark to Henry Amos. 200 acres.
William Roark to John Corothers. 200 acres.
Richard Harrison to Charles [illegible]. 226 acres.
Thomas Davis to Nathan Flemming. 400 acres.
Thomas Russell to John McGinley. 100 acres.
Robert Campbell to Morgan Morgan. 200 acres.
George Weaver to Thomas Pindle. 500 acres.
Richard Harrison to William Postle. 88 acres.
James Denny to Jacob Scott. 200 acres.

1790, Thomas Chipps' District

Samuel Rabbinet to Richard Brandon. 200 acres. 1790.
Stephen Ashby to Neill [?] Cunningham and Joseph Vanmetre. 800 acres. 1790.
Samuel Rabbinett to Robert Forman. 200 acres. No date.
Thomas Neely to Christopher Hays. 354 acres. 1790.
Samuel Rabbinett to Patrick McGrew. 50 acres. 1790.
Joseph Rabbinet to James Rabbinet. 400 acres. 1790.

1791, Henry Barns' District

Joseph Eckleberger to Manis Brown. 34 acres.
James Gibson to Robert and John Davis. 200 acres.
Samuel Canby to John Hood [?]. 200 acres.
Thomas Neely to Matthias and William Vanlear. 1000 acres.
Samuel Canby to Jeremiah and John Warder. 362 acres, 371 acres.

1791, Thomas Chipps' District

Hugh Phelps to Ezekiel Barns. 100 acres. 1792 [sic].
William [illegible] to John Bell. 500 acres. 1791.
Joseph Abbot to David Cooshman. 50 acres. 1791.
Martin Judy to Joseph Corey. 121 acres. No date.
Francis & Wm Deakins to Michael Everheart. 100 acres. July 1790.
Ezekiel Jones to John Fornie. 131 acres. 1791.

Francis & Wm Deakins to Michael Everheart. 100 acres. July 1790.
Ezekiel Jones to John Fornie. 131 acres. 1791.
Daniel Neely to John Gallaspie. Acreage illegible. 1792 [sic].
Thomas Moore to John Kelly. 330 acres. May 1791.
Thomas Moore to Mary Kinkade. 303 acres. No date.
Martin Judy to Joseph Lane. 400 acres. March 1791.
Samuel Frazer to Samuel Martin. 343 acres. December 1791.
Martin Judy to David Morgan. 400 acres. 1786.
Conrad Hogmire to Jacob Meyer. 300 acres. April 1791.
Benjamin Jennins to Thomas Pindle. 300 acres. May 1791.
Francis & Wm Deakins to David Plunket and David Stewart. 500 acres. No date.
Jonathan Casebeer to David Sayres. 400 acres. August 1790.
Samuel Frazier to Elias Soulard. 338 acres. December 1791.
James Robinson to Jeremiah Tawnyhill. 80 acres. 1791.
John Jacob Judy to Robert Thornton. 400 acres. No date.
Ezekiel Jones to Joseph Wolgermut. 269 acres. August 1791.
Ignatius Butler to John Wimp. 123 acres. 1790.

1792, Thomas Chipps' District

Conrad Hogmire to John Burkett. 205 acres. 1792.
Andrew Miller to Augustin Friend. 57 acres. No date.
Godfrey Stemple to Conrad Holston, 59 acres. No date.
William Pettyjohn to [illegible] Whitley. 400 acres. No date.
Conrad Hogmire to John Stout. 254 acres. No date.
Conrad Hogmire to George Stout. 120 acres. No date.
Conrad Hogmire to Jacob Waggoner. 100 acres. November 1792.
Wilday Taylor to Raphael Walthan. Acreage illegible. No date.

1792, ?Hugh McNeely's District

Thomas Dawson to John Brand. 150 acres.
Jacob LuAlen to John Galaspie. 355 acres.
Jacob LuAlen to William Kennedy. 73 acres.

1793, Hugh McNeely's District

Joseph Wilson to Saml Hanway. 48 acres.
Thos Pindle to Geo Hollenbeck. 200 acres
Wm Morgan to Thos Johnston. 200 acres.
Richd Merryfield to Wm Jacobs. 200 acres.
Jno Bishop to Baltzr Kratzer. 400 acres.
Thos Baird to Chas McGill. 166 acres.
Thos Pindle to Jno Stealy. 40 acres.
Wm Buckanon to David Seers Sr. 25 3/4 acres.
Richd Merryfield to David Seers Jr. 200 acres.
Wm Haymond to Alexr Smith. 400 acres.
Thos Evans to Robt & John Stuart. 202 acres.
Thos McKinly to Saml Wilson. 2 lots.

1793, Thomas Chipps' District

William Conner to John Gribble. Acreage not stated. No date.
William Morgan to James Stinson. 126 acres. August.
Thomas Butler to Jarvis Thompson. 132 acres. March.
Elias Layton to William Tannihill. 346 acres. August.
Joshua Worly to John Worly. 400 acres. August.
William Spurgeon to John Willett. 400 acres. August.

1794, Nathan Springer's District

Artha Trader to John Brummage. 200 acres.
George Hollowback to Ezekiel Burrows. 50 acres.
Richd Merrifield to William Bambridge. 95 acres.
Wm McCleery to Wm Ward Burrows. 4690 acres.
John Prickett to James Dunn. 200 acres.
Thomas John to Fidelus Foster. 95 acres.
Robert Petty to Saml Gandy. 400 acres.
John Prickett to Jeremiah Gallahue. 13¼ acres.
Wm Cambell to Abram Gooseman. 400 acres.
James Morgan to Ezra Horton. 94 acres.
Samuel Hanway to Joseph Lane. 4 acres.
Wm McCleery to Michl Leard [?]. 200 acres.
John Prickett to John McGee. 163 3/4 acres.
Zack Morgan to Wm McCleery. 1 lot.
Thomas Pindle to Alexander McIntire. 111 acres.
Adley Ray to Isaac Reed. 117½ acres.
Simon Troy to Jonah Vandivort. 100 acres.
Richd Corson to Christian Wireman. 750 acres.
Richd Corson to Christian Wireman. 250 acres.
John Flock [?] to Christian Wireman. 156 acres.
Ebenezer [illegible] to Christian Wireman. Acreage illegible.

1794, Thomas Chipps' District
Joshua Lowe to David Bayles. 108 acres. No date.
Robert Irwin to William Benson. 98 acres. No date.
Jonas Hogmire to William Deakins Jr. 38 acres. May.
Salathiel Goff to James Goff. 240 acres. May.
William Conner to John Gribble. Acreage not stated. No date.
Richard Morris to Henry Hazle. 150 acres. May.
James Goff to Peter Heckert. 500 acres. May.
Conrad Hogmire to Mary Karr. 50 acres. May.
Andrew Ramsey to Joseph Mires. 200 acres. May.
Squire Frazier to Russel Potter. 200 acres. May.
Moses Trader to Samuel Ruble. Acreage not stated. May.
Thomas Goff to Mathias Ridenover. 133 acres. May.
Job Bacorn to William Squire. 250 acres. May.
Thomas Goff to Adam Shaver. 50 acres. May.
Thomas Goff to Abraham Wotring. 567 acres. May.

1795, Joseph Trickett's District
David Scott to Andrew Arnett. 200 acres.
Richard Merrifield to Robert Bell. 50 acres.
James Prickett to Rubin Boner Jr. 200 acres.
John Moore to Jesse Bayles. 248 acres.
Wm Ward Burrows to Alexr Hawthorn & Jno Brown. 60 [?] acres.
Nicholas Horner to Cias Billingsly. 400 acres.
Joseph Reed to Thomas Doolittle. Acreage not stated.
David Scott to Thos & Lewes Dewese. 200 acres.
John Downer to Peter Fortney. 335 acres.
John Vandivert to Joshua Hickman. 220 acres.
Henry Robinson to Reece Hastings. 109 acres.
Charles Lash to John Husk [?]. 200 acres.
Edward Haymond to William Hoult. 100 acres.
Richard Merifield to Samuel Keener. 200 acres.
John Robins to Charles Lash. 400 acres.
John Cochran to John Lough. 377 [?] acres.
Zack Morgan to Wm McClerry. 2 lots.
David Bradford to Wm McClerry. 2 lots.
Reece Hastings to Wm McClerry. 45 acres.
John Prickett to Moses Musgrave. 200 acres.
Christopher Wireman to Thomas Moole [?]. 2000 acres.
Christopher Wireman to Thomas Moole [?]. 1500 acres.
Samuel Wilson to Thomas McKinley. Acreage illegible.
Thomas Pindle to Thomas McKinley. 6 acres.
William Bambridge to Alexander McIntire. 95 acres.
Thomas Mills to John McFarling. 360 acres.
Reece Hastings to Wm McClerry. 65 acres.

James Robinson to Clemond Merls. 100 acres.
William Dawson to James Morress. 213 acres.
Charles Martin to the Methodist Society. 1 acre.
Wm Pettyjohn to Benjamin Reeder. 100 acres.
John Simpson to Benjn Reeder. Acreage not stated.
Thos Chips to Benjn Reeder. 400 acres.
Thos Chips to Benjn Reeder. 400 acres.
Evan Watkins to Isaac Robins. 310 acres.
Jonas Camp to James Robinson. 150 acres.
Sylvester Keller [?] to John Robins. 500 acres.
Robinson Lucas to Simeon Riggs. Acreage not stated.
David Scott to Jacob Scott. 400 acres.
David Scott to Jacob Scott. 52 acres.
Barney Haney to Philip Shively. 123 acres.
Richard Merryfield to Daniel Sayre. 300 acres.
John Pricket to Reubin Squires. 200 acres.
Peter Parker to Timothy Smith. 143 acres.
Stephen Moylon to Wm Stephen Smith. 2000 acres.
William Crammond to William Smith. 47,000 acres.
Henry Robinson to Hugh Sidwell. 174 acres.
James Daugherty to William Tingle. 1 lot.
Thomas Pindle to Justice Terrel. 1 acre.
John Finch to Jonah Vandervort. 100 acres.
James Jenkins to Widow Watts. 200 acres.
James Pollock to John Wade. 52 acres.
Baltzer Kratzer to Jacob Zinn. 200 acres.

1795, Alex Brandon's District

Charles Donaldson to Martin Able. 200 acres. January.
Joseph Corey to Zopher Blatchley. 121 acres. January.
Anthony Worley to Thomas Baker. 150 acres. January.
Conrad Hogmire to F and William Deacon. 84 lots in the town of Salem. No date.
Francis & Wm Deakins to John Hoye. 310 acres. February.
John Simmes [?] to James Kelly. 300 acres. April.
Jeremiah Tannehill to Alexander McEntire. 120 acres. May.
Joseph Stewart to Patrick McGrew. 100 acres. No date.
Alexander McEntire to John Stealey. 120 acres. June.
James Kelly to Joseph Stewart. Acreage not stated. No date.
James Kelly to John Wolf. 160 acres. July.
Joseph Stewart to Augustine Wolf. 98 acres. No date.

1796, Alexander Brandon's District

Joseph Butler to Thomas Burchenal. 150 acres. February.
Marten Juda to Joseph Brandon. 200 acres. March.
Zopher Blatchley to Joseph Corey. 121 acres. April.
John Richards and Robert Jameson, executors for Henry Richards, deceased, to Andrew Ramsey, and from Andrew Ramsey to Nicholas Casey. 400 acres. May.
Andrew Ramsey to Nicholas Casey. 100 acres. No date.
Andrew Ramsey to Nicholas Casey. 100 acres. No date.
William Jenkins to Christian Cale. 198 acres. No date.
Edward Galagher to David Easton. 600 acres. No date.
James Stinson to James Guthrie. 126 acres. July.
Martin Juda to John Hareeder. 692½ acres. August.
John Fleming to James Hamilton. 100 acres. No date.
Alexr Brandon to Jacob Pindle. 157 acres. August.
David Easton to William Smith. 2000 acres. September.
Thomas Butler to John Shay. 100 acres. No date.
James Scott to William Tannehill. 100 acres. No date.
Marten Juda to Godfrey Wagner. 200 acres. September.
Godfrey Wagner to Robert Woods. 100 acres. No date.
John Aldridge & Rachel his wife to Amos Workman. 100 acres. No date.

1796, Joseph Trickett's District

Richard Marrifield to Wm Bambridge. 150 acres.
Richard Lee to John Baker. 25 acres.
Benjamin Brane to Paul Dewit. 56 acres.
William Ice to James Edgel. 100 acres.
William Worth to David Evans. 1000 acres.
Keziah Virdin to John Evans Jr &ca. 400 acres.
Leonard Titsword to Jesse Hanway. 469 acres.
William Ice to Adam Ice. 100 acres.
John Statler to John Johnson. 100 acres.
Richard Lee to Robert Lee. 2 acres.
Jonathan Downer to Silas Lord. 1 lot.
William Ice to Anthony Mahan. 100 acres.
Benjamin Brane to Thomas McGee. 79 acres.
Thomas John to Simeon Rice. 304 acres.
Thomas Laidley to Benjamin Reeder. 16½ acres.
Thomas Laidley &ca to Thomas Wilson. 4 acres.

Another list of early Monongalia conveyances, not duplicated in the foregoing, was retained by Colonel John Evans. A true copy was submitted as evidence in the

1808 injunction of Rebecca Wilson vs Benjamin and Eleanor Wilson, original papers of which are in the office of the Circuit Clerk of Augusta County, Staunton, VA (copies in my files). If Evans preserved any other such memoranda he did not re-enter them into the public records of Monongalia, and the Land Book kept for the period in question by this particular commissioner of revenue has not survived.

"A list of conveyances and partitions recorded in my office from January 1788 to January 1789 [the years are both overwritten and difficult to read clearly] Within the district of James Daugherty, Commissioner.

Thomas Davey & Mary his wife to Gurdan Hall 400 acres.

Zackll Morgan & Drusilla his wife to William McCleery Lott in Town

From Conrod Walters & Ann his wife to George Stockton Lott in Town.

From John Peirpoint & Ann his wife to William Lanham Lott in Town.

From Hugh McNeely To James Daugherty 5 acres in Town.

From Zackll Morgan & Drusilla his wife to Saml Hanway 4 acres.

From Wm McCleery & Issabella his wife to Francis Brooke Lott in Town

From Thomas Pindall & Judith his wife to Fauquire McCray Lott in Town

From Zackll Morgan & Drusilla his wife to Rees Woolf Lott in Town

From James Wilson to William Wilson 50 acres

From John Peirpoint & Ann his wife to Thomas Boyd 166 acres.

Test James Daugherty, commissioner. Attest John Evans [illegible abbreviation]."

On the reverse of the slip are written several words, of which only "James Daugherty" is legible, and there are some computations in £.s.d values.

INDEX

ABBOTT [Abbot], 69 379
ABEL [Abell Able], 136 251 276 312 384
ABERCROMBY [Abbacrumba Abercrumby ACrumby], 68 78 138 139 186 187 240 370
ABRAHAM, 253
ADAMSON, 276 283 291
ADARE, 365
ADDISON, 81 134 167 168 373
ADKINS [Atkin Atkins], 16 134 176
AGNEW, 377
ALBERTES, 344
ALDRIDGE [Aldredge], 20 385
ALLEBAM [?], 329
ALLEN, 68 128 146 198 199 337 353 357
ALLEY, 138 167 252 304
ALLISON, 107
ALLTON, 355 356
AMMON [Ammons], 15 86
AMOS, 22 53 127 134 199 379
ANDERSON, 18 27 39 62 66 69 93 99 105 124 132 172 181 212 220 228 244 251 282 289 331 369 374
ANDRIS, 107
ANNON [?], 346
ARCHER, 103 322
ARMET [?], 229
ARMISTEAD, 50 52 123 176
ARMSTRONG, 105 192 341
ARNETT [Arnet], 79 96 199-201 245 291 270 316 322 357 383
ARNOLD, 199 220 234 238 278
ARTHUR, 336
ASHBY [Asbey Asby Ashbey], 57 60 83 122 205 261 281 344 359 379
ASHCRAFT [Achcraft], 144 135
ASHFORD, 161 162
ASHTON, 186 187
ATHY, 346
AUSTIN, 337
AYERS [Ayer Ayres], 39 40 78 79 167 196
BACORN, 137 175 177 280 319 367 377 383
BADOLLET, 29 284
BAILEY [Baily Bayly], 88 173 292 368
BAINBRIDGE [Bambridge Banbridge], 1 120 154 221 229 230 311 347 382 384 385
BAINES, 221
BAIRD, 382
BAKER, 11 19 52 60 70 96 151-153 157 161 165 167 168 196 198 213 217 220 222 223 243 251 258 306 313 317 329 333 378 384
BALDWIN [Baldin], 214 216 270
BALL, 123 341 349

BALLAH, 85 95 173 184 214 232 254 351 357
BALLIE [?], 190
BALTZEL, 40 165 289 312 329 363
BALZER, 96
BANKS, 27 40 48 74 88 117 134 146 148 154 222 273 318
BANNON, 320
BARB, 355 362
BARBOUR, 370
BARBROWER [Bearbrow], 280 367
BARCLEY, 3
BARING [Barring], 60 61
BARKER, 12 32 45 48 61 105 106 145 170 178 191 218 229 240 247 252 269 270 272 276 291 298 310 316
BARKSHIRE, 174 177 190 195 197 201 208 239 249 250 254 307 308 311 314-317 324 329 330 337-341 345 349 350 352-355 360 363
BARNES [Barns], 1 26 39 43 78 80 115 171 174 186 192 193 210-212 215 235 251 254 256 260 286 305 306 336 337 379
BARNET, 226
BARR [Bar], 110 139 270 335
BARRACKMAN [Barrakman Barrickman], 85 86 133 136 217 249 251 305 334 366 374
BARRETT, 179 284
BARRY, 15 56 328
BARTLETT, 326
BARTON, 112
BASHORE, 221
BASNETT [Basnet], 230 318 319 331
BATES, 160 167 277
BATTEN [Batton], 6 20 25 37 62

BATTEN (Cont.) 72 132 242 272 285
BAYLES [Bales], 1 61 71 120 167 230 244 252 278 315 328 383
BAYLOR, 58
BEALL [Beale Beel Bell], 1 4 8 17 18 21 28 29 36 39-41 45 49 50 52 55-57 59 64-66 71 74 91 122 129 133 139 145 154 160 162 163 188 191 192 197 211 216 219 232 243 244 262 263 266 284 291 302 304 317 318 331 343 379 383
BEARD, 239
BEASON, 72 297 308
BEATTY [Beattie Beaty], 28 32 123 166 169 207 238 276
BECKET, 313
BEDINGER, 245
BEEN, 222
BENNETT [Bennet], 46 75 98 103 104 112 125 138 147 148 151 158 175 254 296 325 335 352 361 363
BENS [Benns], 28 173
BENSON, 201 383
BENTON, 373
BERGDOLL, 202
BERRY, 22 57 62 78 88 107 112 143 151 182 228 238 254 289 296
BETTILL [?], 243
BETTZ, 283
BEVAN [Bevin Bevins], 46 197 334
BEVERLIN, 98 145 147 166
BEVIER [?], 268
BICE, 134
BIDDLE [Bidle], 10 17 56 96 374
BIGELOW, 211
BIGGS, 23 27 33 45 71 158 159 247 248 261 279 309 340

BIGGS (Cont.)
362 364
BILLINGSLEY [Billingsly Billinsley], 159 160 199 299 348 352 361 365 383
BILLS, 149 174 193 263 278
BINGAMON [Bingaman], 91 225
BIRCH, 229
BIRD, 57 141
BISHOP [Bisshop], 101 132 142 183 301 382
BISSELL, 214 216
BLACK, 313
BLAIKISTON, 229
BLAIR, 345
BLAKE, 36 118
BLATCHLEY, 3 45 384 385
BODLEY, 265
BOGGESS, 175 226 227 240 263 265 289
BOLLING, 36
BOLTINGHOUSE [Boultinghouse], 93 287 371
BOND, 9 10 150
BONES, 222
BOOTH [Boothe], 39 164 206 220 269 270 294
BOSLEY, 41
BOSWELL, 231
BOWEL, 47
BOWEN, 31 246 267 283 292 293 371
BOWERS, 47 90 126 178
BOWIE, 65 360
BOWLBY [Bowlsby], 92 219 247
BOWMAN, 143 219
BOWSER, 274 275 312
BOYCE, 47 71
BOYD, 48 78 112 147 240 278 386
BOYDSTONE [Boydston], 117 150 365
BOYLES [Boyle Boyls], 11 70 71 109 110 116 151 173 179 272 333 369

BOZARTH, 45
BRADFORD, 117 119 179 383
BRADLEY, 162 272
BRAIN [Brane], 10 23 35 67 81 115 152 186 187 244 249 260 385
BRAND [Bran], 17 207 254 380
BRANDON, 13-16 18 22 23 26 27 53 77 78 83 95 97 107 113 121 130 134 142 167 168 175 183 192 197 198 201 210 241 246 264 271 272 277 295 302 303 320 322-324 327 346 348 357 379 385
BRANHAM, 261
BRANNAN, 249
BRANT [Brandt], 205 215-317 308 345 346 366
BRAUCHMYER, 203
BREEDING, 11
BREWER, 71 345 346
BRICE, 64
BRIGGS, 48
BRISCOE, 139
BRITTON, 228 239 276 282 293 298 335 340 341
BROOKS [Brook Brooke], 44 103 104 241 386
BROUGH [Bruff], 12 199
BROUGHTON [Bratton Brauton Broton Brotton], 114 211 215 235 247 265 267 341
BROWN, 9 19 55 58 89 108 128 145 146 153 165 172 181 228 238 245 248 279 280 320 321 324 342 359 379 383
BROWNFIELD [Bromfield Brumfield], 12 23 57 100 179 182 233 238 284 296
BRUMMAGE [Barmejam Bromage Bromigan Brumage Brumagen Brumagh Brumagin Brumegen Brumegin

BRUMMAGE (Cont.)
    Brumingham], 11 127 128
    164 181 185 189 208 251
    270 276 282 300 342 343
    354 382
BRYAN [Briant], 133 205 263
    272
BUCHANAN [Bohannan Buchannan Buchanon Buckannon Buckanon Buckhannan Buckhannon Buckhanon], 24 28 32 39 54 74 85
    114 123 125 148 197 241
    307 319 345 364 371 382
BUCKALEW, 247
BUCKNER, 173
BUFFINGTON, 238 276
BULLAND [Bullan], 8 11 12 76
BULLOCK [Bullick], 1 9 15 139
    156 222 229 358
BUNNER [Boner Bonner], 37 58
    59 97 106 127 132 175 351
    352 383
BURCHINAL [Burchanald Burchenal], 1 2 32 42 215
    227 228 315 340 367 385
BURK, 14 26 43 64 210
BURKETT, 380
BURKHAM, 237
BURNES, 317
BURRELL [Burrel], 61 67 171
    199 345
BURROWS [Burress Burris Burroghs Burroughs], 9 26
    46 59 67 97 99 117 119 134
    157 165 205 212 229 232
    288 290 306 311 312 322
    329 342 349 354 382 383
BURSON, 183
BUSBY, 32
BUSSER [Buser], 38 39 40
BUSSEY, 25 159 161 216 219
    299
BUTCHER [Bucher], 91 124 266
    267

BUTLER [Butlar], 1 2 3 33 37
    39 42 44 52 65 73 74 79 81
    90 93 100 105 118 145 154
    155 170 171 175 177 178
    184 189-192 196 198-201
    203 207 215 218 225 239
    241 243 244 270 276 301
    315 352 380 382 385
BUTTON, 31
BUZZARD, 346
BYERS, 68 254
BYRD, 80
BYRNE [Byrn Byrnes], 68 69 81
    102 123 243 249 250 255
    273 279 308 347 359
CADWALLADER, 61
CAIN, 22 72 73 78 111 112 117
    131 184 186 234 235 258
    283 284 288 292 293 370
CALDWELL, 29 138
CALE, 40 128 385
CALEY, 352
CALFFLESH, 233
CALHOUN, 58 195
CALLAHAN, 3
CALVERT, 315
CAMP [Kemp Vn Camp Van Camp], 14 35 55 92 153 285
    286 373 384
CAMPBELL [Cambell], 4 8 28
    55 64 66 91 103 122 129
    131 177 214 218 221-225
    237 239-241 252 260 273
    286 298 332 379 382
CANBY, 136 320 379
CANFIELD, 240 316 317 322
CANTWELL, 123
CARBERRY, 11 293
CARHART, 215
CARLISLE, 219
CARPENTER, 145 218 220 233
    247 323 353 354
CARROLL [Carrel], 71 106 134
    135 136 208 340
CARSON, 119

CARTER, 117 259
CARTER [?], 378
CARTNEY, 265
CARVER, 202 204
CARY, 334
CASEBEER, 377 380
CASEY [Casy], 3 33 37 74 170 207 238 276 352 368 385
CASLE [?], 313
CASSIDY [Casady Casaty Cassady Cassaty Casseday], 1 80 109 115 186 331
CASTO [Castow], 159 309 362
CASTON, 158
CAVARE, 53
CHADWICK, 199 278
CHALFONT, 334
CHAMBERS, 372
CHANCE, 231
CHANCY, 136
CHANDLER, 32
CHANEY [Cheney Cheny China Chiney], 28 40 46 57 65 74 82 97 103 118 121 144 165 178 208 209 226 254 284 301 339 360 377 378
CHAPMAN, 86 98 115 116 141 144 161 236
CHENOWETH [Chenworth Chinowith Chinworth], 108 153 265
CHERRY, 199
CHEW, 35 205
CHIPPS [Chips], 2 7 9 16 45 48 49 60 81 84 87-90 96 98 105 114 117 130 151 165 204 209 215 228 232 235 238 239 250 256-258 260 266 287 304 305 321 323 324 326 330 331 333 339 341 345 351 353 355 363 370 374 384
CHISLER [Schisler Shisler], 149 198 205 208 266 292 314 359

CHURCHILL, 25
CISCO, see SISCO
CLACKBURN [?], 318
CLAGETT [Clagget], 39 91 132 142 293 303
CLAGG, 231
CLAIBORNE [Clabourn Clayborne Claybourne], 5 10 17 40 60 61 82 88 194 287 328 374
CLARE, 72 125 206 284 326 328 332
CLARK, 4 9 11 12 29 30 31 33 43 49 52 62 75 77 81 96 124 164 166-168 202 203 209 219 228 229 235 241 246 257 261 277 302 308 309 315 326 334 342
CLARKSON, 6 9 10 17 40
CLARY, 258
CLAYTON [Claten], 97 127 136 199 200 244 336
CLEGG [Clagg Cleg], 70 95 110 125 139 218 219 231 237 270 335 342 357
CLELAND [Clelland], 78 111 122 182 191 203 218 233 377
CLOSTER [Cluster], 156 159 252 253
CLUTTER, 162 311
COAIL [?], 149
COALTER, 321
COATES, 96
COBB [Cob], 19 57 62 86 88 100 143 228 234 241 289
COBUN [Coburn], 92 102 134 164 171 244 329 364 373
COCHRAN, 48 64 69 79 84 104 161 212 219 229 265 267 281 359 383
CODDINGTON, 367
COFMAN, 84
COIL, 75
COLDEN, 40

COLDREN, 175
COLE [Coale], 59 140 141 195 220 300 365 366
COLEMAN, 264
COLLINS [Collens], 11 23 48 84 138 169 178 184 188 191 192 194 218 245 332 344 353
COMBS [Combes Coombs], 45 115 239 299
COMEGYS [Comingys], 96 265 286 329
CONAWAY [Conway], 58 259 324
CONLEY, 3 229
CONN, 158
CONNER [Connor], 18 20 26 30 88 160 162 164 166-169 235 298 382 383
CONROD, 137
COOGLE, see KUGAL
COOK [Cooke], 16 96 173 329 333
COOKUS, 92
COON, 64 65
COOPER, 41 49 266 273 289 293 306 312 316 335 363
COPE, 195 368
CORCORAN, 18 64 125 328 360 361 368
CORDRAY [Cordry], 242 338
CORE [Kor], 6 7 85 86 174 193 249 251 270 279 322 330
COREY [Cory], 3 334 379 384 385
COROTHERS [Carothers Crothers], 13 98 115 161 236 319 371 379
CORSON, 382
COSS, 274 275 312
COUNTS, 47 378
COURTNEY, 11 27 108 144 148 150 206 309 325 332
COX, 1 2 22 115 145 171 172 175 187 190 198 232 239

COX (Cont.) 245 284 310 322 371
COZAD, 266 378
CRACRAFT, 310 320
CRAFT, 377
CRALE, 221
CRAMMOND [Cramond], 10 384
CRAMPLIN, 43
CRANE, 16 204 236
CRISS [Christ], 39 61 66 75 83 101 128 156 159 252 253 261
CRITCHFIELD [Crihfield Scritchfield], 84 112
CROLL [Crall Crool Crull], 22 32 37 40 43 64 77 103 143 158 171 197 208 248 255 257 263 268 320 366 378
CROOKS, 144
CROW, 319
CUNANT [?], 162
CUNNINGHAM, 13 70 112 137 142 186 237 250 252 333 379
CUPP [Coob Cup], 246 283 292 353 356
CURRENT [Currant], 39 77 202 237
CURRY [Currey Currie], 93 94 106 239 240 277 334 365
CURTIS, 146
CUSHMAN [Cooshman Coushman], 14 69 107 121 130 163 195 379
CWEY [?], 241
CZIGAN, 150 374
DAILEY, 231
DAKIN, 355-357
DALIS [?], 42
DARBY, 3 63 164 167 168
DARLEY, 241 245
DARLING, 61 232 234 241 261
DARRAH [Dorough Dorrow], 45 193
DARTWILER, 353

DAUGHERTY [Dehorthy], 4 21
  59 61 65 74 109 132 140
  162 170 171 174 177 196
  201 202 205 206 208 219
  232 234 238 241 263 266
  280 298 310 317 320 325
  329 331 336 338 345 349-
  351 360 363 378 384 386
DAVEY, 386
DAVIDSON, 22 234
DAVIES, 73
DAVIS, 8 13 14 24 28 30 31 33
  34 36 44 46 47 51 54 57 60
  61 66 72-74 84 87 89 92 94-
  96 102 112 115-117 123 126
  131-133 140 147 149 150
  156 158 169 170 173 175-
  178 187 201 202 209 213
  223 225 229 234 240 241
  244 249 251 262 279 281
  285 300 308 309 329 340
  349 366 367 374 379
DAVISSON [Davison], 21 62 88
  103 121 151 179 205 206
  213 238 263 318 328 332
  340 345 377
DAWSON, 12 15 16 24 31 33
  34 53-55 67 69 75 77 85-87
  89 109 154 173 188 190 192
  210 222 233 236 239 241
  254 278 305 380 381 384
DE VALCOLIN, 50
DEAKINS [Deakens Deekins
  Dekens Dekins], 3 4 8 17 18
  19 28 30 32 45 50 56 63-66
  76 77 79 83 85 90 91 96 99
  100 101 116 121 122 124
  125 128 129 131 142 164
  183 184 187 193-195 204
  207 225 227 229 281 286
  287 293 301 303 316 328
  360 361 368 372 374 377-
  379 380 383 384
DEAN, 26 46 75 99 112 114
  117 124 130 159 165 168

DEAN (Cont.)
  170 185 186 202 211 229
  232 240 243 250-252 285
  290 304 306 321 349 370
  371
DEARDORF, 267 268
DEASLY [?], 333
DEAVER, 295
DEEL, 73
DEIBLER [Debler], 174 269 305
  347
DELAP, 197
DEMOND, 168
DEMOSS, 216
DENEALE, 53 83
DENNY, 14 379
DENT, 12 21 23 25-27 29 31 32
  35 41 45 48 49 56 59 66 81
  85 93 95 97 100 103 105
  127 136 140 141 152 156
  166 179 183 199 201 207
  212 219 242 245 247 259
  321 327 346 373
DERICK, 377 see also TETER
DERING, 7 8 49 73 81 97 102
  104 107 113 117 123 126
  127 130 132 134 140 147
  158 162 171 182 185 186
  191 199 201 202 208 218
  228 229 232 236 240 243
  244 248 257 260 274 275
  279 282 289 292 294 302
  313 322 327 333 336 347
  350 351 363 370 371
DEVALCOLIN, 51
DEVILY, 293
DEWEESE [Dewees Dewese], 33
  62 169 170 195 258 266 276
  325 383
DEWIT, 10 107 115 187 385
DICE [Dise], 372 377
DICKEN, 217
DICKENSON [Dickinson], 189
  265 267 331 359
DIEL [or DEIL], 365

DIFFENDERFER [Diffendower], 38 39
DIGMAN, 197 334
DILLMAN [Delman Dilman], 64 293
DILLON, 7
DIMMIT, 346
DIMOND, 142
DIXON, 146
DOBBINS [Dobins], 88 143
DODDRIDGE [Dodridge Doldridge], 207 208 244 322 369
DOLLISON, 318
DONALDSON, 5 19 21 25 34 55 71 92 95 126 130 135 136 183 188 193 197 203 208 217 219 223 224 274 276 290 312 313 318 333 344 353 378 384
DONIPHAN, 69
DONLAP, 20
DOOLITTLE, 34 54 61 66 73 120 128 155 218 311 327 348 358 360 383
DORAN, 241 277
DORROW, see DARRAH
DORSEY [Dossey], 153 159 214 240 257 263 358
DOUGLASS [Douglas], 11 68 72 78 81 111 128 144 167 168 213 253 267 318 320 354
DOWDELL, 88
DOWNER [Downar Downard], 3 7 10 25 41 55 70 75 95 98 104 130 138 142 146 149 151 165 191 192 237 238 240 243 265 267 319 321 345 353 364 371 383 385
DOWNING, 21 64 224
DOWTHET, 37
DOYLE, 12 19 29 205 285
DRAGOO [Draga Dragoe], 24 43 55 67 88 162 233 272 284 293 314 324 326 369

DRAKE, 355-357
DRAPER, 154 191 211
DRENKER, 78
DROWN, 108
DROWN [?], 325
DUCHMANN, see TOOTHMAN
DUDLEY, 6 29 44 54 59 66 74 75 80-82 95 97 113 132 135 140 153 168 184 205 312 324
DUELING, 122
DUFFY, 130
DUGAN [Duggan], 21 51
DUNCAN [Dunkin], 4 197 268
DUNHAM, 22 38 45 47 48 65 95 96 99 181 206 251 270 276 282 372
DUNLAP, 303
DUNLAVY, 320 328
DUNN, 54 91 92 145 153 218 220 233 242 344 353 362 363 366 382
DUNWOODY [Dunwoodie], 18 22 167 256
DUQUID, 40
DUVALL [Devall Duval], 19 185 196-198 207 300
DYER, 27 129 213 245
EARHART, 73
EASTBURN, 49 59
EASTON, 9 53 385
EBERT, 81
ECKHART, 99
ECKLEBERGER, 379
EDDY, 63 206 265
EDGELL [Edgel], 1 385
EDWARDS, 107 209 277
ELERTON, 110
ELLIOT [Elliott], 177 196 291
ELLIS, 205 289
ELLZY [Elsey], 28 88
ELY, 164
ENGLAND [Ingland], 86 100 110 112 143 228 233 284 289

ENSAMINGER, 273 307 315
ERVIN, 201 372
ERWIN [Irwin], 151 156 165 166 192 195 214 216 283 288 321 383
ERWING, 275
ESTILL, 109
EVANS [includes only Evans as principals adjoiners and chain of title; Evans witnessings may be found on almost every page of this book], 3 6 9-13 17 25 37 38 43 46 50-53 55 56 67 68 71 73 75 84-86 96 105 109 110 114 117 120 123 127 134 137 149 152 155 157 158 160 162 166 168 175 176 189 190-192 195 197 201-204 207 208 213 214 219 220 231 232 237 238 242-245 258-260 265-267 270-273 276 281 282 285 286 288 290 292 304 310 312-316 319 320 324-326 334 343-345 350 352-354 359 360 371-373 382 385
EVERHEART, 380
EVERLY [Everley], 15 59 73 86 108 127 135 138 188 192 233 252 286 296 316
EVERY, 264
EWELL, 57 66 93 174 279
EWING, 93 188 287
FAIRFAX, 19 41 54 79 102 114 123 172 194 204 205 210 211 225 297 298 304 311 332
FALLS, 136 200
FANCHER [Fanshear Fansher], 152 158 297 337
FARQUER, 82 108
FARRELL, 234
FAST, 256 336

FAUCET [Fauset Fawcet Fosset], 53 181 190 358
FAULKNER, 78
FAW, 56
FAW [?], 224
FELLER, 312
FENNER, 27
FERGUSON [Forguson Fourgusson Furguson Furgusson], 14 18 19 21 24 45 108 127 134 198 212 291 294
FERRELL [Ferrel], 58 62 82 85 95 97 103 107 110 120 131 135 139 146 154 161 163 172 181 221 228 234-236 240 250 282 332 335-337
FERRY [Ferrey], 35 114 245 288 290
FESLER [Feslar], 19 54
FESTER, 99 100 225
FETHER [Fetters], 306 346 347
FICKLE, 167 168 241 277 295 318
FIELD [Fields], 80 229
FIKE, 42 227 228
FIMPLE, 249
FINCH, 384
FINKLE [Tinkle?], 73
FINLEY, 128
FISHER, 176
FITZHUGH, 63 76 131
FLANAGAN, 213
FLAYER [?], 266
FLEMING [Flemming Flemmon], 12 20 34 36 41 45 75 87 88 136 157 211 263 293 308 350 351 379 385
FLETCHER, 293
FLOCK [?], 382
FLOY, 325
FLOYD, 20 39 40 162 214 216 321 368
FLUHARTY, no entries

FOLEY, 9
FORD [Forde], 176 222 249 270 332 340 341 349
FOREMAN [Forman], 159 295 298 320 333 362 379
FORNIE, 380
FORSTER, 52 96 102
FORSYTH, 68
FORTNEY, 55 82 104 181 182 207 258 279 285 306 328 335 357 369 383
FOSTER, 3 4 16 21 48 137 205 230 382
FOUKE, 126
FOULK [Folk Fulk], 110 152 156 164 166 167 214 216 231 232 252 261 316 321 322 328 345 359-361 366 368 372
FOWLER [Fouler Fowlar], 43 48 92 114 130 179 276 378
FOX [Foxe], 72 117 147
FRANCISCO, see Sisco
FRANKHOUSER, 303
FRANKLIN, 300
FRANKS, 25 26 110 111 138 159
FRANZIER, 380
FRAZEE [Frazey], 14 69 130 209 237 360 377
FRAZER [Fraizier Frazier], 61 107 149 257 285 380 383
FREE, 342
FREELAND, 133 331
FREEMAN, 65
FRENCH, 3 66
FRETWELL, 182 201 293 308 340
FRIEND [Freind Frund], 31 60 77 156 157 281 360 361 380
FRITTS [Frits], 39 164
FRY, 48 182
FUKLE [?], 306
FULLEN, 262
FULLER, 27 47

FULLERTON, 130 200 201 275
FULTON, 215
FUNK, 266
FURBEE [Furbay Furbey Furby], 10 155 170 171 187 219 331 351 357 358 373
GADD, 204
GAIER, 79
GALLAGHER [Galagher], 26 53 69 126 150 190 374 385
GALLATIN [Galitan Gallatine Gallaton], 50 51 165 205 216 240
GALLIHUE [Galihew Gallahew Gallahu Gallahue Gallyhew], 114 211 215 233 235 247 353 382
GALLOWAY [Gallaway], 190 195 267 362
GANDY [Ganday], 35 81 133 187 232 256 259 308 323 382
GANS [Gantz], 43 138 192 253 289
GAPEN [Gappen], 69 126 127 135 259 346 373
GARD, 319
GARDNER, 300 324
GARLOW, 23 24 216 233 368
GARRARD [Gerrard], 209 302
GARRETT, 68 72 192 221
GARWOOD, 332
GASS, 264
GASSAWAY, 88
GASTON, 214
GATES, 199
GAY, 166 177 195 199 202 218 239 245 273 305 316 330 343 355 360 363
GEBLER [Gibbler Gibler], 21 59 239-241 256 311
GEFFERS, 215
GEFFS, see JEFFS
GEORGE, 157 198 212 232 302 327 331 343

GETTINGS, 301
GEYER [Gayer Geir Gire Goyre], 79 92 200 245 270
GIBBONS [Gibbon], 131 167 169 170
GIBBONY, 136
GIBBS, 173
GIBSON, 11 35 36 40 63 111 128 332 378 379
GILKEY, 140 148 333
GILL, 53
GILLESPIE [Galaspie Gallaspey Gallaspie Gallespie Gellespie Gillispey Gillispie], 16 21 43 48 54 55 79 92 111 112 119 236 284 285 287-289 348 351 380
GILLINGS, 301
GILLMEYER, 372
GILMAN, 157
GILMORE, 237
GILPIN, 36
GLASSCOCK, 229 269
GLENN, 251 289
GLOVER, 97 357
GODFREY, 279
GOFF [Gough], 17 57 63 66 76 83 90-92 99 101 124 130 131 157 159 163 164 168 204 226 261 277 278 338 374 383
GOLDEN [Golding], 29 71 99
GOODING, 58 246 363
GOODWIN, 81 257 266
GOOSEMAN [Goosman], 26 95 96 98 163 199 210 231 290 382
GOULD, 226
GRADDYS, 288
GRADY, 367
GRAHAM [Grayham], 17 23 55 87 96 114 152 247 341 342 344 370
GRANT, 252
GRATE, 73

GRAVES, 27
GRAY, 20 58 67 79 80 103 120 142 154-156 165 221 222 233-236 280 284 289 324 327 328 333 339 344 350 351 353 354 357 359 363 366 370 371 373
GRAYSON, 288
GREATHOUSE [Gratehouse], 121 208 209 258
GREEN, 31 89 108 109 133 135 232 234 241 304
GREENWOOD [Green Wood], 70 99 108 140 141 161 173 199 257 263 265 266
GREGG [Greggs Gregs Griggs], 58 59 95 115 120 131 139 161 229 236 320 372 373
GRESMER [Gresmore Grismer], 67 332 345
GRIBBLE [Grible], 3 198 224 243 320 346 382 383
GRIER, 336
GRIFFE, 105
GRIFFETH [Griffen Griffith], 42 52 149 153 229 320 352
GRIM [Grimm], 80 109 357
GRIMSLEY, 289
GROVE, 45
GRUBB [Grub], 32 155 163 235
GRUNDY, 148
GUARD, 107 121
GUBER, 68
GUSEMAN [Gooseman Goosman], 26 95 98 163 199 210 231 237 290 339 340 363 370 372
GUSTIN [Gustine], 66 93 140 141 220 299 300 333
GUTHRIE, 2 45 142 264 269 272 323 348 357 385
GUTRIDGE [Goodridge Gutteridge], 15 90 105 113 218 256
GUYTON, 63

GWATHMEY, 277
HADDEN [Haden], 130 136 318
HADDOX, 126
HAGEMAN [Hagaman], 68 113 130 133 134
HAGNEAR, 234
HAINS, 345
HALE, 347
HALL, 14 17 30 31 47 52 53 65 70 76 93 103 112 136 155 158 160 183 190-192 197 201 218 225 226 249 259 276 286 293 295 311 317 324 326 327 332 337 350 351 386
HAMERSLY, 83
HAMILTON [Hamelton Hammilton], 4 12 16 30 31 33 44 53 55 61 62 68 97 100 105 108 116 131 134 136 147 150 152 158 166 167 176 188 191 200 214 216 219 224 225 228 254 258 266 276 296 309 321 325 332 336 361 362 372 385
HAMMOND, 207 334
HAMPTON, 45 48 195 310 358 372
HAND [?], 258
HANEY, 10 11 99 107 173 187 244 266 278 308 384
HANING, 232
HANNA [Hannah], 24 51 176 343
HANNON [Hannan], 77 240
HANTZEL, 366
HANWAY, 2 4 5 7 10 14 15 19 25 26 36 44 47 52 57 61-63 66 71 93 102-108 112 113 120 128 129 140 146 151 153 159 163-165 168 173 175 176 178 182 184 187 188 191-193 195 198 199 201 215-217 219 221 222

HANWAY (Cont.)
230 240 246 249 257 261 268 270 271 281 291-294 311 340 342 343 349 350 363 370 382 385 386
HARBOUGH, 78
HARDAMAN, 373
HARDEN [Hardin], 13 15 20 35 147 159 191 230 238 253 343 365
HARDESTY [Hardisty], 35 36 39 40 68 166
HARDING, 89 148 343
HARGROVE, 374
HARKNESS, 333
HARMAN, 232 233 278 348
HARMENSON [Harmeson Harminson Harmison Harmonson], 16 24 28 32 54 197 201 241
HARNESS, 164
HARP [Harper], 20 87 93 156 168 169 172 182 218 260 269 287 299 371
HARRIS [Harriss], 12 40 41 71 129 130 236 250 271 332 347 348 359
HARRISON, 28 29 109 135 173 188 285 367 368 379
HARROW, 138 207 290
HARRY, 346
HARRYMAN [Hereman Herriman Herryman], 47 57 84 85 171 262
HARSH, 83 101 131 157 183 187 194 204 205 225 227 261 277 368
HART, 269 271 310 320 364
HARTLEY [Heartley], 17 38 86 134 142 196 260 364
HARTMAN, 339
HARTNESS, 2 121
HARTZELL, 320
HARVEY, 329

HASBROUGH, 81
HASLET [Hazlett], 49 97 113
    269 271 272
HASTINGS, 5 30 53 59 114 117
    383 384
HASTON, 242
HASTON [?], 204
HATFIELD, 39 75 77 91 92 119
    124
HAUGHT [Haut Hott Hought],
    104 110 139 206 226 298
    316 322 335
HAVENER, 101
HAWK, 12 207 238 276
HAWKER, 284 353
HAWKINS, 121 176 282 311
    330
HAWTHORN [Hawthorne], 9 19
    21 24 28 32 46 54 58-60 62
    66 75 82 92 95 97 106 109
    127 129 148 162 166-168
    171 176 186 205 232 238
    243 248 263 273 301 312
    324 328 338 342 350 351
    353 383
HAYDON, 71 72 74
HAYES [Hays Hayse], 25 42 72
    104 362 379
HAYHURST, 150 294 297 322
    324
HAYMOND [Haymon], 6 12 17
    19 21 22 24 75-78 82 96
    104 108 114 153 154 198
    201 220 221 233 251 286
    293 295 311 325 341 342
    350-352 370 382 383
HAYNES, 16
HAYTON, 16
HAZLE [Hazel], 121 208 209
    272 383
HEADLEE, 238
HEBBURN, 28
HECK [Hecke], 277 338 378
HECKERT [Heckart], 124 338
    383

HEFFNER, 223
HEINSMAN, 171
HELLEN [Hellin], 64 201 208
    237 279
HELLEN [?], 96
HELMICK [Helmech Helmeck],
    25 26 61 88 138 159 190
HELP, 197
HENDERSON, 75 77 124 209
    249 251 344 345
HENDRIXON [Hendrexson
    Hendrickson], 45 48 171 229
    272 277 300 372
HENKINS [Hinckins Hinkinias
    Hinkins], 151 181 237 243
    335
HENNING, 146
HENRY, 23 41 100 105 152 166
    252 268
HENTHORN, 3 47 69 138 140
HERFORT, 243
HERNDEN, 205
HERREN, 265
HERRING, 262
HERSMAN, 70
HESL [?], 8
HESLET, 46
HESS, 61 333 339 377
HEWES, 175 220
HEWITT, 197
HEYDON, 29
HEYWARD, 60
HICKENBOTTOM, 212
HICKMAN, 12 54 76 88 201
    218 220 221 233 301 311
    317 323 353 354 383
HICKS, 121 176
HIGHSHEW, 354 355
HILDERBRAND [Helderbrand
    Hilterbrand Hylder Brand
    Hylderbrand], 15 105 107
    151 159 219 343
HILEY, 146
HILL, 35 36 39 44 75 109 135
    263 282 283 311 325

HILL (Cont.)
  330-332 372
HILLEGAS, 83
HILLERY [Hillary Hilleary Hillira], 153 165 280 317 324 342
HILTON, 28 209 284
HINES, 221 294
HIRADER [Hareeder Harruder Horader], 15 143 264 327 385
HISON, 294
HITE, 12 13 25 29 44 46 47 52 54 58 61 62 107 120 124 152 162 167 170 171 199 251 294 312
HIXON, 294
HOARD, 87 138
HOBBS, 332
HODGSON, 102
HOERT [?], 268
HOFFMAN [Haufman], 179 264
HOGMIRE, 8 30 41 50 63 76 124 125 131 142 183 184 193 303 344 377 380 383 384
HOGUE [Hoge Hogg Hogge Hougue], 24 32 40 54 92 118-122 125 148 201 208 287 332 377
HOHLET [?], 160
HOLLAND, 94 113 139 151 174 247 269 290 291 294 327
HOLLENBACK [Hollenbaugh Hollenbeck Hollowback], 88 303 291 311 317 329 382
HOLLENGER, 202
HOLLINS, 229
HOLLOMS, 202
HOLLY, 308 317 345 366
HOLMES, 122 123
HOLSON, 24
HOLSTINE [Holestine Holste Holston], 91 204 301 368 380

HOLTSCLAW, 200
HOLT [?], 298
HOOD [?], 379
HOOEY, 222
HOOK, 277
HOOKER, 249 261
HOOVER, 70 132
HOPKINS, 36 41 60 124 278 374
HORNER, 4 51 75 365 383
HORSE, 32 90
HORTON, 12 15 42 61 65 66 81 118 119 124 128 130 132 164 168 170 193 202 209 210 223 228 230 239 246 252 306 308 353 382
HOSKINSON [Hoskins], 14 21 26 35 67 92 107 155 258 312 314 321 334 351 381
HOTTS [?], 261
HOTZ, 261
HOUGH, 126
HOULT [Holt], 12 17 19 25 76 201 303 304 383
HOUR, 98 175
HOUSE [?], 336
HOWARD, 16 24 64 201
HOWELL [Howel], 80 115
HOY [Hoye], 17 56 74 83 85 96 99 101 185 194 234 249 261 281 286 301 328 360 361 368 369 384
HUBLEY, 38 40
HUFF, 313
HUFFMAN [Houghman], 144 161 236 269 270 272 310 333
HUFFRAGT, 31
HUGGINS, 167
HUGHES [Houghes Hughs Huse], 45 48 51 89 142 209 258 293 303 372
HUGHN [?], 11
HULICK, 173
HULINE [?], 373

HULL, 84 213 277
HUMES, 231
HUNER, 78 344 358
HUNT, 27 66 112 174 248 249
    251 374 377
HURLEY, 15 85 86 89 122 148
    188 230 233 316
HURRY [Hurrey], 104 178 184
    372 373
HURST, 80 185
HUSK [?], 383
HUSS [?], 306
HUSTON, 281
HUTCHINSON, 320
HUTS, 326
HUTSON, 59 138
HYLEGS, 84
ICE [Ieyce], 1 2 34 50 61 69 120
    122 135 189 191 213 216
    230 278 324 385
INSKEEPE [Inskip], 262 328
IRVINE, 213
JACKSON, 13 103 119 179 193
    216-218 223 275 278 315
    318 320 342 345 351-353
    381
JACO, 253
JACOBS [Jacob], 5 21 70 71 88
    95 240 382
JAMES, 65 178 225
JAMESON, 40 385
JANES [Jones?], 255
JARRETT, 68 76 78 98 117-119
    130 139 151 164 176 177
    182 188 201 202 208 211
    217 221-224 234 237 243
    249 250 254 259 271 273-
    276 278-280 307 308 315-
    318 324-327 329 331-333
    338-341 345 349-352 354
    363 364 370 374
JARVIS, 340 355
JEANS, 349
JEFFERIES [Jefferiss Jeffers],
    39 78 93 133

JEFFS [Geffs], 19 143 152 158
    168 169 172 182 189 191
    218 250 260 264 269 271
    272 286 287 310 370 371
JENKINS [Jinkins], 4 12 16 26
    35 36 40 43 45 47-49 54 55
    60 67-70 72-76 78 90 94 98
    111 112 118 119 128 130
    137 139 147 151-153 157
    172 182 188 193 196 197
    199 201 203 217 218 239
    248 254 255 263 264 268
    269 274 281 310 317 318
    322 344 347 348 353 366
    370 378 379 384 385
JENKINS [?], 128
JENNINGS [Jenings Jennings],
    35 177 200 328 380
JOBES [Jobs], 150 192 270 322
    367
JOHN, 6-8 16 17 44 47 71 73
    74 87 93 98 104 106 108
    109 112 116 117 119 120
    127 175 182 184 193 195
    211 215 223 267-270 304
    305 321 326 332 340 346
    365-367 370 382 386
JOHNS, 65
JOHNSON, 61 83 90 131 157
    167 204 210 221 222 227
    228 236 242 247 248 251
    252 261 270 286 288 315
    319 322 327 337 342 346
    348 360 361 367 371 374
    385
JOHNSTON [Jonston], 6 9 10
    26 28 88 89 107 109 123
    142 147 161 167 177 190
    235 236 249 251 260 289
    321 335 349 382
JOLLIFFE [Jolliff], 6 30 37 90
    103 293 303 304 362
JONES, 2 4 15 25 51 55 56 64
    68 73 75 79 88 95 105 106
    110 111 127 140 153 154

JONES (Cont.)
160-162 165 167 183 184
191 192 197 198 200 223
236 268 275 279 282 303
309 313 315 327 339 362
373 378 380
JOSEPH, 10 16 44 67 71 75
108 118 155 165 177 243
313 314 325 331 349
JUDY [Juda Judah Judie], 3
13-15 39 43 55 72 83 107
113 124 167 168 184 274
301-303 312 313 327 378
379 380 385
KARR [Kerr], 316 383
KEASAR, 203
KEELER, 2
KEENER, 383
KEITH, 80
KELLAR, 296
KELLER [?], 254 384
KELLUM [Kellam Killam Killem Killum Killums], 84 111 112 158 159 208 212 213 207 309 362
KELLY [Kelley Killee], 7 138 175 239 302 334 380 384 385
KELSO, 211 221 261 335 336
KEMMERER, 215
KENDALL, 122
KENNEDY [Kenedy Kennady Cannedy], 12 69 105 107 110 131 143 148 176 213 219 228 234 241 253 292 296 380
KERNS [Karn Karnes Karns Kearns], 41 74 82 106 107 114 133 136 162 163 170 173 200 212 230 249 260 267 269 270 272 294 305 328 333 339
KERSON, 8
KIDD, 98 145
KIGER [Kyger], 47 177 197 234 250 254 281 282 285 308

KIGER (Cont.)
328 333 340 341 350 359 374
KIMBLE [Kemble Kemiel Kimel Kimmel], 214 226 237 240
KINCADE [Kinkade], 310 380
KINCHALOE, 288
KING, 88 188 222 258 293 314 357
KIRKHART, 91 184 293
KIRKPATRICK [Kirk Patrick Kirk Pattrick Kirkpattrick], 169 172 182 248 283 287 292 334
KITTS, 60
KNIGHT, 165 216 239 299 362 369
KNOP, 122
KNOTTS [Knots], 65 226 231 237 246 325 326
KNOX, 175 285 351
KOOKEN [?], 110
KRATZER [Kratcher Kratser Kresser Kretcher Kretzer], 11 22 37 39 57 95 96 98 141 142 145 181 206 218 306 382 384
KUGAL, 274 275 312
KUHN, 126 205
LACY, 88
LAIDLEY [Laidly], 4 8 13 15 51 53 65 74 87 103 104 106 112 113 116-119 126 127 132 138 144 151 156 157 162 167 170 189 190 200 212 218 231 235 239 241 256 263 265 270 292 294 306 308 309 313 325 328 337 378 386
LAIRD, 230
LAKE, 248 249
LAMBERTH, 177 203
LAMING [?], 119
LANCASTER [Lankester], 33 181

LANE, 61 102 123 124 188 205 292 373 380 382
LANG, 8 11 245
LANGFORD [Lankford], 43 181
LANGHAM, 108
LANHAM, 6 7 9 11 21 54 129 146 152 167 174 185 190 195 198 199 214 216 231 238 291 294 325 374 386
LANTZ [Lance Lanse Lantze Launce Launtz], 38 70 84 110 125 159 208 265 270 303 312 325 327 328 360
LAP, 113
LAROWE, 175
LARSH, 11 12
LASH, 383
LATHAM, 369
LAUFAR [?], 78
LAUGHFORD, 301 302
LAUGHLIN, 68
LAURASON, 9
LAWLER, 177 330
LAWS, 278
LAYCOCK [Lacock], 20 93 269 287 353 371
LAYTON, 71 190 382
LAZZELL [Lazell Lazzel], 108 137 149 153 161 206 257 265
LEACH, 151 173 194 219
LEADY, 232
LEAMAN, 83
LEARD [?], 382
LEARDEN, 138
LEAS, 222
LEATH [Leeth], 41 42 118
LEATON, 13
LEE, 6 9 11 21 25 54 132 168 257 385
LEESON, 310
LEFEVERE, 378
LEGGETT, 224 225
LEGLERG, 157
LEIGHTON [Leghton], 47 60 61

LEMASTERS [Lamaster Lemaster], 23 41 103 152 237 249 260
LEMLEY, 330 342 343
LEMMON [Leman Lemmons Lemon], 42 93 372
LENHAM, 103
LEONARD, 344
LEVY, 142
LEWELLEN [Lewellin Lieuellen LuAllen Luellen], 47 48 52 79 109 160 162 188 344 353 377-380
LEWIS, 69 173 192 209 220 222 230 234
LEWMAN, 191
LIGHT, 344
LIMING, 210 316
LINDSAY [Linsay Linsey Linzey Linzia], 24 82 97 353 373
LINN [Lynn], 109 139 235 258 344 358
LINSLEY [Linsly], 9 57 58 60 81 113 141
LINTON, 3
LITCHFIELD, 301
LITTLE, 6 25 53 66 113 151 165 190 282 283 295 299 332 350
LIVINGOOD, 174
LIVINGSTON [Levingston], 127 146 185 208
LOCK, 221
LOGAN, 44 331
LONDON, 105 176 209 235
LONG, 75 128 149
LONGWELL, 6 12 25 285
LORD, 3 9 109 208 338 385
LOTT, 100 178 184 192 368
LOUDENSLAGER, 70
LOUGH, 99 212 232 336 359 383
LOVE, 32
LOW [Lowe], 52 62 110 136 137 139 190 314 319 328 369

LOW (Cont.)
 378 383
LOWDINSLAGER, 53
LOWRY [Laury Lowery Lowrey],
 71 121 293 302 310 312 329
 335 350 364-366 373
LOYER [?], 176
LUCAS [Lucus], 59 97 98 116
 127 139 154 210 337 341
 384
LYMAN, 306
LYNCH [Linch], 12 16 81 92
 106 115 116 120 126 128
 131 141 144 161 200 201
 211 235 236 246 247 260
 261 269 270-272 291 292
 298 301 310 312 313 333
 367
LYNN [Sym?], 133
LYON, 230
MABERRY, 193
MACOLM, 224
MADERA [Madara Maderia
 Madira Medera Mederia], 19
 34 108 168 205 217 218 250
 283 284 302 319 359 363
 370
MAGEE, 10 54 69 115 133 145
 148 186 187 191
MAGILL [Magell McGill], 68 72
 76 78 95 138 139 143 147
 182 240 248 270 382
MAGRUDER, 5 8 43 91 129
MAHON [Mahon], 1 2 61 120
 122 142 213 385
MAILEY, 128
MAIN [?], 319
MAINES, 335
MANLEY, 196
MANN, 27 293 357 370
MANSFIELD, 150
MARCHANT [Marchand Marchd
 Merchand Merchant], 51 89
 109 114 257 260 316 328
 373

MARKUS, 289
MARRAIN [?], 262
MARSH, 17
MARSHALL [Marshell], 26 44 62
 69 138 146 147 151 237
MARSTILLER, 50 63 65 79 101
 142
MARTIN [Martain], 19 20 26 29-
 33 49 55 58 59 63 64 73 80
 81 89 103 105 107 108 117
 120 123 130 131 133 135
 137 146 151-153 156 158
 159 164 166 173 176 178
 187-190 195 196 205-208
 212 214 219 220 224 242
 252 254 264 265 269 281
 282 288 289 306 307 316
 318 331 332 340 350 362
 363 367 371 380 384
MARVIN, 326
MASON, 85 164 229 240 292
MASON and NAIL, 111
MASTERS, 116 205
MASTERSON, 1 149
MATHENY [Methena Metheny],
 18 20 39 42 78 79 93 129
 161 166 205 247 262 263
 326 327 372
MATHERS, 325
MATHEW [Matthew Matthews],
 121 153 179 186 212 266
 284 296 307 362
MAXSON, 322
MAXWELL, 47 284 289 314
MAYFIELD, 242
MAYNOR, 37
MAYOR, 272
McALESTER, 258
McCARTY [MCarty McCarta],
 114 117 314
McCITTEN [?], 9
McCLAIN [McClane McLain], 3
 18 22 26 45 68 78 129 138
 160 161 166 167 190 198
 209 219 227 228 241 248

McCLAIN (Cont.)
256 268 277 327 328
McCLANAHAN [McClenahan], 7 8
McCLEAN, 253
McCLEERY [McClerry MCleery], 5 9 14 22 35 39 48 49 55 57 59 74 82 88 95 102 110 114 117 121 124 126 127 131 140 144 147 150 163 172 177-179 199 202 208 214 238 240 242 245 273 280 290 294 301 305 339 343 354 379 382-384 386
McCLELAND [McClelan McClelland], 82 92 102 118 119 126 143 144 162 177 193 194 202-204 219 221 222 224 292 307 312 313 315 316
McCLURE, 230
McCOLLUM [McCullum], 34 63 67 95 167 208 303
McCREA [McCray McRay MCrea], 7 21 68 76 98 108 132 146 151 152 212 243 254 282 287 289 291 293 294 309 353 386
McCREERY, 209
McDAID [McDade], 30 107 114
McDANIEL [McDaniels McDonal McDonald McDonnal McDonnald], 61 88 114 248 255 341 360
McDOUGAL, 214 216 275 276 309
McENER [McEnry], 211 246 367
McENRY [?], 247
McEWEN, 373
McFARLAND [McFarling], 73 94 102 111 116 117 125 126 148 151 158 159 171 191 200 215 218 229 240 244 267 269 299 304 327 328 351

McFARLAND (Cont.)
365 384
McFERRAN, 262
McGEE [Megee], 23 88 112 175 186 220 232 244 249 254 260 285 306 310-313 315 317 325-327 341 344 354 361 382 385
McGINLEY, 262 263 379
McGREW [Magraw Magrew Megrew], 22 23 26-38 39 171 334 379 384
McGUIRE, 122 150 207 245 276
McILHENNY, 262
McINTIRE [McEntire], 6 7 9 11 31 36 41 42 45 51 55 131 163 167 168 199 229 257 290 382 384
McIVER, 102 151
McKEEAN, 243
McKEWN [McKune], 72 379
McKINLEY [McKinely McKinly], 12 28 35 41 51 65 144 163 164 173 178 188 216 246 273 282 303 337 338 345 353 363 372 382-384
McKUNE, 72
McLAUCHLIN, 277
McLAW, 367
McLEAN, 184
McMEEKIN, 119
McMULLEN, 316
McMUNN, 32
McNEELY, 1 3 22 25 29 45 48 57 58 66 68 87 90 96 106 109 118 120 132 139 140 154 162 174 190 200 223 230 249 250 310 328 340 386
McPECK, 78 166 264 323
McPHERSON, 179
McVICKER, 276 306 350 351 353
McWILLIAMS, 264

Mc[CLELAND?], 318
MEAD, 131
MEAL, 36
MEANS [Mean], 9 236 303 381
MEAS, 85 188 222 233
MEEKER, 219 262
MEEKS, 236
MELCHER, 115
MELEY, 365
MELLETT, 221
MELROSE, 45 57 61 66 128 146
MENAR, 101
MENZIES, 118
MERCER, 357
MEREDITH [Maradith Maridyth Meridith Meridyth Merrideth Merydith], 11 12 43 98 110 189 257 271 275 312
MERL [Marles Merls], 230 241 242 384
MERRIFIELD [Marrifield Maryfield Merifield Merrefield Merryfield], 1 9 16 18 34 48 62 77 88 89 115 139 144 154 156 203 206 221 233 234 273 305 358 382 383 384
MERRILL [Merrel], 272 342
MERRYWEATHER, 202
MESSENGER, 319 359
METCALF, 346
METHODIST SOCIETY, 384
METZ, 104
MEYER, 380
MICHAEL [Micael Michaels Mike], 64 110 145 256 320 322
MIDDLETON, 235
MILES, 108
MILEY, 70 84 127 164 300 354 355
MILLER [Millar], 1 25 26 27 37 38 53 55 59 60 62 73 74 79 80 87 103 107 111 114 120

MILLER (Cont.)
126 144 145 148 149 157 162 163 166 171 174 189 201-203 212 218-220 224 232 235 237 247 253 255 286 296 313 319 323 339 341 354 361 362 369 370 380
MILLS, 20 45 73 78 111 174 193 197 372 384
MILNE, 330
MINEAR [Manear Maneer Mannear Menear Minnear], 82 102 182 192 197 254 255 308 317 345 366
MINNIS [Minnes], 22 24 25 41 45 48 52 62 63 66 67 75 81 85 93 132 144 146 174 190 199 244 273 281 316 363
MINOR, 28 51 105 139 178 226 249 270 289 322 335
MINTHORN, 160 204 222 242 378
MINTON, 121 161
MISSELL, 184
MITCHEL, 253
MITCHELL, 83 85 302
MONTGOMERY, 108 109 211 367 373
MOODY, 101 102 282
MOOLE [?], 383
MOORE [Moor More], 33 37 43 71 72 78 80 88 89 92 93 111 131 143 144 166-168 171 176 186 189 193 196 216 223 232 239 250 256 259 265 267 278 301 302 308 318 323 334 340 351 359 380 383
MORFORD, 69
MORGAN, 1 6 7 8 13 17-19 21 25 30 33 37 42 48 52 60 61 65-68 72 77 81 82 84 86 87 89 90 93 96 98 103 104 114 117-120 126 127 130 132

MORGAN (Cont.)
134 137 139 144 145 152
154 164 166 167 170 175
177 179 185 189 191 196
200 201 206 211 212 214-
216 218 220-222 229 231-
234 239-242 244 250 251
261 262 266 267 270 281
282 286 287 290-294 299
304 308-311 317-319 321
324 325 328 332 336 339
340 343 345-347 350 352-
354 356 357 360 362 364
366 367 369 370 379 380
382 383 386
MORRIS [Maurice Morress
  Morriss], 3 10 28 31 32 34
  39 41 56 75 85 86 102 103
  110 121 137 150 156 187
  188 208 209 214 255 267
  270 271 277 284 293 305
  340 360 366 367 383 384
MORRISON, 45 244 277 312
  313
MORTON, 198 266 294 295 320
  323 378
MOUNT TABER REGULAR
  BAPTIST CHURCH, 183
MOUNTZ, 36 57 64 74
MOWERER, 122
MOYLAN [Moyland Moylon], 5 6
  10 40 82 88 194 384
MUIR, 194
MULATTO, Luce (Ramsey) 136
MUNHALL, 17
MURDOCK [Moredock Mordock
  Murdoch], 29 52 67 152 284
  301
MURPHY [Murphey], 125 378
MURRAY, 176 177
MUSGRAVE, 62 81 122 155
  161 217 218 224 225 255
  344 357 358 383
MYERS [Mires Myer Myre
  Myres], 43 46 49 58 97 105

MYERS (Cont.)
  142 148 206 213 228 231
  233 261 269 271 301 302
  325 355 356 379 383
NAILOR [Nayler Naylor], 52 238
  276
NAST, 90
NEAL, 110 173 372
NEEL, 20
NEELY, 207 212 232 378-380
NEGRO, Abraham (Martin) 135
  Alexander (Payne) 330 Amy
  (Wilson) 186 Aanderson
  (Mann) 370 Anne (Wilson)
  291 Aurthur (Martin) 135
  Beck (McCleery) 179 Bess
  (Jenkins) 196 Betel (Payne)
  329 Betsy (McIntire) 37 Betty
  (Chipps) 232 Bill (Scott) 157
  Cassay (Scott) 336 Caty
  (Payne) 330 Chaney (Payne)
  329 Charles (Chipps) 232
  Charles (McIntire) 37 Char-
  lott (Scott) 336 Clary (Her-
  fort) 243 Daniel (Piles) 298
  Darcus (Pettyjohn) 295
  Dinah (Ramsey) 136 Diner
  (Wilson) 291 Ellenor (Evans)
  286 Els (Pindall) 255 Flora
  (Ramsey) 136 Glasgow
  (Davis) 131 Harry (Scott) 336
  Isaac (Horton) 223 Isaac
  (McCleery) 179 Isaac (Payne)
  330 Jain (Troy) 300 James
  (McCleery) 178 James (Scott)
  336 Jane (Jenkins) 196 Jane
  (McIntire) 37 Jeff (Wilson)
  291 Jeffery (Wilson) 186
  Joan (Joseph) 16 Leah
  (Jones) 223 Leah (Ramsey)
  Lewis (Wilson) 291 Liz
  (McCleery) 179 Lucy (Britton)
  340 Maria (Payne) 302 330
  Milly (Piles) 298 Mima
  (Ramsey) 136

NEGRO (Cont.)
  Nancy (Davis) 131 Nancy (Gardner) 300 Nancy (Jenkins) 281 Nancy (Payne) 330 Nelly (Chipps) 232 Nelson (Woodrow) 372 Peggy (Martin) 135 Peggy (Payne) 330 Rachel (Herfort) 243 Rachel (Horton) 223 Rachel (Jenkins) 281 Rachel (McNeely) 328 Rachel (Troy) 300 Reuben (Herfort) 243 Rose (Pindall) 255 Sam (Scott) 157 185 Sambo (McIntire) 37 Sarah (Chipps) 232 Sarah (Payne) 330 Selah (Payne) 330 Silvey (Martin) 135 Spencer (Piles) 298 Stephen (McNeely) 328 Suck (Pindall) 255 Susannah (Payne) 330 Tamer (Peirpoint) 268 Tom (McNeely) 328 Toney (Jenkins) 281 Vachel (Payne) 302 Watt (Wilson) 291 Will (Payne) 302 William (Scott) 185 William (Payne) 330
NEIGH, 122
NEIGHBOURS, 19 130 135 136 276 379
NEILL [Neil], 17 295
NEWLON, 100 228 233
NEWMAN, 50
NICHOLAS, 260 308
NICKLIN, 172 174 279 280 282 336 364
NINE, 116
NIXON [Neaxon], 15 18 19 105 107 112 147 148 151 164 193 219 254
NOLAND, 270
NORRIS [Norriss], 4 137 174 175 193 196 197 203 290 317 331 344 351 378 379
NORTH, 10 61 120

NUCE [Neuss Noos Noose Nooz Noze Nuess Nuez Nuse Nusz Nuze], 4 21 22 25 29 30 32 38 53 58 64 73 112 146 158 171 208 223 236 255 261 254 296 353 372
NUZUM, 12 23 124 132 189 195 238 249 276 282 305 306 319 332 358 362
OATLEY, 64 120 230
O'BRYAN, 146
OFFUTT, 207 287
OGDEN [Ogdon], 238 303 309 310
OKELL, 161
OKEY, 42 104
OLIPHANT, 186 275
OLIVER, 358
O'NEILL [Oneal Oneale Oneall Oniall], 4 8 28 66 91 122 129
OREAR, 367
ORMSBY, 25
ORR, 28 71 74 147 284
ORSON, 44 75 339 351 354 363
ORSTON, 212
ORTON, 212
ORTT, 137
OSBORN [Osburn], 124 168
OSWALT, 75
OTT, 91 122 134 232
OVERTON, 148 373
OWEN [Owens], 76 103 262 272 273 373 374
OXLEY, 66
OZSO [?], 96
PAGE, 80 341 349
PALMER, 48
PARISH [Parrish], 70 95 128 336
PARKER, 101 104 273 384
PARKS [Parkes], 13 179 342
PARKYNS, 9

PARR, 143
PARSONS, 352 368
PARTMUS [Partmas], 24 89
PATTERSON, 72 200 316 317
PATTON [Patten], 9 53 115 135 186 244 289 297
PAUL, 38 39 328
PAYNE, 80 89 97 98 102 108 109 130 146 152 159 163 164 166 168 178 181-183 185 186 198 199 202 205 209 210 212 213 218 220 223 232 236 243 244 248 255 258 260 278 285 289 292 293 302 304 305 308 309 321 322 325 326 329 330 342 349 350 355 357 362 370-373
PEACOCK, 86 98 115 116 141 144 154 161 236
PECK, 50 59 177 273 307 315
PECKENPAUGH [Peckenpaw Peckinpaugh Pickenpaw Pickingpaugh], 54 56 241 263 279 303 335 348 363
PEEBLES [Peebels Preples], 213 367 372
PEIRPOINT [Pairpoint Pierpoint], 5 7 26 62 68 71 76 78 98 119 138 139 147 250 268 319 347 370 386
PEIRY, 17
PEMBERTON, 10
PENROSE, 295
PEPER, 243
PERCIVAL [Perceval], 173 372
PERDUE [Perdew], 96 217 329 335
PERRY, 32 189 258
PERRYMAN, 373
PERSONETT, 210 220
PETER, 29 284
PETERS, 38-40 63 90 132 262
PETIT, 69
PETTY, 382

PETTY [PELLY?], 34
PETTYJOHN [Pette John Petty John], 3 7 11 12 14 23 43 47 62 104-106 124 132 134 189 220 221 235 248 249 254 269 282 286 294 295 297 318 350-352 380 384
PEYTON, 9 32 80
PHELPS, 26 43 379
PHIDDY, 269
PHILIPS [Fillips Phillips], 15 31 34 51 55 71 74 83 105 110 112 127 157 158 183 197 203 213 224 226 234 236 237 260 289 308 359 371
PHILSON, 293
PIATT, 36
PICK, 49 336
PICKETT, 60
PIERCE [Pearce Pearse Perce], 16 54 70 88 90 148 186 215 265 299 300 311 317 344 350
PILES, 23 61 146 186 249 258 298 381
PINDALL [Pindel Pindell Pindle], 6 9 11 12 16 23 24 32 35 41 44 45 48 49 51 53 59 61 79 84 98 110 113 115 130 135 138 140 145 163 165 169 177 178 184 206 209 212 214 215 228 231 235 239 241 243 245 250 254 255 257-259 266 282 287 290-293 299 309 312 321 323 324 326 329 331 332 335 341 353 355 363 364 379 380 382 384-386
PITZER, 309
PIXLER [Picksler], 209-211
PLEASANTS, 20 80
PLOM, 155 309
PLUM, 77 132 146 163 350 362
PLUNKET, 380
POE, 289

POLLOCK [Pollick], 23 92 138 247 384
POLSLEY [Palsley Pawsley Pawlsley], 220 233 242 251 270 276 282 294 319 337 362
POOLE, 75
POOR, 66 286 295 344
POPE, 60 277
POPPENO, 29 30
PORSAL [?], 160
PORT, 205 266
PORTER, 40 111 354
POST, 25 166
POST [PORT?], 147
POSTLETHWAITE [Postle Postlethwait Postlewait Postlewaith Postleweight], 33 37 57 85 109 114 133 136 142 189 201 207 217 366 379
POTTER, 3 15 16 22 38 39 45 61 64 72 78 121 124 126 161 166 167 186 190 209 210 264 272 302 303 308 310 327 353 372 383
POTTERLL, 26
POWELL [Powel], 22 24 29 45 48 52 67 71 74 82 89 93 96 97 114 152 189 201 202 226 236 287 290 291 300 357 358 371 372
POWERS [Power], 294 350 351
PRATHER [Brater Prater], 104 326
PRATT, 329
PRICE, 12 116 207 214 265 311 329 357 358 369
PRICKETT [Preckett Pricket], 6 12 17-19 62 90 105 193 215 223 231 242 244 270 289 293 304 309 344 353 354 362 369 382-384
PRIDE, 117 187 188
PRINGLE, 330
PRITCHARD, 310 366

PROLL, 36
PROVINCE, 103
PRUNTY, 62 220 258
PUGH [Pew], 306 367
PURVIANCE [Perviance], 8 49 316
PUTNAM, 199
QUYNN, 5
RABER [Raver Reaver Rever], 51 97 112 141 199 287 348 352 365
RAINES, 234 241
RALSTON, 17 56 374
RAMS, 118
RAMSEY, 3 29 49 50 54 72-74 119 123 136 143 152 161 177 196 199 203 206 216 217 265 268 269 278 285 287 310 316 320 327 345 351 352 378 383 385
RANDALL, 31 49 64 97 99 135 161 361
RANDOLPH, 295
RANKIN, 138
RATCLIFF, 96
RAVENSCROFT [Ravenscraft], 217 268 310 345
RAY [Rea], 15 157 304 318 382
REAM [Reams Reems], 68 154 160 266 302 306 347
REBBLE [?], 289
REDENOUR, 275
REED [Read Reid], 15 16 34 45 56 63 74 103 114 118 125 143 146 147 149 150 163 164 176 192 199 226 290 292 296 303 327 328 340 341 343 349 364 382 383
REEDER, 6 7 9 13 14 19 20 22-25 27 29 30 35 40 51 52 61 66 68 79 80 82 83 87 108 120 127 129 135 146 152 156 163 174 176 178 179 185 190 196 197 204 206 213-217 223 230-233 242

REEDER (Cont.)
  248 250-252 257 261 276
  279 285 293 294 306-308
  312 313 317 319 321 326
  329 339 342 345 350 353
  355 359 361 363 366 371-
  373 384 386
REESE [Rees], 22 58 93 359
REEVES, 81 139 271 291
REILY [Riely], 264 353
REINTZEL [Rantzel], 3 66 83 85
  125 174 195 207 281 287
  301
REISCH [?], 251
RENSHAW, 330
RHODES [Rhoads Road Roads
  Rodes], 43 178 368
RICE [most entries are variants
  for ROYCE], 89 154 215 250
  298 323 386 see also ROYCE
RICH, 354
RICHARDS, 42 170 352 385
RICHARDSON, 153
RICHEY [Richie Richy Ritchey
  Ritchie], 29 40 47 81 194
  224 239 275 284 308 315
  320
RIDDLE, 42 170 352
RIDENOUR [Ridenever Riden-
  hour Ridenover Ridinhour],
  17 57 63 90 91 99-101 194
  204 205 225 274 275 312
  383
RIDGWAY [Ridgeway], 4 53 71
  137 140 167 182 193 196
  223 250-252 266 273 274
  297 308 327 332 342 372
RIGGS, 59 69 70 97 116 117
  127 336 384
RIGHTER, 206
RINEHART, 17 63 168 225 227
RIVER [Rivers], 273 274 307
  315
ROARK, 22 53 79 109 113 379
ROBE, 14 24 74 83 86 94 95
  125 148 162 185 197 198
  202 247 259 300 301 327
  350
ROBERTS [Robbarts], 1 18 33
  39 40 53 62-65 67 73 75 77
  105 124 132 153 154 165
  209 215 224 226 247 248
  255 256 261 265 267 280
  315 318 322-324 326 339
  342 346 348 354 355 357
  370 381
ROBERTSON, 59 373
ROBINETTE [Rabbinet Robbinet
  Robenet Robinnet Robnett],
  23 75 78 83 101 183 197
  209 267 268 306 379
ROBINS, 11 140 141 148 378
  383 384
ROBINSON [Robeson Robison],
  1 5 13 19 27 29 32 40 44 49
  70 103 106 130 142 148 179
  191 199-201 211 221 222
  225 229 246 247 254 306
  320 360 367 371 380 383
  384
ROBY, 178
RODEHEFFER, 321
RODMAN, 119
ROGERS [Rodgers], 17 26 37 49
  68 72 78 88 103 143 147
  164 173 240 268 270 288
  366 370
ROHRER, 91
ROLAND, 78 144
ROLSTON, 255
ROOT, 126 171
ROSE, 27 65 117 288 328 330
ROSS, 6 32 126 176 178 293
ROWLAND, 3 72 81 92 111 126
  128 171 267 271 274 275
  291 301 313 373
ROYCE, [Roice Royse Ryce] 31
  44 59 60 89 93 214 234 235

ROYCE (Cont.)
 241 265 304 305 321 324
 331 367 see also RICE
RUBLE [Rubell], 3 41 52 80 104
 220 320 326 383
RUCKLE, 221
RULE, 209
RUMBLEY, 348
RUMSEY, 36
RUNNER, 246 349
RUNYON [Runnion], 26 42 201
 261 364 378
RUSSEL [Russell], 28 74 81 82
 89 245 262 263 279 305 306
 335 339 363 379
RUTHERFORD, 58 251 283 319
RYNEER [Reinier], 171
SADLER, 210 306
SAFFORD, 157
SALZER, 206
SAMPLE, 373
SAMS, 89 142
SANDERS, 50 106 153 183 303
SAPP, 55 89 142 316 332
SASTO [?], 31
SAVARY, 40 106 153 206 328
SAY [Seay], 16 330
SAYRE [Sayers Sayr Sayres
 Seers], 15 18 20 34 58 74 83
 85-87 95 107 110 114 115
 120 121 125 131 138 148
 154 158 163 172-174 192
 221 233 234 249 260 271
 279 280 282 299 345 360
 380 382 384
SCHEIBLI, 38
SCHNEBLY, 30 39 41 91 122
 134
SCHROEDER, 174 177
SCOTT [Scot], 4 5 10 11 14 18
 20 26 31-35 40 41 46 47 54
 55 59 60 68 69 71 79 81 84
 86 89 90 94 103 105 106
 108 109 114-117 119 126
 127 130 131 134 135 141

SCOTT (Cont.)
 144 145 153 155 157 162
 169 170 185 188 193 195-
 197 200 202 206 207 211
 212 219 220 223 227 228
 232 238-240 242 244-247
 257-260 265 267 270 273
 274 276 280 285 302 303
 305-307 309 311-313 315-
 317 319 321 326 328 330
 331 336-339 342 344 346
 349 351 354 355 357 359-
 361 364 367 371 373 379
 383-385
SCRIPPS [Scrips], 52 137 150
 166 361 362
SCRITCHFIELD, see CRITCH-
 FIELD
SCRYER, 77 307 308
SCULL [?], 157
SEAMAN, 112 192
SEATON, 219
SEDGWICK [Sidgwick], 218 243
SEEGER, 38 40
SELSBY, 229
SEMPLE, 8
SEVEAR, 202
SEVERANS [Severan Severens
 Severins Severns], 18 125
 129 154 160 167 256 298
 315 316 347 358
SEWALL, 56
SEXTON, 120 151 163 164 175
 176 179 185 211 220 228
 238 246 355 356 367
SHACKELFORD, 257
SHADOCK, 278
SHARK, 274
SHAVER [Shafer Shaffer], 18 21
 90 92 101 162 193 237 383
SHAW, 3 8 80 138 219 302 326
 351
SHAY, 1 385
SHEAN [Shahan Shehan], 185
 213 244 266 267

SHEETS [Sheetz], 211 261 324
325 337
SHEILDS, 126
SHERIDAN, 265
SHINN [Shin Shins], 70 95 271
274 275 290 292 321 325
349
SHIOR [?], 284
SHIVELY [Sheibley Shibely
Shibley Shiveley], 14 35 38-
40 59 189 207 212 244 266
271 303 346 365 366 384
SHOBE, 367 372 373
SHOCKLEY, 28 32 86 108 197
201 217 222 232 260 293
325 353 365 366
SHOOP, 274 307 315
SHRADER, 320
SHRIVER [Schriver Shriber
Sriver], 24 179 181 221 310
SHROYER, see SCRYER
SHULL, 224
SHUMAKER, 368
SHUMAN [Shoeman], 170 243
269 367 368
SHUTTLESWORTH [Shackles-
worth Shettlesworth], 66 95
115 181 260 348
SIDWELL, 5 53 59 70 114 117
327 339 354 384
SIGHMAN [?], 6
SILLIG, 177 221
SILLIMAN, 109
SIMESON [Simerson], 130 283
SIMMES [?], 384
SIMMONS, 125
SIMON, 213
SIMPLER, 16 118 177
SIMPSON, 7 27 29 49 57 84
136 142 194 224 244 263
289 302 321 384
SIMS, 30
SINE [Syne], 192 246
SISCO [Cisco Fransisco

SISCO (Cont.)
Francisco Scisco Siscoe], 87
88 114 211 215 235 247 297
SISLER, 326
SISTER, 348
SKEIN, 68
SKINNER [?], 46
SLAUGHTER, 288
SLEDGER [Slidger], 29 58 74
194 195
SLOE, 26
SLYE, 174
SMALLY, 107
SMELL, 67 231 345 361
SMILEY, 267
SMITH, 5 10 19 22 25 27 30 34
38 52 53 55 56 59 67 71 74
92 95-97 104 107 108 116
120 130 131 135-137 139
148-150 161 171 186 191
200 201 210-214 216 217
221 229 231 234 236 237
243 246 247 249 250 253
254 257 259 261 264 268
269 271-273 276 278 279
283 285 287 293 308 309
317 323 325 326 333 338
339 345 347 348 351 366
367 374 382 384 385
SMITHSON, 63 153 159
SMOOT [Smout], 2 31 39 60 93
SMYTH, 40 116 137 173 210
319 320 see also SMITH
SNELL, 231
SNIDER [Snyder], 7 33 81 87 93
96 114 130 169 175 213 216
220 227 230 233 235 236
249 295 296 304 305 330
366 369
SNODGRASS [Snotgrass], 6 20
63 81 110 130 150 151 156
164-166 214 216 271 275
285 292 312 321 322 324
368

SNOWDEN, 125
SOMERVILLE [Sommerville], 46 49 102 280
SOULLARD [Soulard], 138 380
SOUTHER, 297
SOUTHWORTH [Southwerth], 7 19 128 257 325
SOVEREIGN [Soverns], 45 135 198
SOWERHABER, 89 133
SOYERS, 243
SPADER, 280
SPAHR, 237
SPAIR, 367
SPALDING, 16
SPARKS, 195
SPAW, 195
SPENCER, 49 88 173 280
SPRING, 144
SPRINGER, 1 12 17 19 23 25 40 48 54 62 72 87-92 96 104 114 134 145 194 211 212 215 224 229 240 242 253 273 303 305 307 315 318 341 369
SPURGEON [Spurgen Spurgin], 103 133 138 209 272 274 300 312 313 378 379 382
SQUIRE [Squier Squires], 12 18 132 167 168 241 258 277 320 346 383 384
STAFFORD, 9 26 51 55 72 131 143 146 158 182 215 229 230 248 256 304 332 366
STAGG [Stag], 37 56 86 199 305
STAIR, 344
STALEY, 320
STALL, 205
STANBURY [Stanbrey], 45 48 107
STANLEY [Standley], 22 43 64 227 263 264 295 296
STARK, 176
STARKY, 143
STARN, 154
STARTSMAN, 378
STATELER [Statelar Statlar Statler], 6 7 53 54 70 95 146 151 178 181 218 243 279 335 385
STATTON, 329
STEALEY [Stealy], 4 9 11 50 54 58 73 79-81 91 96 102 108 109 113 163 164 168 177 178 190 195 199 202 203 208 209 214-216 234 241 256 259 271 274 275 280 289 290 292 307 308 311-313 315 316 325 327 330 337 338 341 345 354 359-361 382 384
STEEL, 157 260 273
STEMPLE, 57 77 91 99-101 193 204 301 368 378 380
STEPHENS, 23 148 150 167 176 194 225 245 320 378
STEPHENSON [Stevenson Stinson], 2 24 80 142 215 251 267 268 382 385
STERLING, 51 71
STERN, 202 221
STERRETT [Sterret], 265 267 359
STEVENS, 12 59
STEWART [Steward Stuart Swart], 3 23 27 37 60 71 78 79 90 94 102 111 112 132 133 137 143 144 171 175 179 184 189 195 197-200 209 211 217 220 232 233 244 263 267-270 272 281 284 289 300 301 310 314 319 322 333 337 338 347 371 380 382 384 385
STIDGER, 148
STILES, 79 88 154 160 207 208 322 323
STILLWELL [Stilwell], 195 341
STINEBAUGH, 374

STITTS, 236
STOCKTON, 44 46 61 105 117 120 386
STOCKWELL, 254
STODDERT, 36 174
STOKELEY, 109 265
STONEBRAKER, 184
STONEMAN, 18
STONHILL, 86
STOUGH [Stow], 8 63 125 184 193
STOUT, 380
STOVER, 223
STRAIT [Straight Strate Streete Streight], 43 44 67 106 112 165 203 213 233 368 369
STRIBLING, 238
STULL, 378
STURGEON, 39
STUTLER, 262
SULLIVAN [Sullavan Sullevin Sweleven], 25 140 164 205 263 296 337 347
SUMMERS, 15 50 59 224 225
SUMMERVILLE, 151 344 367
SUTER, 374
SUTHERLAND, 120
SUTTON, 30 35 78 144 151 152 175 197 225 241 301 320 330 334 364
SUTTON [?], 320
SWAINE, 102
SWAN, 41 258
SWANK, 162 242 272
SWEARINGEN [Swearengen Sweringen], 50 59 92 183 206 223 347
SWISHER [Swisser Switzer], 74 210 257 263 339
SYPOLT [Sipolt], 39 156 159 252
TANNEHILL [Tanahill Tanehill Taneyhill Tannahill Tannahille Tannihill Tanyhill Taunehill Tawnyhill Tenehill

TANNEHILL (Cont.)
Tonnehill], 4 16 29 42 44 62 77 104 129 131 137 139 188 224 243 256 307 314 315 318 364 378 380 382 384 385
TARLTON, 221
TARNEY [Tearney], 85 152 246 262 279 363
TARRISON [Terrison], 17 56 96 374
TATE, 80 163 214-216 289 290 292 293
TAYLOR, 26 30 41 42 74 90 123 153 165-168 177 191 195 205 235 254 282 304 311 319 347 369 380
TENANT [Tennant Tennent], 70 95 104 146 179 218 265 279 285 316 322 359
TERISE [?], 123
TERREL, 384
TETER [Tetery Tetra], 63 76 99-101 187
TETRICK, 133 221 288
TETSOARD [Titsword Titsworth Titzard], 2 297 325 385
THISTLE, 133
THOMAS, 69 71 73 95 100 105 127 134 148 151 158 160 200 213 219 231 236 237 244 245 253 262 268 284 289 291 326 332 336 356 362 364
THOMPSON [Thomson], 8 14 15 21 28 30 44 91 116 129 137 150 155 188 195 200 214 216 222 252 286 290 309 319 344 346 353 354 373 381 382
THORN, 155 178 319 369
THORNTON, 55 68 224 380
THROCKMORTON, 368
TIBBS, 55 71 74 95 121 126 137 150 153 198 278 279

TUBBS (Cont.)
  327 362
TICHENAL, 326
TICHONOR, 27
TIDBALL [Tiddball], 213 238
TIERNAN, 241
TIFFIN, 108
TILTON, 176
TINGLE, 4 21 29 46 53 54 59
  60 73 74 104 113 120 126
  148 157 162 167 169 194
  195 202 204 205 226 252
  254 263 281 282 292 302
  307 321 324 325 332 337
  340 345 354 359 363 384
TINNEY, 300
TISDALE, 205
TOLBOTT, 64
TOLER, 325
TOMLINSON [Tomlinstone], 118
  378
TOMS, 222 224
TONCRY, 319
TOOTHMAN [Doughman
  Duckman], 228 308
TOPLIFF, 31 33 44
TOUCHSTONE, 315
TRADER, 3 18 21 22 26 52 251
  276 286 314 320 350 378
  382 383
TREMBLY [Trembley Tremley
  Trimbly], 79 155 215 266
TRICKETT [Tricket], 14 22 26
  43 64 85 86 95 98 110 115
  116 139 141 144 161 210
  236 255 287 332
TRIMBLE, 13 228 367
TRIPLETT, 1-3 7 13 14 46 49
  69 163 195 237 265 280 343
  349
TROOP, 9
TROUGAN [?], 271
TROXEL, 378
TROY, 102 121 127 128 144
  145 153 179 185 279 284

TROY (Cont.)
  300 342 355 362 382
TRUMBLE, 310 352
TUCKER, 36 66 79 94 103 107
  113 120 162 163 164 208
  212 235 270 295 318 332
  344
TULL, 44
TUPPER, 199
TURKEYHISER, 334
TURLEY, 173
TURNER, 36
TUSING, 88 91
TYLOR, 27
VAN CAMP, see CAMP
VANCE, 372
VANDEGRIFT [Vandegrapp
  Vandergraft Vandgraft
  Vandigraft], 46 89 189 358
VANDERVORT [Vandavort
  Vandervourt Vandevort
  Vandivert Vandivort], 4 5 71
  74 86 119 125 138 150 153
  158 185 198 217 255 268
  297 310 315 316 320 333
  362 382-384
VANDRUFF [Vandroof], 21 297
VANHORN, 31 43 138
VANKIRK, 40
VANLEAR, 379
VANMETRE [Venmeter], 245
  379
VANUXEN [Vanuxsen], 56 374
VANUXEN [?], 17
VARNER, 226 238 316
VEACH [Veek], 31 34 36 150
  173 211 305
VERDIN [Virdin], 6 25 385
VERPLANCK, 208
VIGERS [?], 373
VIGUS, 308
VINCENT, 134 238
VULGAMOT, see WOLGAMOT
WADE, 23 28 32 138 148 159-
  161 188 213 228 247 298

WADE (Cont.)
    299 366 384
WAGNER [Wagener Waggener
    Waggoner Wagoner], 13 14
    16 78 80 107 113 142 166
    218 222 258 264 283 286
    317 333 334 339 345 362
    370 380 385
WAITE [Wait Wayt], 32 233 243
    371
WALKER, 47 122 125 170 199
    271 316 370
WALLACE, 28 49 50 59 194
    379
WALLER, 88 222 256 311
WALLS, 16 41 118 119 134 194
    226 354 355
WALTER [Walder Walters], 226
    233 261 386
WALTON, 69 293
WARD, 360 361
WARDEN, 272
WARDER, 379
WARE, 220
WARING, 344 354
WARMAN, 3 4 10 19 43 44 54
    60 69 72-74 77-79 90 101
    118 119 137 141 143 152
    153 158 193 203 216 217
    268 276 278 340 341 344
    351 378
WARREN, 264
WATHEN [Walthan Wathan], 30
    235 380
WATKINS [Wadkins], 13 35 59
    97 133 148 157 207 229 230
    384
WATSON, 4 5 89 91 102 123
    142 189 191 244 250 266
    269 271 273 274 297 315
    322 327 336 353 364 368
WATTERS, 289 290
WATTON, 73 340
WATTS, 218 238 278 384
WAYMAN, 56 207

WARE, 53
WEAVER, 7 24 30 42 53 59 71
    98 116 120 127 131 137 139
    142 157 185 206 210 234
    240 251 252 256 260 268
    269 271 276 284 285 332
    333 370 379
WEBB, 47 53 67 77 153 203
    289 314 342
WEBSTER, 18 26 97 129 167
    256 298 346 358
WELCH, 265
WELLS, 14 25 74 187 194 231
    279 285 348-351 358 362
WELTNER, 175
WENDERS, 122
WERNINGER [Warninger], 81
    106 174 231 307 328 330
    331 341 345 347 360 361
    374
WEST, 52 106 132 137 143 144
    188 246 249 269 272 286
    299 306
WESTCOTT, 27
WESTFALL, 50
WEVELY, 261
WHAIM, 56 64
WHARTON, 96
WHATEN, 166
WHESTONE, 142
WHITE, 10 11 55 200 216 308
    309 317 342
WHITEHAIR [Whitehare], 45 79
    101 185 193 265 339
WHITLEY, 380
WHITSON [Whitston], 21 57 86
    88 100 112 143 228 233 289
WICKART, 74 82 339 340
WICKWARE, 70 131 149 160
    174 175 203 248 249 255
    289 317 327 331 332 337
    340 359 360
WIENT, 273 307 315
WILES [Weil Wild Wilds Wile],
    18 57 124 131 132 265 277

WILES (Cont.) 378
WILHELM [Wilhelma Willham Willhlem], 250 283 292
WILKINS [Wilkinson], 115 139 251 252 283 358
WILLACK [?], 258
WILLETTS [Willets Willett Willits], 121 130 227 265 272 295 303 333 382
WILLEY [Wiley Willy Wily], 1 13 18 19 58 59 84 89 97 108 131 157 212 218 229 230 302 317 325 343
WILLIAMS, 1 9 12 13 16 21 23 25 26 29 30 39 41 44 57 58 61 63 66 68 73 75 76 87 90 91 93 95 97 98 109 113 122 123 127 132 134 137 142 149 151 152 156 167 169 170 174 176 190 202 226 230 231 264 271 279 293 303 307 312 313 323 325 358
WILLIAMSON, 109 179
WILMARTH, 108
WILSON [Willson], 4 6 9 11 14 18 20 21 26 32 35 41 43 46 52 54 55 62 67 81 85 94-96 103 105 108-110 113 115 117 120 125-130 134 135 139 143 145 147 149 151 155 156 158 160 163-165 168 171-175 178 181 183-187 189 192 199 202 203 205 206 211-214 216 219 220-224 226 228 234 236 237 239 240 244 245 249 250 253 257 259 262 265 269 277 279 282 283 286 289-294 297 305 307 309-313 323 325-329 331 332 340 341 344 345 348 350-354 358 371-374 382 383 386

WILT, 205
WIMP, 19 38 45 48 51 52 72 83 84 130 380
WINANS, 378
WINCHESTER, 58
WINDSOR [Winsor], 23 45 48 61 87 254 308 381
WING, 288
WINGER, 224
WIREMAN, 39 43 47 91 119 211 301 302 382 383
WISBY [Whisbey Whisby Wisbey], 37 39 46 47 67 86 171 362
WISECOP, 316
WISECUP, 233
WISEMAN, 189 220
WOLF [Wolff Woolf], 16 17 22 23 78 80 83 109 112 150 162 182 201 213 249 261 296 352 379 385 386
WOLGAMOT [Volgamut Vulgamott Wolgermut Wulgamot], 68 124 302 347 380
WOLUMPER [?], 378
WOLVERTON, 218
WOODBRIDGE, 137
WOODROW, 236 238 243 244 245 254 265 276 279 287 308 335 345 346 352 353 357 359-361 363 372
WOODS [Wood], 13 14 22 25 38 106 107 112 113 166 188 192 203 247 264 278 294 302 323 333 357 378 385
WOOL, 27
WOOTTON, 5
WORK, 131
WORKMAN, 20 105 235 298 385
WORLEY [Worly], 2 46 49 97 113 118 133 258 382 384
WORREL [Worall Worell Worl Worrell], 46 97 209 229 269 360 377

WORTH, 3 191 218 229 320 385
WOTRING [Woodring Wootring], 45 50 56 77 90 99-101 128 204 225 368 383
WRIGHT, 230
WYATT [Wayatt Wayett Wayette Wyatte Weatt], 2 44 67 77 153 154 280 324 342
YANCY, 78
YATES, 358
YEAGER, 35
YOHA, 335
YOST, 106 121
YOUNG [Yong], 53 203 271 274 312 328 355-357
YOUNGMAN, 104 163 165 292
ZEAGAN, see Czigan
ZIMMER, 372
ZINN, 7 22 24 58 102 109 123 182 207 255 289 306 321 358 359 369 384